Diagnostic-Prescriptive Reading Instruction

Diagnostic-Prescriptive Reading Instruction

A Guide for Classroom Teachers
Fourth Edition

Martha D. Collins
University of Akron

Earl H. Cheek, Jr.
Louisiana State University

WCB Brown & Benchmark
P U B L I S H E R S

Madison, Wisconsin•Dubuque, Iowa•Indianapolis, Indiana
Melbourne, Australia•Oxford, England

Book Team

Editor *Paul L. Tavenner*
Developmental Editor *Sue Pulvermacher-Alt*
Production Editor *Peggy Selle*
Visuals/Design Developmental Consultant *Marilyn A. Phelps*
Visuals/Design Freelance Specialist *Mary L. Christianson*
Publishing Services Specialist *Sherry Padden*
Marketing Manager *Pamela S. Cooper*
Advertising Manager *Jodi Rymer*

WCB Brown & Benchmark

A Division of Wm. C. Brown Communications, Inc.

Vice President and General Manager *Thomas E. Doran*
Executive Managing Editor *Ed Bartell*
Executive Editor *Edgar J. Laube*
Director of Marketing *Kathy Law Laube*
National Sales Manager *Eric Ziegler*
Manager of Visuals and Design *Faye M. Schilling*
Design Manager *Jac Tilton*
Art Manager *Janice Roerig*
Production Editorial Manager *Vickie Putman Caughron*
Permissions/Records Manager *Connie Allendorf*

Wm. C. Brown Communications, Inc.

President and Chief Executive Officer *G. Franklin Lewis*
Corporate Vice President, President of WCB Manufacturing *Roger Meyer*
Vice President and Chief Financial Officer *Robert Chesterman*

Cover design by Dale Rosenbach

Chapter opening photos courtesy of Edward B. Lasher

Copyedited by Carol Chubiz

A Times Mirror Company

Library of Congress Catalog Card Number: 91-77897

ISBN 0-697-12575-0

Printed in the United States of America by Wm. C. Brown Communications, Inc.,
2460 Kerper Boulevard, Dubuque, IA 52001

10 9 8 7 6 5 4 3 2

To Ben, Courtney, and Collin
Thanks for your patience and encouragement!
MDC

Contents

5 STEP FIVE
Fitting the Parts Together   403

13 The Total Diagnostic-Prescriptive Reading Program   405

Appendixes   413

Preface

Reading instruction in elementary and middle school classrooms is changing. The first edition of this text provided classroom teachers with information on developing a systematic procedure for assessing reading skill performance and providing appropriate prescriptive instruction. Through the years, research in reading has presented new information about reading instruction, the importance of comprehension, the role of word identification in the reading process, the impact of early learning on reading development, and the necessity for developing positive attitudes toward reading as a learning process. With this wealth of new information, each revised edition of this book has attempted to provide the new research to assist classroom teachers as they seek to incorporate these ideas into their world of practice.

This fourth edition reflects the most significant revisions of this text as "diagnostic-prescriptive instruction—revised" is viewed from the perspective of reading as a language process. Classroom teachers are faced with the basal v. whole-language dilemma when attending meetings and reading professional materials. Our philosophy is that the answer to successful reading instruction does not reside in an either-or approach. Effective teachers must develop a sound philosophy as they understand reading as a language process. Using this understanding, students in their classrooms are evaluated through dialogue, observations, and informal and formal assessments to determine instructional strengths and weaknesses in reading. The various student needs then help teachers to determine the most appropriate instructional approaches for reading development.

The first chapter of the text deals with the diagnostic-prescriptive reading model, the role of the school personnel and teacher in providing diagnostic-prescriptive reading instruction, and the impact of parents on the learning process. Understanding the philosophy that underlies this chapter helps teachers identify their roles and responsibilities in implementing the concept of diagnostic-prescriptive reading instruction in the classroom.

The remaining chapters are divided into five steps that outline the diagnostic-prescriptive model. Step 1 (Chapters 2 and 3) is concerned with presenting informal and formal diagnostic procedures for assessing the reading-language performance of each student in the teacher's class. Informal procedures such as observation, attitude and interest evaluation, informal reading inventories, and portfolios are discussed in

Chapter 2. The emphasis is to know the students and their reading-language strengths and weaknesses as they interact with print in a variety of situations. Chapter 3 presents formal assessment instruments used to obtain additional information on students as they are evaluated in relation to the criteria of standardized tests.

Step 2 (Chapter 4) is "Synthesizing Data" and focuses on assisting the classroom teacher in organizing, analyzing, interpreting, and using the diagnostic information. This chapter "Organizing Diagnostic Information", is the crucial link between testing and prescriptive teaching. With properly synthesized diagnostic information, a profile for prescriptive instruction can begin.

In Step 3 (Chapter 5) "Organizing the Classroom for Instruction," techniques for classroom organization are discussed. Various forms of grouping are presented along with information about collaborative learning. Basic teacher concerns such as the organization of groups, the arrangement of facilities and materials, and management procedures are addressed.

Ideas for using prescriptive reading instruction in the classroom are presented in Step 4 (Chapters 6–12). Chapter 6 gives general information about prescriptive teaching by discussing the importance of direct and indirect teaching as reading and language learning activities are used in the classroom. The remaining chapters in this step address the various developmental areas in the reading process including emergent literacy, word identification, comprehension, study strategies, and personal reading. Chapter 12 provides additional information on meeting the needs of the special learner in the regular classroom as students with physical impairments, psychological handicaps, educational differences, and language variations are mainstreamed.

In the final step, Step 5, the need for diagnostic-prescriptive reading instruction is summarized with a review of how the classroom teacher fits the parts together. This is necessary for the successful implementation of a reading program that meets the individual reading needs of each student as reading is developed as part of the language process.

Each chapter is preceded with questions that suggest its objectives, an introductory passage, and vocabulary to be noted as the chapter is read. All vocabulary is defined in the chapter and in the glossary at the end of the book. The chapters close with a summary, exercises for applying the information in a classroom, and a reference list for further suggested readings. The appendixes include a list of reading skills, a list of informal reading inventories, a sample interest and attitude inventory, a sample observation checklist, a select bibliography of children's books, information on the construction of an informal reading inventory, and a sample interpretive report. The instructor's manual, available only to professors using this text in their class, contains sample evaluation questions, suggestions for using the text, and transparency masters that correspond to the figures and tables in the text.

■ New to This Edition

The fourth edition of *Diagnostic-Prescriptive Reading Instruction* represents a revised look at the concept of diagnostic-prescriptive reading instruction. By approaching reading instruction as a part of the language process, the importance of language development and writing as related to reading is an underlying consideration in diagnostic and prescriptive teaching. Each chapter contains an update of research within the chapter and in the suggested reading at the end of the chapter. Revisions were also made within the content of each chapter. For example, Chapter 1, "Diagnostic-Prescriptive Reading Instruction in Today's Classroom," presents the need for diagnostic-prescriptive reading instruction based on student diversity in the classroom looking at language development as a major factor in the reading process. Chapter 2 focuses on the importance of informal evaluation of reading and language by providing classroom teachers with the basic information necessary for prescriptive instruction or further formal evaluation. Chapter 5 incorporates information on collaborative learning as another means of organizing for diagnostic-prescriptive instruction. Chapter 6 approaches prescriptive instruction as integrated reading and language instruction using direct and indirect instructional strategies. The focus of language in the reading process is most evident in the new Chapter 7 on "Emergent Literacy." Within this chapter the importance of early learning in the home and school environment is emphasized with specific ideas as to how this prior knowledge affects oral language, reading, and writing.

The many changes in this edition are a result of our professional growth, experiences, and input of our students, colleagues, and their students. For this, we are most appreciative and we continue to invite comments as you use this fourth edition!

Martha D. Collins
Earl H. Cheek, Jr.

Diagnostic-Prescriptive Reading Instruction

1

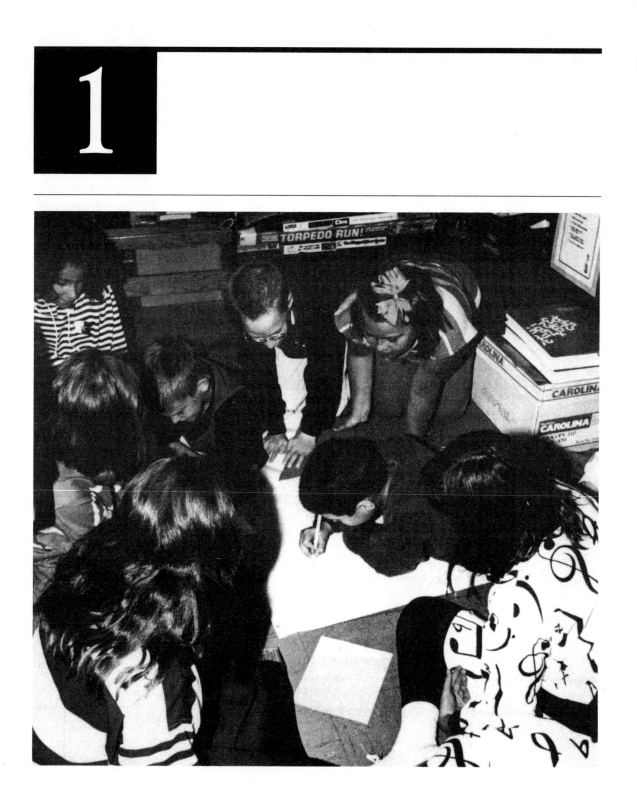

Diagnostic-Prescriptive Reading Instruction in Today's Classroom

As the teachers use their basal readers and the skill tests that accompanied each unit, they sometimes feel that their reading program is not meeting the needs of their students. A typical elementary school population consists of a mix of Caucasian, African-American, Asian, Hispanic, and Native American students from many backgrounds. Some of the students arrive at first grade already reading while others have had little exposure to books. Some students have extensive experiences and computers in their homes, while others have little more than sand lots for play. In addition to the ethnic diversity and different backgrounds of experience, teachers have mainstreamed students from different special education classes.

No wonder teachers sense problems with their existing reading program! Faculty in schools around the nation have realized that reading development is part of language development and when these areas are totally separated for teaching or discussion, student learning is compartmentalized. Although many teachers use a diagnostic-prescriptive process to determine strengths and weaknesses of reading skills, frequently they have not considered the relation of speaking, listening, and writing to the reading process.

Realizing the importance of the other aspects of language to the reading process, especially when dealing with such diverse student populations, teachers formulate many questions about their existing program as they redefine diagnostic-prescriptive reading instruction to include language behaviors demonstrated through listening, speaking, and writing. As these questions develop, teachers discuss students in the context of their language performance, not just skill knowledge; they realize that not only knowledge of reading skill development is important, but that reading is a more complex language process.

These questions, which arise in the mind of any teacher who sees the current information on reading instruction, are addressed in the first chapter of this book. An understanding of this foundation for "diagnostic-prescriptive reading instruction—revised" is necessary before exploring the remainder of the book, which elaborates on the specific steps involved in providing appropriate diagnostic-prescriptive reading instruction.

What is the reading/language process? How does it relate to the reading process?

Why is diagnostic-prescriptive instruction important?

What is meant by the concept of diagnostic-prescriptive instruction?

Why are other areas of language important to the process of diagnostic-prescriptive reading instruction?

How does diagnostic-prescriptive instruction relate to the reading/language process?

What areas of reading are important for inclusion in diagnostic-prescriptive instruction?

Who is involved in a diagnostic-prescriptive reading program?

What can the teacher do to become a more effective teacher of reading?

How does the effective teacher establish an environment to facilitate reading development in the classroom?

As this chapter is read, the following terms are important to note.

Vocabulary to Know

Assessment	Diagnostic-prescriptive instruction	Reading/language process
Basals	Individualized instruction	Scope and sequence
Comprehension	Mainstream	Study skills
Concepts	Personal reading	Teacher effectiveness
Continuous diagnosis	Prereading	Word identification
Diagnosis	Prescription	

■ Reading as a Language Process

A third grade class with thirty-six students including four mainstreamed students (one blind, one visually impaired, one educationally delayed, and one behavior disordered) and one dedicated teacher housed in a small classroom packed with desks—these are the observable features in many classrooms of the '90s. Not as readily observable are the variety of performance levels of these students, the differences in background experiences, especially as related to language development, and the range of students' interests and attitudes.

Much research in reading focuses on theory and reading as a process. Reading is defined as a process used to associate meaning with printed symbols in order to understand ideas conveyed by the writer. It is a process that requires the use of complex thought procedures to interpret printed symbols as meaningful units and comprehend them as thought units in order to understand a printed message. However, realizing that reading is a process does not tell teachers how to meet the variety of needs in today's classroom. Careful analysis of the theory and research provides information to be used in developing instructional practices. To summarize the research at this time the following conclusions may be drawn:

- Reading is part of the language process;
- Diversity in student needs affects learning; and
- Appropriate instruction is necessary for cognitive development.

Using these general conclusions and our knowledge of the current status of reading performance in America's schools, the need for diagnostic-prescriptive reading instruction is obvious. Results from the 1988 National Assessment of Educational Progress reported that while 9- and 13-year-olds were functioning better than those tested on the 1971 assessment, these students continue to lack the knowledge to function competently in today's complex society due to changes in performance made primarily during the '70s.[1] Reading instruction must begin to interface with the language process, recognizing that each student is different and the student's requires instruction geared to background, strengths, and needs. In order to meet this challenge, teachers need to know the levels of performance of each student, individual interests and attitudes toward reading, and techniques to accommodate this range of information within a classroom setting.

The complexity of reading instruction intensifies as one considers the theoretical models of the reading process proposed by many researchers. Accordingly, these various theories and models of reading instruction range from Gray's taxonomic model to the linguistic models of Chomsky, Goodman and Ruddell to Rosenblatt's transactional model.[2] While all of these models have had an impact on reading instruction, as Singer has suggested, a series of models is probably necessary to explain and predict reading performance.[3]

Realizing the diversity in today's classroom, teachers must note the existence of different models and approaches to reading instruction along with how these variations relate to their students. For example, in developing a better understanding of the reading process, researchers have given much attention to linguists, psycholinguists, and sociolinguists. Goodman's ideas that reading is an interaction between thought and language whose major goal is meaning has lead teachers to realize that a reader may not recognize every graphic cue. Indeed, errors in decoding are to be recognized as they affect meaning; the good reader corrects these errors when they interfere with comprehension.[4] Errors which are dialectical and do not interfere with understanding may not be corrected. Goodman suggests that a divergent dialect itself is not an obstacle in learning to read; the problem for the divergent-dialectic speaker is the rejection of the dialect by teachers.[5]

The concept of reading as a language process is further developed by other linguists, such as Frank Smith, when they include the simultaneous interaction of the reader's past experiences, expectations about meaning, and word recognition strategies in assisting with formulating meaning from the printed page. Thus, Smith believes that it is impossible to learn the sound of a word by building up from the sounds of letters. "Reading does not easily lend itself to compartmentalization," Smith states.[6] This statement summarizes a major emphasis of the linguist's concept of the reading process.

On the other hand, there are traditional views of the reading process, such as that of William S. Gray. Gray suggests that reading is a four-step process that includes:

1. *Word Perception*. The reader perceives the printed word.
2. *Comprehension*. The reader understands the meaning of the word as used in the context.
3. *Reaction*. The reader reacts to the idea presented by the writer based on the reader's feelings and past experiences.
4. *Integration*. The reader integrates the new ideas gained from reading into his or her personal perspective and applies the ideas to daily activities.[7]

Reading is a language process. Photo courtesy of Edward B. Lasher.

Gray's definition of the components of the reading process describes the philosophy used in many skill-centered reading programs. This approach to reading instruction is described as a **bottom-up** process of instruction, meaning that reading begins with the printed symbol and moves to a level of understanding. As this process for reading instruction has been used through the years, experience has noted that:

- Compartmentalized instruction is not the natural way students learn to read, and
- The process is not appropriate for many students, especially the language different student whose language and experiences are varied.

The reading process involves much more than the development of skills to facilitate the perception or identification of words and understanding. Readers derive meaning from print based on their past experiences, language, and purpose of reading. Thus, the importance of language understanding and background experiences as aids in comprehension must be recognized. Writers transmit ideas and feelings, using their backgrounds of experiences and their unique language style. Readers must then, in order to obtain meaning from these written words, relate their individual experiences and understanding of language. The extent to which the reader has the background knowledge to relate to the meaning that the writer is presenting determines the degree to which understanding will occur—and understanding is the essential aspect of reading. Because student experiences are so varied, instructional adjustments must accommodate the learner.

Since language and experiences have come to be recognized as crucial to reading success, the **top-down** and **interactive** models of reading have become more accepted definitions of the reading process. Proponents of the top-down model such as Goodman and Ruddell suggest that reading is based on what the reader brings to the printed page. Reading is hypothesis testing that verifies the appropriateness of decoded words and meaning provided by text. The reader begins with an idea about the printed information and monitors understanding.[8]

On a continuum between the bottom-up and top-down models of reading is the interactive model. Rummelhart's work has suggested that the reader and the text must work in concert to obtain meaning from print.[9] The interactive model uses past experiences of the reader combined with new information from the text to gain understanding of the printed page. While these varying models may seem more theoretical than practical, they are indeed very important in planning reading instruction. Literature-based reading programs tend to reflect an interactive model to build on the experiences of the student. The traditional basal program tends to be categorized as a bottom-up model which builds from lower level to higher level skills. Some categorize the use of language-experience as an example of top-down instruction.

While none of these approaches always fits neatly into any of these categories, teachers need to note the global differences in philosophies as they study this text, think of implementing strategies in their classes, and consider their philosophical views about reading. The issue of the "best" philosophy for reading instruction is well summarized from a research perspective by Stanovich. He states:

> Research on the reading process has been undertaken from a variety of perspectives. Too often progress in understanding reading is impeded when researchers working from different perspectives adopt a strong assumption of paradigm incompatibility: that a gain for one perspective is a loss for another. There *paradigm wars* in reading research mirror those that have taken place within the general educational research community during the last decade. It is argued that this assumption of paradigm incompatibility is false, and that progress toward a comprehensive understanding of the reading process would be hastened if we declared an end to the paradigm wars in the reading field and if investigators from all perspectives agreed to peaceful co-existence.[10]

From this discussion of the reading process, language is frequently mentioned as a significant factor in reading development. Reading research, classroom practices, and indeed the 1992 National Assessment of Educational Progress promote reading as a language process.[11] Speaking, writing, and listening are interrelated partners in the development of language literacy. As diagnostic-prescriptive reading instruction is planned, the relationship of language to reading must be viewed as an integrated process—reading as a language process.

■ The Concept of Diagnostic-Prescriptive Instruction

The concept of diagnostic-prescriptive reading instruction has been operationalized in classrooms for many years with attempts to implement programs ranging from testing and teaching isolated skills to putting students into different basal reading books. With the increased understanding of the important relationships among reading, writing, speaking, and listening, the operationalized definition of diagnostic-prescriptive reading instruction must be viewed in a broader perspective. *The concept of diagnostic-prescriptive instruction in reading means that the individual strengths and weaknesses of each student are identified through various diagnostic procedures with appropriate instruction provided based on the diagnosis.*

Diagnosis involves observation of the students' language behaviors when speaking, reading, listening, and writing, review of written work, and discussions with the students and other teachers, supplemented as needed with appropriate informal and formal evaluation procedures. Prescriptive instruction means that students are taught based on their interests and needs. ALL students are involved in a diagnostic-prescriptive reading program—the excellent reader has special needs to be further developed in language, whether it be vocabulary extension or expressing ideas in writing, while the poor reader often has many reading difficulties to be addressed using interests and strengths in language. Implementing the concepts of diagnostic-prescriptive reading instruction requires faculty and administrative commitment with an understanding of the reading/language process. With this leadership, other specific components needed are:

A scope and sequence of reading skills and knowledge expectations in listening, speaking, and writing. The hierarchy of skills is important for teacher knowledge in the diagnostic-prescriptive reading program. While there is no one correct hierarchy in reading and students will not progress through the skills list, teachers must be knowledgeable of the reading skills in order to incorporate appropriate skill development into the instructional program. Likewise, teachers need to be knowledgeable of student expectations in other areas of language development so that proper instruction is planned. Knowing what the students are expected to learn in reading, writing, speaking, and listening, encourages the integration of the areas for language literacy development. Based on the diagnosed need of the student, instruction can be systematically planned using the skills and expectations as guidelines.

Learning about the student as a person. Test information, checklists of behavior, and information from others provide a profile about a student. However, this profile may be affected by other factors such as home environment, stress, siblings, and comfort in the school environment. Teachers need to learn about each student as a person to determine if these other pieces of information contribute to an accurate picture.

Procedures to facilitate continuous diagnosis of each student. Diagnostic information from a variety of sources is another essential component of a diagnostic-prescriptive program. The teacher does not need to spend a great deal of time in testing individual students, but plans must be developed to determine the various sources of information which will be monitored for each student. Chapters 2 and 3 present procedures for obtaining appropriate diagnostic information, i.e., portfolios, observations, and tests.

Providing prescriptive instruction. In a diagnostic-prescriptive program, instruction is provided based on individual needs, although the instruction is usually done in a small group or total class setting. Prescriptive instruction requires carefully planned teaching activities using a variety of strategies and materials to develop the language and reading skills identified as important for each student. Planning and organization are most important in providing appropriate instruction. Chapter 5 gives specific ideas for material organization. Chapters 6–12 contain suggestions for prescriptive teaching.

The concept of diagnostic-prescriptive instruction is based on meeting student's needs. Years ago, this idea was misinterpreted to mean that the student was tested on a particular skill, assigned a material to develop the skill, and tested again at some later date. This is *not* diagnostic-prescriptive instruction—this should be known as the "plug-in approach!" Prescriptive instruction must be carefully planned to maximize effective use of both student and teacher time. One way is to follow a structured guided or direct reading lesson format which is discussed further in chapter 5. Others prefer to use a less structured lesson format to allow students more latitude in experimenting with language. Suggestions for using these procedures are incorporated into chapters 6–12.

Methods for keeping records on each student. As teachers learn more about students, the information must be recorded in some systematic manner. In some school systems, reading skill development is recorded using skill checksheets. However, because reading development is more than skill development, other information is also monitored. What about writing, spelling, and speaking? Strengths or deficiencies in these areas are related to reading and are noted in the development of language literacy. Although these records require teacher time, they are essential components of the program to aid in guiding instruction, conferring with parents and evaluating progress. Chapter 4 provides ideas on how record keeping can be managed by the classroom teacher.

The need for providing diagnostic-prescriptive reading instruction using these five components is evident when one thinks of the diversity in every elementary classroom. Teachers and parents note that no two students in the classroom are exactly alike in their reading development. The teacher may locate six students reading near the same level, but each of these students has different specific needs and interests that must be met through appropriate instruction. As suggested earlier, the reading process is not a simple process but consists of many interrelated components that are integrated by the reader. Thus, readers react to print in different ways based on their abilities and experiences. When teachers understand that the

Figure 1.1
Model for
Diagnostic-
Prescriptive
Reading Instruction

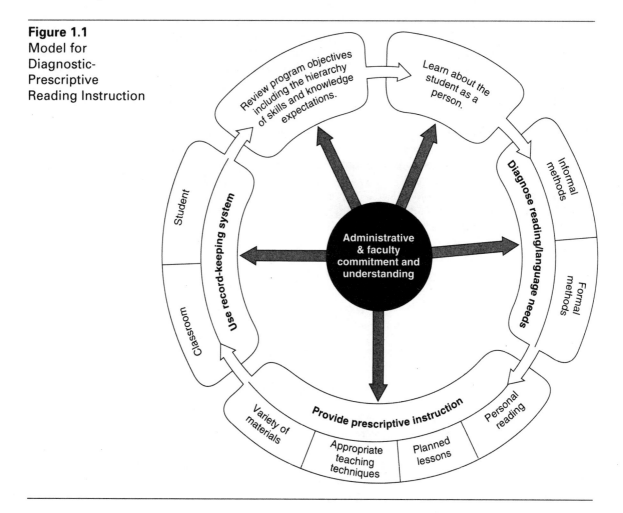

process of reading is not an exact, step-by-step procedure followed in the same way by all students, then differences in learning are better understood. Such understanding helps one to realize that the traditional three-group organizational plan using one set of materials cannot be successful in teaching all students to read. The complex nature of reading as a language process itself shows the need for the concept of diagnostic-prescriptive reading instruction.

■ Staff Responsibilities for Reading Instruction

The school reading program traditionally has required the involvement of all members of the school staff. Implementing a diagnostic-prescriptive program necessitates greater communication among the faculty, planning, and involvement of support staff, such as the librarian, guidance counselor, school reading teacher, teachers of music, art, and physical education, and teachers in exceptional education. The school principal is the instructional leader in the school. The tone, atmosphere, cooperation among faculty, involvement of parents, and general philosophy of the school depends to a great extent upon the involvement of the principal. Howeve., because the purpose of this text is to help teachers become more knowledgeable of the diagnostic-prescriptive reading process, the focus of this section is on the various responsibilities of the teacher with suggestions as to how others may support the teacher in this instructional enhancement.

The teacher in the **self-contained classroom** has the responsibility for a group of students who remain in the same classroom with that teacher for the entire school day. In this role, the teacher instructs all students in this classroom in all the subjects they will encounter for an entire school year. This requires that a self-contained classroom teacher be an expert in many areas of instruction. Such a responsibility has definite advantages, especially for reading instruction. Plans for the coordination of reading instruction with writing and speaking become easier to develop. Social studies and science become more than separate content areas allowing the teacher the opportunity to readily transfer appropriate strategies for reading expository as well as narrative materials.

Historically, many self-contained classroom teachers have not sensed the responsibility for diagnosing reading strengths and weaknesses in the classroom; they feel that students with problems are referred to the special reading teacher for help and believe that reading diagnosis means more testing and is too time consuming. However, as teachers have received more information about reading instruction and have realized that appropriate reading instruction relates to all students in all areas of the curriculum, a more systematic diagnostic approach to monitoring reading/language learning is of major importance to the self-contained classroom teacher. Teachers are realizing that systematic diagnosis is not a clinical testing approach added to the instructional program, but rather the use of appropriate diagnostic procedures as necessary to learn about the student's literacy with language—reading, writing, speaking.

The **departmentalized classroom teacher** has the responsibility for teaching a specific content area or areas to several classes of students during the school day. This teacher is responsible for teaching all students from a particular grade level or levels one or more content subjects, such as social studies, science, or math. Departmentalized classroom teachers are usually trained to teach a specific content area and may not realize their responsibility to integrate reading, writing, listening, and speaking learning into their content instruction. A content teacher is a teacher of language—not beginning reading or language, but the application of language literacy skills to content information to facilitate learning. Following are unique difficulties encountered in using language skills, especially reading, in the content classroom for which the classroom teacher, self-contained and departmentalized, should be prepared as the concept of diagnostic-prescriptive instruction is implemented.

Readiness for Learning. Readiness for learning is an important variable. Departmentalized content teachers need to review information on child growth and development, then spend some time in a primary classroom to fully appreciate the concept of readiness for learning. First-grade teachers face a new group of squirming students each September. A few of these students can already read, some will be ready to read in a few weeks or months, and others will require a year or more of readiness work to develop language competencies before they are ready to read. The mental age of students in a typical first-grade class on the first day of school may range from three to eight years of age; their individual needs must be met. At the end of the first grade, the range has probably increased, with the second-grade teacher finding a range of mental ages from about four to ten. Some students still may not be ready to begin formal reading instruction at the end of the first, second, or third grades. However, social and emotional factors do not permit the students to be held in the first grade for several years! Some students, therefore, reach the middle grades unable to read, write, or speak as well as many feel they should; they enter school without the necessary readiness (prereading) behaviors for academic learning and never catch up. Content teachers must realize how far students have advanced during the primary grades and help them continue to progress.

Individualized Instruction Is Essential for Learning in the Classroom. Teachers at both the elementary and middle school levels not only have these students who approach school with varying levels of readiness for learning, but these students have many different backgrounds of experiences and opportunities for the application of "school" information to their environments. This diversity affects their level of performance and their response to the learning environment. Instruction must be adjusted to meet these individual needs—this does not suggest that each student receives one-to-one instruction, but small group instruction along with large group instruction and some one-to-one instruction is essential for meeting the many individual needs in all classrooms. This topic is dealt with in more detail in Chapter 5. It is sufficient to say at this point that if the individual learning needs of students are not met each year, students slowly fall further and further behind until they become so frustrated that no learning occurs. Teachers often find students who cannot perform in the classroom and who cope with school by appearing not to care about learning. This is characteristic of students who have been frustrated to the point of rebelling or withdrawing from the situation. Content teachers are faced with the challenge of attempting to motivate these students to learn again sometimes with subjects that seem to have little relevancy to their lives.

Departmentalized content teachers also have students who are good readers and writers and who need the challenge offered in content learning. These students are accepted as the good student—whose success is enjoyed by all UNTIL the student becomes bored through the lack of challenges and loses interest in school. Individualized instruction with these successful students allows them to participate in group activities which are more challenging and decreases the likelihood of problems! Meeting individual student needs is essential in motivating the student to learn in the classroom!

Content Reading Is Different from Reading a Basal. Changing from the basal readers used in the elementary grades to the content materials in the upper elementary and middle school levels can be difficult for many students. This transition begins in about the third or fourth grade and presents problems to both good and poor readers. These difficulties arise from the different format, the application of reading and writing skills, the vocabulary load, and the many concepts presented.

In reading content materials, the *transfer of reading skills from basal readers to content materials* is sometimes difficult, especially for the poor reader. Unless teachers show students *how* to apply the skills learned from the basal program, it is difficult for many students to transfer this knowledge. Because of the more consistent language patterns used in basal readers, students not only experience problems in transferring skills, but also become confused when facing the *literary style commonly used in content materials*. Students who are already exhibiting reading difficulties become more confused by this turn of events and develop deeper feelings of inadequacy and frustration.

Content materials also require the application of *higher-level* reading skills. In many basal programs more emphasis is placed on the literal comprehension skills, which primarily require recall of information, than on the interpretive and critical reading skills.[12] However, in content material, the student uses the higher-level comprehension skills in order to understand what is being read. Comprehension and study skills at the inferential, interpretive, and application levels are emphasized in content materials. Unless great care is taken in teaching them, the stress on application creates frustration and leads to a decrease in students' performance as well as a corresponding decline in their self-concept.

Coping with *compact presentation* is another challenge encountered by students studying content materials. Students have difficulty understanding content selection because many new concepts and facts are presented in a very brief span of time as compared to the basal format, which presents a few concepts or ideas. In addition, encountering a *mass of unrelated facts* in content reading poses further problems for students. Although the trend in content reading is toward emphasizing how to learn, rather than simply learning new information, students are often faced with a barrage of unrelated facts from all content areas, whereas in basal readers they encounter a more limited number of concepts to be synthesized. This places severe stress on poor readers, who have difficulty learning even the limited information presented in the basal reader. In order for the student to function and progress at a satisfactory level, the content teacher must emphasize the learning process, rather than the importance of learning facts. Unfortunately, content teachers may not be aware that such problems exist and blame the students for their poor performance, rather than considering the material or the teaching style used.

Another major problem encountered when reading content materials is that of understanding the *many new words introduced*. The vocabulary load suddenly becomes much greater as more new words are introduced over a shorter span of time. This is especially true in the beginning sections of content materials when new vocabulary seems to fill every page. Again, in the basal, the student is accustomed to having fewer new words introduced and devoting time to discuss them. Although content teachers sometimes introduce new vocabulary in class, they may require students to become familiar with the words on their own. Content teaching implies much more independence in the student; but content teachers note—students must be taught HOW to learn on their own. Teachers cannot assume that students will select the appropriate vocabulary necessary for learning; guidance from content teachers is needed when new vocabulary is being introduced.

Closely related to understanding new words is the problem of *introducing technical and specialized vocabulary in each of the content areas*. Many of these words are familiar to the students, but the appropriate or precise meaning may not be clear and need introduction if students are to comprehend the material. Without question, such new vocabulary is on a level of difficulty much higher than that encountered in basal readers. While all teachers help students to develop their vocabulary, each content teacher is responsible for the development and clarification of the specialized and technical vocabulary appropriate to the particular content.

Specialized vocabulary is vocabulary that changes in meaning from one content area to another. For example, the word *mass* means a collection of data in mathematics, the weight of some material in science, or a religious ceremony in literature or social studies. As a result of these various definitions, students need to be taught the special meaning of this word in relation to the appropriate content area to which it pertains. *Technical vocabulary* is vocabulary that is essential to the understanding of a specific content area. Since it relates to only one field, technical vocabulary is usually critical to the understanding of concepts in that content area. An example of a technical vocabulary word is *genes*. In order for students to comprehend the concept of genetics, they must first understand the meaning of this technical word. The student's comprehension of content materials is dependent upon understanding the meaning of content specific words.

Comprehending the numerous concepts presented is another difficulty in reading content materials. So many new concepts are introduced in such a short span of time that students often experience frustration. Content teachers must understand the need to adjust instruction so that those students with reading problems and limited experiences have the opportunity to learn the concepts being introduced. Unless they grasp the introductory concepts in content areas, students become totally lost as the year progresses, because many concepts within the content areas build on one another. The poor reader needs more time and adjusted instruction in order to gain some knowledge of the basic concepts being introduced. Without these basic concepts, such students have little chance for success in the content areas and are sometimes regarded as non-learners. At this point, frustration mounts and the self-image becomes more negative, increasing the likelihood that these students will become dysfunctional readers.

Reading in a variety of sources causes difficulty in dealing with content materials when students have worked previously with only one text at a time. At the upper levels in the content areas, students are encouraged to supplement their textbook

Figure 1.2
Factors Contributing to the Difficulty of Content Reading

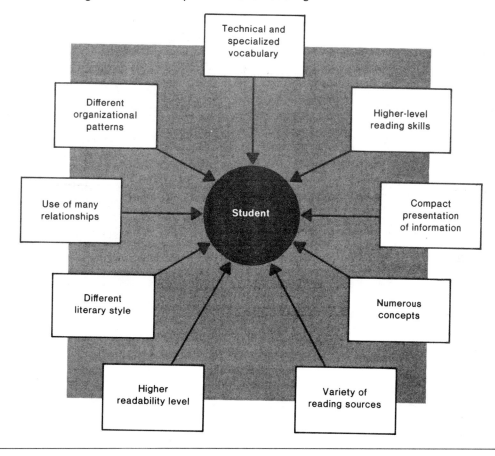

material with information from outside sources, and are expected to use many sources in their quest for information relating to specific topics. They switch from one type of material to another and may be unfamiliar with the use and format of these other resources. In addition, different types of materials have various levels of reading difficulty, causing the poor readers to be unable to use them. These difficulties need to be taken into consideration by the content teacher so that poor readers will not be expected to work with some types of sources as efficiently as good readers.

The *readability level of the content material* itself often causes the poor and average reader great difficulty. Teachers use basal readers written on a variety of readability levels. In the content areas, however, usually only one book is available for each grade level; these texts are frequently two or more grade levels higher in read-ability than they purport to be.[13] Thus, content teachers need to locate various texts and library books on different readability levels.

Understanding the relationships among the content area subjects may be difficult for students changing from basal readers. The concept that all content learning is similar should be stressed. For example, although each content area has its own technical and specialized vocabulary, the methods for learning this vocabulary are the same. In a similar fashion, inferential comprehension is inherent in all content areas; the same method of inference used in learning one can also be used in learning another. Content teachers working together to stress the similarity of learning methods for all content areas will benefit the students and offset many inconveniences experienced by the teachers.

The integration of reading and language with the content areas greatly assists all students in understanding content materials. Many departmentalized content teachers integrate these areas into their total instructional program realizing the importance of integrated learning experiences. Noting which areas are needed to read the content materials and using a diagnostic-prescriptive approach to teaching allows teachers to adjust their instruction to meet the individual needs of each student. The poor readers then have a reasonable chance for success while the better readers will be challenged in their learning experiences.

The self-contained and departmentalized teachers are primarily responsible for the direct instruction of students in their classes. However, this instructional process is facilitated as others on the school faculty become an integral part of this process. As suggested earlier, the **principal** is the key to a successful diagnostic-prescriptive reading program. The principal forms the foundation for a successful reading program by understanding the reading process and the concepts of diagnostic-prescriptive instruction, providing necessary staff time for planning, locating materials for instruction, supporting the faculty as they face the initial frustrations of change, and helping parents and students understand the changes occurring in the reading program. An enthusiastic principal with a positive attitude toward the program evokes a positive response from teachers, students, and parents.

The school **media specialist** or **librarian** also has an essential role in the diagnostic-prescriptive reading program. Media specialists have at their disposal an extensive collection of reading materials that are essential to motivate students to read and add to the instructional program. Sharing these materials with the students through book reviews, storytelling, creative dramatics, and displays makes them aware of the wealth of information found in books. The media specialist reinforces the development of reading by helping the students to apply their knowledge in reading as they read for enjoyment and to locate information.

The role of the school **reading teacher** varies, depending on the job description provided for the position. In some schools this person is a resource teacher who works in the classroom helping teachers to meet their students' reading needs. In this capacity, the reading teacher in a diagnostic-prescriptive program helps the classroom teacher to develop diagnostic skills, such as observation and informal testing, and also provides ideas for prescription development based on the diagnosis. In other schools, this person may have the role of a special reading teacher who works only with the poorer readers. In this capacity, the reading teacher must coordinate instruction with the classroom teacher. The reading teacher works with the classroom teacher in diagnosing and providing prescriptive instruction.

Music, art, and physical education teachers are also members of the diagnostic-prescriptive reading program team. These persons work with the classroom teacher in identifying students with specific reading deficiencies, and assisting with prescriptive instruction in their related areas. For example, the music program can be a great help to the student with poor auditory skills by providing instruction in the identification of various instruments by their sounds. The art teacher can design instruction to help younger students develop their tactile senses and visual perception. The physical education teacher can work with the classroom teacher to design specific exercises to develop in young students the necessary motor skills such as eye-hand coordination. With older students, the physical education teacher can often recommend books, activities, or assignments, and elicit a more positive response than the classroom teacher. Together with the classroom teacher, these special area teachers can develop student interests that enhance reading.

Teachers in exceptional education may have some self-contained classes of students at either extreme of the mental ability scale; or they may serve as resource teachers as their students are mainstreamed in regular classes. The exceptional education teacher whose students are mainstreamed provides assistance in the reading program by helping the classroom teacher diagnose specific needs, but assists more significantly in prescription development. Students with handicaps such as hearing and vision impairments need additional teaching assistance in order to develop in reading. This exceptional education teacher, like the reading instructor, must continuously coordinate with the classroom teacher in providing the most appropriate instruction for these learners.

Guidance counselors at all levels have major responsibilities in the diagnostic-prescriptive reading program. While they do not necessarily deal with direct instruction in the classroom, they serve to support the teacher in providing reading instruction. The responsibilities of counselors include helping to develop positive attitudes toward school and reading, helping the student to develop a positive self-concept, helping the teacher investigate personal problems that may impede learning, promoting communication among the faculty, and aiding in parent-teacher conferences to communicate the student's strengths and weaknesses as identified in the program.

In providing appropriate instruction for all students, teachers may find that the services of noninstructional school personnel are necessary. The **school nurse** can help with students suspected of having physical problems that are health related, such as poor nutrition or diseases. The nurse can also help in diagnosing vision and hearing problems that so frequently affect learning. Certainly in providing diagnostic-prescriptive instruction the physical well-being of the student is a major concern as learning is hindered with poor health.

Figure 1.3

Roles in the Diagnostic-Prescriptive Reading Program

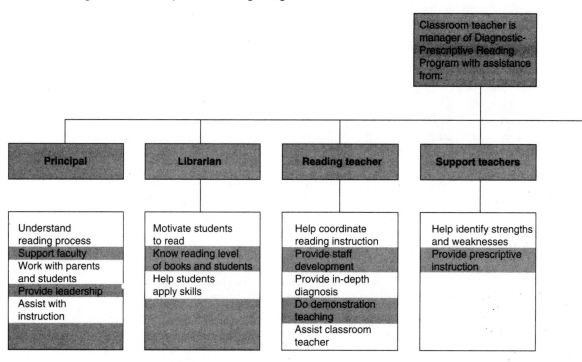

The **school psychologist** provides assistance in evaluating students suspected of having learning problems. Referrals to the school psychologist can bring assistance through observation of behaviors, testing, and recommendations for changes in the instructional program.

As these descriptions suggest, everyone in the school is involved in the diagnostic-prescriptive reading program. Teamwork is essential! The entire staff continuously shares their observations and collaborates in designing all areas of the curriculum to enhance students' learning. Parental involvement is most significant in this coordination with the staff and is discussed later in this chapter. The leadership of the principal, cooperation of the parents, and collaboration of the faculty are all parts of a complex puzzle which, when put together, will create a program that produces students who can read and who enjoy reading (see figure 1.3)!

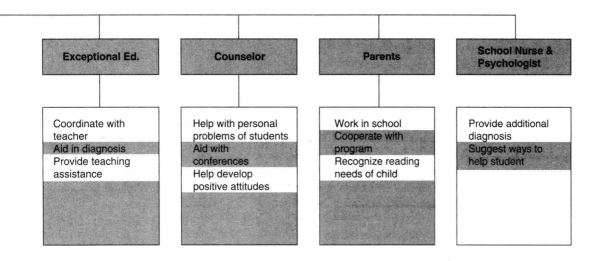

Exceptional Ed.	Counselor	Parents	School Nurse & Psychologist
Coordinate with teacher Aid in diagnosis Provide teaching assistance	Help with personal problems of students Aid with conferences Help develop positive attitudes	Work in school Cooperate with program Recognize reading needs of child	Provide additional diagnosis Suggest ways to help student

■ Parental Involvement in Reading/Language Development

Parents are an essential element in language development and likewise in the diagnostic-prescriptive reading program. Parental involvement in learning is a topic of many articles and texts with its importance emphasized in each. The brief treatment of this topic at this point in this book does not indicate a lack of importance, but rather serves as an introduction to an important area which will be discussed repeatedly throughout the book. Educators tend to identify activities or duties that parents perform in the school to be contributions, such as serving as volunteers or aides and attending parent-teacher organization meetings. While these are important activities, parental involvement in the reading/language process begins before school entrance and continues with many activities outside the school environment. Parents are the child's first teachers. Not only are they role models for their child, but parents establish a home literacy environment—an environment that supports or discourages literacy learning.

The literary-rich home is "reader friendly" with books for children throughout the house. The children visit the library on a regular basis and are aware of the many different forms of print in their environment, including the telephone book, catalogs, newspapers, cookbooks, and their own mail in the form of the abundance of advertisements and other junk mail received each day. Writing is encouraged and modeled as lists are made, bills paid, and letters mailed to friends. Children in the literacy-rich home assist in sending birthday invitations, making cards and writing thank-you notes (using pictures, invented spelling, or the computer) for gifts. They have a variety of writing tools—paper in all shapes and colors along with crayons, pencils, pens, markers, and paints. Reading and writing are viewed as important forms of communication with others.

In the literary-rich home, children are read to on a regular basis and allowed to experiment with language through conversation, asking questions, doing pretend reading with pictures and story memory, along with writing using invented spelling and pictures. As parents encourage children to play with language, children become free to use a variety of means to communicate and realize the benefits of communication with others. Such an attitude about language is very important to prepare children for school. However, parental involvement in language learning must continue after the child is in school. Encouragement for reading and writing activities are expanded by sharing information about what is being read at home and at school as parents talk about reading and writing in their adult world.

Parents are also involved with school activities. They may serve as a school volunteer or a guest resource person, visit the class to share a story with several children on a periodic basis, attend open house or work on school committees. Parents and teachers must communicate through conferences, phone conversations, and notes—the more face-to-face discussions the better. Teachers get to know the parent while parents gain a new understanding of their child! Communication between parents and teachers needs to be honest, open, and frequent to avoid misunderstandings and to help the children realize that these two significant adults know each other and are concerned about providing the best educational opportunities for them.

Parent-teacher conferences occur in many ways. At the beginning of the school year, contact between the parent and teacher is needed. A phone call or note of introduction is important if the parent and teacher are unable to meet to discuss the common goal of providing instruction and guidance that are best for the child. Experienced teachers often comment that the parents who need to be more involved with their child's school progress seem not to be available for conferences while other parents are always at school or involved with school activities. For some parents, conferences can be frustrating and even threatening. These unavailable parents may know that their child is having problems in school; the parents may have had problems in school years before—school was frustrating and this frustration reappears as they hear about the "inadequacies" of their child. Especially for these parents, teachers need to consider ways to develop parent-teacher conferences which focus on team building. Berger provides a few basic tips:

- Send notes to parents asking their time preferences.
- Offer schedules for conferences at varying times allowing for parental preferences. Phone calls as a follow-up to the invitation can serve to confirm the time, clarify questions, and welcome parents.
- Provide a private and comfortable meeting place that is away from the children and post a note on the door to avoid interruptions. Arrange the furniture so that tables and chairs do not separate the teacher from the parent.
- Have samples of the child's work so that references to specific strengths and weaknesses can be discussed.
- Encourage two-way communication in the conference—warmth, an attitude of caring, smiling, and empathy are needed as the ability to listen and respond develops a sense of respect.
- Understandable language is essential. Education jargon leads to misunderstanding and stops communication.
- Be prepared. Practice what needs to be said before meeting the parents and determine the best way to present the information. Organize the information to make efficient use of parent and teacher time.[14]

Parental involvement is a significant part of the diagnostic-prescriptive program. Teachers need opportunities to share their knowledge of the child with parents while parents provide related information from a different perspective. This type of communication is an essential component that serves as the basis for a diagnostic-prescriptive reading program.

■ School/Class Environment for Diagnostic-Prescriptive Reading Instruction

Teachers, like children, approach tasks positively or negatively dependent on the environment—the school climate. Positive school climates encourage risk taking while a negative environment fosters status quo or doubtful behavior in learning and attitudes for students and teachers. Language literacy, especially reading, requires risk taking with printed words in a safe environment. This environment presents opportunities for literacy development if activities are functional, relevant, and meaningful for individuals and relate to their own social purposes and goals.[15] As Shirley Brice Heath so wonderfully described in *Ways with Words*, as children learn to use language, children reflect greater differences than the formal structure of language and need much more than parent-child interaction to learn to use language.[16] Language socialization in the home and school requires appropriate environments to develop positive feelings about speaking, listening, reading, and writing. Teachers help parents understand the importance of environment for learning in the home and have major responsibility in establishing the school environment. But what is the appropriate school environment for diagnostic-prescriptive reading instruction?

From the wealth of research with at-risk and disadvantaged learners, many beliefs about appropriate instructional procedures have changed. These changed beliefs significantly affect the classroom environment as philosophies and instructional activities are adjusted. The first report by the Study of Academic Instruction for Disadvantaged Students suggests the following alternatives for improving conventional practice. Schools should have:

- An emphasis on the knowledge students bring to school;
- Explicit teaching of how to function in the "culture" of the school;
- Early emphasis on appropriate "higher order" tasks;
- Extensive opportunities to learn and apply skills in context;
- A combination of teacher-directed and learner-directed instruction;
- Variation in classroom management approaches depending on the kind of academic work being done;
- Some use of grouping arrangements that mix ability levels; and
- More flexibility in grouping arrangements.[17]

Environmentally speaking, this translates into a classroom which is rich, stimulating, and interactive with purposeful print and language activities. Teachers encourage learning in a natural, noncompetitive, risk-taking setting. This is a literate classroom environment which has a physical arrangement to encourage student dialogue, an instructional curriculum consisting of literacy activities rich with quality literature and writing opportunities, and an organizational arrangement that facilitates meeting individual student needs.[18] Diagnostic-prescriptive reading instruction exists within this type of environment. Diagnosis through on-going observation, dialogue, and evaluation with students provides the base for prescriptive instruction using appropriate literacy activities and grouping students to learn from one another and the teacher. Meeting the variety of learning needs helps create an environment which facilitates diversity and encourages relevancy for learning. Language literacy thrives as students experience enjoyment and success in the world of print.

■ The Effective Teacher

Program characteristics, parental involvement, positive classroom environments, and an appropriate philosophy for diagnostic-prescriptive reading instruction are all part of a quality language literacy curriculum. However, the crucial element of the instructional program is the effective teacher. As research through the years has identified the significant role of the classroom teacher, researchers in the last decade have focused on identifying the characteristics of the effective teacher. Duffy and Roehler suggest that the effective teacher is an instructional decision maker who demonstrates the following characteristics:

- Effective teachers think in terms of what students must learn, rather than the tasks to be completed.
- They view reading broadly rather than as a series of skills or a discrete subject.
- These teachers understand the motivational aspect of learning to read— liking to read is as important as learning to read.
- Effective teachers emphasize cognitive processing and awareness, rather than rote memory and accurate answers.
- These effective teachers, are not dependent on basal texts viewing them as tools, rather than an instructional imperative.
- They recognize the teacher's guide as initial suggestions for tasks and activities to be expanded and explained—as teachers they must show students HOW to do a task and apply a concept appropriately.
- Effective teachers understand the complexity of reading instruction and do not look for a panacea. "The answer" for solving the complexities of reading instruction, classrooms, and students and teachers is as evasive as gold at the end of the rainbow!
- In the classrooms of effective teachers, change is always occurring. As their professional knowledge grows, they are continuously thinking, changing, modifying, and innovating—ways to improve are always experimentations.[19]

Related to the characteristics of the effective teacher proposed by Duffy and Roehler are the findings of Guzzetti and Marzano's summary of teacher effectiveness research, which indicates that teacher beliefs and perceptions about themselves, students, and teaching, in general, are as important as their instructional practices. These beliefs are manifested in three areas that appear to be strongly related to student achievement: (1) high expectations on the part of the teachers toward the success of their students; (2) a belief in the basics; and (3) dissatisfaction with the status quo, which translated into constructive behavior as teachers alleviated dissatisfaction by implementing new and more effective instructional programs.[20]

Other factors that appear to assume major roles in providing effective reading instruction are organization, time on task, peer interactions, and type of instruction. Organizational ability is a trait that is highly regarded by both students and peers. Teachers who are well-organized are not only highly regarded by their students, but also appear to be more effective teachers than disorganized teachers.[21] Perhaps the primary characteristics exhibited by organized teachers are the ability to plan effectively and being well-prepared to teach the lesson.[22]

One of the variables that consistently indicates a direct impact on effective instruction is time on task. Rosenshine and Berliner[23] found that students who spent more time on tasks directly related to the teacher's objective will learn more of the content of a lesson than those spending less time on the content presented in the lesson. Clearly, both research and personal experience indicate that more time spent on a task will result in higher student achievement. Thus, it is important for teachers to plan instructional activities to facilitate on task behavior.

Another important factor to consider in providing effective instruction is peer interaction. Research indicates that students are aware of their ability in the reading class in relation to other students. Rosenholtz[24] believes that students' perception of their ability in reading classes has an impact on self-concept, which is directly related to the amount of interaction by any given student. In other words, interaction is directly related to the student's perceived ability in the reading class. Students who perceive themselves as good readers will interact more, while those students who perceive themselves as poorer readers will interact less. This *status characteristic* is a process that students use to make decisions about how bright other students are in relation to themselves. In addition, Cohen[25] found that group work is affected in a similar manner. Group members who perceived other group members as better readers were less likely to participate in group work. For these reasons, a variety of language activities are needed using flexible grouping procedures.

These research findings are particularly important to teachers of reading, since student interaction is an important aspect of a diagnostic-prescriptive program. Without sufficient student participation in the reading process, it is difficult to determine student's progress or to provide instruction appropriate to that student's needs. Students with lower self-concepts are encouraged to interact more in class through literature and language activities such as activities that emphasize oral abilities, dramatization, artwork, and discussions. Success in these activities improve the student's perceived status in the reading class, thus ensuring a more successful transition to print.

A final factor of considerable importance in the examination of effective teaching is the type of instruction provided in reading classes. One model of teaching reading that has gained support is the direct instruction model.[26] Direct instruction is predicated on the mastery of skills keyed into specific objectives. It features such principles as immediate feedback, a structured learning environment, and repetition and reinforcement. It has gained widespread popularity in recent years because of its apparent success in teaching students basic reading skills. Others believe that the direct instruction model focuses too much on skill development, and should be tempered by more holistic approaches emphasizing language development and social interaction. This lack of a consensus may appear confusing to teachers; however, it seems safe to assume that a teaching model emphasizing the more effective aspects of direct instruction and the holistic approaches will result in positive student gains in reading.

The effective teacher of reading understands the nature of reading and views reading as a language process. Effective teachers are knowledgeable and use their knowledge to be decision makers as they exercise control in the learning environment. They expect their students to be successful and provide opportunities for the students to see their success as they enjoy experimenting with language. These teachers help students learn what reading is all about and how it works as related to their world. Effective teachers are dedicated to knowing the needs of their students and providing appropriate instructional activities to expand their strengths as they overcome their weaknesses. Teacher's guides and tests do not dictate the curriculum for the effective teacher—the needs and motivation of the students are the challenges of these knowledgeable teachers!

■ Summary

The concept of diagnostic-prescriptive reading instruction is changing as current literature approaches reading as part of the language process. Speaking, listening, reading, and writing are integrated parts of the language learning process. This process begins with young children and parents as literacy emerges—talking, listening, reading together, and experimentations with writing are essential in the developmental process. Parents are the first teachers.

As children enter school, their backgrounds of experience and home learning environment are most important as progress in academic activities. While parents must stay involved in the learning process, the teacher becomes another significant model in providing an appropriate learning environment and effective instruction. The effective teacher is the classroom manager and a knowledgeable decision maker. This teacher recognizes the strengths and weaknesses for each student to facilitate positive cognitive social and emotional growth opportunities. This teacher also has a philosophy about reading instruction, which provides learning experiences in accord with these beliefs and the needs of the students. The concept of diagnostic-prescriptive reading instruction is part of this basis for instructional development. Diagnostic-prescriptive reading instruction requires administrative and faculty commitment to and understanding of the learning process. Specifically, the concept of diagnostic-prescriptive instruction in reading is defined in this chapter to mean that the individual strengths and weaknesses of each student are identified through various diagnostic procedures with appropriate instruction provided based on the diagnosis. The components are:

- A scope and sequence of reading skills and knowledge expectations in listening, speaking, and writing to guide teachers as they plan for students.
- Procedures to facilitate continuous diagnosis of each student using informal and formal diagnostic strategies.
- Use of a variety of materials and teaching techniques to meet individual student needs and encourage the use of the reading/language process for enjoyment and learning.
- Planned lesson procedures to make maximum use of student and teacher time as the individual needs of students are met in the instructional program.
- Methods of keeping records on each student through checklists, portfolios, and files.

Each faculty member is involved in the implementation of a diagnostic-prescriptive reading program. Additionally, the administration provides the leadership for the program, and helps parents understand the program and get involved in giving necessary assistance at home. The diagnostic-prescriptive reading program requires teamwork to develop better readers who are able to function in a complex society.

■ Applying What You Read

You are selected as a faculty representative to discuss changes needed in the school district reading program. During the first meeting, some say that they have read about a concept known as diagnostic-prescriptive reading instruction; however, no one seems to know very much about it. Outline the information you could share with the committee on the concept of diagnostic-prescriptive reading instruction.

The principal in your school has asked that you lead a discussion on the involvement of the faculty in a diagnostic-prescriptive reading program. Outline your ideas.

Some teachers in your school use the basal materials while others promote the concept of whole language instruction in their reading program. How does diagnostic-prescriptive instruction relate to these philosophies?

Compare the reading program in the elementary or middle school that you attended or last observed with the diagnostic-prescriptive reading program described in this chapter.

In your present or future role as a content teacher, reading specialist, or administrator, how do you see the reading-language process relating to content instruction?

Select several basal readers and compare them with content textbooks used.

Continuous diagnosis is a very important part of a diagnostic-prescriptive program. What is continuous diagnosis? Why is it so important? How could a diagnostic-prescriptive program function without it? Is continuous diagnosis done in your classroom or school? How?

■ Notes

1. Ina V. S. Mullis and Lynn B. Jenkins, *The Reading Report Card, 1971–1988: Trends from the Nation's Report Card.*

2. William S. Gray, "Reading and Physiology and Psychology of Reading," in *Encyclopedia of Educational Research*, edited by E. W. Harris; Noam Chomsky, *Language and Mind*; Kenneth S. Goodman, "Behind the Eye: What Happens in Reading," in *Theoretical Models and Processes in Reading*, 2nd ed., edited by Harry Singer and Robert Ruddell; Robert B. Ruddell, *Reading-Language Instruction: Innovative Practices*; Louise M. Rosenblatt, "Towards a Transactional Theory of Reading," *Journal of Reading Behavior*.

3. Harry Singer, "Theoretical Models of Reading," *Journal of Communications*.

4. Goodman, "Behind the Eye," p. 5.

5. Kenneth S. Goodman with Catherine Buck, "Dialect Barriers to Comprehension Revisited," *The Reading Teacher*.

6. Frank Smith, *Understanding Reading: A Psycholinguistic Analysis of Reading and Learning to Read*, p. 8.

7. William S. Gray, *On Their Own in Reading*, pp. 35–37.

8. Kenneth S. Goodman, "Unity in Reading," in Harry Singer and Robert Ruddell, eds., *Theoretical Models and Processes of Reading* (3rd ed.).

9. David Rummelhart, *Toward an Interactive Model of Reading*.

10. Keith E. Stanovich, "A Call for an End to the Paradigm Wars in Reading Research," *Journal of Reading Behavior*, pp. 221–31.

11. Robert Rothman, "NEAP Board Adopts Blueprint for 1992 Reading Test," *Education Week*, March 14, 1990, p. 4.

12. Frank Guszak, "Teacher Questioning and Reading," *The Reading Teacher*.

13. Barbara K. Clarke, "A Study of the Relationship Between Eighth Grade Students' Reading Ability and Their Social Studies and Science Textbooks."

14. Eugenia H. Berger, *Parents as Partners in Education* (3rd ed.).

15. Bambi B. Schieffelin and Marilyn Cochran-Smith. "Learning to Read Culturally: Literacy Before Schooling," in *Awakening to Literacy*.

16. Shirley Brice Heath, *Ways with Words*.

17. Michael S. Knapp and Brenda J. Turnbull, "Better Schooling for the Children of Poverty: Alternatives to Conventional Wisdom," *Study of Academic Instruction for Disadvantaged Students, Vol. 1*.

18. Jeanne B. DeGrella, "Creating a Literate Classroom Environment," *Resources in Education*.

19. G. G. Duffy and L. R. Roehler, *Improving Classroom Reading Instruction: A Decision-Making Approach* (2nd ed.).

20. Barbara J. Guzzetti and Robert J. Marzano, "Correlates of Effective Reading Instruction," *The Reading Teacher*.

21. M. Trika Smith-Burke, "Classroom Practices and Classroom Interaction during Reading Instruction: What's Going On?," in James R. Squire, ed., *The Dynamics of Language Learning*.

22. Donald J. Leu, Jr. and Charles K. Kinzer, *Effective Reading Instruction in the Elementary Grades*.

23. Barak V. Rosenshine and David C. Berliner, "Academic Engaged Time," *British Journal of Teacher Education*.

24. S. J. Rosenholtz, "Modifying a Status-Organizing Process of the Traditional Classroom," in J. Berger and M. Zelditch, Jr., eds., *Pure and Applied Studies in Expectation States Theory*.

25. Elizabeth G. Cohen, "Expectation States and Interracial Interaction in School Settings," in R. H. Turner and J. F. Short, eds., *Annual Review of Sociology*.

26. Fran Lehr, "Direct Instruction in Reading," *The Reading Teacher*; James F. Baumann, "Teaching Third-grade Students to Comprehend Anaphoric Relationships: The Application of a Direct Instruction Model," *Reading Research Quarterly*.

■ Other Suggested Readings

Adams, Marilyn Jager. *Beginning to Read: Thinking and Learning about Print*. Cambridge, Massachusetts: The MIT Press, 1989.

Blanton, William E., Gary B. Moorman, and Karen D. Wood. "A Model of Direct Instruction Applied to the Basal Skills Lesson." *The Reading Teacher* 40 (December 1986): 299–305.

Duffy, Gerald G., and Laura R. Roehler. "Teaching Reading Skills as Strategies." *The Reading Teacher* 40 (January 1987): 414–21.

Hoffman, James V. *Effective Teaching of Reading: Research and Practice*. Newark, Delaware: International Reading Association, 1986.

Loughlin, Catherine E., and Mavis D. Martin. *Supporting Literacy: Developing Effective Learning Environments*. New York: Teachers College Press, 1987.

Mosenthal, Peter B. "Research Views: Defining Reading: Freedom of Choice but Not Freedom from Choice." *The Reading Teacher* 39 (October 1985): 110–12.

Pritchard, Robert. "The Effects of Cultural Schemata on Reading Processing Strategies." *Reading Research Quarterly* 25 (Fall 1990): 273–95.

Richards, Janet C., Joan P. Gipe, and Bruce Thompson. "Teacher's Beliefs about Good Reading Instruction." *Reading Psychology* 9 (1987): 1–6.

Squire, James R. (ed.). *The Dynamics of Language Learning*. Urbana, Illinois: National Conference on Research in English, 1987.

Diagnosis

STEP 1

Step 1 revolves around knowledge of the many informal and formal diagnostic procedures that teachers may use as they implement diagnostic-prescriptive reading instruction strategies in their classes. To determine the most appropriate procedures, teachers must first know the students—their interests, backgrounds, and attitudes toward learning. With this basic knowledge, teachers then begin to make diagnostic decisions. With the emphasis placed on reading tests in today's educational society, classroom teachers sometimes fail to realize the vast array of additional procedures for use in learning about students reading behaviors. Chapters 2 and 3 summarize this information.

2

Informal Diagnostic Procedures

Informal diagnostic procedures are the primary tools used by classroom teachers to assess student proficiency in reading. These informal assessments include non-standardized, commercial-informal tests and naturalistic assessments developed by the teacher using classroom reading materials and closely related to the instructional program. Informal procedures are simple to administer, inexpensive, and as accurate as many standardized tests for meeting the instructional planning needs of the teacher. As reading instruction has become more language-based, integrating reading and writing processes with literature with less emphasis on testing and teaching many isolated skills, teachers have questioned the use of standardized reading skills tests. Questions have been raised about reading tests with many classroom teachers now making greater use of informal assessment procedures as they plan reading instruction with their students.

Because classroom teachers are realizing the valuable information that can be obtained about their students as they teach, more attention is being given to informal classroom diagnosis. Some of the common questions asked by classroom teachers regarding informal diagnosis are discussed in this chapter.

Why are informal measures so important?

What are the different informal diagnostic procedures?

What is an Informal Reading Inventory (IRI) and how is it used?

How can informal procedures be used to greater advantage in the classroom?

How does informal diagnosis fit with the use of a literature-based reading program?

What does a teacher look for when using observation as a technique for informal diagnosis?

What informal diagnostic procedures can a content teacher use to assess reading?

What informal procedures are useful in diagnosing comprehension difficulties?

How is word identification assessed using informal diagnosis?

How does writing and listening proficiency relate to informal reading assessment?

As this chapter is read, the following terms are important to note.

Vocabulary to Know

Attitude inventory	Informal Reading Inventory (IRI)	Objective-based tests
Cloze procedure	Insertions	Observations
Comprehension	Instructional level	Omissions
Content Reading Inventory	Interest inventory	Portfolios
Criterion-referenced tests	Interpretive comprehension	Prior knowledge
Critical reading	Literal comprehension	Readability
Frustration level	Literature-based reading	Repetitions
Graded basal series	Miscues	Substitutions
Hesitations	Mispronunciations	Whole language assessment
Independent level	Naturalistic assessment	Word recognition inventories
Informal diagnosis		

■ An Overview

Informal diagnostic procedures are nonstandardized techniques used by teachers to determine their students' strengths and weaknesses in reading. Areas measured are: (1) *prereading*, which includes oral language and auditory and visual perception skills; (2) *decoding* or *word* identification, more specifically, knowledge of sight words, phonic, contextual, and structural analysis skills, and dictionary skills; (3) *context processing* or *comprehension*, including literal, interpretive, and critical reading; (4) *study skills*, such as reference skills and using parts of a book; and (5) *personal reading*, which involves the application of the other areas via reading for information and enjoyment.

Informal diagnosis is also the most appropriate procedure for use in assessing student performance in language, writing, and listening to determine how reading proficiency relates to these areas. Language development is demonstrated through oral language, listening, writing, and comprehension performance. Writing skills relate not only to language development but also to word identification, comprehension, and study skills such as organization of information. Informal diagnostic procedures allow the teacher to interrelate classroom performance in all areas of language by monitoring behaviors such as oral reading, discussion, writing, following directions, and general attitude toward reading. Whether using a language-based, skill-based or combination approach in the classroom, the teacher should know the skills involved in reading. An extensive listing of the specific skills in each of the reading areas is provided in appendix A.

As informal diagnostic data is obtained, more than academic performance information is needed to gain the appropriate knowledge about students. Awareness of the students' prior knowledge and experiences are important in understanding reading and language proficiency. Physical, intellectual, and emotional factors along with the students' interests and attitudes toward reading are significant parts in understanding reading performance. Because various facets of the students' reading behaviors need to be seen as they are integrated into daily reading experiences, informal diagnostic procedures are preferred—especially for initial diagnostic information. Using the variety of informal procedures, teachers can easily observe and evaluate behaviors during instruction to obtain data that more accurately reflects the students' strengths and weaknesses in reading. Informal procedures yield much qualitative data whereas formal diagnostic tests provide quantitative information. Informal procedures encourage teacher interpretation of responses allowing greater flexibility in scoring responses. Harlin and Lipa suggest that informal measures are better predictors of reading performance with young children than formal assessment methods.[1]

With the diversity of informal diagnostic reading/language procedures used by classroom teachers and the flexibility encouraged in designing and interpreting the procedures, different informal techniques are created each day. However, the basic informal strategies are presented in this chapter and with these, teachers can combine, redesign, and create appropriate procedures as they informally diagnose their students. The more common techniques presented in this chapter include observations; informal instruments including attitude and interest inventories, informal reading inventories, word recognition inventories, criterion referenced/objective-based tests, cloze procedure, and content reading inventories; and oral and written language assessments including miscellaneous sources such as workbooks, learning centers, and classroom activities (see figure 2.1). Some of these informal instruments are developed by the individual classroom teacher while others are designed by the school district or purchased through commercial sources. Regardless of the procedure or the source, informal diagnostic strategies can provide essential information for:

- Grouping students for reading/language instruction,
- Determining students' strengths and weaknesses in reading as related to the school curriculum,
- Selecting teaching techniques and resources appropriate to the students' levels, needs, and interests,
- Monitoring students' reading development,
- Providing specific information to parents, and
- Determining how a student interacts with print and the language process.

Informal diagnostic procedures provide excellent sources of information about students' interaction with reading/language. To maximize the information that can be learned from this data, teachers must be good listeners—lookers—interpreters!

Figure 2.1
Informal Diagnostic
Procedures

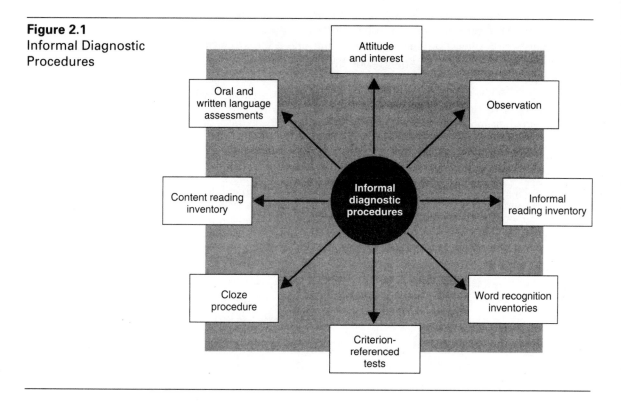

◼ Process Assessment

Reading is a language process used to interpret printed symbols—this interpretation occurs as a student interacts with print in books, newspapers, brochures, advertisements, and the environment. One of the major advantages identified in using informal diagnostic procedures is that teachers are encouraged to look, listen, and interpret as students interact with print in a natural way, i.e., while reading their social studies text or reviewing information to use in a group presentation. This naturalistic assessment facilitates process assessment, which is an examination of the influences of reading, writing, listening, and speaking upon each other. Process assessment requires that reading be viewed as a part of the language process. The assessment is so related to instruction that they are basically indistinguishable. Assessing the reading/language process also requires the teacher to be knowledgeable of the interrelated process, along with the components of the separate reading, writing, listening, and speaking areas.

As language and reading instruction have developed in a more integrated style during the last ten years, process assessment using naturalistic reading experiences to gain diagnostic information is a significant new direction in reading diagnosis. Informal diagnostic procedures are the basis for this process assessment. Integrating the procedures outlined in this chapter and devising appropriate ones for individual classroom circumstances facilitates the concept of process assessment allowing language-based teachers to evaluate reading as part of the language process. As the various informal diagnostic procedures are discussed, ideas for incorporating them into process assessment are suggested. To organize process assessment information into a useable form for sharing with students and parents, portfolios are discussed.

Observation

Teacher observation is one of the most important methods of informal diagnostic evaluation, especially as one views reading as a language process. Used alone or in conjunction with other informal procedures, observation of students in work and play situations allows the teacher to note their traits and attitudes while involved with print and non-print activities. Changes in behavior are clues to the astute teacher that progress is occurring or problems loom on the horizon! Teachers have many opportunities during the school day to observe the reading and language patterns of students; observations of silent reading as well as oral reading, textbooks and fiction, computer screen reading and workbook activities, writing and discussions provide valuable information to the teacher interested in learning more about students' reading behaviors. Depending on the type of reading they are doing, students change their reading styles and act differently. Further observation of students working in reading groups as compared to reading or writing alone is helpful for the teacher in developing a diagnostic profile. Although characteristics such as over-aggressiveness in play, hyperactivity, propensity to distractions, or passiveness in class participation are easily observable behaviors signifying reading problems, there are many less noticeable signals for the teacher. For example, the student who looks long and hard to find an appropriate book for leisure reading frequently saying that he doesn't really have time to read or the eight-year-old who selects a huge volume on Greek mythology is saying that there is a problem with reading. The student who finishes first but doesn't participate in discussions may be frustrated with too difficult materials or bored with the repetition of information she already knows. Important questions remain:

- What is the specific problem?
- What is the cause?
- What will correct the problem?

More structured observations are needed to address these questions.

Figure 2.2
Sample Anecdotal Record

Joe Smith

9-28   Joe played in the game area during free reading time. He had a fight with Sam about one of the games.

10-2   Joe looked at books during free reading time. He could not tell me what he read.

10-5   During the reading group Joe pronounced all the words correctly but he could not answer any of the comprehension questions.

10-8   Joe refused to come to the reading group and spent the time sleeping on his desk.

Structured observation takes either of two forms—a checklist or anecdotal records. Anecdotal records are detailed notes concerning individual students with dates recorded for each observation. These records often reveal consistent patterns of behavior which may be significant for instruction. Anecdotal records are most helpful in observing a student with a severe reading disability, in order to gain more insight into the student's reading behaviors. Some teachers keep an anecdotal record card box or notebook to note significant events of individual students each day. Such information is of great assistance in parent conferences and referrals for further evaluations. Having factual records of observations along with date (time may also be helpful) provide teachers with a handy reminder guide.

Anecdotal records require the teacher to note carefully the behavior and reactions of the student during a specified time. The most difficult problem for an observer using the anecdotal record is to keep fact separate from opinion. Only the actual facts or events are to be recorded; no interpretations or opinions are added until all observations for the student are complete (see figure 2.2).

Checklists allow teachers to keep information on large groups of students. A checklist is a versatile instrument of one or more pages listing specific reading/ language behaviors about which the teacher wants to know student performance. The checklist does not lend itself to in-depth observations of students over a long period of time; this is the function of the anecdotal record.

To guide classroom observation, checklist record forms need to follow a consistent criteria: (1) items address a specific behavior that can be observed; (2) space for additional observations and comments; and (3) limited number of specific items so that the checklist is not too lengthy. Teachers must be familiar with the items to be evaluated on the observational checklist. Some of the standard items may be:

- Understands facts in materials read,
- Fluent in oral reading,
- Participated in classroom discussion,
- Enjoys reading assigned material,
- Enjoys reading self-selected material,
- Ability to recognize new words, and
- Uses variety in oral vocabulary.

Checklist observations take place during a scheduled reading time or any time the student is reading. The teacher informally observes designated students for a few minutes during the selected time over a period of days to note the designated information. Specific steps in using an observation checklist are

1. Design a checklist that meets the needs of your classroom.
2. Make copies of the checklist to provide one per student to be observed.
3. Become familiar with the checklist to ease its use during observation time.
4. Schedule short periods of time to observe the student while reading.
5. Select one or two specific areas on the checklist, then observe the student to note strengths and weaknesses in these areas.
6. Note the results of your observations.
7. Select other areas to be observed at different times.

Observation checklists are developed by the classroom teacher. Possible items which may be included on a checklist are listed in appendix D. Items must be limited to facilitate ease of use.

Perhaps the most difficult phase of the observation process is interpreting the results. It is one thing to record a student's actions and statements during the day, but quite another to identify the underlying reasons for the behavior observed. An example of behavior that may be very difficult to interpret would be consistent emotional reactions recorded during the observation period. Use a cautious approach in determining the reasons for such an emotional upheaval and discuss ideas with another knowledgeable person.

Observations of reading and writing activities provide the teacher with many new insights into a child's difficulties, learning patterns, and avoidance strategies.[2] To further the use of observations of language behavior through more informal procedures, Y. Goodman suggested using a naturalistic assessment procedure called "kid-watching." Kid-watching involves: (1) observing, (2) interacting, (3) documenting, and (4) interpreting. Observation is done while interacting with the students; documentation and interpretation are done following an anecdotal record format.[3] Using this less structured procedure allows the teacher to use checklists and ancedotal records for documentation of the results of their naturalistic assessment. Before drawing any conclusions or making decisions based on observation, note the frequency with which the problem seemed to appear and the consistency of the problem from day to day. Remember that observation checklists involve less subjective evaluation than anecdotal records; thus, it may be helpful to use one to support or reject the findings of the other. Observation should be viewed as a beneficial part of all areas of diagnosis; however, teachers must be very aware of their students, and cautious in interpreting the information gained from observing them.

Observation is only one of many tools needed in diagnosing behaviors during the reading process; observation provides general information needed to direct further investigations. Observation is a natural assessment procedure used by teachers as they monitor reading and language development and adjust instruction as they see learning occur in the classroom. Remember, students are always changing and growing, necessitating that up-to-date observations be used to direct teaching and conferencing rather than six-month-old notes. Teachers should continuously note the reading behaviors of all students focusing on a few students at one time for more in-depth review. Using information gleaned from the observations can guide the teacher to sources of additional information, however, the teacher must be cautious of forming conclusions based on limited information from a few observations—attitudes and values of teachers may easily affect evaluations of a student. Stick to the facts; reserve opinions and hasty conclusions! With the influx of formal tests—state assessments, achievement tests, standardized tests, end-of-book tests—teachers must continue to trust their intuition and observe students as they interact with print and one another in the classroom environment. This form of process assessment is the beginning of diagnostic-prescriptive reading instruction.

■ Informal Instruments

Many informal diagnostic procedures use some type of printed instrument to assist in gaining insight as to how students process information. These instruments or inventories can be developed by the teacher, purchased from a commercial source, or provided by other professionals. They are not timed, norm-referenced standardized tests but rather are additional resources which can be adapted by the classroom teacher to gain more information about students' reading behaviors. These instruments are discussed in the following categories:

Attitude and interest inventories
Informal reading inventories
Word recognition inventories
Criterion-referenced/objective-based tests
Cloze procedure
Content Reading Inventory
Oral and written language assessments

Attitude and Interest Inventories

Research studies consistently link reading interest, attitude, and reading success.[4] Athey cites evidence that "tends to support the view that good readers are likely to be more intellectually oriented, and to exhibit higher aspirations and drive for achievement, and show more curiosity, and more positive attitudes toward school in general and reading in particular."[5] Attitude and interest toward reading create feelings, both positive and negative, that become habitual. As Smith suggested, "the emotional response to reading . . . is the primary reason most readers read, and probably the primary reason most nonreaders do not read."[6] Consequently, teachers need to be familiar with a variety of procedures to assess students' interests and attitudes toward reading. Obviously, the observation techniques previously discussed are quite helpful. However, other procedures compatible with observation may also be used with individuals or groups. This section reviews these various procedures beginning with teacher generated inventories and moving to student generated narrative responses to language and reading. A sample interest and attitude instrument is found in appendix C.

Inventories. One of the more common ways to determine students' reading attitudes and interests is the inventory. Interest inventories are regarded as effective tools for determining areas in which students exhibit specific interests. Some inventories are in a question or incomplete sentence format, while others use a rating scale allowing the student to indicate the degree or extent of feelings about an idea. A Likert scale rating of 1–5 may be used with older students, or younger students may respond by marking the shape of a face. McKenna and Kear have developed a rating scale for teachers in grades 1–6 to measure attitude using Garfield poses.[7] A sample of this instrument is provided in figure 2.3.

The interest and attitude inventory is easy to develop and use, since the only criterion to be followed is to develop questions designed to explore the interests of the student. The teacher can determine the types of questions to be asked, put them

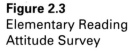

Figure 2.3
Elementary Reading
Attitude Survey

Reprinted with permission of GARFIELD: © 1978 United Feature Syndicate, Inc.

into a questionnaire format, and administer the inventory individually or in groups. After administering the inventory, the teacher interprets the results and uses the information gained to structure the students' learning activities around their interests in an effort to improve attitude toward reading.

Autobiography. Another way to learn more about a student is through a reading autobiography. This autobiography can be formulated orally or in writing, dependent upon the student's age and skill. Disabled readers who dislike writing usually prefer the oral autobiography or to record their message on a tape recorder. The procedure may be developed in various formats ranging from the checklist form of autobiography to a series of open-ended questions that the student uses as the basis of a narrative response. A checklist of descriptors can be easily written and quickly administered as the students mark the words or phrases that best describe them as a reader. This format, however, does not allow students to express their feelings due to the constraints of pre-selected ideas. More meaningful information may be obtained using leading questions with the students and asking them to write about their feelings toward reading. Questions such as:

- How would you feel at the end of your birthday party if all your gifts were books?
- Describe your idea of a great day at the library.
- How do you feel when you have to read?
- What do you think when your teacher says it's time for reading?
- What is your favorite subject in school? Why?
- What is your least favorite subject in school? Why?
- When did you read your first book? How did you feel?
- What do you like most (or least) about reading?

Using a few stimulating questions that are not to be answered directly, students will recount a developmental history of their reading experiences giving the teacher a more in-depth look at individual students, their attitudes toward other students in the class, their feelings about themselves in relation to their peers, their sentiments about reading, and perhaps even their reactions toward the teacher. The teacher also gains insight into the various forms of spelling and grammar used, vocabulary development, sentence structure, organizational pattern, and overall skill in written expression. With older students, the reading autobiography allows students to gain insight into their reading strengths or weaknesses and put them into perspective. With this self-evaluation and teacher guidance, personal goals for reading are set and steps are taken for further development.

Book Title Rating. Another effective method of determining interests is to provide students with book titles and ask that they rate the titles according to their interest. Individual students can evaluate a series of titles according to personal likes and dislikes. From this rating, the teacher determines the areas of interest for each student.

Discussions and Interviews. Group discussions or one-to-one interviews encourage free expression of personal frustrations or successes related to reading and language activities. Interaction provides poor readers with an opportunity to verbalize their feelings and allows students to learn how others deal with the printed word, how they decode a word, how they use clues to determine the appropriate meanings of an unfamiliar word, or how they locate the answer to a specific question. Using a discussion, the teacher has an opportunity to study how the students' thought processes work and gain insight into ways of adjusting instruction to better meet individual needs.

Class discussions may be initiated using student responses to questions related to the reading material or emerge as students discover how peers located or remembered information. This strategy helps students realize that people learn in different ways and that they are not alone with problems in reading—all students experience successes and failures.

Individual student interviews with the teacher provides the frustrated, hostile reader a private period of time to express feelings and begin to set short range goals for feeling success. Perhaps this short period of time with a teacher or other adult will provide the student, who obviously wants and desperately needs individual attention, an opportunity to verbally express feelings towards school before hostile actions lead to labels such as behavior disordered, emotionally disturbed, or juvenile delinquent!

A classroom atmosphere conducive to expression of true feelings is essential if interviews or discussions are used to determine students' interests and attitudes toward reading. Close teacher-student relations and a feeling of trust contribute to this openness.

Reviews and Journals. Teachers and students need to write each day about special happenings. This may relate to a positive reaction about the story the teacher reads to the class, a book checked out of the library, the frustration of being asked to read from the social studies book, or the teacher's observation of an improved attitude of a group of students. Students who write brief reviews of their reading also provide teachers an opportunity to see what kinds of materials they enjoy. This activity should in no way be construed as a "book report," which students say is a major negative action that teachers use to turn them off to reading.[8] These written or oral reviews are for the purpose of gaining an understanding of the student's interest. Young readers may be encouraged to "sell" a book to a friend after reading it. In order to "sell" the book, the student tells enough of the story to interest the friend in reading it. The teacher learns much about a student's interest by keeping a record of the books being "sold."

Another means of eliciting student response to books is to establish a graffiti board. Cover a bulletin board with heavy paper and encourage students to write book titles and their reactions to help others in selecting books for leisure reading. Again, teachers can determine students' interests by observing their response to various books.

Personal journals encourage students to write about daily activities. Frequently, such activities include events of the day which are particularly pleasant or frustrating. For the astute teacher, these are important messages that suggest interests and feelings about reading to be addressed through related learning activities in the classroom. The student who writes of his excitement after finishing *Charlotte's Web* may be invited to share the story with peers or develop a science project on spiders. Likewise, the student who enters the same line in her journal each day saying "I hate to write." needs to be provided with other options of self-expression while developing a more positive feeling about her skills in writing.

Free writing is yet another way of learning about the reading interests and attitudes of students. Teacher creativity is the only limit when using written language as a diagnostic tool in this area.

Information gained from inventories, autobiographies, discussions, interviews, reviews, and journals provide the teacher with insight into the student's likes, dislikes, and attitudes, and possibly some insight into the student's values, peer interaction, and self-concept. With this type of information, a word of caution is needed regarding the interpretation of these instruments. Results on any of these instruments need periodic review due to quickly changing interests and peer pressures which impact reading, positively or negatively. Students develop more diverse interests, have more experiences, encounter changes in the peer group, and are influenced by various teachers and adults. Thus, current diagnostic information is needed in using data related to interests and attitudes. Poor readers frequently respond positively to the question, "Do you like to read?" Realizing that this is often an effort not to offend the teacher, to create a favorable impression and sometimes even an effort to hide guilt feelings, provides the teacher with more insight into the student's feelings.

Teacher awareness of student interests and attitudes in relation to reading is of great value in providing appropriate learning activities to overcome reading problems or prevent their development. Teachers cannot generalize as to the interests and attitudes of students towards reading—all first graders do not come to school eager to learn to read just as all sixth grade boys do not enjoy books about sports. Know your students and try to use this personal knowledge of their feelings as your guide in creating an atmosphere conducive to good instruction.

Informal Reading Inventories (IRI)

One of the most informative diagnostic procedures is the Informal Reading Inventory. An IRI is a compilation of graded reading selections arranged in sequential order from easiest to most difficult with comprehension questions to accompany each selection. The selections used may be passages from graded basal reading series, graded passages from miscellaneous materials, graded passages written by the teacher, or one of many published inventories. Many school districts have developed their own IRIs and most publishing companies provide an IRI to accompany their basal series. Appendix B contains a listing of published IRIs.

An IRI is administered individually, enabling the teacher to determine the student's specific word identification and comprehension strengths and weaknesses, while observing both oral and silent reading habits. This instrument is also helpful to the teacher in analyzing the processes used by the student to deal with print (see figure 2.4).

The IRI is frequently used during the beginning weeks of school to diagnose more carefully those students for whom the teacher needs more specific information. The instrument is also used to place new students and to continuously monitor the progress of all students as their reading proficiency develops.

Figure 2.4

Basic Steps in Using an Informal Reading Inventory

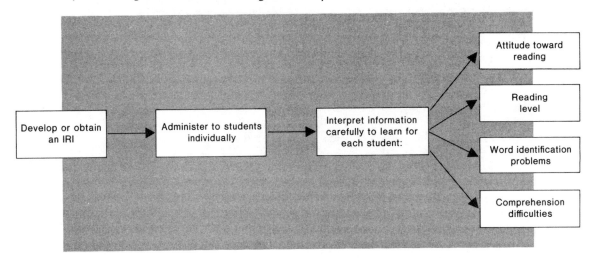

Since many published Informal Reading Inventories are available, teachers must be aware of their advantages and disadvantages. Jongsma and Jongsma found variety among these instruments in the content, style, and length of the passages, with readability estimates used as the primary means of passage validity and scaling. Differences in directions to the examiner were noted, as well as discrepancies on what constituted an error in oral reading. Factual recall questions were the dominant type of comprehension assessments. Additionally, they found no data on any of the eleven tests evaluated to validate the correspondence between reading levels established through informal reading inventory testing and classroom performance.[9]

Other evaluations of commercial IRIs suggest that there is a reasonable amount of agreement between IRIs constructed by teachers using teaching materials and some commercial IRIs.[10] In evaluations of commercial IRIs the questions of reliability and validity are always raised—there are more questions in this area than answers, although Helgren-Lempesis and Mangrum found that these instruments were "by no means as unreliable as some critics have suggested."[11]

Pikulski reviewed four current published IRIs to help teachers identify those that best suit their needs.[12] His findings are given in table 2.1.

Published inventories offer the teacher complete word lists, passages, and questions in a ready-to-use format. Most inventories provide multiple passages at each level to assess oral and silent reading and to determine a listening level. Although there are many IRIs available for teacher use, such an instrument can be developed by the teacher. Appendix G describes the construction of an IRI. Administration and interpretation information for use of the IRI in the classroom is provided in the following pages.

Table 2.1

Characteristics of Four Informal Reading Inventories

Inventory	Grade Levels	Forms of Inventory	Length of Passages	Source of Passages	Use of Pictures	Use of Purpose Setting Questions	Number of Comprehension Questions Per Passage	Types of Comprehension Questions	Criteria for Instructional Level	Time Needed for Administration
Analytic Reading Inventory (ARI)	Primer to 9th, 1st–9th for science and social studies	3 equivalent narrative forms; 1 social studies and 1 science form	Varies: 50–352	Written for inventory. Some science and social studies passages from textbooks.	No	Discourages discussion before reading, but allows examiner discretion	6 for levels primer–2nd; 8 for levels 3rd–9th	main idea factual terminology cause and effect inferential conclusion	95% for word recognition; 75% comprehension	not stated
Basic Reading Inventory (BRI)	Preprimer to 8th	3 Forms; A for oral, B for silent, C as needed	50 words at preprimer; 100 words primer to 8th grade	Revised from earlier editions; original source not stated.	No	Uses prediction from titles	10 for all levels	main idea fact inference evaluation vocabulary	95% for word recognition (only "significant" miscues counted); 75% comprehension	not stated
Classroom Reading Inventory (CRI)	Preprimer to 8th	4 forms in all; A & B for students in grades 1–6; C for junior high students; D for high school and adults	Varies; 24 words to 157 words	Written for inventory based on readability	Yes	Yes	5 for all levels	factual inferential vocabulary	95% for word recognition; 75% comprehension	12 minutes
Informal Reading Inventory by Burns & Roe (IRI–BR)	Preprimer to 12th	4 forms; all interchangeable	Varies; 60 words to 220 words	Primarily from graded materials in basal readers & literature books	No	Yes	8 for all levels	main idea detail inference sequence cause/effect vocabulary	85% word recognition for grades 1 & 2; 95% word recognition for grades 3 & above; 75% comprehension	40–50 minutes

Source: John J. Pikulski "Informal Reading Inventories," *The Reading Teacher 43* (March 1990): 515. Reprinted with permission of John J. Pikulski and the International Reading Association.

The many published Informal Reading Inventories require careful teacher review. Photo courtesy of Edward B. Lasher.

Administration of an IRI

One of the practical aspects of the IRI, if designed properly, is that it can be easily and quickly administered by the classroom teacher. For this purpose the teacher needs the appropriate passages for the student, a response sheet for recording and summarizing information, and the teacher copies which contain the comprehension questions and on which the teacher can mark word identification errors. The teacher

Table 2.2

Criteria Used in Scoring Informal Reading Inventories

Powell Differentiated Criteria

Book Level (1–2)	Word Pronunciation	Comprehension
Independent	94% or more	81% or more
Instructional	87% or more	55%–80%
Frustration	86% or less	54% or less
Book Level (3–5)	Word Pronunciation	Comprehension
Independent	96% or more	86% or more
Instructional	92% or more	60%–85%
Frustration	91% or less	59% or less
Book level (6+)	Word Pronunciation	Comprehension
Independent	97% or more	91% or more
Instructional	94% or more	65%–90%
Frustration	93% or less	64% or less

Betts Criteria

Level	Word Pronunciation	Comprehension
Independent	99% or more	90% or more
Instructional	95% or more	75% or more
Frustration	90% or less	50% or less

Source: William R. Powell, "Measuring Reading Performance," ERIC, November 1978, ED 155 589; Emmett A. Betts, *Foundations of Reading Instruction* (New York: American Book Company, 1957), p. 449. Copyright © 1957, American Book Company.

is now ready to administer an IRI to determine the individual's independent, instructional, and frustration levels in reading as well as strengths and weaknesses in comprehension.

Specific criteria for each of the levels of reading have been debated for several years, but the question of which criteria are most accurate remains unresolved. The most commonly used criteria are those provided by Emmett Betts in 1957. Further research regarding the criteria has been done by William Powell. Studies by Pikulski, Hays, and Ekwall present evidence that supports retaining the traditional Betts criteria.[13] Johns and Magliari suggest rethinking the use of Betts' criteria for primary students.[14] Thus, the teacher needs to be aware of this discrepancy and be consistent in the use of a selected criteria. When using a published IRI, note the criteria used in determining reading levels. The specific criteria given by both Powell and Betts for each of these levels are found in table 2.2. The levels are defined below.

Independent level: The level on which students read for recreational purposes. The material is easy enough to read quickly with maximum comprehension of the information.

Instructional level: The level on which instruction in reading is provided. The student can read the material, but has some difficulty with the recognition of words and comprehension to the extent specified in the criteria.

Frustration level: At this level, the student has extreme difficulty in pronouncing words and comprehending the material. This is the level at which the student should *not* be reading for instructional purposes, and certainly not for leisure.

Researchers and practitioners generally agree on the following steps in the administration of an IRI.

1. Rapport is established with the student. This is done through a discussion of what the student is to do and enhanced by developing readiness for reading each of the selections. During this time the student's prior knowledge of topic is activated.

2. The teacher uses a word list to ascertain the student's word identification level. If the *Dolch Basic Sight Word List* is used, the following criteria assist in determining the grade placement.[15]

Dolch Words Known	Equivalent Reader Levels
0–75	Preprimer
76–120	Primer
121–170	First reader
171–210	Second reader or above
Above 210	Third reader or above

   If the teacher has developed a graded word list from other lists, the grade placement is determined using the general criterion that the student should miss no more than one of every five words. This is the student's instructional level on the word list portion of the IRI. With this information or teacher knowledge of the student, the teacher proceeds with the IRI reading selections.

   The word list measures instantaneous recognition of words (sight vocabulary) and word analysis ability. A word is first shown rapidly in a timed presentation of approximately three seconds to determine if the student recognized the word by sight. If a correct response is given, the teacher moves to the next word. If the response is incorrect, the word is presented again for the student to further examine. This presentation is not timed and no clues are provided by the teacher, allowing the student to use word analysis skills to pronounce the word. The teacher records the pronunciations of the word from the timed presentation as well as the untimed exposure. A marking system such as the following can be used:

   √ = correct response
   — = no response
   ? = don't know
   ē-ver-rē = pronunciation of sounds or word units

3. The teacher chooses a selection approximately two grade levels below the student's estimated instructional level. Readiness for reading the selection is developed by introducing the selection and giving the student a purpose for reading the material.

4. The student reads the paragraph orally. The teacher marks the oral reading errors on the response sheet as the student reads. The following marking procedure is suggested.

words pronounced by the teacher =   over the word

mispronunciation =   over the word with the word written above as mispronounced (Mispronunciations affect the meaning of the selection.)

substitution =   through the word with new word written above (Substitutions do not affect meaning.)

omission = ⬭ circle the words or punctuation omitted

hesitation = | between words on which hesitation of more than 5 seconds occurs

repetition = 〰〰〰 over the word

insertion = ∧ with word written in

A sample marked paragraph appears in figure 2.5 and figure 2.6. Another way of noting word identification errors is through the use of a miscue analysis. The general types of miscues proposed by Goodman and Burke are substitutions, omissions, insertions, reversals, and repetitions.[16]

5. The teacher asks comprehension questions following oral reading, and indicates correct and incorrect responses on the sheet. For this comprehension check, the student does not refer back to the selection but rather answers from what is remembered. When a response is incomplete, the teacher may probe for more information by questioning further, asking the student to give more information or to explain what was meant by the response. Responses to these questions are recorded in this way.

√ = correct response
x = incorrect response with the response recorded
Q = further questioning needed
? = don't know

6. The teacher counts and records the words pronounced for the student, the mispronunciations, substitutions, omissions, insertions, and repetitions. Using the criteria for word identification as outlined in table 2.2, the teacher determines whether the passage is on the student's independent, instructional, or frustration level.

7. Another passage is used for silent reading. The teacher introduces the passage and gives the student a purpose for reading.

8. The student reads the passages silently, while the teacher records the words the student asks while reading.

9. The teacher asks the comprehension questions following the silent reading and indicates on the response sheet the correct and incorrect answers.

Figure 2.5
Sample Marked Selection

The swimming pool was ~~beautiful~~ *very pretty*. The sun was ~~reflecting off~~ *shining on* the blue water.

People were swimming and splashing (around) . Hours passed quickly and (soon) the pool
was empty of people. Lights were turned on and the pool looked different. *mp (distant)* No longer
was the sun (shining) on the water. Now the */ mp(sounds)* reflections were from the lights underwater.
Still, the pool was ~~beautiful~~ *very pretty*.

   ✓   1. What was this paragraph about?

        (a swimming pool)

   ✓   2. How do you think the pool looked during the day?

        (beautiful with the sun reflecting off the water and people playing around

        the pool)

   X   3. What made the pool look different at night?
not very many
people *swimming* (the sun was not shining and the lights under the water were turned on)

   X   4. When did the people enjoy the pool?
when it's
hot   (during the day)

   X   5. Why do you think the writer thought the pool was beautiful?
he liked
pools   (because of the sunlight shining on the water and then the lights

        reflecting under the water)

10. The teacher counts and records the words asked by the student, and the
satisfactory or unsatisfactory responses are indicated.

    Once again using the criteria for comprehension in table 2.2, the teacher
determines whether the student's comprehension of the material indicates
the independent, instructional, or frustration level. If the errors on either
the word identification portion of the oral reading or the comprehension
section of the silent reading indicate the frustration level, an easier passage
should be selected. If the passage is at the student's instructional level, the
teacher moves to the next higher level and attempts to ascertain the
student's frustration level. Few errors in both areas, as outlined in the

Figure 2.6

Word Identification Types and Coding System

> Word pronounced by the teacher: Write p over the word.
>
> $\overset{p}{\text{Now the reflections were from the lights underwater.}}$

> Mispronunciations: Write the incorrect word over the correct word in the text with mp written over the correct word in the text.
>
> $\overset{mp\ (distant)}{\text{Lights were turned on and the pool looked different.}}$

> Substitution of a word: Write the incorrect word over the correct word in the text with a line through the correct word in the text.
>
> $\overset{pretty}{\text{The swimming pool was }}$ ~~beautiful~~.

> Omission of a word or phrase: Circle the omitted words.
>
> People were swimming and splashing (around.)

> Hesitation: Put a / between words on which there is a pause of more than 5 seconds.
>
> Now the / reflections were from the lights underwater.

> Repetition: Put a wavy line over the word or phrase.
>
> No longer was the sun shining on the ~water~.

> Insertion of a word: Use a small arrow and write the word.
>
> $\overset{very}{\text{Still, the pool was}}{}_{\wedge}\text{beautiful.}$

criteria, indicate the student's independent reading level. The teacher then moves to more difficult passages in an effort to determine the student's instructional and frustration levels. Several levels may be skipped if the material seems extremely easy for the student.

11. Using alternate passages, read selections to the student to determine a listening comprehension level. The teacher may begin with the passage at the student's grade level or the passage one level higher than the instructional reading level passage. The selection is read to the student and questions asked to determine the information recalled. The student's listening comprehension level is the highest passage at which 80 percent or better is achieved on the comprehension questions. Passages of increasing

difficulty are read until the student achieves less than 80 percent comprehension. When the student falls below this level, the assessment is discontinued. This listening comprehension level indicates to the teacher what can be expected of the student when specific word identification or comprehension difficulties are overcome.

Interpretation of an IRI

Through experience in administering IRIs and observing students' reading habits, the teacher gains much diagnostic information about each student. The following discussion introduces the significant factors to note in administering the IRI with suggestions for interpretation. As the teacher becomes more familiar with the IRI, observational and interpretive skills are greatly enhanced.

General Observations When interpreting the errors made in oral reading, the teacher should consider these points:

Dialectical or regional pronunciations are not counted as errors. This type of mis-pronunciation does not affect comprehension, although the teacher may wish to note the pronunciation.

Young students often hesitate while reading orally. The teacher may wish to mark these hesitations, but not count them as errors. Fluency in reading comes with practice, which the young reader has not had.

Repetitions are noted, but the teacher may elect not to count them as errors. This is a habit that can be corrected. Repetitions slow the rate of reading but usually do not indicate a lack of comprehension. Rereading is a comprehension monitoring strategy.

Substitutions, omissions, and insertions are marked and counted as errors, however, teachers must also note whether these changes hinder comprehension. Errors that could fit the context of the sentence and do not affect comprehension are less severe than those that have no relationship to the sentence. For example:

1. The ~~cat ran~~ car got _around_ under the ~~house~~ home.
2. The ~~cat ran~~ kitten went under the ~~house~~ porch.

While both sentences have many errors, those in the first sentence are more serious because of their effect on comprehension.

Word Identification Errors noted in the identification of words on the word list and in the oral reading section of the IRI reveal significant information about the student's word identification skills. Teachers need to note that few persons read orally without making errors or miscues. The most significant word identification errors are those that affect meaning. Gillet and Temple distinguish these errors through a tabulation made by calculating a *gross* oral reading accuracy score and a *net* oral reading accuracy score. The gross score reflects the total of all word iden-tification errors—those that affect meaning as well as those that do not affect meaning. The net score is the total of only those errors that affect the meaning of the passage. The net score is used to determine reading levels "if the teacher tolerates a number of miscues or if the material is to be read silently."[17]

Responses to note, for possible interpretation of word identification strategies include:

Does the student make more word identification errors on the word list or in oral reading? Fewer errors during oral reading indicate that context clues are being used. However, numerous errors on the word list and during oral reading sug-gest that the student is lacking in word analysis strategies including contextual analysis.

Does the student attempt to pronounce words that he is not sure of or ask that they be pronounced? Failure to attempt to pronounce a word indicates that the student has poor word analysis skills and does not know how to divide words to determine their correct pronunciation.

Does the student frequently hesitate prior to pronouncing a word? This indicates that the student is analyzing the word because of uncertainty. Word analysis is an essential skill in proper decoding of words; however, if this is a frequent oc-currence, the student may become a very slow reader and have poor comprehen-sion. Easier materials and assistance in developing a basic sight vocabulary are needed to overcome the problem.

Does the student often repeat a word several times before going on to the next? Students use this as a way to gain time when they do not know the next word. Note how the word following the repetition is pronounced. Usually the student who uses this technique is unsure and needs to be encouraged to move on more quickly. Activities that encourage the student to pronounce each word in a sen-tence only once may be used to overcome the problem.

Does the student mispronounce the words? This may indicate one of several different problems:

The student calls the word another word that differs by only one letter or sound. This is an indication that the student is not looking at the entire word and using context clues as a word identification technique. Note whether the errors seem to be with the initial, medial, or final sounds, then assist the stu-dent in looking at the entire word as it is read.

The student calls the word an entirely different word—unrelated in meaning and with only a vague resemblance in sounds. This is an indication that the stu-dent is not using context clues or knowledge of sounds. This requires help in all aspects of word identification and comprehension monitoring.

Does the student more frequently miss basic sight words for which most phonic gen-eralizations do not apply or miss words that can be easily analyzed? Many students have great difficulty in recognizing the basic sight words and confuse them with one another. If this error is noted, one way of assisting the student is by using activities that require identification of words in context. If, on the other hand, the student consistently misses words that can be analyzed by using either phonetic analysis, structural analysis, or a combination, then the teacher should note the strategy used and expand this knowledge to use more multiple strategies.

Does the student make consistent insertions or omissions? Students who make these errors and do not correct themselves are not attending to the context of the information. Because of their errors, these students usually have difficulty in comprehending the material. If omissions are the problem, the teacher must determine whether the student knows the word and is just skipping it or if the word is skipped because it is not known. These are two entirely different problems. The student who continuously inserts words may do so in an effort to keep words flowing when a specific word is not known. Students who consistently either insert or omit words should be carefully screened to determine whether a vision problem is contributing to the errors.

Comprehension Often the student who has difficulty with word identification will also have difficulty with comprehension. However, some students have little difficulty in recognizing the words, but are unable to process the information for comprehension. When interpreting the data reflecting comprehension, the teacher must determine whether comprehension errors occur because the student does not recognize the words or because the material is not understood. Lack of understanding may be the result of poor language development, limited background experiences, or difficulty in processing the information.

Recent research related to comprehension questions on the IRI suggests that main idea questions be used cautiously as ". . . student's performance is just as likely to be a reflection of ill suited passages as of the student's inability to comprehend main ideas."[18] Further study of vocabulary questions on IRIs points out that ". . . the vast majority of vocabulary questions did not function properly . . . because they had an unacceptable level of passage independence."[19] Keeping these cautions in mind, however, much evaluation of comprehension processing strategies can be determined through careful interpretation.

Does the student not understand the material because of word identification errors? If this is the problem, the student should be able to respond to questions about materials in which no word identification errors occurred. If easier materials seem to improve comprehension significantly, the student may be diagnosed as having word identification difficulties that contribute to the comprehension problems. Correcting the word identification problem should improve the comprehension skills. If the student makes few errors in word identification, but continues to have difficulty comprehending the material, then further diagnosis is needed to determine the cause(s) of the comprehension errors.

Does the student respond better to questions measuring literal, interpretive, or critical reading skills? If the teacher has appropriately labeled each question according to the area and skills being measured, a rapid review of the errors may indicate a pattern. With this information, the teacher can provide appropriate instruction.

Is there a difference in the comprehension levels when reading orally versus silently? Some readers need to hear themselves say the words in order to comprehend—this is especially true with younger readers and students whose reading experiences have been primarily through oral reading. For these students, silent reading involves mumbling or voicing the words in a soft manner. As students get older, their silent reading comprehension level usually becomes higher than their oral reading comprehension level because silent reading is emphasized more as students leave the primary grades.

Is there a difference in the listening comprehension level and the instructional reading level? If these levels are the same, this suggests that the student may be reading as well as possible at this time; however, a discrepancy in these levels indicates to the teacher that corrective help with the identified reading problems will help the student achieve at this potential level (listening comprehension level). A few students may have a listening comprehension level that is below their instructional reading level. This type of discrepancy suggests several things: (1) the student may have a hearing acuity problem, (2) the student may not have the prior knowledge to understand the concepts presented in the listening passage, (3) the student may not be an auditory learner, or (4) the leveling of the passages may be inaccurate, causing an inaccurate estimate of the instructional level or listening level.

While most IRIs use a format involving questions following the passage, recent research suggests that teachers allow students to retell the story prior to questioning. Retellings provide an opportunity for the students to relate the facts of the story as well as to tell how he understands the interactions of the various components of the passage. The experiences and prior knowledge of the reader become more evident to the teacher along with the strategies used by the student to understand the author.[20] Thus, using retellings as another measure of comprehension adds to the diagnostic information available from the IRI.

IRIs have become a part of the age of computer technology and will likely be more involved in reading software development in the future. The *Computer-Based Reading Assessment Instrument*[21] is available for use in microcomputer format. The *Computer-Based Reading Assessment* is another IRI based on John's *Advanced Reading Inventory*.[22] Further use of the computer is made through the *Computer Assisted Reading Achievement* which interprets general information about students, IRI results, and offers a diagnosis.[23] While all of these instruments are new in the area of reading diagnosis, Henk proposes that the reading diagnosis assessments of the future must become more precise, and to achieve this end one possibility for incorporating our knowledge into a highly diversified assessment instrument would be through the use of computers.[24] With this storage capacity an enormous set of diverse reading materials that reflect narrative and expository text could be developed based on the directions of the teacher. These materials would consider the prior knowledge and interests of the student, with either considerate or inconsiderate text with differing paragraph structures or types of verbal illustrations. A hardcopy of the passages could be provided for use with students. Certainly, the IRIs of the future must reflect changes suggested by our research today—computerized IRIs may be a bridge for putting research into practice!

Informal reading inventories are valuable diagnostic instruments that furnish much insight into the strengths and weaknesses of each student. By following the guidelines outlined in this section, the teacher can determine the student's independent, instructional, and frustration reading levels as well as the listening comprehension level. However, these levels only represent a small portion of the information that can be gleaned from an IRI. Careful analysis and interpretation allow the teacher to note the types of word identification errors made by the student, the impact of these errors on meaning, the relationship of prior knowledge to comprehension, as well as many characteristics of the student's language and strategies used in reading.

■ Word Recognition Inventories

Teachers develop word recognition inventories based on their needs. Specific directions for developing inventories using word lists are provided in appendix G. This section presents information on the various word lists that teachers may review for use in devising a word recognition inventory.

Many word lists are available for use in developing a word recognition inventory. One of the more widely used word list is the *Dolch Basic Sight Word List,* developed in 1941 from three lists in wide use at that time: a list published by the Child Study Committee of the International Kindergarten Union, the first 500 words from the Gates Lists, and the Wheeler and Howell List.[25] The Dolch List consists of 220 basic sight words comprising those words occurring most frequently in basal readers on the first, second, and third grade levels. Although this list is still used by classroom teachers and reading specialists, the relevancy of the Dolch List has been studied by Johnson and by Hillerich.[26] Johnson's study suggested that the Dolch List has become outdated compared to the Kucera-Francis word list. Hillerich, however, in reviewing fourteen different studies, arrived at the following conclusions:

1. The recentness of a list is no assurance of its importance.
2. The language base of the word count is more important than the date it was compiled.
3. The structure words in our language tend to remain constant, although the language is continually changing.
4. The Dolch List does not seem particularly outmoded.

A more recent but similar word list is the *Fry New Instant Word List* revised in 1980. This list consists of the 300 most frequently used words in the English language, with students needing to recognize these words instantly in order to achieve fluency in reading, writing, or spelling. Interestingly, the first 10 words make up about 24% of all written material; the first 100 words make up about 50%, and the first 300 words make up about 65% of all the words written in English.[27] The Fry New Instant Word List is provided in table 2.3.

Table 2.3

Fry's List of "Instant Words"

First Hundred Words (approximately first grade)

Group 1a	Group 1b	Group 1c	Group 1d
the	he	go	who
a	I	see	an
is	they	then	their
you	one	us	she
to	good	no	new
and	me	him	said
we	about	by	did
that	had	was	boy
in	if	come	three
not	some	get	down
for	up	or	work
at	her	two	put
with	do	man	were
it	when	little	before
on	so	has	just
can	my	them	long
will	very	how	here
are	all	like	other
of	would	our	old
this	any	what	take
your	been	know	cat
as	out	make	again
but	there	which	give
be	from	much	after
have	day	his	many

Second Hundred Words (approximately second grade)

Group 2a	Group 2b	Group 2c	Group 2d
saw	big	may	fan
home	where	let	five
soon	am	use	read
stand	ball	these	over
box	morning	right	such
upon	live	present	way
first	four	tell	to
came	last	next	shall
girl	color	please	own
house	away	leave	most
find	red	hand	sure
because	friend	more	thing
made	pretty	why	only
could	eat	better	near
book	want	under	than
look	year	while	open
mother	white	should	kind
run	got	never	must
school	play	each	high
people	found	best	far
night	left	another	both
into	men	seem	end
say	bring	tree	also
think	wish	name	until
back	black	dear	call

Third Hundred Words (approximately third grade)

Group 3a	Group 3b	Group 3c	Group 3d
ask	hat	off	fire
small	car	sister	ten
yellow	write	happy	order
show	try	once	part
goes	myself	didn't	early
clean	longer	set	fat
buy	those	round	third
thank	hold	dress	same
sleep	full	tell	love
letter	carry	wash	hear
jump	eight	start	yesterday
help	sing	always	eyes
fly	warm	anything	door
don't	sit	around	clothes
fast	dog	close	through
cold	ride	walk	o'clock
today	hot	money	second
does	grow	turn	water
face	cut	might	town
green	seven	hard	took
every	woman	along	pair
brown	funny	bed	now
coat	yes	fine	keep
six	ate	sat	head
gave	stop	hope	food

Source: Edward Fry, "A New Instant Word List," *The Reading Teacher 34* (December 1990):286–288. Reprinted with permission of Edward Fry and the International Reading Association.

As teachers use more literature-based materials in reading instruction, the word list of high frequency words used in children's literature levels K–3 is helpful in forming word recognition inventories. Examining 400 books for beginning readers, Eeds developed a list of 227 high frequency words for use in teaching beginning reading through literature books rather than basals.[28] This list of Bookwords is presented in table 2.4. Eeds does not recommend presenting these words in isolation but rather that this list be used by teachers as professional knowledge of the types of words occurring most frequently in literature books. Again high frequency words are in all contexts—magazines, newspapers, textbooks and children's books!

Other valuable word lists are: *Kucera-Francis Corpus*, by Henry Kucera and W. Nelson Francis; *Basic Reading Vocabularies*, by Albert Harris and Milton Jacobson; *A Revised Core Vocabulary: A Basic Vocabulary for Grades 1–8, An Advanced Vocabulary for Grades 9–13*, by Standford Taylor, Helen Frackenpohl, and Catherine White; *Word Frequency Book*, by John B. Carroll, Peter Davies, and Barry Richman; "Sight Words for Beginning Readers" by Wayne Otto and Robert Chester; and *The Ginn Word Book for Teachers* by Dale Johnson, Alden Moe, with James Baumann.[29] These and other word lists may be used to develop word recognition inventories.

Formal word recognition inventories are available to assist teachers who do not wish to develop their own lists. One of the more commonly used lists is the *Slosson Oral Reading Test* (SORT), which is discussed in chapter 3.[30] Another formal instrument that has an oral reading section designed as a word recognition inventory is the *Wide Range Achievement Test* (WRAT); this can be used for ages five through adult and can provide a grade equivalent score.[31]

Word identification can be evaluated informally through a variety of other activities used continuously in the classroom. Activities such as workbook pages, games, and writing assignments provide additional insight into word identification difficulties. Informal assessments of word identification strategies are an integral part of any ongoing diagnostic-prescriptive program, especially at the elementary school level. As teachers diagnose through observation and occasional informal appraisal, appropriate instructional adjustments are made to develop necessary word identification strategies.

Word lists assist the classroom teacher in the identification of sight word deficiencies. In addition, they give the teacher insight into techniques used by students to decode words. Teacher notes indicate whether students have difficulty with initial, medial, or final sounds, or if they do not use strategies in analyzing words; such information is essential for prescriptive instruction. Word recognition inventories assess only one area of reading; they *do not measure comprehension*, thus the scores cannot be used to provide a reading level for the student.

Criterion-Referenced/Objective-Based Tests

Criterion-referenced and objective-based tests are designed to measure what a learner knows or can do relative to a specific objective. The criterion-referenced test is based on objectives that contain the specific conditions, outcomes, and criteria

Table 2.4

Bookwords

the	look	love	new	tell	door
and	some	walk	know	sleep	us
a	day	came	help	made	should
I	at	were	grand	first	room
to	have	ask	boy	say	pull
said	your	back	take	took	great
you	mother	now	eat	dad	gave
he	come	friend	body	found	does
it	not	cry	school	lady	car
in	like	oh	house	soon	ball
was	then	Mr.	morning	ran	sat
she	get	bed	yes	dear	stay
for	when	an	after	man	each
that	thing	very	never	better	ever
is	do	where	or	through	until
his	too	play	self	stop	shout
but	did	let	try	still	mama
they	could	long	has	fast	use
my	good	here	always	next	turn
of	this	how	over	only	thought
on	don't	make	again	am	papa
me	little	big	side	began	lot
all	if	from	thank	head	blue
be	just	put	why	keep	bath
go	baby	read	who	teacher	mean
can	way	them	saw	sure	sit
with	there	as	mom	says	together
one	every	Miss	kid	ride	best
her	went	any	give	pet	brother
what	father	right	around	hurry	feel
we	had	nice	by	hand	floor
him	see	other	Mrs.	hard	wait
no	dog	well	off	push	tomorrow
so	home	old	sister	our	surprise
out	down	night	find	their	shop
up	got	may	fun	watch	run
are	would	about	more	because	own
will	time	think	while		

Source: Eeds, Maryann, ''Bookwords: Using a Beginning Word List of High Frequency Words from Children's Literature K–3,'' *The Reading Teacher 38* (January 1985):420. Reprinted with permission of Maryann Eeds and the International Reading Association.

that are expected for satisfactory completion of the task. The objective-based test is also based on specific objectives, but no predetermined criteria for achievement are provided. This lack of specific criteria is the technical difference between criterion-referenced and objective-based tests.

These tests, in contrast to norm-referenced or standardized tests, do not compare one student's performance with that of another. Students are evaluated on their individual ability to perform the specific skill being measured, rather than in comparison to established norms on a group of related test items. Thus, the criterion-referenced or objective-based test is becoming more popular as a diagnostic tool used by local and state testing programs.

In order to evaluate the use of criterion-referenced reading instruments more easily, examine the contrast between them and norm-referenced instruments, as outlined by Otto.

1. Standardized tests have a low degree of overlap with the objectives of instruction at any given time and place. The overlap for criterion-referenced measures is absolute, for the objectives are the referents.
2. Norm-referenced tests are not very useful as aids in planning instruction because of the low overlap just mentioned. Criterion-referenced measures can be used directly to assess the strengths and weaknesses of individuals with regard to instructional objectives.
3. Again, because of their nonspecificity, norm-referenced tests often require skills or aptitudes that may be influenced only to a limited extent by experiences in the classroom. This cannot be so for criterion-referenced measures because the referent for each test is also the referent for instruction.
4. Standardized tests do not indicate the extent to which individuals or groups of students have mastered the spectrum of instructional objectives. Again, there is no such problem with criterion-referenced measures because they focus on the spectrum of instructional objectives in a given situation.[32]

Table 2.5 provides a further contrast of the two types of tests.

The primary advantage of criterion-referenced tests is that they get directly at the performance of individuals with regard to specified instructional objectives; thus they aid in the management of a skill based diagnostic-prescriptive system of instruction.

There are, however, some limitations inherent in criterion-referenced tests. Otto describes such problems as the following:

1. Objectives involving hard-to-measure qualities, such as appreciation or attitudes, may be slighted.
2. Objectives involving the retention and transfer of what is learned may become secondary to the one-time demonstration of mastery of stated objectives.

Table 2.5

Contrast of Norm-referenced and Criterion-referenced Tests

Point of Comparison	Norm-referenced	Criterion-referenced
Purpose	Determines a student's grade level achievement.	Determines extent to which student objectives are being achieved.
Testing Procedures	Each student takes a complete test.	Items may be randomly assigned as purposes dictate.
Achievement Standard	Comparison with other students of the same age.	Performance of the individual in regard to the objective.
Reporting of Results	Grade-level achievement norms for individuals or groups.	Percentage score on the number of items correct for specific objective.
Implications for Teaching	Teaching for the test constrains classroom activity and invalidates the test.	Teaching for the objectives is desirable and expected if the objectives have been carefully formulated.

3. Specifying the universe of tasks (determining critical instructional objectives) to be dealt with is of extreme importance. Good tests will do nothing to overcome the problem of bad objectives. But note that the problem here is no different from norm-referenced testing.
4. Determining proficiency standards can be troublesome. Perfect or near-perfect performance should be required if: (a) the criterion objectives call for mastery; (b) the skill is important for future learning; (c) items are of the objective type and guessing is likely. Less demanding performance may be adequate if any of the three conditions do not prevail.[33]

Instead of attempting to choose between either norm-referenced or criterion-referenced instruments, teachers should use them to complement each other, choosing the most appropriate instrument for their particular purpose and testing situation. Teachers interested in knowing how students are performing in relation to national standards should use a standardized or norm-referenced test. Teachers who want diagnostic information about a student's performance on a specific skill will find a criterion-referenced or objective-based test to be helpful.

Criterion-referenced tests are being used frequently in schools that have management systems that aid in reading skill diagnosis. In addition, statewide testing programs use objective-based tests to determine student performance on specific minimum objectives or standards. As a result, these tests have become readily available for teacher use. Many current basal reading programs contain criterion-referenced tests to aid in classroom diagnosis. These tests are based on the scope and sequence of skills for the series and are used as part of a management system for evaluating skills taught in the basal.

Teachers must exercise caution in using criterion-referenced tests in a management system for reading. Two suggestions for the proper use of such tests are: 1) follow the scope and sequence of skills outlined for the school, as many management systems are not outlined according to a horizontal and vertical hierarchy of skills; and 2) do not fall into the trap of the "test-teach-test" syndrome, which encourages the development of reading skills in isolation.

The overuse of skills testing via local school and state testing programs has resulted in the teaching of isolated reading skills in many classrooms.[34] Teachers, administrators, and the public must understand that reading is a language process, which is more than the teaching of isolated reading skills. While criterion- or objective-based tests can provide diagnostic information, they must not form the basis of the reading curriculum.

Teachers can prepare their own criterion- or objective-based tests to measure specific objectives. The specific steps to follow in doing so are listed below.

1. Identify the objective that will become the basis for the test item.
2. Specify the objective so that you define exactly what is to be measured.
   Example A: *To understand what is read.* This objective is incorrectly stated. It is not specific; it gives no idea of the outcome or what is to be done to achieve the objective.
   Example B: *After reading a paragraph, the student will identify the main idea of the paragraph.* This objective is more specific and could be used to develop an objective-based test item.
   Example C: *Given three reading selections, each containing a stated main idea and followed by four choices of response, the student will underline the choice that states the main idea for each selection. The student must correctly answer two of the three.* This is the type of objective often used in criterion-referenced test items. It is very specific, leaving little room for doubt as to what is expected. The problem is that the objective is so cumbersome that teachers often find it not very practical for classroom use. Thus, the objective in Example B is more commonly used.
3. Develop the test items to measure the objective as specified. If the teacher uses objectives as specific as the one in Example C, then the item is already designed. However, if a more general objective is used, as in Example B, then the teacher must determine the format, the number of selections to use, the procedure to be used in administration, and criteria for the performance expected for each student. Teachers may use selections from readers and library books or selected items from workbooks to aid in developing test items. An assessment to measure a specific objective usually consists of from three to eight items that measure the specific skill as outlined in the objective. Some assessments are designed for use with individuals, but most can be administered to small groups.

Criterion-referenced tests are helpful components of a skill based diagnostic-prescriptive reading program. They are easy to administer and are excellent for determining the specific skill needs of students in the classroom. However, the concept of objective-based testing should not be limited to assessing reading skills. As teachers approach reading and language development, objectives are specified to guide planning. For example, teachers using a literature-based reading program share a variety of types of literature with students. One objective of this teacher may be that the student can write a four line verse using a rhyming pattern after reading several poems with rhyming verse. This objective can be measured as students develop writing projects. Similarly objectives can be specified and evaluated for other areas of oral and written language through observation, writing activities, informal discussions, and group presentations.

The use of criterion-referenced/objective-based tests cannot be limited to paper-pencil testing of isolated reading skills. While the two concepts have traditionally been discussed together, reading instruction and evaluation are changing. Regardless of the approach to reading instruction, teachers have objectives which are to be evaluated—this evaluation can be done informally using the concept of objective-based assessment in concert with observation, instruction, and learning activities.

Cloze Procedure

The cloze procedure is a versatile, informal instrument for use in determining students' reading levels, determining their use of context while reading, and gaining knowledge about their vocabulary. Developed by Wilson Taylor in 1953, the cloze procedure was initially used as a tool for measuring readability.[35] Further research has suggested that the cloze procedure can also be used as an alternative to the Informal Reading Inventory for determining reading levels.[36]

Research involving a qualitative analysis of the cloze suggested this procedure as an invalid test of reading comprehension because it measures a set of thinking processes related to reading and writing. Ashby-Davis further suggests that cloze probably favors students who are not only good readers but also good writers. While the scores of this student are inflated in terms of reading comprehension, the scores of good, average, or poor readers are underestimated when they are deficient in writing skills, particularly in those skills needed to complete cloze.[37] However, Jonz and McKenna and Layton reported the cloze to have a high level of sensitivity to intersentential ties and concurrent validity with DeSanti finding the semantically and syntactically sensitive scoring procedure to have acceptable concurrent and predictive validity for use with a variety of passages and grade levels.[38] With continuing research as to the acceptable use of the cloze procedure being encouraging, this instrument offers another informal procedure to aid in classroom diagnosis.

A cloze test can be developed without special training in test construction. To develop and administer a cloze test, gather reading selections from textbooks, basal readers, or any other material that is appropriate and unfamiliar to the students, and follow the steps listed below.

1. Select a passage of approximately 250–300 words on a level at which the student is or should be reading.
2. Check the readability level of the passage using a readability formula as outlined in chapter 6.
3. Retype the passage. Beginning with the second sentence, delete every fifth word. Replace each deleted word with a line, making sure that each line is of the same length. Place a number under each line to ease scoring and student responses. Do not delete words from the first or last sentence. There should be approximately fifty blank spaces in the selection.
4. Make copies of the test for students to complete.
5. Direct the students to fill in each blank with the words they think best complete the sentences.
6. Score the papers by counting as correct only those responses that exactly match the original selection. Using a percentage score of correct responses, determine the student's reading level:
   58%–100% correct = Independent level,
   44%–57% correct = Instructional level, and
   0%–43% correct = Frustration level.[39]

Teachers find this technique quite useful in learning more about their students' reading levels and skill in reading incomplete text. To use the cloze procedure, passages at several different reading levels need to be assembled into a booklet for students to work through as an assignment. The objective of using this procedure is to gain an estimate of the level of material the student can satisfactorily read and to gain more diagnostic information through alternative interpretation of responses. As a method of evaluating comprehension, the teacher evaluates each word used in responses. If the student fills in the blanks with totally irrelevant words, the material is probably not understood. On the other hand, if the student completes the blanks with meaning appropriate words which fit the context but are more frequently used words rather than the technical or multi-syllabic word used in the text, the teacher has information indicating a limited student vocabulary.

More diagnostic information can be gathered by examining the types of words substituted in the blanks and the use of other words in the sentence to assist in figuring out the omitted words. Students unable to use these context clues need instructional assistance with this reading strategy.

Activities using a modified cloze format also provide diagnostic information. To determine the extent of the student's vocabulary, students may be asked to list as many words as they can think of to complete each blank. Students with limited vocabularies will encounter difficulty in completing the assignment, indicating to the teacher their need for further vocabulary study.

Another activity using a modified cloze format provides choices of visually or meaning similar words to complete the blank, requiring the student to use context, vocabulary knowledge, and decoding strategies to determine the correct response. Teachers may also design passages omitting all adjectives or other parts of speech allowing students to create their own selections. Activities with a modified cloze format not only provide the teacher with varying types of information but they also provide students with experience in using the cloze format and context clues. This experience is important in comprehension development especially when taking standardized tests which measure comprehension using a modified cloze format.

The value of the cloze procedure, like an IRI, depends on teacher analysis with information regarding reading levels being of secondary importance. The cloze procedure is a good diagnostic technique for use in content classes at all levels. It can be administered to groups of students, thereby minimizing the loss of teaching time in diagnosis, and maximizing the amount of information gained from the instrument. A sample cloze test is provided in figure 2.7.

Content Reading Inventory

A Content Reading Inventory (CRI) is a procedure used by content teachers to diagnose the specific reading skills necessary to learn the concepts in a content area lesson. The teacher must first *identify the concepts* or content to be taught during a particular period of time. Using these concepts, the teacher then *identifies the reading skills* needed to learn the content. The CRI can be developed when these two aspects, concepts and reading skills, are identified as in the example below.

Concept Generalizations
To determine the location of Pearl Harbor.
To understand the meaning of the quote "I shall return."
To understand the significance of the Battle of the Coral Sea.
To understand the term "unconditional surrender."
To realize the impact of the use of the atomic bomb on Hiroshima and Nagasaki.
Reading Skills
Using the atlas
Interpretation
Cause-effect relationships
Main idea
Word meanings
Prefixes
Drawing conclusions
Anticipating outcomes
Evaluation

For each of the identified reading skills, three to five questions are generated using the content materials at an appropriate reading level for the students. The student uses the materials to answer the questions. Sample questions developed from the previous example appear in the following outline.

Figure 2.7
Sample Cloze Selection

What factors affect local climate?

Mountains affect the local climate in a region. They change the movement _____ air masses. Mountains also
(1)
_____ patterns of precipitation. The _____ shows air being forced _____ over a mountain. As _____
(2)   (3)   (4)   (5)
rising air cools, water _____ in the air condenses _____ forms clouds. Rain or _____ falls on the side
(6)   (7)   (8)
_____ the mountain where the _____ is rising. By the _____ the air reaches the _____ of the mountain,
(9)   (10)   (11)   (12)
it _____ lost most of its _____ . So the air that _____ down the other side _____ the mountain is dry.
(13)   (14)   (15)   (16)
_____ bodies of water affect _____ climate of nearby land. _____ near water often have _____ rain
(17)   (18)   (19)   (20)
or snow than _____ far from water. Places _____ large bodies of water _____ have smaller differences
(21)   (22)   (23)
between _____ summer and winter temperatures _____ do places far from _____ . Water heats and cools
(24)   (25)   (26)
_____ slowly than does land. _____ the water is cooler _____ nearby land, the air _____ the land is cooled.
(27)   (28)   (29)   (30)
_____ the water is warmer _____ nearby land, the air _____ the land is warmed.
(31)   (32)   (33)
_____ prevailing winds over an _____ affect climate. Regions where _____ prevailing winds _____
(34)   (35)   (36)   (37)
from over the oceans _____ a lot of precipitation.
(38)
_____ affects climate. Altitude is _____ distance above sea level. _____ high altitudes the air _____
(39)   (40)   (41)   (42)
tends to be lower _____ at low altitudes. The _____ tree and the mountain _____ are both near the _____ .
(43)   (44)   (45)   (46)
Yet the top of _____ mountain, which is almost _____ km (about 3.5 mi) _____ sea level, is covered _____
(47)   (48)   (49)   (50)
snow. What does that tell you about the temperature at the top of the mountain?

Source: Mallinson, G. G. et al, *Science* Horizons (Morristown, New Jersey: Silver Burdett & Ginn, 1991). Reprinted with permission of Silver Burdett & Ginn, Morristown, New Jersey.

Sample Questions for Content Reading Inventory

I. Vocabulary Development
    A. Word Meaning: Directions—Turn to page 30. Write a brief definition of the term "unconditional surrender."
    B. Prefixes: Directions—Turn to page 30. Now that you have defined the term "unconditional surrender," what does the prefix *un* mean?
II. Comprehension
    A. Author's purpose: Directions—Turn to page 25. What does MacArthur mean by the quote, "I shall return"?
    B. Cause-effect relationships: Directions—Turn to page 28. What is the significance of the Battle of the Coral Sea?
    C. Evaluation: Directions—Turn to page 31. How important was the decision to use the atomic bomb on Hiroshima and Nagasaki?
    D. Anticipating outcomes: Directions—Turn to page 32. How has this decision to use the atomic bomb in World War II affected present-day relationships between countries?
III. Reference Skills
    Using the atlas: Directions—Turn to the map on page 35. Locate the Pearl Harbor naval base.

Thus, the student is asked to read specified materials and provide written responses to the questions prior to beginning the unit. With information gathered about each student's knowledge of necessary reading skills, the teacher can determine alternative teaching procedures to help each student develop better skills and learn the content material more easily.

One of the advantages of the CRI is that it can be administered several times during the year, using different material each time. Because it is important to ascertain the students' progress throughout the year, and because the CRI is a group test, it has obvious advantages over other informal and standardized instruments, especially for the content teacher. Using this instrument, the teacher can assess the progress students have made in learning to apply reading skills in content reading. An important point to remember is that not all students are reading at the same level; therefore, materials at various levels are needed to assess the skills. Usually the textbook is used with those reading at or above level, a textbook from a lower level with those who are two or three years below grade level, and an elementary textbook for those greatly below level. Unless this differentiation is made, the teacher will be unable to determine whether the student cannot apply the skill or just cannot read the material.

The CRI provides teachers an informal way to determine the extent to which their students apply their knowledge of reading to their content materials. This inventory evaluates strategies used as students are reading to learn as compared to many other informal procedures, which measure how well students are learning to read. The CRI has a place in every classroom that students are asked to read informational materials.

Oral and Written Language Assessments

As teachers are faced with sorting through the maze and myths relating to reading instruction in today's schools, the basic questions are: Is it whole language? Should I teach skills? Similarly, teachers may shy away from the concept of diagnostic-prescriptive reading instruction equating this to skills instruction. Teachers whose reading instruction is viewed as 'whole language' or literature-based or language-based are continuously involved in evaluation. Among the myths relating to whole language, Newman and Church have identified three dealing specifically with evaluation:

- There's no evaluation in whole language.
- In whole language classrooms there are no standards; anything goes.
- Whole language teachers deal just with process; the product doesn't matter.[40]

These myths are, of course, fallacies; whole language teachers evaluate throughout their instruction based on the specific objectives established striving for an enhanced product—a child who can read and loves to read! These teachers are continuously using informal procedures to evaluate the language process in order to provide appropriate activities that capture interests, improve attitudes, encourage learning, and explore the unknown. Although all of the previously discussed informal diagnostic procedures can provide information about the students' oral and written language skills, there are other informal strategies which focus directly on reading as a language process. Teachers using a language approach to reading instruction realize that "learning is too complex and assessment too imperfect to rely on any single index of achievement."[41] They use many forms with many different labels such as observation or "kid-watching", checklists, written records, objective or performance-based assessments, portfolios, and holistic assessment procedures. In the following pages, additional informal assessment procedures that focus on language assessment are presented.

Think-Alouds. Comprehension monitoring is the purpose of using the think-aloud. This procedure requires readers to provide verbal self-reports about their thinking process to obtain information about how they construct meaning from text. Using prior knowledge of the text information, the student uses his schema to develop a hypothesis of what the text will say and then reads to test the hypothesis. Responding to one hypothesis leads to the development of another and reading becomes an interactive process between the text information and the background knowledge of the reader. Ideally, readers process text in this manner, allowing new information to affect their existing knowledge and enhancing their schema or storage of information. However, poor comprehenders rely only upon the text for information seeming to forget that they may have prior knowledge in the area. Poor comprehenders may also be identified as those who rely exclusively on their background knowledge and allow new information to have little impact on what they already believe—these students develop an understanding according to their definitions, learning little from the author.

The think-aloud procedure is a form of verbal reporting that requires the student to read short selections and talk about what comes to mind as the reading occurs.

Table 2.6

Procedure for Administering and Scoring a Comprehension Think-Aloud

I. **Preparing the text**
    Choose a short passage (expository or narrative) written to meet the following criteria:
    1. The text should be from 80 to 200 words in length, depending on the reader's age and reading ability.
    2. The text should be new to the reader, but on a topic that is familiar to him or her. (Determine whether the reader has relevant background knowledge by means of an interview or questionnaire administered at a session prior to this assessment.)
    3. The text should be at the reader's instructional level, which can be determined by use of an informal reading inventory. Passages at this level are most likely to be somewhat challenging while not overwhelming readers with word identification problems.
    4. The topic sentence should appear last, and the passage should be untitled. Altering the text in this way will elicit information about the reader's strategies for making sense of the passage and inferring topic.
    5. The text should be divided into segments of one to four sentences each.
II. **Administering the think aloud procedure**
    1. Tell the reader that he or she will be reading a story in short segments of one or more sentences.
    2. Tell the reader that after reading each section, he or she will be asked to tell what the story is about.
    3. Have the student read a segment aloud. After each segment is read, ask the reader to tell what is happening, followed by nondirective probe questions as necessary. The questions should encourage the reader to generate hypotheses (what do you think this is about?) and to describe what he or she based the hypotheses on (what clues in the story helped you?).
    4. Continue the procedure until the entire passage is read. Then ask the reader to retell the entire passage in his or her own words. (The reader may reread the story first.)
    5. The examiner might also ask the reader to find the most important sentence(s) in the passage.
    6. The session should be tape-recorded and transcribed. The examiner should also record observations of the child's behaviors.
III. **Analyzing results**
    Ask the following questions when analyzing the transcript:
    1. Does the reader generate hypotheses?
    2. Does he support hypotheses with information from the passage?
    3. What information from the text does the reader use?
    4. Does he/she relate material in the text to background knowledge or previous experience?
    5. Does the reader integrate new information with the schema he/she has already activated?
    6. What does the reader do if there is information that conflicts with the schema he/she has generated?
    7. At what point does the reader recognize what the story is about?
    8. How does the reader deal with unfamiliar words?
    9. What kinds of integration strategies does the reader use (e.g., visualization)?
    10. How confident is the reader of his hypotheses?
    11. What other observations can be made about the reader's behavior, strategies, etc.?

Source: Suzanne E. Wade, "Using Think Alouds to Access Comprehension," *The Reading Teacher 43* (March 1990): 445.

This is done one-to-one with the teacher providing vague probes such as "Is there anything else?" or "Can you tell me more?" The information is tape-recorded with non-verbal actions such as signs of frustrations or puzzled looks recorded via teacher notes. As a teacher hears what the student is thinking as reading occurs, analysis of comprehension strategies can occur. Table 2.6 provides a summary of the procedures for administering and scoring a comprehension think aloud.

From analysis of think-aloud assessments, Wade categorizes comprehenders as:

- The good comprehender who constructs meaning and monitors comprehension while interacting with text;
- The non-risk taker who tries to remember what the text says but never goes beyond the text to hypothesize;
- The non-integrator who uses text clues and prior knowledge and continuously forms new hypotheses never relating previous hypotheses to the information presented;
- The schema imposer who holds on to an initial hypotheses regardless of the information presented; and
- The storyteller who draws more on prior knowledge than information presented.[42]

The think-aloud procedure allows the teacher to assess the comprehension process through personal dialogue with the student. Knowing how students think as they read greatly assists the teacher in providing appropriate instructional guidance to expand comprehension.

Portfolio Assessment. As teachers have attempted to evaluate the oral and written language development of their students through the years, they have used samples of the student's work over a period of time. The concept of a collection of the best work in various areas being brought together as a portfolio has long been used with artists, designers, and other professionals needing to show their products. This concept is now being translated into education, elementary through university programs, as teachers organize a variety of samples of student's work to evaluate learning. Valencia suggests that a portfolio approach to reading assessment is well founded intuitively, theoretically and pragmatically. She summarizes with four guiding principles.

1. Authenticity is basic to sound assessment and portfolios are comprised of authentic tasks, texts, and contexts experienced by the student.
2. Assessment is an on-going, continuous, process which must reflect development. Portfolios are formed from a collection of the best work of students over a period of time.
3. Reading is a multifaceted process requiring assessment via a variety of means that reflect the cognitive processes, attitudinal interaction with print, and literacy activities reflective of the reading-language process.
4. Students and teachers must be active participants in the assessment process which encourages collaboration and reflection by both participants.[43]

Portfolios are another approach to obtaining diagnostic information about a student's performance in reading and language. The contents of a portfolio are dependent upon the ideas of the teacher and student, however, the information could be organized in an expandable file folder and include (a) samples of the student's work selected by the teacher or the student, (b) the teacher's observational notes, (c) periodic self-evaluations done by the student, and (d) progress notes of the student and teacher.[44] Variety is the essential element when considering the contents of the portfolio, however, the student and teacher must be selective about what is included so that the portfolio is reflective of the best of the student's work and not a collection of all of the student's work.

■ Miscellaneous Sources

Teachers sometimes overlook many sources from which they can informally obtain much diagnostic information without ever testing a student. These sources include the daily work of the student, such as workbook pages, learning center activities, and instructional games. Additionally, the teacher can use information from parent conferences and discussions with the students' other teachers to assist in a diagnostic-prescriptive reading program. These miscellaneous sources of data exist in every classroom and are necessary in order to provide continuous diagnosis in reading.

Daily classroom activities are used to assess progress in language and specific skill development, and to note strengths and weaknesses as well as feelings toward the tasks. Observant classroom teachers make notes regarding individual student errors. Errors such as difficulty with specific word identification skills or responding to literal comprehension questions are noted so that appropriate instruction is provided. Workbook pages can serve as a source to reinforce observations made in the reading group or to alert the teacher to look for particular difficulties. The *workbook exercises* are excellent criterion-referenced tests for the teacher who has identified the specific tasks to be taught in the reading class. Thus, in a diagnostic-prescriptive reading program, workbook pages are not used for busywork, but are an integral part of the diagnostic procedures.

Likewise, *learning centers* are used as informal diagnostic resources. As students participate in the prescribed activities of the learning centers, teachers note, through observation and student feedback, the areas of strengths and weaknesses. For example, a learning center devoted to the study of contractions allows the teacher to determine which students have no understanding of contractions, which can understand simple contractions, and which use contractions in their oral and written communication.

Instructional games, whether purchased or teacher-made, provide the same types of diagnostic information as the learning centers. Teachers may group students to work as teams with specific games and ask them to report the difficulties encountered in the activity. Using these diagnostic procedures will assist the classroom teacher in several ways.

1. Less teaching time is spent in administering paper-pencil tests.
2. More diagnostic data is continuously being used to assist in providing appropriate instruction.

3. Students are not continuously facing testing situations and developing a careless attitude toward tests.
4. Evaluation is an integral part of the instructional program, a fact that enhances the concept of diagnostic teaching.

In addition to these sources of data, remember that the students' *parents* provide excellent information that aids in diagnosis. Brief conversations with parents give answers to questions such as:

- Does the student spend any time reading at home?
- Do the parents read at home or do they read to the student?
- What is the family's attitude toward reading?
- How does the mother or father feel about the student's performance in school?
- What kind of family life does the student have?
- Are there reading materials in the home?

Parents are valuable sources of information. They assist by answering these general types of questions; for students with severe reading difficulties, parents can provide information as to possible physical or emotional difficulties that may have contributed to the reading problem. In a diagnostic-prescriptive reading program, everyone and everything is used to assist in supplying the appropriate instruction to the individual student.

■ Tips on Informal Testing

Teachers rely to a great extent on informal testing procedures in order to provide appropriate instruction. As mentioned previously, experience is one of the best teachers in interpreting the various informal assessments. However, there are some suggestions that may help the teacher who is just beginning to use informal diagnostic procedures in the classroom.

Make these testing situations as informal as possible. Much diagnosis can be made by using observation techniques and analysis of classroom work.

Check the readability levels of all materials used in informal testing. Unless the teacher knows the approximate level of the materials, the level on which the student succeeds or fails cannot be determined.

Various instruments should be used in informally diagnosing reading difficulties. No one instrument can provide all the needed data.

Limit the testing time according to an individual student's interest and attention span.

Verify data from one instrument by using your opinion, or another form or procedure for testing a given area. Do not draw conclusions based on limited information from one observation or test.

Ask for assistance from fellow teachers. Consult with others as you reveiw the diagnostic information on students. It is quite likely that another person can assist you in obtaining more information from the informal tests.

■ Physical Factors

The previous sections of this chapter have focused primarily on the assessment of cognitive performance in reading with some information related to the affective areas. However, to properly diagnose and prescribe effective learning activities, teachers must be aware of the many physical factors which may hinder learning. Physical problems are formally diagnosed by a medical doctor but the initial observation and informal diagnosis is frequently noted by the classroom teacher. The physical factors commonly related to reading difficulties are discussed in three categories: (1) Visual and auditory acuity, (2) Alcohol and drugs, and (3) Nutrition.

Visual and Auditory Acuity

Physical factors such as poor auditory and visual acuity account for many difficulties diagnosed in reading. The teacher who suspects a reading problem should first determine whether the problem is in part caused by a physical handicap that can be corrected. Because teachers may not have the necessary equipment to properly diagnose these acuity problems, careful observation is very valuable until a more thorough diagnosis can be made. The following lists present signs of vision and hearing problems.

Indicators of Visual Acuity Problems

Headache in forehead or temples
Rubbing eyes frequently
Tilting head
Holding book too close to face
Losing place in reading
Blinking excessively
Frequent errors in copying
Tense during visual work
Squinting or covering one eye
Nausea or dizziness
Reddened eyes
Poor sitting position
Excessive head movement in reading
Avoiding close visual work
Frequent styes or encrusted eyelids
Blurring of print while reading
Excessive tearing
Fatigued and distraught while reading

Indicators of Auditory Acuity Problems

Monotonous voice pitch
Cupping hand behind ear
Turning ear toward speaker
Misunderstands directions frequently
Requests speaker to repeat statements
Generally inattentive
Poor pronunciation abnormal to age
Turning record player/radio to unusually loud volume
Difficulty in auditory discrimination tasks
Hears ringing or buzzing sounds in ear
Has blank expression
Strained posture in listening
Excessive amounts of wax in ears

Visual Acuity

There is disagreement about the exact degree to which vision contributes to reading achievement. There seems, however, to be a correlation. In a survey of sixty-nine students referred to the university reading clinic, the authors noted that twenty-three, or exactly one-third, were referred for further visual examinations. Technical terms used to describe various types of visual problems include:

Amblyopia: commonly called "lazy eye." This is lowered acuity in one eye, possibly because of suppression.

Aniseikonia: the image of an object is formed in a different size or shape in each eye.

Astigmatism: a blurring vision due to an uneven curvature of the front of the eye. Not usually related to reading problems.

Convergence: the degree to which the eyes turn in to focus on the same object.

Fixation: skill in holding fusion on a given object.

Fusion: the ability of both eyes to align so that the object is centered. Without proper fusion, double vision results.

Hyperopia: farsightedness, or the ability to see objects at a distance but not close.

Myopia: nearsightedness, or the ability to see objects close but not at a distance.

Strabismus: lack of binocular coordination due to a muscular imbalance of one or both eyes.

In assessing visual acuity, schools have previously used the *Snellen Chart* or the *E Chart.* These charts measure only distance vision. In addition, vision is tested in only one eye at a time; this is unnatural. These tests are not recommended for use in determining whether a student has a vision problem contributing to a reading difficulty. Other instruments that provide a more accurate diagnosis are listed on the following pages. While this list is not exhaustive, it gives information on the various types of visual screening instruments available. Additional information on visual screening can be found in *Screening Vision in Schools.*[45]

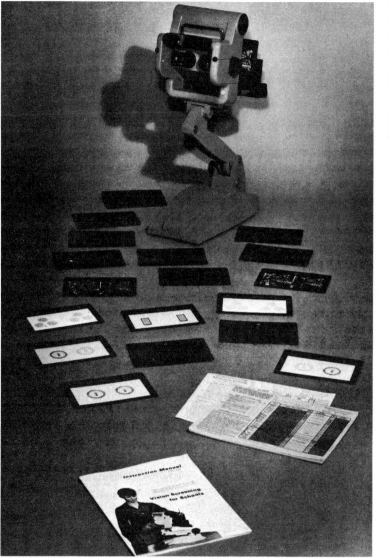

Figure 2.8
Keystone Telebinocular Reproduced by permission of Mast Keystone 4673 Aircenter Circle, Reno, NV 89502.

Keystone Visual Survey Tests
Mast Keystone, Reno, NV

The *Keystone Telebinocular* (figure 2.8) is a viewer used with a series of slides to measure the following areas: Simultaneous Perception, Vertical Imbalance, Lateral Posture at Far Point, Fusion at Far Point, Usable Vision of Both Eyes at Far Point, Stereopsis, Color Blindness, Lateral Posture at Near Point, Fusion at Near Point,

Visual Acuity of Both Eyes at Near Point, Visual Acuity of Right Eye at Near Point, and Visual Acuity of Left Eye at Near Point. These tests are used to screen for possible nearsightedness, farsightedness, astigmatism, muscular imbalance, lack of fusion at the near and far points, binocular efficiency, stereopsis level or depth perception, and color blindness.

Teachers need no specialized training to administer this test, but care is needed in recording and interpreting the record form. This screening instrument, like others, tends to over-refer for further analysis. However, it is a very thorough screening device in reading diagnosis.

Ortho-Rater
Bausch and Lomb Optical Company, Rochester, New York

The *Ortho-Rater* is a vision screening device originally designed for adult and industrial use. The subtests were restandardized by Helen M. Robinson for use in schools and clinics. This instrument, like the *Keystone Visual Screening Tests*, tends to over-refer students, especially young children.

The tests included with this instrument are Acuity Far (right eye), Acuity Far (left eye), Far Sightedness (right eye), Far Sightedness (left eye), Phoria Far, Phoria Near, Depth Perception, and Color Blindness.

Auditory Acuity
Auditory or hearing acuity is the ability to hear pitches of sounds at varying levels of loudness. The different degrees of loudness are measured in decibels, while the pitch or frequency of sounds is measured in cycles per second or hertz.

Auditory acuity is measured by an instrument known as an audiometer. There are many different types of audiometers; however, they all function in basically the same way.

The teacher places earphones on the student and faces the student away from the instrument. Setting the audiometer at the correct decibels according to the manual, the teacher begins testing at various frequencies. The student is directed to signal when a sound is heard. The tones are cut off by an interrupter switch to allow the teacher to change the frequencies and decibels, if necessary. The teacher records the responses on an audiogram. When testing is complete, the marks are joined by a line to provide a profile of the student's hearing in each ear. The frequencies to be tested range from about 125 to 8000 cycles per second. Students with a hearing loss between 500 and 2500 cycles per second in one or both ears should be referred for a closer examination. These students may experience difficulty in school because the female teacher's voice tends to be at a higher frequency. Additionally, some consonant sounds are at higher frequencies.

Note that some slight hearing losses may be transitory, because of ear infections and other temporary conditions. Therefore, the teacher may recheck the student in several weeks before referring for further testing. More specific information on the administration and interpretation using various audiometers is contained in the manuals that accompany the instruments. Several companies that provide the more frequently used audiometers are listed below. It should be noted that, although some companies provide tests that can be administered in a group situation, they are not as reliable as individually-administered tests.

Auditory Instrument Division
Zenith Radio Corporation
6501 W. Grand Avenue
Chicago, Illinois 60635

Beltone Electronics Corporation
Hearing Test Instruments Division
4201 W. Victoria Street
Chicago, Illinois 60646

Maico Hearing Instruments
7375 Bush Lake Road
Minneapolis, Minnesota 55435

Other companies such as Grayton Electric, Audiometer Sales Corporation, Royal Industries, Precision Acoustics Corporation, and Sonotone Corporation provide audiometers that are adapted for school use.

Alcohol and Drugs

As changes occur in society so do the schools. Alcohol and drug use has skyrocketed resulting in school-related issues: (1) Children whose mother was a substance abuser during pregnancy, (2) Children born with alcohol or drug addiction due to use by the mother, and (3) Children using alcohol and drugs. Chronic substance abuse of the mother during pregnancy results in several types of abnormality which affect learning. Central nervous system development is maximal during the first 3 months of pregnancy and protein starvation (which occurs with substance abuse) during this period is devastating for future intellectual development. If brain tissue does not receive proper nourishment at this time, repair cannot be achieved later. Thus, children will likely have lower intelligence or a learning disability. Techniques for teaching these students are discussed in a later chapter.

Schools are seeing more children born with a substance abuse addiction. These children, while no longer addicted, have mental, physical, and emotional problems caused by the addiction. Crack cocaine babies become students in the classroom evidencing behavior such as severe mood swings, short attention spans, difficulty in processing information, delayed mental and physical development, to mention only a few of the noted behaviors. Research is lacking as to the best ways to teach these children, but as part of the diagnostic process, the teacher must attempt to determine the cause of these behaviors and be assured that the problem is indeed birth-related rather than current.

Substance abuse with alcohol and drugs seems to begin at earlier ages each year. Drugs are available to many young children making it necessary for teachers to be aware of the symptoms of drug use. They are:

- Mood swings from lethargic to silly high.
- Inattentive in group and individual situations.
- Social disruptions in class.
- Keeps distance from acquaintances—tends to work alone.
- Poor nutrition and sleep habits.
- Regularly late or sick.
- Dilated pupils.
- Does not keep promises.
- Looks for sources of money.
- Seems depressed.

While all of these symptoms may not be observed, teachers should seek assistance if several symptoms appear or there is an overall change in a student's behavior. The first person to contact is the school counselor who should be able to do the necessary follow-up to obtain assistance for the student.

Nutrition

The effect of nutrition on learning was once described briefly by saying that the hungry child cannot concentrate on learning. While this is an accurate statement, the impact of nutrition on learning is an area of intense investigation. Children need food and they need food on a regular basis, i.e. breakfast, lunch, snacks, dinner. However, the types of food provided have a significant impact on learning, an impact that varies from student to student. Basically, we know that diets high in sugar products tend to decrease attention spans. Some students become hyperactive, unable to control their physical movement and focus on learning tasks. Diets high in sugar and refined carbohydrates negatively effect eye movements, including fixations and regressions.[46]

As more is learned about the impact of diet on learning, learning deficiencies can be traced to food allergies ranging from flour to red meat. In diagnosis, teachers need to be aware of changing behaviors in students and determine if these behaviors are related to a need for food or types of food eaten. Students with low blood sugar levels may blank out when in need of food while students with an allergy to flour may zoom around the room after a lunch of pasta and bread.

■ Summary

Many informal diagnostic procedures were presented in this chapter. Because of the growing importance of the teacher in the diagnostic-prescriptive process, informal measures are becoming the basis for instructional planning. Using informal diagnostic procedures, the teacher learns much about each student in the class.

Informal assessment procedures in reading are focusing on how students process information as they read in addition to their specific knowledge of reading skills. Observation was discussed as a valuable diagnostic tool. Using the two observational techniques of anecdotal records and checklists, teachers gain much information about the reading behaviors of students.

Informal instruments were also discussed. These included attitude and interest inventories, the Informal Reading Inventory, word recognition inventories, criterion-referenced/objective-based tests, cloze procedure, and Content Reading Inventory. Procedures for developing, administering, and interpreting these instruments were discussed.

Informal strategies for assessing oral and written language were also presented, including think-alouds and portfolios as well as miscellaneous classroom activities such as games and learning centers. In presenting the informal assessment strategies, the teacher was reminded to continuously assess using many sources of information to more adequately identify the student's reading behaviors when interacting with language in different situations.

Although the primary focus of this chapter was on the informal assessment of cognitive and affective behaviors related to reading, the last portion of the chapter reminded the teacher of the importance of physical factors in determining the instructional needs of a student. Visual and auditory acuity behaviors indicating difficulties that would affect reading were presented. Other physical factors which affect reading performance such as alcohol and drug use and nutrition were also included in this chapter.

■ Applying What You Read

Administer an informal reading inventory to five students and identify their areas of strengths and weaknesses. Then spend time observing these same five students to determine what additional information you glean from observation.

Using a checklist, observe several students and record your observations. From this data, determine what other informal assessment procedures may be needed to more specifically diagnose their reading needs.

Develop your own interest inventory. Administer this inventory to several poor readers and several good readers. Compare the results.

Determine several specific objectives of your reading program. Develop objective-based assessment procedures to measure the objectives.

Make a list of sources of informal diagnostic data currently available in your classroom. How are you using this informaton? What other information do you need?

Identify three ways that writing is used daily in the elementary classroom. How can diagnostic information be obtained in each of these situations?

Portfolios sound like an interesting concept to incorporate into your informal assessment procedures. How would you initiate the development of portfolios and how would you maintain the information during the year? How would you introduce this information to parents?

■ Notes

1. Rebecca Harlin and Sally Lipa, "Emergent Literacy: A Comparison of Formal and Informal Assessment Methods," *Reading Horizons*.

2. Courtney B. Cazden, "Contexts for Literacy: In the Mind and in the Classroom," *Journal of Reading Behavior*.

3. Yetta M. Goodman, "Kid Watching: An Alternative to Testing," *National Elementary School Principal*.

4. A. C. Purves and Richard Beach, *Literature and the Reader: Research in Response to Literature, Reading Interests, and the Teaching of Literature*; Herbert J. Walberg and Shiow-Ling Tsai, "Correlates of Reading Achievement and Attitude: A National Assessment Study," *Journal of Educational Research*; M. Cecil Smith, "A Longitudinal Investigation of Reading Attitude Development from Childhood to Adulthood," *Journal of Educational Research*.

5. Irene Athey, "Reading Research in the Affective Domain," in *Theoretical Models and Processes of Reading*, 2nd ed., edited by Harry Singer and Robert Ruddell.

6. Frank Smith, *Understanding Reading: A Psycholinguistic Analysis of Reading and Learning to Read*, 4th ed.

7. Michael C. McKenna and Dennis J. Kear, "Measuring Attitude Toward Reading: A New Tool for Teachers," *The Reading Teacher*.

8. Charles Bruckerhoff, "What Do Students Say About Reading Instruction?" *The Clearing House*.

9. Kathleen S. Jongsma and Eugene A. Jongsma. "Test Review: Commercial Informal Reading Inventories," *The Reading Teacher*.

10. John J. Pikulski and Timothy Shanahan, eds.; "Informal Reading Inventories: A Critical Analysis," in *Approaches to the Informal Evaluation of Reading*; Page Bristow, John Pikulski, and Peter Pelosi, "A Comparison of Five Estimates of Instructional Level," *The Reading Teacher*.

11. Valerie A. Helgren-Lempesis and Charles T. Mangrum II, "An Analysis of Alternate-Form Reliability of Three Commercially-Prepared Informal Reading Inventories," *Reading Research Quarterly*.

12. John J. Pikulski, "A Critical Review: Informal Reading Inventories," *The Reading Teacher*.

13. Eldon E. Ekwall, "Informal Reading Inventories: The Instructional Level," *The Reading Teacher*; Eldon Ekwall, "Should Repetitions Be Counted as Errors?" *The Reading Teacher*; Warren S. Hays, "Criteria for the Instructional Level of Reading," 1975, Microfiche ED 117 665; John Pikulski, "A Critical Review: Informal Reading Inventories," *The Reading Teacher*.

14. Jerry L. Johns and Anne Marie Magliari, "Informal Reading Inventories: Are the Betts Criteria the Best Criteria?" *Reading Improvement*.

15. Maud McBroom, Julia Sparrow, and Catherine Eckstein, *Scale for Determining a Child's Reader Level*.

16. Yetta M. Goodman and Carolyn L. Burke, *Reading Miscue Inventory*.

17. Jean Wallace Gillet and Charles Temple, *Understanding Reading Problems: Assessment and Instruction*.

18. Frederick A. Duffelmeyer and Barbara Blakelly Duffelmeyer, "Are IRI Passages Suitable for Assessing Main Idea Comprehension?" *The Reading Teacher*.

19. Frederick A. Duffelmeyer, Susan S. Robinson, and Susan E. Squire, "Vocabulary Questions on Informal Reading Inventories," *The Reading Teacher*.

20. James R. Kalmbach, "Getting at the Point of Retellings," *Journal of Reading*; Karen D. Wood, "Free Associational Assessment: An Alternative to Traditional Testing," *Journal of Reading*.

21. Jay S. Blanchard, *Computer Based Reading Assessment Instrument*.

22. Jerry L. Johns, *Computer-Based Graded Word Lists*.

23. Michael McKenna, *Computer Assisted Reading Achievement*. Southern Micro Systems, Burlington, NC.

24. William A. Henk, "Reading Assessments of the Future: Toward Precision Diagnosis," *The Reading Teacher*.

25. Child Study Committee on the International Kindergarten Union, *A Study of the Vocabulary of Children Before Entering First Grade*; Arthur I. Gates, *A Reading Vocabulary for the Primary Grades*; H. E. Wheeler and Emma A. Howell, "A First Grade Vocabulary Study," *Elementary School Journal*.

26. Dale D. Johnson, "The Dolch List Re-Examined," *The Reading Teacher*; Robert L. Hillerich, "Word Lists: Getting It All Together," *The Reading Teacher*.

27. Edward Fry, "A New Instant Word List," *The Reading Teacher*.

28. Maryann Eeds, "Bookwords: Using a Beginning Word List of High Frequency Words from Children's Literature K–3." *The Reading Teacher*.

29. Henry Kucera and W. Nelson Francis, *Computational Analysis for Present-Day American English*; Albert J. Harris and Milton D. Jacobson, *Basic Elementary Reading Vocabularies*; Stanford E. Taylor, Helen Frackenpohl, and Catherine White, *A Revised Core Vocabulary: A Basic Vocabulary for Grades 1–8, an Advanced Vocabulary for Grades 9–13*; John B. Carroll, Peter Davies, and Barry Richman, *Word Frequency Book*;

Wayne Otto and Robert Chester, "Sight Words for Beginning Readers," *Journal of Educational Research*; Dale D. Johnson, Alden Moe, with James Bauman, *The Ginn Word Book for Teachers*.

30. Richard L. Slosson, *Slosson Oral Reading Test*.

31. J. F. Jastak, S. W. Bijou, and S. R. Jastak, *Wide Range Achievement Test*.

32. Wayne Otto, "Evaluating Instruments for Assessing Needs and Growth in Reading," *Assessment Problems in Reading*, pp. 17–18.

33. Otto, "Evaluating Instruments," p. 18.

34. April 1987 issue of *The Reading Teacher*.

35. Wilson L. Taylor, "Cloze Procedure: A New Tool for Measuring Readability," *Journalism Quarterly*.

36. Eugene R. Jongsma, "The Cloze Procedure: A Survey of Research."

37. Clarie Ashby-Davis, "Cloze and Comprehension: A Qualitative Analysis and Critique," *Journal of Reading*.

38. John Jonz, "Another Turn in the Conversation: What Does Cloze Measure?" *TESOL Quarterly*; Michael C. McKenna and Kent Layton, "Concurrent Validity of Cloze as a Measure of Intersentential Comprehension," *Journal of Educational Psychology*; Roger J. DeSanti, "Concurrent and Predictive Validity of a Semantically and Syntactically Sensitive Cloze Scoring System," *Reading Research and Instruction*.

39. John Bormuth, "The Cloze Readability Procedure," *Elementary English*.

40. Judith M. Newman and Susan M. Church, "Myths of Whole Language," *The Reading Teacher*.

41. Sheila W. Valencia, "Alternative Assessment: Separating the Wheat from the Chaff," *The Reading Teacher*.

42. Suzanne E. Wade, "Using Think Alouds to Assess Comprehension," *The Reading Teacher*.

43. Sheila W. Valencia, "A Portfolio Approach to Classroom Reading Assessment: The Whys, Whats, and Hows," *The Reading Teacher*.

44. Valencia, "A Portfolio Approach," p. 339.

45. Fred W. Jobe. *Screening Vision in Schools*.

46. Patricia K. Hardman, Judith A. Clay, and Allan D. Lieberman, "The Effects of Diet and Sublingual Provocative Testing on Eye Movements with Dyslexic Individuals," *Journal of the American Optometric Association*.

■ Other Suggested Readings

Blanchard, Jay, and Jerry Johns. "Informal Reading Inventories—A Broader View." *Reading Psychology* 7 (1986): iii–vii.

Farr, Roger, and Robert Carey. *Reading: What Can Be Measured?* 2nd ed. Newark, Delaware: International Reading Association, 1986.

Johnson, Marjorie S., Roy A. Kress, and John J. Pikulski, *Informal Reading Inventories*, 2nd ed. Newark, Delaware: International Reading Association, 1987.

McKenna, Michael C. "Informal Reading Inventories: A Review of the Issues." *The Reading Teacher* 36 (March 1983): 670–79.

Schmitt, Maribeth Cassidy. "A Questionnaire to Measure Children's Awareness of Strategic Reading Processes." *The Reading Teacher* 43 (March 1990): 454–61.

Smith, Edwin H., Billy M. Guice, and Martha C. Cheek. "Informal Reading Inventories for the Content Areas: Science and Mathematics." *Elementary English* 46 (May 1972): 659–66.

Swanson, Beverly B. "Strategic Preferences of Good and Poor Beginning Readers." *Reading Horizons* 28 (Summer 1988): 255–62.

Valencia, Sheila W. "You Can't Have Authentic Assessment without Authentic Content." *The Reading Teacher* 44 (April 1991): 390–91.

3

Formal Diagnostic Procedures

Formal diagnostic procedures are defined as those instruments that are administered using specific guidelines and that provide norms to compare a student's scores with those of other students of the same age or grade level. Classroom teachers are typically most familiar with the formal testing procedures associated with administering group achievement tests. Although these are formal testing procedures, unfortunately they usually do not qualify as diagnostic reading tests. This chapter is designed to familiarize the teacher with other formal diagnostic procedures that may be used in conjunction with the informal diagnostic procedures presented in chapter 2.

Teachers should use formal diagnostic procedures to further explore students' reading problems in order to provide more appropriate prescriptive instruction. They realize that some formal diagnostic instruments are administered to groups of students, while others must be administered individually. Most of these tests are relatively simple to administer. The teacher needs only to review the materials and administer the instrument several times under the supervision of a trained person prior to using it in the classroom.

This chapter reviews a variety of formal diagnostic procedures, including oral reading tests, diagnostic reading tests, auditory discrimination tests, intelligence tests, and survey reading tests. Specific questions addressed in the chapter include:

What are formal diagnostic procedures?

Why are formal procedures important in reading diagnosis?

What types of formal diagnostic procedures are available to evaluate reading difficulties?

What are some differences between individually-administered and group-administered formal diagnostic procedures?

How does the teacher select appropriate tests for use with given students?

What are the various individually-administered formal diagnostic instruments? How do they compare?

What are the various group-administered formal diagnostic instruments? How do they compare?

How are the different tests administered?

These terms should be noted as this chapter is read.

Vocabulary to Know

Formal diagnostic procedures
Group achievement tests
Group-administered formal tests
Group diagnostic tests

Group survey tests
Individual auditory discrimination
  tests
Individual diagnostic reading tests

Individual intelligence tests
Individual oral reading tests
Individually-administered formal
  tests

■ An Overview

Formal diagnostic procedures are the standardized techniques used by teachers and reading specialists to learn more about students' strengths and weaknesses in reading. However, as suggested by Bussis and Chittenden, "Although research of the past thirty years has fundamentally reshaped conceptions of language and language learning, these changes have yet to find expression in reading tests."[1] Likewise, Squire and Valencia and Pearson say that our research in reading reflects the importance of reading as a process, emphasizing cognitive processing, yet our assessment in the classroom continues at the skills level.[2] This contrast is vividly represented in table 3.1. Current literature is filled with descriptions of how reading is a holistic process with prior knowledge and language being essential to comprehension. However, the tests on today's market represent a more traditional view of reading as a skills-oriented procedure for which tests can provide data as to the strengths and weaknesses in the various specific areas, especially word identification and general comprehension. Thus, this chapter on formal diagnostic procedures presents information on instruments currently available to teachers—some of the newer instruments are attempting to incorporate our research knowledge while others continue to reflect tradition. In viewing formal diagnostic testing at this time, it must be said that reading educators are at a crossroads. Hopefully with the next edition of this text, more tests will be available that better reflect our current knowledge, and alternate methods for gathering diagnostic data will be more widely accepted.

One major change has already occurred as we suggest that formal diagnostic procedures be used to supplement informal procedures. Informal procedures, as outlined in chapter 2, allow more latitude in the testing situation; they are not bound by the standardization procedures required of formal tests. Teacher use of formal diagnostic tests should be limited to the use of select tests to gain more information on a specific problem area identified by informal diagnostic procedures. Thus, neither large amounts of teacher nor student time is necessary for formal diagnostic procedures; they are administered only as the teacher needs more information.

Table 3.1

A Set of Contrasts between New Views of Reading and Current Practices in Assessing Reading

New views of the reading process tell us that . . .	**Yet when we assess reading comprehension, we . . .**
Prior knowledge is an important determinant of reading comprehension.	Mask any relationship between prior knowledge and reading comprehension by using lots of short passages on lots of topics.
A complete story or text has structural and topical integrity.	Use short texts that seldom approximate the structural and topical integrity of an authentic text.
Inference is an essential part of the process of comprehending units as small as sentences.	Rely on literal comprehension test items.
The diversity in prior knowledge across individuals as well as the varied causal relations in human experiences invite many possible inferences to fit a text or question.	Use multiple choice items with only one correct answer, even when many of the responses might, under certain conditions, be plausible.
The ability to vary reading strategies to fit the text and the situation is one hallmark of an expert reader.	Seldom assess how and when students vary the strategies they use during normal reading, studying, or when the going gets tough.
The ability to synthesize information from various parts of the text and different texts is a hallmark of an expert reader.	Rarely go beyond finding the main idea of a paragraph or passage.
The ability to ask good questions of text, as well as to answer them, is a hallmark of an expert reader.	Seldom ask students to create or select questions about a selection they may have just read.
All aspects of a reader's experience, including habits that arise from school and home, influence reading comprehension.	Rarely view information on reading habits and attitudes as being important information about performance.
Reading involves the orchestration of many skills that complement one another in a variety of ways.	Use tests that fragment reading into isolated skills and report performance on each.
Skilled readers are fluent; their word identification is sufficiently automatic to allow most cognitive resources to be used for comprehension.	Rarely consider fluency as an index of skilled reading.
Learning from text involves the restructuring, application, and flexible use of knowledge in new situations.	Often ask readers to respond to the text's declarative knowledge rather than to apply it to near and far transfer tasks.

Sheila Valencia and P. David Pearson, "Reading Assessment: Time for a Change," *The Reading Teacher* 40 (April 1987): 731. Reprinted with permission of Sheila Valencia and P. David Pearson and the International Reading Association.

Formal diagnostic procedures, like informal diagnostic procedures, have both advantages and disadvantages. Realistically for the teacher, the chief disadvantages may be the time needed for the individually-administered instruments and the acquisition of a sufficient number of copies of a test for use as necessary. To deal with these problems, teachers (1) use group tests whenever possible and request the assistance of the reading teacher if numerous individual tests are needed, and (2) select initially only one or two formal tests that seem to best meet the general needs of students, then build a test file in the school over several years.

The advantages of formal diagnostic procedures definitely outnumber the disadvantages. Although the time factor for individual testing may be viewed as a disadvantage, the one-to-one testing situation is an advantage in itself, because the teacher learns more about the student. Additionally, formal diagnostic procedures provide the teacher with a more complete profile of the student, as well as with some comparison of the student with others of a similar age. Although diagnosis is not based on this comparative data, this data assists in communicating with parents.

The tests presented in this chapter are classified as group or individual tests with further breakdowns according to types. The tests classified as individual formal diagnostic procedures are administered to only one student at a time. These are more time consuming and require increased proficiency and experience on the part of the examiner to interpret the information. However, they yield much valuable information and assist in determining more accurately students' strengths and weaknesses.

Group-administered formal tests can be used to test large or small groups of students; however, these tests may not yield as much information on the individual student, and the teacher does not learn the helpful personal information gained in an individual testing situation. This lack of specific information combined with the time factor involved in scoring and interpreting test results may dissuade teachers from using these tests.

Because of the various factors involved in implementing diagnostic-prescriptive instruction, a concern of the classroom teacher is when to use these formal tools. Practically speaking, using group tests is probably a more realistic objective than using individual tests. As already stated, group tests are relatively easy to administer since the time involved is minimal and an entire class can be tested at one time. The teacher's schedule can be adjusted for several hours to accommodate this type of testing.

Individual formal instruments are time consuming to administer, because students must be tested on a one-to-one basis. These instruments require time as well as more specialized training for administration, scoring, and interpretation. Thus, they are best used as supplements to informal measures and formal group measures. However, individual formal instruments play an important role in an in-depth diagnosis of a small number of students in the classroom.

Because of the constraints associated with individual formal instruments, a classroom teacher's testing time may be more wisely spent using group tests in conjunction with the informal procedures already discussed in chapter 2. Nevertheless, in the case of a severely disabled reader, the teacher may use one or two well-chosen, individually-administered instruments. The teacher needs a workable knowledge of these instruments in order to better understand reports from the reading specialist or to request further testing from other outside sources. *Regardless of the pros and cons of using formal diagnostic procedures, teachers must be familiar with them in order to provide better prescriptive reading instruction in their classes.* To assist the teacher in selecting appropriate formal diagnostic procedures, the tests discussed in this chapter

Table 3.2

Formal Group Tests

Test	Appropriate Levels	Subtest Scores
Survey Tests		
Boehm Test of Basic Concepts— Revised	Grades K–2	Total Score of Concept Knowledge
Gates—MacGinitie Reading Tests	Grades K–12	Vocabulary, Comprehension, Total
Iowa Silent Reading Test	Grades 6–12, College	Vocabulary, Comprehension, Directed Reading, Reading Efficiency
Diagnostic Reading Tests		
MAT6 Reading Diagnostic Tests	Grades K.5–9.9	Varies with form—Visual Discrimination, Auditory Discrimination, Sight Vocabulary, Reading Comprehension, Rate of Comprehension
Stanford Diagnostic Reading Test	Grades 1.6–13	Varies with form—Auditory Vocabulary, Phonetic Analysis, Structural Analysis, Comprehension
Test of Reading Comprehension	Ages 7.0 to 7.11	General Reading Comprehension Core, General Vocabulary, Syntactic Similarities, Paragraph Reading, Sentence Sequencing
Achievement Tests		
California Achievement Test	Grades K–12	Reading, Spelling, Language, Mathematics, Reference Skills
Comprehensive Test of Basic Skills	Grades 0.1–13.6	Reading, Language, Arithmetic, Study Skills
Metropolitan Achievement Test	Grades K–12.9	Reading Comprehension, Language, Mathematics, Science, Social Studies
Stanford Achievement Test	Grades 1.5–9	Reading Comprehension, Language, Mathematics, Science, Social Science, Auditory Skills

are summarized in table 3.2 (group tests) and table 3.3 (individual tests). Using these tables as references, teachers can select those testing instruments that best meet their needs at a given time. A further resource that assists in selecting tests is provided by Mavrogenes, Hanson, and Winkley.[3] Reviews for many of these tests are found in the *Mental Measurements Yearbook*.

■ Group Test Procedures

The first section of this chapter deals with those instruments generally referred to as group-administered tests. There are many types of group tests used for varying purposes; what they have in common is that they all can be administered in a group situation. The various types include survey reading tests, diagnostic reading tests, and achievement tests. Each type has a specific purpose, different from the others. The use of each is dependent upon the testing conditions and information desired. Both types are discussed in this section.

Survey Reading Tests

Survey reading tests are used to determine reading levels in several general categories, i.e., vocabulary, comprehension, and rate. The primary reason for their popularity is the ease by which they are administered by classroom teachers. Moreover, the manuals for these instruments are usually quite clear and concise in describing the appropriate manner for administering, scoring, and interpreting the data. Other reasons for their popularity include the time factor, norms, and test construction. Survey reading tests can be administered and scored in a relatively short period of time, especially as compared to individually-administered tests. They are standardized, using national norms, and some, such as the *Gates-MacGinitie Reading Tests*, provide local norms. In most instances, these instruments are carefully constructed by persons with expertise in test construction and in the area of reading.

Survey reading tests have disadvantages as well. One disadvantage, which is actually a characteristic of a survey test, is that the information obtained lacks depth. For example, only two or, at the most, three scores are obtained from these instruments. The scores are in the general areas of vocabulary, comprehension, and rate of reading. The results are reported in either grade equivalents, stanines, percentiles, or perhaps all three. Although a survey instrument is designed to provide general information, it is also considered a limitation. Even though scores in only these general areas are obtained, one suggestion for turning this disadvantage into an advantage is to analyze each item in the instrument so that more detailed diagnostic information about a student can be obtained. While this procedure can be used to obtain diagnostic data, such an analysis is quite time consuming and there are other instruments that provide the data in less time.

Another disadvantage of survey reading tests is that the scores obtained are frequently inflated, representing the students' frustration levels; teachers should note that the scores do not indicate the students' instructional or independent levels. However, if scores represent the most accurate information available, use them as a starting point for diagnosis in conjunction with an Informal Reading Inventory.

The advantages and disadvantages of survey reading tests are presented for review to aid teachers in determining whether or not such instruments would be beneficial in their classrooms. One important consideration is that their primary purpose is to serve as a *screening device*. The most appropriate way to use this instrument in a classroom situation is to administer it to the entire class, determine grade equivalent scores for each student, make an item analysis to obtain more diagnostic information, set up initial groups using the results of this instrument and any other available information, and then begin to administer other diagnostic tests to students about whom more in-depth information is desired. Used in this manner, the survey reading test can provide helpful information. These survey reading tests are frequently used in special reading programs in which general data is needed to measure progress of all enrolled in the program. No diagnostic data is needed for such reports. However, in such circumstances teachers should use other instruments for diagnosis.

Boehm Test of Basic Concepts—Revised (Boehm-R)
Ann E. Boehm
The Psychological Corporation, San Antonio, Texas, 1986
(Grades K–2)

This test is designed to measure children's mastery of basic concepts considered important for following teacher verbal instructions and for success during the first years of school. Because language knowledge is so essential for success in reading, teachers may want to use this test, which can be administered to small groups or individuals, with their class to determine the concept knowledge of young students. Students who do not understand these basic concepts will experience difficulty in early reading.

Forms C and D measure the same 50 concepts with 26 additional concepts measured at the Applications level for Grades 1 and 2.[4] Information from this test can be used by kindergarten and primary level teachers to provide prescriptive instruction based on items answered incorrectly on the test. The *Boehm Resource Guide for Basic Concept Teaching* may be used as a guide for prescriptive teaching of these basic concepts.

Gates-MacGinitie Reading Tests, Third Edition
Walter H. MacGinitie and Ruth K. MacGinitie
The Riverside Publishing Company, Chicago, Illinois, 1989
(Grades K–12)

The Gates-MacGinitie Reading Tests are among the better-known group survey reading test batteries. This instrument was developed in 1965 by Arthur Gates and Walter MacGinitie; however, it was primarily a revision of the *Gates Primary Reading Tests*, the *Gates Advanced Primary Reading Tests*, and the *Gates Reading Survey*. A second revision occurred in 1989 with the publication of the third edition expected in 1993.

The 1989 battery uses a booklet format, which facilitates test administration and hand-scoring. One of the main advantages of this instrument is that a classroom teacher can administer the instrument one day, hand-score the booklets, and have the grade equivalents, stanines, or percentiles available for use the next day. All items are in multiple choice format.

Another useful feature of the third edition is that the test materials are new and relate to current experiential patterns of students. This edition was field-tested with students of various socio-economic and racial backgrounds in order to develop items that decrease cultural bias in the instrument. As a result, new national norms were developed. Out-of-level norms are also available.

The *Gates-MacGinitie Reading Tests*, Third Edition, consist of nine tests for Grades K–12. A new Level PRE (pre-reading) has been added for kindergarten and the beginning of the first grade. This test is untimed and measures literacy concepts, reading instruction relational concepts, oral language concepts, and letters and letter-sound correspondences. Level R, also untimed, is designed for use with first graders and assesses knowledge of initial consonants and consonant clusters, final consonants and consonant clusters, vowels, and use of context.

Interesting comprehension passages that correspond in difficulty and suitability of the material to the specified grade level are provided in Levels 1–10/12, which include two tests—a vocabulary test and a comprehension test.

The third edition uses scoring keys or self-scoring answer sheets, which enable the teacher to score the booklets much faster. Another useful service provided by the publisher is the machine-scored profile sheet which not only reports the testing data, but also includes a brief diagnostic evaluation of the student. For those school systems using The Riverside Scoring Service, this is an added advantage.

The nine levels of the *Gates-MacGinitie Reading Tests* have two forms at each level except for Levels PRE, R, and 1. Each level, with the exception of PRE and R, provides three scores: vocabulary, comprehension, and total reading score. The levels are divided as follows:

- Level PRE, Grade K–1.1
- Level R, Grade 1.0–1.9
- Level 1, Grade 1.5–1.9
- Level 2, Grade 2
- Level 3, Grade 3
- Level 4, Grade 4
- Level 5/6, Grade 5–6
- Level 7/9, Grade 7–9
- Level 10/12, Grade 10–12[5]

The teacher's manual includes information on raw scores, standard scores, grade equivalents, percentile ranks in grade, NCE scores, and stanines. This test is widely used as a screening device in reading, and has proven to be a valuable instrument for use with groups of students.

Iowa Silent Reading Test (ISRT)
Roger Farr, Coordinating Editor
The Psychological Corporation, San Antonio, Texas, 1973
(Grades 6–12, College)

This test battery was originally published in 1927 and included grades 4–8 in the elementary section, and grades 9–14 in the advanced section. The latest revision, published in 1973, has three levels: Level 1, Grades 6–9; Level 2, Grades 9–Community College, and Level 3, above-average readers in the eleventh and twelfth grades. Since the focus of this book is on elementary and middle school students, Level 1 is the primary level of interest; Levels 2 and 3 are mentioned only for informational purposes.

Several areas are tested on the ISRT: vocabulary, reading comprehension, directed reading, and reading efficiency. With this instrument, reading skills are assessed through the use of various types of reading material rather than only the basic textbook. Testing for literal information is minimal with more stress placed on applying skills and knowledge.

For example, in the vocabulary section of Level 1, Grades 6–9, word knowledge is measured with words carefully selected as to level of difficulty and frequency of use. Another feature in the Comprehension section of Level 1 is the use of high-interest materials emphasizing various reading styles and content. Inferential comprehension is tested in conjunction with literal meaning. In the Directed Reading section of Level 1, also referred to as work-study skills, proficiency in the use of the dictionary is tested, using imaginary words that follow phonemic principles. Library skills and knowledge of other sources of information are also tested. The skills of skimming and scanning are assessed using materials from encyclopedias. The final area measured in Level 1 is Reading Efficiency, also referred to as rate with comprehension. This test is designed to indicate a student's speed and accuracy using a modified cloze item procedure.

The "Guide for Interpretation and Use" is designed to inform the instructor of the rationale for the ISRT and to assist in the interpretation of the test data.[6] The ISRT is another screening instrument for teachers at the middle school levels and above. Remember, however, that these instruments should be evaluated by teachers in relation to the objectives of their school's reading program.

Diagnostic Reading Tests

Group diagnostic reading tests are used quite extensively in school systems throughout the country. They have a valuable role in assisting teachers in gathering diagnostic information about their students in minimal time. Their popularity is further enhanced because they are easy to administer.

Detailed manuals and norms further enhance the time factor and ease of administration. The manuals that accompany these instruments are easily understood and facilitate the successful administration, scoring, and interpretation of the tests. For example, the manual that accompanies the *Stanford Diagnostic Reading Test* is extremely thorough and quite detailed. The time required for administering these instruments is relatively brief compared to that required for individually-administered instruments. A classroom teacher's time is so valuable that speed is imperative in considering diagnostic instruments. Of equal importance are the norm factors. These instruments are standardized using national norms. Therefore they allow school systems to compare their school population with others.

The primary advantage of the group diagnostic reading test is that a great deal of information is obtained during a relatively brief expenditure of time. In contrast to group survey reading tests, which yield only vocabulary, comprehension, and rate-of-reading scores, group diagnostic reading tests furnish much more in-depth information. They provide several subtest scores that aid in ascertaining areas of strengths and weaknesses. The *Stanford Diagnostic Reading Test* yields scores in several areas, including structural analysis, auditory discrimination, auditory vocabulary, and literal and inferential comprehension. The basic difference between the two types of instruments, other than subtest information, is the time and expense involved. Usually, group survey reading tests require less time than group diagnostic reading tests and are less expensive.

The primary disadvantage of group diagnostic tests is the lack of teacher-student interaction during testing. While diagnostic tests are administered, teachers obtain much diagnostic data when they observe individual students. This individual observation and interaction, of course, is not possible when tests are group administered. Other limitations of the various tests are explored in the discussions in the following pages. Teachers should note, however, that the primary objective of the group diagnostic reading test is to provide as much in-depth information in as short a period of time as possible.

Metropolitan Achievement Tests: Sixth Ed. (MAT6) Reading Diagnostic Tests
Roger C. Farr, George A. Prescott, Irving H. Balow, and Thomas P. Hogan
The Psychological Corporation, San Antonio, Texas, 1986 (Grades K.5–9.9)

The MAT6 *Reading Diagnostic Tests* are designed to provide classroom teachers with detailed, criterion-referenced, prescriptive information needed to diagnose student strengths and weaknesses in reading. The levels of the tests include Primer (Grades K.5–1.9), Primary 1 (Grades 1.5–2.9), Primary 2 (Grades 2.5–3.9), Elementary (Grades 3.5–4.9), Intermediate (Grades 5.0–6.9), and Advanced 1 (Grades 7.0–9.9). Each level of the instrument contains tests that reflect the curriculum generally taught at that level.

Primer: Visual discrimination, letter recognition, auditory discrimination, sight vocabulary, phoneme/grapheme: consonants, vocabulary in context, and reading comprehension.

Primary 1: Auditory discrimination, sight vocabulary, phoneme/grapheme: consonants, phoneme/grapheme: vowels, vocabulary in context, word part clues, and reading comprehension.

Formal reading tests are used to provide diagnostic data on individuals and groups. Photo courtesy of Edward B. Lasher.

Primary 2: Sight vocabulary, phoneme/grapheme: consonants, phoneme/grapheme: vowels, vocabulary in context, word part clues, and reading comprehension.

Elementary: Phoneme/grapheme: consonants, phoneme/grapheme: vowels, vocabulary in context, word part clues, rate of comprehension, and reading comprehension.

Intermediate: Phoneme/grapheme: consonants, phoneme/grapheme: vowels, vocabulary in context, word part clues, rate of comprehension, skimming and scanning, and reading comprehension.

Advanced 1: Vocabulary in context, rate of comprehension, skimming and scanning, and reading comprehension.

The information provided by this group diagnostic test includes the student's overall reading achievement, an estimate of the student's Instructional Reading Level, and diagnostic information regarding performance on each of the objectives assessed. The reading comprehension subtest measures literal and inferential comprehension as well as critical analysis. The Primer level has only 1 form (Form L), while Primary 1 through Advanced 1 levels have two forms (Form L and Form M).

The Instructional Reading Level (IRL) is derived from silent reading passages on the Reading Comprehension Test. From this information, the teacher is provided with a report listing the students suggested for each instructional group. Each passage on the Reading Comprehension Test also has a purpose-setting question to assist the reader in activating prior knowledge about the given topic.

The detailed Teacher's Manual provides criterion-referenced information, teaching suggestions, a table noting the importance of the various reading skills, and tables that provide a full range of derived scores, including scaled scores, percentile ranks, stanines, grade equivalents, and normal curve equivalents. Norms are also provided for national and local school populations.[7]

The *MAT6* is a welcome addition as a group diagnostic reading instrument. Classroom teachers should find it very useful, especially those employed in school systems using the *Metropolitan Achievement Test*.

Stanford Diagnostic Reading Test (SDRT)
Bjorn Karlsen and Eric F. Gardner
The Psychological Corporation, San Antonio, Texas, 1984 (Grades 1.5–12)

The *SDRT* is one of the more widely used group diagnostic reading tests. This instrument was first published in 1966. In 1974, Level III for grades 10–12 was added. The latest revision was published in 1984. The four levels are Red Level (Grades 1.8–3.8), Green Level (Grades 3.1–5.8), Brown Level (Grades 5.1–9.8), and Blue Level (Grades 8.8–12.8). Each level has two forms (G and H), thus facilitating its use in a pre- and post-test situations, if desired. The areas measured on each level are:

Red Level: Auditory vocabulary, auditory discrimination, phonetic analysis, word reading, and comprehension.

Green Level: Auditory vocabulary, auditory discrimination, phonetic analysis, structural analysis, and comprehension.

Brown Level: Auditory vocabulary, comprehension, phonetic analysis, structural analysis, and reading rate.

Blue Level: Comprehension, vocabulary, word parts, phonetic analysis, structural analysis, scanning and skimming, and fast reading rate.

The primary purpose of the *SDRT* is to assist in diagnosing strengths and weaknesses. Scores are reported in stanines, percentile ranks, scaled scores, and grade equivalents. By using the student profile sheet, the teacher is able to discern immediately the areas in which each student exhibits strengths or weaknesses in reading.[8]

One of the strengths of the *SDRT* is the excellent manual. The manual for the 1966 edition was adequate, but the manuals since the 1976 edition are outstanding. For example, the Red Level manual has detailed information for administering the test, scoring, interpreting the results, and using the student profile. The section on interpreting the data is one of its best features.

Another strength of the *SDRT* concerns the distribution of the items in the curve. There is a greater concentration of scores in the lower end of the distribution. This instrument is directed toward poor readers, which "makes *SDRT* scores more reliable for students scoring below the 50th percentile . . . and means that pupils with reading problems will find *SDRT* less frustrating and less threatening than most tests."[9]

Other strengths of the *SDRT* include such factors as teacher time for administration and interpretation, silent reading as well as auditory subtests, and ideas for prescription development. Since the *SDRT* is a group instrument, it does not require a great deal of the teacher's time. It can be administered in a total of about two hours and generates much useful information in this relatively brief period. Like other group diagnostic tests, the *SDRT* does not require the classroom teacher to be a testing specialist in order to administer and interpret it. The directions in the manual are quite clear and specific as to proper administration. The interpretive section of the manual, as already mentioned, is excellent.

The *SDRT* contains a good mixture of listening and silent reading subtests, allowing students to demonstrate their capabilities either through auditory or visual modes. The information provided in the manual greatly facilitates the preparation of instructional strategies based on diagnostic data.

The *SDRT* evaluates decoding (phonetic and structural analysis) through the high school (Blue) level. Additionally, this test provides separate scores for comprehension of textual, functional, and recreational reading passages along with a traditional skills breakdown. Many scoring services are provided with this instrument, including an Individual Diagnostic Report with summaries for each class, grade in school, and grade in system. If teachers or school systems have a NCS Model 3000 scanner, a scoring and reporting package is available for use on an IBM PC or compatible computer. This quickly provides the teacher with diagnostic information for a class. An Instructional Placement Report sorts pupils by instructional priority into remedial, developmental, enrichment, decoding, vocabulary, comprehension or rate groups to aid in grouping for instruction. This instrument is linked statistically with the *Stanford Achievement Test Series*.

This test is obviously well-suited for use by the classroom teacher, and is an excellent group diagnostic tool for obtaining initial diagnostic information.

Test of Reading Comprehension (TORC)
Virginia L. Brown, Donald D. Hammill, and J. Lee Wiederholt
Pro-Ed, Austin, Texas, 1986-Revised Ed. (Ages 7-0—17-11)
(Also may be purchased through The Psychological Corporation)

Using references addressing the psycholinguistic and cognitive components of reading, the authors have developed a diagnostic test that measures general reading comprehension and specialized reading comprehension for various content areas. The four subtests that form the General Reading Comprehension Core are General Vocabulary, Syntactic Similarities, Paragraph Reading, and an optional subtest of Sentence Sequencing. These subtests are relatively free from the influences of specific content area vocabulary. Four diagnostic supplements provide additional information about the students' comprehension abilities in dealing with content area vocabularies (mathematics, social studies, and science) and in reading directions for schoolwork.

The *TORC* is a silent reading test with no time limits. The format of each subtest varies in accord with the area being assessed:

General Vocabulary: Twenty-five items with each item consisting of three stimulus words related in some way. The student is asked to select two words from the set of four provided which are related to the three stimulus words.

Syntactic Similarities: Twenty items composed of five sentences in each item. The student chooses two of the sentences that have the same or nearly the same meaning.

Paragraph Reading: The six paragraphs followed by five questions for each paragraph have a multiple-choice format. The same type of question is used for the five questions following each paragraph; i.e., #1 best title, #2 and #5 story details, #3 inference, and #4 negative inference. This format would allow the teacher to determine if a pattern exists in the errors.

Sentence Sequencing: This optional subtest has ten items consisting of five randomly ordered sentences. The student must place the sentences in order to develop a meaningful paragraph.

Mathematics Vocabulary, Social Studies Vocabulary, and Science Vocabulary: Twenty-five items are used on each of these three subtests to measure the student's understanding of sets of vocabulary items related to the various content areas. Using a format like that in General Vocabulary, the student selects the appropriate words that form a relationship with the given stimulus words. The subtests are scored separately by content area.

Reading the Directions of Schoolwork: This is another optional subtest designed for younger and remedial readers to determine their comprehension of written directions encountered in schoolwork. These twenty-five items require that the item be read and the directions carried out on the answer sheet.

The manual that accompanies *TORC* provides careful directions for administration, information on interpreting the results, the answer key, and normative tables including percentile ranks and standard scores. Additionally, the test materials include a summary and profile sheet that can be used to review diagnostic data on an individual student and to compute the Reading Comprehension Quotient (RCQ), which is comparable with other indices such as general intelligence and language ability.[10]

This norm-referenced test of reading comprehension is relatively easy to administer and is comparable to other group diagnostic reading tests in the amount of time required for administration (1–3 hours). Given the amount of new knowledge regarding comprehension in the last ten years and the difficulties expressed in the research regarding traditional reading comprehension test formats, this reading comprehension test represents a good beginning in adjusting the content and format. Teachers wanting more information on the comprehension abilities of their students may find this a helpful instrument.

Achievement Tests

Achievement tests are designed to measure student knowledge in various broad areas of the curriculum, the extent to which specific information has been acquired, or the extent to which certain skills have been mastered. These tests are intended to determine whether instruction in the broad areas of the curriculum has been effective.

Achievement tests are rigidly standardized, using norms developed from a large sampling of the appropriate school-age population. They are group-administered instruments that survey several curriculum areas taught in the schools. The information elicited is similar to that obtained from survey reading tests, in that it is not in-depth diagnostic information. By their very nature, achievement tests are not designed to be diagnostic instruments. They provide information that is general rather than specific. Scores are reported in grade equivalents, stanines, or percentiles.

The majority of achievement tests basically measure the same curriculum areas: language, mathematics, reading, science, and social studies. School systems are anxious to determine how effective their instruction is and to test as many areas of instruction as possible; it appears that achievement tests are the least expensive manner of obtaining this general information. Thus, they account for a large percentage of the standardized instruments used in the school systems.

Four of the more widely used achievement tests and their subtest areas are outlined below.

California Achievement Tests, Forms E and F
CTB/McGraw Hill, Monterey, California 1985, 1986, 1987 (Grades K–12)

Measures reading, spelling, language, mathematics, and study skills. Includes science and social studies at Level 12 and above; optional end-of-course tests in many areas.

Comprehensive Test of Basic Skills
CTB/McGraw Hill, Monterey, California, 1981, 1982, 1983, 1984, 1985 (Grades K–12)

Measures reading, language, mathematics, reference skills, science, social studies, and spelling.

Metropolitan Achievement Test, 6th ed.
The Psychological Corporation, San Antonio, Texas, 1985, 1986 (Grades K–12)

Measures reading, mathematics, language, science and social studies through the survey battery, and reading, mathematics, and language through diagnostic batteries.

Stanford Achievement Test
The Psychological Corporation, San Antonio, Texas, 1982, 1983, 1984, 1986, 1989 Norms in *Stanford 7 Plus* (Grades K–13)

Measures reading, language, mathematics, listening; science and social studies measured from Primary 3 up; optional writing test.

All types of instruments have strengths and limitations, and achievement tests are no exception. Some of these are listed below.

Strengths

School systems receive information covering a wide range of curriculum areas.
Classroom teachers can easily administer these tests.
Strict norming procedures are followed.
Data assists in evaluating students' progress over a period of time.
Some tests provide criterion-referenced test data on specific reading areas.

Limitations

Lack of depth in information necessitates an item analysis to ascertain diagnostic data.
Scores received are on the students' frustration level.
Improper administration procedures, such as massing large groups of students together in the cafeteria or auditorium, may occur; these circumstances often result in fallacious data.
Requires the use of silent reading skills, thus reflecting, in many instances, a reading problem rather than knowledge of the material being tested.
Test results are not promptly returned to classroom teachers.
Local norms may not be available.

With proper use, under appropriate conditions, and with recognition of their strengths and limitations, achievement tests can fulfill a useful role as broad, group survey instruments providing valuable assistance to school districts in evaluating their total curriculum. If the criterion-referenced or diagnostic test data is available and requested by the school district, achievement tests can provide some individual diagnostic data on students' strengths and weaknesses in specific areas.

■ Individual Test Procedures

Different types of individually-administered instruments are discussed in the following section of this chapter. These tests are categorized as oral reading tests, diagnostic reading tests, auditory discrimination tests, and intelligence tests.

Each category is treated in detail, and the various instruments are described. An attempt is made to discuss instruments most useful to the classroom teacher. Tests were chosen according to what the authors believe to be the frequency of their use, though conceding that some outstanding instruments may be omitted.

Oral Reading Tests

In the nineteenth century, oral reading was the most important aspect of reading. Proper enunciation and pronunciation of words were the mark of an educated person. Students were taught to read through emphasis on oral activities; schools stressed such activities as round-robin oral reading and choral reading. It was assumed that a person with good oral skills likewise possessed good silent reading skills; this assumed correlation between oral and silent reading went virtually unchallenged for many years.

Table 3.3

Formal Individual Tests

Test	Appropriate Levels	Subtest Scores
Oral Reading		
Gray Oral Reading Test, Revised	Grades 1–12	Oral Reading Quotient, Passage Score; Comprehension Score
Slosson Oral Reading Test, Revised	Grades 1–8 and High School	Reading Level
Diagnostic Reading		
Diagnostic Reading Scales	Grades 1–6	Independent, Instruction, Frustration Levels, Eight Phonic Tests
Durrell Analysis of Reading Difficulty	Grades 1–6	Oral Reading, Silent Reading, Listening, Flash Words, Word Analysis, Spelling, Handwriting, Visual Memory, Hearing Sounds
Formal Reading Inventory	Grades 1–12	Standard Scores, Percentile Ranks
Gates-McKillop-Horowitz Reading Diagnostic Tests	Grades 1–6	Oral Reading, Words—Flash, Words—Untimed, Phrases—Flash, Knowledge of Word Parts, Visual Form of Sounds, Auditory Blending, Four Supplementary Tests
Sipay Word Analysis Test	Grades 2–12	Sixteen Tests of Word Analysis Skills
Test of Early Reading Ability, Second Edition	Ages 3.0 to 9.11	Total Score
Tests of Language Development, 2nd ed.	Ages 4.0 to 12.11	Twelve tests of Oral Language Concepts
Test of Written Language, 2nd ed.	Ages 7.0 through 17.11	Nine subtests of written language concepts
Woodcock Reading Mastery Tests, Revised	Grades K–12	Letter Identification, Word Identification, Word Attack, Word Comprehension, Passage Comprehension, Total
Auditory Discrimination		
Wepman Auditory Discrimination	Ages 5–8	Satisfactory/Unsatisfactory
Intelligence		
Peabody Picture Vocabulary Test, Revised	Ages 2.6 to 18	I.Q., Mental Age
Slosson Intelligence Test, Revised	Ages 4 and above	I.Q., Mental Age

Questions about the use of oral reading tests have surfaced; researchers have noted that the relationship between oral and silent reading is not great enough to use one type of instrument to predict success in the other.[11] Thus, when teachers want diagnostic data on oral reading performance, they must use some oral reading test. However, as these instruments are used, teachers need to consider Goodman's notion about oral reading when administering and interpreting such a test: There are periods in the development of reading competence when oral reading becomes very awkward. Readers who have recently become rapid, relatively effective silent readers seem to be distracted and disrupted by the necessity of encoding oral output while they are decoding meaning. Ironically, then 'poor' oral reading performance may reflect a high degree of reading competence rather than a lack of such competence.[12]

In the early 1900's, the ideas of Parker and Huey began to influence reading instruction.[13] Huey suggested that reading in daily life was done silently, while students were taught oral reading at school. Parker considered oral reading, like speech, to be a means of expression, while silent reading was a matter of attending to the printed material. These comments prompted research into the areas of oral versus silent reading. The results suggested the superiority of silent over oral reading, and led to changes in testing procedures. Some felt so strongly about the importance of silent reading that they urged that oral reading not be taught.[14] The debate has continued; most teachers now realize that both oral and silent reading must be taught, and that oral reading is an excellent means of diagnosing a student's word difficulties in context.

In administering oral reading tests, the teacher asks the student to read aloud, then marks the errors made, carefully noting such difficulties as mispronunciations, omissions, repetitions, substitutions, unknown words, and sometimes hesitations. Comprehension questions are asked in order to measure the student's understanding of material when reading orally. With this information, the teacher can assist in correcting many reading difficulties. Each oral reading test has its own marking and scoring procedures, which the instructor should review. The marking system is usually similar to that presented in the discussion of Informal Reading Inventories in chapter 2.

The two oral reading tests to be discussed in this section are the *Gray Oral Reading Test*, Revised Edition, and *Slosson Oral Reading Test*.

Gray Oral Reading Test, Third Edition (GORT-3)
Revised by J. Lee Wiederholt and Brian R. Bryant
Created by William S. Gray, edited by Helen M. Robinson
Pro-Ed, Austin, Texas, 1992
Also sold by The Psychological Corporation, San Antonio, Texas
(Grades 1–12)

The original *Gray Oral Reading Test* was a major revision of the *Standardized Oral Reading Paragraphs* first published by William S. Gray in 1915. *GORT-3* is a third edition reflecting minimal changes from *GORT-R*. The *GORT-R* is a major revision based on current research and theoretical ideas. The principal purposes of this test are to assess oral reading speed and accuracy, and to assist in diagnosing oral reading miscues and comprehension. This revised test has two equivalent forms each containing thirteen increasingly difficult passages.

The *GORT-R* has new normative, reliability, and validity data based on new passages designed with careful attention given to story structure and content, comprehension questions in a multiple-choice format, and modifications in the scoring criteria. Time in seconds (Rate) and oral reading errors (Deviations from Print) are combined to give an overall Passage Score. Any deviations from print or miscues are counted as errors but, of course, normal speech variations are acceptable. Five types of miscues that are classified for further diagnosis include meaning similarity, function similarity, graphic/phonemic similarity, multiple sources, and self-correction. The Passage Score is combined with the Comprehension Score to provide the Oral Reading Quotient, which is the primary score for interpreting oral reading performance on the *GORT-R*. Grade equivalent scores are not provided (see figure 3.1.).

In revising the passages, the authors gave considerable attention to the text structure and content rather than just to the readability levels as determined by a readability formula. The content reflects more general reading types of passages as compared to content related passages. The complexity of the sentence structure, logical connections between sentences and clauses, as well as density of words and other related factors, were considered in the text structure. This attention given to content and text structure rather than to readability levels resulted in passages that do not make a smooth progression from level to level when readability formulas are applied and has raised questions from a reviewer. Radencich suggested that "the lack of a smooth progression from grade to grade in the readabilities . . . [combined with] low alternate form reliabilities . . . indicate that [it] cannot be used with confidence for documenting progress nor for research which requires alternate forms."[15] However, for individual diagnosis of oral reading strengths and weaknesses this test seems to be adequate.

The change in comprehension questions represents another major revision in the *GORT-R*. The questions are literal, inferential, critical, and affective using a multiple-choice format. The vocabulary used in the questions is carefully controlled and the questions are passage-dependent.[16]

The scores provided on this instrument give only general information; teacher interpretation of miscues and other oral reading behaviors are the necessary diagnostic data. Assistance in this interpretation is available in the examiner's manual along with detailed information on test administration and scoring, and data on the development of the test.

Figure 3.1
Gray Oral Reading Test

Summary of GORT-3 Test Results

Section I. Identifying Information

	Year	Month	Day
Date tested	____	____	____
Date of birth	____	____	____
Chronological age	____	____	____

School ____________________ Grade ________

Examiner's name ____________________

Examiner's title ____________________

Section II. Record of GORT-3 Scores

PRETEST: ________ POSTTEST: ________

Story	Rate	Accuracy	Passage Score	Comp. Score
1				
2				
3				
4				
5				
6				
7				
8				
9				
10				
11				
12				
13				
Raw Score				
Grade Equiv.				
%ile				
Std. Score				

Sum of Std. Scores ________

%ile ________

Oral Reading Quotient (ORQ) ________

Section III. Record of the Test Scores

	Test Name	Test Date	GORT-3 Equiv.
1.			
2.			
3.			
4.			
5.			

Section IV. Profile of Scores

Std. Score	Rate	Accuracy	Passage Score	Comp. Score	ORQ	1	2	3	4	5	Quotient
	GORT-3 Scores					Other Scores					
20	•	•	•	•	•	•	•	•	•	•	150
19	•	•	•	•	•	•	•	•	•	•	145
18	•	•	•	•	•	•	•	•	•	•	140
17	•	•	•	•	•	•	•	•	•	•	135
16	•	•	•	•	•	•	•	•	•	•	130
15	•	•	•	•	•	•	•	•	•	•	125
14	•	•	•	•	•	•	•	•	•	•	120
13	•	•	•	•	•	•	•	•	•	•	115
12	•	•	•	•	•	•	•	•	•	•	110
11	•	•	•	•	•	•	•	•	•	•	105
10	•	•	•	•	•	•	•	•	•	•	100
9	•	•	•	•	•	•	•	•	•	•	95
8	•	•	•	•	•	•	•	•	•	•	90
7	•	•	•	•	•	•	•	•	•	•	85
6	•	•	•	•	•	•	•	•	•	•	80
5	•	•	•	•	•	•	•	•	•	•	75
4	•	•	•	•	•	•	•	•	•	•	70
3	•	•	•	•	•	•	•	•	•	•	65
2	•	•	•	•	•	•	•	•	•	•	60
1	•	•	•	•	•	•	•	•	•	•	55

Slosson Oral Reading Test, Revised (SORT-R)
Richard L. Slosson
Slosson Educational Publications, Inc., East Aurora, New York, 1990
(Grades 1–8 and High School)

The *Slosson Oral Reading Test—Revised* "is based on the ability to pronounce words at different levels of difficulty. The words have been taken from standardized school readers and the Reading Level obtained from testing median or standardized school achievement."[17]

This oral reading test consists of ten lists of twenty words each and measures only word pronunciation in isolation. It makes no attempt to ascertain comprehension of oral reading. The test is not timed, except that hesitation on a word for more than five seconds counts as an error. The test should take from three to five minutes to administer. The student's raw score, the total number of words correct, can be converted to a Reading Level using the tables provided.

If the teacher selects the *SORT* as a diagnostic tool, it should be viewed as a test of word recognition techniques rather than as an oral reading test. Thus, the teacher should note the mispronunciations made by the student, as well as the types of word analysis skills employed in attempting an unknown word. Information obtained from this test depends on the teacher's knowledge and skill in observing and interpreting student responses.

Diagnostic Reading Tests

Standardized diagnostic reading tests are designed to provide in-depth analysis of reading difficulties. The individual diagnostic reading tests discussed in this section provide the most thorough diagnosis of reading problems. These tests are used with students who exhibit more severe reading difficulties on informal or group tests or for whom the teacher desires more detailed information.

The individual standardized diagnostic tests are time consuming to use with a large number of students; however, the teacher can use these instruments with selected students as needed. These tests have various subtests, which assist the teacher in identifying individual reading problems.

In this section, individual diagnostic reading tests are discussed. There are many more such tests; however, these were selected because they seem to be the most commonly used.

The following tests are presented in this section:

- *Diagnostic Reading Scales*
- *Durrell Analysis of Reading Difficulty*
- *Formal Reading Inventory*
- *Gates-McKillop-Horowitz Reading Diagnostic Tests*
- *Sipay Word Analysis Test (SWAT)*
- *Test of Early Reading Ability*
- *Tests of Language Development (TOLD-2)*
- *Tests of Written Language (TOWL-2)*
- *Woodcock Reading Mastery Tests (WRMT)*

Diagnostic Reading Scales
George D. Spache
CTB/McGraw Hill, Inc., Monterey, California, 1981
(Grades 1–6 and Disabled Readers in Grades 7–12)

The *Diagnostic Reading Scales* consist of a series of tests designed to analyze oral and silent reading skills as well as auditory comprehension. The testing materials include an examiner's manual, an examiner's record book, and a student's reading book. The examiner's record book is expendable. This test was revised in 1981. The purpose of this revision was

> . . . to update, expand, and facilitate use of the test. The major thrust of the revision centered around reassigning grade levels to the reading selections. The new level assignments were based on analyses of revised readability formulas and results from the national study for the revision of the DRS.[18]

Additionally, the word analysis and phonics tests were revised and expanded with nonsense words used instead of isolated letters and their sounds. The manual for the examiner was revised and a cassette provided to aid in training in the use of the DRS. A 1982 technical report provides data from studies of the earlier editions as well as the 1981 edition.

The test book contains three word-recognition lists, two sets of eleven graded reading passages, and twelve supplementary word-analysis and phonics tests. The word-recognition lists form the first part of the test battery. These lists have three basic purposes:

- To function as a pretest, indicating the entry level for testing in the reading selections.
- To reveal the student's methods of decoding words in isolation.
- To evaluate the student's sight-word vocabulary.

Using the level from the word recognition list, the teacher selects a passage to be read orally. The passages range in difficulty from a grade placement of 1.4 to 2.5. There are two passages at each level. The student's oral reading performance is evaluated according to word recognition and comprehension errors. The specific number of errors allowed is indicated for each paragraph. As the student reads, the teacher marks the following errors: omissions, additions, substitutions or mispronunciations, repetitions (two or more words), and reversals.

Hesitations and self-corrections are not counted as errors. Words are not pronounced for the student. When the student fails, either in word recognition or comprehension, the oral reading should stop. Spache considers the Instructional Level a measure of oral reading and comprehension and is usually one level below the point of failure in the oral reading selections.

The main caution concerning this instrument is that it uses the terms Instructional and Independent Levels in a way that is different from their customary use in the Informal Reading Inventory. The authors remind teachers to be cognizant of the difference in terminology and to avoid using the terms to mean the same as in other instruments. Perhaps it would be easier to note the levels as Oral Reading Level and Silent Reading Level in order to avoid confusion.

Once the Instructional Level (or oral reading level) is determined, the student's Independent Level (or silent reading level) is ascertained by means of silent reading. Spache contends that "the majority of children can read silently with adequate comprehension at levels above the Instruction Level."[19] Thus, the student reads silently until more than the allowed number of comprehension questions are missed. The Independent Level is the final level at which the student shows the minimal level of comprehension.

The reading passages are also used to determine the student's Potential Level, or the level at which the student can listen and respond satisfactorily to questions. The Potential Level is determined by reading the next passage above the Independent Level to the student and then asking questions. The Potential Level is the last level at which the student gives the appropriate number of correct responses.

Following the use of the reading passages, the twelve supplementary word analysis and phonics tests are administered. The content of the tests are:

1. Initial Consonants
2. Final Consonants
3. Consonant Digraphs
4. Consonant Blends
5. Initial Consonant Substitution
6. Initial Consonant Sounds Recognized Auditorily
7. Auditory Discriminations
8. Short and Long Vowel Sounds
9. Vowels with r
10. Vowel Diphthongs and Digraphs
11. Common Syllables or Phonograms
12. Blending[20]

The revised edition of the *Diagnostic Reading Scales* was reviewed by Lipa who questioned the "advantage in using the DRS in preference to other published IRIs now available." She specifically had difficulty with the length and complexity of the Examiner's Manual, the releveling of passages in the revised edition, the interest level of the passages, and the factual nature of some questions.[21]

Questions regarding the reliability and validity of the test were addressed by Spache in the *Technical Bulletin*[22] with other comments in *Diagnosing and Correcting Reading Disabilities*.[23]

This test is useful for the classroom teacher or the reading clinician at the elementary and middle school levels. The detailed information provided can be used with data from other instruments to obtain an in-depth profile of the reader.

Durrell Analysis of Reading Difficulty, 3rd edition
Donald D. Durrell and Jane H. Catterson
The Psychological Corporation, San Antonio, Texas, 1980 (Grades 1–6)

The *Durrell Analysis of Reading Difficulty* is a series of tests and situations in which the various aspects of a student's reading may be observed. It consists of a manual of directions, a booklet of reading paragraphs, a tachistoscope, various cards for use with the tachistoscope, and an individual record blank. Approximately thirty to forty-five minutes of testing time are necessary to administer this test, which is composed of the following subtests:

Eight Oral Reading paragraphs with comprehension questions are provided. The student is to read at least three selections. The teacher should find the "basal paragraph" or paragraph in which no more than one error is made. The "upper level" is found when seven or more errors are made in a single paragraph, or the student takes more than two minutes to read the paragraph. During the oral reading, the teacher is to mark omissions, mispronunciations, repetitions, words pronounced for the student, insertions, punctuation marks ignored, and hesitations. Each paragraph is timed. Following the oral reading of each paragraph, comprehension questions are asked. The checklist of errors is marked at the completion of this section. Three kinds of data are collected on these passages: oral reading errors, comprehension, and time for reading. Scoring includes the time element as the most important factor.

The Silent Reading subtest uses the second set of eight paragraphs. The student is timed as the designated paragraph is read silently. When the paragraph has been completed, the student is asked to tell everything remembered about the story. Following this unaided recall, the teacher asks questions to assist the student in remembering more about the story. The grade norms are based on time and memory scores.

The third subtest is Listening Comprehension, which consists of nine paragraphs. The teacher begins reading the paragraph appropriate for the student's grade or chronological age. After listening to the material read, the student responds to comprehension questions. The listening comprehension level is determined when no more than one question in eight is missed.

The tachistoscope is used on the Word Recognition and Word Analysis subtests. Lists of words are printed on strips of cardboard. A word is flashed for the student to recognize and if the word is missed, it is shown again with time provided for word analysis. The teacher must note carefully the responses during the flash and the analysis. The test is stopped when seven successive errors are made in each area. All or part of these tests may be administered as necessary to learn more about the performance of the student.

A Listening Vocabulary subtest is provided to furnish a second index of reading capacity, using the same words that appeared in the Word Recognition and Word Analysis subtests. The scores obtained on the Listening Vocabulary subtest are compared to the scores on the Word Recognition and Word Analysis subtests.

Sounds in Isolation is a subtest designed to require students to produce the sounds of isolated letters, letter groups, and word parts. Included in the word parts are affixes.

Other subtests include Spelling, Phonic Spelling of Words, Visual Memory of Words (primary and intermediate), and Identifying Sounds in Words. An additional subtest also included to aid in diagnosing the kindergarten age student is the Prereading Phonics Abilities subtests, which measures knowledge of letter names, ability to write letters, knowledge of letter sounds, and skill in matching written and spoken words.[24]

This test provides numerous checklists to assist in deriving maximum information from each subtest. These checklists, used in conjunction with the Profile Chart on the front of the test booklet, will provide much diagnostic data on the student. The main criticism of the earlier edition of this test, as well as this edition, is its lack of information on reliability and validity. Regardless of this criticism, the test has proven over the years to be an excellent source of diagnostic information on poor readers. Teachers should, however, be aware of the lack of technical information on this test, and consult such reviews as Schell and Jennings[25] before deciding to use the entire instrument.

Formal Reading Inventory
J. Lee Wiederholt
Pro-Ed, Austin, Texas, 1986
(Grades 1–12)

The *Formal Reading Inventory* is designed to provide data on silent reading comprehension as well as oral reading miscues. This test was developed in response to concerns about the lack of normative data, as well as reliability and validity information on informal reading inventories. Four forms (A, B, C, D), each consisting of thirteen stories with five comprehension questions per story, make up the basic components of the test. Form A can be used for diagnosing silent reading and Form B, for oral reading. Forms C and D can be used in the same way or for reassessments. The Student Record Form is used for recording answers to the questions and for summarizing other information about the student. Teacher worksheets are used for coding oral reading miscues as per the five types specified: meaning similarity, function similarity, graphic/phonemic similarity, multiple sources, and self-corrections. This miscue analysis provides detailed diagnostic data. The examiner's manual gives background information on the test, test administration and scoring procedures, and suggestions for interpreting the results.

Scores obtained on this test include standard scores and percentile ranks with no information provided that relates to grade equivalents or independent, instruction, and frustration reading levels.[26] Thus, this test provides diagnostic information via teacher interpretation and analysis of errors, rather than through separate types of scores. The *Formal Reading Inventory* shares some of the same weaknesses as the *Gray Oral Reading Test-Revised*,[27] however, this test is a step forward as the informal reading inventory format is now available with normative data along with reliability and validity information.

Gates-McKillop-Horowitz Reading Diagnostic Tests, 2nd edition
Arthur I. Gates, Anne S. McKillop, and Elizabeth Cliff Horowitz,
Teachers College Press, New York, New York, 1981 (Grades 1–6)

The *Gates-McKillop-Horowitz Reading Diagnostic Tests* consist of a detailed manual of directions, the test materials, and the pupil record booklet. The teacher uses one copy of the pupil record booklet for each student since individual responses are recorded in the booklet. As with all tests, the teacher needs to be very familiar with the manual prior to using the instrument. Since the purpose of this instrument is to obtain as much diagnostic information as possible on the student, the manual suggests the following:

- Data from other tests should be used for information and correlated with this instrument.
- There is no specific order for the administration of these subtests.
- Not all subtests must be given to the students.
- After following the specified procedures in administering the tests, the teacher may gain more diagnostic data by allowing the student to work independently on the items not completed on a specific subtest. Care should be taken to keep this record separate from the original recording so that errors in scoring will not result.

The test is composed of eight basic parts, two of these being further divided into more specific subtests. These are briefly described in the order of their presentation in the manual.

The Oral Reading subtest has seven paragraphs, which increase in difficulty. These readings are designed to assess the student's use of context and meaning clues, as well as word-form clues, in word recognition. Both phonetically regular and irregular words appear in the paragraphs. Also included in this subtest are four individual sentences, primarily containing phonetically regular words, which are intended to measure the student's use of meaning or word-form clues. During the oral reading, the teacher is to mark the following types of errors: hesitations, additions, omissions, repetitions, mispronunciations, and self-corrections. The student reads until eleven or more errors are made on each of two consecutive paragraphs. The total number of errors is expressed as a raw score, which can then be converted into a grade norm.

The next two subtests are Words: Flash and Words: Untimed, which are designed to determine the student's ability to decode isolated words. The Flash subtest measures instant recognition of words, while the Untimed subtest allows for the application of word analysis skills. The test information can be converted to a grade score.

The subtests in Knowledge of Word Parts: Word Attack proceeds from the largest units, nonsense words, to the smallest units, individual letters. The nonsense words are used to determine skill in syllabication, employing two or more frequently used syllables. The next parts of this subtest measure the decoding skills of recognizing and blending common word parts and reading words. One-syllable words containing consonant combinations are used in recognizing and blending common word parts, while one-syllable words without consonant combinations are used in the reading words test. The student's performance on these two parts determines whether or not the remainder of the test should be given. Knowledge of isolated sounds is assessed on the letter sounds section by asking the student to give the sound corresponding to each of the individual printed letters or letter combinations. The student's ability to recognize and name upper- and lowercase letters is measured in the portions naming capital letters and lowercase letters.

Vowel knowledge is assessed on the Recognizing the Visual Form of Sounds subtest. The student is required to associate a graphic symbol with the vowel sound heard in words pronounced by the test administrator.

Auditory Blending and Auditory Discrimination are two subtests in which no visual component is involved. Auditory Blending measures whether a student can orally combine given sounds to make a word. The ability to hear the difference between similar-sounding phonemes, which are presented orally, is assessed on the Auditory Discrimination subtest.

Subtests are also included to evaluate spelling of isolated words (both phonetically regular and irregular words) in informal writing. The Informal Writing Sample subtest assesses the student's facility in written verbal expression as well as in handwriting.[28]

The *Gates-McKillop-Horowitz Reading Diagnostic Tests* are measures of the oral reading, writing, and spelling skills of students in grades 1–6. Evaluation of word analysis skills is stressed with no attention given to silent reading or comprehension. The Manual of Directions refers the examiner to the *Gates-MacGinitie Reading Tests* for information on comprehension and vocabulary.

This test is very comprehensive in its identification of word analysis difficulties, however, the teacher must be quite familiar with the instrument in order to use it appropriately. Additionally, the test must be carefully interpreted by a person who is trained in reading test interpretation. The teacher may wish to use some of these subtests with select individuals in the classroom, but the time element would prohibit its wide usage as a classroom diagnostic tool.

Sipay Word Analysis Test (SWAT)
Edward R. Sipay
Educators Publishing Service, Inc., Cambridge, Massachusetts, 1974
(Grades 2–12)

The *Sipay Word Analysis Tests* are criterion-referenced tests consisting of sixteen subtests designed to measure word analysis skills. There is also an initial test, the Survey Test, which is administered to help decide which of the subtests need to be administered. The test components include a general test manual, a mini-manual for each subtest, test cards, answer sheets, and an individual report form.

The subtests of the *SWAT* include:

- Test 1—Letter Names
- Test 2—Symbol-Sound Association: Single Letters
- Test 3—Substitution: Single Letters
- Test 4—Consonant-Vowel-Consonant Trigrams
- Test 5—Initial Consonant Blends and Digraphs
- Test 6—Final Consonant Blends and Digraphs
- Test 7—Vowel Combinations
- Test 8—Open Syllable Generalization
- Test 9—Final Silent E Generalization
- Test 10—Vowel Versatility
- Test 11—Vowels Plus R
- Test 12—Silent Consonants
- Test 13—Vowel Sounds of Y
- Test 14—Visual Analysis
- Test 15—Visual Blending
- Test 16—Contractions

Much emphasis is placed on summarizing and interpreting the findings of each subtest; the mini-manual provides necessary information as well as suggestions for follow-up testing. In addition, an individual report form can be used in summarizing and reporting the findings for each student.

The *SWAT* provides two types of scores. Specific strengths and weaknesses scores are used following the criteria of:

68–100% correct: can or probably can perform the task,
51–67% correct: may be able to perform the task, and
 0–50% correct: cannot or probably cannot perform the task.

Performance objective scores are also given using a criterion of at least 95% accuracy.[29]

This test is extremely specific in providing diagnostic data on word identification skills. The results provide information for the teacher to use in prescriptive teaching in this area. Sipay seems to have given careful thought to providing a test that measures these skills as they are actually used in reading, and attempts to test the skills in an activity-oriented setting.

The Test of Early Reading Ability, Second Edition
D. Kim Reid, Wayne P. Hresko, and Donald D. Hammill
Pro-Ed, Austin, Texas, 1989
(Ages 3.0 to 9.11)

TERA is designed to identify children who are significantly behind their peers in the development of reading, to suggest instructional practices for overcoming their difficulty, and to document their progress. Thus, the young students with whom this instrument is used must be able to understand the directions for the items, provide some type of response for these items, and have some facility in the English language. Children who have limited exposure to the socio-cultural experiences in the United States will be penalized on this test.

The three areas specifically measured on this test are construction of meaning in print, knowledge of the alphabet and its functions, and conventions of written language. The measurement of these areas provides one test score to reflect the child's level of reading development; there are no subtest scores. Items relating to construction of meaning are of three types: (1) awareness of print in environmental contexts (identifying signs, logos, and words frequently found in context; selecting words that go with other words, story retellings, anticipation of written language, and a cloze task); (2) knowledge of relations among vocabulary items (letter naming and alphabet recitation, oral reading, and proofreading); and (3) awareness of print in connected discourse (book handling and response to other print conventions). Fifty items are used to measure these three areas and to provide three kinds of normative scores: Reading Quotients, Percentiles, and Reading Ages. No grade equivalents are given.[30]

The Examiner's Manual provides directions for administering and scoring the test, as well as suggestions for analyzing the results. To facilitate diagnostic-prescriptive reading instruction, an item profile is offered to assist the teacher in obtaining an idea of the child's functioning across the three areas and to provide guidance in determining what further diagnosis may be needed.

Tests of Language Development, 2nd Edition (TOLD-2)
Phyllis L. Newcomer and Donald D. Hammill
Pro-Ed, Austin, Texas, 1988
(Ages 4.0 to 12.11)

TOLD-2 is designed to identify children who have language disorders and to isolate the particular types of disorders they have. This instrument is especially adept at analyzing those language problems relating to semantics, syntax, and phonology.

The *Tests of Language Development* are divided into primary and intermediate sections. The primary section has seven subtests that measure different components of spoken language. Picture Vocabulary assesses the understanding of words from a semantics perspective, while Oral Vocabulary assesses defining words, also from a semantics perspective. The third, fourth, and fifth subtests assess understanding sentence structures, generating proper sentences, and using acceptable morphological forms from a syntax perspective. These subtests are Grammatic Understanding, Sentence Imitation, and Grammatic Completion. Word Discrimination is the sixth subtest and assesses noticing sound differences from a phonology perspective, and the seventh subtest is Word Articulation which assesses saying words correctly, also from a phonology perspective.

The intermediate section of *TOLD-2* has six subtests that assess components of spoken language. These include: Sentence Combining which assesses constructing sentences from a syntax perspective, Vocabulary which assesses understanding word relationships from a semantics perspective, and Word Ordering which assesses constructing sentences from a syntax perspective. The final three subtests are: Generals which assess knowing abstract relationships from a semantics perspective, Grammatic Comprehension which assesses recognizing grammatical sentences from a syntax perspective, and Malapropisms which measure ability to correct ridiculous sentences from a semantics perspective.

The Examiner's Manual provides directions for administering and scoring the test as well as other pertinent information that would help facilitate diagnostic-prescriptive reading instruction.

Test of Written Language, 2nd edition (TOWL-2)
Donald D. Hammill and Stephen C. Larsen
Pro-Ed, Austin, Texas, 1988
(Ages 7.0 to 17.11)

TOWL-2 is designed to assess various aspects of written language and uses both essay analysis (spontaneous) formats and traditional test (contrived) formats. This instrument has two alternative equivalent forms and is intended for use with individuals or small groups.

The subtests that use an essay or spontaneous format are:

- Thematic Maturity—the number of content elements that are included in the student's story.
- Contextual Vocabulary—the number of nonduplicated long words used in the story.
- Syntactic Maturity—the number of words in the story that are used in grammatically and syntactically correct sentences.
- Contextual Spelling—the number of words in the story that are spelled correctly.
- Contextual Style—the number of different capitalization and punctuation rules that are used by the student in composing an essay.

Those subtests using a traditional or contrived test format include:

- Vocabulary—Sentences that show knowledge of stimulus words are written by the student.
- Style and Spelling—Dictated sentences are written by the student and checked out for proper spelling, capitalization, and punctuation.
- Logical Sentences—Students correct sentences that contain common illogicalities.
- Sentence Combining—Students combine the ideas expressed in simple sentences to write compound or complex sentences.

The Examiner's Manual provides directions for administering and scoring the test. It also has a section that provides suggestions for assessing written language informally and suggests ideas for teachers to use in improving their students' writing capabilities.

Woodcock Reading Mastery Tests–Revised (WRMT-R)
Richard W. Woodcock
DLM Teaching Resources, Allen, Texas, 1987 (Grades Kindergarten–12)

The *Woodcock Reading Mastery Tests-Revised* is available in two alternative forms, with Form G consisting of six subtests and Form H including only the four reading achievement tests. The six subtests included in Form G are Visual-Auditory Learning, Letter Identification, Word Identification, Word Attack, Word Comprehension, and Passage Comprehension. The materials needed for this test include a manual, response forms, and an easel notebook containing all the test materials.

The six tests of the *WRMT-R* are organized in three clusters. The Visual-Auditory Learning and Letter Identification tests compose the Readiness Cluster. The Basic Skills Cluster consists of the Word Identification and Word Attack tests. The Reading Comprehension Cluster is made up of the Word Comprehension and Passage Comprehension tests. This revised edition of the *WRMT* has an added readiness section and an expanded Word Comprehension test. Scoring procedures have also changed along with additional options for interpretation. To allow for differing degrees of precision, there are three options for interpreting the *WRMT-R*.

The lowest level allows the examiner to plot raw scores from the *WRMT-R*, the Goldman-Fristor-Woodcock Auditory Skills Test Battery, and the Woodcock-Johnson Psychoeducational Battery on an Instructional Level Profile and/or on three diagnostic profiles. When this is completed, approximate grade equivalents and instructional ranges can be seen with strengths and weaknesses identified from these various measures.

The next level of interpretation involves using the norm tables to obtain a total reading score along with percentile ranks and relative performance indices (RPIs) for each of the subtests.

The highest level of interpretation also uses the norm tables to determine exact grade equivalents, age equivalents, a variety of standard scores, confidence bands for RPIs, and percentile ranks.[31] The manual suggests a fourth level of interpretation, however, the procedure is not described in this book because the authors believe that it is too time consuming for teacher use.

The six tests that form the *WRMT-R* battery and their descriptions are as follows:

Visual-Auditory Learning: This test is the same as the Visual-Auditory Learning subtest of the Woodcock-Johnson Psychoeducational Battery, which requires the student to associate unfamiliar visual stimuli (rebuses) with familiar oral words and then to translate sequences of rebuses into sentences.

Letter Identification: This test has forty-five items to assess the student's skill in naming or pronouncing letters of the alphabet. Upper- and lowercase letters in four styles of type (Roman, sans serif, cursive, and a speciality typeface) are used.

Word Identification: Skill in pronouncing words in isolation is measured on this test. One-hundred fifty words ranging in levels of difficulty are pronounced until five or more consecutive words are missed.

Word Attack: This test provides fifty items to determine the student's ability to identify nonsense words, using phonic and structural analysis skills. The nonsense words proceed from simple to complex, and the test stops when five or more consecutive errors are made.

Word Comprehension: This test consists of three subtests to measure Antonyms, Synonyms, and Analogies. Separate scores can be obtained for comprehension of words in the different content areas of general reading vocabulary, science-mathematics vocabulary, social studies vocabulary, and humanities vocabulary.

Passage Comprehension: The modified cloze procedure is used with the eighty-five items on this test. The student reads silently a sentence or short passage that has a word missing, and then provides the word that goes in the blank space. The passages range in difficulty from first grade to college level.[32]

The revised edition of the *WRMT-R* has more sample items and includes a Short Scale, which requires only the administration and scoring of the Word Identification and Passage Comprehension tests. This edition of the test includes additional diagnostic aids and provides more guidance in presenting scores. In addition to the special microcomputer scoring program, a report is also available to parents that gives test results, explains student performance, and describes each of the tests.

Auditory Discrimination Tests

Auditory discrimination may be defined as the ability to distinguish likenesses and differences in sounds. It is only one aspect of an area known as auditory perception. The correlation of auditory discrimination skill development with reading proficiency relates at best with the student's ability to discriminate between various combinations of sounds. However, the importance of this area has long been disputed in the field of reading. Writers such as Robeck and Wilson and Durrell and Murphy contend that auditory discrimination skills are extremely important and are directly related to reading.[33] Others, like Smith, and Deutsch and Feldman, have found no evidence that auditory discrimination training has any positive impact on reading achievement.[34] In addition to this debate over the importance of auditory discrimination skills, there is also concern regarding the procedures used to assess them. Dykstra maintains that the various auditory discrimination tests are not equivalent in prescriptive ability or in their relationship to reading. He found the most effective test for predicting reading achievement to be one that requires the student to select a picture of an object with the same initial sound as a spoken word.[35] Oakland concluded that phonemic auditory discrimination tests correlated better with reading achievement than nonphonemic tests.[36]

More recently, Newman found that auditory training produces superior growth in auditory skills; these gains did not transfer to reading achievement among the experimental group and, in fact, the control group that practiced various reading exercises had greater growth in reading.[37]

Koenke's study of three auditory discrimination measures, Wepman's *Auditory Discrimination Test*, the Goldman-Fristoe-Woodcock *Test of Auditory Discrimination*, and the Kimmell-Wahl *Screening Test of Auditory Perception*, found great differences in performance on the various measures with only two of fifty-two subjects passing all three tests and only twelve failing all three tests.[38] Thus, there is little consistency in what is considered auditory discrimination from one test to another. This complication may exist due to factors such as dialect differences, vocabulary range, prior knowledge, varying views of the directions for the task, examiner bias, and the lack of visual cues.[39]

Research offers teachers no clear-cut answer to the question regarding the value of auditory discrimination testing or teaching. However, the authors support Ekwall and Shanker's suggestion that "teachers and reading specialists test and teach auditory discrimination skills to young children (ages five to seven) when such an approach appears to be warranted. All children in a particular class will not require this instruction, and for those who do the amount of time spent should not be so great as to detract from other, more important reading-skill areas."[40] An auditory discrimination test may be administered as a separate instrument or as a part of another test, such as the *Stanford Diagnostic Reading Test* or the *Gates-McKillop-Horowitz Reading Diagnostic Tests*. The most commonly used separate auditory discrimination test is the Wepman *Auditory Discrimination Test*.

Auditory Discrimination Test
Joseph M. Wepman
Language Research Associates, Chicago, Illinois, 1973
(Ages 5–8)

The revised *Auditory Discrimination Test* consists of forty pairs of words on each of the two forms. The teacher pronounces each pair, and the student states whether the words are the same or different. The teacher has the student face in another direction, so that the possibility of lip reading does not enter into the score.

Before administering this test, the teacher should be sure that the student understands the meaning of the terms same and different. Some examples are provided for practice. Teachers must be careful to pronounce the words correctly and not to overemphasize likenesses and differences in the pairs.

The score is based on the number of correct responses. Norms are provided for ages five to eight, but the test may also be used with older students.

Intelligence Tests

The use of intelligence tests as aids in reading diagnosis or predictors of reading success can be either supported or discredited by research. However, the general conclusion is that group intelligence tests are more a measure of reading ability than intelligence. Individual intelligence tests seem to be better indicators of potential. Verbal mental ability tests, such as the verbal section of the *Wechsler Intelligence Scale for Children—Revised (WISC-R)*, correlate more highly with reading comprehension. Studies like that of Bond and Dykstra suggested that at the first-grade level, correlation between mental ability and reading comprehension is generally in the .40's and .50's.[41] Allen indicated that this correlation rose into the .70's by the fourth grade.[42] Thorndike found that the .70 correlation tended to remain into the freshman year of college.[43] Spache and Spache conclude that an I.Q. score may be a fairly good predictor of reading ability for students with an extremely high I.Q. or for those who are mentally retarded.[44] Sewell found that the I.Q. correlated moderately with achievement for both black and white first graders, but was a more reliable predictor for whites than for blacks.[45]

An I.Q. test is not an essential measure in diagnosing a reading problem. In fact, intelligence tests usually provide little information beyond that gained by observation or by the administration of an individual reading test. The intelligence tests with subtests that seem to be most helpful in reading diagnosis are the *Wechsler Intelligence Scale for Children—Revised*, the *Wechsler Adult Intelligence Scale—Revised*, and the *Stanford-Binet Intelligence Scale*. These tests are administered by a specially certified person and take a great deal of time; thus, teachers are unable to use them for diagnostic purposes. If, however, these tests are administered, the teacher should request information on each of the subtest scores. This information may assist in determining strengths and weaknesses in learning and in providing better prescriptive instruction. Sources such as *How to Use WISC-R Scores in Reading/Learning Disability Diagnosis* by Searls are most helpful in making maximum use of the information.[46]

Should the teacher believe that an intelligence measure may provide more necessary information, and if individual I.Q. test data are not available, there are two individual intelligence measures that can be administered by the teacher: the *Peabody Picture Vocabulary Test—Revised* and the *Slosson Intelligence Test—Revised*.

Peabody Picture Vocabulary Test—Revised (PPVT-R)

Lloyd M. Dunn and Leota M. Dunn
American Guidance Service, Inc., Circle Pines, Minnesota, 1981
(Ages 2.6 to Adult)

The *PPVT-R* is designed to provide an estimate of a student's verbal intelligence by assessing hearing vocabulary. This is done using 150 sets of four pictures: the student selects the named picture for each set. The kit includes a spiral-bound book containing the pictured plates, a manual, and individual test record booklets. There are two forms, Forms A and B, which are included in one kit. The test requires about ten to fifteen minutes for administration. An I.Q., a percentile score, and a mental age indication can be obtained from the raw score.

Validity, reliability, and relationship with reading success are the points often questioned relative to the *PPVT*. Spache has suggested that the reliability of the estimate is improved if both forms are administered.[47] He states that the influence of socioeconomic or linguistic handicaps on the score is not significant. Ekwall's research, however, indicated that the *PPVT* is a highly unreliable measure of intelligence for individual students.[48] Pikulski reported that the *PPVT* and *Slosson Intelligence Test* correlated equally well with the *WISC* for students with reading disabilities.[49] Thus, the teacher should recognize that the studies regarding this instrument provide varying information dependent upon the population, and that this test is strictly a measure of intelligence based on the student's vocabulary knowledge. Because vocabulary and language knowledge are so important to success in reading, this test is better used as a predictor of reading success than of intelligence.

Slosson Intelligence Test—Revised (SIT-R)

Richard L. Slosson; Revised by Charles L. Nicholson and Terry L. Hibpshman
Slosson Educational Publications, Inc., East Aurora, New York, 1990
(Ages Preschool to Adult)

The *SIT-R* is a verbal measure of intelligence that was developed to emulate the *Stanford-Binet*. Many items were adapted from the *Stanford-Binet* (Form L-M) with this test being used as the criterion validity for the *SIT-R*. The test follows a question-answer format. The manual suggests that the test can be administered in ten to twenty minutes, however, the experience of the authors is that about fifteen to thirty minutes are necessary.

This test was developed as a short screening instrument for teachers and others without extensive training in test administration. Armstrong and Mooney found that the results were equally valid when the test was given by a teacher or a test administrator.[50]

The *SIT-R*, like all other verbal measures of intelligence, penalizes the student with limited experiences in language. Thus, the classroom teacher must exercise caution.

A number of changes were made in the 1990 edition of the *SIT*, but it remains very similar in content to the other editions. This edition contains sections on validity, independent sampling, other research findings, as well as an extended bibliography. Moreover, an item analysis can be purchased as a Supplement to aid in screening for strengths and weaknesses in various areas.

■ Summary

This chapter presented an overview of various formal diagnostic procedures available for use by the classroom teacher. Some of the instruments discussed require special training; others do not. However, classroom teachers willing to devote a minimum amount of time to the study of the tests can administer and interpret the instruments mentioned.

Two broad categories of diagnostic procedures were discussed with several types of instruments in each category. The major categories were group and individual testing procedures.

There were three types of group-administered tests presented:

Survey reading tests
Diagnostic reading tests
Achievement tests

Under individually-administered procedures, four types of tests were presented:

Oral reading tests
Diagnostic reading tests
Auditory discrimination tests
Intelligence tests

These instruments, with their individual strengths and limitations, were presented to assist teachers in becoming more knowledgeable of tests that may help in diagnosing student needs in reading.

■ Applying What You Read

Under what circumstances would an individually-administered diagnostic instrument be preferable to a group-administered diagnostic instrument?

What type of instrument would be better suited for screening a fourth-grade class for specific word identification and comprehension skills? Why?

Your school is selecting some formal diagnostic tools to use in the reading program. What individual tests would you recommend? Why? What group tests would you recommend? Why?

Are there any instances in which you as a classroom teacher might want to use the results from group I.Q. tests? Why or why not?

A second-grade student in your classroom has a reading problem and exhibits difficulties with sight words, auditory and visual perception, as well as word identification. What type of formal diagnostic instrument could you use with this student? What specific tests would you recommend? Why?

Identify a battery (2 or 3 tests) of formal tests that you would like to have available in your classroom. Tell why you selected each.

■ Notes

1. Anne M. Bussis and Edward A. Chittenden, "Research Currents: What the Reading Tests Neglect," *Language Arts*.

2. James R. Squire, "Introduction: A Special Issue on the State of Assessment in Reading," *The Reading Teacher*; Sheila Valencia and P. David Pearson, "Reading Assessment: Time for a Change," *The Reading Teacher*.

3. Nancy A. Mavrogenes, Earl F. Hanson, and Carol K. Winkley, "A Guide to Tests of Factors that Inhibit Learning to Read," *The Reading Teacher*.

4. Ann E. Boehm, *Examiner's Manual: Boehm Test of Basic Concepts-Revised*.

5. Walter H. MacGinitie et al., *Gates-MacGinitie Reading Tests Teacher's Manuals*, 1989.

6. Roger Farr, ed., *Iowa Silent Reading Test, Manual of Directions*.

7. Roger C. Farr, George A. Prescott, Irving H. Balow, and Thomas P. Hogan, *MAT6 Reading Diagnostic Tests: Teacher's Manual*.

8. Bjorn Karlsen, Richard Madden, and Eric F. Gardner, *Stanford Diagnostic Reading Test: Manual for Administering and Interpreting*.

9. The Psychological Corporation, *1987 Catalog*, p. 88.

10. Virginia L. Brown, Donald D. Hammill, and J. Lee Wiederholt, *Manual: Test of Reading Comprehension, Revised Edition*.

11. Connie Juel and B. Holmes, "Oral and Silent Reading of Sentences," *Reading Research Quarterly*.

12. Kenneth S. Goodman, "Behind the Eye: What Happens in Reading," in *Theoretical Models and Processes in Reading*, 2nd ed., edited by Harry Singer and Robert Ruddell.

13. Francis W. Parker, *Talks on Pedagogies*; Edmund B. Huey, *The Psychology and Pedagogy of Reading*.

14. Nila Banton Smith, *American Reading Instruction*, 3rd ed., pp. 158–64.

15. Marguerite C. Radencich, "Test Review: Gray Oral Reading Tests-Revised and Formal Reading Inventory," *Journal of Reading*.

16. J. Lee Wiederholt and Brian R. Bryant, *Manual: Gray Oral Reading Tests*, Third Edition.

17. Richard L. Slosson, *Slosson Oral Reading Test*, 1990, p. 1.

18. George D. Spache, *Diagnostic Reading Scales*, Examiner's Manual, p. 10.

19. George D. Spache, *Diagnostic Reading Scales*, revised, p. 18.

20. George D. Spache, *Diagnostic Reading Scales*, Examiner's Manual, pp. 9–16.

21. Sally Lipa, "Test Review: Diagnostic Reading Scales," *The Reading Teacher*.

22. George D. Spache, *Diagnostic Reading Scales: Technical Bulletin*.

23. Spache, *Diagnosing and Correcting Reading Disabilities*, pp. 203–14.

24. Donald D. Durrell and Jane H. Catterson, *Durrell Analysis of Reading Difficulty: Manual of Directions*.

25. Leo M. Schell and Robert E. Jennings, "Test Review: Durrell Analysis of Reading Difficulty," 3rd ed., *The Reading Teacher*.

26. J. Lee Wiederholt, *Formal Reading Inventory*.

27. Radencich, "Test Review: Gray Oral Reading Tests-Revised and Formal Reading Inventory," *Journal of Reading*.

28. Arthur I. Gates, Anne S. McKillop, and Elizabeth Cliff Horowitz, *Gates-McKillop-Horowitz Reading Diagnostic Tests*, 2nd ed., Manual of Directions.

29. Edward R. Sipay, *Sipay Word Analysis Tests*.
30. D. Kim Reid, Wayne P. Hresko, and Donald D. Hammill, *Manual: Test of Early Reading Ability*, 1989.
31. Richard W. Woodcock, *Woodcock Reading Mastery Tests-Revised: Manual*, p. 1.
32. Woodcock, *Woodcock Reading Mastery Tests-Revised: Manual*, pp. 1–5.
33. Mildred C. Robeck and John A. R. Wilson, *Psychology of Reading: Foundations of Instruction*; Donald D. Durrell and Helen A. Murphy, "The Auditory Discrimination Factor in Reading Readiness and Reading Disability," *Education*.
34. Frank Smith, *Psycholinguistics and Reading*; Cynthia P. Deutsch and Shirley C. Feldman, "A Study of the Effectiveness of Training for Retarded Readers in the Auditory Skills Underlying Reading," Title VII, Project No. 1127 Grant.
35. Robert Dykstra, "Auditory Discrimination Abilities and Beginning Reading Achievement," *Reading Research Quarterly*.
36. Thomas D. Oakland, "Auditory Discrimination and Socioeconomic Status as Correlates of Reading Ability," *Journal of Learning Disabilities*.
37. Susan B. Newman, "Effect of Teaching Auditory Perceptual Skills on Reading Achievement in First Grade," *The Reading Teacher*.
38. Karl Koenke, "A Comparison of Three Auditory Discrimination-Perception Tests," *Academic Therapy*.
39. Mary Ann Geissal and June Knafle, "A Linguistic View of Auditory Discrimination Tests and Exercises," *The Reading Teacher*.
40. Eldon E. Ekwall and James L. Shanker, *Diagnosis and Remediation of the Disabled Reader*, p. 297.
41. Guy L. Bond and Robert Dykstra, "The Cooperative Research Program in First Grade Reading Instruction," *Reading Research Quarterly*.
42. M. Allen, "Relationship Between Kuhlmann-Anderson Intelligence Tests and Academic Achievement in Grade IV," *Journal of Educational Psychology*.
43. Robert L. Thorndike, *The Concepts of Over- and Underachievement*.
44. George D. Spache and Evelyn B. Spache, *Reading in the Elementary School*, 4th ed.
45. Trevor E. Sewell, "Intelligence and Learning Tasks as Predictors of Scholastic Achievement in Black and White First-Grade Children," *Journal of Psychology*.
46. Evelyn F. Searls, *How to Use WISC-R Scores in Reading/Learning Disability Diagnosis*.
47. Spache, *Diagnosing and Correcting Reading Disabilities*, p. 88.
48. Eldon E. Ekwall, *Diagnosis and Remediation of the Disabled Reader*, p. 177.
49. John Pikulski, "The Validity of Three Brief Measures of Intelligence for Disabled Readers," *Journal of Educational Research*.
50. Robert J. Armstrong and Robert F. Mooney, "The Slosson Intelligence Test: Implications for Reading Specialists," *The Reading Teacher*.

■ Other Suggested Readings

Chall, Jeanne S. and Mary E. Curtis. "What Clinical Diagnosis Tells Us About Children's Reading." *The Reading Teacher* 40 (April 1987):784–88.
Coleman, M. and W. R. Hermer. "A Comparison of Standardized Reading Tests and Informal Placement Procedures." *Journal of Learning Disabilities* 15 (1982): 396–98.
Farr, Roger and M. Beck. "Validating the 'Instructional Reading Level' of the Metropolitan Achievement Tests." *Journal of Research and Development in Education* 17 (1984):55–64.

Farr, Roger and Robert F. Carey. *Reading: What Can Be Measured?* Newark, Delaware: International Reading Association, 1986.

Gunning, Thomas G. "Wrong Level Test: Wrong Information." *The Reading Teacher* 35 (May 1982):902–5.

Harris, Albert J. and Edward R. Sipay. *How to Increase Reading Ability*, 9th ed. New York: Longman, 1990.

Johnston, Peter H. *Reading Comprehension Assessment: A Cognitive Basis*. Newark, Delaware: International Reading Association, 1983.

Johnston, Peter H. "Prior Knowledge and Reading Comprehension Test Bias." *Reading Research Quarterly* 19 (Winter 1984):219–39.

Koenke, Karl and Jane McClellan. "ERIC/RCS Report: Teaching and Testing the Reading Disabled Child." *Language Arts* 64 (March 1987):327–30.

Mason, George E. and Beverly B. Swanson. "Why First Graders Err on Standardized Reading Tests." *Reading World* 23 (October 1983):60–68.

Pikulski, John J. "The Role of Tests in a Literacy Assessment Program." *The Reading Teacher* 43 (May 1990):686–88.

Smith, Lawrence L. and Jerry L. Johns. "A Study of the Effects of Out of Level Testing with Poor Readers in the Intermediate Grades." *Reading Psychology* 5 (1984):138–43.

Synthesizing Data

STEP 2

Step 2 is a key link in using the diagnostic information for prescriptive teaching. Classroom teachers realize that much time can be wasted in diagnosis if the data are not properly organized, interpreted, and summarized. Thus, chapter 4 provides suggestions for teachers to use in order to obtain maximum information from data on each student.

4

Organizing Diagnostic Information

Classroom teachers realize that synthesizing data from the diagnostic information gathered on each student is an essential step in the development of a diagnostic-prescriptive reading program. Since students are continuously diagnosed during the school year, large amounts of data are collected. However, the information gained is little more than a series of test scores, observational information, and miscellaneous data gathered about each student. In order for information to have any significance to the teacher, student, parents, or others involved in the program, the teachers must synthesize the data. To accomplish this, teachers should identify a series of tasks to be carried out. These include organizing the data, analyzing and interpreting it, providing recommendations for instruction, and summarizing the findings (see figure 4.1).

The completion of these four tasks is essential if the diagnostic information obtained is to have a meaningful impact on the teaching process. Synthesizing the data to form a meaningful whole enables the teacher to prescribe adequately the most effective techniques and materials to use with each student. It allows other school personnel to better understand the reasons for the use of specific procedures in dealing with the reading development of individual students.

During the period when the diagnostic information is obtained, the teacher gains valuable insights into the student's personality, attitude, value system, peer relationships, and, perhaps to some extent, cultural and environmental factors that affect a student's performance in reading. These affective aspects of diagnosis are extremely important in the synthesizing process, and are as relevant as the cognitive information obtained through informal and formal testing procedures. Both cognitive and affective determiners go hand-in-hand in developing the most effective prescription for teaching a student to read. As teachers consider these determiners, they should ask themselves these questions:

What procedures should be used in synthesizing data?

How are data organized for teacher use?

What are the interrelationships between analysis and interpretation of diagnostic information?

Why are these interrelationships so vital to the diagnostic-prescriptive process?

How are diagnostic data analyzed and interpreted?

How does the teacher effectively summarize diagnostic information to enhance the instructional process?

How can the diagnostic information be organized for daily classroom use to provide prescriptive instruction?

What do the various terms used on the test instruments, such as raw score, stanine, and grade equivalent, mean to the teacher?

As this chapter is read, the following terms are important to note.

Vocabulary to Know

Analysis	Interpretation	Raw score
Correlation	Mean	Reliability
Data	Median	Standard score
Grade equivalent	Normal curve	Stanine
Grade level	Percentile	Summarizing
Grade placement	Range	Validity

Figure 4.1
Four Basic Tasks in
Synthesizing
Diagnostic Data for
Prescriptive
Instruction

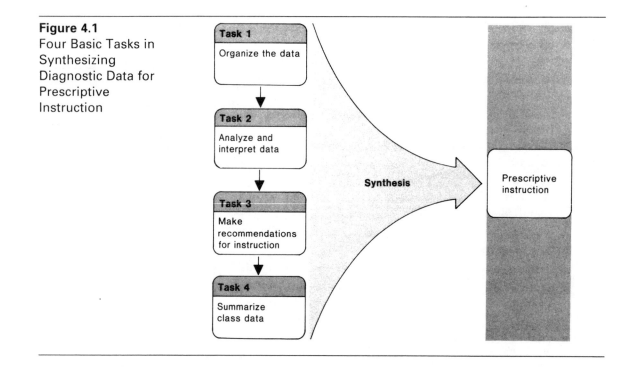

■ Knowing What We Have

After the diagnostic information has been gathered, it is essential for teachers to determine what they have and to organize this data in a way that will enhance its usefulness. This information should be recorded in a logical sequence so that the teacher may refer to it as needed. An important aspect of diagnosis is to have data that is both accessible and useful. This enables the teacher to provide a more appropriate learning environment for students.

Knowing what we have in terms of diagnostic information about students requires organization which in turn enhances instruction and is indispensable in synthesizing data. Data can be organized in many ways; as teachers become more accustomed to gathering and interpreting diagnostic information, they will develop and refine their own ideas for organizing this information. Since it is crucial that diagnostic data be organized initially in some usable format and since this concept may be unfamiliar to some teachers, the following suggestions may be helpful in organizing diagnostic data.

It may be helpful to use a folder for each student so that the information can be readily available for the teacher's use. The folder may contain tests, observations, and other pertinent data useful for prescriptive instruction. Remember that the information should be objective and factual. Personal opinions concerning the student's behavior or home life should not be recorded in a student's folder, which is open for review by many people.

As data are collected, the teacher may wish to consider a four-step organizational plan used by the authors. The categories or steps in this plan are concerned with basic information about the student, her background, identifying diagnostic information, interpretation of the data, and listing recommendations for prescriptive instruction. These steps are outlined in figure 4.2.

The first step is concerned with recording *basic information*, such as the student's name, chronological age, and the dates during which diagnostic information was obtained. Another important factor is whether or not the student is in the correct grade level; some students may have been retained in previous grades. Although this step may appear somewhat simplistic, it is crucial that it be reported correctly, as many test norms use this information. The teacher may record this basic information on the front of the student folder or on a separate sheet of paper inside the folder. For students with severe reading problems, for whom more formal case reports are developed, the instructor would use this as introductory information.

In the second step, the *student's background* is explored. This is valuable because of the many factors that affect a student's reading ability. Such variables as physical condition, cultural and socioeconomic background, educational factors, the home environment, interests, experiential background, and prior knowledge are all useful in developing an appropriate instructional program for the student. This is an area that perhaps influences the student's educational progress more than any other. The

Figure 4.2
Organization of Data

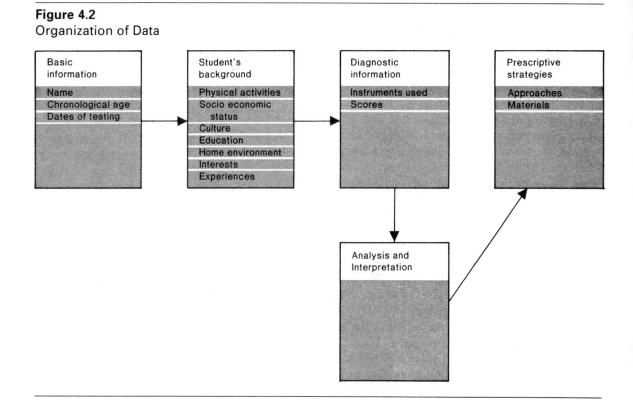

authors have seen many students with adequate reading skills and cognitive abilities who theoretically should have been able to read, but could not because of a number of other factors that adversely affected them. Foremost among these are unstable homes, poor experiential backgrounds, lack of prior knowledge, cultural differences, and language differences. Unfortunately, there are so many factors that adversely affect a student's ability to read that the teacher experiences great difficulty in dealing effectively with them. Learning to read is not always contingent upon the improvement of oral language abilities, learning phonetic and structural analysis skills, and improving comprehension; many outside forces heavily influence reading progress. For this reason, it is imperative that as much background information as possible be available to the teacher. This not only allows teachers to be better informed about their students, but further enhances the prospect for success in improving the student's reading capabilities. To organize this data, the teacher may find it useful to list significant information about the student as obtained from parent conferences or from the student. Possible leading questions that might be asked are listed on the next page.

Parents

Were there any difficulties with the pregnancy, the birth process, or development
 of the child?
How many children are in the family?
How does this child get along with others in the family? Father? Mother? Siblings?
Have you noticed that your child has difficulty with reading?
When did you first notice the difficulty?
What kind of activities does the family enjoy together?
How much reading does each of the family members engage in during the week?
What is the longest trip that your child has taken?
Do you take your child with you when you go shopping, visiting, or on trips?
How does your child feel about school? Reading?

Student

Do you like to read? What types of material?
Do you have your own books at home? What is your favorite book?
Do your parents read to you? When?
What is your favorite activity after school?
What do you like to do best with your father? Mother? Brother(s)? Sister(s)?
Have you been to the zoo? Grocery store? On trips to other states?

In addition, the teacher may wish to use parent information sheets and interest
inventories such as that in appendix C to gather more information regarding the
student's background. This information should be listed on the inside of the student's folder or on a separate sheet kept in the folder. The teacher should remember
that the purpose of this information is to assist in better diagnosing the student's
reading problem and providing appropriate prescriptive instruction.

The third step in organizing data deals with the *identification of the diagnostic information*. The teacher should list on a summary page the instruments used and their
scores. Other informal diagnostic information such as portfolios, journals, observation checklists, interest and attitude surveys, criterion-referenced tests, and notes on
daily work, should also be listed with the necessary information. The teacher should
arrange or formulate the information so that data are readily accessible and easy to
use. This step is essential to the task of *analysis and interpretation* of the data, discussed
in the following section.

The fourth step in organizing the data is concerned with *listing prescriptive or instructional strategies* for the student. After the data has been interpreted in terms of
the student's strengths and weaknesses, and the background information analyzed,
the teacher is ready to recommend the instructional strategies to be used in teaching.
This can be accomplished by using either a list format or a narrative format for
enumerating materials and approaches for teaching. A list format saves time and
presents the information in such a manner that the teacher need only turn to the
prescriptive section in the folder to locate the procedures recommended for instruction. The instructor should list the appropriate approach or method of teaching for

Portfolios require teachers and students to conference frequently as progress is monitored.

each student and the materials to be used. Once this is done, the teacher may easily refer to each student's folder to determine the skills to be developed or the appropriate methods or procedures to be used in the instructional process. It is important to remember that prescriptions can and do change. This is a characteristic of the diagnostic-prescriptive instructional process and, in fact, one of its underlying principles. Chapters 6–12 deal specifically with prescriptive instruction for the students.

Knowing what we have in the way of diagnostic data and effectively organizing this data into a usable format is an essential first step in the process of synthesizing and using diagnostic information. Data that is both accessible and useful enhances the instructional process and enables teachers to more effectively use the facilities and materials available to them.

■ Using What We Know

After the data have been organized and we know what we have, the next step in synthesizing diagnostic information involves analyzing and interpreting this information. Analysis is crucial to the process of determining a student's strengths and weaknesses and involves the objective evaluation of the diagnostic information that has been gathered. For example, a primary student might exhibit difficulties in directionality and left-to-right sequencing in his/her daily journal recordings. An examination of this journal by the teacher would indicate problems in these areas and the necessity for providing appropriate instruction without adversely affecting the student's interest in this journal writing activity.

An example of analysis using a formal testing instrument might involve the inferential comprehension subtest of the *Stanford Diagnostic Reading Test*, Red Level. An analysis of this subtest reveals a third stanine score, which is slightly below average. On further analysis of this subtest score, the teacher realizes that the student experienced great difficulty with activating his schema in regard to the information asked in many of the questions. In other words, the student has little or no prior knowledge and depth of experiences to enable her to answer the questions satisfactorily.

Another example of analyzing data may involve the results obtained from an informal reading inventory such as the *Sucher-Allred Reading Placement Inventory*. In this particular example, a third grade student's performance on the *Sucher-Allred* yields an instructional reading level of 2^1 (equivalent to second grade, first semester). An analysis of this data indicated that this student's actual classroom reading level (instructional level) is below that of the student's grade placement level. This information alerts the teacher to a potential problem involving this student's instructional program. Thus, objective analysis involves evaluating the types of errors made by the student without interpreting the consequences of these errors.

Analysis of the scores taken from test data enables the teacher to look at the individual phases of the total picture, so that essential questions about particular problems can be raised and answered. Looking at a total score is not likely to reveal the information needed for prescribing an appropriate instructional program. For example, two students may score at a low, third-year level on an informal reading inventory, however, a closer analysis of the data may indicate that one student showed strengths in word identification skills, while the other was stronger in comprehension.

By analyzing the individual test scores, a teacher can gain a better understanding of the student's strengths and weaknesses. Does the student exhibit strengths in sight vocabulary, literal comprehension, and word identification skills? Does the student experience difficulty in the area of inferential comprehension? Does the student show an interest in certain reading materials but not in others? These are types of questions that can be answered in diagnosing reading difficulties. Without looking at all the individual components, it is difficult for the teacher to arrive at an adequate understanding of the student's capabilities. Thus, analysis of the test data is of major importance in determining why a particular student does or does not experience difficulty in reading.

For many students, an analysis can be made rather briefly; or it can be an indepth interpretation of a student's strengths and weaknesses. Since the teacher's time is so valuable, an in-depth evaluation of each student is not always possible. For most students, a brief, but thorough examination of the data should suffice for

Figure 4.3
Brief Analysis
of Data

```
            Name: Joe Hunter                              Grade: 3
       Interests: Racing cars, motorcycles, and machine guns
                  Likes to make things with tools
                  Likes to watch television


Sucher-Allred Reading Placement Inventory
     Satisfactory comprehension; poor sequencing skills
     Poor phrasing—ignores punctuation
     Omits word endings
     Weak in medial sounds
        Independent level:    Primer
        Instructional level: 2²
        Frustration level:    3¹


Stanford Diagnostic Reading Test—Red Level
     Difficulty in auditory discrimination
     Poor vocabulary
     Unsure when tested using a cloze format
        Auditory Discrimination:
           Stanine 4—Grade equivalent 1.9
        Phonetic Analysis:
           Stanine 6—Grade equivalent 3.2
        Auditory Vocabulary:
           Stanine 5—Grade equivalent 2.6
        Word Reading:
           Stanine 5—Grade equivalent 2.8
        Reading Comprehension:
           Stanine 5—Grade equivalent 3.1
        Total Comprehension:
           Stanine 5—Grade equivalent 2.6
```

the development of an appropriate prescription. In fact, the teacher may wish to briefly summarize the data on a half-page for each student, to be referred to as needed. Figure 4.3 gives an example of one way to briefly analyze the data for an individual student.

Interpretation is a necessary adjunct to analysis of the data. In this procedure, the data are further evaluated, while the strengths and weaknesses of each student are interpreted with an exploration of the underlying causes for poor test results. Adequate interpretation is essential to prescription. Without it, strengthening a poor reader's skills becomes almost impossible.

In interpreting test data, certain patterns from the various tests are normally observable. These give valuable clues to the development of a complete diagnosis to serve as a basis for appropriate instruction. It is important to note that when diagnostic information is obtained from a variety of sources, specific patterns of strengths and weaknesses for individual students become more evident and identifiable.

There are many difficulties that may enter into the interpretation of a student's reading problems. These difficulties may be manifested in various reading skills, behavior patterns, and attitudinal tendencies that influence classroom reading performance. Other primary areas that provide positive and/or negative influences on reading performance are language factors, prior knowledge, experiential factors, socioeconomic factors, environmental factors, and physical conditions.

When interpreting diagnostic information, not only should the data be interrelated, but also it is essential to consider every aspect that could affect the student's reading performance. For example, a student is observed experiencing difficulty in recognizing certain vocabulary while working with a basal group, and has also scored below level on the informal reading inventory in word identification. However, the student's performance on the comprehension subtest of the *Stanford Diagnostic Reading Test* and the reading passages of the *Sucher-Allred Reading Placement Inventory* is below level, but considerably better. Although this data yields somewhat conflicting results, the teacher is aware of other primary factors that affect the student's reading performance. These factors include a limited experiential background and language-base, which has resulted in a lack of prior knowledge, thus depriving the student of encoded schema[1] with which to appropriately decode certain vocabulary. Thus, the teacher correctly concludes that the student is compensating for deficiencies in encoded schema through the efficient use of contextual analysis and interactive comprehension strategies. The teacher's primary responsibility in this situation is to assist in strengthening the student's experiential background and language-base in order to expand the student's schema.

When analyzing information derived from formal, informal, and naturalistic procedures, it is critical to the development of students as successful readers to be aware of a number of factors that must be considered in conjunction with the teacher's diagnostic data. Some of these factors are:

- Print awareness
- Prior knowledge and experiential background
- Language acquisition, both oral and written
- Cognitive ability
- Sociocultural factors
- Interest and motivation
- Physical factors including visual, auditory and motor
- Home environment
- Maturation
- Ability to interact with text materials

Because accurate interpretation is so vital to the development of an appropriate instructional program, the following section is devoted to the analysis and interpretation of the reading capabilities of a student in a typical classroom setting. Also, an in-depth case report of another student is presented in appendix E. Both of these students are in normal classroom settings, and their teachers have summarized the diagnostic information according to the steps outlined in the section on "Knowing What We Have" and have followed the case report format presented on page 141.

For the first student, a minimal number of tests were administered and intended as a guide for classroom teachers who would not write a detailed analysis and interpretation of each of their students. The second student (see appendix E) receives reading instruction as a member of a special reading pullout program in addition to the reading instruction provided by the classroom teacher. Since more in-depth diagnostic information is helpful in providing an appropriate instructional program for this student, a more extensive case report is presented. Both reports have a prescriptive component in order to demonstrate the application of the analysis and interpretation of information to the classroom instructional program.

Developing Interpretive Reports

Student 1 (Classroom)

I.   Student Data

Student's Name:	*John*
Date of Birth:	*October 16, 19—*
Sex:	*Male*
Chronological Age:	*Ten Years*
School:	*Oaks Elementary*
School District:	*Baton Rouge Parish*
Grade:	*3.2*
Examiner:	*Debbie Smith*
Dates Tested:	*October 30, 19—*
	October 31, 19—
	November 1, 19—
	November 6, 19—
	November 7, 19—

II.   Background Information

Family History

John is a ten-year-old male who lives with his mother and siblings in Baker. John is one of three children and was the third born. He has an older sister, Alice, age twelve and an older brother, Sam, age eleven.

John's parents are divorced. His father completed his education through the tenth grade and his mother through the twelfth. His mother works as a custodian.

Social History

John is a friendly, quiet child with a rather serious demeanor. He enjoys playing football with his brother and going to the mall with his mother. John does see his father and likes to go bowling with him.

John has been on vacations to the beach in Florida. He has been to the circus, the zoo, a museum and has visited a farm, but has never been on an airplane.

Educational History

Currently, John attends Oaks Elementary, a neighborhood school. He was retained in first grade and again in second grade. John is presently in third grade. His grades for the first nine weeks of this year were as follows: "F" in reading; "D" in language; "C" in spelling; "C" in mathematics; "C" in science and "B" in social studies. John received "A" in both conduct and work habits. Recently, however, he has become discouraged and doesn't try. He also does not complete homework assignments. A review of John's most recent *California Achievement Test* scores revealed total stanines of "2" in reading, "2" in language, and "2" in math.

Physical Factors

John exhibited no apparent physical problems during any of the testing procedures.

General Behavior During Testing

John seemed to enjoy being tested. He maintained a relaxed and friendly attitude throughout all procedures.

III.   Diagnosis

Test Administered:	*Sucher-Allred Reading Placement Inventory*
Test Date:	*October 31, 19—*
Word Recognition:	*2*
Independent Level:	*Primer*
Instructional Level:	*1*
Frustration Level:	*2*[1]
Listening Capacity:	*3*[2]

Analysis and Interpretation of Data

The Elementary Interest Inventory

In the first section of the inventory, entitled Home Relationships, John indicated that he gets along well with his sister and brother. They enjoy playing football together. John helps out at home by taking out the trash. In his spare time he enjoys playing outside.

In the Personal Life area of the Elementary Interest Inventory, John indicated that he is happy when he gets to go places with his father. He worries most about his mother working late and leaving him home alone. John stated that he wants to be a professional football player when he grows up.

In the third section of the Elementary Interest Inventory concerning reading, John stated that he enjoys reading and thinks it is fun and important. He indicated that he has lots of books at home, but had a difficult time naming any of them.

When questioned about school, John revealed that he liked school. His favorite subject is math and his least favorite is language. He said that he does not enjoy copying from the language book. John likes the fact that lots of his friends are in his room. He acknowledged that he gets in trouble at school for not having done his homework, but he then contradicted himself by saying that he does his homework in the living room every day after school.

John indicated in the Peer Relationship section of the Elementary Interest Inventory that he has a best friend who is nice to him. John would rather play with a friend than be alone, but wishes that his friends were nicer.

The Interest section of the Elementary Interest Inventory revealed that John most enjoys playing sports outdoors. His favorite indoor activity is playing with his car collection. He enjoys making things and would like to make his own car. He admires his mom the most and wishes he could spend more time with her.

John added no further information about himself in the Unaided Question section of the Elementary Interest Inventory.

Sucher-Allred Reading Placement Inventory

On the word recognition subtest, John achieved a grade equivalent of 2. John made one error on List A (Primer). He read "begin" for "began". On List B (First Reader) John made three errors. He read "lunch" for "laughed", "watch" for "watched" and he did not attempt "surprise". Finally, on List C (2.1), John had six errors. He read "small" for "smell", "watch out" for "without", "climb" for "climbed", "buttoned" for "button", "ground" for "garden" and he did not attempt "middle". These errors are evidence of difficulty with vowel sounds and structural analysis.

John's independent reading level as indicated by the Oral Reading section of the Sucher-Allred was at the Primer level. John had three word recognition errors. They consisted of two mispronunciations and one substitution. He had one comprehension error.

John attained an instructional level of grade one on the Sucher. He made five word recognition errors at this level. The errors consisted of two mispronunciations, one nonpronunciation, one substitution, and one regression. John correctly answered all of the comprehension questions.

The frustration level for John was determined to be at a grade level of 2. There was a marked increase of word-recognition errors with a total of eighteen. John's listening capacity was determined to be at the 3^2 level.

Synthesis

Overall analysis of the data indicates that John is a remedial reader, functioning well below level for his current grade placement and chronological age. On all tests, John exhibited weaknesses with basic vocabulary recognition and decoding skills. Word identification skills are limited. He has no apparent method for decoding unfamiliar words and therefore seems reluctant to attempt decoding. John's instructional program should include approaches which would provide him with strategies for analyzing words and improving his word identification skills.

John's comprehension ability is somewhat stronger. When he reads material that is not too difficult, his comprehension and recall are good. With more difficult reading material, John's numerous word-recognition errors severely impede his comprehension.

IV.   Prescription

Because of John's severe limitations in reading, combined with his chronological age and grade placement, extensive instruction with the basal should be limited. An eclectic approach utilizing a variety of methods would be most appropriate for John. A language-experience approach to expand John's experiential background combined with a multi-sensory approach would be beneficial.

Through the language-experience approach of providing John with experiences he has never had and then using his own words to discuss and write about the experience would be meaningful and relevant for him. After experience with this approach, John should then be instructed through process writing. He should use process writing and read from his own writing frequently. Through these modalities, John's reading, writing, speaking and listening skills should be enhanced.

The multi-sensory approach would incorporate words John wants to learn and those words in turn would be used for writing stories. By following the VAK (visual-auditory-kinesthetic) procedure John's senses of hearing, vision, touch and muscle movement would be stimulated in learning those new words.

John should receive direct instruction in word identification techniques. Following basic procedures such as discussing a particular skill (for example: contractions) and explaining how it is used to determine an unknown word and then providing opportunities to develop the skill through games and other activities would help John develop independent decoding strategies. John should be provided with ample opportunity to apply these skills in the context of meaningful reading selections.

To increase his comprehension skills, John should be provided with activities which encourage him to draw conclusions, predict outcomes and identify main ideas. This should be accomplished in the context of John's own reading.

John apparently lacks motivation for reading. His personal reading skills should be expanded and developed by providing him with various types of reading material specifically related to his abilities and interests. Art and writing activities should be used as a means for self-expression with John.

Because of John's lack of motivation and low self-esteem one-to-one or small group instruction should be employed whenever possible. Individual counseling might also be recommended. John's previous retention and lack of success have, no doubt, contributed greatly to his current problems. His instruction should be designed and paced in such a manner that allows John to experience success on a frequent and continuous basis.

The following section presents a proposed outline of a case report, which teachers may wish to use as a guide in preparing reports. In this outline, note that four primary areas are suggested for inclusion in a case report. These are student data, background information about the student, diagnosis, and prescription. Some tips that will assist the teacher in writing reports such as this, and the one presented in appendix E are given below:

Follow an organized procedure for presenting the information. The teacher may wish to use the steps outlined in this chapter or some other plan that provides the necessary information. It is much easier to organize information when a basic outline or planned procedure is followed.

Give specific data first, including the name of the test, date administered, and scores. This basic information is essential for future reference and communicating with others. Be sure to check the information carefully as it is transferred from the primary source.

Provide a brief analysis and interpretation of the data, using only the information obtained from the diagnostic assessments. Teachers must carefully study the test scores, the correct and incorrect answers of the items, as well as the actions of the student, and interrelate this information to properly diagnose strengths and weaknesses in reading.

Prepare a summarized list of the information, giving both the reading strengths and weaknesses of the students. Diagnostic information is more usable when it is succinctly presented. Thus, significant findings from the analysis and interpretation of the discussion should be listed for easy reference.

List specific recommendations for instruction to help improve the student's reading. Using the diagnostic data, the teacher must give specific suggestions for providing prescriptive instruction. These suggestions should be listed in order to aid the teacher in giving appropriate instructions.

Case Report

I. **Student Data**

Student's Name: _____

Date of Birth: _____ Sex: _____

Chronological Age: _____ School: _____

School District: _____ Grade Level: _____

Parents: _____ Home Phone: _____

Address: _____

Examiner: _____

Dates Tested: _____

II. **Background Information**
Family, Birth and Developmental History
Social History
Educational History
Physical Factors (Vision, Hearing, other)
General Behavior During Testing

III. **Diagnosis**
Test Data (Instruments Administered and Scores)
Analysis and Interpretation of Data (Each instrument should be analyzed and interpreted.)
Synthesis (Data from various instruments should be briefly summarized, focusing on the student's strengths and weaknesses.)

IV. **Prescription**
Approaches
Methods
Techniques
Materials (Published and Teacher-made)

Communicate the ideas so that other teachers as well as parents will understand the information. This is a professional report that should be beneficial not only to the classroom teacher but also to others who are interested in the student's reading progress. Keep the information objective and present it in a positive manner. Reports such as these may stay in the student's folder for many years.

■ Recommendations for Using Data

After organizing, analyzing, and interpreting the diagnostic information, the teacher is ready for the third task, which is to use the data for recommending specific instructional strategies. Since these recommendations or prescriptions are based on the strengths and weaknesses revealed in the diagnostic data, it is essential that the

Figure 4.4
Skills Chart

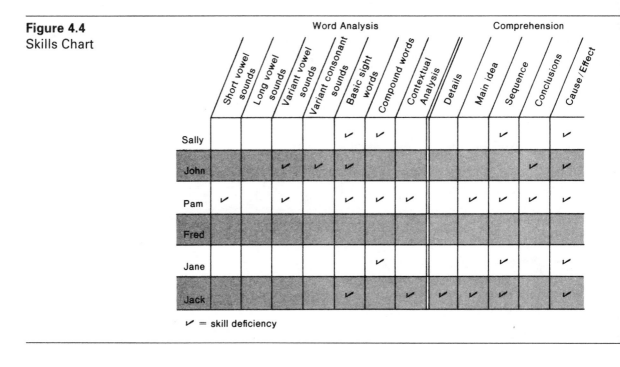

teacher use them to the greatest advantage. In order for diagnostic-prescriptive instruction to be successful, appropriate recommendations must be based upon adequate diagnosis.

Because recommendations and prescription development are such essential elements in the diagnostic-prescriptive reading program, specific information and techniques are presented in more detail beginning in chapter 6. It should be noted at this time, however, that when specific suggestions are provided for prescriptive teaching, they should be summarized and listed in a usable manner. The teacher usually does not read a lengthy narrative set of recommendations that give only general suggestions. Specifics presented in a succinct and organized manner greatly assist the teacher in providing appropriate instruction.

■ Summarizing Information for Classroom Use

The primary purpose of this chapter is to further develop the teacher's capabilities in organizing, analyzing, and interpreting diagnostic information. However, the diagnostic information gathered, analyzed, and interpreted for each student in the classroom is almost totally ineffective without some techniques for summarizing it for classroom use. Information that is not summarized will not be used. Thus, the

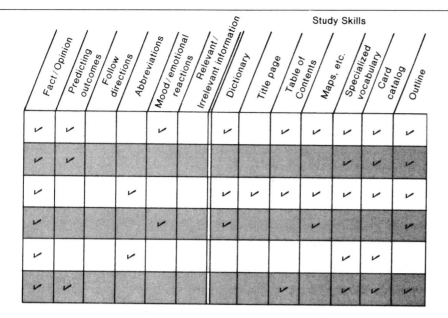

teacher's fourth task is to summarize the data so that it is readily accessible for daily use in classroom instruction. To be used effectively for developing prescriptions, diagnostic information must be available in a format that is clear and easy to use, allowing the teacher to determine immediately the strengths and weaknesses of each student, along with relevant information such as interests and instructional level.

Diagnostic information should be used for developing reading groups and interest groups as well as for individualizing instruction. Because these groups are very flexible, the teacher should have the data available to shift students to appropriate activities during the school day. The authors have used different formats for organizing the information; classroom charts seem to be the easiest to use.

A chart with the scope and sequence of skills listed across the top and students' names down the side is one way to summarize the students' strengths and weaknesses in skill development (see figure 4.4). The information can be determined from the various informal and formal tests and observations; this constitutes an integral part of managing diagnostic-prescriptive instruction for a classroom of students.

The teacher will also need a chart that lists the scores and other data from the tests. This chart has the students' names down the side and the instruments listed across the top (see table 4.1). This provides the necessary summary information regarding general strengths and weaknesses.

Table 4.1

Summary of Classroom Diagnostic Data

Stanford Diagnostic Reading Test, Green Level						Sucher-Allred Reading Placement Inventory		
	Auditory Vocabulary	Auditory Discrimination	Phonetic Analysis	Structural Analysis	Comprehension		Word List Instructional Level	Oral Reading	
					Literal	Inferential		Instructional	Independent
			Stanines						
Lucy	6	6	7	6	6	5	H4	H4	M3
Juan	5	5	5	5	5	4	M3	M3	L2
Bettye	6	6	6	6	6	6	M4	M4	M3
Sam	2	3	3	2	2	1	M1	M1	P
Delores	5	4	5	4	5	4	H2	H2	H1
Frank	5	6	5	5	5	5	M3	M3	M2

Some diagnostic-prescriptive reading systems provide other means of summarizing classroom data. School systems or individual schools may computerize the information and furnish a classroom summary sheet to each teacher. This type of summary saves teacher time, but necessitates continuous updating.

Still another way of gathering and summarizing data is through the use of portfolios. Portfolios are a way of collecting diagnostic information each day from the students. This includes such information as stories, journals, daily reading and writing activities, and any other reading/writing material generated by the students. This information can be kept in brown envelopes, expandable folders, or any other collection device deemed appropriate by the teacher. This material can be examined periodically by the teacher in order to determine the progress of each student.

Measurement Terms Defined

As teachers review diagnostic information and analyze and interpret the data, they should be familiar with the terminology used in the test materials. The authors have defined fifteen terms that seem to be most frequently used in diagnostic data.

Correlation: The degree of relationship between two variables expressed by the coefficient of correlation, which extends along a scale from 1.00 through 00.00 to −1.00; 1.00 denotes a perfect positive relationship; a coefficient of 00.00 denotes no relationship, and a coefficient of −1.00 denotes a perfect negative relationship.

Durrell Analysis of Reading						Wepman	Slosson I.Q.
Oral Reading	Silent Reading	Listening Comprehension	Word Analysis	Visual Memory	Sounds		
L1	L1	H3	M1	L1	L1	20/30	Low Average

Grade equivalent: A derived score converted from the raw score on a standardized test, usually expressed in terms of a grade level divided into tenths. The grade equivalents in sixth grade, for example, range from 6.0 to 6.9, with 6.9 indicating six years, nine months or the end of the sixth grade. Remember that this score represents the student's frustration level or level at which he should not be taught, and should be viewed with caution. It may or may not accurately reflect a student's actual reading level (see figure 4.5).

Grade level: The actual grade in which the student is enrolled.

Grade placement: The level at which the student is placed for instruction. The student in the fourth grade with a low second-grade reading level may have a grade placement of 2.3 at the fourth-grade level. This term may also be used on some tests as a synonym for grade equivalent.

Mean: The average of a set of numbers derived by taking the sum of the set of measurements and dividing it by the number of measurements in the set.

Median: The central number in a set. There are equal numbers of scores that fall above and below the median number in a set.

Normal curve: Same as the bell curve, which has more scores at the mean or median and a decreasing number in equal proportions at the left and right of the center (see figure 4.6).

Percentile: The percentage score that rates the student relative to the percentage of others in a group who are below the score. A student at the 47th percentile has

Figure 4.5
Misuse of Grade Equivalents

WHEREAS, standardized, norm-referenced tests can provide information useful to teachers, students, and parents, if the results of such tests are used properly, and

WHEREAS, proper use of any standardized test depends on a thorough understanding of the test's purpose, the way it was developed, and any limitations it has, and

WHEREAS, failure to fully understand these factors can lead to serious misuse of test results, and

WHEREAS, one of the most serious misuses of tests is the reliance on a grade equivalent as an indicator of absolute performance, when a grade equivalent should be interpreted as an indicator of a test-taker's performance in relation to the performance of other test-takers used to norm the test, and

WHEREAS, in reading education, the misuse of grade equivalents has led to such mistaken assumptions as: (1) a grade equivalent of 5.0, on a reading test means that the test-taker will be able to read fifth grade material, and (2) a grade equivalent of 10.0 by a fourth grade student means that student reads like a tenth grader even though the test may include only sixth grade material as its top level of difficulty, and

WHEREAS, the misuse of grade equivalent promotes misunderstanding of a student's reading ability and leads to underreliance on other norm-referenced scores which are much less susceptible to misinterpretation and misunderstanding, be it

RESOLVED, that the International Reading Association strongly advocates that those who administer standardized reading tests abandon the practice of using grade equivalents to report performance of either individuals or groups of test-takers and be it further

RESOLVED, that the president or executive director of the Association write to test publishers urging them to eliminate grade equivalents from their tests.

Resolution passed by the Delegates Assembly of the International Reading Association, April 1981.

done better on the test than 47 percent of the other people taking the test. Percentile scores may be reported in *quartiles* and *deciles*, in which case a 50th percentile is in the second quartile and the fifth decile. Percentiles, quartiles, and deciles cannot be averaged, added together, subtracted, or treated arithmetically in any manner.

Range: The distance between the largest and smallest numbers in a set, calculated by subtracting the smallest score from the largest score. For example, the scores on a test may be 10, 8, 15, 22, 36, and 20; the range, calculated by subtracting 8 from 36, would be 28.

Raw Score: An untreated test score usually obtained by counting the number of items correct. The raw score is used to determine the other scores, such as grade equivalent and percentile.

Reliability: A term that refers to the consistency with which the test agrees with itself or produces similar scores when readministered over a period of time by the same individual.

Figure 4.6

Various Types of Standard Score Scales in Relation to Percentiles and the Normal Curve

Percent of cases under portions of the normal curve   0.13%   2.14%   13.59%   34.13%   34.13%   13.59%   2.14%   0.13%

Standard deviations	−4SD	−3SD	−2SD	−1SD	0	+1SD	+2SD	+3SD +4SD

Cumulative percent rounded   0.1%   2.3%   15.9%   50.0%   84.1%   97.7%   99.9%
                              2%   16%   50%   84%   98%

Percentile equivalents   1   5   10   20 30 40 50 60 70 80   90   95   99
                                         Q₁   Md   Q₃

Typical standard scores

z-scores   −4.0   −3.0   −2.0   −1.0   0   +1.0   +2.0   +3.0   +4.0

T-scores   20   30   40   50   60   70   80

CEEB scores   200   300   400   500   600   700   800

AGCT scores   40   60   80   100   120   140   160

NCEs   1   10   20   30   40   50   60   70   80   90   99

Stanines   1   2   3   4   5   6   7   8   9

Percent in stanine   4%   7%   12%   17%   20%   17%   12%   7%   4%

Standard deviation: A term used to describe the deviations of scores from the mean, which varies with the range in a set of scores. Thus, the greater the range in scores, the larger the standard deviation can be.

Standard score: A raw score expressed in some form of standard deviation units. They can be dealt with arithmetically and are easier to interpret than raw scores. Various types of standard scores include z-scores, T-scores, CEEB scores, and stanines.

Stanines: A 9-point scale that is another form of a standard score with a mean of 5 and a standard deviation of about 2. The 9 stanines fit along the base of the normal curve with Stanines 1, 2, and 3 considered below average, Stanines 4, 5, and 6 average, and Stanines 7, 8, and 9 above average.

Validity: The extent to which a test measures what it is designed to measure. A test may be reliable but not valid, in that it does not measure what it purports to measure.

To provide further assistance in visualizing these various terms in relation to the normal curve, the teacher should carefully study figure 4.6. In selecting as well as interpreting tests, teachers should note the types of data provided as well as the reliability and validity of the instruments.

■ Summary

Synthesizing diagnostic information is an important aspect of the diagnostic-prescriptive process. In order for diagnostic information to be used effectively, it must be as clear and well organized as possible. This can be achieved more readily by using specific guidelines for synthesizing data. The data must be organized, analyzed, and interpreted before recommendations for instruction can be developed. From this information teachers should organize a usable summary format.

Perhaps the key to the successful implementation of diagnostic-prescriptive instruction is the analysis and interpretation of the diagnostic information, since this leads directly to the recommendations for prescriptive instruction. It is primarily the responsibility of the classroom teacher to detect the strengths and weaknesses of each student. By achieving this objective, the teacher is able to effectively implement a prescriptive program for the student.

■ Applying What You Read

In your classroom, you have administered a group reading test and an individual test to the five lowest students. How would you summarize this data for your daily use?

As a middle school teacher, you have two students for whom you need to write in-depth reports regarding their performance. Outline the information that should be included in the report.

How would you, as an elementary or middle school teacher, summarize and use diagnostic information in your classroom?

■ Note

1. David E. Rummelhart, "Understanding Understanding," in *Understanding Reading Comprehension,* edited by James Flood.

■ Other Suggested Readings

Dechant, Emerald. *Diagnosis and Remediation of Reading Disabilities*. Englewood Cliffs, New Jersey: Prentice-Hall, 1981, Chapters 1 and 13.

Farr, Roger, and Robert F. Carey. *Reading: What Can Be Measured?* Newark, Delaware: International Reading Association, 1986.

Gentile, Lance M., and Merna M. McMillan. *Stress and Reading Difficulties: Research, Assessment, Intervention*. Newark, Delaware: International Reading Association, 1987.

Jongsma, Kathleen Stumpf. "Portfolio Assessment." *The Reading Teacher* 43 (December 1989): 264–65.

Strang, Ruth. *Diagnostic Teaching of Reading*, 2nd ed. New York: McGraw-Hill Book Company, 1969, Chapter 14.

Valencia, Sheila. "A Portfolio Approach to Classroom Teaching Assessment: The Whys, Whats, and Hows." *The Reading Teacher* 43 (January 1990): 338–41.

Wilson, Robert M., and Craig J. Cleland. *Diagnostic and Remedial Reading for Classroom and Clinic*, 6th ed. Columbus, Ohio: Charles E. Merrill Publishing Company, 1989.

Organizing the Classroom for Instruction

STEP 3

Diagnostic information is most effectively used for prescriptive instruction in reading when the classroom is properly organized and managed. Teachers should recognize that Step 3 is crucial to the success of their program. Therefore, they must carefully consider the ways in which their classes are organized and arranged in order to meet the diagnosed needs of the students. The ideas in chapter 5 are provided to share their findings.

5

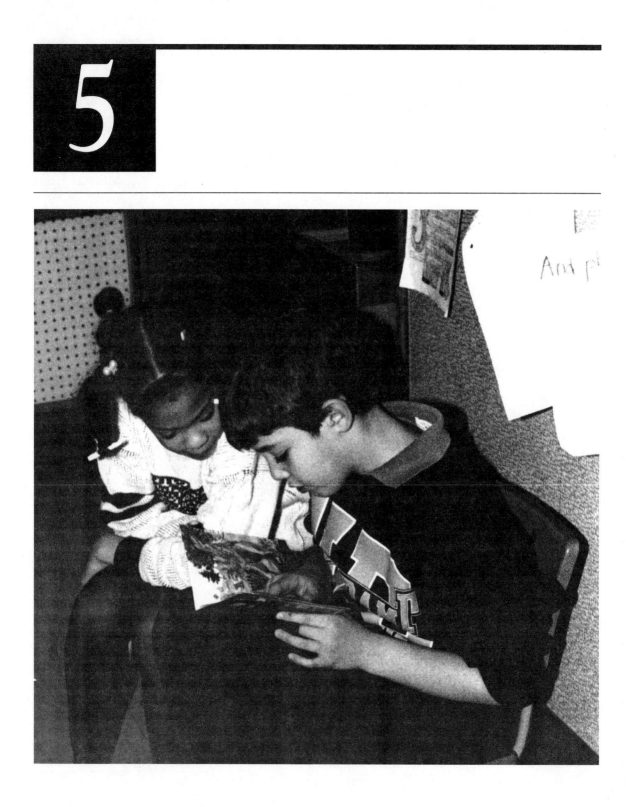

Organizing for Diagnostic-Prescriptive Reading Instruction

Classroom teachers at the elementary and middle school levels continuously ask how they can use all of the diagnostic-prescriptive information to provide appropriate instruction for thirty students in one classroom without additional assistance. Teachers often ask for smaller classes, aides, or volunteers—anything to lower the adult-pupil ratio. This assistance may be helpful, but research does not support their request.[1] Lower adult-pupil ratios do not directly result in increased student achievement. (The well-organized teacher who has thirty students and manages the classroom can produce students with higher performance levels than the teacher who has an unorganized classroom with fifteen students.) There are many factors in the classroom that affect a student's ability to learn: one of the most important deals with classroom organization and management. While this area is extremely important to successful teaching, often it is not dealt within pre- and in-service training programs. Teachers then find themselves assigned to the classroom, not knowing how to deal effectively with their time, resources, facilities, and students. Therefore, this chapter is provided to share some ideas on ways to organize and manage elementary and middle school classrooms. The major limitation of this description is that ideas about classroom organization and management lend themselves more to demonstration than to presentation by means of the printed word. Nevertheless, the following questions will be addressed in this chapter.

What are the various procedures for grouping?

How does a teacher determine who goes into which group?

How is the furniture arranged in the classroom to facilitate diagnostic-prescriptive instruction?

How is diagnostic-prescriptive information organized to aid the teacher in instruction?

What does the teacher do with the other groups while working with one group?

How are materials selected and used in a diagnostic-prescriptive reading program?

In selecting materials, how does the teacher determine if the reading level is appropriate to the students?

As this chapter is read, the following terms are important to note.

Vocabulary to Know

Achievement groups	Grouping procedures	Management
Assessments	Heterogeneous	Organization
Collaborative learning (Cooperative learning)	Homogeneous	Peer tutoring
	Indirect instruction	Readability
Cross-age tutoring	Individualization	Skills groups
Direct instruction	Integrated instruction	Teacher effectiveness
Facilities	Interest groups	Use of material

■ Overview

Each classroom teacher develops organizational procedures that help in managing reading instruction. There is no magic list that will work for everyone. However, as teachers think about classroom organization and plan for the implementation of diagnostic-prescriptive reading instruction, they must accept the responsibility of becoming an instructional decision-maker. Teachers who are effective decision-makers demonstrate the following characteristics:

1. They think first of what students must learn not of the tasks that must be accomplished. Rather than focus on completing skill exercises, decision-makers are concerned with reading materials from the "real" world.
2. These teachers view reading in a broad perspective—as a component of the total language process involved with communication rather than as a series of skills.
3. The motivational aspect of reading is important to effective decision-makers. They want students to learn how to read but they also want them to *like* reading.
4. Cognitive processing and awareness are emphasized rather than correct answers and rote memory in the classes in which teachers are decision-makers. While correct answers are important, the measure of accomplishment is that the students understand how they got the correct answer.
5. Teachers who are effective decision-makers do not depend on basal readers. These materials are considered a guide and a tool to be used to initiate instruction. From there, the teacher acts as an effective decision-maker by adjusting, changing, adapting, and modifying to direct instruction toward the appropriate goals for the individual student.

6. These teachers cautiously use teacher's guides for their basals, realizing that the guides seldom explain *how* to do a task. Thus, the teacher must create the explicit instructions that are necessary for helping the student understand the task or activity.

7. Effective teachers realize that there is no panacea for teaching reading. Reading instruction is complex as are the classrooms, students, and teachers. A teacher's instructional competence is constantly developing—*the* answer may never be found.

8. These teachers also realize that there is no perfect way to teach reading. Their instruction is constantly under review, as they look for ways to improve.[2]

Outstanding teachers provide a feeling of responsibility for helping their students learn, expend efforts to use alternative classroom strategies, and develop a system of classroom management in which responsibility and control are shared with students. These teachers design their own activity-based curriculum and develop environments for ensuring that students know how to work independently, because the students are responsible for accomplishing what is expected of them.[3] As Duffy and Roehler so honestly state:

". . . teachers who are effective decision makers are in control because they use professional knowledge rather than follow someone else's prescriptions. They are professionals who make their own decisions, not technicians who follow directions."[4]

Teacher effectiveness studies[5] have consistently indicated that teacher organization relates to the nature of the on-task behavior of students. Furthermore, the studies have concluded that reading achievement depends on reading instruction and that teachers improve behaviors through direct instruction and reinforcement.

We have stressed that students are different in many respects: chronological age, maturity, interests, experiential background, and environmental background. For these very reasons, the classroom teacher's responsibility is awesome and ever-changing. In order to achieve optimum results from each student and from the learning environment, the effective teacher considers all the factors that affect a student's ability to benefit from the instruction received, and provides a literate environment for student development. Duffy and Roehler provide an excellent description of the literate environment that facilitates effective classroom organization and management. They suggest that:

"In a literate environment a classroom is permeated with examples of literacy and language in action—*real* language and *real* literacy. For instance, instead of the traditional situation in which the teacher talks and everyone else is quiet, a literate environment encourages various kinds of student communication, both oral and written. Similarly, instead of limiting written material to textbooks, many other kinds of printed materials are used, including trade books, magazines, comic books, catalogs, recipes, and newspapers. Also, rather than teaching writing as a separate subject with an emphasis on neatness and accuracy of script, writing is integrated into reading activities along with speaking and listening."[6]

This literate environment provides indirect and direct instruction that facilitates learning based on the needs of the individual student.

■ Integrated Instruction

The development of a literate environment is essential to the success of a diagnostic-prescriptive program. A crucial component of this program is integrated instruction. Integrated instruction involves the simultaneous implementation of reading, writing, expressive and receptive language, studying, researching, and using content strategies in the classroom. Expanding the students' schemata, using their experiences and prior knowledge, and developing their interests, are all part of integrated instruction. This is crucial to the total effort to make learning more of a naturalistic process that is spontaneous and real to students.

Reutzel and Cooter[7] suggested that the classroom environment and daily routine must encourage reading as a primary activity integrated with other language modes such as writing, speaking, and listening. Students should be encouraged to write, respond, discuss, and become thoroughly involved with books, not to complete worksheets in social isolation. It is further essential that teachers communicate the importance of reading, by reading for their own purposes and reading with the students in order to set a positive example. Teachers also need to provide opportunities for demonstrating reading strategies, for sharing in the reading process, and for evaluating individual reading progress.

In a discussion closely related to this topic, Cheek, Flippo, and Lindsey[8] suggested several guidelines for facilitating reading instruction in an integrated instructional setting. These guidelines provide parameters within which teachers can contemplate, conduct, and evaluate their reading programs. They are indicative of student-centered learning and can be used by teachers throughout the various grade levels.

1. Reading is a language-based process.
2. Reading is a complex process with many variables that can affect it.
3. Reading instruction should meet the needs of each student.
4. Teachers should assess their students' reading abilities both quantitatively and qualitatively, and use this information as a basis for instruction.
5. Reading is closely related to the other language arts; thus, listening, speaking, and writing are crucial to the reading process because these processes enable students to make the connection between what they hear, see, speak, and read.
6. Integrating reading into the content areas is essential for effective instruction.

7. Personal reading is a crucial element of the total reading program.
8. Reading should be a positive experience for students.
9. Learning to read is a continuous developmental process.
10. Students with special needs must be provided for within the regular classroom program.
11. Students should understand that the ultimate goal of reading is comprehension.
12. Facilitative teachers that emphasize principles of student growth and development within a student-centered classroom environment are essential to effective reading instruction.

Organized teachers know their students, establish clear and reasonable expectations, have rules and procedures that are consistent with student needs and are consistently followed; they also communicate this information to the students. As a part of the classroom organization, students not only receive instruction, but also are involved in explanations, feedback, monitoring, and continuous reinforcement. To help these ideas become more practical in the elementary or middle school classroom, let us for a moment imagine that the first day of school is near, and each teacher is preparing to teach a group of thirty or more students. Imagine the confusion as one attempts to prepare for the opening of school. There are many things to be done to organize reading instruction for the coming year. Books, supplies, desks, tables, etc., must be organized; but most importantly, the organizational techniques for instruction must be decided upon with preparation to implement these plans when the students arrive.

The teacher must decide which management procedures will be used in the classroom. How many groups will there be? How will the groups be organized? What procedures will be used with the groups? These are the initial questions to be answered before confronting the eager faces on the first day of school.

■ Management Procedures

Teachers have their own styles of managing a classroom; some styles are quite effective, while others create additional work. The management of a classroom is perhaps one of the more difficult tasks confronting the teacher. It is a task that requires an innovative and creative mind, a knowledge of the content to be taught, an understanding of the various needs of the students, skills in organization and planning, as well as a willingness to modify procedures based on student response.

Kounin identified six behaviors that were involved in effective classroom management. They include:

1. Withitness—The students are aware of what is happening in all parts of the room at all times.
2. Overlapping—The teacher is able to deal with two or more activities or issues simultaneously.

3. Smoothness—The teacher ends one activity and moves directly to another activity without abrupt changes or deviations. This also relates to the teacher's ability to deal with minor management problems without interrupting the instruction or attention of the students.
4. Momentum—The pace is maintained throughout the activity, with quick, efficient transitions.
5. Accountability—The teacher makes sure that all students are providing responses, and provides corrective feedback when necessary.
6. Alerting—All students are attentive to the responses of others during activities.[9]

With this general introduction on management procedures, the remainder of this section will present some specific techniques for managing a classroom. Included are suggestions for individualizing instruction to meet student needs, various techniques for grouping students, and ideas as to how management systems may be used to aid in organizing instructions.

Individualization

Individualized instruction is a topic that has been discussed at some length in the past few years. At one point during this discussion, many educators believed that individualized instruction was limited to one-to-one instruction. Each student had to be working on a different assignment in order for instruction to be considered individualized.

Research, however, found that more effective instruction is provided from the teacher and this occurs more effectively via group instruction.[10] Thus, the term individualization is now used to mean that every student is working on tasks geared to her instructional level and specific needs. Quite possibly a student will receive individualized instruction within a grouping format, since there are probably others in the class who need instruction in the same area. Information from various informal and formal assessments is used to assist the teacher in making these decisions.

Of the various ways of providing individualized instruction, working with groups is the most common. Grouping is discussed in detail later in this chapter. Note that in individualized instruction students are grouped because diagnostic information indicates that all in the group need the same type of instruction in the same area, not because it's easier for the teacher to work with a group!

Another technique used in individualized instruction is to allow periods of independent reading. Again, students do not have to do this alone and apart from the class. This activity encourages students to make some independent decisions about what they like to read. Students participating in independent reading activities are allowed some flexibility and given an opportunity to express themselves in activities that grow out of independent reading. Perhaps the student would enjoy writing a poem or short story, working with a group of other students in role-playing activities, presenting a play, making a pretend movie with real cameras (or, if not too expensive, a real movie), or developing a series of short stories for publication on the school press (ditto machine). These types of indirect instructional activities promote growth and the ability to make decisions; they also augment the learning environment. In addition, they add interest to the school environment, often developing an eagerness to learn. This technique used in individualizing instruction is not to be confused with the individualized reading approach, which uses library books as the main source of instruction. This approach is discussed in chapter 6.

An interesting technique for individualized instruction for select students is contracts. These contracts assign tasks for instruction and provide flexibility in classroom organization. Teachers have successfully used this technique, especially in middle school classes. The theory behind the use of contracts is that the teacher and the student will arrive together at a logical starting point for instruction. They will agree upon a goal to be reached and specific objectives to be accomplished. A period of time for completion of the task, as well as the specific tasks, will be agreed upon, with both parties more or less bound to abide by their part of the contract. Sometimes the student and teacher will actually sign the contract in order to instill a more formal sense of responsibility. Another facet of this agreement is that students may contract for the grade they wish to receive for their work. Of course the grade received, if grades are given, will depend upon the quality of the work. Teachers should note, however, that when this technique is used, the student must have some direct instruction. Students do not improve their reading by being assigned materials; effective teachers first provide instruction, then contract with students for reinforcement activities.

This arrangement can be used with some poor readers, but there are limitations to consider. Such elements as the student's ability to work independently for the period of time specified in the contract, the reading skills required by the student, and the availability of appropriate materials and activities must be weighed before the teacher decides to use a contract with a student. The poor reader will need a short-term contract in order to feel a sense of accomplishment before becoming frustrated. In addition, the contract usually works better with older students than with younger ones. However, used in moderation, this technique is a good motivating device for the more gifted student and sometimes also for the slower student. A sample contract is provided in figure 5.1.

Paraprofessionals and volunteers can greatly assist the instructor in implementing an individualized program. The trained paraprofessional can work with individuals or small groups carrying out the plans made by the teacher. This allows the teacher extra time to work with individual students, to do more direct instruction with groups, and to serve as a manager of instruction. However, in effectively using aides in the classroom, teachers must be well organized. Hiatt found that teachers with

Figure 5.1
Sample Contract

Name: *Wendy Crowden*   Grade: *5th*
Starting Date: *Feb. 1, 19--*   Ending Date: *Feb. 5, 19--*

Objectives:

1. To decode words containing vowel sounds represented by the letters *oi, oy, ou,* and *ow*.
2. To recognize fact from opinion in reading selections.
3. To follow directions independently in completing this contract.

Assignments:

Objective #1:

– Work with the teacher in Group 3 to review the vowel sounds.
– Select 2 of the following tasks. Complete and give them to the teacher. – *The New Phonics We Use,* Book D, pp. 47-50, 56-57.
   – *Phonics Workbook,* Book B, pp. 147-149, 151-154.
   – *Reading Booster Code Book,* pp. 71-76.
   – Learning Center A.

Objective #2:

– Work with the teacher in Group 1 to discuss distinguishing between fact and opinion.
– Select 1 of the following tasks. Complete and give it to the teacher.
   – *Basic Reading Skills,* pp. 106-109.
   – *Study Skills for Information Retrieval,* Book 1, p. 75; Book 2, p. 75; Book 3, p. 72.
– Complete the activities in Learning Center C.

Objective #3:

– Check your work to be sure that you followed directions!

Wendy Crowden   *Mrs. Bailey*
     Student   Teacher

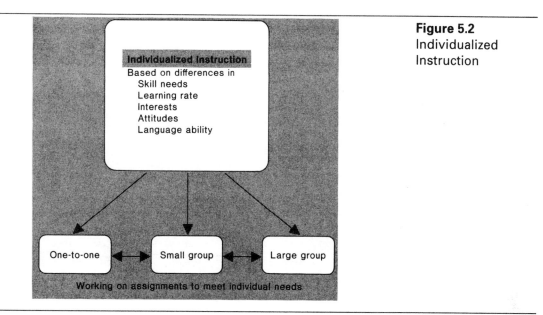

Figure 5.2
Individualized
Instruction

aides spent twenty-nine minutes per day in disciplining students while those without aides spent approximately forty minutes. Eleven minutes may seem significant until a final statistic is noted—only six of the eleven minutes were used for instruction![11] Organized teachers who individualize instruction tend to provide more instruction, with or without aides.

Teachers realize that some one-to-one instruction is essential. When a student fails to progress in a small group or has difficulty in some particular area, individual attention is needed. Yet, instruction on a one-to-one basis is neither needed nor desirable with every student on a continuous basis. Students need the social interaction developed by working in large and small groups (see figure 5.2). Musgrave provides many ideas for teachers to consider in individualizing instruction in elementary or middle school classrooms. Among the ideas in this book are specific suggestions for individualizing instruction through whole-class and small-group discussions, role-playing and sociodrama, simulations, and textbook dramatizations. Musgrave also suggests some independent study methods, such as resource centers, learning packets, and modules, to meet the unique needs of students.[12]

Further ideas about individualized instruction in reading are available in books or articles by Wallen, Slater, Reeves, and by Kaplan, Kaplan, Madsen and Taylor.[13] Although individualized instruction on a one-to-one basis has declined during the last few years, teachers recognize the value of this management technique and note that with the availability of computers in the classroom, the use of this technique will expand.

Developing Instructional Groups

In elementary schools, grouping is the most frequently used instructional management procedure. Grouping allows the classroom teacher considerable flexibility in implementing the instructional program, permitting the teacher to devote more time to individuals than would ordinarily be possible in a whole-class type of format. Grouping also facilitates better adaptation of materials and resources to individual needs.

Research during the last fifteen years has contributed much information about the issues related to grouping. Grouping is supported in all studies. Grouping allows the teacher or another adult to spend more time working with students, which seems to be the critical component in improving achievement. Kean, Summers, Ravietz, and Farber found that achievement was improved when students were taught via small-group and whole-group class combinations as compared to students who received individual instruction only, small-group instruction only, or whole-class instruction only.[14] Related to this are the findings of the Beginning Teacher Evaluation Study, which suggested that students working with a teacher or another adult were usually engaged about 84% of the time while those students working alone were on task only 70% of the time.[15] As Rosenshine and Stevens summarize the research related to this area: ". . . three general instructional procedures have frequently been correlated with reading achievement: teacher-directed instruction, instruction in groups, and academic emphasis."[16]

Various types of grouping procedures are used in schools and classrooms. Procedures differ from classroom to classroom, and especially from the elementary to the middle school levels. The two main types of grouping often debated are *homogeneous* and *heterogeneous*.

Homogeneous grouping puts students together in a class based on their ability or achievement levels. For example, Ms. Brooks has the top group of fifth graders this year, or all of the students reading at the fifth grade or higher, while Ms. Cox has the middle group and Ms. Day has the low group. On the other hand, heterogeneous grouping mixes all ability or achievement levels in each class. Usually through random or alphabetical assignments, Ms. Brooks, Ms. Cox, and Ms. Day would each get some of the top group, middle group and low group of readers. While many teachers argue that a homogeneous grouping arrangement is easier and that they can do a better job of meeting needs when the students are not so diverse, this argument is not supported by research. Kulik and Kulik concluded from a review of studies on homogeneous grouping that homogeneous or ability grouping is often beneficial for high-ability students but not for low-ability students.[17] This finding was supported by Persell in a review of studies of ability grouping from which the conclusions were that a slight improvement in achievement occurred for the high-ability groups; however, the gain was negated by the substantial losses of the middle- and low-ability groups.[18]

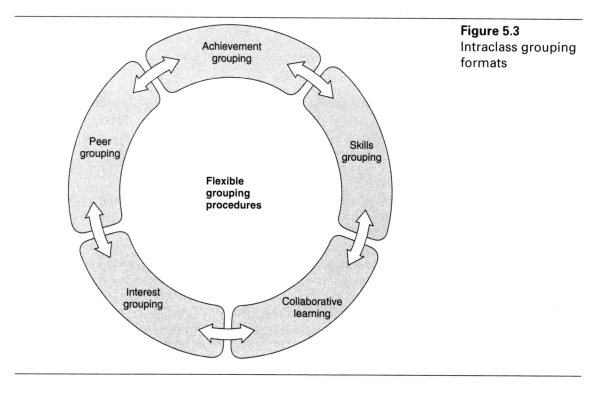

Figure 5.3
Intraclass grouping formats

Homogeneous grouping is used more at the upper levels when students are ability-grouped or assigned to tracks. At the elementary level, more heterogeneous grouping patterns are usually found. One of the greatest problems is the idea that homogeneous grouping alleviates the need for smaller groups within the individual classroom. Whether a classroom is homogeneously or heterogeneously grouped according to the school management design, further grouping within the classroom is essential. Few classrooms would contain thirty students whose performance is exactly the same and who need exactly the same instruction.

Intraclass Formats

The population of a classroom may be grouped in two ways—intraclass and interclass. In an intraclass format, students can be grouped within the class in various ways for instructional purposes. These are basically achievement groups, skills groups, interest groups, cross-age or peer groups, and collaborative or cooperative learning groups. Each of these techniques for grouping will be examined more carefully.

Achievement Grouping The most widely used grouping technique is achievement grouping. In this technique, a classroom of students is divided into several groups based on their level of achievement. Those performing at the highest level are grouped together and those performing at the lowest level are grouped together, with one or more groups organized between the highest and the lowest level. A rather common practice is for the classroom teacher to use this method in forming three reading groups. However, the authors suggest that the instructor have three achievement groups initially and, as soon as management procedures permit, that these be expanded to perhaps as many as five.

Other types of groups, as discussed in the following sections, may be added in order to meet the needs of the students. Remember, that in a typical fifth-grade classroom that is heterogeneously grouped, reading levels may range from low-first to ninth-grade level. Therefore, more than three achievement groups are needed to accommodate this wide variation in levels.

Since achievement grouping is, as a general rule, the most widely used grouping procedure, one should exercise caution in designating student placement. Through continuous evaluation of the student, try to avoid a situation in which the student is labeled a poor reader and not given an opportunity to improve his position in the classroom. Teachers must be flexible in their grouping techniques, encouraging students to move from one group to another as their needs dictate. Research indicates that students frequently are not moved into other achievement groups during the school year.[19] Once placed in a certain reading group, they usually remain with it. This is unfortunate, as students' learning rates change during the school year, and all within a group do not progress together.

In addition, caution is to be exercised in determining what instruments are used to place students in achievement groups. Many times achievement tests do not accurately reflect the student's knowledge or skill. Thus, using these tests as a basis for grouping is very dangerous. If used for grouping purposes, achievement test results should be considered in conjunction with teacher observations and other individualized measures. No one instrument alone can serve as the tool for grouping students. However, test scores are a valuable aid in grouping. Instructional grouping based only on teacher judgment tends to create greater socioeconomic segregation than grouping based on test scores alone.[20]

Teachers also seem to praise lower ability groups more than the higher achievement groups, although the students read on a lower level and answer more questions incorrectly.[21] Moreover, in teaching achievement groups, instructors tend to treat the group as a teaching unit, rather than considering individual student needs. Low level groups generally receive highly structured instruction in decoding and basic comprehension skills, while the top level group enjoys more flexibility in procedures and assignments, as well as instruction in the more sophisticated comprehension skills.[22]

Obviously, there are differences that exist in the instruction provided to various ability groups. Hiebert and Peterson, Wilkinson, and Hallinan summarized many research studies that addressed reading instruction for low- and high-ability groups. Their conclusions are:

1. Decoding tasks were the focus of instruction for students in the low-ability groups, while high-ability groups were involved with meaning-related activities.
2. Silent reading was the predominant means of reading for the good readers, with poor readers spending the majority of their time reading orally. Errors made by poor readers were corrected using graphophonic cues. When cues were recommended to good readers, which was less frequently than to poor readers, they were syntactic and semantic cues.
3. Low-ability groups were less attentive to instructional activities and spent more time off task for administrative and disciplinary reasons than students in high-ability groups.
4. Low-ability students were less popular with their peers, had a poorer self-concept, and more negative feelings toward reading and their reading groups than did the high-ability groups.[23]

To alleviate some of these negative feelings of students in low-ability groups, Peterson, Wilkinson, and Hallinan suggest that teachers be more flexible in moving students to different groups, attempt to provide good instruction to all groups, use alternative grouping procedures to encourage low-ability students to interact more with others, avoid labeling groups, and be aware of the long-range impact of grouping on the educational and emotional development of students.[24] Thus, teachers must consider other grouping patterns in addition to achievement groups in managing reading instruction.

Skills Grouping A second grouping technique involves the use of reading skills for the purpose of student placement. Skills grouping is used to place students in specific groups for instruction in a given skill. It is entirely possible that this placement will be different from the achievement grouping placement. For example, a student may be in the high reading group but have difficulty with a reading skill that others in the group seem to have learned. Such a student would work in a skill group that may be composed of students from several other achievement groups who also have difficulty with this skill. The primary method of implementing this type of management procedure is to group the students on the basis of their needs in a specific reading area.

Although research as to the pros and cons of skill group instruction has not been conducted, studies that deal with grouping in general recommend that grouping formats other than ability grouping be used to provide flexibility in the classroom and to allow students in the various ability groups to interact. Those who are opposed to skills instruction in reading would, of course, also oppose this type of grouping

format. However, because skills and strategies for using these skills, form the content to be developed in reading, the authors believe that such groups are vital to a diagnostic-prescriptive reading program. Crucial to the success of using such groups are the procedures used in developing or reinforcing the skills. Students in skill groups need to first receive direct instruction from the teacher who demonstrates the process for using the skills to enhance reading. Once students show that they have an understanding of the skill, the teacher moves them into the application of the skill in various reading situations in conjunction with other skills already known. Various strategies including study techniques, think aloud processes, reciprocal questioning, and study guides are incorporated into this instructional process. Instruction in skills groups is not to focus only on passing a test on an isolated skill but rather to focus on the understanding and application of skills to the total reading process.

When one or more students exhibit difficulty in using a specific skill, corrective instruction is needed from the teacher either through skill grouping or one-to-one instruction. This type of grouping is usually for a short period of time, since the primary purpose is to strengthen a skill deficiency. When the skill is learned, the student leaves this skill group and moves to another, as needed.

Interest Grouping Another type of grouping that has been used rather successfully is interest grouping. This allows students who have similar interests to work together in order to explore their interests in greater depth. A positive aspect of this type of grouping is that students from all achievement levels are intermingled, which provides for considerable interaction without regard to reading level. Used interchangeably with achievement and skill grouping, this type of instructional grouping format has proven to be highly successful, since it motivates students to learn and work together. One of the weaknesses of achievement grouping is the lack of opportunity for students from different levels to interact and discuss subjects of importance to them. Interest grouping provides this opportunity, thus overcoming one of the reasons students become disenchanted with learning to read. In addition, interest grouping helps to make reading enjoyable and interesting as students are encouraged to read materials related to their unique interests. Therefore, interest grouping helps motivate students who never seem to become enthusiastic over any of the reading material assigned to them. The use of interest grouping also will allow students from deprived backgrounds to learn by interacting with their peers from more diversified experiential backgrounds. Learning about other students' experiences helps to improve the oral language development of the poorer readers and, in turn, improves their reading. Interest grouping is a useful procedure that teachers should use continuously in their classes, inasmuch as internal social processes in groups contribute to subsequent differential opportunities for students;[25] social development and reading groups are related!

By allowing students to read materials of special interest to them, comprehension is enhanced. Asher found that when students indicated a high interest in a passage, their comprehension was greater than when they had a low interest in the material.[26] This may be explained by several factors: 1) interest in a topic suggests more knowledge about the topic, thus the student has a better developed schema and 2) interest in a topic means that the students have a greater attention span and become more involved in learning. Anderson, Hiebert, Scott, and Wilkinsen have suggested that students can read at a higher level when interacting with materials on topics of special interest as compared to the level at which they typically read.[27] For all of these reasons, interest grouping is a viable option for the teacher who is concerned about the reading development of individual students. Procedures are outlined in chapter 2 to determine student interests—use this information as an aid in personalizing reading instruction!

Peer Grouping A fourth type of grouping, which has proven most helpful in elementary and middle school classrooms, is the concept of student or peer tutoring.

Peer tutoring uses one student in a class to help another student who needs assistance in a particular area. Teachers may use this grouping procedure to allow a student who needs to practice oral reading to do so with another student rather than with the teacher or an entire group. Another way of using peer tutoring is by asking a student who has learned a skill or has strength in one area to help a student who is not as proficient. In peer tutoring, the tutor usually progresses as much as, if not more than, the person being tutored. Although the tutor may already "know" the skill, through tutoring, a higher level of understanding is achieved. This type of grouping may also be referred to as cross-age tutoring when an older student works with a younger student in an effort to improve the reading skills of the latter. It has been found that in many cases the older students also improve their reading skills, especially if they are poor readers.[28] Labbo and Teale[29] conducted a recent study using lower-achieving fifth graders to tutor kindergarten children. In this study the fifth graders prepared and read storybooks to kindergarten students. Both quantitative data and qualitative results gathered suggested that a cross-age reading program is a promising way of helping poor readers in the upper elementary grades to improve their reading.

An example of a successful cross-age tutoring program is the one implemented by Morrice and Simmons[30] in which older and younger students became "Reading Buddies." In this program, fifth graders and primary grade students collaborated in a whole language, cross-age program developed around activities using Big Books, special holidays, and outdoor science.

Therefore, an added advantage of this program is that students who would not ordinarily read books they consider childish, will read them so that they can be better able to help "their" student. Thus, in peer tutoring everyone seems to benefit—the student, the tutor, and the teacher!

In experiences with peer tutoring, the authors have found this to be an effective way to motivate the poor reader. This procedure has an overall positive effect on reading; students exhibit increased interest in learning to read and have a more positive attitude toward themselves. Furthermore, students doing the tutoring develop a more positive self-image and show greater interest in their school work. The classroom develops an atmosphere of helping and caring for one another.

One way the authors have used the peer tutoring concept is with fifteen-year-old nonreaders tutoring kindergarten and first graders in an adjoining school. The older students had a dual incentive for reading "easy" materials; they had to learn to read them in order to provide the story hour for these classes. One of the most amusing, yet beautiful occasions was the day these older boys had to learn to read "The Three Bears" because of a request from a little kindergarten girl. They could not let her down, and they could not read the story with only a two-day notice! So, they decided to tell the story via a play and only learned to read certain parts! We drew straws for the Goldilocks part, put on wigs and costumes, and created a smash hit with these younger students. The boys were so pleased with themselves that they began to take requests for stories! Needless to say, they had a very proud teacher!

Collaborative Learning
Collaborative or cooperative learning utilizes group dynamics within a classroom setting by emphasizing shared learning experiences to reach a common goal or to solve a common problem. In this setting, students of varied abilities, interests, and experiences are grouped together and given the responsibility for completing a particular task. It is incumbent upon the students in a particular group to organize, plan, guide each other, and to complete individual assignments within the group in order to reach their common goal.

Proponents of collaborative or cooperative learning believe that these small group configurations not only increase interest among students, but also promote

Collaborative learning activities allow students to learn from each other as they work together. Photo courtesy of Edward B. Lasher.

critical thinking. For example, Johnson and Johnson [31] found that cooperative teams achieve at higher levels of thought and retain information longer than students working individually.

Another proponent, Robert Slavin [32], believes that there are a number of advantages to students in this collaborative setting. He suggested that these advantages can be demonstrated in the following statements.

1. Students are more highly motivated to learn with greater intrinsic motivation.
2. More academic improvement in both tutor and tutee is demonstrated.
3. An increase in the student's self-esteem is evident.
4. Students develop more positive perceptions about the intentions of others.
5. Negative competition among student decreases.
6. Students accept differences among themselves more readily.
7. Dependence upon the teacher is decreased significantly.
8. Higher achievement test scores result.

There are any number of ways to implement collaborative or cooperative learning in the classroom. Bromley [33], for example, suggested using a "buddy journal," which is a diary that a pair of students keep together in which they write back and forth to each other. It serves three basic functions for students. These include setting a purpose for communication (sharing an idea in writing), providing an opportunity to compose a message, and feedback from a peer who answers with a response in the journal.

Keegan and Shrake[34] implemented literature study groups in their classrooms as a way to foster collaboration and as an alternative to ability grouping. These groups are comprised of seven or eight students who sit in a circle around a tape recorder, and one member begins the discussion by reading an open-ended quotation. This initiates a brief period of sharing ideas using their books for reference. Next, students read the pages they have assigned themselves. Then, in their literature logs, they react to their stories and to the preceding group discussion using a friendly letter format. This creates a situation in which the student and teacher can pursue a dialogue about literature.

There is growing evidence to indicate that collaborative or cooperative learning is an effective way to teach in an integrated instructional environment. We believe that this type of grouping format encourages more collaboration among students, heightens interest, results in better learning, and is an effective alternative to achievement grouping.

The various procedures for intraclass grouping discussed in the preceding pages will be of assistance to teachers in organizing their classroom learning environments. The teacher serves as manager of the instructional program, and must use a variety of intraclass grouping procedures in order to provide the most appropriate instruction for each student. A student may be involved in all five types of groups during one day.

Needless to say, no instructional plan yet devised can compensate for poorly organized classroom settings and ineffective teaching; good diagnostic-prescriptive procedures can only be implemented by means of good management and organizational techniques!

Interclass Formats

Interclass or cross-class grouping is the second major grouping procedure. With this type of grouping, students from several classes are integrated in common reading classrooms according to their achievement levels. In other words, parallel scheduling among classes is used to facilitate reading instruction. The purpose of interclass grouping is to permit the teachers involved to develop homogeneous units. Several groups are formed, as determined by the reading levels of the students involved, then each teacher works with a specific group. This type of grouping may be limited to one grade level or may cross several grade levels. For example, all the students in the fifth grade would be divided into groups according to their reading levels. Then each fifth-grade teacher would work with a particular group during the time designated for reading. Crossing grade levels would involve dividing students from several grade levels into groups according to their reading levels, regardless of age or maturity. Teachers then work with students from mixed grade levels. Since this grouping procedure may create a poor self-concept for older students reading on a lower-level, great caution must be exercised in using it.

An assumption often made concerning this type of grouping is that it reduces the range of abilities in each classroom. In reality, however, it does not reduce the range

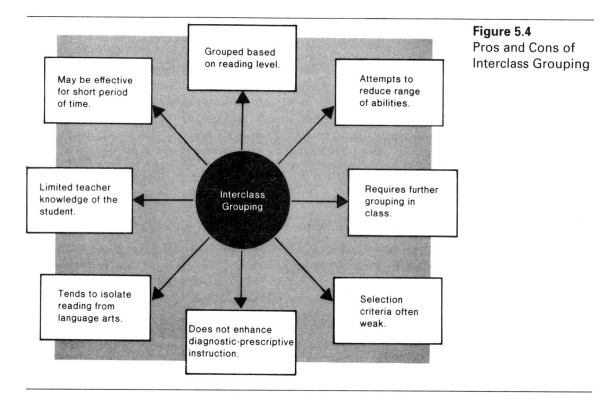

Figure 5.4
Pros and Cons of
Interclass Grouping

of abilities significantly, since the selection criteria used are often relatively weak. This type of grouping has been found to be useful in short-term periods, but its effectiveness is greatly reduced over longer periods of time. When this procedure is used, teachers must realize that it does not preclude the need for grouping within the classroom. As was pointed out in the discussion on homogeneous grouping, no matter how a classroom of students is grouped, further small groupings are needed.

Another significant problem with interclass grouping is that the teacher assigned to a particular student may know little about that student because this teacher has contact with the student for only about an hour per day. This creates some difficulties in correlating appropriate activities for the student. Also, reading becomes separated from the other learning activities. The effectiveness of instruction is reduced, since reading is not integrated into the broad spectrum of learning.

Although interclass grouping is used in many schools, caution must be exercised in dealing with the problems that have been identified. Students can readily be "lost" in the shuffle from teacher to teacher. More importantly, it is extremely difficult for the teacher to diagnose reading problems and provide effective prescriptive instruction with such limited teacher-student contact time.

Regardless of the grouping format used in the school, intraclass or interclass, obtaining and using diagnostic information is a major responsibility of the classroom teacher. This information is essential in determining how to group students to provide the best prescriptive instruction. The teacher is responsible for evaluating, organizing, synthesizing and updating diagnostic data. Because a student's learning is not constant, adjustments in grouping assignments must be made during the year. *These adjustments require that classroom teachers use continuous diagnosis as a basis for change.* This is stressed because the tendency in the elementary and middle school grades is to make an initial grouping assignment, allow a routine to set in, and forget to re-evaluate the student's group placement. For many students, this has meant that they remain in the same achievement group for their entire elementary school life!

Organizing Groups

One of the more critical aspects of grouping is the manner in which these groups are organized. Since the type of groups generally used has been discussed, let us now examine ways to develop these groups in the classroom. Because the majority of classroom teachers have a three-group instructional format, the sample design will use three groups.

Table 5.1 presents a basic design for implementing an instructional program in reading in the elementary and middle school grades. This design uses three groups and a Directed Reading Activity format; the design can be easily expanded and adapted for use with more than three groups as long as the basic organization is kept intact. The three groups are achievement groups, with other grouping patterns to be used as needed within the design. The time variable may be adjusted by the instructor to reflect hours actually spent in reading and language arts. This plan will be used for several days, since an entire reading lesson for three groups cannot be completed in the limited time provided for reading instruction each day.

In order to effectively manage groups and use a design such as the one presented in Table 5.1, the following basic suggestions are offered as guides for management:

1. *Time the activities* for each group so that one group does not finish its assignment while the other groups have much longer to work. Try to keep the time for various assignments for the groups about the same.
2. *Provide alternatives* for the students when they finish their assignments. Because it is impossible to have all students finish their work at exactly the same time, it is necessary for the teacher to provide activities when the assigned work is completed. For example, a reading center provides an opportunity for the student to enjoy independent reading activities, or an activities center can give additional assistance in developing reading skills. Students need to be aware of their alternatives as they finish assignments so that they will not need to disturb the teacher's work with another group, or others in the class.

Table 5.1

Organizational Format for Reading Instruction

Time*	Group 1	Group 2	Group 3
—to—	*Review/apply previously learned skills.* As a group, individualized into smaller skill groups, or using peer tutoring, these students are provided activities in which they apply skills or strategies taught in earlier lessons. Students from the other groups may be included as necessary.	*Language development.* Writing, listening, or other language activities are done by the group or individualized according to the needs or interests of the students. Students from the other groups may be included as appropriate.	*Readiness and skill development.* (Teacher)**Introduce the new concepts to develop background knowledge and provide direct instruction for the skills needed for what is to be read. May include students from Groups 1 and 2.
—to—	*Language development.*	*Readiness and skill development.* (Teacher)	*Skill application.* Through various activities, the students apply the newly introduced skills.
—to—	*Readiness and skill development.* (Teacher)	*Skill application.*	*Language development.*
—to—	*Skill application.*	*Personal reading.* Specific time is provided for students to read books of their choice. Activities such as dioramas, designing book jackets, letters to the author, etc., are included to encourage the sharing of information.	*Review and introduce material.* (Teacher) Concepts, vocabulary, and skills (new and previously taught) needed to read the material are reviewed and a purpose for reading is established.
—to—	*Personal reading.*	*Review and introduce material.* (Teacher)	*Silent reading.* Using the purpose(s) established, the students read all or a portion of the material silently. Suggest that they read it at least 2 times.
—to—	*Review and introduce material.* (Teacher)	*Silent reading.*	*Read along.* Because this group needs many opportunities to review reading materials, they are allowed to work together to interact about the material. This can be done by peer grouping of partners to read aloud with, reading into a tape recorder, or discussing what they have read using teacher-generated questions.

*Times vary, but generally range from ten to twenty minutes per time block.

**Group 3 is considered the low achievement group in this class; thus, the teacher begins with this group to get them working from the start.

Table 5.1

Continued

Time*	Group 1	Group 2	Group 3
—to—	*Silent reading.*	*Read along.*	*Guided reading.* (Teacher) Based on silent readings and other interactions with the materials, the teacher discusses the information with the students via questions, retellings, and oral reading of selected parts. This serves as a way of obtaining ongoing diagnostic data.
—to—	*Student guided reading.* Via teacher-designed activities, the students review the information read to assess their comprehension and to clarify points. Questions and discussions are used well here.	*Guided reading.* (Teacher)	*Follow-up.* Activities to extend the concepts presented are included at this time via various art, music, creative dramatics, or other language activities. Teachers can also use this time to reteach information that the students do not seem to understand. This can be done via skill groups, peer groups or the achievement group as appropriate to the situation.
—to—	*Guided reading.* (Teacher)	*Follow-up.*	*Follow-up.* Because these students so frequently spend their follow-up time doing more skill work, two periods of time are included so that they will have an opportunity to be involved with some "fun-type" extension activities.
—to—	*Follow-up.*	*Follow-up.*	*Readiness and skill development.* (Teacher) New material.
—to—	*Language development.*	*Readiness and skill development.* (Teacher) New Material.	*Skill application.*

The Direct Reading Lesson procedure is followed again with new material.

*Times vary, but generally range from ten to twenty minutes per time block.

**Group 3 is considered the low achievement group in this class; thus, the teacher begins with this group to get them working from the start.

3. *Appoint a leader* for each group. If students have questions as they work, they can direct them to the leader; in this way they will not disturb the other groups or the teacher. If neither the leader nor the group can answer the questions, then the leader may ask the teacher. This procedure also helps control the student who constantly seeks attention by asking questions of the teacher.
4. *Provide interesting activities* to develop language skills. Realize that paper-pencil tasks become very boring to students; thus, manipulative activities are essential. In addition, games and learning centers can be used to furnish other activities when students finish their assignments. In far too many classrooms, students are expected to spend their time doing worksheets and copying from the board. This is a waste of student time and paper, and leads to boredom, frustration, and disruptive behavior!
5. Use some time for *total class activities*. At the beginning of each school day or each class, take a few minutes for a total class activity. This may include listening to a record or story, singing a song, or playing a game. Social skills, as well as language skills, are developed through such activities.

    During this time, the teacher may give group assignments, making certain that students understand what they are to do as well as what they can do when they finish assignments. Depending on the students' age level and attention span, the teacher will need to bring the class together as a total group every ten to thirty minutes for a brief break. Otherwise, students become confused as they move from area to area and tend to lose interest in their work.
6. *Provide activities that are appropriate* to the student's level and needs. Do not provide the same listening activity or skills activities for several groups. In table 5.1, the headings are the same for each group, but the activities for each group must be designed to meet individual levels and needs. Although it takes time to develop centers, games, and activities, this is necessary for maximum learning to occur.

In an effort to demonstrate the usefulness of grouping procedures in the content area, a format for implementing these procedures in a content-classroom was also developed. More effective instruction can take place in the content areas if attention is given to individual students through some grouping procedures. The role of the content teacher, has changed from that of a conveyor of information to one of facilitating instruction and attending more to the individual needs of students. Necessity has dictated this change because of the increased problems that students have had in coping with content material. Therefore, it is hoped that an instructional design for content-area teaching will help content teachers to incorporate reading instruction in their classes at the elementary and middle school levels.

Figure 5.5 presents the basic design for implementing reading instruction in the content areas. Three groups are used, and various activities presented to provide the classroom teacher with a choice of activities in classroom instruction. This format

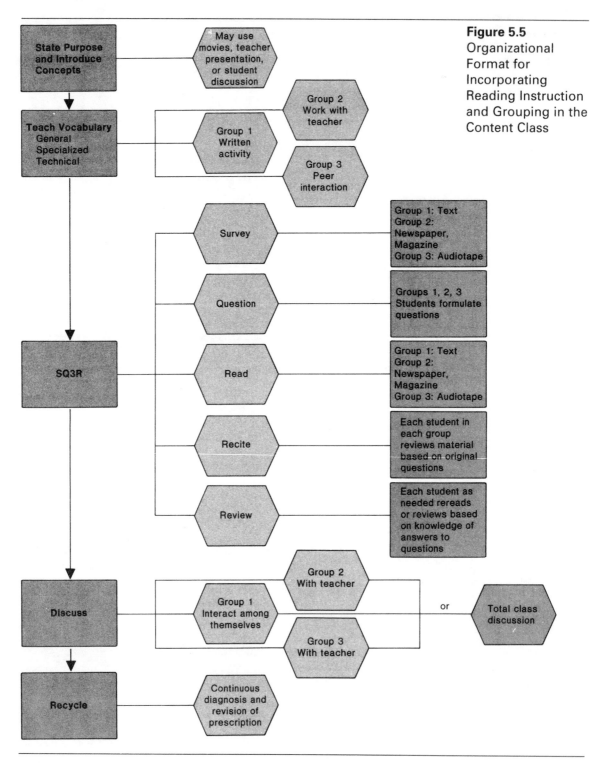

Figure 5.5
Organizational Format for Incorporating Reading Instruction and Grouping in the Content Class

can be easily expanded for use with more than three groups. Since some activities require more time than others, the content specialist should determine the average amount of time that the activities will require in order to establish a framework for presenting them. This design follows the Directed Reading Activity format and the SQ3R procedure for reading the material.

Content teachers may benefit from the organizational suggestions previously discussed. By adjusting instruction to the reading levels and interest of the students, content teachers will find that students gain more information about the content area and show more interest in the classroom. Thus, organizing and managing the classroom becomes an easier task.

Arranging Facilities

As teachers use various ideas in organizing and managing their classrooms, they will need to consider how the classroom facilities may be arranged to assist in instruction. The kinds of space and facilities needed depend on the particular management styles of each teacher. However, certain limitations are always involved in considering physical arrangements. Regardless of the teachers' ideas or needs, time, space, finances, and the goals of the individual school are to be considered.

Given the limitations imposed, each teacher is obligated to derive maximum advantage from the facilities available. For example, thirty desks in a room do not require the teacher to forego all grouping and individualization ideas in developing teaching plans. Desks must be rearranged to provide instruction that meets the needs of the students. In an effort to assist the classroom teacher in arranging the facilities properly, two diagrams indicating possible arrangements that stress grouping and individualization procedures are shown in figures 5.6 and 5.7. These represent two of many ways to arrange the classroom for optimum instruction.

These two diagrams represent classrooms that may be in the traditional school or in a more modular-structure school. Regardless of wall arrangement, such a classroom setup provides for flexible groupings and freedom of movement in the room. Ideally, the teacher needs some individual student desks, as well as tables for group work. Ample storage space is helpful since the teacher needs to store the materials, activities, games, and centers when not in use. As indicated in the diagrams, quiet reading and activity areas are necessary, especially in the elementary grades. If the classroom is not carpeted, it is possible to obtain carpet squares from carpet stores to cover those small areas. Using a little carpet, and adding a few big cushions and a rocking chair will encourage students to visit the reading corner in their leisure time.

In addition to the availability of desks, tables, chairs, book cases, and storage areas, the attractiveness of the facilities is another concern. A clean, attractive room is very useful in motivating students to learn. Facilities alone do not create a learning environment; their arrangement, usefulness, cleanliness and attractiveness are the key factors. Thus, the teacher who provides a variety of attractive bulletin boards containing activities for the students to use in developing various reading skills, as

Figure 5.6
Room Arrangement

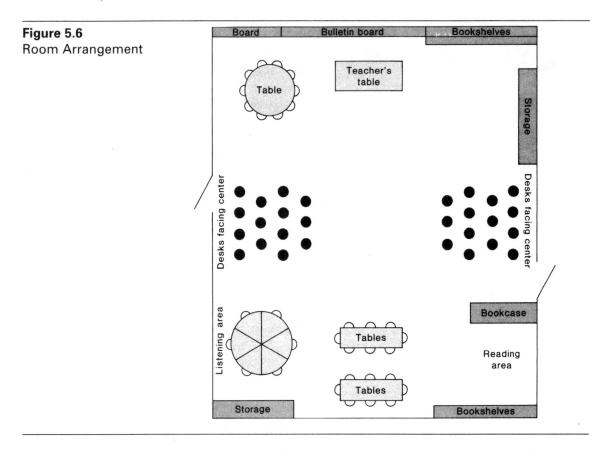

well as areas to display the students' work is motivating learning through facilities. Teachers may also ask students to be responsible for developing bulletin boards during the year and displaying their work. This encourages the students to feel that they are an important part of the classroom. Attractive bulletin boards and displays add much to the classroom, and sometimes a little paint can brighten old desks and tables to help create a better feeling about the room. Students need to feel at home in the classroom in order to benefit most from instruction.

In this example, changes in the classroom facilities certainly had a positive effect on learning. A first-year teacher was placed in an inner-city school with fifth and sixth graders who had been "going through" an average of three teachers a year. He was told to teach them to read. He tried. The students had no respect for the school, the room, the materials, or the teacher, and the teacher felt most uncomfortable in the room. One day after school as he sat dejected, the idea occurred to him that something had to be done with the room. He presented the idea to the classes the next day, and they were all quite excited—after all, it meant putting away the books for a few days! With the principal's agreement, the classes obtained paint, old carpet, curtains, and tables, and made their classroom into what they wanted. The teacher

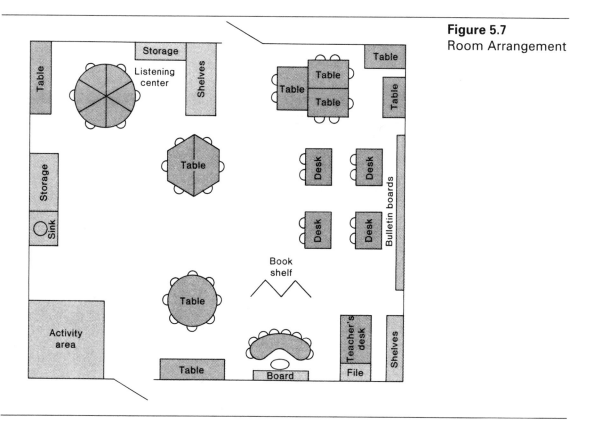

Figure 5.7
Room Arrangement

made some cushions for the reading corner, and the students turned the old closet space into individual study carrels. Needless to say, these students were proud of their room. This pride was definitely reflected in the changes in their attitude and achievement. The teacher even asked to come back the next year!

Facilities do make a difference. The teacher can arrange the classroom so that it is comfortable, and provide students with the opportunity to adjust the facilities for their individual needs. A warm, comfortable room makes coming to school an enjoyable experience for both the teacher and the students.

Selecting and Using Materials

The students are assessed, the groups determined, and the facilities comfortably arranged. Now it is time to begin to work with the students. The first question that teachers must ask is, "What materials do we have?" This is an essential question, because teachers need a variety of materials in order to provide appropriate prescriptive instruction. However, variety does not mean just a large number of materials, but rather materials that meet the various needs in the classroom.

Students' needs as revealed by diagnostic testing are the teacher's first consideration in selecting materials. A second consideration in selecting appropriate materials is to learn what skills they include as well as their level. Suppose that a teacher has a class of third graders who are mostly reading below grade level and have much difficulty in recognizing words. If all the materials are written at about a third-grade level and emphasize comprehension skills, then there is not much variety of materials. In this case, the teacher would require additional materials to meet the students' needs. Another necessary consideration before beginning to review materials carefully for possible selection is to know the students' interests. As discussed in the previous section, considering the students' interests results in improved learning for the student and easier instruction for the teacher. When these basic ideas have been considered, instructors can more thoroughly evaluate the reading materials available. One evaluation form that may be used is provided in figure 5.8. Other evaluation procedures are available from Kaufman, Burns and Roe, Harris and Smith, Cunningham, and Dixon.[35]

One factor to consider in evaluating reading materials is the readability level. Publishing companies may provide a readability level for their materials; however, these levels usually reflect an average for the entire set of materials or a level determined in some unknown manner. Thus, teachers can check the readability levels of materials and recognize the limitations of readability formulas. Before discussing the various readability formulas, their general limitations should be reviewed.

Readability formulas furnish only an estimate of the level of a given selection. Because the formulas are based on the word difficulty and sentence length, or number of syllables and sentence length, the complexity of the concepts in the selection is not considered. There is no formula at this time that measures concepts; thus, the teacher is the judge of whether the level provided by the formula is appropriate for the given student population. Recognize too, that different formulas provide slightly different levels for a material because the formulas are calculated differently. Therefore, no material has an exact level according to the readability formulas. This lack of exactness is further noted as teachers check various passages within a textbook. It is generally observed that each portion of each story in a basal reader has a different readability level. Thus, the level is usually reported by averaging or stating the range of levels.

In using readability formulas to review content materials, note that they do not accurately measure mathematics or other materials that have an abundance of equations. Moreover, the specialized vocabulary that is so essential in all content areas tends to raise the readability levels of the material. It is suggested, therefore, that the instructor be aware of the more difficult terms and teach them prior to asking the students to read the material. Do not try to eliminate specialized vocabulary in the content areas merely to lower the readability level of the material; it is the responsibility of the teacher to prepare the students by teaching the difficult words and concepts. Further considerations regarding readability are provided by Maxwell, Tibbetts, Hittleman, Nelson, and Lange.[36]

Figure 5.8
Guidelines for Use in Evaluating Instructional Materials

Title of material or series: _____

Author(s): _____

Publisher:_____ Copyright date:_____

Address: _____

Price for one unit or part of unit (specify): _____

Price for teacher's guide or edition: _____

Grade levels: _____

	Check Yes	No
A. Content		
1. meets needs and interests of intended student population	___	___
2. contains balanced representation of different socioeconomic and ethnic groups	___	___
3. provides review and reinforcement of skill	___	___
4. is up-to-date and relevant to the times	___	___
5. is relevant to assessed needs of district/school/classroom	___	___
6. has a clear, concise style	___	___
B. Scope		
1. is compatible with other materials and techniques being used	___	___
2. coordinates well with other subject areas	___	___
3. complements objectives of district programs	___	___
4. facilitates continuous progress	___	___
5. strengthens systematic development of reading skills	___	___
6. is adaptable for varying types of teaching	___	___
C. Readability		
1. is evident in vocabulary load for appropriate level	___	___
2. is strengthened by concepts	___	___
3. is aided by language structure and length of sentences	___	___
4. The approximate readability level is _____		
D. Format (For printed material only)		
1. includes appropriate type size and spacing	___	___
2. shows adequate margins	___	___
3. has quality binding	___	___
4. provides for individual replacement of consumable parts	___	___
5. has quality illustrations	___	___

Reproduced by permission of Florida Department of Education, "Guidelines for Evaluating Instructional Materials" Florida Right to Read Effort.

Figure 5.8
(continued)

	Check	
	Yes	No
F. Teacher's Guide		
1. provides sufficient direction	___	___
2. provides adequate lesson plans	___	___
3. provides suggestions for further skill development	___	___
4. indexes specific skills	___	___
5. defines terms	___	___
G. Supplementary Materials		
1. are available to implement program	___	___
2. are valuable addition to program	___	___
H. Evaluation		
1. provides individual or group informal inventory	___	___
2. provides diagnostic tests	___	___
3. provides mastery tests	___	___
4. suggests prescriptive/reteaching activity	___	___

General Rating: Check appropriate line and indicate a reason for your rating.

1. ___ Recommend without reservation
2. ___ Recommend with reservation
3. ___ Accepted as best of limited choice
4. ___ Unsuited for this school at this time
5. ___ Not recommended

_____
Evaluator

After reviewing all of these limitations, teachers may wonder why readability formulas are used. They are used primarily to provide an estimate of the readability level of a selection. This level used in conjunction with the teacher's judgment helps determine if a material is suitable for a student or group of students.

There are many readability formulas that teachers may use. Some of the more common formulas are the Fry Readability Graph, the Flesch Reading Ease Test, Aukerman's readability formula, the SMOG formula, Dale-Chall readability formula, and the Spache readability formula.[37] The Spache formula is designed to be used with lower elementary level materials, while the Dale-Chall, SMOG, Aukerman and Flesch formulas are for upper elementary, secondary and adult level materials. The Fry formula can be used with materials at all levels. Because this formula is so flexible and easy for the teacher to use, it is provided in figure 5.9.

Figure 5.9
The Fry Readability Graph

GRAPH FOR ESTIMATING READABILITY — EXTENDED

by Edward Fry, Rutgers University Reading Center, New Brunswick, N.J. 08904

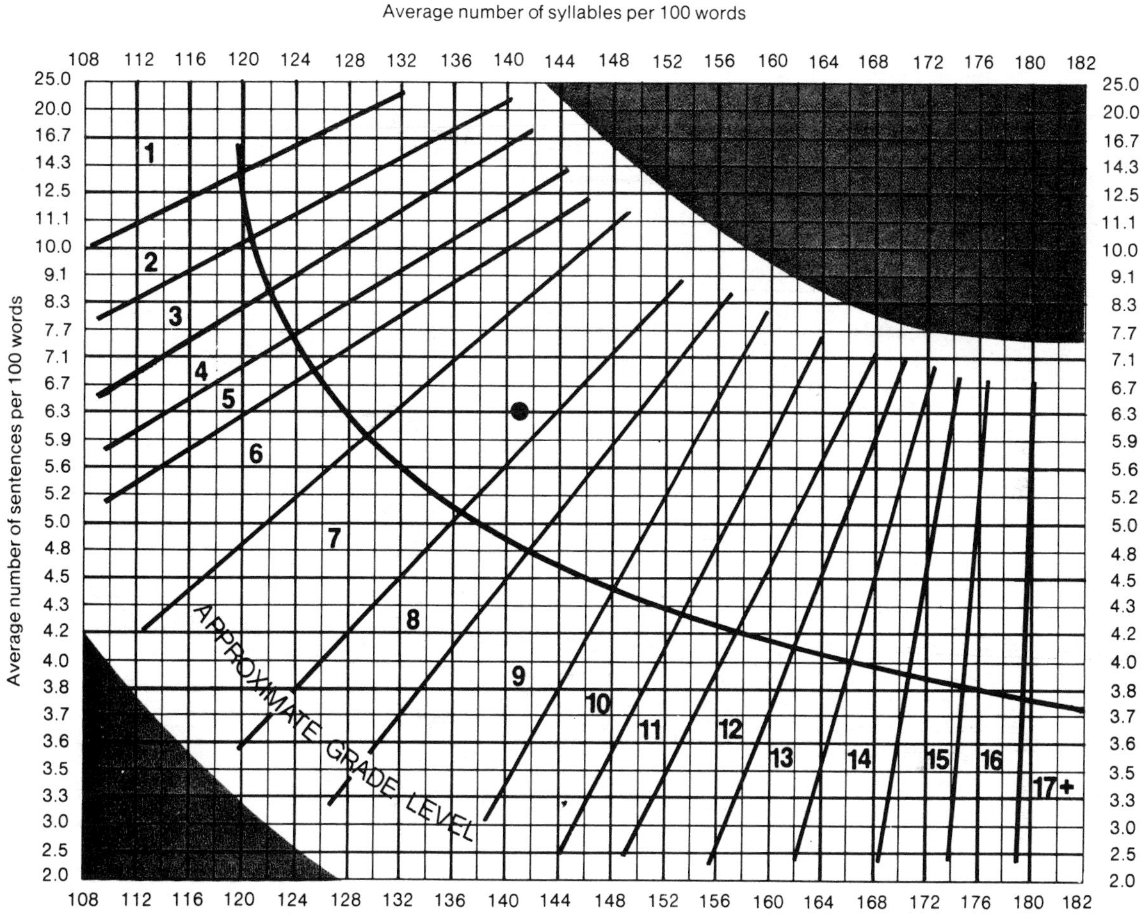

Average number of syllables per 100 words

DIRECTIONS: Randomly select 3 one hundred word passages from a book or an article. Plot average number of syllables and average number of sentences per 100 words on graph to determine the grade level of the material. Choose more passages per book if great variability is observed and conclude that the book has uneven readability. Few books will fall in gray area but when they do grade level scores are invalid.

Count proper nouns, numerals and initializations as words. Count a syllable for each symbol. For example, "1945" is 1 word and 4 syllables and "IRA" is 1 word and 3 syllables.

EXAMPLE:

	SYLLABLES	SENTENCES
1st Hundred Words	124	6.6
2nd Hundred Words	141	5.5
3rd Hundred Words	158	6.8
AVERAGE	141	6.3

READABILITY 7th GRADE (see dot plotted on graph)

For further information and validity data see the Journal of Reading December, 1977.

Careful attention is needed in selecting reading materials. There is such an abundance of resources on the market that teachers must evaluate the materials very thoroughly before purchase. Some of the materials are excellent and well worth the money, while others are only gimmicks. In addition, realize that if the materials do not meet the needs of the students, then they are of no value in the classroom. This means that periodic evaluations of the materials available in the classroom must be done in relation to student needs, and materials must be exchanged with other classes as necessary. Funds are usually not available to purchase new reading materials each year; thus, maximum usage must be made of existing materials. To assist teachers and administrators in their evaluation of reading materials, the Educational Products Information Exchange Institute (EPIE) has produced product reports that analyze basic and supplementary reading materials. These reports are available from EPIE Institute, 463 West Street, New York, New York 10014. The reviews assist in the thorough evaluation of reading materials, but cannot replace the teacher's analysis, which considers individual student needs.

In discussing reading materials, administrators need to recognize that more than one set of basal readers is helpful in teaching reading. Although materials alone do not enable students to read (and it is well known that many teachers do not need even a set of basals to teach), the fact remains that reading materials help the teacher by providing more abundant resources from which to develop prescriptions. Therefore, the assumption made in this section is that in implementing a diagnostic-prescriptive reading program, the teacher will have basal readers as well as a variety of other materials. However, teachers must be aware of the varying readability levels within basal materials. Eberwein, in a study of three series of basal readers, found that the average readability range was 2.1 grade levels for preprimers to 7.6 levels for fourth-, fifth-, and sixth-grade textbooks. The books did not become progressively more difficult from beginning to end.[38]

Although basal readers remain the dominant teaching material used in most school districts, the current trend is toward a greater reliance on children's literature. We believe that greater emphasis on literature in the classroom will expand the students' experiences, develop schema for learning that was not present, and result in a more well-rounded child with increased chances of being a better reader.

There are a great number of materials available for teaching children to read. Some are more effective than others. Two types of materials that appear to be particularly effective with primary students are predictable books and Big Books.

Predictable books are books that have no ending and allow students to activate their schema and experiential base in order to suggest an ending. These books are particularly effective in activating critical thinking.

Big Books are books that are larger than normal in size and print. The primary advantage of Big Books is that they closely approximate family storybook reading. These children's books feature language that is predictable and presented in patterns that make them easier to read and understand for young children. Children can read them over and over and not grow tired of them. After the student has read the books a number of times and feels comfortable with it, language activities such as thinking along, tracking print with your hand during all significant parts of the story, and examining text features such as letters and punctuation marks can be integrated into the lesson.[39]

Organizing and Arranging Materials

The arrangement of materials facilitates instruction and motivates students. Thus, the wise teacher displays different materials during the year rather than putting everything out in August or September. The change in materials is in itself a motivating factor for students. Students feel that they have something new to work with, when in fact it has just been pulled from storage. After using a material for a month or six weeks, give it to another teacher or put it away for a few weeks; variety is provided.

Book shelves or racks are excellent means of displaying library books, basals, and other texts. The materials in the classroom library are changed periodically, but the basal readers remain in the classroom throughout the year. To supplement these materials, the teacher may obtain old basal texts from the school system's surplus material warehouse. These books may be left intact, or taken apart to make mini-stories. The mini-stories can be put in construction paper covers to form an interesting section for the classroom library. Another way to supplement this resource area is through the use of language-experience story books. As the language-experience approach is used with various students, their story collections can be illustrated, bound, and placed in the room for others to read. Racks for displaying these materials sometimes may be obtained from department or grocery stores as they remodel or discard material. Students, especially at the upper levels, seem to read more materials when they are attractively displayed on racks.

Kits arranged in various parts of the room or on a table in the far corner of the room allow students an opportunity to move around to obtain materials. Only a few kits displayed at one time avoid the confusion and boredom of doing the same type of work.

For the language-experience approach, a section of the room could contain materials such as a large chart (for primary grades), paper, pictures, and possibly a tape recorder to allow students the opportunity to dictate a story for transcription when no one is available to write.

Selecting appropriate materials from the wealth of children's books, media, basals, and other forms of print is a challenge for teachers. Photo courtesy of Edward B. Lasher.

Materials such as tapes, recorders, and headphones may be placed in a central location for use at the listening center. In addition, paper, pencils, and crayons should be readily available for use in follow-up activities.

In introducing materials for classroom use, it is best to go over them with a small group, so that students will know where the materials are and how they are organized. This alleviates some of the problems of giving various assignments, working in small groups, and putting the materials back. Students are of great assistance in keeping materials in order if taught how to use them and if they enjoy the classroom atmosphere.

Developing Materials

Although teachers use commercial materials for 94% of their reading instruction,[40] they still need to make games, tapes, or skills kits to better meet students' needs and accommodate their teaching style. Many instructors tend to avoid teacher-made material and rely on the commercial materials for some good reasons. In a study, Shannon states:

- Administrators believed that commercial materials are based on research.
- Classroom teachers felt that they were meeting administrative expectations when they used commercial materials.
- Administrators, reading teachers, and classroom teachers believed that teachers might not be involved in teaching reading and that teachers truly believe the materials can teach students to read.[41]

Furthermore, teachers frequently believe that the time and money invested in developing materials may not be worth the return. This idea is supported in part by Snyder.[42] However, there are times when teachers must develop their own materials in order to provide appropriate instruction or reinforcement activities. Some ideas for developing materials are given to assist the teacher in providing prescriptive instruction.

To develop listening comprehension skills, the classroom teacher needs a variety of tapes available for independent student activities. Though some teachers may have commercially prepared tapes available, they are usually limited in number and must be supplemented to address the wide range of levels and interests. Thus, over the years, the teacher accumulates a variety of listening comprehension activities. These can be easily developed, using a short story from the library or one of the stories provided in the various issues of teacher magazines. On the tape, the teacher first provides a purpose for listening, then reads the story, and finally indicates follow-up activities using questions about the story. By properly labeling these tapes as to emphasize the listening comprehension skills as well as their levels, the instructor soon has a listening library in the classroom.

Workbooks are best used when they are set up as skill kits in the classroom. Only three copies of each workbook are needed when used as outlined below.

1. Collect all available workbooks; have at least two copies of each, three if possible.
2. Take two of the workbooks apart, leaving the third intact for reference.
3. Label each page as to its level and the skill developed.
4. If possible, laminate each page or put it in a plastic sheet on which the students can mark; this will also protect the pages as students handle them.
5. Develop a file by placing the pages in folders arranged according to skills. This file may be a metal file cabinet or a box covered with contact paper.
6. The teacher then selects pages on the appropriate levels, as needed for individual or group skill reinforcement.

Games and activities developed by teachers are valuable sources of independent work to develop and reinforce skills. These materials may be made from scraps of paper, juice cans, egg cartons, fruit baskets, or bits of material around the house. Teachers can always think of ways to recycle materials to create usable learning activities. Figure 5.10 provides a summary of the advantages and disadvantages of teacher-made and commercially developed materials; these are to be considered as teachers develop materials for prescriptive instruction.

Teachers frequently want many materials, but sometimes they do not use them effectively. Materials do not teach students to read—the teacher must do that—but they can greatly assist when effectively used to meet the individual student's needs.

Figure 5.10
Pros and Cons of
Hard-Produced and
Commercially
Produced Materials

Pros and cons of hand-produced and commercially produced materials

Hand-Produced		Commercial	
Pros	Cons	Pros	Cons
1) Can be designed to meet specific needs and interests of target group.	1) Durability of the constructed material is sometimes questionable.	1) Material can be geared to specific needs of children.	1) May use a too difficult vocabulary or a different approach to skill development.
2) Use an appropriate vocabulary and level of difficulty.	2) Constant remaking or mending may be required.	2) Material is durable, legible, and colorful. Looks professional and may be long-lasting.	2) May be limited in usefulness.
3) Children can be actively involved in game production.	3) Construction *must* reflect high standards of neatness and legibility.	3) A wide variety already available on the marketplace.	3) Require much time to locate, evaluate, purchase.
4) Kits and activity game files can be expanded as needed.	4) Directions must be carefully thought out.	4) If teacher time is a factor, may be less expensive than "home made."	4) Lost items are expensive to replace.
5) Favorite "old" games can be easily adapted.	5) Construction sometimes requires more time than is warranted.		5) Frequently considered too expensive.
6) Materials are sometimes more economical.	6) Easily available commercial materials are sometimes more economical.		

Geraldine V. Snyder, "Learner Verification of Reading Games," *The Reading Teacher* 34 (March 1981): 689. Reprinted with permission of Geraldine V. Snyder and the International Reading Association.

Since teachers use a variety of materials in teaching reading, it is essential that they coordinate the materials used to avoid giving duplicate assignments or assignments in materials with conflicting philosophies. More information is provided in chapter 6 regarding various approaches for teaching reading; at that time a discussion on correlating the various approaches is presented. Accordingly, this topic will not be dealt with in detail here. We will only state that the teacher must know the materials and the students in order to provide the most appropriate prescriptive instruction.

■ Summary

The topics dealt with in this chapter were the optimum use of classroom organization and management procedures, as these can facilitate diagnostic-prescriptive instruction.

The proper use of classroom management techniques improves not only the learning environment, but also the quality of teaching. Good individualization and grouping procedures are vital to the educational growth of students. Various methods of grouping were discussed, with some emphasis on organizing the classroom in order that these grouping procedures may be implemented. Models of grouping formats for both elementary and content area classrooms were included. Since the arrangement of classroom facilities is so critical, models were presented that suggest some alternatives to the traditional classroom arrangement.

After the organizational and management procedures were outlined, the next step involved actual implementation of the learning process through the selection and use of materials that are either commercially published or teacher-made. When all of the steps that have been discussed—classroom organization and management, individualization and grouping, arrangement of facilities, and the use of materials—are integrated into a total picture, the process of helping students learn to read through prescriptive instruction can begin.

■ Applying What You Read

You are teaching a fourth-grade class. Draw a schema, arranging the furniture as you would like to have it. Outline the types of groups that you may have.

As a new teacher in a middle school, how would you organize your classroom for instruction? What would you do to manage this class?

Develop a grouping procedure for teaching reading to twenty-eight second graders whose achievement levels range from a nonreader to two students reading on a fourth-grade level.

As a content teacher, develop a grouping procedure that can be used in your classroom to develop certain concepts. Identify the concepts and the exact procedures that can be used.

■ Notes

1. Richard D. Arnold, "Class Size and Reading Development," in *New Horizons in Reading*, edited by John E. Merritt; Richard L. Harris, "Research Evidence Regarding the Impact of Class Size on Pupil Academic Achievement"; Howard K. Holland and Armand J. Galfo, *An Analysis of Research Concerning Class Size*; Robert L. Thorndike, *Reading Comprehension in Fifteen Countries*; Nello Vignocchi, "What Research Says About the Effect of Class Size on Academic Achievement," *Illinois School Research and Development*.

2. Gerald G. Duffy and Laura R. Roehler, *Improving Classroom Reading Instruction*, pp. 14–15.

3. Janet Kierstead, "Outstanding Effective Classrooms," in *Claremont Reading Conference Forty-Eighth Yearbook*, edited by Malcolm P. Douglas.

4. Gerald G. Duffy and Laura R. Roehler, *Improving Classroom Reading Instruction*, p. 15.

5. Carolyn M. Evertson and Linda M. Anderson, "Beginning School," *Educational Horizons*; Gerald G. Duffy, *Teacher Effectiveness Research: Implications for the Reading Profession*; John T. Guthrie, "Effective Teaching Practices," *The Reading Teacher*; William H. Rupley and Timothy R. Blair, "Specifications of Reading Instructional Practices Associated with Pupil Achievement Gains," *Educational and Psychological Research*.

6. Gerald G. Duffy and Laura R. Roehler, *Improving Classroom Reading Instruction*, p. 100.

7. D. Ray Reutzel and Robert B. Cooter, Jr., "Organizing for Effective Instruction: The Reading Workshop," *The Reading Teacher*, pp. 548–55.

8. Earl H. Cheek, Jr., Rona F. Flippo, and Jimmy D. Lindsey, *Reading for Success in Elementary Schools*, pp. 40–47.

9. J. S. Kounin, *Discipline and Group Management in Classrooms*.

10. C. W. Fisher, N. N. Filby, R. Marliave, L. S. Cahen, M. M. Dishaw, J. E. Moore, and D. C. Berliner, *Teaching Behaviors, Academic Learning Time, and Student Achievement: Final Report of Phase III-B, Beginning Teacher Evaluation Study*.

11. Diana Buell Hiatt, "Time Allocation in the Classroom: Is Instruction Being Shortchanged?" *Phi Delta Kappan*.

12. G. R. Musgrave, *Individualized Instruction*.

13. Carl J. Wallen, "Independent Activities: A Necessity, Not a Frill," *The Reading Teacher*; Mallie Slater, "Individualized Language Arts in the Middle Grades," *The Reading Teacher*; Harriet Ramsey Reeves, "Individual Conferences-Diagnostic Tools," *The Reading Teacher*; Sandra Nina Kaplan, Jo Ann Butom Kaplan, Sheila Kunishima Madsen, and Bette K. Taylor, *Change for Children*.

14. M. Kean, A. Summers, M. Ravietz and I. Farber. *What Works in Reading*, p. 9.

15. C. W. Fisher, N. N. Filby, R. Marliave, L. S. Cahen, M. M. Dishaw, J. E. Moore, and D. C. Berliner, *Teaching Behaviors, Academic Learning Time, and Student Achievement*.

16. Barak Roseshine and Robert Stevens, "Classroom Instruction in Reading," in *Handbook of Reading Research*, edited by P. David Pearson, p. 758.

17. C. C. Kulik and J. A. Kulik, "Effects of Ability Grouping on Secondary School Students: A Meta-analysis of Evaluation Findings." *American Educational Research Journal*.

18. C. Persell, *Education and Inequality: The Roots and Results of Stratification in American Schools*.

19. Linda L. Brown and Rita J. Sherbenou, "A Comparison of Teacher Perceptions of Student Reading Ability, Reading Performance, and Classroom Behavior," *The Reading Teacher*; Chris Moacdieh, "Grouping of Reading in the Primary Grades: Evidence on the Revisionist Argument," Paper presented at the Annual Meeting of the American Educational Research Association, Los Angeles, California, April 13–17, 1981; John J. Pikulski and Irwin S. Kiroch. "Organization for Instruction," in *Teaching Reading in Compensatory Classes*, edited by Robert C. Calfee and Priscilla A. Drum.

20. Emil J. Haller and Sharon A. Davis. "Does Socioeconomic Status Bias the Assignment of Elementary School Students to Reading Groups?" *American Educational Research Journal.*

21. Jeanne Martin and Carolyn M. Evertson, *Teachers' Interactions with Reading Groups of Differing Ability Levels.*

22. Linda Grant and James Rothenberg, *Charting Educational Futures: Interaction Patterns in First and Second Grade Reading Groups*; Paula R. Stern and Richard J. Shavelson, "The Relationship Between Teachers' Grouping Decisions and Instructional Behavior: An Ethnographic Study of Reading Instruction." Paper presented at the annual meeting of the American Educational Research Association, Los Angeles, California, April 13–17, 1981.

23. E. H. Hiebert, "An Examination of Ability Grouping for Reading Instruction," *Reading Research Quarterly*; P. Peterson, L. Wilkinson, and M. Hallinan, *The Social Context of Instruction: Group Organization and Group Processes.*

24. P. Peterson, L. Wilkinson, and M. Hallinan, *The Social Context of Instruction.*

25. Linda Grant and James Rothenbert, *Charting Educational Futures.*

26. S. Asher, "Topic Interest and Children's Reading Comprehension," in *Theoretical Issues in Reading Comprehension*, edited by R. Spiro, B. Bruce and W. Brewer.

27. R. C. Anderson, E. H. Hiebert, J. A. Scott, and I. A. Wilkinsen, *Becoming A Nation of Readers.*

28. Jack Cassidy, "Cross-age Tutoring and the Sacrosanct Reading Period," *Reading Horizons*; Hal Dreyer, "Rx for Pupil Tutoring Programs," *The Reading Teacher*; Joan L. Fogarty and Margaret C. Wang, "An Investigation of the Cross-Age Peer Tutoring Process: Some Implications for Instructional Design and Motivation," *The Elementary School Journal.*

29. Linda D. Labbo and William H. Teale, "Cross-Age Reading: A Strategy for Helping Poor Readers," *The Reading Teacher*, pp. 362–69.

30. Connie Morrice and Maureen Simmons, "Beyond Reading Buddies: A Whole Language Cross-Age Program," *The Reading Teacher*, pp. 572–79.

31. Roger T. Johnson and David W. Johnson, "Action Research: Cooperative Learning in the Science Classroom," *Science and Children*, pp. 31–32.

32. Robert Slavin, *Cooperative Learning.*

33. Karen D'Angelo Bromley, "Buddy Journals Make the Reading-Writing Connection," *The Reading Teacher*, pp. 122–129.

34. Suzi Keegan and Karen Shrake, "Literature Study Groups: An Alternative to Ability Grouping," *The Reading Teacher*, pp. 542–47.

35. Maurice Kaufman, *Perceptual and Language Readiness Programs: Critical Reviews*; Paul C. Burns and Betty D. Roe, *Teaching Reading in Today's Elementary Schools*; Larry A. Harris and Carl B. Smith, *Reading Instruction* (4th ed.); Patricia M. Cunningham, "A Teacher's Guide to Materials Shopping," *The Reading Teacher*; Carol N. Dixon, "Selection and Use of Instructional Materials," in *Teaching Reading in Compensatory Classes*, edited by Robert C. Calfee and Priscilla A. Drum.

36. Martha Maxwell, "Readability: Have We Gone Too Far?" *Journal of Reading*; Sylvia-Lee Tibbetts, "How Much Should We Expect Readability Formulas to Do?" *Elementary English*; Daniel R. Hittleman, "Seeking a

Psycholinguistic Definition of Readability," *The Reading Teacher*; Joan Nelson, "Readability: Some Cautions to the Content Area Teacher," *Journal of Reading*; Bob Lange, "Readability Formulas Second Looks, Second Thoughts," *The Reading Teacher*.

37. Edward Fry, "Fry's Readability Graph: Clarifications, Validity, and Extension to Level 17," *Journal of Reading*; Rudolph F. Flesch, "A New Readability Yardstick," *Journal of Applied Psychology*; Robert C. Aukerman, *Reading in the Secondary School Classroom*; Harry G. McLaughlin, "SMOG Grading—A New Readability Formula," *Journal of Reading*; Edgar Dale and Jeanne Chall, "A Formula for Predicting Readability," *Educational Research Bulletin*; George D. Spache, *Good Reading for Poor Readers*.

38. Lowell D. Eberwein, "The Variability of Readability of Basal Reader Textbooks and How Much Teachers Know About It," *Reading World*.

39. Dorothy S. Strickland and Lesley Mandel Morrow, "Emerging Readers and Writers: Sharing Big Books," *The Reading Teacher*, pp. 342–43.

40. Educational Products Information Exchange, *Report of A National Study of the Quality of Instructional Materials Most Used by Teachers and Learners*.

41. Patrick Shannon, "Some Subjective Reasons for Teachers' Reliance on Commercial Reading Materials," *The Reading Teacher*.

42. Geraldine V. Snyder, "Learner Verification of Reading Games," *The Reading Teacher*.

■ Other Suggested Readings

Anderson, L. "The Environment of Instruction: The Function of Seatwork in a Commercially Developed Curriculum." in *Comprehension Instruction: Perspectives and Suggestions*. Edited by G. G. Duffy, L. R. Roehler, and J. Mason. New York: Longman, 1984.

Au, Kathryn (ed.) "A Special Issue on Organizing for Instruction." *The Reading Teacher* 44 (April 1991): 534–624.

Baumann, James F. "Implications for Reading Instruction from the Research on Teacher and School Effectiveness." *Journal of Reading* 28 (November 1984): 109–15.

Crocker, Robert K., and Gwen M. Brooker. "Classroom Control and Student Outcomes in Grades 2 and 5." *American Educational Research Journal* 23 (Spring 1986): 1–11.

Duffy, Gerald G., and Laura R. Roehler. "Improving Reading Instruction Through the Use of Responsive Elaboration." *The Reading Teacher* 40 (February 1987): 514–20.

Felmlee, Diane, and Donna Eder. "Contextual Effects in the Classroom: The Impact of Ability Groups on Student Attention." *Sociology of Education* 56 (April 1983): 77–87.

Gettinger, Maribeth. "Time Allocated and Time Spent Relative to Time Needed for Learning as Determinants of Achievement." *Journal of Educational Psychology* 77 (February 1985): 617–28.

Haller, Emil J. "Pupil Race and Elementary School Ability Grouping: Are Teachers Biased Against Black Children?" *American Educational Research Journal* 22 (Winter 1985): 465–83.

Haller, Emil J., and Margaret Waterman. "The Criteria of Reading Group Assignments." *The Reading Teacher* 38 (April 1985): 772–81.

Hallinan, Maureen, and Aage B. Sorensen. "Class Size, Ability Group Size, and Student Achievement." *American Journal of Education* 94 (November 1985): 71–89.

Haskins, Ron, Tedra Walden, and Craig T. Ramey. "Teacher and Student Behavior in High- and Low-Ability Groups." *Journal of Educational Psychology* 75 (December 1983): 865–76.

Hoge, Robert D., and Robert Butcher. "Analysis of Teacher Judgments of Pupil Achievement Levels." *Journal of Educational Psychology* 76 (October 1984): 777–81.

Jongsma, Kathleen Stumpf. "Questions and Answers: Collaborative Learning." *The Reading Teacher* 43 (January 1990): 346–47.

Pittman, Sherry I. "A Cognitive Ethnography and Quantification of a First-Grade Teacher's Selection Routines for Classroom Management." *The Elementary School Journal* 85 (March 1985): 541–57.

Smith, Carl. "ERIC/RCS: Shared Learning Promotes Critical Reading." *The Reading Teacher* 43 (October 1989): 76–77.

Thurlow, Martha, Janet Graden, James E. Ysseldyke, and Robert Algozzine. "Student Reading during Reading Class: The Lost Activity in Reading Instruction." *Journal of Educational Research* 77 (May–June 1984): 267–72.

Unsworth, L. "Meeting Individual Needs Through Flexible Within-Class Grouping of Pupils." *The Reading Teacher* 38 (December 1985): 298–303.

Prescriptive Instruction

As teachers consider the revised concept of diagnostic-prescriptive reading instruction recognizing that diagnosis is a continuous process attuning to the language processes of all students, more questions arise as the topic of prescriptive instruction is approached. In the traditional sense, prescriptive reading instruction is done by teaching deficient skills identified through the testing procedures. However, teachers approach prescriptive instruction in a more holistic manner in today's classroom.

Teachers realize that quality instruction is the key component in the successful school reading program. Using informal and formal diagnostic data and daily evaluations along with their skill in organizing and managing reading instruction, teachers direct their attention to providing appropriate reading instruction that meets the needs of individual students. Chapters 6–11 are designed to help teachers provide better prescriptive reading instruction for each student. In these chapters, prescriptive teaching and prescriptive instruction are used interchangeably as suggestions are offered to assist in the teaching/learning process.

6

Prescriptive Teaching of Reading

Teachers are the instructional leaders in the classroom. As instructional leaders, classroom teachers realize that they have the tremendous responsibility not only of identifying the reading strengths and weaknesses of each student, but also of providing appropriate instruction to meet each student's needs. Instruction based on the diagnosed needs of each student is referred to as prescriptive instruction.

This chapter provides an overview of prescriptive reading instruction as related to actual classroom practice. Some basic principles underlying prescriptive instruction, together with various approaches for teaching reading, and ideas on developing prescriptions for individuals and groups are discussed. More specifically, the following questions are addressed.

What is prescriptive teaching or instruction?

What are some basic guides for the teacher to follow in providing prescriptive instruction?

How does prescriptive instruction differ in self-contained and departmentalized classrooms?

What does the teacher need to consider before beginning prescriptive reading instruction?

What are the various reading approaches used in prescriptive instruction?

How do the diagnostic data relate to prescriptive instruction?

How does the teacher develop prescriptions? When does a teacher plan for prescriptive reading instruction?

As this chapter is read, the following terms are important to note.

Vocabulary to Know

Approaches	Directed Reading Activity	Language experience approach
Basal reader approach	Electic approach	Literature-based reading
Computer-assisted instruction	Indirect instruction	Multi-sensory approach
Direct instruction	Individualized reading approach	Prescriptive instruction
Directed Learning Activity	Language-based instruction	Skill development

■ Philosophy of Prescriptive Teaching

In thinking further about the concept of diagnostic-prescriptive reading instruction, it is necessary to review and extend the discussion of prescriptive teaching in chapter 1. Prescriptive teaching is reading instruction provided to meet the diagnosed reading needs of each student. This is not to imply that it must be one-to-one instruction. The definition does mean, however, that individual student needs are met through either individual, small group, or large group instruction.

Teachers need to remember that in providing reading instruction, diagnostic data directs the instructional program for each student. One teacher summarized the idea of prescriptive teaching by defining it as *"teaching what you know the student needs rather than what the publishing companies tell you to teach."* This is one way of thinking about prescriptive teaching. As long as teachers follow some type of scope and sequence or reading continuum, whether from the school or publishing company, they will have continuity in learning experiences and development from level to level.

In prescriptive reading instruction, teachers are the decision makers and directors of the learning process. Knowing the needs of the students, they plan appropriate lessons to capture interests and develop skills using appropriate materials and strategies.

Basic principles or guides for prescriptive instruction that give the teacher direction in implementing prescriptive teaching in the classroom are discussed in the following pages.

Prescriptive teaching can be implemented in many ways; there is no one best way. Each teacher using the concepts of prescriptive reading instruction determines the best way to put them into effect in the classroom. Just as each student is unique, so also is each teacher's style of teaching, classroom arrangement, and confidence in providing reading instruction. Teachers use ideas provided in this text, from other teachers, past experiences and other sources, adapting them to their classrooms. The element that must always exist in prescriptive instruction is that it be based on the students' diagnosed needs.

Varied approaches and techniques must be used in prescribing instruction for a specific reading problem. Many approaches for teaching reading have been identified, and research dealing with the different approaches is voluminous. However, as was found in the First Grade Studies, there is no one best approach for teaching reading.[1] Likewise, there is no one technique that is always successful in dealing with diagnosed reading problems. Each student is unique in her learning style, reading habits, background experiences, and self-expectations. Thus, a guide that tells a teacher what to do with each student cannot be provided; only suggestions can be made. The teacher must, through careful thought and in some cases trial and error, determine what works best with different students.

Prescriptive instruction should follow a developmental continuum. In order for prescriptive reading instruction to provide for continuity in skill development, a defined scope and sequence of reading skills is needed. Without a continuum of skills, whether from a publishing company or developed within the school system, teachers lack structure for guiding skill development, and gaps or inconsistencies may develop. The hierarchy of skills serves as a guide to the teacher; it is not to be followed rigidly.

Teachers using a basal reader as their primary reading material have a scope and sequence of reading skills as a base to their instructional program. Teachers using a language-based approach do not have a hierarchy of skills directly associated with their materials, but may find that there is such a skills continuum used as part of their local or state testing programs. Skills instruction must not be equated to good reading instruction as "mastery" of skills is not the goal of reading nor is it the major descriptor of a good reader. However, teachers must be aware of some developmental order of reading and language skills in order to recognize how well students are learning and to plan appropriate instruction.

Prescriptive instruction must be based on continuous diagnosis. The diagnosis made by the classroom teacher serves as a guide in identifying students' reading needs. In order for teaching to be truly prescriptive, teachers re-evaluate and diagnose their students continuously. This is not to imply that formal tests are frequently administered. The ongoing diagnosis is done through observation of the students' performance of assigned tasks, other informal procedures, and possibly some formal diagnostic tests, if necessary. Regardless of how the information is obtained, the classroom teacher continuously assesses changes in reading performance in order to provide instruction based on the needs of the student.

Instruction should be flexible in prescriptive teaching. In following diagnostic-prescriptive procedures for reading instruction, teachers need to be aware that the diagnostic information suggests indications of strengths and weaknesses in reading, and that the prescriptive instruction is based upon these indications. Thus, the teacher may begin instruction in an identified area of need only to become aware that the actual need is a lower-level skill or that the student has developed beyond what is being taught. Flexible teachers make changes in the prescriptive instruction being provided. This may mean moving the student to another group for instruction or offering some individual instruction for a period of time. Flexibility is an essential element of good prescriptive instruction.

Prescriptive teaching requires that all school personnel work together as a team. As discussed in chapter 1, the entire school staff must work together not only in the continuous diagnosis of students, but also in providing prescriptive instruction. The librarian may assist in developing personal reading skills by encouraging students to read books at their independent reading level. She may also aid in the teaching of study skills by assisting the teacher in developing the specific library and reference skills as necessary. Content teachers can identify the reading skills necessary for learning the content materials and help develop these skills as related to content reading. Reading or language arts teachers should share with the content teachers all diagnostic data available in order to facilitate prescriptive reading instruction in all classes.

The principal and guidance counselor facilitate prescriptive reading instruction by locating materials and teaching ideas to assist in meeting special student needs. Additionally, they provide much positive reinforcement to students as they improve in reading and to teachers as they strive to improve learning opportunities.

In order for prescriptive reading instruction to have the greatest impact, school faculty recognize that reading is a tool used in all school work, that each student improves according to diagnosed needs, and that each faculty has responsibility for helping students to improve. When a principal and school faculty understand their roles in the school reading program and work together for the benefit of the student, then a prescriptive reading program functions at its best.

Prescriptive teaching aids students in applying their knowledge of reading skills to the reading of content as well as other printed materials. In prescriptive teaching, specific reading needs are identified and appropriate instruction is provided. This is the first step in prescriptive instruction. The essential second step is that the student is taught how to use his knowledge in reading materials for enjoyment and to gain information. Students do not automatically transfer reading skills developed in isolation to their reading tasks. Thus, the development of reading skills does not improve reading performance unless the student is taught how to apply the skills as necessary. Teachers assist in this transfer by showing the student how skills are to be used in a given situation. For example, the student who has been taught the skill of sequencing ideas or events should be shown how to use this skill in recalling ideas from a story, in remembering the steps in a science experiment, or in determining the chronological order of events in a social studies lesson.

In developing reading skills as well as in teaching their application, the teacher provides direct instruction and uses materials to reinforce and review. Reading skills are not developed by "plugging" students into materials, but rather by explanation from the teacher, with reinforcement as needed, using various activities or materials. When students demonstrate a basic understanding of the reading process, teachers then show them how "school" reading is an integral part of their daily life experiences.

Prescriptive reading programs are designed to foster a positive self-image and enjoyment of reading as well as the development of the reading process. Reading instruction that meets identified needs and is on the appropriate level for the student not only enhances the development of reading but also helps students to have a more positive attitude toward themselves due to their success in learning. A basic knowledge of the language process and a good self-concept provide an excellent foundation for the enjoyment of reading. Thus, teachers should remember that the end product of the school reading program is a student who can read, and who enjoys reading as a leisure-time activity as well as for informational purposes.

Most teachers at the elementary and middle school levels believe in these basic principles of prescriptive reading instruction, yet some teachers have difficulty implementing the concept. The classroom teacher in a self-contained situation implements prescriptive reading instruction in a self-contained situation differently from the teacher in a departmentalized classroom. Likewise, the reading specialist or resource teacher working with small groups of students having severe reading problems may provide prescriptive instruction through means that differ yet reinforce those used in the classroom.

Using the diagnostic data from the classroom teacher, supplemented by any additional information from the language arts teacher, the content area teachers and the reading specialist or resource teacher, classroom teachers can work together to develop a class profile of areas of reading—language development and determine how to best meet the individual student needs.

These basic principles provide only general directions for implementing prescriptive instruction. Teachers must interpret and apply them according to their individual teaching styles and classroom needs.

■ Approaches for Prescriptive Reading Instruction

In order to provide prescriptive reading instruction, the diagnosed needs, interests, and learning styles of the students are to be considered. Thus, teachers need familiarity with various approaches that may be used in prescriptive teaching.

Many approaches have been presented by different writers; for some the term "methods" is synonymous with "approaches." Burns and Roe identify the major approaches as basal reader approach, language experience approach, individualized reading approach, linguistic approaches, intensive phonics approaches, changed alphabet approaches, systems approaches, and eclectic approaches.[2] Fry discusses various methods of teaching reading, including the basal reader, reading systems, individualized reading, programmed instruction, different alphabetic approaches, audiovisual reading materials, language experience approach, and kinesthetic approach.[3] Other authors, including Vacca, Vacca, and Gove and Miller and McKenna identify slightly different listings of approaches for teaching reading.[4]

As teachers read current professional materials, attend professional meetings, and talk about reading instruction in their classes, two basic approaches are prominent. In the elementary and middle school classrooms of the '90s, teachers use a *basal*

Figure 6.1
Basic Principles of
Prescriptive
Reading Instruction

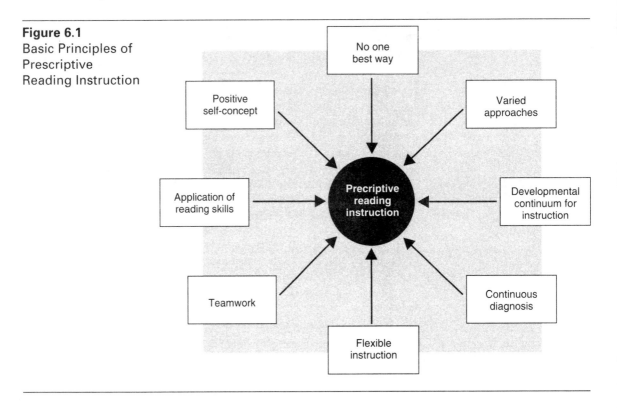

approach or a *language-based approach* for reading instruction. While these approaches do not exist in complete isolation and certainly are not mutually exclusive, current literature may lead one to think of the "two approaches to reading!" To appropriately represent the trends and to provide information needed by the teacher to best meet individual student needs, these two major approaches are discussed first with other secondary approaches presented that are used to modify these primary approaches to meet student needs.

When selecting the appropriate reading approach to use with students, teachers consider certain basic factors. These factors include: (a) the teacher's philosophy and definiton of reading and language instruction; (b) the characteristics of the students (e.g., cognitive and linguistic abilities, prior knowledge, experiential background and socio-cultural background); and (c) school and classroom environmental conditions (e.g., class size, equipment and materials, etc.).[5] Although the majority of school districts in this country have used basal readers, many of which are eclectic in nature, literature/language-based instruction is becoming very popular and influencing the use of basal readers.

Jagger[6] believes that several important themes regarding the essential role of language in learning to read have emerged in recent years. Included in these themes are the following essential concepts inherent in language development:

1. *Language-learning is a self-generated, creative process.* Children learn language without direct instruction. They learn it in a variety of ways (e.g., through experience or by listening to others) and experiment with and practice their language in situations where language is purposeful.

2. *Language-learning is holistic.* The language components of function, form, and meaning are learned simultaneously. Children acquire new and more complex forms and functions for language when they have a need for new and more complex meanings. Through this process they learn that the forms used to express meaning and intention may vary according to purpose and context.

3. *Language-learning is social and collaborative.* Language is acquired by children in meaningful interactions with others who provide models. These individuals also support children's language-learning by responding to what children are trying to say and do, rather than to form.

4. *Language-learning is functional and integrative.* Children do not first learn language and then second, learn how to use it. Language acquisition and the ability to communicate are simultaneous functions. This process also stimulates children's ability to use language to think and learn.

5. *Language-learning is variable.* Because language-learning is inherently variable, the meanings, the forms, and the functions of children's language are dependent upon children's personal, social, and cultural experiences.

Although the selection of appropriate approaches to meet the needs of the students is essential to effective reading instruction, developing and expanding the language base of the students is one of the most important responsibilities of the teacher. The development of language as a communication skill is necessary for students to effectively interact with print. Not only do students need to have good language capabilities, but they need awareness of the relationship between language and reading. This awareness enables them to more clearly understand the correlation between language, reading, and writing. Thus, it is essential that an emphasis on the development of language permeate the overall reading instructional program without regard to the approach or approaches selected to meet an individual student's needs.

However, as teachers consider approaches to develop language while involved in reading instruction, the significant element is instruction rather than approaches. Durkin suggests this definition of instruction: "Instruction refers to what someone or something does or says that has the potential to teach one or more individuals what they do not know, do not understand, or cannot do." This definition of instruction suggests the importance of success in that learning occurs and pertinence in that the something that is learned is important to know. Durkin further suggests

Students are placed in basal reader groups based on their reading level. Photo courtesy of Edward B. Lasher.

that in order for appropriate instruction to occur, three elements need to exist: objectives, instruction, and application.[7] As approaches are discussed in relation to prescriptive instruction, the elements of objectives, purpose for instructing and application, or use of what is learned will be incorporated.

Basal Approach

In previous editions of this book, the authors have not discussed the basal approach in a separate category but have incorporated basal materials as a part of the eclectic approach to reading. However, in current information relating to approaches to reading instruction, two basic categories (1) basal approach and (2) language-based approach are discussed. While all instruction in reading does not fit neatly into these two categories, it is appropriate to consider the use of basal materials as an approach to reading that emphasizes the sequential development of reading skills. As discussions of basal v. language-based approaches cause changes to occur in the classroom, teachers are using basal materials in several ways:

- Use the basal reader and workbook to develop the reading skills as outlined in the teacher's manual;
- Use the developmental continuum of skills from the basal to plan instruction using the basal and various materials to implement an eclectic approach to reading instruction; and
- Use the basal materials as extras in the class while library books and children's literature become the primary sources for reading experiences.

Teachers using basal materials in the first two ways consider themselves as using a traditional basal approach in that their instruction is skill driven from the developmental continuum of skills in the basal. Teachers using basal materials in the third way are attempting to use a language-based approach yet feel compelled by parent, principal or peer pressure to allow students to read the basal. Although many current basal series are language oriented using story content of children's literature books, variety of characters, and less rigidly controlled vocabulary, and manuals encourage teachers to incorporate writing activities and language experiences into their teaching plans, basals have a skills continuum as their foundation. This skills continuum is a series of individual skills taught through the basal lessons and often reflect the testing programs of the school district or state. Thus, teacher use of basal materials as an approach to reading is frequently encouraged, directly or subtly, as a rationale to ensure better test scores on skills-oriented local and state tests.

As an example of this skill/test emphasis, one of the authors had an interesting personal experience when moving to a new area. In searching for a school district that had a good primary level reading program for a language fluent, ready-to-read, learning is fun five-year-old, several schools were identified with one teacher singled out as being one of the best kindergarten teachers. With further investigation, it was learned that this teacher used a language-based approach that resulted in good readers with positive self-concepts and a love for reading—UTOPIA! Upon moving into this school area and learning that the teacher was a neighbor, the author got to know her much better and had the opportunity to work in her classroom. All reports were accurate! One day as her teaching was praised, this teacher lamented, "I'm not sure my children are learning their reading skills well enough to go into some of the first-grades so I'm giving them the kindergarten end of the book [basal] test this week." As would be expected, the students did very well on the test, but this teacher with twenty years of experience providing developmentally appropriate language instruction to kindergarten students, recognized by peers in the school system as being the best, and with living results throughout the neighborhood, had doubts about how well her children would do on a skills-based test. Therefore, as teachers consider philosophies of reading as related to how they will approach reading instruction, the realities are the pressures of tests. With this reality, the basal will continue to be a major approach for incorporating reading skill instruction.

Another advantage of the basal approach is that it encourages continuity for students as they progress through the grades and as they transfer to various schools using the same basal series. Continuity in skill development is important in a program using a skills approach. Without the continuity provided by a continuum of skills, there is a risk of teachers emphasizing some skills repeatedly and overlooking other significant skills. In addition to this continuity, the basal reader is accompanied by a teacher's manual which provides directions to the teacher for instructing the students in reading a story and developing the necessary skills. This lesson plan follows a guided or directed reading format using teacher-directed and student-directed activities. Teachers and administrators frequently feel more comfortable when such planned lessons from the publishing company are followed believing that the lessons are developed by reading specialists who know what needs to be taught.

The basal approach may also be a favored material because of the availability of related supplemental activities to reinforce the lesson. Workbooks, charts, skills sheets, computer programs and other manipulatives are available to supplement the basal reader, thereby freeing the teacher of the added responsibility of locating other materials. This time-saving element is especially attractive to the teacher with thirty squirming second graders!

Many teachers, administrators, and parents believe a basal approach to be the best alternative to providing good reading instruction in the elementary grades. For some teachers, this is the appropriate approach in that it supports their philosophical belief about reading instruction, relates to their experiences, and provides them with the necessary plans and materials to implement this philosophy in the classroom.

However, in implementing prescriptive instruction, teachers who use the basal approach should note that prescriptive instruction means addressing the individual reading needs of the student. This sometimes parallels the basal lesson but the teacher may need to make instructional changes to better meet student needs. As teachers get to know their students, they identify those who have developed the necessary skills to function independently with minimum skill instruction from the teacher, those who have minimum skill knowledge but need the language foundation prior to learning skills, and those who need to continue to develop reading skills in a structured manner. The instructional needs of all these groups of students may not be met through the exclusive use of a basal approach. A basal approach may serve to meet some of their instructional needs, but incorporating other approaches through the year will be necessary to maximize the learning potential of all students.

Student needs, teacher philosophy, and materials form the base for prescriptive instruction. When the teacher realizes this, another factor must be mentioned as the basal approach is discussed. Some students need a structured program that follows the same lesson format each day and allows them to see how many pages they have read during a specified time. Other students are totally bored with this approach needing more variety in lesson format and materials. Knowing the reading needs and interests of the students is necessary, but the added dimension of learning style is equally important in motivating students to enjoy reading. For these reasons, teachers must be flexible in their teaching approach, adapting the approach to their philosophical belief about reading instruction. There is no one best approach for teaching reading—teacher style, student needs, and learning environment are the crucial elements.

Language-Based Approach

Whole language, literature-based, language experience and whole literacy instruction are the unique, widely defined terms used to describe instruction which connects reading and writing, and uses literature. Bergeron suggests that whole language is the response of any approach or program supportive of literature-based or integrated instruction.[8] Inconsistencies in the literature as to what this instructional strategy includes have caused confusion in classroom implementation. To exemplify this confusion about whole language, in a review of the literature, Bergeron found whole language to be an approach (Mosenthal, 1989), a belief (Farris & Kaczmarski, 1988), a method (Hajek, 1984), a philosophy (Brountas, 1987), an orientation (Richards, Gipe, & Thompson, 1987), a theory (Reutzel & Hollingsworth, 1988), a theoretical orientation (Edlesky, Draper, & Smith, 1983), a program (Slaughter, 1988), a curriculum (Mersereau, Glover, & Cherland, 1989), a perspective on education (Watson, 1989), and an attitude of mind (Rich, 1985).[9] Although many teachers would suggest that they use a whole language approach in their instruction, the confusion of the definition of whole language and its base in early research on oral and written language development cause the authors to discuss this concept of teaching reading as a *language-based approach*. For purposes of this discussion, the language-based approach is defined as instructional procedures which facilitate a naturalistic development of oral and written language skills used in speaking, listening, reading, and writing.

With this broad definition, how does a teacher implement a language-based approach? According to Bergeron, the concept of whole language ". . . includes the use of real literature and writing in the context of meaningful, functional, and cooperative experiences in order to develop in students motivation and interest in the process of learning."[10] Ridley in comparing whole language to text-based reading suggests that "whole language teaching incorporates authentic materials such as newspapers, literature, notes, recipes, student's books, and other writing, [and] . . . is learner-centered [as] students choose topics, audiences, purpose, and books and they manage their own time [with] whole language activities . . . as varied as the teachers who implement them."[11] Added to these descriptions of whole language instruction are Hiebert and Colt's three patterns of incorporating literature-based reading instruction into the classroom. They suggest:

- Pattern 1: Teacher-selected literature in teacher-led groups;
- Pattern 2: Teacher- and student-selected literature in teacher- and student-led small groups; and
- Pattern 3: Student-selected literature read independently.[12]

Using a combination of these three patterns, they suggest that children will develop as thoughtful, proficient readers.

Two approaches previously considered individually as different ways of teaching reading are now part of the language-based approach. The *Language Experience Approach* and the *Individualized Reading Approach* are strategies discussed as teachers talk about implementing a whole language or language-based approach in their classes.

The language-experience approach is defined by Hall as "a method in which instruction is built upon the use of reading materials created by writing down children's spoken language."[13] Allen has provided another definition that presents the students' concept of the language-experience approach:

- What I can think about, I can talk about.
- What I can say, I can write—or someone can write for me.
- What I can write, I can read.
- I can read what I can write and what other people can write for me to read.[14]

These definitions reflect the importance of using the students' language as the basis for the development of reading materials. This approach integrates all areas in order to strengthen the communication skills of reading, speaking, writing, and the listening skills for each student.

The basic idea of developing story or experience charts has been used in schools since the early 1900s. However, through the work of Allen, Stauffer, and Hall, this approach has become better understood and accepted for teaching reading to students of any age, preschool through adult.[15] The rationale for the use of this approach is that by using the student's own oral language as dictated, reading can be a successful experience.

In using the language-experience approach in the classroom, the teacher can follow these steps:

- Use the approach with an individual student, a small group, or a large group, depending on the purpose of the lesson.
- Discuss some experience that is common to the group or that seems important to the individual student, using a stimulus such as a field trip, an object, or a picture.
- Prepare the student(s) for telling a story by having them summarize ideas from the discussion or give a title to the ideas discussed.
- Allow each student to contribute to the story by sharing ideas about the experience.
- Write each sentence on the board or a chart.
- Read each idea after it is written, sweeping your hand under each line to emphasize left-to-right progression.
- Read the story together (teacher and students) when it is complete.
- Discuss the story, pointing out capital letters, names, ideas, etc.
- Copies of the story are made either by the students or duplicated by the teacher.
- On the following days, the story is reread and skill development is accomplished by means of the vocabulary and ideas in the story. This last step is extremely important in the development of reading skills, yet it is often overlooked when using the language-experience approach.

Table 6.1

Language-Experience Approach

Advantages	Limitations
—The students' language is the basis for the reading material. —Several learning modalities are used—auditory in dictating the story, visual in seeing the words, and kinesthetic in copying or writing the story. —Students are motivated to read because the information is interesting to them. —Self-concept is enhanced as the student realizes that others think his ideas are important. —Older students with poor reading skills are interested in the content of the material. —Concepts such as left-to-right orientation, capitalization and punctuation, word boundaries, etc., can be easily taught. —Oral language skills, which are especially beneficial to the student from an educationally deficient environment, are developed.	—The approach is unstructured; thus, there is no sequential development of skills. —The teacher must assume major responsibility in using this approach as there are no prepared materials. —The lack of repetition of vocabulary and vocabulary control may be troublesome for some students. —Like any other approach, the overuse of this format in teaching may become boring to the student. —The development of the charts is time consuming for the teacher.

This skill development may deal with word parts, letter sounds, capitalization and punctuation, word endings or any other skills needed by the student. Word cards with new vocabulary words may be developed to aid in other reading and writing experiences.

Language-experience, as a strategy or approach, has advantages and limitations that must be recognized. These are summarized in table 6.1.

Individualized reading, as in previous literature, closely resembles a literature-based approach as discussed in current literature. This approach is based on Olson's philosophy about child development, which promotes the ideas of seeking, self-selection, and pacing.[16]

This concept was used by Veatch in describing her own views about reading, and has become known as the individualized reading approach.[17] In implementing this approach in the classroom, the teacher should follow these steps:

- Know the reading levels and interests of the students with whom this approach will be used. These can be determined using procedures discussed in chapter 2.
- Obtain library books or other materials of interest for the students to read. A large number of books that represent a variety of topics and reading levels is needed. The teacher must select the books very carefully, keeping in mind that different literary forms should be represented.

- The readability levels of the books should be determined either by using a readability formula or library source such as *Children's Catalog*.[18] The books should be organized according to levels so as to aid students in locating material that they can read.
- The student selects a book that he wants to read. The student is not limited to the books at his readability level, as the teacher must realize that interest in a book goes a long way in motivating the student to read. However, the student should be allowed to read several pages to determine whether the book is too difficult and whether it is interesting, before selecting the book to read.
- When the book is selected, the student should realize that he is expected to read the entire book and then sign up for a conference with the teacher to discuss the story. However, if help is needed while reading, the teacher must be flexible enough to give assistance. During the silent reading, the student may list words not recognized or understood.
- After completing the story, the student notifies the teacher that he is ready for a conference. During the conference, which may last from five to twenty minutes, the teacher asks questions about the story, listens to the student read a short passage in order to diagnose word identification difficulties, provides some individual skill development instruction, and summarizes the results of the discussion. The conference requires that the teacher be very familiar with the stories read in the classroom and also with the reading continuum used in the school.

Literature-based reading can be used with an entire class of students or an individual student. It is not necessarily designed to supplement the basal readers, although it may be used with some students while others use the basal reader, or to add variety to reading instruction. To assist the reader to visualize this approach in the classroom, a description of the author's use of it is provided. Initially this approach was used because there were no other materials in an overcrowded elementary school. The parents insisted that the students have books, and most of the students hated reading!

On the first day of school I was met by thirty-seven second graders who were not ready for school to begin. With no basal readers, kits, or any instructional material, I had decided to use the language-experience approach with a few students and children's books from the library with most of the class.

My first task was to determine the reading levels of the students, which I soon discovered ranged from preprimer to the sixth-grade level. With this information I went to the library to check out books for the students who were reading from low, second-grade to sixth-grade level. There I met my first obstacle—the librarian, who allowed me to keep books for only two weeks. As a first-year teacher, I continued to smile, took my books to the room, checked the readability levels, put a piece of colored tape on each to denote the level, and arranged them on the shelf.

Students develop an understanding of reading as a language process as they read the books they write. Photo courtesy of Edward B. Lasher.

The students were directed to select books from those at their level. They were allowed to read those below their level during extra time and those above their level with permission.

To assure continuity of skill development because of local testing procedures and raised eyebrows from the third grade teachers, I used the skills continuum for the basal series being used in most of the classes in the school. A large chart containing the students' names and the skills was made, laminated and taped on my desk. Using observations and other informal procedures, I determined skill strengths and weaknesses and used the chart as my guide for grouping and conference discussions.

As the students read their books, they kept a word bank of unknown words. When they finished a book, they placed a name card in a box on my desk to notify me of their need for a conference. They proceeded to another book until they were called for a conference.

During the conference, we discussed words that were difficult, and I asked comprehension questions based on the needs of the student. Following the conference, I placed a note in my notebook that summarized our discussions. The student was given a gummed label with the title of the book just completed to put on his individual reading record poster, which decorated the wall.

Each day the students worked in small groups to develop skills that needed to be strengthened. Many games and activities were used to reinforce this group work.

Table 6.2

Literature-Based Reading

Advantages	Limitations
—Flexibility and freedom in grouping and adjusting instruction.	—Time consuming for the teacher, in that much planning, diagnosis, record keeping, and knowledge of the reading process is essential.
—The teacher has regular interaction with the student on an individual basis.	—Schools may not have enough library books to loan for an extended period of time.
—Students read materials that meet their interests.	—Teachers must be knowledgeable of children's literature in order to have effective conferences.
—Students read in a manner that resembles real-life reading situations.	—Vocabulary is not controlled.
—Students build a more positive self-concept, as success in reading comes with working at the appropriate level.	—Poor readers have difficulty attending to a book on their own.
—Students are exposed to a variety of children's books.	—Easy books for students with a limited vocabulary are difficult to locate.

Every two weeks, the class and I loaded our little red wagon, dressed in favorite character costumes, paraded the books to the library, and checked out a new group of books. This procedure continued the entire school year. The results—a group of students who enjoyed reading.

In retrospect, the question arises as to how the teacher could manage this hectic schedule over a long period of time. The response is that when students are excited about reading and are improving, the teacher is rewarded, and energy seems to come from unknown sources.

Another response to the management of literature-based reading in the classroom is that each child does not have to read different books at all times. As suggested by Hiebert and Colt,[19] in addition to this totally individualized procedure allowing students to select all literature, teachers can select the literature for groups of students to read and lead discussions with the groups, or teachers and students can jointly select the literature with teacher and student led small group discussions. Implementation of literature-based reading allows for teacher flexibility; the key is that the students are reading a variety of quality children's literature and developing an enjoyment for reading as they progress into mature readers.

The advantages and limitations of literature-based reading seem apparent from these descriptions. They are summarized in table 6.2.

To implement a language-based approach in an elementary classroom, the teacher needs an understanding of children, child development, and language development. An understanding of children and child development helps the teacher to determine appropriate learning experiences in accord with the interests and behaviors of the student. Attention span, personality traits, and peer interactions are important in planning. Teachers also need an understanding of language development. Oral and written language develops in relation to listening and psycho-motor skills. Teachers knowing the interactions of these areas are better able to provide appropriate language-based instruction. In addition to these student behaviors, teachers need a knowledge of the writing process, children's literature, and classroom organization. A language-based approach does not use a text and teacher's manual; the instructions for implementing such an approach are based on the teacher's knowledge of content and children, creativity, and willingness to take risks in providing students with appropriate instruction.

Bergeron has further suggested " . . . that many of the components of traditional reading instruction, such as ability grouping, controlled texts, or isolated exercises, no longer are consistent with the whole language concept. When one begins to contrast the overall concept of whole language with those approaches that have come to be defined in the construct of traditionalism, a conflict between whole language and tradition may be inevitable."[20] However, Farr has suggested that while some aspects of the two approaches, traditional and whole language, are incompatible such as separate skills instruction and the lack of freedom of choice by teachers who misuse teacher's manuals, other issues such as the use of quality literature and writing activities coincide with whole language.[21]

However, teachers implementing a prescriptive instructional program recognize that meeting the instructional needs of students requires the use of appropriate elements of a traditional basal approach and a language-based approach along with other approaches and techniques. For example, the inner-city youngster who comes to school with poor oral school language, distrust of authority figures, and a low self-concept is not likely to become a successful school statistic if placed in a program using only a traditional basal approach with stories that have little relation to the child's background of experiences and words that have no meaning. This child needs a program with a language-based approach that involves her in speaking and listening activities that expand her language and develops a feeling of success with teachers and peers. On the other hand, the child from middle-class America who has school-related experiences and a positive self-concept, can read but has some difficulty, may profit from a more structured basal approach that develops the lacking skills to move the student from average to above-average reading performance. Proponents of the basal approach say that the language-based approach lacks structure for practical implementation in the classroom; proponents of the language-based approach retort that the basal approach is too structured and takes the fun out of learning and the creativity out of teaching.

Both of these approaches offer different learning experiences for students. Teachers must follow their philosophical beliefs to determine the best approach for their teaching style and be willing to incorporate other approaches that benefit the student's instructional program.

Figure 6.2
Approaches for
Reading Instruction

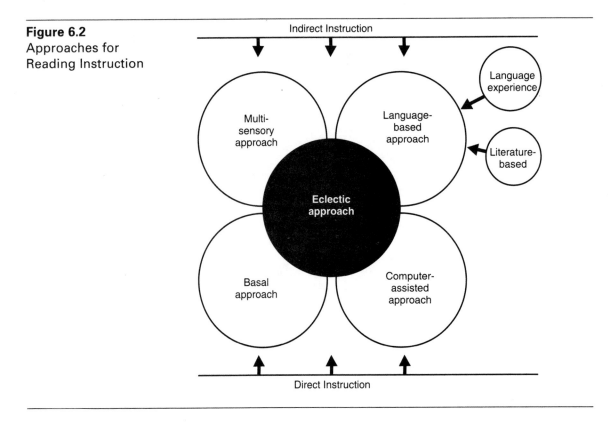

In addition to these two primary approaches used in elementary schools today, other approaches exist and teachers need an understanding of these different approaches in order to meet the variety of student needs in their classes. For students with severe reading problems, teachers may use a *multi-sensory approach*. All school districts are becoming involved with computers and teachers need to recognize the *computer-assisted approach* as another means of teaching and motivating students to read and write. These two approaches are viewed as secondary approaches to enrich the basal or language-based approaches.

Multi-Sensory Approach

The multi-sensory approach involves the sense of touch and muscle movement along with the senses of vision and hearing. Most students learn to read using the basic receptive senses of the eyes and ears. Some learn better through the visual mode than the auditory mode, or vice versa, but these are considered the primary senses necessary for reading. However, some students must have other stimulation

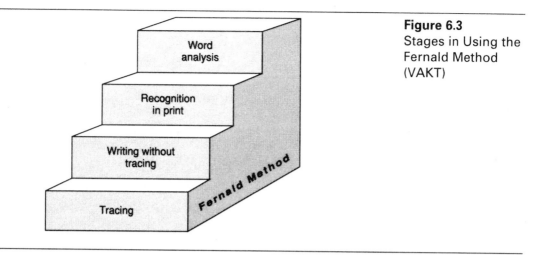

Figure 6.3
Stages in Using the
Fernald Method
(VAKT)

in order to learn words in reading. For these individuals, the multi-sensory approach is used. If the classroom teacher recognizes that this approach is necessary, there are several methods that may be used:

- Kinesthetic (VAKT)
- VAK
- Neurological impress

The kinesthetic method was developed by Grace Fernald as a way of teaching nonreaders.[22] This method, also known as the Fernald method or the Visual Auditory Kinesthetic Tactile (VAKT), follows four basic stages in teaching words to the nonreader (figure 6.3). The teacher begins with words the student wants to learn, then proceeds to build a story with the words when the student is ready. Words are taught using the following stages.

Stage 1: Tracing. The word is written for the student. The student traces the word and says each part of the word as it is traced. This is repeated until the student can trace the word from memory. The student then writes the word, saying each part as it is written.

Stage 2: Writing Without Tracing. When the student seems familiar with the word, he looks at the word and writes it from memory without tracing.

Stage 3: Recognition in Print. The student looks at a word, is told the word, pronounces it, and writes it from memory.

Stage 4: Word Analysis. The student is taught to look for familiar parts of a word and to try to identify new words from the known parts.

This method is designed for use with the student who is experiencing great difficulty in reading.

A similar method is the VAK or visual-auditory-kinesthetic. This method, also developed by Fernald, is a modified VAKT procedure in which Stage 1 has been altered. The major change is that the student pronounces the entire word rather than the word parts as she writes. Like the VAKT, this should be used with students who experience difficulty in learning through other approaches.

Neurological impress is another method designed to assist the student with reading problems. In this method, the teacher reads a selection and points to the words, while the student reads along, pronouncing as many words as possible. This method has been adapted for group instruction through the use of earphones and tape recorded stories used while the student looks at the words in the story. As suggested by Harris and Sipay, this method seems to have more promise as a supplementary procedure, since "the teacher can neither control nor observe where the child's eyes are focused, [and] the child may or may not be looking at the right word, on the right line, as he hears the spoken word."[23]

Thus, examining the methods included within the multi-sensory approach, the classroom teacher should note that they are used primarily with students having difficulty in reading. However, this approach may be used on occasion to assist any student in remembering troublesome sounds, syllables, or words.

Computer-Assisted Approach

Technology is a current trend in today's elementary and middle school classrooms with computers in the classroom, closed-captioned television for poor readers, and telecommunication forming a basic array of classroom options. While all of these options can enhance prescriptive instruction, the most available technological option is computer-assisted instruction which provides a secondary approach for teachers using a basal approach or a language-based approach.

The four basic options for using the computer-assisted approach include:

- Basic skills software, sometimes referred to as electronic ditto sheets, the first type of programs made available for assisting reading instruction;
- Word processing programs designed to encourage students to write by easing the writing process by providing assistance in rewriting, spell checks, and grammar analysis;
- Student-directed, open-ended software that encourages the student to think and make decisions as they work through the program; and
- Telecommunication, hypertext, and hypermedia which serve as resources that bring information about all topics as close as the phone and computer screen.

Teachers using a basal reader approach usually have available several types of computer software to accompany their series. This software may include a computer-management system that helps the teacher with record-keeping by administering objective-based tests on the computer and recording student performance. This helps with instructional planning but is not considered computer-assisted instruction. However, other software with the basal series which allows students to practice skills previously taught by the teacher is computer-assisted instruction. While these skill programs have been criticized by some as being an irrelevant time-filler which may be today's slick answer to basals and workbooks,[24] Wepner found that at-risk eighth graders dealt well with this drill-and-practice software as long as the content was relevant to their interests and level.[25] Because of the abundance of this type of software (due to the ease of developing such programs) and questions about its usefulness for some students, teachers are encouraged to identify student needs and plans for instruction prior to selecting programs for follow-up use. Remember, for some students, the best skills software is a significant improvement over traditional paper-pencil worksheets while for others computer drill-and-practice is no different than the traditional procedures. Teacher judgment of students and software are essential in making this selection of materials for use as part of a computer-assisted instructional approach.

Word-processing programs are also abundant with the basic programs such as AppleWorks and Microsoft Word available for adult and student use. There are, however, many word-processing programs designed for student use to make the writing process easier. The motivation of using the computer combined with assistance from the spell check and a grammar analysis along with the ease of rewriting using the delete key and moving text helps many students learn that writing is indeed a process that relates to communicating meaning to a reader. Programs such as *Language Experience Recorder Plus* (LER+) uses a speech synthesized word processor with primary print that speaks what students record.[26] *Magic Slate* is another word processor program with a fill-in feature to create cloze-like stories for use with primary level students.[27] *The Children's Writing and Publishing Center* allows the students to insert graphics into their writing.[28] *Success with Writing* models the writing process by moving the student through the stages of writing: prewrite, arrange, compose, and evaluate/edit modules.[29] These are but a few of the word-processing programs available for use with computer-assisted instruction. In implementing this approach in the classroom, teachers will need word-processing software to encourage the natural linkage between reading and writing and the development of writing using a process approach.

As teachers become more involved in using a language-based approach in their classes, they need to be aware of the many types of programs available to allow students to interact with language, literature, and writing as they enjoy learning. Software such as *The Semantic Mapper* and *The Literacy Mapper* facilitate the use of prior knowledge as students brainstorm their related experiences and develop printed copies of maps.[30] *The Comprehension Connection* provides on-screen assistance with each selection to encourage students to monitor their comprehension and implement metacognitive strategies as they read.[31] *Super Story Tree* is a program with the multimedia capability of using graphics, fonts, sound, and music to create interactive branching stories that allow students to develop or retell stories according to their own ideas.[32] *Success with Reading* is a literature-based software package that allows students to monitor their comprehension through the use of a

cloze procedure.[33] Programs such as *Create with Garfield* allows students to develop their own comic strip ideas interrelating word processing and comprehension to present their ideas.[34]

Extending these student-directed software packages, telecommunication systems are using computers to transfer information from one place to another. These systems provide teachers with up-to-date professional information and allow students to have access to resource information without days of thumbing through the library. Developing a database for organizing, saving, and accessing information is an aid to reading and a tool needed in daily life in the 21st century.[35]

Hypertext programs are being developed to allow students to create their own scenarios as they interact with pictures or print. While this form of computer-assisted instruction is in its beginning stages, these programs facilitate student thinking as they explore various relationships and sequences of activities through their choices on the screen. *Amanda Stories* are short, animated, and wordless stories about the adventures of a camel and a cat whose journeys are charted by the reader as choices are made on the computer screen.[36] *The Manhole* and *Cosmic Osmo* are similar programs that use text, graphics, speech, and sound effects allowing students to explore the universe.[37] Hypertext offers students the opportunity to control their own learning through investigations of information in a nonsequential or nontraditional manner.[38] However, because the use of hypertext and hypermedia require hardware resources beyond that available to many classroom teachers (i.e. large random access memories and hard disk drives with laserdisc/videodisc, compact disc and player, and high resolution color monitors for hypermedia), teachers may not consider this as a viable option at this time when implementing a computer-assisted approach in the classroom.

Computer-assisted instruction is another approach available to the classroom teacher when implementing prescriptive reading instruction. Computers are in schools or are available for the asking from many computer companies or foundations willing to assist in getting technology into the classroom. Teachers are encouraged to use this approach as they develop cognitive and affective learning areas with their students.

Eclectic Approach

Teachers have long recognized that there is no one best way of teaching reading. If there were, this section of the book would be much shorter and there would be far fewer reading materials on the market. The need for a combination of approaches must be stressed in discussing prescriptive instruction, since a major component of prescriptive teaching is the use of the appropriate approach with each student. Thus, the eclectic approach, which combines the desirable aspects of other approaches to meet student needs, becomes the approach most frequently used in the prescriptive reading program.

In discussing the eclectic approach, the authors are including the basal materials as a structured type of eclectic approach. This is because the current basal reader materials have changed significantly in the last decade and use various strategies for developing the skills. For example, the story content more closely reflects the children's literature used in literature-based teaching. The controlled vocabulary and the limited story characters have disappeared. Language-based philosophies have had a definite impact on the basal materials. Incorporated into most teachers' guides, which accompany the basal materials, are suggestions for using language experience, ideas for furthering reading through literature-based instruction, techniques for using the multi-sensory approach to teach letters and words, and specific activities for word identification and comprehension skill development. The basal reader is no longer designed to function as a self-contained unit but rather as a structured way to guide teachers in the use of various approaches to teach reading. Unfortunately, the basal is often misused, and these ideas are not incorporated into the lessons; instead, the student may be limited to the reader and a workbook. When used in this manner, the basal is not considered to be a part of the eclectic approach.

As teachers use the eclectic approach, it is important to match the appropriate approach to the student's needs. For example, overemphasizing isolated skills with an above-average reader may impede the student's progress in such areas as reading rate, comprehension, and interest.

To teach reading effectively, teachers are familiar with and use a variety of approaches. Thus, the strength of the eclectic approach is that the students' needs can be met. The limitations are that careful planning and coordination on the part of the teacher are essential, and an assortment of materials is necessary. The teacher who believes in diagnostic-prescriptive teaching will overcome these two limitations by taking time to plan and to locate materials, either from other places or by making them. The First-Grade Studies and the follow-up research leave no room for doubt that teachers must use the eclectic approach in order to meet the reading needs of all students.[39]

■ Teaching for Student Needs

Regardless of differences in approach used when providing prescriptive instruction, there are many commonalities involved in the prescriptive teaching process. Essential to all teachers is the need for diagnostic data summarized for each student and organized into a usable format. This information indicates the students' interests, strengths and weaknesses in reading, and instructional reading level. The teacher can then use the student's interests and strengths to improve areas of weakness. For example, the teacher has a student who is interested in baseball, has a collection of baseball cards, and remembers all the details from each card along with the card's value to a card collector. Yet, the student cannot organize ideas in the social studies lesson on the Industrial Revolution, so the teacher can help this student in several ways by using his interest. The teacher may associate the trading of baseball cards to the development of the country during the Industrial Revolution or more concretely design the information on each phase of the Industrial Revolution in a card format allowing the student to complete the information on each card as he reads. The Industrial Revolution will, of course, not be as exciting to a baseball lover as baseball cards but using a strategy in which he can associate his organization of information to new knowledge develops his comprehension of new information.

Teachers using a skills continuum as a part of their instructional approach need to relate diagnostic data to the skills continuum to determine starting points for instruction. In using a basal approach or a language-based approach, students develop skills in word identification, comprehension, and study skills with continuous opportunities for their application. Extreme skill deficiencies in any of these areas is a signal to the teacher that direct instruction is needed in a small group or on an individual basis. More specific information on prescriptive instruction in the areas of emergent literacy, word identification, comprehension, study, and personal reading skills is provided in chapters 7–11.

The content teacher in a departmentalized situation implements prescriptive reading instruction in several ways. Instruction may be needed in the reading skills that the students do not know, yet must use in order to learn content information. In addition, the content reading teacher can assist in reading development, cognitive and affective, by using literature to supplement the content lessons. Not only does this provide additional information in a different manner, it shows students that reading social studies or science content develops knowledge as well as enjoyment of new information. Content teachers need to use the diagnostic data of the reading and language arts teachers along with their own information to develop a class profile of reading skill needs and interests. This profile serves as a valuable resource to use in planning units of study in the content classroom.

Providing prescriptive instruction in the self-contained or content classroom using any approach requires planning for direct and indirect instruction. *Direct instruction* is when the "teachers assume a highly structured, active, and dominant role in which teacher talk is relied upon to ensure that students interpret the work in the intended way and achieve the desired outcome."[40] Creating process and content outcomes requires the use of direct instruction.

Indirect instruction depends more on a structured environment than on teacher talk. Students discover outcomes through activities which shape the student's interpretations.[41] Although these two types of instruction may seem at opposing ends of a continuum, indeed they rely on one another to communicate information to the learner.

For example, in a lesson in which the teacher wants to teach a strategy of interpreting a story, she may guide the student through the story by directly or deductively teaching the parts and showing how to interpret each part. She may then allow for more indirect instruction as the student practices this strategy using other works of literature and reports his interpretations to the teacher. The Directed Reading Activity and Directed Learning Activity outlined in the following pages reflect the use of direct instruction followed by indirect instruction.

Teachers using a language-based approach may use more indirect instruction followed by direct instruction as needed. For example, as students select their books in literature-based reading, they may only be guided to select fairy tales. After reading and discussing their books, the teacher will guide the students to identify the characteristics of fairy tales and possibly to write their own brief fairy tale using these characteristics. The teacher provides direct instruction only when necessary in a lesson planned for students to do more discovery or inductive learning. All prescriptive lessons need some direct and some indirect instruction. How this instruction is implemented depends on the goals of the teacher, level of the student, and information to be conveyed.

Directed Reading Activity

To facilitate direct prescriptive instruction in both self-contained and departmentalized classrooms, the teacher needs to follow a plan. The most commonly used design in reading instruction is the Directed or Guided Reading Activity (DRA). This procedure has been followed for many years by elementary teachers using the basal reader. However, any classroom teacher can use this procedure with or without the basal reader.

The five basic steps of the DRA are described below and should be followed in all reading lessons.

Readiness: Establish readiness for reading material by introducing the topic and the skills needed to read the material. Teach vocabulary words as well as concepts necessary to understand the material to be read relating the new information to the student's prior knowledge.

Figure 6.4
Steps in the Directed Reading Activity

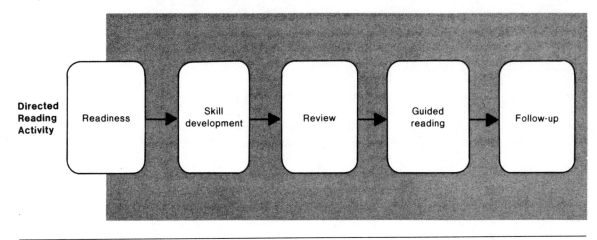

Skill Development: Using the diagnostic data, provide students with instruction to develop the skills necessary to understand the material to be read. This may be done individually or in small groups.

Review: The vocabulary, concepts, and skills necessary to be successful should be reviewed. At this time, the teacher gives the student a purpose for reading the material and asks for silent reading.

Guided Reading: With a purpose for reading clearly stated, the student begins to read the designated material (basal reader, newspaper, library book, experience story, etc.) silently. Following silent reading, ask comprehension questions that relate to the purpose given for reading and to the diagnosed comprehension skill needs of the individual students. For example, the student who has difficulty with the comprehension skill of distinguishing fact and opinion would be asked questions relating to this skill as a review of information taught during the Skill Development portion of the lesson. Following the comprehension check of silent reading, the student may be asked to read portions of the story orally to locate specific information or for some other definite purpose.

Follow-Up: Do additional follow-up after the guided reading to develop skill deficiencies, to extend knowledge on a given topic, and to allow students to apply the information learned from reading to some activity. This Follow-up session will vary from lesson to lesson and from student to student. It may be used to motivate some students to read; for others it is a time for further skill development. The Follow-up session is a valuable time for providing additional prescriptive instruction.

Directed Learning Activity

The departmentalized content teacher can use an adapted DRA to provide prescriptive reading instruction in the content areas. The authors refer to this plan as the Directed Learning Activity (DLA). This technique is for students using material written at their instructional reading level. The procedure is designed for use with small groups or a whole class. The following steps present ideas on providing prescriptive reading instruction in the content areas. Step 4 of this plan incorporates the Directed Learning Activity.

Step 1: Determine the concepts to be stressed in the content material and relate the reading strategies needed to understand these concepts. In order to meet individual student needs and various learning styles, the content teacher must teach concepts rather than just a textbook. Thus, for a given topic, the content specialist identifies the specific concepts to be taught. This way of looking at content material is used for several reasons.

1. With the wealth of knowledge, facts, and materials available today, it is impossible for one textbook to provide all the information students need. Thus, the teacher identifies key concepts and assists students in learning how to use materials to increase their knowledge.
2. No one textbook meets the reading level of every student in a classroom. Therefore, the content teacher uses a variety of materials in order to provide students with printed information they can read. If the content specialist is using concepts rather than one textbook, then many materials can be used.

Step 2: Identify the reading strategies/skills that are necessary for understanding the content materials. After the concepts have been identified, the content specialist selects the reading strategies that are essential to understanding them. Usually there are four to six reading skills that students use if they are to understand the concepts. Content teachers may wish to refer to the list of skills in appendix A to identify the many reading skills that relate to their content area. This may be a rather lengthy list, as different strategies and skills are necessary in order to teach various concepts. At a later time, the content specialist will select appropriate skills from this list, which will help the student to understand the material.

An example of a concept and related reading skills is shown below:

Social Studies Concept: Freedom of speech is an essential component of a democracy.
Related Reading Skills: Vocabulary Development
                             Generalizations
                             Cause-Effect
                             Contrast-Comparisons
                             Relationships

Figure 6.5
Diagnostic Chart for Content Teachers

Student name	Concept					Concept					Concept					Concept					Concept				
	Skill	Skill	Skill	Skill	Skill																				
Ginger	X			X																						
Lance	X	X	X	X	X																					
Kristy			X																							
Wendy		X	X		X																					
Joe	X																									
Harry					X																					
Carmen																										

X denotes need for additional instruction in the skill.

Once teachers have identified this information, their instructional program will begin to take shape.

Step 3: Assess student strengths and weaknesses in the reading strategies and skills. There are several procedures that may be used to diagnose strengths and weaknesses. One procedure, the Content Reading Inventory, is presented in chapter 2.

With the identified concepts and reading skills as well as the diagnostic data on the students, the content specialist may use a file folder or sheet of paper to develop a class chart like the one in figure 6.5. This will assist in organizing the information and aid in prescriptive teaching.

Step 4: Outline teaching strategies for the development of the concept need skills, and reading strategies. At this point, the teacher puts together materials that meet the students' diagnosed needs, in order to teach the concepts necessary for learning the content. Using the DLA format as a guide, this is not difficult. The DLA follows this procedure:

Introduce the concepts and vocabulary. The content teacher introduces the concepts to be studied. This may be done directly, using questions or a movie, or in a more indirect manner based on previous classes. Regardless of the procedure used, the concepts to be studied for a unit or designated period of time need to be carefully introduced. Because the entire class is probably studying the same concepts, this would be a total class activity. In introducing the concepts and materials to be studied, the content specialist also teaches the vocabulary necessary for reading the materials. This includes the general vocabulary as well as the specialized and technical words. Teachers should realize that although a student may be able to pronounce a word, its special meaning as related to the content area may cause difficulty. The responsibility for teaching vocabulary rests with each content teacher. With various reading abilities in the classroom and various materials in use, it may be necessary to teach vocabulary development skills to small groups. Some of the groups can use written activities, while others work with the content teacher or discuss the terminology with one another. Examples of written vocabulary activities follow:

Science *Vocabulary Development:* Give the antonyms for these words:

exhale _____ ventricle _____

Social Studies *Vocabulary Development:* Fill in the missing word:

1. A body of advisors of a head of state is a _____ .
2. Refusal to trade with another country is an _____ .
3. The title of the highest ranking official of the United States residing in another country is _____ .

Teach/review reading skills. This phase of the instructional process depends not only upon the identification of those reading skills that are relevant to the student's understanding of the content material, but also includes demonstrating the application of these reading skills appropriately. Although content teachers are not reading specialists, they assist students in adapting previously learned skills to content materials, as well as learning how to apply new skills to these materials.

Outline the purposes for study. Students are more willing to accept some of the requirements made in content areas if they are given specific purposes for study. Teachers usually receive negative responses when they give students a chapter to read with no specific reason for studying it. In addition, students need to know how studying this material relates to their present or future lives. Having a purpose helps students relate to the material and motivates them to study it.

Read and study the material. The students have been introduced to the concept, taught the vocabulary, and given a purpose for reading by this time. Now we are ready to ask them to read the material. At this point the content specialist may help the student use the SQ3R or other appropriate study techniques. The teacher must remember that students are to read only the material directly related to the concepts introduced. This may or may not be an entire section of the text or other sources. The teacher should also remember to use various materials that are appropriate to the students' levels. This may mean that other instructional tools such as films, tapes, newspapers, magazines, records, etc. will also be used. Thus, all students will not finish at the same time. This will allow the content specialist to begin the next step at different times to allow for more small group work.

Discuss the information learned. As the students complete their reading assignments, the content specialist begins discussions relating to the concepts being studied. These may be stimulated by written questions or they may be group discussion sessions. As these discussions are developed, the content teacher must keep in mind the specific reading skills that need to be developed with the various students. This information is obtained from the diagnostic instruments discussed in chapters 2 and 3 and recorded in some format such as the chart in figure 6.5. Sample written activities that may be used to promote discussion and develop appropriate learning skills are outlined below.

Social Studies *Details:* Read the following passage and answer these questions. (A short passage on "The Gettysburg Address")

Who wrote "The Gettysburg Address?"
What is the meaning of this passage?
Where was it delivered?
When was this passage delivered?

Mathematics *Following Directions:* Give the students directions for factoring polynomials carefully and slowly. Then have them write the directions in their own words, going through it step-by-step.

Follow-up activities. After small group and total class discussions of the concepts, some follow-up activities should be used to reinforce the subject. These activities may be in the form of other outside readings, reports, special skill development, or art activities. The content specialist can provide additional assistance in developing the reading skills at this time.

Step 5: Recycle Steps 1, 2, 3, and 4 continuously. It is essential that diagnosis be a continuous part of prescriptive teaching. If students are to learn content material, content teachers must assume the responsibility of teaching. Teaching students at the appropriate level does not end in the primary grades. If content teachers want students to learn the content presented, they must take students as they are and develop the reading skills they need.

This chapter has addressed basic ideas concerning prescriptive instruction, procedures to use in providing instruction, and the different approaches that should be used in prescriptive teaching. The next specific task confronting the teacher is that of developing prescriptions for instruction. Teachers should remember that in prescriptive instruction, each student has an assignment based on diagnosed needs. This prescription may be written for the student each day or only outlined in the teacher's plans, but it must be designed with the individual in mind.

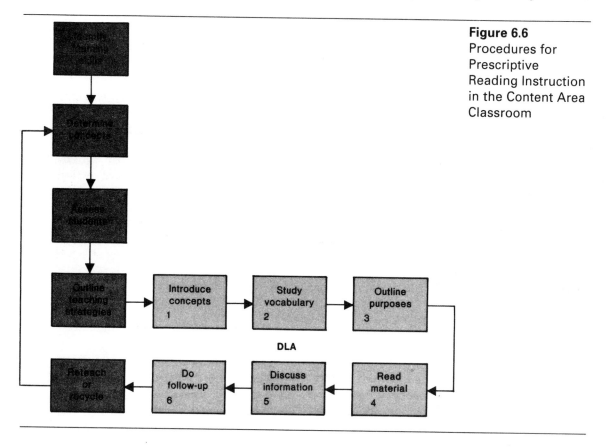

Figure 6.6
Procedures for Prescriptive Reading Instruction in the Content Area Classroom

As teachers develop prescriptions, these ideas need to be kept in mind:

- The prescription should guarantee success. Tasks that are performed while working with the teacher should be at the student's instructional reading level, while tasks to be performed alone should be at the independent reading level.
- In prescriptive instruction, the teacher should provide direct instruction before asking the student to work alone or with a group. Individual work is done to reinforce the ideas taught by the teacher.
- The student is directed to tasks requiring the application of skills that have been taught in isolation.
- Prescriptive instruction allows the students opportunities for decision-making. This includes the selection of a learning task from several choices, and the opportunity to express their feelings toward the tasks.

- Teachers continuously analyze the student's performances in order to gain the diagnostic information needed to re-evaluate the prescriptive teaching assignments.
- Directions given on all tasks need to be specific and clearly stated.

In developing prescriptions, the teacher outlines plans for the entire class and writes individual prescriptions as needed. To organize the instructions for a class, the teacher should have an outline of all tasks going on at the same time. This planning procedure helps the teacher in grouping students, arranging students in the different centers, and planning for other variables such as changes in the noise levels in the room. In addition, the teacher can use this "master plan" for instruction as a daily record of the students' activities in order to plan for future instruction. This overall plan is outlined in the teacher's lesson plan booklet and used as a record for directing students in the various tasks. Evaluation notes are added as observations are made.

There are many approaches to prescriptive instruction and ways to organize students to enjoy reading. The essential element is that the instruction provided is planned to meet the diagnosed needs of the students.

■ Summary

This chapter has provided the classroom teacher with an introduction to prescriptive reading instruction. It includes some basic principles for prescriptive instruction to serve as guides for the teacher. The underlying philosophy is that there is no one best way to implement prescriptive teaching in the classroom; the teacher must adjust these ideas to individual situations.

To present additional instructional ideas, five approaches to reading instruction were discussed. These included the basal approach, language-based approach, multi-sensory approach, computer-assisted approach, and eclectic approach. Advantages and limitations are discussed for each approach to assist the teacher in determining the best techniques to use with each student.

Because the teachers in a self-contained classroom and a departmentalized classroom must approach prescriptive reading instruction with a slightly different emphasis, directed teaching procedures were outlined for each. The Directed

Reading Activity format was provided for self-contained classroom teachers, while an adaptation of this procedure, the Directed Learning Activity, was furnished for departmentalized content teachers seeking to integrate prescriptive reading instruction into the content areas. Moreover, some specific techniques were given in order to assist teachers in using prescriptions in reading.

Ways of prescribing for specific difficulties in emergent literacy, word identification, comprehension, study skills, and personal reading will be presented in chapters 6–11.

■ Applying What You Read

You are a new teacher in a school that is beginning a diagnostic-prescriptive reading program. The diagnostic data has been summarized, and you are not ready to organize yourself to provide prescriptive instruction. What would you do?

In your preservice training program you had two reading courses. One professor presented information as though reading skills were the major ingredient in reading instruction. The other professor discounted reading skills as unnecessary parts of the reading process and presented strategies for involving students in literature and writing activities. Now, with your first teaching assignment in a low-income neighborhood with seven of your third graders speaking English as a second language and the principal and teachers talking about the new basal program, what will you do? How will you determine the best approaches for your students?

The principal in your school has asked that every teacher use a variety of approaches in providing prescriptive instruction. To make sure that an effort is made in this direction, each teacher is asked to describe the three most common approaches used in his classroom. What three approaches would you identify and why?

A friend of yours teaches sixth-grade social studies. The students need help in reading, so the faculty is moving toward the use of diagnostic-prescriptive reading instruction throughout the school. Your friend doesn't understand how prescriptive reading instruction can fit into the social studies class. How could you explain?

■ Notes

1. Guy L. Bond and Robert Dykstra, *Final Report, Project No. X-001.*
2. Paul C. Burns and Betty D. Roe, *Teaching Reading in Today's Elementary Schools,* pp. xii–xiii.
3. Edward B. Fry, *Elementary Reading Instruction,* pp. 134–227.
4. JoAnne L. Vacca, Richard T. Vacca, and Mary K. Gove, *Reading and Learning to Read,* pp. 234–372; John W. Miller and Michael McKenna, *Teaching Reading in the Elementary Classroom,* pp. 373–404.
5. Earl H. Cheek, Rona F. Flipps, and Jimmy D. Lindsey, *Reading Success in Elementary Schools,* p. 288.
6. Angela Jagger, "On Observing the Language Learner: Introduction and Overview," in *Observing the Language Learner,* edited by Angela Jagger and M. Trika Smith-Burke, pp. 1–7.
7. Dolores Durkin, "Dolores Durkin Speaks on Instruction," *The Reading Teacher,* p. 472.
8. Bette S. Bergeron, "What Does the Term Whole Language Mean? Constructing a Definition from the Literature," *Journal of Reading Behavior,* p. 301.
9. Peter B. Mosenthal, "The Whole Language Approach: Teachers Between a Rock and a Hard Place," *The Reading Teacher,* pp. 628–29; P. J. Farris and D. Kaczmarski, "Whole Language, a Closer Look," *Contemporary Education,* pp. 77–81; E. Hajek, "Whole Language: Sensible Answers to the Old Problems," *Momentum,* pp. 39–40; M. Brountas, "Whole Language Really Works," *Teaching K-8,* pp. 57–60; J. C. Richards, J. P. Gipe, and B. Thompson, "Teachers' Beliefs about Good Reading Instruction," *Reading Psychology,* pp. 1–6; D. R. Reutzel and P. M. Hollingsworth, "Whole Language and the Practitioner," *Academic Therapy,* pp. 405–16; C. Edlesky, K. Draper, and K. Smith, "Hookin' 'em in at the Start of School in a 'Whole Language' Classroom," *Anthropology and Education Quarterly,* pp. 257–81; H. Slaughter, "Indirect and Direct Instruction in a Whole Language Classroom," *The Reading Teacher,* pp. 30–34; Y. Mersereau, M. Glover, and M. Cherland, "Dancing on the Edge," *Language Arts,* pp. 109–18; D. J. Watson, "Defining and Describing Whole Language," *The Elementary School Journal,* pp. 129–41; S. J. Rich, "Restoring Power to Teachers: The Impact of 'Whole Language'," *Language Arts,* pp. 717–24.
10. Bergeron, p. 319.
11. Lia Ridley, "Enacting Change in Elementary School Programs: Implementing a Whole Language Perspective," *The Reading Teacher,* pp. 640–46.

12. Elfrieda H. Hiebert and Jacalyn Colt, "Patterns of Literature-Based Reading Instruction," *The Reading Teacher*, pp. 14–20.

13. Mary Anne Hall, *The Language Experience Approach to Teaching Reading*, 2nd ed., pp. 1–2.

14. Roach Van Allen, "The Language-Experience Approach," in *Perspectives on Elementary Reading*, edited by Robert Karlin, p. 158.

15. Roach Van Allen, *Language Experiences in Communication*; Russell G. Stauffer, *The Language-Experience Approach to the Teaching of Reading*; Mary Anne Hall, *Teaching Reading as a Language Experience*.

16. Willard C. Olson, *Child Development*.

17. Jeanette Veatch, *Individualizing Your Reading Program*.

18. Rachel Fidell and Estelle A. Fidell, eds. *Children's Catalog*.

19. Hiebert and Colt, pp. 14–20.

20. Bergeron, p. 320.

21. Roger Farr, "Trends: A Place for Basal Readers under the Whole Language Umbrella," *Educational Leadership*, p. 86.

22. Grace M. Fernald, *Remedial Techniques in Basic School Subjects*.

23. Albert J. Harris and Edward R. Sipay, *How to Increase Reading Ability*, 6th ed., p. 403.

24. C. Doyle, "Creative Applications of Computer-Assisted Reading and Writing Instruction," *Journal of Reading*, pp. 236–39; J. Hancock, "Learning with Databases," *Journal of Reading*, pp. 582–89.

25. Shelley B. Wepner, "Holistic Computer Applications in Literature-based Classrooms," *The Reading Teacher*, pp. 12–19.

26. George E. Mason, *Language Experience Recorder Plus*.

27. Sunburst Communications, *Magic Slate*.

28. The Learning Company, *The Children's Writing and Publishing Center*.

29. Scholastic, *Success with Writing*.

30. Gloria Kuchinskas and M. C. Radencich, *The Semantic Mapper* and *The Literary Mapper*.

31. David Reinkling, *The Comprehension Connection*.

32. G. Brackett, *Super Story Tree*.

33. M. Balsam and C. Hammer, *Success with Reading*.

34. Developmental Learning Materials, *Create with Garfield*.

35. Robert J. Rickelman and William A. Henk, "Telecommunications in the Reading Classroom," *The Reading Teacher*, pp. 418–19.

36. Voyager Company, *Amanda Stories*.

37. Activision, *The Manhole* and *Cosmic Osmo*.

38. Jay S. Blanchard and Claire J. Rottenberg, "Hypertext and Hypermedia: Discovering and Creating Meaningful Learning Environments," *The Reading Teacher*.

39. This research can be found in the following issues of *The Reading Teacher*: May 1966, October 1966, May 1967, October 1967, January 1969, and March 1969.

40. Gerald G. Duffy and Laura R. Roehler, *Improving Classroom Reading Instruction*, 2nd ed., p. 76.

41. Duffy and Roehler, p. 76.

■ Other Suggested Readings

Altwerger, B., C. Edelsky, and B. M. Flores. "Whole Language: What's New?" *The Reading Teacher* 41 (1987): 144–54.

Bagford, Jack. "What Ever Happened to Individualized Reading?" *The Reading Teacher* 39 (November 1985): 190–93.

Barr, Rebecca and Marilyn W. Sadow. "Influence of Basal Programs on Fourth-Grade Reading Instruction." *Reading Research Quarterly* 24 (Winter 1989): 44–71.

Bauman, James F. "How to Expand a Basal Reader Program." *The Reading Teacher* 37 (April 1984): 604–7.

Beazley, M. R. "Reading for a Real Reason: Computer Pals Across the World." *Journal of Reading* 32 (1989): 598–605.

Blanton, William E., Karen D. Wood, and Gary B. Moorman. "The Role of Purpose in Reading Instruction." *The Reading Teacher* 43 (March 1990): 486–93.

Durkin, Dolores. "Is There a Match Between What Elementary Teachers Do and What Basal Reader Manuals Recommend?" *The Reading Teacher* 37 (May 1984): 734–44.

Gunderson, Lee and Jon Shapiro. "Some Findings on Whole Language Instruction." *Reading-Canado-Lecture* 5 (Spring 1987): 22–26.

Mason, George E. "Technology Development: It's Not the Hardware of the Software; It's How You Use It." *The Reading Instruction Journal* 29 (1986): 2–7.

Pinnell, Gay Su, Marh D. Fried, Rose Mary Estice. "Reading Recovery: Learning How to Make a Difference." *The Reading Teacher* 43 (January 1990): 282–95.

Sebasta, Sam Leaton. "Commentary: Miss Smith and the Traditional Method." *The Reading Teacher* 33 (February 1980): 516–18.

Shannon, Patrick. "Some Subjective Reasons for Teachers' Reliance on Commercial Reading Materials." *The Reading Teacher* 35 (May 1982): 884–89.

Spiegel, Dixie Lee. "Six Alternatives to the Directed Reading Activity." *The Reading Teacher* 34 (May 1981): 914–20.

Templeton, Shane. "Literacy, Readiness and Basals." *The Reading Teacher* 39 (January 1986): 403–9.

7

Emergent Literacy

Teachers who know young children and are aware of their cognitive development, recognize that the wealth of information in emergent literacy carries an important message. The foundation for reading is established during the preschool years as literacy emerges through language and writing development. Home and school environments rich in oral language, print materials, and writing activities create a literate environment in which the necessary early learning occurs.

The importance of conversations with adults and children to explore topics of interest, drawing and writing, listening and responding to literature, and awareness of environmental print are important components in the preparation of children for school reading experiences. This chapter presents information about each of the language areas of literacy development and suggests the impact of this learning on reading. Ideas for diagnosing and developing emergent literacy are presented to assist the preschool and elementary teachers in understanding the developmental nature of the reading process and the integral role that language plays in this development.

The chapter is organized to address the following questions.

What is emergent literacy?

Why is emergent literacy so important in reading development?

Why has the terminology changed from prereading to emergent literacy?

What does research tell us about this area?

How can the teacher diagnose emergent literacy development?

What ideas can be used to develop emergent literacy or to provide assistance to the student who is identified to have problems in this area?

As this chapter is read, the following terms are important to note.

Vocabulary to Know

Auditory discrimination	Environmental print	Retelling
Auditory memory	Invented spelling	Visual comprehension
Bookhandling	Language development	Visual discrimination
Booksharing	Listening comprehension	Visual memory
Dictation	Oral language	Visual-motor skills
Emergent literacy	Phonemic awareness	Word boundaries
Environment	Prereading skills	Writing

■ The Importance of Emergent Literacy

Emergent literacy as a way of thinking about early development in reading and writing is a relatively new way of viewing the language processes of young children. Formerly, educators viewed language development in the early years as relating to listening and speaking and then later development at the ages of 5 or 6 of developing the necessary "prereading skills" associated with reading and writing. Research in the last decade has confirmed that the conditions which aid in the development of first language learning are the same conditions that promote literacy development. Teale and Sulzby suggest that the new research in emergent literacy has unique dimensions:

1. The age range studies have been extended to include children 14 months and younger.
2. Literacy is no longer regarded as simply a cognitive skill but as a complex activity with social, linguistic, and psychological aspects.
3. Since literacy learning is multidimensional and tied to the child's natural surroundings, it is studied in both home and school environments.
4. Researchers are now studying literacy learning from the child's point of view.[1]

In an extensive review of the literature, Mason and Allen[2] found that certain specific communication patterns and practices, parent-child interactions, parent-child literacy activities, societal and parental expectations, linguistic contexts, story literacy concepts, home reading patterns, language interactions, and meaningful literacy events contribute to the acquisition of reading concepts. They further concluded that:

1. Social and linguistic contexts for learning play profound roles in the development of early literacy.

2. Phonological awareness and story understanding are the primary components around which literacy concepts revolve. These are acquired through informal as well as formal home and school activities.
3. Literacy goals, both personal and public, affect learning.
4. Parents who assist in the development of literacy at home have children who come to school prepared for reading instruction.
5. Experiences that emphasize phonological awareness, knowledge of print-speech relations, and story-reading contribute to future reading success.

Thus, it is important to note that the acquisition of print appears to be a developmental process that begins at birth and continues into the school-age years. The foundation for successful reading must clearly be laid during a child's preschool developmental stage, not only after a student enters school.

Thus, the understandings of what happens in learning with young children as reading prerequisites are developed has changed from the cognitive prereading skills' focus to a realization that learning, requiring communication, has a relation to the development of the language process. As Strickland and Morrow suggest:

> We now have new understandings about the origins of literacy development. Reading and writing start much earlier than we had suspected. The toddler's insistence on having "the ducky book" and no other, the two-year-old's uncanny ability to recognize all the sugar-laden cereals in the supermarket, and the three-year-old's persistence in writing her own shopping list are now valued as evidence of ongoing literacy development.[3]

Oral language, reading, and writing develop concurrently in young children. Children in literacy-rich environments learn as they observed, play, have dialogue with adults and peers, and receive encouragement. This is not cognitive instruction; experience is the teacher! **Emergent literacy then is the natural development of the language process with young children.** This concurrent development of oral language, reading, and writing form the basis for formal reading instruction in school. This perspective on learning to read and write focuses on the active use of language and print in a rich environment as compared to the notion of prereading skills or reading readiness which suggests that children are not ready to read until a certain age or until discrete subskills are taught.

Teachers of young children diagnose levels of performance with emergent literacy behaviors and plan the learning environment to develop and expand the student's understanding of print. Observation of students as they have access to reading and writing materials, opportunities to write messages, encouragement to keep logs and records in the classroom, and experiences in sharing their books and writings provide teachers with necessary diagnostic information about individual students.[4] Teachers need to know if young students understand the functions of reading and writing, have developed a sense of story structure and how to comprehend a story, and make attempts at reading and writing in their own way before beginning conventional reading and writing.[5] Roney[6] suggests that the major concepts inherent in the early reading process are print awareness, language development, story structure, and the usefulness of reading.

Print Awareness

A basic concept that influences reading is print awareness. An essential aspect of this concept is the child's awareness of how print functions. Clay[7] suggested that children must understand numerous concepts about print that include, but are not limited to, the following:

1. Books have a specific orientation with an identifiable front and back, and pages have an identifiable top and bottom.
2. Print is important since it, not the pictures, is to be read.
3. The ability to identify the 26 letters of the English alphabet, both lower- and upper-case, is essential to successful reading.
4. Directionality is essential to successful reading. For example, print on the left page is read before print on the right page. And print on a page progresses from left to right and from top to bottom.
5. The concept of linearity is important. This involves the knowledge that letters in a word and words in a sentence are ordered from left to right, and that by changing the order you alter the meaning.
6. A word as a cluster of letters surrounded by space is a necessary concept for word identification.
7. An awareness of the basic elements of capitalization and punctuation is important.

Print awareness begins as children scribble to communicate a message and read "McDonald's" when they see the golden arches. This aspect of emergent literacy usually begins by the age of 2 and develops naturally according to the stimulation provided in the home environment.[8] Children whose home environment provides limited opportunities to experiment with books, paper, markers, pencils, and environmental print will be less ready to interact with print in the school environment.

Understanding the interrelatedness of the reading and writing processes is important in providing literacy development experiences for young children. Parents need to be educated to understand this relationship. As important and more basic to the development of print awareness is the parents' understanding of the schools theory of literacy. As Fitzgerald, Spiegel, and Cunningham reported, low-literacy parents tend to view language learning from a skills perspective while high-literacy parents reflected on language learning from a cultural practice perspective.[9] This difference in perspective may cause problems when trying to transfer a language-based philosophy to parents who believe in skill-based learning or skill-based learning to parents who believe in language-based learning. However, print awareness experiences need to begin with all children in the home environment at an early age in order to allow literacy learning to emerge.

Language Development

An extension of the concept of print awareness is that children must become aware of the relationship between oral language and print very early in their development. As Roney[10] noted, the simple act of recognizing that speech can be translated into print, and print into spoken language, enables children to begin to understand the symbol system of our language.

Children have many experiences with both oral and written language as they progress through the various developmental stages. They are exposed to many types of communication devices such as television, radio, print media, traffic signs, and billboards. Parents and others have read stories to children with varied themes and topics. Children are exposed to written language in familiar situations, and in the process of learning to read and write they learn about its purposes, the processes by which others read and write, and the specific visual features that characterize print.[11]

Students who come from educationally deficient environments are often lacking in the area of oral language. Oral language is vitally important in the reading process, in as much as language must be spoken first before it is understood on the printed page. Much more is said about oral language development in a later section of this chapter. It is sufficient to say here that poor oral language skills have a tremendous impact on reading; thus, the prime objective of many preschool programs is to develop oral language skills.

Halliday identifies seven functions evident in the language of young children:

1. Instrumental: children use language to satisfy personal needs and to get things done.
2. Regulatory: children use language to control the behavior of others.
3. Personal: children use language to tell about themselves.
4. Interactional: children use language to get along with others.
5. Heuristic: children use language to find out about things, to learn things.
6. Imaginative: children use language to pretend, to make believe.
7. Informative: children use language to communicate something for the information of others.[12]

In order for children to become effective readers and understand the relationship between spoken and written language, it is essential to expose them to a wide variety of printed materials. Children are then more able to develop a sense of print and language awareness that will enhance their potential for success as effective readers.

Story Structure

Another type of early experience that affects a child's potential success as a reader is story structure. When initially interacting with print, children with a variety of story experiences are aware of the type of story that they are reading. They are able to recognize stories as being nursery rhymes, animal stories, or how-to books. However, children with limited story experiences are more likely to have a narrow sense

Figure 7.1
Tree Structure of
Categories of
Classification
Scheme for
Emergent Reading
of Favorite
Storybooks

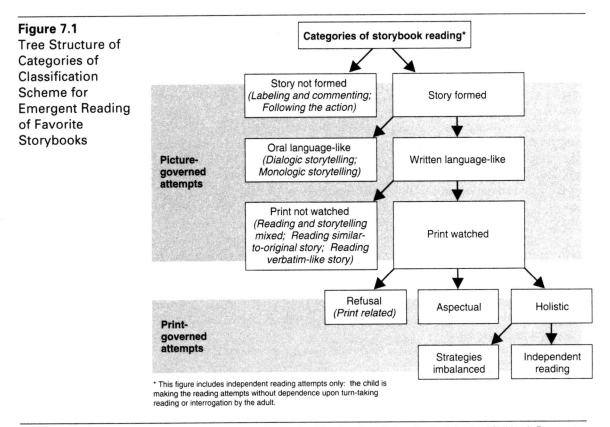

Categories of storybook reading*

Story not formed
(Labeling and commenting;
Following the action)

Story formed

Picture-governed attempts

Oral language-like
(Dialogic storytelling;
Monologic storytelling)

Written language-like

Print not watched
(Reading and storytelling
mixed; Reading similar-
to-original story; Reading
verbatim-like story)

Print watched

Print-governed attempts

Refusal
(Print related)

Aspectual

Holistic

Strategies
imbalanced

Independent
reading

* This figure includes independent reading attempts only: the child is
making the reading attempts without dependence upon turn-taking
reading or interrogation by the adult.

Reprinted with permission of Elizabeth Sulzby and the International Reading Association. Elizabeth Sulzby, "Children's Emergent Reading of Favorite Storybooks: A Developmental Study," *Reading Research Quarterly,* 22(Summer 1985):464.

of a story's structure. These children tend to experience more difficulty in interacting with various types of literature. Developing this sense of story structure, which involves learning under what circumstances various characters, settings, and linguistic idiosyncrasies can appear in various types of literature, enables children to become more successful readers.[13]

As young children become involved with books and story structure, the essential element is their understanding. Listening comprehension is often measured by the student's skill in answering questions about what has been read. However, recent research suggests the use of story retellings to determine the listener's (or reader's) understanding of the information. Sulzby suggests that in retelling stories, children use different sources for the message beginning with pictures and moving toward print as the child develops greater familiarity with the story and the language process (see Figure 7.1). This concept of story reading is based on the presence of a storylike unit or structure with some indication of past, present, and future.[14]

Reading to young children is the best language development/ reading readiness activity provided by parents. Photo courtesy of Edward B. Lasher.

Reading Usefulness

Roney[15] believes that one of the most important aspects of learning to read is the ability of children to develop the knowledge that reading is both enjoyable and immediately useful. Unless the children's interest can be maintained, it will be more difficult for them to derive enjoyment or benefit from their reading activities. Failure to instill this enjoyment of reading into the child's early print experience may result in the identification of reading as a negative experience, which could impede the child's development as a successful reader. Children experiencing enjoyment and pleasure from reading activities, however, are more likely to continue developing into life-long readers.

Relevancy of reading to the environment in the home and at school is extremely important in learning to read. Students from environmental conditions that are conducive to learning to read are more likely to experience success than students from less favorable environments. Some specific aspects that contribute to the environmental factor include social/cultural awareness, experiential background, prior knowledge, oral language development, and interest in reading.

Students from homes in which reading is not important often enter school with little expertise in school literacy areas. These students may have few experiences with a book, newspaper, magazine, or any type of printed material. They have not been read to nor have they seen others read in the home. Moreover, experiences outside their culture are usually nonexistent, a condition that limits their understanding of many of the materials and ideas confronting them in school. These conditions contribute to the students' lack of interest in learning to read, which means that the teacher not only must develop the prerequisite knowledge, but also must motivate the students to learn.

In teaching children to read, it is important to remember that each child brings a different set of experiences to the reading process. Such differences as socio-cultural background, parental expectations, values, interests, and language tend to create a wide disparity in the developmental base of each student. Many students will clearly understand the connection between spoken and written language while others will be unaware of this relationship. This degree of understanding will be manifested in the children's knowledge of the symbol system of American-English, and gaps in the experiential background of children may create some difficulties for the teacher. Although these gaps in experiences and knowledge are important, instruction that is both appropriate and effective for each child must be provided.

■ Developing Emergent Literacy

Linguistic awareness is the critical area developed as literacy emerges with young children. This linguistic awareness develops as children experiment with all aspects of language. Emergent literacy involves the accumulation of information about tasks such as reading and writing in order to demonstrate an understanding of or literacy in the area. The base of this understanding is oral language. However, emergent literacy as a natural process cannot be separated into language compartments. The research focus in recent years consistently discusses how young children develop the language process and points out how listening, speaking, reading and writing are integrated rather than separated in learning. However, teacher awareness of the various components as separate parts is necessary. For this reason, this section is organized to provide ideas for use in the classrooms that have integrated language instruction as well as those that separate the areas for language development.

Specific subskills described in discussions of prereading are developed in a language-based program through daily activities as children learn about language or through designated skill activities in the skills-based program. As discussed earlier, skills-based programs teach according to a specific continuum of skills while programs designed to foster an emergent literacy point of view develop skills according to the level and experiences of the student as the teacher provides learning activities that enhance language development. To implement an emergent literacy program, the teacher knows the skills necessary to design activities to use skills that the students know and to develop new skills. This section presents the three major areas for language development in the emergent literacy curriculum and incorporates the related subskills so that these ideas can be developed in either a skill-based or language-based program for young children. The three areas are: oral language, writing, and reading.

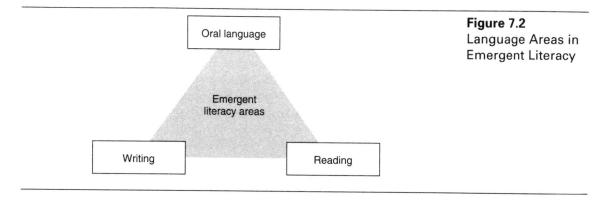

Figure 7.2
Language Areas in
Emergent Literacy

Oral Language

Oral language is a most important area in the development of early reading and writing. Students learn language by listening and speaking, and interpret this knowledge through reading and writing. Understanding language enables the child to use scribble to represent words or to read pictures in books. Early studies by Loban and Strickland indicate that reading can be influenced either adversely or positively by the language of the reader.[16] Students with good oral language skills tend to have advantages in reading over those with poor oral language skills because of the content of the materials and the language patterns used.

As Britton explains, the culture from which the student comes is another important consideration in developing oral language. Students from a particular culture and dialect group learn to speak not only the language of that group, but also learn to think and organize their ideas in accordance with the views of their closest contacts.[17] A serious error teachers sometimes make is attempting to change a student's language without understanding their culture and dialect. Teachers need to develop an understanding of students' backgrounds and cultures in order to encourage them to extend their learning and expand their language.[18]

Another essential component of language is syntactic ability. Chomsky examined the relationship between students' knowledge of complex syntactic structures and the amount of reading done by them as well as the amount of material read aloud to them. She found that students who were read to and who read more on their own had a much better knowledge of complex structures than students who heard and read fewer books.[19]

It is essential that teachers provide an atmosphere that is conducive to the development of oral language skills. An environment of acceptance and respect will encourage students to share their experiences with the teacher and with other students. As students share their various experiences, the teacher will have an opportunity to learn more about their modes of learning, language development, and the socio-cultural factors that affect their learning in a positive or negative manner.

Teachers and parents need to provide activities such as creative dramatics, group discussions, child-adult conversations, storytelling and retelling, group recitations of poems and chants, and shared reading experiences to help children become effective language users. Strickland and Morrow further suggest that the classroom environment that supports oral language is one that:

- Values the language children bring to school and use it as a basis for growth and development.
- Provides a variety of firsthand experiences within the child's environment.
- Allows children to express themselves in a variety of ways.
- Values individual uniqueness.
- Encourages children to focus on events and materials that have meaning to their lives.
- Provides opportunities for children to communicate with a variety of people including peers and adults.
- Recognizes and values the natural desire to communicate.
- Gives opportunities to express what they know and what they feel.
- Allows experimentation with language.[20]

While these suggestions are designed for classroom teachers, the first teachers that assist with oral language development are parents who need to be made aware of their role and ways of encouraging the development of oral language. Oral language is an integral part of the reading-writing process. Because of this important relationship between oral language and the printed word, teachers and parents must consider carefully the ways oral language development is encouraged in the child's environments.

Reading

Prereading and reading readiness have been discussed as major areas of cognitive development with young children for many years. What must a child know in order to read? When should a child begin to read? How do you teach a child to read? These questions have been asked and answered in a variety of ways. In learning the answers to these questions, much has been learned about language, the language process, and the relationships among listening, speaking, reading, and writing.

Reading develops as children learn to interpret messages provided through pictures in books, symbols on signs and labels in their environment as they ride down the road or help with grocery shopping, as they read favorite books according to their interpretation, and as they respond to nursery rhymes and stories read by others. Reading begins before the child picks up a book and decodes the symbols exactly as printed. The acts have been referred to as prereading or reading readiness activities but are recognized as early reading activities. Regardless of the label, children who engage in these activities are using their oral language along with visual and auditory awareness of language.

Visual awareness of elements needed in the reading process involve an understanding of directionality, discrimination of symbols, and memory of symbols, both letters and pictures. Directionality is sometimes considered a visual-motor skill and involves the mastery of left-to-right progression and top-to-bottom orientation. Children develop an understanding of directionality as they have experiences with print and see letters and words read to them. Directionality is also considered as students learn to recognize and form letters with the common confusions of b and d, p, q and g, m and w, n and u. While students sometimes reverse letters and words as they read, more frequently these occur as they write. These confusions are more of a maturation problem than a reading problem although parents and teachers become anxious tending to rush a diagnosis of a reading problem. The authors experiences suggest that immature children are more likely to have this reversal problem and that as they mature, the problem takes care of itself unless there is a learning disability or someone has made the issue a problem. An anxious parent called asking one of the authors how she might have her child evaluated for dyslexia. The author asked for more information as to why the mother was concerned and was told that the child reversed letters, could not remember words when told, was hyperactive, and could not write letters on the line. While these are some characteristics of a learning disability, the real problem was uncovered when the parent was asked the age of the child. The mother responded, "Matt will be five in three months." Reversals are common with children to the age of eight.

Understanding left-to-right and top-to-bottom progression of print is a basic concept of the reading process and is necessary for independent reading to occur. Students develop this understanding as they see print being read to them when reviewing their language experience stories or as the reader follows the line of print with the hand using a left-to-right sweeping motion while reading. The same development occurs in learning to read from the top of the page to the bottom. Another example of student confusion of this concept occurred in a second grade class as a bright little girl wrote her spelling words. Half the words were written perfectly from left-to-right while the other half were written perfectly but from right-to-left. The child was asked why she wrote the words differently. Her quick response was, "The teacher told me to." Puzzled by the response, she was asked to tell how the teacher told her to do this. The wonderful little girl said, "The teacher said to start writing at the red line on the side of your paper and write toward the middle so I started at this red line (indicated the one on the left side of the notebook paper) and wrote my words. When I did the next side, I started at the other red line (indicated the one on the right side of the paper) and did just like the teacher said." What a complex task to write words and letters backwards just to follow the directions of the teacher! A prescription for this problem was quickly provided.

Successful readers also learn to distinguish letters and words. With practice this discrimination leads to memory of the symbols which facilitates reading. For example, children learn to recognize the difference in the letter "a" and the letter "o" and combinations of letters such as "cat" and "dog" as they are beginning the reading process. There is no question of the importance of knowing how to visually discriminate and remember symbols; however, research has questioned the relationship of exercises using pictures to the visual discrimination of symbols.[21] Durkin and Ollila suggest that the most appropriate instructional procedures for direct instruction of visual discrimination involve the use of letters and words, rather than pictures, shapes, and numerals.[22] Again, this discrimination skill usually develops as students are exposed to print and language without the use of specific workbook activities.

Visual memory of letters and words develops as students learn to discriminate and is important as students recognize letters, as well as the basic sight words such as *the, what, come, and, with*. Learning to recognize unique features of letters and words in order to distinguish one from another and aid in memory enables students to identify them quickly as they read. From a summary of the research, Adams suggests ". . . the speed with which they can name individual letters both strongly predicts success for prereaders and is strongly related to reading achievement among beginning readers."[23] She further explains that speed and accuracy in naming letters indicates the prereader's familiarity with letter identities while it provides confidence and a basis as letter sounds are associated.

Reading pictures and words using pictures in the environment help young children recognize that symbols communicate a message. This reading of environmental print is one way of developing an understanding of what is seen. For environmental print to be more than the recognition of the golden arches to indicate a nearby McDonald's or Tony the Tiger to identify a box of Frosted Flakes, letters in words and associated sounds need to be pointed out to children. Going beyond this basic identification of visual symbols develops an understanding of how to use environmental print to interpret letters. Labeling items in the classroom, displaying daily messages or directions in the room, and identifying topics of discussion using cards with names to communicate to young children the association between oral and written language uses environmental print to develop a visual comprehension of information. Allowing a young child to locate his name from several cards and use another card to "sign in" each morning helps the child learn to visually recognize his name and connect this reading process to writing using scribbles and letters as he develops.

Just as visual processing of information is important in emergent literacy, auditory processing is essential. Children develop an awareness of oral language and talk, initially using one word to communicate an idea and quickly putting words together

Books help children
unlock mysteries of the
world and their
language. Photo
courtesy of Edward B.
Lasher.

to form phrases and sentences. Regardless of the number of words spoken, the child
is using words to convey a message, not a sound or syllable, but a meaningful message. Children begin to develop the concept of individual words as the words are
pointed out when they are interacting with print. Words become a series of squiggly
marks with a space in front and a space at the end. Visual and auditory processing
of language occur together. As children hear and see words they develop the concept
of isolated words and then can begin to relate to the association of letters and sounds
within the word. Every primary level teacher has had the experience of being asked
how to spell "onceuponatime" by the young writer beginning his own fairy tale.
Auditorily the student has comprehended one word used to begin a story and when
the teacher begins to spell four separate words, the child is confused.

Just as children learn to visually discriminate one letter from another, they also
learn to auditorily discriminate these sounds. Research investigations into just how
children should be taught to identify letters and learn sounds suggests that letters
and sounds are best learned together.[24] Adams states that "functional understanding of the alphabetic principle depends equally on knowledge of letters and on explicit
awareness of phonemes because it depends so closely on the association between
them."[25] Thus, as we teach auditory discrimination of sounds it is important to teach
visual discrimination of letters to assist students in associating the sounds and symbols of their language.

Developing this phonemic awareness of their language is important to a child's
success in learning to read. In her analysis of research, Adams suggests that students

possess phonemic awareness as evidenced through their speech production and understanding of oral language; however, this functional knowledge is not the same as the conscious knowledge needed to understand the phonological process.[26] As literacy emerges, teachers develop the phonemic awareness of language as they help students associate the sounds and letters of their oral and written language. This need for knowledge of the association of sounds and symbols is not to suggest that teachers of young children initiate an intensive phonics program to develop phonemic awareness. Indeed, if children are to learn this association in a manner in which they can continue to develop in later years, schools need programs rich in experiences providing for linguistic awareness using story reading, songs, nursery rhymes, oral language activities including discussions, free play in structured situations, and dramatizations, and language games encouraging both oral and written language expression. Developing this phonemic awareness assists the student as they encounter words and additional instruction in associating sounds and symbols.

All students will not learn to recognize or discriminate sounds at the ages of four, five, or six. Children who have not been involved with language activities in the home environment will not be ready for this phase of emergent literacy. Some children, particularly little boys, have difficulty with high-frequency sounds (/f/, /v/, /d/, /p/, /t/, /g/, /k/, /sh/, and /th/), due to auditory acuity problems[27] caused by ear infections or delays in the formation of their middle or inner ear structure.

The most important activity that parents and caretakers of young children can engage in with children from birth to school-age is reading to the child. Repeatedly, researchers have concluded that the single most important activity for developing the skills and knowledge needed for success in reading is reading aloud to children.[28] In addition to learning concepts about print and sounds as discussed earlier, children learn about story structure and develop an understanding of the meaningful messages conveyed through stories and poems. Auditory or listening comprehension expands vocabulary and develops oral language as parents encourage comments and have dialogue with the child as the story is read.[29]

In a study of literacy events in home environments lacking value in literacy, Teale found that events categorized as "storybook time" occupied, on the average, less than two minutes per day with many children having no storybook reading time at all.[30] As Adams suggests, if these children continue this pattern throughout their preschool years, they will have received about sixty hours of storybook reading as compared to about 1,000 hours of storybook reading to the child in a literacy-rich home environment.[31] The differences in the language awareness and listening comprehension performances of these two groups of children will be miles apart with little opportunity for this difference to be made up when they enter school.

The wealth of children's literature in libraries, schools, and some homes must be put in the hands of all parents if literacy is to emerge with all young children. In a study of reading interests of three-year-old children, Collins found that definite preferences in story content exists with differences in preferences of girls and boys as well as children from different socioeconomic levels (see table 7.1).[32] This

Table 7.1

Comparison of Reading Interests of Three-Year-Olds from Two Socioeconomic Levels

	Male	**Female**
Middle-income	Informational books Pattern books	Story books
Lower-income	Pattern books	Pattern books Story books

Martha D. Collins. "How Do Three-Year-Olds Select Favorite Books." Paper presented at the College Reading Association, Philadelphia, PA, October 1989.

difference in reading preferences is important as stories are read to young children. As their language becomes better developed, their reading interests tend to veer away from pattern books toward books with greater content. Girls prefer story books about people or animals, real or fictional characters while boys want informational books about trucks, dinosaurs, or animals. The less well-developed the child's language, the more they enjoyed pattern books including nursery rhymes and repetitious verses. Initial data from a follow-up study with five-year-olds suggests that middle-income girls develop a preference for pattern books (parents reported that these girls enjoyed pattern books prior to the age of three) as they try to read the book independently or with an adult reader and middle-income five-year-old boys have a preference for storybooks and informational books.[33] This change in reading interests appears to reflect the development of language literacy with age, oral language development, literacy experiences, and environment leading to reading.

For understanding information obtained by listening, students should have some command over key components of the language, namely phonology (sound structure), syntax (sentence structure), semantics (word meaning and the relationships among meanings), and text structure (conventions about how events and assertions within a text are typically structured). Various researchers have found that the lack of facility in any one of these components leads to either reduced comprehension or increased processing time. Thus, a good listener orchestrates all of these components simultaneously.[34]

In a literature summary related to teaching listening comprehension, Pearson and Fielding concluded that:

1. Listening training in the same skills typically taught in reading comprehension curricula tends to improve listening comprehension.
2. Listening comprehension is enhanced by various kinds of active verbal responses on the part of students during and after listening.

3. Listening to literature tends to improve listening comprehension.
4. Certain types of instruction primarily directed toward other areas of language arts may also improve listening comprehension.
5. Direct teaching of listening strategies seems to help students become more conscious of their listening habits.[35]

For many years, auditory comprehension has been identified as an indicator of potential reading ability. In a review of studies that compared reading and listening comprehension at various levels, Sticht et al., found that in the elementary grades (one–six), almost all of the comparisons favor the listening comprehension mode. However, in grades seven through twelve, the proportion of studies showing an advantage to reading comprehension increases.[36] Although this summary would suggest that in the elementary grades students can rely on their already well-developed listening comprehension abilities to assist their less well-developed reading abilities, Schell cautions against using a listening comprehension level to determine the reading potential of students in grades 1–3. In a review of research, he found that students were overreferred for help in reading when listening comprehension was used as an indicator of potential.[37] Regardless, students are often able to attend more critically to material read to them than to material they read silently. It is not uncommon for students to be able to comprehend these passages on a higher readability level than their silent reading level. This interesting correlation between listening and reading has resulted in the investigation of this phenomena over a period of several years.

Numerous studies have examined the relationship between listening and reading. Ross found that good listeners rated higher than poor listeners on intelligence, reading, socioeconomic status, and achievement, but not on an auditory acuity test.[38] This study indicates that auding (listening) requires a finer degree of discrimination than acuity.

Deutsch et al., found that children from lower socio-economic backgrounds were at a distinct disadvantage in learning to read because their language patterns interfered with the comprehension of both oral and written materials.[39] In a related study, Clark and Richards found a significant deficiency in auditory discrimination in economically disadvantaged preschool students.[40]

Parents of young children are usually intensely interested in the reading success of their child. Many investigations have been done to determine what factors in the home environments contribute to success in reading. McGee and Richgels summarize this research with six factors that support literacy learning.[41]

1. Availability and variety of reading and writing materials appropriate to the age and interests of the children.[42]
2. Parents who are readers and writers.[43]

3. A daily routine for storybook reading and use of writing as a part of the daily activities.[44]
4. Discussions with children as stories are read and talk about written language when they write together.[45]
5. A feeling of responsibility toward literacy development.[46]
6. A sensitivity to children's interests and experiences when reading and sharing books as well as an acceptance of the level of the child's performance.[47]

In a study of parents' perceptions of factors affecting the reading development of preschool intellectually superior accelerated readers and intellectually superior non-readers, Burns and Collins found all parents involved in literacy development activities with their children. However, mothers of accelerated readers provided more opportunities for their children to discuss, recall, and interact with information from stories or story-related materials than mothers of nonreaders. Mothers of accelerated readers also provided more opportunities in the home environment to interact directly with pictures, letters, sounds, words, sentences, and book-related concepts than nonreaders. There was no difference in opportunities provided the two groups to interact with words in the context of signs, newspapers, magazines, labels, and television or in the number of opportunities provided to scribble, draw, form shapes, form letters, copy words, spell words, and write messages.[48]

While the length and detail of information presented in this section may suggest that reading is the most important aspect of emergent literacy, a review of the information should clearly indicate that oral language and writing are integral parts of this discussion.

Writing

As a mother tried to explain to her young daughter that writing under her special message from Bill Martin in her *Brown Bear, Brown Bear* book is not a good idea because it messes up her favorite book, the child responded: "He put his name in it 'cause he wrote the book; I put my name in it 'cause I read the book." Who can argue with this logic? This exemplifies Donald Graves message suggesting that as young children mark with chalk, pens, or crayons, "The child's marks say 'I am'."[49]

As literacy emerges, children express their developing language through writing and reading activities. Writing has been viewed for many years as a process that begins after reading although current research shows that emphasis on writing activities in early reading programs results in special gains in early reading achievement.[50] Young children experiment with writing, just as they experiment with reading, using lines and marks to communicate a message. Maria Montessori promoted the idea of write first, read later[51] with current studies of children who read early supporting her theory that many of these children wrote before reading.[52]

Writing begins with scribbles, progresses as children write as they paint or play with clay and builds to making stories or journals. Photos courtesy of Edward B. Lasher.

With young children writing begins with lines and scribbles, progresses to drawings, then to letterlike forms, reproduces well-known word units, uses invented
spelling, and finally begins to write using conventional spelling. Writing emerges
just as other areas of language in varying continuums dependent upon the child's
background, experiences, and needs. For example, the two-year old makes marks on
a paper to experiment with a marker on paper (or walls, sheets, clothes, arms, etc.).
He is not trying to communicate a message, however, as he observes others using a
pen to write a message his purpose for using the marker changes. These lines become
more than marks, they are interpreted by the young writer to carry a specific message.

This relation of writing to the reading process with young learners represents a
significant change in thinking in the last ten years. Previous discussions of prereading included no discussion of writing as being related to early literacy development. Indeed, writing has been viewed as a way of communicating a message after
the student learns to read and spell. With the wealth of new information to support
what primary teachers and parents have long believed, writing development is integrated as part of all discussions of emergent literacy.

As children begin to associate sounds and symbols, they begin to use this knowledge to write using invented spelling to communicate their ideas. Chomsky has summarized common features of invented spelling:

- Children incorporate whole letter names into their spellings: YL (while),
  THAQ (thank you), PPL (people).
- Consonants tend to contribute part of their names although sometimes
  unconventionally: KAN (can), JRIV (drive).
- Long vowels generally speak for themselves: BOT (boat), AGRE (angry).
- Short vowels come close: BAD (bed), LUKS (looks), or are omitted
  altogether.
- Letters such as I and r tend to lose their vowels: GRL (girl), PKN (picking).
- N and M before stop consonants often go unrepresented: WOT (won't),
  PLAT (plant).[53]

Teachers sometimes have concerns about the impact of invented spelling on correct spelling. Clarke found that in classes encouraging invented spelling the students
wrote longer stories, had greater success in spelling regularly spelled words and words
on a standardized spelling test, performed better on reading regularly spelled nonsense words and on reading lists of high-frequency irregular and lower frequency
regular words.[54] With the greater use of computers in classrooms, students need to
be allowed to experiment with writing using the word processor. Letter recognition
and discrimination are enhanced as sounds and symbols are associated to communicate a meaningful message.

Encouraging young children to write to communicate a message is the important
part of the writing process in emergent literacy. Spelling, spacing, penmanship, and
punctuation are mechanical skills that can and will be developed once children
learn the real purpose for writing—to convey meaning.

Figure 7.3
Sean Demonstrates an Excellent Understanding of the Reading and Writing Processes at the End of Kindergarten as He Writes "I Liked the Cat Story and *Wacky Wednesday*."

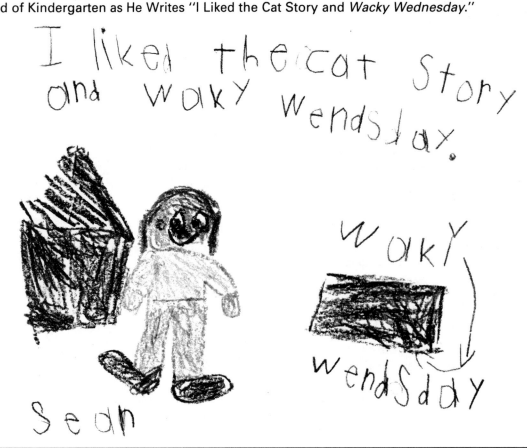

■ Prescriptive Strategies for Emergent Literacy

As classroom teachers plan ways of incorporating diagnostic-prescriptive instruction into their emergent literacy development, attention needs to be given to diagnostic procedures for use with young students. As mentioned earlier, observation is the best evaluation technique for noting what children know; however, teachers must know the behaviors being observed and keep specific records of their findings. Other procedures are outlined in table 7.2 (see page 254).

I like the books you read to us.

Figure 7.4
Ronnie is also Completing Kindergarten and is Using His Understanding of Invented Spelling to Write "I Like the Books You Read to Us."

To provide prescriptive instruction, teachers of young children realize the importance of language development as the foundation of the reading and writing processes. Few children enter kindergarten or first-grade at the same point because of the differences in their environment and experiences. Strickland and Morrow suggest ideas for teachers to use daily to develop language and literacy (see figure 7.5). Additional ideas are given in Table 7.3 (see page 255).

Although these prescriptive ideas are separated into the three categories of oral language, reading, and writing, the activities reflect the integrated nature of the language process. Many of the reading activities require oral language and writing while the writing activities require the use of oral language or reading. Thus, the activities can be used to aid in the development of several areas of language development.

Table 7.2

Diagnostic Procedures for Evaluating Emergent Literacy Areas

Oral Language	Observation checklist
	Peabody Picture Vocabulary Test
	Test of Early Language Development–2
	Test of Early Reading Ability–2
	Test of Language Development–2
	Criterion/Objective-based tests
Reading	Observation checklist
	Criterion/Objective-based tests
	Test of Early Reading Ability–2
	Informal Reading Inventory
	Gates—MacGinitie, Pre-reading
Writing	Observation checklist
	Test of Early Written Language
	Test of Written Language–2

Figure 7.5
Daily Language
and Literacy
Opportunities

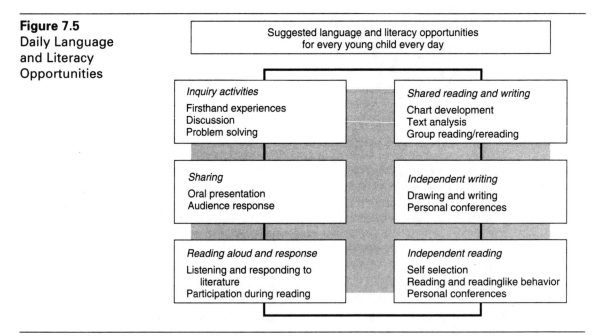

Suggested language and literacy opportunities for every young child every day

Inquiry activities
Firsthand experiences
Discussion
Problem solving

Shared reading and writing
Chart development
Text analysis
Group reading/rereading

Sharing
Oral presentation
Audience response

Independent writing
Drawing and writing
Personal conferences

Reading aloud and response
Listening and responding to literature
Participation during reading

Independent reading
Self selection
Reading and readinglike behavior
Personal conferences

Reprinted with permission of Dorothy Strickland and Leslie Mandel Morrow and the International Reading Association. Dorothy Strickland and Leslie Mandel Morrow, "Creating curriculum: An emergent literacy perspective," *The Reading Teacher,* 42(May 1989):723.

Table 7.3

Prescriptive Techniques for Emergent Literacy Development

Area	Prescriptive Technique
Oral Language	—Ask students to say a specified number of words to describe an object or picture. —Using a topic of interest, develop word walls containing as many words as the students can think of about the topic. Add to this each day. —Following a field trip, film, or story, ask students to use appropriate words to tell about their experience. —Using various objects, ask students to point to them according to a specified color, shape, size, etc. —Ask students to show or tell where objects are located when hearing such prepositions as over, under, in, out, etc. —Label objects, pictures, or art work in the room and have students dictate a sentence or phrase about their work. —Ask students to dictate stories about pictures from newspapers or magazines. —Ask students to tell about their favorite pet using complete sentences. —Invite students to give the recipe for making their favorite food. —Ask students to tell the sequence involved in making a garden, getting dressed to come to school, or in going on a field trip. —Read a story and ask students to retell the story in proper order or with necessary characters. —Let students work in small groups to discuss their favorite foods, TV programs, pets, etc. —With an assigned topic, ask each student to contribute at least one related idea about the topic.
Reading	—Have students string colored beads directionally from left to right in a given pattern. —Give students cards containing their names written with sand and ask them to trace their name with their finger. —Give students a letter and ask them to select from a set of letters, one that is exactly like the given letter; then select one that is different. —Give students an alphabet board containing lower-case letters and a set of cards containing the upper-case letters to be matched. —Give each student several cards containing names of students in the room. One card should have the student's own name to be selected by recognition. —Show a picture of an event and list words that represent things that the students identify in the picture. —Have students draw a picture of their home in as much detail as possible. Then ask them to dictate a story that describes to the class what their picture shows. —Give students a series of photographs of an event and ask them to arrange the photographs in the correct sequence. Once properly arranged, ask them to dictate a story telling about the pictures. —Play a tape of an automobile horn, a fog horn, and a boat horn. Then ask students to identify the sounds they heard.

Table 7.3

Continued

Area	Prescriptive Technique
Reading *(continued)*	—Using three paper bags, put rocks in one, sand in another, and coins in the last one. Allow students to shake the bags, describe what they hear and dictate a story about these different sounds. —Give students a series of two letters such as /b/ and /s/. Ask the students to clap or raise their hands when the two sounds are the same. —Say several pairs of words, some with the same sounds and some different. Ask students to clap when the words sound the same and stand when they are different. —Read students a story containing rhyming words. After reading a short portion of the story, ask them to supply the rhyming word as you read using a modified cloze procedure. —Play a game with students in which directions are given such as "Stand up and shake your foot." As the task is performed, give additional directions making each longer and more complex. —Give students a specific sound. Then say several words containing the specific sound and ask students to clap when the sound is heard in each word. —Give students two words with the same beginning sound. Ask them to give the sound with which both words begin. —Say two words with different ending sounds (can, pop). Ask students to repeat the ending sounds. —Show pictures of several animals. Say two words and ask students to select the picture that begins with the same sound as the two given words. —Tell a story about the beach using descriptive words such as sifting sand, fat fish, etc. Ask students to name the pairs of words that begin with the same sound. —Show a picture of an object. Ask students to name as many objects as possible that begin or end with the same sound. —Say several simple words with medial sounds such as fat and big. Ask each student to say at least one word with the same medial sounds as the examples. —Give students two words with the same medial sound (sit, trip). Ask each student to say at least one word with the same medial sound as the examples. —Read a sentence that has the last word deleted. Ask students to say the missing word that rhymes with another word in the sentence. (The ham was better than _____ .) —Give the students a word. Ask them to make up a sentence in which the last word rhymes with another word in the sentence. For example: "The big cat ate a *rat.*" —Ask a student to give a simple direction to another student and see that the direction is correctly followed. Then ask the second student to give a different direction to another student. Follow this procedure letting everyone experiment with giving directions. —Describe an object and ask students to tell what it is and to find a picture of the object. —Have a student describe an object. Ask the students to attempt to determine what the object is from the student's description. When the task is completed, have each student draw a picture of the object.

Table 7.3

Continued

Area	Prescriptive Technique
Reading *(continued)*	—Read a story to the students and ask them to retell their favorite part of the story. —After reading a short story, ask students to draw a picture of how the main character looks in their minds. —Have a student tell a story containing four events. Ask the other students to illustrate in order the four events that were described. —Tell a story using pictures depicting the sequence of events. Place the pictures on a table in random order and ask the students to put them in the correct order. —Read a portion of a predictable story and ask the students to predict what will happen next telling why they think as they do. —After reading a short sentence using descriptive language, ask students to illustrate their impression of the sentence. —Read a short story that is emotionally descriptive. Ask students to tell how the characters felt in the story. —Read a story and ask the students to tell why the story ended as it did. —After hearing a story, ask students to illustrate the conclusion. —Read part of a story and ask students to tell or illustrate how they think the story should end.
Writing	—Give students a basket containing various colors and shapes of paper along with markers, crayons, and pencils. Ask them to select their favorite and write their favorite letter of the alphabet on it. —Put a small pad of paper in the housekeeping center to encourage students to make shopping lists or take messages from the phone. —In the writing center put labeled mailboxes for each child. Using the writing materials and envelopes in the center, encourage students to correspond with each other using pictures and invented spelling and putting the message in the appropriate mailbox. —After making popcorn or some other food, ask the students to work in teams to list the steps followed or tell how the food was prepared. —Encourage students to use the word processor and type or copy words or ideas that they wish to share with others. —Use a graphic software package on the computer and help students develop their own invitations or announcements. —Help students write the letters of the alphabet and draw pictures of objects that begin with the designated letter. —Invite the students to write a thank-you note to a visitor to the class. —Make booklets of dictated stories about a field experience or some exciting adventure of the week.

■ Summary

Emergent literacy forms the foundation for developing the language skills necessary for success in reading and writing. The research and discussions presented in this chapter reiterate this idea in many different ways. The research summaries provided in the discussion of the three categories of literacy development, oral language, reading, and writing, emphasize the need for parents and teachers to assist in providing the necessary experiences in an interrelated manner.

Language development is affected by the child's home and school environments. Parents are the first teachers that stimulate language and begin literacy development through exposure to print materials. When children enter school, their learning in this new environment is significantly affected by the experiences provided in the home environment.

The diagnostic information from the previous chapters was related directly to the emergent literacy areas through a chart indicating the most appropriate specific diagnostic techniques. The concept of prescriptive teaching was related to the areas of emergent literacy through a chart of prescriptive activities.

■ Applying What You Read

You are asked to talk with the kindergarten and first grade teachers at a local elementary school about the concept of emergent literacy. What would you tell them? Why do we discuss emergent literacy now when discussing young children and not prereading skills?

Design a program for evaluating the language development skills of children entering your first grade class. Be specific as to the behaviors that you would evaluate.

You have been hired as a kindergarten teacher in an inner-city school. How would you begin to determine the needs of your students? In what areas of emergent literacy would you suspect their development would be the weakest? Why?

Teachers in your school read to the students and encourage the students to discuss the stories and other daily activities. However, they do not see how writing fits into the scenario of emergent literacy. How would you explain this relationship?

Half of the kindergarten and first grade teachers in your school have "thrown away the basals" and decided to implement a 'whole language program' (each define whole language a little differently). All of the second grade teachers use a basal and do not wish to use anything else. How could this dilemma be resolved in the best interest of the students? Consider that a child could experience two different philosophies in the first two years of school.

■ Notes

1. William Teale and Elizabeth Sulzby, *Emergent Literacy: Writing and Reading.*
2. Jana M. Mason and J. Allen, "A Review of Emergent Literacy with Implications for Research and Practice in Reading," in *Review of Research in Education*, edited by E. Z. Rothkopf, pp. 3–47.
3. Dorothy S. Strickland and Lesley Mandel Morrow, "New Perspectives on Young Children Learning to Read and Write," *The Reading Teacher.*
4. Dorothy S. Strickland and Lesley Mandel Morrow, "Assessment and Early Literacy," *The Reading Teacher.*

5. William Teale, Elfrieda Hiebert, and Edward Chittenden, "Assessing Young Children's Literacy Development," *The Reading Teacher*.

6. R. Craig Roney, "Background Experience is the Foundation of Success in Learning to Read," *The Reading Teacher*.

7. Marie Clay, *The Early Detection of Reading Difficulties: A Diagnostic Survey*.

8. L. A. Kaster, N. L. Roser, and J. V. Hoffman, "Understandings of the Forms and Functions of Written Language: Insights from Children and Parents," in *Research in Literacy: Merging Perspectives*, edited by J. E. Readence and R. S. Baldwin, *36th Yearbook of the National Reading Conference*, pp. 85–92; Marilyn M. Manning and Gary L. Manning, "Early Readers and Nonreaders from Low Socioeconomic Environments: What Their Parents Report," *The Reading Teacher*; Lesley Mandel Morrow, "Home and School Correlates of Early Interest in Literature," *Journal of Educational Research*.

9. Jill Fitzgerald, Dixie Lee Spiegel, and James W. Cunningham, "The Relationship Between Parental Literacy Level and Perceptions of Emergent Literacy," *Journal of Reading Behavior*.

10. R. Craig Roney, "Background Experience is the Foundation of Success in Learning to Read."

11. Anne H. Dyson, "'N Spell My Grandmama: Fostering Early Thinking about Print," *The Reading Teacher*.

12. M. A. K. Halliday, *Learning How to Mean: Exploration in the Development of Language*, pp. 19–21.

13. R. Craig Roney, "Background Experience is the Foundation of Success in Learning to Read."

14. Elizabeth Sulzby, "Children's Emergent Reading of Favorite Storybooks: A Developmental Study," *Reading Research Quarterly*.

15. R. Craig Roney, "Background Experience is the Foundation of Success in Learning to Read."

16. Walter Loban, *The Language of Elementary School Children*; Dorothy Strickland, "Black is Beautiful vs. White is Right," *Elementary English*.

17. J. Britton, *Language and Learning*.

18. Kenneth Goodman, "Let's Dump the Uptight Model in English," *Elementary School Journal*.

19. Carol Chomsky, *The Acquisition of Syntax in Children from 5 to 10*.

20. Dorothy S. Strickland and Lesley Mandel Morrow, "Reading, Writing, and Oral Language," *The Reading Teacher*, pp. 240–1.

21. Thomas C. Barrett, "The Relationship Between the Measures of Pre-reading Visual Discrimination and First-Grade Achievement: A Review of the Literature," *Reading Research Quarterly*; Albert J. Harris, "Practical Applications of Reading Research," *The Reading Teacher*; Robert E. Liebert and John K. Sherk, "Three Frostig Visual Perception Sub-tests and Specific Reading Tasks for Kindergarten, First, and Second Grade Children," *The Reading Teacher*; Arthur V. Olson and Clifford I. Johnson, "Structure and Predictive Validity of the Frostig Developmental Test of Visual Perception in Grades One and Three," *Journal of Special Education*; Edward Paradis, "The Appropriateness of Visual Discrimination Exercise in Reading Readiness Materials," *Journal of Educational Research*.

22. Dolores Durkin, *Teaching Them to Read*, 3rd ed., pp. 181–82; Lloyd Ollila, "Reading: Preparing the Child," in *Reading: Foundations and Instructional Strategies*, edited by Posel Lamb and Richard Arnold.

23. Marilyn Jager Adams, *Beginning to Read: Thinking and Learning about Print*, p. 43.

24. D. C. Ohnmacht, "The Effects of Letter Knowledge on Achievement in Reading in the First Grade," *Reading Research Revisited*, edited by L. M. Gentile, M. L. Kamil, and J. S. Blanchard, pp. 141–42.

25. Adams, *Beginning to Read*, p. 54.

26. Adams, p. 54.

27. Henry P. Smith and Emerald V. Dechant, *Psychology in Teaching Reading*.

28. Richard C. Anderson, Elfrieda H. Hiebert, Judith A. Scott, and Ian A. G. Wilkinson, *Becoming a Nation of Readers*; Carol Chomsky, "Stages in Language Development and Reading Exposure," *Harvard Educational Review*; Dolores Durkin, *Children Who Read Early: Two Longitudinal Studies*.

29. Lesley Mandel Morrow, *Literacy Development in the Early Years*; G. J. Whitehurst, F. Falco, C. J. Lonigan, J. E. Fischal, B. D. DeBaryshe, M. C. Valdez-Manchaca, and M. Caulfield, "Accelerating Language Development through Picturebook Reading," *Developmental Psychology*.

30. William H. Teale, "Home Background and Young Children's Literacy Development," in *Emergent Literacy: Writing and Reading*, edited by W. H. Teale and E. Sulzby.

31. Adams, p. 47.

32. Martha D. Collins, "How Do Three-Year-Olds Select Favorite Books?" Paper presented at College Reading Association, Philadelphia, PA, October 1989.

33. Martha D. Collins, "Reading Interests of Five-Year-Olds: Effects of Language Development," in process.

34. P. David Pearson and Linda Fielding, "Research Update: Listening Comprehension," *Language Arts*, pp. 617–18.

35. Pearson and Fielding, "Research Update: Listening Comprehension," pp. 619–21.

36. Tom G. Sticht, L. J. Beck, R. N. Hanke, G. M. Kleiman, and J. H. James, *Auding and Reading: A Developmental Model*.

37. Leo M. Schell, "The Validity of the Potential Level Via Listening Comprehension: A Cautionary Note," *Reading Psychology*.

38. Ramon Ross, "A Look at Listeners," *Elementary School Journal*.

39. Martin Deutsch et al., *Communication of Information in the Elementary School Classroom*.

40. Ann D. Clark and Charlotte J. Richards, "Auditory Discrimination Among Economically Disadvantaged and Nondisadvantaged Preschool Children," *Exceptional Children*.

41. Lea M. McGee and Donald J. Richgels, *Learning How to Mean: Exploration in the Development of Language*, pp. 70–82.

42. Lesley M. Morrow, "Home and School Correlates of Early Interest in Literature," *Journal of Educational Research*; William H. Teale, "Positive Environments for Learning to Read: What Studies of Early Readers Tell Us," *Language Arts*; Denny Taylor, *Family Literacy*.

43. Lesley Mandel Morrow, "Relationships Between Literature Programs, Library Corner Designs, and Children's Use of Literature," *Journal of Educational Research*; J. A.

Schickedanz and M. Sullivan, "Mom, What Does U-F-F Spell?" *Language Arts*; M. Clark, *Young Fluent Readers*.

44. Dolores Durkin, *Children Who Read Early*; J. A. Schickedanz and M. Sullivan, "Mom, What Does U-F-F Spell?"; Shirley B. Heath, *Ways with Words: Language, Life, and Work in Communities and Classrooms*; Shirley B. Heath and C. Thomas, "The Achievement of Preschool Literacy for Mother and Child," in *Awakening to Literacy*, edited by H. Goelman, A. A. Oberg, and F. Smith, pp. 51–72; H. J. Leichter, "Families as Environments for Literacy," in *Awakening to Literacy*, edited by H. Goelman, A. A. Oberg, and F. Smith, pp. 38–50.

45. David B. Yaden, Jr. and Lea M. McGee, "Reading as a Meaning Seeking Activity: What Children's Questions Reveal," in *Thirty-third Yearbook of the National Reading Conference*, edited by Jerry Niles, pp. 101–09; R. Gundlach, J. B. McLane, F. M. Scott, and G. D. McNamee, "The Social Foundations of Children's Early Writing Development," in *Advances in Writing Research: Vol. 1, Children's Early Writing Development*, edited by M. Farr, pp. 1–58.

46. N. E. Dunn, "Children's Achievement at School-Entry as a Function of Mothers' and Fathers' Teaching Sets," *Elementary School Journal*; Marcia Baghban, *Our Daughter Learns to Read and Write: A Case Study from Birth to Three*; C. E. Snow, "Literacy and Language: Relationships During the Preschool Years," *Harvard Educational Review*; J. C. Harste, C. I. Burke, and V. A. Woodward, *Children, Their Language and World: Initial Encounters with Print*.

47. A. Ninio, "Picture Book Reading in Mother Infant Dyads Belonging to Two Subgroups in Israel," *Child Development*; E. Hiebert and C. Adams, "Fathers' and Mothers' Perceptions of Their Preschool Children's Emergent Literacy," *Journal of Experimental Child Psychology*.

48. Jeanne M. Burns and Martha D. Collins, "Parent' Perceptions of Factors Affecting the Reading Development of Intellectually Superior Accelerated Readers and Intellectually Superior Nonreaders," *Reading Research and Instruction*.

49. Donald H. Graves, *Writing: Teachers and Children at Work*.

50. Robert D. Aukerman, *Approaches to Beginning Reading*, 2nd ed.; M. A. Evans and T. H. Carr, "Cognitive Abilities, Conditions of Learning, and the Early Development of Reading Skill," *Reading Research Quarterly*.

51. Maria Montessori, *The Secret of Childhood*.

52. Durkin, *Children Who Read Early*, p. 137.

53. Carol Chomsky, "Approaching Reading Through Invented Spelling," in *Theory and Practice of Early Reading*, edited by L. B. Resnick and P. A. Weaver, pp. 43–65.

54. L. K. Clarke, "Invented versus Traditional Spelling in First Graders' Writing: Effects on Learning to Spell and Read," *Research in the Teaching of English*.

■ Other Suggested Readings

Cunningham, Patricia M., Dorothy P. Hall, and Margaret Defee. "Non-Ability Grouped, Multilevel Instruction: A Year in a First-Grade Classroom." *The Reading Teacher* 44 (April 1991): 566–71.

Gibson, L. *Literacy Learning in the Early Years Through Children's Eyes*. New York: Teachers College Press, 1989.

Harste, Jerry. "Jerry Harste Speaks on Reading and Writing." *The Reading Teacher* 43 (January 1990): 316–18.

Lartz, Maribeth Nelson, and Jana Mason. "Jamie: One Child's Journey From Oral to Written Language." *Early Childhood Research Quarterly* 3 (June 1988): 193–208.

McGee, Lea, Rosalind Charlesworth, Martha Collins Cheek, and Earl H. Cheek. "Metalinguistic Knowledge: Another Look at Beginning Reading." *Childhood Education* 59 (January/February 1983): 123–27.

Mason, Jana M. "Early Reading from a Developmental Perspective." In *Handbook of Reading Research,* pp. 505–44. Edited by P. David Pearson. New York: Longman, Inc., 1984.

Pinnell, Gay Su, Mary D. Fried, and Rose Mary Estice. "Reading Recovery: Learning How to Make a Difference." *The Reading Teacher* 43 (January 1990): 282–95.

Rasinski, Timothy. "The Role of Interest, Purpose, and Choice in Early Literacy." *The Reading Teacher* 41 (January 1988): 396–400.

Roskos, Kathy. "An Inventory of Literate Behavior in the Pretend Play Episodes of Eight Preschoolers." *Reading Research and Instruction* 30 (Spring 1991): 39–52.

Strickland, Dorothy S., and Leslie Mandel Morrow. *Emerging Literacy: Young Children Learn to Read and Write.* Newark, Delaware: International Reading Association, 1989.

——— . "New Perspectives on Young Children Learning to Read and Write." *The Reading Teacher* 42 (October 1988): 70–71.

Strickland, Dorothy S., Leslie Mandel Morrow, and Tammye Mensh Pelovitz. "Emerging Readers and Writers: Cooperative, Collaborative Learning for Children and Teachers." *The Reading Teacher* 44 (April 1991) 600–602.

Tovey, Duane R., and James E. Kerber (eds.) *Roles in Literacy Learning: A New Perspective.* Newark, Delaware: International Reading Association, 1986.

8

Word Identification

Word analysis, decoding, word identification, word processing, word recognition—these terms name the category of skills used to determine how a set of printed symbols is pronounced to form a word to which a meaning can be associated. These skill areas include the use of sight word knowledge, phonic analysis, contextual analysis, and structural analysis.

Word identification receives considerable attention in the classroom and is often the most controversial in the public domain. Teachers and parents too often associate good reading with good word identification.

Thus, classroom emphasis is sometimes diverted toward the development of the word identification skills, with little time remaining for the other reading areas, such as comprehension and study skills. The result may be that students become good word callers, but have little understanding of what they read.

The public controversy regarding word identification centers on whether students should be taught to read through the use of phonics or the look-say or sight approach. Teachers must help the public understand that learning to recognize words is not a matter of learning one set of skills *or* another, but involves learning to use *all* of the word identification skills, as appropriate.

Because of the importance of this area and the controversies apparently resulting from a lack of understanding of the word identification skills, classroom teachers have asked the following questions, which will be addressed in this chapter.

What are the word identification skills?

What does research say about the development of word identification?

How does the teacher assist students in learning to use the various word identification strategies?

What are some basic principles for teaching this area?

Which diagnostic instruments are most appropriate for use in this area?

What prescriptive strategies can be used in developing word identification skills?

As this chapter is read, the following terms are important to note.

Vocabulary to Know

Accent

Affix

Analytic phonics

Automaticity

Compound words

Consonant cluster

Consonants

Context clue

Contextual analysis

Contractions

Inflectional ending

Phoneme-grapheme correspondences

Phonic analysis

Picture clue

Prefix

Sight words

Structural analysis

Suffix

Syllables

Synthetic phonics

Variant patterns

Vowels

Word identification

■ Word Identification and Reading

Students enter school with a speaking and listening vocabulary as extensive as their background experiences, and exceeding their reading vocabulary. In order to develop a reading vocabulary, students must be taught to recognize printed words. Thus, teachers in the primary grades help students to acquire the strategies necessary to identify words, while teachers at higher levels must continue to extend and reinforce the application of these strategies.

Before beginning a discussion of the four areas of word identification, a broader issue needs to be considered. The issue deals with the development of word identification via a whole language process or through the teaching of word identification skills. Without question, young children develop an awareness of print through their experiences—trips to the grocery store develop an awareness of labels and lead to the identification of words such as "peanut butter." As children listen to nursery rhymes and stories, they memorize the order of the words, the sounds, and the unique features of a word in order to recognize it in print. Reading this "talk written down" goes further as parents and teachers write the words and sentences of young children and encourage them to read "their story." This whole language approach to decoding words is recommended by proponents of naturalistic reading who say that reading will occur as children are exposed to print in meaningful situations. Goodman and Goodman, and Mason[1] suggest that awareness of print in the environment is the first stage children pass through when developing written language abilities.

Children who seem to read naturally prior to school entrance have been studied to determine how they develop their decoding process. Durkin, Plessas and Oakes, Price, and Burns[2] found that these accelerated young readers had been provided some instruction to develop letter/sound/word concepts and encouraged to respond during story reading episodes. Thus, some word identification instruction appears to help these natural readers to focus on the necessary features of print. Beginning

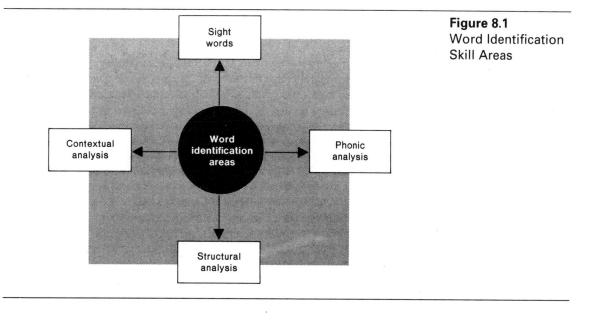

Figure 8.1
Word Identification
Skill Areas

reading instruction cannot be viewed as a philosophical debate of whole language versus skills instruction. Parents and teachers must begin with the child's language and relate new words to the known language. Word identification instruction in the areas of sight word vocabulary, phonic analysis, structural analysis, and contextual analysis is not going to leave the school curriculum, nor should it. However, teachers must provide appropriate instruction in these areas using the child's language as a basis, and realize that some readers develop their own system of decoding while others need more structured instruction.

In developing word identification skills, teachers assist students in learning a variety of techniques so that they are prepared to decode unknown words. Students must develop a *sight word knowledge* consisting of the words they see most frequently in their reading. Readers of all ages continuously expand their sight word knowledge as words are added to their reading vocabulary. However, initially students begin with a limited sight vocabulary consisting of words that cannot be decoded by any other procedure except memory. Another procedure that students are taught to use in recognizing words is *phonics*. Phonics knowledge involves learning to associate specific phonemes or sounds with the appropriate graphemes or symbols. Phonic analysis can be used as one procedure for recognizing unknown words but this is not the only strategy needed for adequate word identification.

Structural analysis skills are taught as other procedures for decoding unknown words. These strategies help the students to look at word parts such as syllables, affixes, contractions, and compound words to determine the correct pronunciation. *Contextual analysis* skills use the meaning of the phrase, sentence, or passage in conjunction with the other word identification skills to decode the unknown word. Using all of these strategies, students are able to recognize the many words they see in reading material.

Learning to identify the many words in the English language is complicated by many factors. One major factor relates to the language itself. Because our language is composed of so many other languages and dialects, students often encounter difficulties understanding the irregularities. This factor becomes more complex for the student in a program that teaches phonic analysis as the primary word identification strategy. Thus, word identification instruction should provide a variety of strategies to help the students decode the words read in the English language.

There are many factors that affect reading development. These factors—intelligence, environment, and maturation—also are to be considered as the teacher provides instruction in the word identification skills. Intelligence, or the mental age of the student, has an impact on readiness for beginning to learn the various word identification skills. Parents and teachers realize that the chronological age of six does not automatically indicate that the student is ready for instruction in the word identification strategies taught in reading.

Readiness for learning the word identification skills is also affected by environmental factors. As discussed in the previous chapter, many prereading skills are developed before formal reading instruction is begun. These are frequently started in the home, but when students do not develop some skills in auditory and visual discrimination prior to school entrance, this instruction is provided in school. Many students who enter school with these deficiencies seem to have difficulty in overcoming them and learning the various word identification skills. The difficulty stems from a home environment that has not stimulated language or provided experiences that motivate learning and interest in reading. This factor is further complicated when teachers do not consider the impact of environment on language development and fail to expand language as words are taught.

Maturation is another factor affecting the development of word identification skills. In addition to the impact of physical and emotional maturation on the learning of word identification skills, maturation in terms of speech or language development also plays an influential role in this process. Students who are unable to pronounce a sound, or who do not auditorially distinguish certain sounds in the language, often have immature speech patterns. This immaturity in speech may make learning phonics difficult; thus, the teacher emphasizes other word identification strategies, i.e., sight vocabulary, while developing the speech skills.

Another element to be considered in providing prescriptive instruction in this area is the learning style of the student. Most students learn equally well through the visual or auditory modes. For this reason, students are taught to use a variety of word identification skills in unlocking words. However, some students have perception or discrimination problems that create difficulty in using either the visual or auditory mode in learning. These are not acuity difficulties, but perception problems that may not be physically corrected. Teachers must note these difficulties and adjust instruction accordingly. Students with strength in the visual mode and weakness in the auditory mode experience more success in learning words by sight or the look-say method. Conversely, students with strength in the auditory mode and weakness in the visual mode learn to sound out words using phonics. To assist these students in learning words, teachers may need to use the VAKT method discussed in chapter 6.

Developing word identification skills is a complex process often complicated by the factors of maturation, learning styles, environment, and intelligence. Teachers who consider these factors to be important in learning to identify words have begun prescriptive teaching. The following sections present a more in-depth discussion of the word identification areas with a summary of research findings that affect prescriptive teaching.

Sight Word Knowledge

In defining sight word knowledge as a procedure for identifying words, note that this strategy may be considered a method for teaching beginning reading. The look-say method is based on the premise that the student is taught to recognize words by sight rather than through an analytic process such as phonics or structural analysis. However, as a procedure for word identification, sight word knowledge is remembering words that occur most frequently in reading and are not easily analyzed through other procedures.

Teachers usually associate sight word knowledge with the Dolch Basic Sight Word List, the Fry New Instant Word List, or the word lists that accompany the basal series. These lists are composed of high-frequency words that should be identified quickly in order not to slow the reading rate and interfere with comprehension. Sight words are taught as whole units. Later, these words may be analyzed in parts after they are known to help students recognize other words with similar components. This is known as analytic phonics and is discussed in the next section.

Teachers find that students have difficulty remembering the more abstract words included on many sight word lists. In a study regarding the learning of words with a high concrete visual imagery level as compared to words with low imagery level (abstract words), Hargis and Gickling found that high-imagery words were easier to learn than low-imagery words and were remembered longer. Studies by Jorm, and Kolker and Terwilliger had similar results, indicating that both good and poor readers' memories of words is enhanced by word imagery.[3] Classroom teachers experience more difficulty in teaching these low-imagery words, such as *was* and *the*, than they do the high-imagery words, such as *cat*, *mother*, and nouns that can be visualized.

Teachers also realize that words with similar shapes and sounds seem more difficult for the students to remember. McNeil and Keislar found that students had greater difficulty identifying test words that were similar in letter configuration.[4] Thus, teachers should provide much variety and repetition in helping students learn low-imagery words that are similar in sound and shape. The most common groups include words such as *who, what, where, was, when, were, the, this, them, then, that, there, these,* and *those*.

To assist in learning these essential but difficult words, teachers use many different strategies. King and Muehl found that the appropriate methods for teaching sight words varied with the similarity of the words.[5] Cues such as pictures were helpful in remembering similar words. The use of auditory or visual cues provided faster learning of the similar words, but had little impact on learning words that were not similar.

Goodman, Dallmann, Rouch, Chang, and DeBoer, Wood and Brown, Allington and McGill-Franzen, Adams and Huggins, and Hudson and Haworth suggest that sight words should be taught in the context of other words.[6] This idea is refuted by Singer, Samuels, and Spiroff, who concluded that "efficiency in learning to associate responses to graphic stimuli is significantly greater when the word is presented in isolation than when presented in sentence context or in association with a picture, or both."[7]

However, as teachers, the authors have found that students tend to remember the more abstract words better when they are within the context of a sentence. This technique of learning sight words combines sight word recognition with contextual analysis and places the word in the context of normal reading. This seems to be a more realistic way of learning sight words. In practice activities with these sight words, flash cards need the context clues of phrases or sentences with the word underlined for emphasis. *Was* and *saw* look less similar in *"I saw your dog yesterday."* When introducing new sight vocabulary, teacher-student discussions help the student focus on the word, assist in clarifying misconceptions of meaning, and tend to improve memory of the word. Using an inductive procedure to introduce a new word involves providing a sentence with the new word underlined. Students then provide their pronunciations and definitions of the word with the teacher raising questions to clarify their understanding, leading to the conclusion of an appropriate response. This procedure focuses attention on the word and aids the students in expanding their vocabulary.

Further research regarding sight word learning has investigated the correlation of the interest of the words with the speed of learning. Harris concluded that kindergarten children from low socioeconomic backgrounds learned high-interest words and words not of high interest equally well. However, Braun found significant differences favoring interest-loading of words for both boys and girls.[8]

In developing knowledge of sight words, teachers may consider the results of a study by Lahey and Drabman.[9] Using token reinforcement consisting of verbal feedback and tokens that could be exchanged for pennies, they found that the no-token subjects took about twice as long to learn the words as did the token group. This technique may be adapted to help students learn the more difficult sight words. In a study of the use of games to reinforce sight vocabulary, Dickerson found that games serve as better reinforcements than worksheets, and that those games involving the most movement were more effective than the more passive games.[10] Using these various procedures to teach and reinforce sight vocabulary will enhance word identification.

Teachers realize that most words become a part of the students' sight vocabulary as they become more experienced readers. Initially, sight word learning involves

Word identification strategies are developed individually, in groups, or with the total class as needed. Photo courtesy of Edward B. Lasher.

primarily the Dolch Basic Sight Words or some similar list, along with words from the students' environment; however, other words are continually added. Although there has been some debate during the last fifteen years as to whether the Dolch Basic Sight Word List will be useful as a valid core list,[11] Johns, Edmond, and Mavrogenes have found that this list still accounts for more than fifty-five percent of the words used in materials written for students in grades 3–9.[12]

Though research seems inconclusive as to exactly how sight words should be taught, teachers need to consider these findings in relation to individual student needs and develop instructional procedures accordingly.

Students need good visual discrimination skills in order to see likenesses and differences in the sight words. Moreover, it is helpful if the student knows the names of the letters, so that specific letter differences in words can be discussed.

Much practice is necessary to remember sight words. How much practice is needed for students to achieve "automaticity?"[13] It varies from student to student and from word to word.

In beginning reading instruction, teachers sometimes encourage students to focus on words by noting clues that distinguish the words. One such procedure involves noting word shape or configuration to call attention to unique features and to aid in distinguishing between two confusing words. This "crutch" may be useful for some troublesome words; however, it is not a primary strategy for teaching sight words. Similarly, colors have been used as clues for helping students note the difference in long and short vowel sounds, i.e. red for the long vowel sound and blue for the short vowel sound. This is not a good technique as students tend to rely on the color clues and when they see the words in print without the colors, there is no transfer of learning.

Many follow-up games and activities are needed to reinforce the initial teaching activity. Specific ideas are provided in table 8.4. Other word identification strategies such as phonic, structural, and contextual analysis are necessary in expanding sight vocabulary. The best strategy for expanding and reinforcing sight vocabulary is practice—read—Read—READ! As Durkin suggests, "a sizeable sight vocabulary is one of the most important instructional outcomes in the beginning years."[14]

Phonic Analysis

Phonics is the association of phonemes or sounds with graphemes or symbols. Since the publication of *Why Johnny Can't Read* and *Learning to Read: The Great Debate*, both teachers and the public have renewed their interest in phonics instruction.[15] Prior to this, instruction in the word identification skills had turned from phonics to the look-say or sight method. The basic issue in the debate over the teaching of word identification was not whether to teach phonics, but rather whether beginning reading should be taught through the use of synthetic or analytic phonics. As discussed in chapter 6, analytic phonics begins by teaching an entire word and then teaching the sounds within the word. Synthetic phonics is taught by presenting the isolated sounds in the word and blending them to form the entire word.

The findings of Chall's research indicated that a mode-emphasis method using intensive synthetic phonics produced better results than the teaching of analytic phonics. Similar findings were reported by Bond and Dykstra in the First Grade Studies.[16] However, further follow-up research by Dykstra showed that by the second grade the students taught through a synthetic method were not superior in reading comprehension.[17]

Becoming a Nation of Readers, a report from the Commission on Reading, has provided the latest wave of interest in phonics. The two recommendations regarding phonics instruction were the only recommendations made about word identification instruction; thus, many interpreted the report to suggest a return to structured phonics instruction and the exclusion of other word identification skills. The recommendations are:

- Teachers of beginning reading should present well-designed phonics instruction.
- Reading primers should be interesting and comprehensive, and give children opportunities to apply phonics.[18]

The authors warn against such a literal interpretation of the recommendations of this report and strongly urge teachers to aid students in using a variety of techniques in identifying words.

Regardless of the method used for teaching phonics, the teacher must be cognizant of the research regarding what should be taught. Although basal materials and phonics work texts present some organization of phonics skills, there is no one "best" sequence or hierarchy.

Each reading material or basal reading series has its own philosophy about phonics instruction. An analytic approach is used in some materials while others present synthetic phonics. Some present phonics instruction as a part of the readiness or preprimer materials while other materials do not introduce phonics until the first reader. There is also a discrepancy as to how much is introduced at each level and whether consonants or vowels (long or short) are presented first. In considering the development of phonics skills, Boyd found that the most rapid growth in phonics was at the second and third grades, while development at the higher grades was slower.[19] Thus, some sequence for teaching phonic analysis must be followed during the first two or three years of school to provide continuity of approach and instruction.

Note that students at the upper levels not only learn phonics at a slower rate, but also seem to lose some phonics skills that were previously learned. Plattor and Woestehoff found that performance on tests of skills such as letter sounds and rhyming word knowledge seemed to decrease as the students advanced from grades three to six. Yet reading performance remained good.[20] This finding has significant implications for diagnostic-prescriptive reading programs and state testing programs. Students at the upper levels may reveal deficiencies in the phonics skills because they have already internalized them into their reading practices and have no use for the isolated skills. A need for prescriptive instruction is not always indicated.

In teaching analytic phonics, rules or generalizations are presented in order to assist the student. Clymer identified some 45 generalizations that were presented in reading materials. He found only 18 of them to be useful according to the specified criteria. Further research concerning these generalizations by Emans and Bailey had similar conclusions.[21] In a replication of Clymer's study with more recent reading materials, Collins[22] suggests that the generalizations in table 8.1 are appropriate. Spache identified 121 different phonics rules in the literature and found only 10 to meet the criteria at least 75 percent of the time. They are:

- Vowels—When *y* is the final letter in a word, it usually has a vowel sound. When there is one *e* in a word that ends in a consonant, the *e* usually has a short sound.
- Vowel digraphs—In these double-vowel combinations, the first vowel is usually long and the second silent: *oa, ay, ai, ee.*
- Vowel with *r*—The *r* gives the preceding vowel a sound that is neither long nor short. (True also for vowel with *l* or *w*.)
- Consonants—When *c* and *h* are next to each other, they form only one sound. *Ch* is usually pronounced as in *kitchen, catch,* and *chair,* not as *sh.* When the letter *c* is followed by *o* or *a,* the sound of *k* is likely to be heard. When *c* is followed by *e* or *i,* the sound of *s* is likely to be heard. When two of the same consonants are side by side, only one is heard.[23]

The usefulness of teaching specific rules has been further researched by Hillerich and Harris, Serwer and Gold, and Glass and Burton. Hillerich found that students taught vowel rules showed no superiority in word recognition and were, in fact,

Table 8.1

Generalizations Taught in Basal Reading Materials Grades 1–6

Generalization	Percent of Utility
Vowels	
—A vowel between two consonants in a word produces a short sound. The pattern CVC and CVCC produce the short V sound.	50
—Two or more consonants between vowels suggests that the first vowel represents the short sound.	95
—One vowel sound can be represented by many spellings.	100
—An *e* at the end of a word, and the only vowel in the word, represents the long *e* sound.	86
—In words with two or more syllables that end with letter *y*, the *y* usually stands for the long *e* sound.	93
—Two vowel letters can stand for one vowel sound.	77
—If the letter *a* stands for the long vowel sound, the letter *e* at the end of the word is a marker to indicate that in these words the letter *a* stands for the long vowel sound.	99
—The letters *ai* and *ay* also represent the long *a* sound.	83
—When *o* is followed by a *w*, the *o* and the *w* together sometimes stand for the sound you hear in *flow* and *how*.	99
—The two letters *o* and *a* together stand for a single vowel sound.	100
—The two vowel letters *ea* usually stand for the sound of short *e*.	77
—The two vowel letters *oo* represent one sound in the middle or end of a word.	99
—The letter *r* following a vowel letter changes the vowel sound represented by that letter.	93
—Unstressed vowels usually have the schwa sound.	100
Consonants	
—Two letters in the English language can represent one sound.	100
—The *ch* spelling for *ch* may occur at the beginning, middle, or end but *tch* comes generally at the end of the word and the *t* in the middle of the word.	
ch for ch—beginning, middle, end	99
tch for ch—end	82
t for ch—middle	88
—The letter *c* can represent two sounds. The sound of *s* as in celery and *k* as in came.	98
—The letter *g* is followed by *e, i,* or *y* usually stands for the sound heard in gem. When *g* is followed by *a, o,* or *u* it usually stands for the sound heard in game.	
g followed by e, i, or y	84
g followed by a, o, or u	90
—The letter *qu* represents the sound heard in quite.	94
—A consonant cluster is two or more consonant letters commonly blended.	95
—Digraphs consist of two letters that represent one sound.	91
—The *c* spelling and the *k* spelling for *ck* may appear at the beginning, middle, or end of a word, while the *ck* may appear at the middle or end.	
c/k for ck—beginning, middle, end	100
ck for ck—middle, end	100
Syllabication	
—The number of vowel sounds in a word represent the number of syllables found in that word.	100
—A word with a vowel followed by two consonant letters and another vowel letter, the syllables are usually divided between the two consonants.	86
—A word has a vowel followed by a single consonant letter and another vowel letter is usually divided after the first vowel letter. The first vowel letter represents the long sound.	65
—When the second syllable of a word ends in *-le*, the word is divided between the vowel and the consonant preceding the *-le*.	33

Martha D. Collins, "Evaluating Basals: Do They Teach Phonics Generalizations?" Evaluation in Reading-Learning-Teaching-Administering, *Sixth Yearbook of the American Reading Forum*. Muncie, IN: Ball State University Press, 1986.

inferior in reading comprehension when compared with students who had been taught first to discriminate short and long vowel sounds. Harris, Serwer and Gold suggest a negative correlation between the time devoted to instruction in phonics and the performance in comprehension. In addition, the second- and fifth-grade students in Glass and Burton's study made practically no use of phonics rules in decoding unfamiliar words; yet the teaching of these rules continues to be a major portion of the reading instruction in many schools.[24]

As reading educators have analyzed the findings of research in phonics, they have realized the importance of the work of the linguists. Although many of the phonics generalizations seem to be relatively useless in decoding the English language, Hanna and Moore found English to be 86.9 percent phonetic.[25] Linguists approach the teaching of decoding through the association of letter patterns with sound patterns. Individual sounds are not analyzed as in traditional phonics. Additionally, linguists are concerned with the language process involved in decoding words, rather than just the sounds and pronunciation of words. Decoding, as defined by the linguist, includes meaning.

Research by linguists regarding the teaching of phoneme-grapheme correspondences is extensive. Bloomfield and Barnhart suggested that the beginning reader should be given material designed for teaching the orthographic-phonic regularities of English and that irregular relationships should be introduced later.[26] Contrary to this belief, Levin and Watson, and Williams have suggested that multiple phoneme-grapheme correspondences should be introduced early in reading instruction in order to develop a more useful problem-solving approach to reading.[27]

Research in the areas of phonics and linguistics is quite extensive. As linguists and reading specialists work together, the vast amount of knowledge regarding the teaching of sound-symbol relationships is being translated into classroom practice. With renewed emphasis on phonics instruction, textbook publishers and researchers have incorporated the ideas of linguists into materials to help the beginning reader develop more successful word identification skills.

Regardless of approach, phonics, as all other reading skills, should be taught **directly** through teacher demonstration of how the strategy is used. Specifically, as teachers introduce new vocabulary words, a system of decoding should be taught. Show how the vowel sounds are analyzed, the ways the consonants and vowels work together to represent various sounds, and how phonic analysis is used with other word identification skills to decode a new word. The learning of phonics should be a realistic process, developed through the application of appropriate principles as needed to decode words.

Structural Analysis

Structural analysis relies on the use of word elements or parts to aid in recognizing unknown words. Skills such as syllabication, prefixes, suffixes, contractions, and compound words are included in this area. Structural analysis differs from phonic analysis in that larger meaningful units or morphemes are dealt with by critically examining the structure of the word.

As in other areas of word identification, research is inconclusive. The skill area that has received the most attention is syllabication. In the studies done by Clymer, Emans, and Bailey, eight generalizations were identified that related to syllabication. Six of these met the criteria of 75 percent usefulness:

- In most two-syllable words, the first syllable is accented.
- If *a, in, re, ex, de,* or *be* is the first syllable in a word, it is usually unaccented.
- In most two-syllable words that end in a consonant followed by y, the first syllable is accented.
- If the last syllable of a word ends in *le,* the consonant preceding the *le* usually begins the last syllable.
- When the first vowel element in a word is followed by *th, ch,* or *sh,* these symbols are not broken when the word is divided into syllables and may go with either the first or second syllable.
- When the last syllable is the sound *r,* it is unaccented.[28]

In a review of current basal reading materials, Collins found these principles of syllabication to exist in at least three of the five series reviewed.

- The number of vowel sounds in the word represent the number of syllables found in that word.
- When the second syllable of a word ends in *le,* the two syllables are divided between the vowel and the consonant preceding the *le.* (Clymer found 97% utility.)
- When a word has a vowel followed by a single consonant letter and another vowel letter, divide the word after the first vowel letter. (Clymer found 44% utility.)
- When a word has a vowel followed by two consonants and another vowel, the syllables are usually divided between the two consonants. (Clymer found 72% utility.)[29]

Syllabication seems to be a skill that is better used after the student can pronounce the word, rather than as an aid in pronunciation.[30] Courtney reinforces this belief as he notes that syllabication principles are of decreasing value above the elementary grades, because of the increase in exceptions.[31] Canney and Schreiner found that intensive instruction in syllabication did not improve the word attack or reading comprehension skills of second graders, although the students could verbalize and apply the syllabication principles being taught.[32]

Additional questions are raised regarding the use of syllabication as a word recognition device, after reviewing a study by Marzano et al.[33] Comparing gains in syllabication and comprehension in middle school students, the authors found little correlation.

Harris and Sipay believe that syllabication knowledge can provide students with some guidelines for dividing polysyllabic words into units that can be analyzed phonetically.[34] Gleitman and Rozin advocate the use of the syllable as a unit for initial acquisition in reading, although this idea is not supported by psycholinguists such as Goodman.[35]

In considering syllabication, one must also address the use of accents. Winkley studied the various accent generalizations and identified seven general conclusions that apply to multisyllabic words.[36] Harris and Sipay identify only two accent generalizations as important for teaching:

- Usually accent the first syllable in a two-syllable word.
- Affixes are usually not accented.

They further suggest that the good reader primarily uses trial and error in determining the appropriate syllable to accent.[37]

In research regarding other structural analysis skills, Spache questions the teaching of isolated prefixes, suffixes, and roots, in that these units vary within the context of the word, and students seem to use these analytic skills infrequently.[38] Thus, it is suggested that they be taught primarily as visual units or letter clusters.

Schell and McFeely have reviewed the various areas of structural analysis and caution teachers that these skills must be taught in a realistic reading situation, rather than as isolated or independent rules.[39]

The instructional sequence of structural analysis skills in reading materials is organized in many different ways. One possible sequence is: 1) inflectional endings, 2) compound words, 3) prefixes, 4) suffixes, and 5) contractions. Of course, within each of these categories the subcomponents are outlined to move from the most frequently used word parts to the least frequent ones at higher grade levels. Such an organization of the structural analysis skills provides some assurance that all areas will be addressed. However, teachers must use their judgment to be sure that words containing the components being taught are included in the reading material. Teacher's manuals that accompany reading materials frequently present structural analysis units as isolated features and provide the student with no application in the text material read for that lesson. These skills assist students in decoding some unfamiliar words, but will be useful only to the extent that they are taught through application in context.

Contextual Analysis

Contextual analysis is defined by Spache as the ability "to determine word recognition and word meaning by the position or function of a word in a familiar sentence pattern."[40] This is the one area of word identification about which there is no debate. Emans identifies four uses of context clues in word recognition:

1. To help children remember words that they may have forgotten.
2. To use with other word-recognition skills such as phonics and structural analysis to check the accuracy of words.

3. To assist in the rapid recognition of words by anticipating from other words.
4. To aid in the correct pronunciation of words with multiple meanings and pronunciations.[41]

While other word identification skills seem to become less useful as the reader matures, the contextual analysis skills become more valuable. Spache concludes that adult readers use letter sounds or word structure very little and rely on contextual analysis as their main tool for understanding strange words.[42] Goodman found that while first-grade students used context to some extent to recognize words, third-graders greatly increased their use of this skill.[43]

The idea of using context clues to aid in word identification begins with young children as they use picture clues to gain meaning from their picture books. Later, they use the picture clues to assist in determining words. As students move into materials with more words and fewer picture clues, they look for other means of figuring out unknown words not in their sight vocabulary. Schwartz and Stanovich found that better readers tend to automatically look at other words in the sentence for assistance while poorer readers are more likely to look at individual sounds to analyze the word.[44] Similarly, Juel investigated the extent to which good, average, and poor readers in second and third grade identify words of varying difficulty by a text-driven (decoding or sight recognition) or a concept-driven (context clues) method. She found that good readers are predominately text-driven, while poor readers are concept-driven, and average readers fluctuate.[45]

Most research regarding context clues relates to the classification of the various types of clues. The most generally accepted classification is that of Ames, who has identified fourteen types of clues:

1. Language experience or familiar expression
2. Modifying phrases or clauses
3. Definition or description
4. Words connected in a series
5. Comparison or contrast clues
6. Synonym clues
7. Tone, setting, and mood clues
8. Referral clues
9. Association clues
10. Main idea and supporting detail pattern
11. Question-answer pattern in paragraph
12. Preposition clues
13. Nonrestrictive clauses or appositive phrases
14. Cause-effect pattern of sentence or paragraph.[46]

Using Ames's classification scheme, Rankin and Overholzer attempted to rank the clues from easiest to most difficult. Their findings suggest the order of difficulty as numbered above is 4, 2, 1, 14, 9, 8, 6, 3, 12, 11, 5, 10, 13, with 4 being the easiest and 13 the most difficult.[47]

Contextual analysis clues most frequently used as word identification aids are titles or themes of a passage, syntactic clues, semantic clues, or a combination of these clues with phonic and structural analysis clues. Syntactic clues are used by noting the function of the unknown word in a sentence. For example, in this sentence:

Courtney accidentally _____ on Clem's tail,

the unknown word tells what Courtney did to Clem's tail. Possible words that could be determined from the syntax are *fell, stepped, pulled.* By combining this syntactic clue with a phonic clue, the correct word can be pronounced.

Courtney accidentally s _____ on Clem's tail.

By combining clues, the student decides that *stepped* is a reasonable choice that fits the pronunciation and meaning of the sentence.

When students ignore syntax in reading, they miscall words and use inappropriate words that make no sense in the sentence. Comprehension is adversely affected by these errors. To improve the use of syntactic clues, teachers may use modified cloze sentences for instructional and reinforcement exercises.

Erin has a _____ , white cat named Snowball.
large   black   furry   foot

Through class discussions, students can identify various options for completing the sentence, with the teacher showing them how to select words that fit the structure and make sense in the context of the sentence.

Semantic clues relate more directly to meaning and often function in conjunction with syntactic clues. Syntactic clues deal with the arrangement of words in the sentence, while semantic clues depend on the other words in the sentence or adjoining sentences to assist in determining the meaning of the unknown word. For example, in the sentence given above the unknown word is easier to determine if a second sentence is read.

Erin has a _____ , white cat named Snowball. This cat is small but she feels like silk.

Teaching context clues seems complex, but these skills must be taught if students are expected to use them. Emans and Fisher have suggested some simple ways of beginning to develop use of context clues: (1) giving no clue except the context, (2) giving the beginning letter, (3) giving the length of the word, (4) providing the beginning and ending letters, (5) giving a four-word choice, and (6) giving all the consonants in the word.[48]

In reviewing the research in these various areas of word identification, it is evident that students must be provided with a background in using all the different word identification strategies. The importance of each of these areas is summarized by Frenzel in table 8.2.

Table 8.2

Four Word Recognition Approaches: Their Dependences, Uses, and Limitations

	Dependent Upon	Uses in Word Recognition	Limitations
Sight words	Visual memory of words and shapes. Configuration skills. Using high-utility words. Discrimination skills. Associating words and images.	Needed to build initial vocabulary. Foundation for other attack skills. Provides cues in concert with other strategies. Bank of sight words on individual basis.	Impossible to learn thousands of words by sight. Similar configurations are confusing. Detached from meaning. Visual memory inefficient in learning large numbers of words. Pronouncing isolated words is not true reading. Some may not learn well from visual approach.
Phonics	Knowledge of sight words. Ability to associate certain sounds with certain symbols. Synthesizing skills. Analyzing skills. Following a sequential development of decoding skills. Ability to use visual and auditory discrimination skills. Good speaking and listening vocabularies.	Used systematically to attack words, with general commonalities. Used in blending, patterning, and substituting skills. Used to manipulate sounds to obtain acceptable results. Used best in conjunction with other attack options. Operates in reading, spelling, and writing. Applied best to familiar words.	Generalizations may have low utility value. English is inconsistent; irregularities cause problems. Sounding letters in isolation is unrealistic and confusing. Laborious letter-by-letter sounding is slow; child can become overly analytical. Some may not learn well from auditory approach. Piecemeal identification tends to lose bigger meaning.
Structural analysis	Knowledge of sight words. Synthesizing skills. Analyzing skills. Visual cues to word parts. Good speaking and listening vocabularies. Knowledge of semantic effects of word parts. Following a structure-meaning sequence.	Used along with context, phonics, and sight words. Used in getting meaning via word parts. Aids in building words from known words. Operates in reading, spelling, and writing. Uses structure to determine root, inflection, or derivative. Applied best to familiar bases.	Generalizations may be erroneous or inapplicable. May get meaning without pronunciation. Not all words can be analyzed structurally. Cannot memorize lists of affixes. Some may not transfer structural analysis skills. Overanalysis tends to make each syllable a word. Cannot look for little words in big words.

Table 8.2

Continued

	Dependent Upon	Uses in Word Recognition	Limitations
Context clues	Speaking and listening vocabularies. Awareness and use of syntactical and semantical signals. Prediction and anticipation skills. Intuitive knowledge of language and its patterns. Comprehension skills. Visual skills.	Used along with phonics and structural analysis skills. Identifies words in a realistic and meaningful setting. Some words must be in context to obtain proper pronunciation and meaning. Might be first consideration in attacking an unfamiliar word. Forces thinking while reading; aids understanding.	Unknown words must be familiar. Guessing may produce incorrect words. Material may not have sufficient or strong context clues. Reliance on one type of signal may produce problems.

Norman J. Frenzel, "Children Need a Multipronged Attack in Word Recognition," *The Reading Teacher* 31 (March 1978): 627–31. Reprinted with permission of Norman J. Frenzel and the International Reading Association.

■ Prescriptive Teaching of Word Identification

Because word identification is so necessary in the development of comprehension, personal reading, and study skills, appropriate prescriptive instruction is needed to develop specific areas. To assist in the diagnostic-prescriptive process, table 8.3 reviews the diagnostic procedures that are appropriate for evaluating specific strengths and weaknesses in the various word identification areas.

The informal diagnostic procedures of the Informal Reading Inventory, observation checklist, and criterion-referenced tests are proper tools to be used in all areas of word identification diagnosis. In addition to these informal procedures and the formal diagnostic tools listed in table 8.3, the teacher may wish to add other instruments to the list. The procedures included are only those discussed in chapters 2 and 3.

In using the Informal Reading Inventories, *Gray Oral Reading Test*, and *Reading Miscue Inventory* to diagnose the word identification errors, teachers should note that there are no specific scores in the various word identification areas; teacher must use their knowledge of the skills and observe the types of errors made in oral reading.

Using the diagnostic data, the teacher then provides prescriptive instruction in the areas of need. In diagnostic-prescriptive instruction, direct instruction is imperative. The teacher spends time explaining the skill and working with the students prior to assigning activities that use the skill. This is especially essential in developing word identification skills, since students tend to learn the skills in

Table 8.3

Diagnostic Techniques for Evaluating Word Identification

Skill Areas	Procedures
Sight Vocabulary	*Botel Reading Inventory* (word recognition test) Criterion-referenced test *Diagnostic Reading Scales* (word recognition lists) *Durrel Analysis of Reading Difficulty* (word recognition) *Gates-McKillop-Horowitz Reading Diagnostic Tests* (words-flashed, untimed) *Gray Oral Reading Test* Informal Reading Inventory Observation checklist *Reading Miscue Inventory* *Slosson Oral Reading Test* *Stanford Diagnostic Reading Test,* Red Level (word recognition) *Woodcock Reading Mastery Tests* (word identification) Word Recognition Inventory
Phonic Analysis	*Botel Reading Inventory* (phonemic inventory test) Criterion-referenced test *Diagnostic Reading Scales* *Durrell Analysis of Reading Difficulty* (word analysis, sounds of letters, hearing sounds in words, phonic spelling of words) *Gates-McKillop-Horowitz Reading Diagnostic Tests* (oral reading test, knowledge of word parts) *Gray Oral Reading Test* Informal Reading Inventory Observation checklist *Reading Miscue Inventory* *Sipay Word Analysis Tests* (Tests 1–15) *Stanford Diagnostic Reading Test* (phonetic analysis) *Woodcock Reading Mastery Tests* (word attack test)
Structural Analysis	*Botel Reading Inventory* (phonemic inventory test—syllabication) Criterion-referenced test *Gates-McKillop-Horowitz Reading Diagnostic Tests* (oral reading test, syllabication test) *Gray Oral Reading Test* Informal Reading Inventory Observation checklist *Reading Miscue Inventory* *Sipay Word Analysis Tests* (test 16—contractions) *Stanford Diagnostic Reading Test,* Green, Brown, Blue Levels (structural analysis)
Contextual Analysis	Cloze procedure test Criterion-referenced test *Gray Oral Reading Test* Informal Reading Inventory Observation checklist *Reading Miscue Inventory*

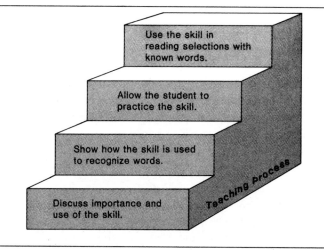

Figure 8.2
Steps in Teaching
Word Identification
Skills

The steps shown in the figure (bottom to top):
- Discuss importance and use of the skill.
- Show how the skill is used to recognize words.
- Allow the student to practice the skill.
- Use the skill in reading selections with known words.

Teaching process

isolation and are unable to use them in reading materials because they do not understand how to transfer skill knowledge from the worksheet to a written selection. This problem can be dealt with by using carefully planned instructional procedures:

Discuss the skill with students, explaining how it is used in determining an unknown word. For example, in teaching contractions, explain that shortened word forms are used in reading just as in speaking. Use a conversation with the students to note the contractions.

Show students how to use the skill in decoding words. Using the contractions from the conversation, the teacher could write the abbreviated form of the word and the two complete words to show how to recognize the contraction.

Provide opportunities for students to develop the skill. Games, worksheets, and various group activities are ways to provide practice in developing the skill.

Arrange occasions for students to use the skill in the context of a reading selection. The teacher may need to remind students of the appropriate skill to use in the situation; however, the skill is not mastered until students have it at their command for application when needed.

Singer identified ten principles of teaching word identification:

1. Proceed from the familiar to the unfamiliar.
2. Help the student become independent in using word identification skills.
3. Teach a variety of ways to identify words.
4. Provide instruction in analyzing new words and much repetition to learn the skill.
5. Use interesting ways to practice learning new words.
6. Use variety in the drill exercises.
7. Let the students know as they make progress.

8. Maximize the probability of success in each lesson.
9. Coordinate instruction among teachers when working with the same student.
10. Follow a sequence of skills in developing word identification skills.[49]

As teachers work with students in using the various word identification strategies, the focus needs to be on using appropriate strategies as the situation dictates. For example, one possible procedure which may facilitate such an integrated use of the various word identification strategies is:

1. Look at the word to see if it is a part of your sight vocabulary.
2. If not, look at the first letter or letters to see if this phonic analysis along with the use of context trigger a pronunciation.
3. Think about the type of word that would complete this sentence. Is it the name of something? Is it a describing word? Is it an action word? Think of words which fit this category and begin with this sound.
4. Look at the vowel. How many vowels are in the word? In a short word, one vowel at the beginning of a word or between two consonants usually represents a short vowel sound. One vowel at the end of a word usually represents the long sound. When two vowels are together, try the long sound of the first vowel—if that doesn't sound right, then try the short sound. Teach students to use the generalizations which are most frequently correct!
5. Consider the ending sound. Blend the beginning sound, vowel sound(s), and ending sound to see if a sensible word is produced.
6. If not, try the other sound of the vowel. Again blend the sound to see if the new attempt makes sense in the context.
7. While the above steps usually work well with short words, multisyllabic words require the use of other strategies. Identify the base word using the above procedures to decode it appropriately. Then look at the prefix, suffix, or inflectional ending. Pronounce the base word plus the affix.
8. If these steps don't result in an appropriate pronunciation, skip the word and continue to read for the meaning. If you are reading aloud, ask the teacher for assistance. REMEMBER: Meaning is the important aspect of reading—every word does not have to be pronounced exactly as long as the reader understands the message the writer is trying to convey.

Table 8.4 gives specific suggestions for developing the different word identification skills. These ideas are to aid the teacher in providing reinforcement as prescriptive instruction is given for specific word identification skill needs.

The diagnostic procedures and prescriptive teaching ideas included in the preceding tables are suggested to assist the classroom teacher in providing instruction in word identification to meet each student's needs. Teachers must always remember that students need to know a variety of word identification techniques in order to analyze unfamiliar words in reading. Thus, there is no one best way of analyzing words; there is only a best way for analyzing an individual word in a specific situation.

Table 8.4

Word Identification Skills

Skill	Prescriptive Techniques
Sight Vocabulary	
Identify familiar words	Label familiar objects in the room such as chair, table, etc., then ask students to identify the familiar word in a sentence.
	Give students cards containing familiar words and let them hold up the cards when an object or action is shown by another student.
Identify basic sight words in context	Use a tape recorder or machine such as a Language Master with cards containing the sight words and ask the student to record the words. The pronunciation can be checked with another tape or the instruction channel of the Language Master.
	Give students a flannel board with cards containing the sight words in a sentence. Let a student put a card on the board and another student pronounce the word and use it in another sentence.
Phonic Analysis	
Reproduce from memory upper- and lower-case letter symbols	Select one student to be the "letter caller." Ask this student to call the letter and the others to write the designated letter on their individual slates (made from cardboard sprayed with black enamel) or paper.
	Write the upper- or lower-case letter form on the board and ask students to write the form not given by the teacher.
Associate concept of consonants with appropriate letters	Tape *A-B-C* letter strips to the floor and ask a student to toss a bean bag on a consonant.
	Place each letter of the alphabet in upper- and lower-case form on individual squares of paper. Ask students to place all of the consonants in a jar.
Associate concept of vowels with appropriate letters	Ask designated students to hold up individual letter cards. When the letter card contains a vowel the group stands up.
	Play a card game similar to "Old Maid," using cards containing vowels. One card should contain a consonant. The student left with this card is the "Vowel Villain."
Associate sounds and symbols for initial, medial, and final consonant sounds	Pronounce a word and ask students to write the letter or another word containing the designated sound in a given position.
	Use unfamiliar or nonsense words and ask students to pronounce a part of the word or the entire word. This may be done as a game with points given for each correct response.
Recognize sounds and symbols of variant consonant patterns	Give students small cards containing the variant consonant patterns. Have them group patterns that represent the same sounds and label the patterns with the sound.
	Pronounce a word containing a designated sound represented by a variant consonant pattern such as sig*n* /n/. Ask the students to name other words containing this variant pattern or other variant patterns representing the /n/ such as *know*.
Associate sounds and symbols for initial, medial, and final long and short vowel patterns	Use words containing a certain vowel sound. Ask students to identify the vowel and vowel sound prior to pronouncing the word. Then give an unfamiliar or nonsense word containing the same sound and ask students to pronounce the word.
	Give students three word cards and a clue, such as "The word I am thinking of has a long *a* sound." Then ask a student to select the word or words that fit the clue. That student may then give a clue to the next student.
Recognize sounds and symbols of variant vowel patterns	Play a game whereby a vowel sound is given and students identify words containing the vowel sound spelled in different ways.
	Ask students to hold cards representing the various vowel sounds. Give other students word cards containing words with variant vowel patterns. The student matches the word with the appropriate vowel card.

Table 8.4

Continued

Skill	Prescriptive Techniques
Phonic Analysis *(continued)* *Blend sounds to form words*	Begin with words containing two sounds. Give two students big cards with the appropriate letters. Ask the others to pronounce the letter sounds. As the two students move closer together, the letters are blended more closely until the word is formed. Pronounce the sounds that must be blended to form a word and write them on the board as they are pronounced. The student must blend these sounds to form the word. For example, /c/ - /a/ - /t/ to form cat.
Substitute initial, medial, and final sounds to form new words	Give students a word such as *sit* and ask them to substitute designated letters in certain positions to form new words. This can be done by using letter cards and changing the letter as directed. Use a word wheel or tachistoscope idea and change parts of the word by turning the wheel or sliding the tachistoscope card. As the new word is pronounced points may be given.
Structural Analysis *Recognize compound words*	Select sets of words, some that form compound words and some that do not. Give the words to the students written as compound words, showing them how to look at the two known words to determine the unknown word. When the words are pronounced, ask students to identify the real compound words. Give students sections of the newspaper and marking pens. Ask them to circle each compound word that they find. The student with the most compound words wins the "Compound Detective Award of the Day."
Recognize contractions and original word forms	Read the students a story containing contractions. Each time they hear a contraction they may stand or hold up a word card containing the two words forming the contraction. Use a game board in which each square contains a contraction. When the student "lands" on the square, the two words that form the contraction must be given.
Analyze affixes	Give students selections containing words with prefixes or suffixes. Ask them to identify the affix that has been added. Then write several of the sentences, using the words without the affix. Discuss how the meaning is changed. Use sentences containing words whose meaning can be changed by adding prefixes or suffixes. After the student reads the sentence, ask that the meaning be changed by adding a suffix or prefix.
Recognize inflectional endings	Give students sentences in which the inflectional endings are omitted. Ask them to add the endings and tell why they are needed. Distribute magazines or newspapers and ask students to cut out or mark words with inflectional endings.
Divide unknown words into syllables	Write several unknown words on the board from a textbook or other reading material. Ask the students to identify the number of vowel sounds in each word. Then ask them to use the list of syllabication generalizations to divide the word into syllables. Divide the group into teams and let them select words for one another.

■ Summary

This chapter has presented many ideas on developing word identification. There are four major word identification areas: sight word knowledge, phonic analysis, structural analysis, and contextual analysis. Within each of these areas, there are specific skills to be developed to aid students in recognizing words.

Much research has been conducted to determine which word identification skill is most important in reading and which techniques are the most valuable in teaching the skills. This chapter presented many of the research findings and the conclusive evidence that there is no word identification skill that can function alone. Knowing various strategies, the students can select the appropriate one to use in a particular situation. Likewise, a variety of techniques may be used to help students learn the word identification skills.

The tables included in this chapter present a summary of the diagnostic procedures that were most appropriate for the categories of word identification skills and suggestions for reinforcing these specific skills. As with all skill areas in reading, the teacher first diagnoses areas of need prior to providing prescriptive instruction in word identification. Some general procedures for prescriptive word identification instruction were also given.

■ Applying What You Read

You are teaching in the upper elementary grades. Through diagnostic test data, you find a group of students in your class who have very limited structural analysis skills. What would you do? Design a program for them.

There are several parents in your school who believe that phonics instruction is the answer to all reading problems. How would you explain the importance of the various word identification strategies to them?

Three students in your second-grade class have very poor phonics skills. They also have difficulty with the auditory discrimination skills in prereading. What would you do about teaching the phonics skills to these students? What about the other word identification skills?

As a first-grade teacher, you have five students who are having difficulty with their sight vocabulary. They can learn the nouns and the more concrete words, but abstract words such as *the, and, what* give them great difficulty. What ideas could be used in developing a prescriptive program for these students?

Contextual analysis requires the use of the meaning of other words in the passage. As a sixth-grade teacher, you have some students who have poor comprehension skills and do not use context clues at all when they read. How could you help them learn to use context clues? How do you think this will affect their comprehension development?

■ Notes

1. Yetta M. Goodman and Kenneth S. Goodman, "Spelling Ability of a Self Taught Reader," *The Elementary School Journal*; Jana M. Mason, "Preschoolers Concept of Reading," *The Reading Teacher*.

2. Dolores Durkin, "An Earlier Start in Reading?" *The Elementary School Journal*; G. Plessas and C. R. Oakes, "Prereading Experiences of Selected Early Readers," *The Reading Teacher*; L. Price, "How Thirty-Seven Gifted Children Learned to Read," *The Reading Teacher*; Jeanne M. Burns, "A Study of Experiences Provided in the Home Environment Associated with Accelerated Reading Abilities as Reported by Parents of Intellectually Superior Preschoolers," Ph.D. dissertation.

3. Charles H. Hargis and Edward F. Gickling, "The Function of Imagery in Word Recognition Development," *The Reading Teacher*; Anthony F. Jorm, "Effect of Word Imagery on Reading Performance as a Function of Reading Ability," *Journal of Educational Psychology*; Brenda Kolker and Paul N. Terwilliger, "Sight Vocabulary Learning of First and Second Graders," *Reading World*.

4. J. D. McNeil and E. R. Keislar, "Value of the Oral Response in Beginning Reading: An Experimental Study Using Programmed Instruction," *British Journal of Educational Psychology*.

5. Ethel M. King and Siegmar Muehl, "Different Sensory Cues as Aids in Beginning Reading," *The Reading Teacher*.

6. Kenneth S. Goodman, "A Linguistic Study of Cues and Miscues in Reading," *Elementary English*; Martha Dallmann, Roger L. Rouch, Lynette Chang, and John J. DeBoer, *The Teaching of Reading*, 4th ed; Martha Wood and Mavis Brown, "Beginning Readers' Recognition of Taught Words in Various Contextual Settings," in *Reading Research: Studies and Applications*, edited by Michael L. Kamil and Alden J. Moe, *28th Yearbook of the National Reading Conference*, pp. 55–61; Richard L. Allington and Anne McGill-Franzen, "Word Identification Errors in Isolation and In Context: Apples vs. Oranges," *The Reading Teacher*; M. J. Adams and A. W. F. Huggins, "The Growth of Children's Sight Vocabulary: A Quick Test with Educational and Theoretical Implications," *Reading Research Quarterly*; J. Hudson and J. Haworth, "Dimensions of Word Recognition," *Reading*.

7. Harry Singer, S. Jay Samuels, and Jean Spiroff, "The Effect of Pictures and Contextual Conditions on Learning Responses to Printed Words," *Reading Research Quarterly*.

8. Larry A. Harris, "Interest and the Initial Acquisition of Words," *The Reading Teacher*; Carl Braun, "Interest-loading and Modality Effects on Textual Response Acquisition," *Reading Research Quarterly*.

9. Benjamin Lahey and Ronald Drabman, "Facilitation of the Acquisition and Retention of Sight-Word Vocabulary Through Token Reinforcement," *Journal of Applied Behavior Analysis*.

10. Dolores Pawley Dickerson, "A Study of Use of Games to Reinforce Sight Vocabulary," *The Reading Teacher*.

11. John N. Mangieri and Michael S. Kahn, "Is the Dolch List of 220 Basic Sight Words Irrelevant?" *The Reading Teacher*; Dale D. Johnson, Richard J. Smith, and Kenneth L. Jensen, "Primary Children's Recognition of High-Frequency Words," *The Elementary School Journal*.

12. Jerry L. Johns, Rose M. Edmond, and Nancy A. Mavrogenes, "The Dolch Basic Sight Vocabulary: A Replication and Validation Study," *The Elementary School Journal*.

13. S. Jay Samuels, "Automatic Decoding and Reading Comprehension," *Language Arts*.

14. Dolores Durkin, *Teaching Young Children to Read* 4th ed., p. 168.

15. Rudolf Flesch, *Why Johnny Can't Read and What You Can Do About It*; Jeanne Chall, *Learning to Read: The Great Debate*.

16. Guy L. Bond and Robert Dykstra, "The Cooperative Research Program in First Grade Reading Instruction," *Reading Research Quarterly*.

17. Robert Dykstra, "Summary of the Second Phase of the Cooperative Research Program in Primary Reading Instruction," *Reading Research Quarterly*.

18. Richard C. Anderson, Elfrieda H. Hiebert, Judith A. Scott, Ian A. G. Wilkinson, and Members of the Commission on Reading, *Becoming a Nation of Readers: The Report of the Commission on Reading*, p. 118.

19. R. D. Boyd, "Growth of Phonic Skills in Reading," in *Clinical Studies in Reading III,* edited by Helen M. Robinson.

20. Emma E. Plattor and Ellsworth S. Woestehoff, "Specific Reading Disabilities of Disadvantaged Children," in *Reading Difficulties: Diagnosis, Correction and Remediation,* edited by William Durr.

21. Theodore Clymer, "The Utility of Phonic Generalizations in the Primary Grades," *The Reading Teacher;* Robert Emans, "The Usefulness of Phonic Generalizations Above the Primary Grades," *The Reading Teacher;* Mildred H. Bailey, "The Utility of Phonic Generalizations in Grades One Through Six," *The Reading Teacher.*

22. Martha D. Collins, "Evaluating Basals: Do They Teach Phonics Generalizations?" in *Evaluation Reading-Learning-Teaching-Administering,* edited by Donavan Lumpkin, Mary Harshberger, and Peggy Ransom, *6th Yearbook of the National Reading Conference.*

23. George D. Spache, *Diagnosing and Correcting Reading Disabilities,* p. 219.

24. Robert L. Hillerich, "The Truth About Vowels," in *Insights into Why and How to Read,* edited by Robert Williams, pp. 63–68; Robert L. Hillerich, "Vowel Generalizations and First Grade Reading Achievement," *Elementary School Journal;* Albert J. Harris, Blanche Serwer, and Laurence Gold, "Comparing Approaches in First Grade Teaching with Disadvantaged Children Extended into Second Grade," *The Reading Teacher;* Gerald G. Glass and Elizabeth H. Burton, "How Do They Decode? Verbalizations and Observed Behaviors of Successful Decoders," *The Reading Teacher.*

25. Paul R. Hanna and James T. Moore, "Spelling—From Spoken Word to Written Symbol," *Elementary School Journal.*

26. Leonard Bloomfield and Clarence Barnhart, *Let's Read: A Linguistic Approach.*

27. Harry Levin and J. Watson, "The Learning of Variable Grapheme-to-Phoneme Correspondences: Variations in the Initial Consonant Position," *A Basic Research Program on Reading;* Joanna P. Williams, "Successive vs. Concurrent Presentation of Multiple Grapheme-Phoneme Correspondences," *Journal of Educational Psychology.*

28. Clymer, "The Utility of Phonic Generalizations in the Primary Grade"; Emans, "The Usefulness of Phonic Generalizations Above the Primary Grades"; Bailey, "The Utility of Phonic Generalizations in Grades One Through Six."

29. Collins, "Evaluating Basals: Do They Teach Phonics Generalizations?"

30. Ruth F. Waugh and K. W. Howell, "Teaching Modern Syllabication," *The Reading Teacher;* Ronald Wardhaugh, "Syl-lab-i-ca-tion." *Elementary English;* L. V. Ruck, "Some Questions About the Teaching of Syllabication Rules," *The Reading Teacher.*

31. Brother Leonard Courtney, "Methods and Materials for Teaching Word Perception in Grades 10–14," in *Sequential Development of Reading Abilities,* edited by Helen M. Robinson.

32. George Canney and Robert Schreiner, "A Study of the Effectiveness of Selected Syllabication Rules and Phonogram Patterns for Word Attack," *Reading Research Quarterly.*

33. Robert J. Marzano, Norma Case, Anne DeBooy, and Kathy Prochoruk, "Are Syllabication and Reading Ability Related?" *Journal of Reading.*

34. Albert J. Harris and Edward R. Sipay, *How to Increase Reading Ability,* 6th ed., p. 377.

35. Lila R. Gleitman and Paul Rozin, "Teaching Reading by Use of Syllabary," *Reading Research Quarterly;* Kenneth S. Goodman, "The 13th Easy Way to Make Learning to Read Difficult: A Reaction to Gleitman and Rozin," *Reading Research Quarterly.*

36. Carol Winkley, "Which Accent Generalizations are Worth Teaching?" *The Reading Teacher*.

37. Harris and Sipay, *How to Increase Reading Ability*, p. 379.

38. Spache, *Diagnosing and Correcting Reading Disabilities*, p. 223.

39. Leo M. Schell, "Teaching Structural Analysis," *The Reading Teacher*; Donald C. McFeely, "Syllabication Usefulness in a Basal and Social Studies Vocabulary," *The Reading Teacher*.

40. Spache, *Diagnosing and Correcting Reading Disabilities*, p. 402.

41. Robert Emans, "Use of Context Clues," in *Reading and Realism*, edited by J. Allen Figurel, pp. 76–82.

42. Spache, *Diagnosing and Correcting Reading Disabilities*, p. 404.

43. Kenneth S. Goodman, "A Linguistic Study of Cues and Miscues in Reading," *Elementary English*.

44. R. M. Schwartz and Keith E. Stanovich, "Flexibility in the Use of Graphic and Contextual Information by Good and Poor Readers," *Journal of Reading Behavior*.

45. Connie Juel, "Comparison of Word Identification Strategies with Varying Context, Word Type, and Reader Skill," *Reading Research Quarterly*.

46. W. S. Ames, "The Development of a Classification Schema of Contextual Aids," *Reading Research Quarterly*.

47. Earl F. Rankin and Betsy M. Overholzer, "Reaction of Intermediate Grade Children to Contextual Clues," *Journal of Reading Behavior*.

48. Robert Emans and Gladys Mary Fisher, "Teaching the Use of Context Clues," *Elementary English*.

49. Harry Singer, "Teaching Word Recognition Skills," in *Teaching Word Recognition Skills*, edited by Mildred A. Dawson, pp. 2–14.

■ Other Suggested Readings

Carnine, Douglas, Edward J. Kameenui, and Gayle Coyle. "Utilization of Contextual Information in Determining the Meaning of Unfamiliar Words." *Reading Research Quarterly* 19 (Winter 1984): 188–204.

Ceprano, Maria A. "A Review of Selected Research on Methods of Teaching Sight Words." *The Reading Teacher* 35 (December 1981): 314–22.

Durkin, Dolores. "Is There a Match Between What Elementary Teachers Do and What Basal Reader Manuals Recommend?" *The Reading Teacher* 37 (April 1984): 734–44.

Dyson, Anne H. "N Spell My Grandmama: Fostering Early Thinking about Print." *The Reading Teacher* 38 (December 1984): 262–71.

Eeds-Kniep, Maryann. "The Frenetic Fanatic Phonic Backlash." *Language Arts* 56 (November/December 1979): 909–17.

Ehri, Linnea C. "Movement into Reading: Is the First Sign of Printed Word Learning Visual or Phonetic?" *Reading Research Quarterly* 20 (Winter 1985): 163–79.

Goodman, Kenneth S. "What's Whole in Whole Language?" Ontario: Scholastic-TAB, 1986.

Groff, Patrick. "A Test of the Utility of Phonics Rules." *Reading Psychology* 3–4 (July–December 1983): 217–26.

Juel, Connie. "The Development and Use of Mediated Word Identification." *Reading Research Quarterly* 15 (Fall 1983): 305–27.

Juel, Connie. "The Influence of Basal Readers on First Grade Reading." *Reading Research Quarterly* 20 (Winter 1985): 134–152.

Nagy, William E., and Richard C. Anderson. "How Many Words Are There in Printed School English?" *Reading Research Quarterly* 19 (Spring 1984): 304–30.

Nagy, William E., Richard C. Anderson, Marlene Schommer, Judith Ann Scott, and Anne C. Stallman. "Morphological Families and Word Recognition." *Reading Research Quarterly* 24 (Summer 1989): 262–282.

Nemko, Barbara. "Context Versus Isolation: Another Look at Beginning Readers." *Reading Research Quarterly* 19 (Summer 1984): 461–67.

Rash, Judy, Terry D. Johnson, and Norman Gleadow. "Acquisition and Retention of Written Words by Kindergarten Children Under Varying Learning Conditions." *Reading Research Quarterly* 19 (Summer 1984): 452–60.

Samuels, S. Jay, Gerald Begy, and Chaur Ching Chen. "Comparison of Word Recognition Speed and Strategies of Less Skilled and More Highly Skilled Readers." *Reading Research Quarterly* 11 (1975–76, No. 1): 72–86.

Trachtenburg, Phyllis. "Using Children's Literature to Enhance Phonics Instruction." *The Reading Teacher* 43 (May 1990): 648–655.

Watson, Dorothy. "Watching and Listening to Children Read." In *Observing the Language Learner*. Edited by Angela Jaggar and M. Trika Smith-Burke. Newark, Delaware: International Reading Association, 1985.

West, Richard F., Keith E. Stanovich, Dorothy J. Feeman and Anne E. Cunningham. "The Effect of Sentence Context on Word Recognition in Second- and Sixth-Grade Children." *Reading Research Quarterly* 19 (Fall 1983): 6–15.

White, Thomas G., Joanne Sowell, and Alice Yanagihara. "Teaching Elementary Students to Use Word-part Clues." *The Reading Teacher* 42 (January 1989): 302–309.

Williams, Joanna P. "Teaching Decoding with an Emphasis on Phoneme Analysis and Phoneme Blending." *Journal of Educational Psychology* 72 (February 1980): 1–15.

9

Comprehension

Teachers realize that comprehension is an indispensable aspect of reading instruction, and is essential to a student's success in reading. They are also aware of the current research interest in reading comprehension. Although their school has a skills hierarchy and they have taught comprehension skills in an orderly progression from beginning reading through high school, these teachers are beginning to wonder what the research implications are for their instructional practices.

Therefore, this chapter presents the current research implications for comprehension instruction. It also seeks to aid classroom teachers in using their knowledge of the comprehension skills as well as the research to provide the best prescriptive instruction to improve students' comprehension. Because most materials and testing programs in reading continue to identify individual comprehension skills, a comprehensive list of these skills is provided, together with ideas to assist classroom instruction in reinforcing the skills as necessary to meet individual student's needs. Additionally, from current information on comprehension instruction the many new strategies are presented as other ways of developing comprehension. Also included are suggestions for using appropriate diagnostic techniques discussed in previous chapters. Some questions addressed in this chapter are:

What factors influence the development of comprehension?

How do the various taxonomies of learning theory relate to comprehension?

What does research tell us about this area?

What is comprehension?

How can comprehension be assessed by the teacher?

What are some ideas that may be used in providing prescriptive instruction in comprehension?

How is comprehension developed through prescriptive teaching?

As this chapter is read, the following terms are important to note.

Vocabulary to Know

Acronyms	Interactive model	Schema
Advance organizer	Interpretive skills	Semantic mapping
Cause-and-effect relationships	Literal skills	Signal words
Cognitive development	Miscomprehension	Story grammar
Comparisons	Organization patterns	Story structure
Comprehension	Questioning	Structured overview
Contrasts	Reciprocal questioning	Synthesis
Critical skills	Reciprocal teaching	Taxonomy
Discourse analysis	Relevant and irrelevant information	Text structure
Figurative language		

■ Factors That Influence Comprehension

The importance of comprehension in learning to read is seldom questioned. True reading is comprehending or understanding the printed word. Reading does not stop after a word has been analyzed and pronounced; the process is only begun. Pronunciation is evaluated on the appropriateness of the meaning in the context. As the meaning is understood in relation to the other words or ideas, connected discourse is formed allowing for the communication of information to the reader.

This, in turn, facilitates written communication between the writer and the reader. Because the primary purpose of reading is the communication of ideas to the reader, students must have the skills or strategies that will enable them to receive information from the printed page.

Unfortunately, some programs place so much emphasis on the development of word identification skills, especially phonetic analysis, that decoding the word has become paramount in the reading process. As a result, a student is able to pronounce words in isolation, but when the word is placed in context, many of these same students will have difficulty pronouncing the word and will not know its meaning. Likewise, many reading programs have placed an emphasis on the "mastery" of individual comprehension skills. The result has been students who pass tests on individual skills, i.e. cause-effect relationships, main idea, fact-opinion, but who cannot put these skills together and apply them as needed to understand what they read.

The concept of comprehension is somewhat more difficult to understand because we cannot observe the ongoing neurological processes. While we know that comprehension occurs, it is also necessary to understand how it occurs, and in some cases, why it does not occur. In contrast to word identification, which is more easily monitored, the secrets of comprehension are more mysterious and difficult to unlock. Why do some students exhibit more strength in comprehension than others? This is a question that has troubled teachers for quite some time. Obviously, there are many answers to this question, and yet, even with answers, a few students still do not comprehend well in spite of the teacher's best efforts. When examining this complex question, a closer look at students exhibiting weaknesses in comprehension is warranted. There are probably one or more factors interacting to create this difficulty. These factors have been studied by various writers and are summarized on the following pages.

Durkin identifies seven basic factors that affect ability in comprehension. These are oral language, intelligence, features of the material read, motivation, interest, familiarity with the content being read, and the relevance of correspondence between the dialect of the reader and that of the author.[1]

Harris and Smith identified six factors they believe are the primary determinants of reading comprehension. These factors include background experience, language abilities, thinking abilities, affection (including such areas as interests, motivation, attitudes, beliefs, and feelings), reading purposes and text.[2]

In addition to these sources, some of the factors outlined in chapter 7 that influence prereading also apply to the area of comprehension—intelligence and environment. The environmental factors can be further subdivided into sociocultural awareness, background of experiences, oral language, and interests in reading.

Because of the numerous factors that interact with the comprehension process, definite agreement cannot be reached as to one list that provides the exact reasons for comprehension difficulties. However, some of the more common factors that are generally accepted as contributing to comprehension or miscomprehension of information are discussed in the following pages. These are given in an effort to examine their impact on the comprehension process and to assist teachers in providing better comprehension instruction.

Intelligence is a critical factor in every area of learning, especially in comprehension. Recalling simple details from a story, while considered by some to be a lower-level comprehension skill, requires a rather complex thinking process. Inferential and analytical understanding often necessitate more intelligence in comprehension. A student must use deductive and inductive reasoning capabilities for comprehension at all levels; therefore, intelligence plays a key role in the comprehension process.

Other key factors, categorized as environmental, include sociocultural awareness, background of experience, oral language, and interests in reading. Sociocultural factors are extremely important to comprehension. Often students from lower socioeconomic backgrounds have had very little opportunity to familiarize themselves with printed material. Generally, verbal rather than written stimuli are used for communication, making it difficult for these students to comprehend printed materials with any depth of understanding. Another unfortunate aspect is that comprehending the printed page may have little or no status in some neighborhoods where little reading is done. An integral part of the sociocultural factor is related to dialectical differences. Many linguists have voiced concern that students using nonstandard American-English orthography, or divergent speakers, experience so much difficulty in reading materials written in standard American-English that comprehension of the printed material is virtually impossible. However, Gemake has suggested that the dialect pattern of nonstandard black English does not interfere in the reading comprehension process of the third grade black student. It does however, interfere with oral reading. Gemake further suggests that comprehension of complex sentence patterns is more difficult for students speaking nonstandard black English.[3]

Oral language is crucial to comprehension. In order to understand written words, they must be a part of the student's oral and listening vocabulary. This is, of course, the premise upon which the language-experience approach is built. In a review of research, Christie found that students have difficulty comprehending written materials that contain syntactic structures not found in their oral language. This is significant when instructing those who speak English as a second language, those whose dialect differs substantially from standard English, as well as language-delayed children who have been mainstreamed into the regular classroom.[4] The language experience approach as well as an intensive language development program are necessary to develop oral language to the point that it is not a major obstacle to reading comprehension.

A broad foundation of experiences is important as children enter school, since comprehending the reading material is often contingent upon having experiences related to the information encountered. An example of this is noted when an inner-city student is asked to read a story about a vacation at the beach, an experience of which the student has no prior knowledge. This lack of experience increases the difficulty level of the material and decreases the student's chances for success. Stevens found that prior knowledge is a significant factor in comprehension of information read by all ability groups of ninth graders.[5] Stahl, Jacobson, Davis, and Davis conducted a series of three studies that suggested that the ability of sixth graders to comprehend certain social studies materials was affected by prior knowledge and vocabulary difficulty.[6] Therefore, a variety of experiences are essential aids to comprehension. Information for which students have an established schema or extensive prior knowledge can usually be read more rapidly than material filled with new concepts.

Another essential factor is the interest level of the material. Assuming that the level of the material is appropriate, comprehension is better when a student is interested in the subject. Research suggests that passages of high prior knowledge and passages of high topic interest in relation to the reader's experiences have a significant effect on comprehension.[7]

Some materials are difficult for students to comprehend because of specific features such as vocabulary, the presentation of too many complex ideas, and the rate at which they occur.[8] Thus, related to the interest of the material, the written message itself must be considered as a critical factor affecting comprehension. Sentence structure and text structure, as well as the organization of ideas can enhance or deter a student's comprehension of information.

Purpose-setting, either by the teacher or the student, is another factor that facilitates comprehension. When students are aware of why they are reading, they derive more information and enjoyment from the selection.[9] Although this has been a common assumption about reading instruction, current research in schema theory reiterates the need to have students recall what they know about a topic before they begin to read about it. The idea of establishing readiness for reading is further supported by many studies investigating the use of advance organizers and graphic organizers for use in content reading.[10] Research has established the value in aiding students to relate their present knowledge to what they are expected to learn from new materials.

Another factor affecting comprehension is the reading rate. Teaching students to adjust their reading rate to the type of material read and to their purpose for reading will improve comprehension. Difficult material will require slower reading for better comprehension, while easier material will allow the student to increase their rate without impairing their comprehension.[11]

In addition to these factors, a study conducted by Zabrucky and Ratner suggested that reading ability affected the students' evaluation and regulation of comprehension.[12] This is an important point since cognitive monitoring by students is crucial to comprehension.

Many factors affecting comprehension also influence other areas of reading; therefore, the primary purpose of this discussion is to focus the teacher's attention on the major factors involved in comprehension. When students do not read well because of one or more of these factors, frustration and hostility result. Consideration of these factors in the diagnostic-prescriptive process will assist in providing appropriate comprehension instruction.

■ Relating Taxonomies and Comprehension

Comprehension is a thinking process, a process that Carey suggests is difficult to define, is not easily quantified, is ultimately not precisely observable, and that begets other processes.[13] For many years comprehension has been viewed as a process involving the development and application of a variety of subskills. These subskills were arranged in some systematic sequence according to various taxonomies of learning. The hierarchies progress from the lower levels of thinking to the higher levels. Frequently, teachers and materials are criticized because elementary grade students are not given the opportunity to develop their cognitive abilities as highly as possible. This is due, in part, to the questioning strategies used by some teachers. Often elementary students are asked low-level, literal questions that require only basic knowledge and result in one- or two-word answers. These literal-level questions force students to read strictly for main ideas, specific details, and other such information. In too many classes, students are rarely asked to synthesize and evaluate the information read. As a result, their thinking abilities are not developed to process more complex ideas.

Taba found that teachers tend to pour out information to students and, as a result of the low level of questioning, encourage them to recite this material back almost word for word. She felt that thinking was incorrectly perceived "as a global process which seemingly encompassed anything that goes on in the head, from daydreaming to constructing a concept of relativity."[14]

A later study by Guszak further substantiated the theory that levels of questioning used in elementary grades were primarily of the literal type. He found that recognition and recall or memory questions formed 78.8 percent of all questions in the second grade, 64.7 percent in the fourth grade, and 57.8 percent in the sixth grade. Questions at the higher levels such as translation and evaluation were used only 20 percent of the time and in many cases required only a yes or no response.[15] As a result of these and other studies, many elementary teachers are becoming more aware of the need to enhance their students' development in cognition by improving their questioning strategies.

While criticism has been voiced regarding the tendency to use more literal type questions than higher level questions, research has shown that asking higher level questions is not the more effective procedure for mastering factual or higher level learning.[16] Experimental studies found that the asking of recall questions resulted in better student performance on recall tests, with all classes doing equally well on tests that contained higher level questions regardless of the number of higher level questions asked during the classes.[17] With the confusion existing in this area, we suggest that teachers attempt to include all levels of questions in their instructional programs and assist students in understanding the processes involved in answering various types of questions. Indeed, Wixson found that students recall information based on the level of questions used during their instructional time.[18]

In an effort to help teachers improve learning, several important taxonomies, indicating how the learner progresses from the lowest levels of thinking to the highest, have developed. The primary purpose of these taxonomies is to enable the teacher to examine the learning process and to assist in the development of more appropriate questioning strategies for students.

Three of the more widely used taxonomies and their correlations to the three levels of comprehension skills suggested by the authors are presented in table 9.1. The taxonomies depicted were developed by Bloom, Sanders, and Barrett.[19]

However, current research is questioning whether these taxonomies do indeed reflect actual level of questioning difficulty for students. Pearson and Johnson propose another classification of questions. They suggest that questions whose answers are exclusively text-based are called textually explicit, while those that depend primarily on the text with some prior knowledge are called textually implicit. Their third category is scriptually implicit. Scriptually implicit questions rely more on prior knowledge with some input from the text.[20] Moreover concern is being voiced about the teaching of subskills as a means of improving comprehension. The discussions as to the levels of thinking as well as the teaching of subskills have divided reading researchers into three groups who debate whether the reading process is best described through a top-down, bottom-up, or interactive model.

Table 9.1

Relating Taxonomies to Levels of Comprehension

Levels of Comprehension	Taxonomies		
	Bloom	*Sanders*	*Barrett*
Literal	Knowledge	Memory	Recognition
	Comprehension	Translation	Recall
Interpretive	Application	Interpretation	Inference
(Inferential)	Analysis	Application	
	Synthesis	Analysis	
		Synthesis	
Critical	Evaluation	Evaluation	Evaluation
			Appreciation

Those who believe that reading is a top-down process suggest that the student brings more information to the page than the page brings to him. This prior knowledge is used to make good guesses about the nature of the text. The student reads to confirm or modify the hypothesis as well as to appreciate the style and ideas of the author. In the top-down model, the student starts with a hypothesis and attempts to verify it by reading. Theorists who support this model maintain that students even use this hypothesis testing procedure in recognizing words they sample a few features of the word and confirm its identity. In this model, the higher levels in the taxonomies are used by the students in unlocking new information that is often considered as lower levels of thinking.[21]

Another hypothesis of thinking is called the bottom-up model. Researchers who adhere to this position believe that the page brings more information to the student than the student brings to the page. This position is also referred to as text-driven, because the student begins with little information about the text, but as the print is sequentially processed the message is understood. The bottom-up model was the first used to depict information as a series of discrete stages that agree to a great extent with the levels in the learning taxonomies.[22]

Because many researchers have not agreed with either of these models as being descriptive of the reading process, particularly the comprehension phase, a third hypothesis has emerged: the interactive model. This theory is based on the work of Rummelhart; it involves the reader and text working in concert to reveal a meaning. Strange contends that the interactive model begins as the student first attends to print. Then prior knowledge is used to make decisions about the print; these are decoding and comprehension decisions. These, plus other sources such as past experiences, help the student derive a unique meaning. This idea of an interactive model using past experiences (concepts) combined with new information from the text, leads to further research in reading comprehension under the label of schema theory, which attempts to describe how old information is combined with new ideas to enhance comprehension.[23]

Schema theory is not a totally new idea nor is it a new name for an old idea; it is an old idea that has been expanded. Schema theory, as discussed by Mason

> . . . has two key components: (1) that skilled readers draw simultaneously on several different sources of knowledge as they peruse text sources ranging from letter information and words to high-level concepts and from interpreting facts to constructing strategies and planning how to read; and (2) that skilled readers construct progressively refined hypotheses about a text in order to understand, learn, or remember it.[24]

However, schema theory research offers more to aid in developing comprehension. According to schema theory research, the ability to infer and the nature of the inference depend on the reader's knowledge; even explicit text is interpreted in different ways when the student constructs meaning from the text as well as from his previous knowledge. Schema theory supports our common sense about reading: "the more we know before we read, the more we learn when we read."[25]

The concepts of taxonomies, levels of questions, and specific subskills in comprehension acquire a different meaning as these new research areas become better understood.

Mason, Osborn, and Rosenshine suggest: "General reading comprehension cannot be reliably subdivided into subskills, not even into the skill of deriving implicit meaning and the skill of deriving explicit meaning."[26] Sheridan argues that schema theory provides evidence that comprehension is a holistic process. Comprehension skills instruction is necessary, but in relation to the schemata rather than to isolated skills.[27] The way students organize information in their minds is an aid as they organize new information.

Different researchers have investigated the organization of text materials, using a procedure known as discourse analysis. By identifying the text structure of materials, students can be taught to identify various organizational patterns of text in order to better understand new information. Meyer identified five basic patterns: response, comparison, antecedent/consequent, description, and collections.[28] Although these organizational patterns have been identified from an analysis of students' writing, the concept of identifying the organizational patterns in text is not new. As early as 1917, Thorndike reported that one reason for failure in reading is the student's inability to organize and to understand organizational relationships in written materials.[29] In 1964, Smith and McCallister maintained that different patterns of writing exist in various content areas and serve as aids to understanding.[30] However, here too, schema theory research has provided additional insight into the use of organizational patterns to aid comprehension. Cheek and Cheek analyzed content textbooks and identified four organizational patterns commonly used in content writing. These patterns are enumeration, relationship, problem-solving, and persuasion.[31] Further, Collins found that by teaching those organizational patterns to middle school students, comprehension is significantly improved.[32]

Schema theorists suggest that if students were taught to recognize the organization of materials and if materials were written so as to follow the logical patterns that students understand, then comprehension would be a natural process of understanding. Rosenshine goes further to suggest that there is no clear evidence for distinct reading skills or for a skills hierarchy.[33] Readance and Harris have more cautiously considered those skills that seem essential to comprehension. They studied nine comprehension subskills—identifying main ideas, identifying outcomes, drawing conclusions, determining sequence, identifying pronoun referents, deriving meaning from context, using punctuation clues, understanding syntax, and affixes. One skill, affixes, was determined to be a false prerequisite for comprehension. Identifying outcomes, using punctuation clues, and understanding syntax were found to be necessary, but insufficient in themselves to assure comprehension. The five remaining skills were deemed to be associated with competency.[34]

Much of the current research in comprehension questions the teaching of comprehension skills and proposes various strategies for developing comprehension. Many of these strategies offer classroom teachers excellent alternatives for teaching comprehension to students with different needs. Teachers cannot ignore the need to view comprehension as the goal of reading instruction and as an integral part of the language process. However, neither can teachers escape the real world of state and local assessments of isolated comprehension skills and dealing with reading tests that continue to measure comprehension according to specific skill areas. Thus, the remainder of this chapter will discuss various strategies that can be used to develop comprehension, along with activities for teaching the specific comprehension skills.

■ Strategies for Teaching Comprehension

Comprehension Development

The comprehension skills are divided into three basic areas: literal, interpretive (inferential), and critical. The specific skills within the areas are listed later in this chapter and are summarized in appendix A. This section provides a discussion on each of the basic areas and furnishes some insight into the importance of the area according to research findings.

Literal Skills
Developing literal comprehension skills is an integral part of the total reading process. Some teachers believe that students must deal with these basic, low-level comprehension skills, developing proficiency in their use in order to progress to more difficult interpretive and critical skills. Such subskills as finding the main idea, recalling details, contrasts and comparisons, interpretation of abbreviations, symbols and acronyms, and several others, are classified as literal skills.[35]

Other subskills of particular importance to literal comprehension are identifying the main idea and reading for details. Dechant states that the ability to identify the main idea is essential to the understanding of what is written. Dawson and Bamman suggest looking for a definite sequence of details when learning to follow directions.[36] Without an understanding of these skills, comprehension would be very difficult. Organizing words in meaningful units such as phrases, clauses, and sentences further assists in the comprehension process.[37] The overall organization of skills into some meaningful order is valuable for teacher direction and to assure that students are taught the comprehension skills included not only in the literal area, but also in the interpretive and critical areas as well.

Interpretive (Inferential) Skills

Interpretive skills are believed by some to require a higher level of cognition and perception than literal skills. Drawing inferences and interpreting the language and mood of the writer become vitally important in comprehending the inner meaning of the material read. Interpretation involves examining more than the superficial aspects of a selection; it involves drawing conclusions, making generalizations, predicting outcomes, and synthesizing ideas, as well as using other inferential skills.

In order to facilitate comprehension at a higher cognitive level, the reader must delve further into the meaning of the material. A closer examination of language patterns and syntax indicates that these contribute to successful comprehension. This closer examination of language patterns will enhance the perception of the deep structure of a sentence.[38] Deese reinforced this concept by describing the syntax of a language as the bridge between the sound system and the semantic or meaning system in the language.[39]

The use of context clues in grasping the meaning of selections is an essential interpretive comprehension skill. Reading teachers once felt that the student's use of these clues was beneficial only to comprehension. However, Burmeister felt that word meaning was aided by the use of context clues, while Allen stated that a student's experiential background plays a major role in gaining information from material through the use of context. Emans found that context clues could aid students in identifying words they had forgotten, checking the accuracy of words identified through the use of other clues, anticipating words (thus increasing the rate of recognition), and identifying totally unfamiliar words.[40]

Another valuable ally in promoting interpretive comprehension is to understand the proper use of signal words. These conjunctions enable students to determine the meaning of sentences and passages.[41] Teaching students to interpret figurative language and puctuation are two additional skills that assist students in acquiring meaning from materials. Figurative language is most helpful to elementary students, enriching their vocabulary and improving their ability to gain meaning from materials they encounter.[42] Punctuation is frequently used to replace the intonation pattern in speech, necessitating the understanding of this skill as quickly as possible.[43] Teaching the proper use of punctuation as an aid in comprehension, while seemingly an easy skill to learn, certainly becomes an instructional challenge with some students.

Reading is a process used to gain information. Photo courtesy of Edward B. Lasher.

As with literal skills, many factors interact to influence interpretation of printed materials; however, every student needs the opportunity to develop these skills in order to go beyond superficial understanding to a deeper understanding of the meaning of that material.

Critical Reading Skills

Just as interpretive skills sometimes are more difficult for students to master than literal skills, critical reading skills are believed to require an even higher level of cognition than either literal or interpretive skills. Critical reading skills require that evaluative judgments be made about the material read and the reader's reasoning abilities be used.

The importance of the development of critical reading skills is further emphasized by the numerous efforts to reach a comprehensive, yet specific, definition of this area. Durkin views critical reading as both reading and reacting to printed material. Ives defines critical readers as those who, in addition to identifying facts and ideas accurately as they read, engage in interpretive and evaluative thinking. Burns and Roe state that critical reading is the evaluation of written material.[44] There seems to be little doubt that critical reading is the application of specific criteria such as validity, accuracy, and truthfulness in evaluating material.[45]

Teaching students to read critically is essential because of the various types of printed material that they will deal with in school and throughout their adult life. Perceiving bias, identifying relevant and irrelevant information, differentiating between fact and opinion, understanding fallacies in reasoning, and dealing with other situations that require critical evaluations of printed material form the basis for mature decision making. To enhance the learning of these skills, teachers should condition their students to read critically by expanding their knowledge, showing them how to question and use sound judgment in applying logic to all situations, then instruct them to reach a decision based on the analysis of all the data.[46]

Unfortunately, critical reading has not been emphasized as much in the lower elementary grades as it should have been,[47] even though research has shown that students at this level can read critically when given the opportunity and the appropriate instruction.[48] To include critical reading skills in the instructional programs, good questioning techniques, discussion, analysis of propaganda, and sound reasoning must be included in order to provide for a broader range of expression and ideas in the classroom. These techniques have been quite successful in improving critical reading skills.[49]

Perhaps the skill most widely used in teaching critical reading is that of analyzing propaganda. Since the Institute of Propaganda Analysis released its list of techniques for influencing opinion in 1937, teachers have taught these techniques extensively. Those techniques identified by the Institute are: (1) name calling, (2) glittering generalities, (3) transfer, (4) plain folks, (5) testimonials, (6) bandwagon, and (7) card stacking. Although instruction using these techniques has been effective,[50] the perception of propaganda does not ensure that students will always be able to resist its more insidious aspects.[51]

As the research clearly indicates, developing the ability to read critically is an essential part of comprehension. Unless this ability is developed to its fullest, students will be unable to distinguish between important and unimportant information, unable to detect bias, or may fall prey to a fast-talking salesman or to others who do not have their best interests at heart. Good evaluative judgments are based on good critical thinking.

Tips on Teaching Comprehension

The concept of using prescriptive techniques to provide instruction in the various comprehension skill areas is based on evaluating students' strengths and weaknesses in the skill areas. Several methods of evaluation are presented in table 9.2. Table 9.3 provides some techniques for implementing prescriptions for reinforcing comprehension skills.

As in other chapters, diagnostic procedures for evaluating each area are presented. In using table 9.2, please note that several of the instruments listed do not separate comprehension into various skill area subtests; therefore, it is necessary that the teacher evaluate these tests more carefully, using an item analysis technique if you wish to deal with specific skills. The instruments or procedures that fall into this category are listed under each skill area to which they apply, with no subtest specified. The informal procedures that are included, as well as the *Reading Miscue Inventory*, depend upon the teacher's questioning techniques for diagnosing the three categories of comprehension; thus, they are listed under all three skill areas.

In using various instruments to diagnose comprehension, great caution should be taken to avoid making decisions about the students' strengths and weaknesses in

Table 9.2

Diagnostic Techniques for Evaluating Comprehension Skill Areas

Skill Areas	Procedures
Literal and Interpretive	Cloze test
	Criterion-referenced tests
	Diagnostic Reading Scales (Instructional Level; Independent Level)
	Durrell Analysis of Reading Difficulty (Oral Reading; Silent Reading)
	Formal Reading Inventory
	Gates-MacGinitie Reading Test (Comprehension)
	Gilmore Oral Reading Test (Comprehension)
	Gray Oral Reading Test (Comprehension)
	Group Reading Inventory
	Informal Reading Inventory
	Iowa Silent Reading Test (Reading Comprehension)
	Observation checklist
	Reading Miscue Inventory
	Stanford Diagnostic Reading Test (Red Level—Comprehension;
	Green Level—Literal and Inferential Comprehension;
	Brown Level—Literal and Inferential Comprehension;
	Blue Level—Literal and Inferential Comprehension)
	Test of Reading Comprehension
	Woodcock Reading Mastery Tests (Word Comprehension Test; Passage
	Comprehension Test)
Critical	Criterion-referenced tests
	Group Reading Inventory
	Informal Reading Inventory
	Observation checklist
	Reading Miscue Inventory

comprehension, especially on the basis of too limited information. Niles and Harris[52] recommend that teachers consider the following when reading diagnosis is conducted in comprehension:

Method of measurement: Are the questions oral or written? Is a recall or multiple-choice format used? What is the level of the question? Is the question a quality question?

Instructional environment: Does the environment provide a quality setting for reading? Is reading done orally or silently? What is the teacher's attitude toward reading?

Text: What is the content and style of presentation?

Reader: What does the reader bring to the situation in terms of interests, experiences, and intelligence?

Each of these factors will affect the results of diagnosis in comprehension. For example, Wilson found that average readers in the sixth and seventh grades performed significantly better but there was no difference between the two groups on responses to factual questions.[53] Thus, test scores, especially in comprehension, should be analyzed to determine the validity of the information.

In providing prescriptive instruction in comprehension, teachers must be sure that they are instructing and modeling the behavior that is desired. Durkin has characterized the state of instruction in reading comprehension as basically no instruction.[54]

While there is not one way of teaching comprehension skills, there are some basic guidelines that should be followed:

1. *The teacher should introduce the skill by telling and showing examples of the skill as used in the reading situation.*
2. *The teacher should show the students how to use the skill in their reading.*
3. *Opportunities should be provided for the students, working together, to demonstrate their understanding of the skill.*
4. *Once the students demonstrate an understanding as they work with the teacher and peers, their individual knowledge can be evaluated through individual activities.*

For instructors who continue to be troubled by the teaching of isolated comprehension skills and who view the current research in comprehension as a glimmer of hope of being able to approach comprehension instruction as a language process, Strange offers seven uses of the schema theory that will aid in prescriptive teaching by allowing the newer ideas to be immediately implemented along with existing skills instruction.

1. *Prereading instruction.* Continue to motivate and provide purposes for reading. Add to your prereading instruction the notion of schema theory by helping students organize their related past experiences and make predictions about what will be learned from the new information.
2. *Vocabulary instruction.* Provide more instruction in vocabulary, helping students learn specific labels for their schemata.
3. *Analyze question/answer relationships.* Consider the lower and higher levels of questioning as outlined in the taxonomies, but also consider the text material to determine if, indeed, the question responses require literal, inferential, or critical thinking skills.
4. *Recall important details.* Noting details or recalling factual information is only valuable in helping students add to or change their existing schemata. Thus, minimal time should be spent on recalling details, and more time spent on helping students infer new ideas.
5. *Compare stories.* Help students learn to compare stories by looking at the plots, characters, setting, events, etc. Story grammar research indicates that stories should not be dealt with as isolated units but should be interrelated to note similarities and differences.

6. *Model/stimulate.* Modeling is an important instructional element in teaching comprehension. Teachers can stimulate students to think of the stories they read by talking about the story, comparing it to another, or predicting what will happen. This modeling of the comprehension process helps students realize that understanding information goes beyond the answering of isolated questions.

7. *Understand miscomprehension.* There are many reasons for incorrect or different answers to comprehension questions. Answers are not merely right or wrong; some answers that differ from those given in the teacher's manual may actually appear more correct when the students' schemata is considered. Possible explanations, which may help the teacher better understand miscomprehension, include:

- No existing schemata when students lack background in an area;
- Naive schemata when the students have only limited experiences to relate to the topic;
- No new information when a story adds nothing to the students existing knowledge, thus causing them to ignore the details because they are predictable and well-understood;
- Poor story that does not assist the students in integrating or relating the new ideas to their schemata;
- Many schemata are appropriate in some stories, which allows for different interpretations;
- Schematic intrusion allows a response to a question to come from the student's mind with no plausible line of reasoning;
- Textual intrusion is used to respond incorrectly to a question when students give a response based on information from the text but the response is unrelated to the question.

The idea of miscomprehension provides another way of looking at answers to comprehension questions, just as miscues have added a dimension to the analysis of word identification errors.[55] Both consider the student, his background of experience, and the impact of the error on the reading process.

These ideas regarding comprehension instruction should be considered when classroom teachers are planning their prescriptive teaching. Instruction by means of modeling is essential; teaching isolated comprehension skills must be related to practical situations in order for students to view reading as a helpful process that may be used to gain new information or for enjoyment.

Table 9.3 presents ideas for reinforcing instruction with each of the comprehension skills.

The preceding tables and table 9.3 present informal and formal diagnostic procedures, along with prescriptive techniques for each comprehension skill area, in an effort to facilitate the teachers' use of this information. Their purpose is to enable the teachers to use the activities and to develop additional activities that will enhance the effectiveness of the diagnostic-prescriptive reading programs in their classrooms.

Table 9.3

Comprehension Skills

Skill	Prescriptive Techniques
Literal Skills	
Understand concrete words, phrases, clauses, and sentence patterns	Give students pictures of objects or situations and words or sentences that correspond. Ask them to match the picture to the word or sentence it represents.
	List several words from a book, magazine, or newspaper for which students may not know the meaning. Begin a word chain that contains the word and a sentence on one side of the strip of paper and the dictionary definition on the other side. Each student may have a paper chain or a group may develop one to hang in the classroom.
Identify stated main idea	Ask students to read a paragraph and circle in red the sentence that tells what the paragraph is about.
	Let each student in a group read one sentence from a paragraph containing a stated main idea. The student who reads the main idea sentence and identifies it as the main idea is crowned "Mr. or Ms. M. I." for most important sentence or main idea.
Recall details	Give students a paragraph to read. Ask them to circle the details that answer who, what, when, where, and how in green ink.
	Use a newspaper article and ask students to underline details that tell more about the title of the article.
Remember stated sequence of events	Give students a short story to read that contains a sequence of events. Ask them to retell the events in the proper sequence. If an event is skipped, the group must begin the sequence again.
	Ask students to read a story that has a sequence of events. Cut the story into sentence strips, giving each student one or more strips. Let them reconstruct the story in sequence. This is especially fun with a language-experience story and big sentence strips that can be taped to the floor.
Select stated cause-effect relationships	Give students a story with a stated cause-effect relationship. Ask them why the effect occurred or what caused something to happen. For example, "Why was the store owner angry?" or "What caused the bike tire to go flat?"
	After reading a story containing cause-effect relationships, ask students to identify each cause-effect situation. Help them relate these to real life situations.
Contrast and compare information	Use two or more ideas in a story and ask students to tell how each is like or unlike the other. For example, compare a bear and a dog in the story.
	Give students two sentences in which ideas or objects are being compared. Ask them to underline the things that are being compared.
Identify character traits and actions	After reading a selection containing characters, ask students to act out designated characters, noting specific habits, behaviors, or actions.
	Ask students to read a story about a famous person. Then list the traits of the person that they think helped make him or her famous.

Table 9.3

Continued

Skill	Prescriptive Techniques
Literal Skills *(continued)*	
Interpret abbreviations, symbols, and acronyms	Ask students to list abbreviations or acronyms from a selection. Then write the meaning of each.
	Make a list of abbreviations, symbols, and acronyms that students find as they read. Develop a class dictionary or card file.
Follow written directions	Give students sets of written directions. As they follow the directions, a picture of some object will be formed.
	Ask students to read directions for playing a game, tell the directions to another student, and follow the directions in playing the game.
Classify information	Give students lists of items and ask them to classify or group them according to some appropriate title or heading.
	Ask students to take sentences from various stories and group them according to some topic. They may use some as topic sentences and others as supporting sentences.
Interpretive Skills	
Predict outcomes	Tell students to read a story to a designated point. They should stop and predict what will happen next or how the story will end. This may be done orally, as a written paper, or through illustrations.
	Give students a comic strip with the last frame missing. Ask them to predict how the comic ends.
Interpret character traits	After reading a story that contains different characters, ask students to describe how they think a character would act in a given situation.
	Use puppets and let students write a script for them based on the characters they have read about in another story.
Draw conclusions	Give students several sentences that could be the beginning of a story. Ask them to develop a conclusion for the story from the given information.
	After reading a story, ask students questions that require them to reach some conclusions from the information.
Make generalizations	Let students read a story and ask them to respond to questions that require them to make generalizations such as these: Do the people in the story like each other? Which ones? Why do you think so? Could this story have happened in our city? Why?
	After reading a story, ask students to decide when the story took place and to say why they think it happened at that certain time. They may also make generalizations about the story setting and characters.
Perceive relationships	Give students a selection that shows a relationship between two ideas. Ask them to identify the relationship such as the way a little girl acted at a party and the way her mother acted.
	Using several selections, ask students to identify the relationships of some similar ideas such as the time at which the various ideas occurred, or the different ways the characters responded to problems.

Table 9.3

Continued

Skill	Prescriptive Techniques
Interpretive Skills *(continued)*	
Understand implied causes and effects	Give students a story that contains the cause of a situation and ask students to decide the possible effects. For example, the law says that dogs cannot be loose in the city, but Mr. Jones refuses to put his dogs in a pen. What may happen? Why will these things happen?
	Give students a list of effects of situations and ask them to identify the possible causes. For example: the ship spilled oil; the house burned down; the boy got a new bike. Tell why these things may have happened.
Identify implied main ideas	Ask students to read a selection in which the main idea is not stated. Have them relate the main idea.
	After reading a story, have students decide on a good title for the story.
Interpret figurative language	Develop a class file of figurative expressions found while reading. Use these expressions to create a booklet that depicts the expression in a literal manner and in its intended way.
	Have students read a selection containing figurative language. Each expression should be underlined, and groups of students asked to discuss them to interpret the meaning.
Interpret meaning of capitalization and punctuation in a selection	Give students some sentences without capitalization or punctuation and ask them to read the sentences. As a group, add the correct capital letters and marks. See how much easier the sentences are to read.
	Give students two sentences that are alike except for punctuation. Discuss the differences in meaning. For example: "Vicki," said her mother, "is nice." Vicki said her mother is nice.
Understand mood and emotional reactions	After reading a story, ask students to identify the emotions expressed through the actions of the characters and the words used by the author.
	Ask students to read a poem containing emotion. Let some students act out the various lines, while others guess which line is being dramatized.
Interpret pronouns and antecedents	Give students several sentences containing pronouns and antecedents. Ask them to identify the appropriate antecedents for each pronoun.
	Select a passage containing pronouns and antecedents. Delete the pronouns and have students try to interpret the ideas and add the correct pronouns.
Understand author's purpose and point of view	Have students read letters from the editorial page of the newspaper and decide the writer's point of view.
	After reading a story, ask students to decide why the author wrote the story and how she felt about the topic.
Construe meaning by signal words	Give students a selection containing signal words, e.g. *first, last, in summary, therefore.* Ask them to underline each signal word and tell what the word is signaling in this selection.
	Play a game giving clues about signal words. Ask students to identify the appropriate signal word from a given selection. For example, which word in the last paragraph tells you the story is almost finished?

Table 9.3

Continued

Skill	Prescriptive Techniques
Interpretive Skills *(continued)*	
Understand meaning of abstract words	Ask students to circle all words in a paragraph that cannot be defined through concrete objects or actions. Then discuss the meanings of these abstract words. Use a list of abstract words such as democracy, freedom, love, and identify concepts that help define these words. See how many ideas students can list to assist a person from outer space in understanding the words.
Summarize information	Give students a story and ask them to summarize it to send as a telegram to a friend. Tell them that it costs 5¢ for each word used, so the message must be short but complete. Ask students to take a newspaper article and underline the key parts. They should summarize the article in several sentences to share with the class.
Recognize implied sequence	Use information from various sources and ask students to organize the ideas into a logical sequence. Give students a story that uses a flash-back technique and ask them to identify the actual sequence of events.
Use context clues to determine meaning	Use sentences containing comparisons, antonyms, or synonyms that can aid in determining the meanings of other words in the sentence. Ask the students to underline the context clue word and circle the word it defines. Select a list of multiple-meaning words and use them in sentences. Ask students to read the sentences and tell how the meanings are different.
Synthesize data	Use the summary statements from various sources and ask students to synthesize all of them to formulate their own statement. Give students some information regarding a topic and ask them to synthesize it to form their own story.
Critical Reading Skills	
Identify relevant and irrelevant information	Give students a passage that contains some information that does not belong. Ask them to mark through the irrelevant information. Ask students to organize some information from materials that you give them. In order to complete the task, they must discard some material that does not belong and use only the relevant information.
Interpret propaganda techniques	Show students samples of literature from various groups who promote their beliefs through propaganda. Identify specific parts of the material and discuss the ideas or possible reasons for the statements. Give students some statements that are fact and others that are propaganda. Discuss how they differ.
Perceive bias	Give students selections to read that contain bias regarding local or national events. Ask them to identify the bias and to debate the issue with another student of a different opinion. Use the editorial page of the newspaper or magazine and ask students to locate articles or letters that reflect a bias.

Table 9.3

Continued

Skill	Prescriptive Techniques
Critical Reading Skills **(continued)**	
Identify adequacy of materials	Ask students to review several materials and determine which is adequate to answer a list of questions that have been provided.
	Assign topics to the students. Give each four books and ask them to select two that provide the most information on the topic.
Understand reliability of author	Look at the information provided on the author and the topic of the material. Ask students to evaluate the qualifications of the author in terms of the topic.
	Give students a list of book titles and a list of authors with information on each. Ask them to match the title with the most appropriate author.
Differentiate facts and opinions	Give students a list of facts and opinions. Ask them to circle each opinion statement and tell why it is an opinion.
	Ask students to read several short selections on a topic and determine which is factual and which is opinion.
Separate real and unreal information	Give students a list of ideas. Ask them to identify the ideas that are real and to tell why they are real.
	Read passages to the students and ask them to stand up or clap when the information is unreal or cannot happen.
Understand fallacies in reasoning	Give students paragraphs that contain fallacies in reasoning, such as name calling, the bandwagon technique, stereotypes, etc. Ask them to underline the sentences that show these fallacies and to explain them.
	Use the advertisements in a newspaper to identify the fallacies in reasoning that attempt to lure people into buying merchandise.

Developing Vocabulary

Vocabulary is an essential element in the comprehension process. While this fact has been recognized for many years, its importance has been reinforced with the wealth of research in the last decade. As Johnson suggests, "The decade of the 1980s could be characterized as the period of rediscovery of the importance of vocabulary instruction to reading comprehension."[56] Students with adequate vocabularies find that understanding the meaning of material is generally less difficult for them than for students with inadequate vocabularies. Vineyard and Massey found this to be true even when intelligence was held constant; they supported a continuation of teaching strategies for improving comprehension through the improvement of vocabulary.[57] Although the importance of vocabulary to comprehension has not been questioned, there has been debate as to the impact of various types of vocabulary instruction on comprehension. Thus, Ruddell, and Carr and Wixson[58] have provided guidelines that may assist teachers in determining vocabulary development strategies that increase vocabulary knowledge as well as improve reading comprehension. The guidelines proposed by Carr and Wixson are summarized as follows:

1. Instruction should help students relate new vocabulary to their background knowledge. This helps vocabulary to develop a personal meaning that aids in remembering and improves comprehension.
2. Instruction should help students develop elaborate word knowledge. Strategies that help students develop more than a single definition of a word in one context serve to enhance vocabulary knowledge and comprehension by providing a broader knowledge base for more extensive learning.
3. Instruction should provide for active student involvement in learning new vocabulary. The age old strategy of locating the meaning of a word in the dictionary has not worked. Students remember what they are actively involved in learning—creating definitions of words from context is a more active process than copying a definition. Student-directed rather than teacher-centered instruction is important in vocabulary learning.
4. Instruction should develop students' strategies for acquiring new vocabulary independently. Effective vocabulary strategies help students become independent learners or strategic readers who monitor their reading.[59]

In teaching vocabulary to enhance comprehension, the understanding of concepts cannot be ignored. Sometimes concepts and the vocabulary to be learned are the same or the understanding of the vocabulary is crucial to acquiring new information. Regardless, concepts, vocabulary, and comprehension do not operate in isolation, they represent an interwoven process that results in learning. When vocabulary instruction is related to the concepts to be learned with the students' knowledge and past experiences incorporated, active learning occurs. Two similar strategies used to relate concepts and vocabulary are the *graphic organizer* and *advance organizer*. Ausubel suggested the advance organizer to help students establish a mental anticipation of the information to be read.[60] To establish this readiness for learning new information, short reading selections, verbal introductions, or graphic displays are provided to develop a point of reference for the reader to begin to associate prior knowledge with the information to be read. They serve to activate prior knowledge. Graves, Cooke, and LaBerge suggested using an advance organizer as a preview procedure for reading difficult selections.[61]

The graphic organizer is also used to help the student relate old information to new information or concepts. The information is usually presented as a chart that shows the relationships among the vocabulary and concepts. While the teacher may provide a complete chart to introduce the new vocabulary, greater learning

Figure 9.1
Graphic Organizer in Science

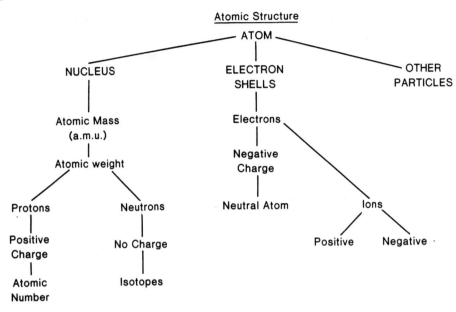

The following questions can be used to guide students in using the structured overview.

1. Of what basic components is an atom composed?
2. How were electrons discussed?
3. What type of charge do electrons possess?
4. What is a neutral atom?
5. Why is the term ions used in relationship to electrons?
6. Of what basic components is the nucleus of an atom composed?
7. What is the relationship between protons and neutrons?
8. Why does mass play a significant role in atomic theory?

Developed by Mary Hamilton, East Baton Rouge Parish School System, Louisiana.

occurs when a chart with limited information is presented along with the new words or concepts to be learned; through discussion the students are involved in completing the diagram. Figure 9.1 provides an example of a completed graphic organizer and sample questions that may be used to guide the students in understanding the information.

To further interrelate the learning of concepts and vocabulary, Gillet and Temple suggested the use of a *concept ladder*. A concept ladder is designed to show how the word is related to other words and concepts that are already known. Using several

Figure 9.2
Concept Ladder for "The Shoe"

A. Kind of?	B. Part of?	C. Function of?
clothing	*cover for foot*	*protection*
Shoe	Shoe	Shoe
leather	*complete outfit*	*made of strong material*
Kinds of it?	Parts of it?	Functions of it?
(name 2)	(name 3)	(what does it do?)
tennis shoe	*toe*	*protects foot from*
boat	*heel*	*sharp objects*
	sole	

basic questions, the students complete the concept as a small group to pool their knowledge or individually as they read.[62] An example of a concept ladder is given in figure 9.2.

Semantic mapping or *webbing* is another strategy for involving students as concepts and vocabulary are presented. This strategy visually displays the relationship among words and helps to categorize words. Smith and Johnson suggest following these basic steps in using this strategy:

1. Select a word that is central to what is to be learned.
2. Write the word in the center of the board.
3. Through class discussion, ask appropriate questions to elicit information that students know about this word.
4. Group the responses in appropriate categories and write them around this central word.
5. Ask the students to help label the categories.[63]

An example of a completed semantic map is given in figure 9.3. This strategy, which is similar to some graphic organizers, makes use of the students' prior knowledge while developing new vocabulary and concepts.

Another strategy that notes the semantic aspects of material for teaching vocabulary and concepts is the *semantic feature analysis* (SFA). Anders and Bos propose this strategy to help "students to learn the relationships between and among the conceptual vocabulary and the major ideas in the text."[64] Based on schema theory, which uses the students prior knowledge for learning new information, the SFA can be developed and used in the following way:

1. The teacher thoroughly reads the assignment to be given to the student to determine the major ideas in the assignment.

Figure 9.3
A Semantic Map

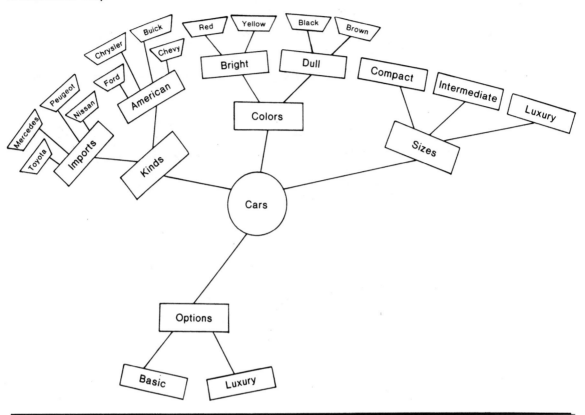

2. List (using a phrase or single word) the vocabulary that the students need to know.
3. List the words that represent the major ideas (superordinate concepts) and then those that represent details related to these major ideas (subordinate concepts).
4. Organize the vocabulary into a relationship chart with the superordinate concepts as headings across the top and the related vocabulary down the side. This relationship chart becomes the instructional tool.
5. Give each student a copy of the chart. As the topic of the assignment is given, provide a definition of each superordinate word, encouraging students to add information that involves their personal experiences or understandings.

6. Then introduce each subordinate term and discuss how it is related to the superordinate concept.
7. If there is a positive relationship, use a +, a negative relationship use a −; a 0 indicates that there is no relationship between the superordinate and subordinate idea.[65]

Again, this strategy involves the student in the learning experience and relates new learning to what is already known. Many strategies exist for developing vocabulary. Don't forget the importance of using context; this simple strategy is most frequently used by mature readers and requires no teacher assistance. Teacher reinforcement of this technique is done using modified cloze passages that omit select words. Teachers are only limited by time and their creativity. However, as we move from listing words on the board for students to locate in the dictionary or giving the student a guide to complete as they read, remember the criteria provided for evaluating vocabulary strategies—involve the students, use their prior knowledge, and help them become independent learners who use a variety of ways in discovering the meaning of words.

Building Schema

Previous discussions have been based in part on using the students' past experiences and activating their knowledge of an area in order to build vocabulary. But what about the student with very limited or no knowledge of an area? How is schema activated? Spiro and Myers suggest that one major problem, which has been overlooked in the research on schema theory, is that "One cannot have a prepackaged knowledge structure for everything!" They suggest "that the best approach for such a situation is to tentatively encode as much information as possible in as many ways as possible."[66] That is, students should be told that when they have no knowledge of an area and have no way of obtaining this knowledge, they should remember everything. Acknowledging that this may not be possible, however, they propose some new research questions.

In the meantime, what can the classroom teacher do to help students with few background experiences to build schema? Barnes, Ginther, and Cochran suggested that students taught schemata and given a specified purpose were able to learn new vocabulary from context significantly better than those students not receiving such instruction.[67]

Obviously, the best way to build these experiences is via firsthand visits or activities. Given that this is not always possible, how then do we realistically develop this knowledge that is so vital to comprehension? For some situations the use of an *advance organizer, graphic organizer,* or *semantic map* would help students learn from other students and visualize relationships. These strategies can also be designed to delve into the existing knowledge of the student to find something that remotely relates to the concepts and to build on this limited knowledge. Such probing requires teacher skill in questioning and leading a discussion, as well as patience combined with much positive reinforcement.

Student questioning is a good way of eliciting information from students to help them determine what they know and don't know about a word or idea. Through such strategies as *active comprehension* and *reciprocal questioning,* students learn to ask questions in order to gain more information. Active comprehension according to Singer requires that the teacher ask questions that elicit questions in return. Asking the students what they would like to know about a picture or an introductory paragraph that you read serves to arouse curiosity and involve the student in what is being taught.[68] Reciprocal questioning or ReQuest, designed by Manzo, is a similar procedure that encourages students to ask questions about their reading material. To use this strategy, the teacher may follow this procedure:

1. The teacher and students read silently the first sentence of the passage to be studied.
2. The students then ask as many questions about the passage as they can think of with the teacher answering the questions clearly and completely.
3. The teacher then asks questions about the same sentence with the students answering as completely as possible. In this way, the teacher is modeling good questioning strategies.
4. When these questioning sessions are complete, the students and teacher read the next sentence and proceed as before.
5. When the teacher feels that the students have a basic understanding about the information in the text and can understand the passage, they are asked to read the remainder of the passage.[69]

This procedure can be modified to use with an individual student or with small groups; and the teacher may use paragraphs instead of sentences for each reading.

Another student-centered strategy that aids in building schema is *reciprocal teaching.* Reciprocal teaching is based on teaching students to use four activities to improve their comprehension: question generating, summarizing, predicting, and clarifying. Teaching these activities involves the teacher providing explicit instruction, modeling, and giving corrective feedback for each of the activities. In this strategy, the question generating is similar to the ReQuest procedure outlined previously. Summarization involves allowing students to monitor their own comprehension by telling the basic information gained from reading the material. Following this summary, the students are then asked to predict what they believe will happen in the passage (text-based prediction) or what they believe will be discussed (content-based prediction). The students then read to prove or disprove their hypotheses. In the last activity, the students seek to clarify information in the text by discussing the information, the text presentation, unclear sentences or vocabulary,

Organizing information is a study procedure which needs to be taught. Photo courtesy of Edward B. Lasher.

or other points of confusion.[70] This strategy encourages continuous dialogue for teachers to diagnose difficulties that students are having with concepts and vocabulary due to inadequate schemata, and allows for students to learn from their peers and the teacher as questions are answered.

Teacher-student interaction with text seems to be crucial to building schema. The *Directed Reading-Thinking Activity* (DRTA) involves the student in predicting, verifying, judging, and extending thinking as teachers pose open-ended questions. Using logical stopping points in a passage, the teacher poses questions for which the student provides a hypothetical answer based on his general knowledge. Class discussion extends or limits these ideas with the student reading to verify the information. Reading is halted at the next logical stopping point with the student addressing the correctness of the hypothetical answer, and raising further questions and possible answers to be verified by reading the next portion of the passage. This process is continued through the passage.

These strategies, which use continuous teacher-student interaction, help build schema by developing a readiness for reading short portions of information, discussing and clarifying the information and providing additional pre-reading information for further reading. Presenting smaller units of information allows for the continuous schema development through discussing and reading as compared to the more traditional procedure of giving students information on a larger unit of material at one time. These small steps help students as they process new information and allow them to develop and relate their understandings as they build the schemata!

Using Text

Recent research in comprehension is filled with terms like considerate and inconsiderate text, text organization, story structure, and story grammar. Prior to this research, few considered the extent to which text could help or deter comprehension; if comprehension difficulties existed, the student was the problem. However, with the wealth of new information and a better understanding of the comprehension process, teachers, parents, and researchers are accepting what students have known—some texts are easier to read than others. This ease has little to do with readability level or student interest in the passage (although this is a consideration to be discussed later), but instead is due to the way the text is put together. Because all reading occurs with some type of text or material, teacher awareness of ways of teaching students to deal with text is an important component in developing comprehension.

Considerate text is organized to aid the reader in understanding the information. Sentences and paragraphs are put together for ease of communication, typographical aids are used, ideas flow in a logical order—the writer is considerate of the reader and communicates ideas as directly as possible. Inconsiderate text, on the other hand, appears unorganized and without a clear purpose. This type of text seems to be put together in haste without regard to communicating a message to the reader. As teachers preread materials that students are expected to study, they can readily identify considerate and inconsiderate text and plan instruction accordingly.

Various ways have been identified for approaching text analysis; however, one must remember that the structure of the text differs from one reader to another due to the individual's background experiences. Complex text analysis procedures have been outlined by Meyer, Kintsch, and Frederiksen, while Mandler and Johnson, Rummelhart, Stein and Glenn, and Thorndyke have developed systems for narrative prose or story analysis.[71]

Beginning reading materials usually are presented in a narrative style; thus, students need a knowledge of *story structure* or *story grammar*. Teachers cannot use the complex story analysis procedures due to time limitations, yet they need to know how to evaluate the basic framework of stories so they determine the extent to which stories follow a regular format and are prepared to help students deal with stories that deviate.[72] In order to assist students' understanding of the story's framework, Marshall further suggests that teachers draw from the structure of the story for their comprehension questions.[73] Story grammar involves students' knowledge of the basic elements of the story. These include:

- *Theme*—What is the major point? What is the moral point? What did _____ learn at the end?
- *Setting*—Where does the story happen? When did it happen?
- *Character*—Who is the main character? What is he like?
- *Initiating events*—What is _____'s problem? What does _____ have to try to do?
- *Attempts*—What did _____ do about _____? What will _____ not do?

- *Resolution*—How did _____ solve the problem?
  What would you do to solve _____'s problem?
- *Reactions*—How did _____ feel about the problem?
  Why did _____ do _____ ? How did _____ feel at the end?
  Why did _____ feel that way? How would you feel about _____ ?[74]

As teachers understand story grammar and use their knowledge to guide their instruction, students will become more aware of the importance of story grammar.

Strategies for developing story grammar have been used successfully to improve reading comprehension of narrative information.[75] Smith and Bean suggest several specific strategies that teachers can use to improve student awareness of story grammar.[76] *Story patterns* are developed when the teacher draws scenes from the top to the bottom of the page to represent major events in the story and uses these pictures to show students how to create a story. The students then make up a story to go with a new set of illustrations, using the structure just demonstrated by the teacher. Another strategy is the *visual diagram* for which illustrations are provided in a circular format to represent the adventures of the main characters or events in the story. The student uses this information to write a story that represents the key elements of the story's structure. A third strategy is the *tree diagram*. The students are provided with a tree containing questions to determine who, where, doing what, story begins, does what, and end. Using these questions as the story frame, the students write their own story using story structure to organize their ideas.

Story mapping is another strategy that has been used successfully to develop story grammar.[77] A story map uses a chart format to help students understand the relationships among the major events in the story. Once students understand the information in their general framework, broader, more in-depth questions can be addressed. An incomplete framework for a story map is presented in figure 9.4.

Story grammar seems to be automatically developed with some students, just as they learn to put words together to form a sentence. Other students do not possess this natural ability and must be shown how to use story structure to improve their understanding of narrative information. However, story grammar should not be taught as an isolated unit, but rather in relation to developing comprehension for a story. Just as reading skills are not taught as isolated components of the reading process, story structure instruction needs to be taught in the context of usable situations.

As students move out of the primary grades, more of their reading materials are presented in an expository style. To understand the text structure of these materials, students need to be aware of the various organizational patterns of text. As mentioned previously in this chapter, expository text is written according to several basic patterns. Meyer has identified five patterns:

1. Enumeration
2. Time Order
3. Comparison-Contrast
4. Cause-Effect
5. Problem Solution.[78]

Figure 9.4
A Story Map Frame

Theme:

Major Point:

Moral Point:

Setting:

Time:

Place:

Character:

Main Character:

Other Characters:

Sequence of Events:

Initiating Events:

Attempts:

Resolution:

Reaction:

Although units and chapters within a text may contain several different patterns, students need to be taught how to use clues or signal words to determine what the author is presenting. Vacca, Vacca, and Gove have identified words that signal the different organization patterns.[79] These are presented in figure 9.5.

The *pattern guide* is a useful strategy for helping students understand text structure. The pattern guide is designed by the teacher to help the student identify the organizational pattern used in the selection and to remember the significant information. An example of a pattern guide is given in figure 9.6.

Using these various strategies, students will become more aware of the organization of text, both narrative and expository. As a result of this knowledge, comprehension should improve.

Figure 9.5
Signal Words for Organizational Patterns in Text

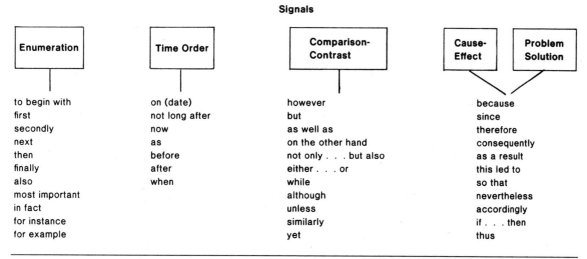

Signals

Enumeration	Time Order	Comparison-Contrast	Cause-Effect	Problem Solution
to begin with	on (date)	however	because	
first	not long after	but	since	
secondly	now	as well as	therefore	
next	as	on the other hand	consequently	
then	before	not only . . . but also	as a result	
finally	after	either . . . or	this led to	
also	when	while	so that	
most important		although	nevertheless	
in fact		unless	accordingly	
for instance		similarly	if . . . then	
for example		yet	thus	

From *Content Area Reading*, 3/e by Richard T. Vacca and JoAnne L. Vacca. Copyright © 1989, 1986 by Richard T. Vacca and JoAnne L. Vacca. Reprinted by permission of Harper-Collins Publishers.

Questioning

The traditional way of developing comprehension is by asking questions. However, there has been much criticism of questioning strategies used in the elementary and middle school classes. This criticism ranges from Durkin's statement that comprehension is continuously assessed, via questioning, rather than taught,[80] to a concern as to how teacher-generated questions compare to student-generated questions.

Many alternative ideas have been proposed through the years to improve questioning. Because questioning is frequently developed via individual skills, information and examples of different types of questions are given in the previous section of developing comprehension skills. Teacher direction is the primary strategy considered in that section. However, consideration should be given to using *student-generated questions* to provide direction to reading and as a follow-up after reading. As teachers model effective questioning patterns through teacher-directed questions or the *ReQuest* strategy discussed earlier, students learn how to pose questions prior to reading, as they read, and following reading. Thus, teachers will find that learning is greatly enhanced as students are more involved in the question developing process.

Figure 9.6
A Pattern Guide

Pattern Guide for Relationship Pattern

Topic: Development of Communities

Part I: Cause-Effect Relationships
In the chapter on the "Development of Communities" in the text, find the effects of the following causes.
Write your answer in the space provided.

1. Cause: Communities with the same life forms
    Effect: _____

2. Cause: Geography and climate
    Effect: _____

3. Cause: Low average temperature and low annual precipitation
    Effect: _____

4. Cause: Moderate rainfall, damp and acidic soil with no permafrost
    Effect: _____

5. Cause: Above average rainfall and temperature climate
    Effect: _____

6. Cause: Heavy rainfall and high temperature
    Effect: _____

7. Cause: Very low rainfall and hot, cold, or temperate climates
    Effect: _____

Part II:

What do you think the author was trying to say? Write your answer in the space below each question.

1. Why should we be concerned about the development of communities?

2. How does the development of communities affect our quality of life?

3. Why has the future of our world's forests become a major concern to us?

Guides such as the three-level study guide and concept guide also offer students a framework for response as they read. Using either questions or statements, these guides provide direction to students to note important information when reading. While these tend to be more teacher-directed than student-directed, they may be a strategy that works with some students who need continuous direction as they read. An example of a concept guide is given in figure 9.7.

Questioning will always be a primary strategy for developing comprehension. Teachers should use questions to monitor comprehension, being sure to use a variety of questions at different levels. Teacher questioning forms the basis for what students learn in a class—they learn to read in order to answer the teacher's questions!

Impact of Affect on Comprehension

Though many strategies exist for developing the cognitive facets of comprehension, sometimes comprehension remains poor. Why? The one component that has frequently been ignored is the affective domain as it relates to comprehension. Teachers and parents have recognized that interests, attitudes, feelings, and overall motivation are essential ingredients in the learning process. When students read information that interests them, their comprehension is better than when they are directed to read a story because it comes next in the book! In fact, many times students can read material that is written at a higher level when the topic is of interest to them. One of the authors had an experience with an older student who was reading at a very low level, yet saw his basketball hero pictured on the cover of *Sports Illustrated.* The student asked if he could take the magazine and read the story. Of course, the response was in the affirmative. This student labored through the article for a week, stopping his peers and teachers in the hallway to ask a word. At the end of the week, he brought the magazine back and said, "Now, let me tell you about this story!" He understood every detail, had learned many basic sight words that teachers had tried to pound in for the last seven years, and came to the door every Monday morning looking for the new issue of the magazine! Had this student's reading level suddenly jumped about six years? Absolutely not, but he had found something to read that related to his interests and he now viewed reading with a new attitude.

Chapter 11 deals with developing the personal aspect of reading, and chapter 2 presented ways of assessing attitudes and interests; therefore, that information will not be repeated here. However, the purpose of this section is to focus on the impact of the affective domain on comprehension. Higher level comprehension skills are best developed when students are asked to compare the feelings of the main character in the story to their feelings about a particular situation. Additionally, helping students deal with emotions can be developed through reading comprehension. Encouraging students to try to feel what the author is saying or to put themselves

Figure 9.7
A Concept Guide

Concept Guide in Social Studies

Topic: The Historical Development of Canada

Part I: As you preview pages 422-435, complete these statements.

1. Energy produced by water power is _____.

2. A _____ is a group of nations that includes Great Britain and many former British colonies.

3. Because both French and English are official languages in Canada, the country is referred to as being _____ .

Part II: Put the words in the list below into their proper group based on their relationship to the concept.

Jacques Cartier	Quebec	Hudson Bay
Samuel de Champlain	New France	Newfoundland
John Cabot	Roman Catholic	Protestant
Henry Hudson	Montreal	New Brunswick

                French Canada   British Canada

1. _____   _____

2. _____   _____

3. _____   _____

4. _____   _____

5. _____   _____

6. _____   _____

7. _____   _____

8. _____   _____

9. _____   _____

10. _____   _____

11. _____   _____

12. _____   _____

in Hannah's shoes in *One Hundred Dresses* is teaching students to comprehend what the author is trying to communicate. The comprehension process is a communication process between the author and reader; it is not complete when students simply recall the information printed on the page. Feelings, attitudes, emotions, and beliefs must be communicated for students to truly experience the full meaning of reading. For many students, this emotional relation with reading first occurs when their teacher reads *Charlotte's Web* and they experience Fern's feelings about Wilbur, and later Wilbur's feelings when Charlotte dies. Why do students love this story and seem to never tire of it? It is a book of feelings, emotions, and beliefs that form the basis of the story and for which the details only add more meaning. Most narrative stories evoke some reaction from students, be it positive or negative. Teachers cannot overlook this aspect of comprehension—use questioning strategies to get students involved in this affective part of the comprehension process!

The wealth of information on comprehension becomes more voluminous each day. Spache and Spache have provided an excellent summary of what works in comprehension instruction based on research. This information is presented in table 9.4.

Table 9.4

Comprehension Instruction[81]

What Works	What Does Not Work
Providing direct instruction on meanings of words in the reading[82]	Chalkboard prereading presentation of new words
Learning multiplicity of word meanings by categorizing words	Teaching most common meanings of words
Asking pupils to attempt to define new words, eliminating study of those already known[82]	Previewing all new words in the selection
Teaching meaning and effect of signal words	Teaching connectives and signal words as sight words
Using cloze to promote development of contextual analysis; following with discussion of choices and training in hypothesis testing	Teaching contextual analysis as a group of terms
Teaching interpretation of paragraph types above fourth grade[83]	Assuming that author's style is not significant
Beginning assessment with factual questions—who, what, when, where[83]	Following basal manual in questioning
Moving from factual to explanatory questions—how, why[84]	Mixing questions to test thoroughly
Moving then to higher level questions—generalization, evaluation, and inferences[84]	Covering facts read as completely as possible
Confining imagery questions to grades above primary, expecting that some pupils cannot use it[85]	Teaching children to use imagery

Table 9.4

Continued

What Works	What Does Not Work
Discussing pictures in the text may help recall[85]	Failing to discuss and react to pictures
Spending time relating pupil knowledge to content of selection by discussion, pretests, spelling out purposes, and previewing[86]	Getting into the reading as soon as possible
Reinforcing recall by writing pupil concepts on chalkboard, reorganizing this with aid of pupils[87]	Testing comprehension by questioning only
Teaching post-primary children to write a summary sentence after each paragraph in content material[85,88]	Using teacher questioning and printed exercises for assessment
Recognizing that main ideas include most important idea, ideas related to theme, and what could be expressed in a new title[88]	Teaching main ideas as central thought
Realizing that a comprehension difficulty may require indirect treatments, as vocabulary, informational background, word analysis, etc.[88]	Curing comprehension difficulty by direct teaching of comprehension strategies
Using tests and discussion of correct answers, information feedback and reviews[88]	Giving tests to measure comprehension
Direct teaching of these comprehension strategies[89]	Using printed exercises to practice main ideas, details, etc.
Using children's prior experiences as related to selection as a basis for predicting probable ideas in the selection[90]	Talking with children about their experiences as they might be related to the title of the selection
If children answer a question correctly, they may ask one of the teacher or other children[90]	Having all questions come from the teacher
Teaching pupils how to summarize, outline, raise questions to be answered in the reading; providing practice in these skills[91]	Reserving study skills instruction only for subject matter lessons
Recognizing that comprehension is not really promoted by oral reading	Expecting oral readers to show more than bare, literal recall
Using inferential prereading questions that require a good deal of reading before answering, above primary grades	Using factual prereading questions
Supplying glosses or marginal headings on ditto sheets before reading to guide students	Assuming pupils can use present headings
If content of selection is beyond pupil informational background, helping them by prereading preparation with explanation and discussion[88]	Using an audiovisual aid to prepare students for new, difficult materials
Allowing at least five seconds after each question for think time[92]	Continuing to expect rapid responses to your questions
Recognizing that there may not be correct answers to some questions because they are a matter of opinion or judgment[93]	Expecting and demanding correct answers

Giving feedback by asking for elaboration or explanation or by pointing out why answer is correct[94]

Recognizing answer is correct by saying so

■ Summary

Comprehending printed material is the purpose and goal of reading. For a student to be a successful reader, comprehension must occur. However, comprehension occurs at various levels. For example, some students may comprehend well at the literal level, but experience great difficulty in interpreting information or evaluating material. Thus, it is essential that students be taught to read on all three comprehension levels: literal, interpretive, and critical.

Why some students comprehend well at all levels of reading and others do not has always puzzled teachers. Some of the reasons include the various factors that affect reading comprehension; among those mentioned were experiences, language capabilities, intelligence, motivation, interests, attitudes, dialect, and purposes for reading. One or more of these may prevent many students from realizing their potential.

Another important factor in teaching students to comprehend materials is related to cognitive development. Many teachers do not assist students in reaching their highest level of cognition because of the types of questioning they use. It is essential to question students at interpretive and critical levels, not just at the literal level. Taxonomies have been developed in an effort to assist teachers in achieving this goal. Three taxonomies developed by Bloom, Sanders, and Barrett were presented.

Current research in comprehension questions the teaching of specific subskills and encourages comprehension development using the student's knowledge structure or schema. Although new ideas are provided in this research, much of the information only amplifies many of the present classroom practices.

To assist classroom teachers in applying these new research findings as well as coping with current requirements for instruction in comprehension, strategies for developing vocabulary, building schema, dealing with text, and developing the affective area were also presented.

■ Applying What You Read

You have been transferred to a new school to teach the second grade. Your students have had very limited experiences and have poor oral language skills. How important are these impediments to the development of comprehension? How can these factors be partially nullified or reversed?

Using the taxonomies presented in this chapter as a model, develop your own taxonomy for teaching comprehension. Discuss the role that taxonomies have in the reading comprehension process.

Design a program for diagnosing comprehension. Apply this diagnostic program to your classroom by selecting those procedures best suited to your students' needs.

After obtaining accurate diagnostic information about your students' strengths and weaknesses in comprehension skills, design appropriate prescriptive techniques for each student. Implement these prescriptions as early as possible.

■ Notes

1. Dolores Durkin, *Teaching Them to Read*, 3rd ed., pp. 393–95.
2. Larry A. Harris and Carl B. Smith, *Reading Instruction: Diagnostic Teaching in the Classroom*, 4th ed., p. 256.
3. Josephine Gemake, "Interference of Certain Dialect Elements with Reading Comprehension for Third Graders," *Reading Improvement*.
4. James F. Christie, "Syntax: A Key to Reading Comprehension," *Reading Improvement*.
5. Kathleen C. Stevens, "The Effect of Background Knowledge on the Reading Comprehension of Ninth Graders," *Journal of Reading Behavior*.
6. Steven A. Stahl, Michael G. Jacobson, Charlotte E. Davis, and Robin L. Davis, "Prior Knowledge and Difficult Vocabulary in

the Comprehension of Unfamiliar Text," *Reading Research Quarterly*, pp. 27–43.

7. R. Scott Baldwin, Ziva Peleg-Bruckner, and Ann H. McClintock, "Effects of Topic Interest and Prior Knowledge on Reading Comprehension," *Reading Research Quarterly*.

8. Durkin, *Teaching Them to Read*, pp. 394–95.

9. Harris and Smith, *Reading Instruction*, pp. 87–89.

10. Dolores Durkin, "What is the Value of the New Interest in Reading Comprehension?" *Language Arts*.

11. George D. Spache and Evelyn B. Spache, *Reading in the Elementary School*, 4th ed., pp. 450–51.

12. Karen Zabrucky and Hilary Horn Ratner, "Effects of Reading Ability on Children's Comprehension Evaluation and Regulation," *Journal of Reading Behavior*, pp. 69–83.

13. Robert F. Carey, "Toward a More Cognitive Definition of Reading Comprehension," *Reading Horizons*.

14. Hilda Taba, "The Teaching of Thinking," *Elementary English*.

15. Frank J. Guszak, "Teacher Questioning and Reading," *The Reading Teacher*.

16. J. A. Stallings and D. Kaskowitz, *Follow-through Classroom Observation Evaluation*.

17. M. D. Gall, B. A. Ward, D. C. Berliner, L. S. Cahen, K. A. Crown, J. D. Elashoff, G. C. Stanton, and P. H. Winne, *The Effects of Teacher Use of Questioning Techniques on Student Achievement and Attitude: Stanford Program on Teacher Effectiveness, A Factorially Designed Experiment on Teacher Structuring, Soliciting, and Reacting*.

18. Karen K. Wixson, "Level of Importance of Postquestions and Children's Learning from Text," *American Educational Research Journal*.

19. Benjamin Bloom, et al., *Taxonomy of Educational Objectives-Handbook I: The Cognitive Domain*, pp. 168–72; Norris M. Sanders, *Classroom Questions-What Kinds?* p. 3; Thomas C. Barrett and R. Smith, *Teaching Reading in the Middle Grades*.

20. P. David Pearson and Dale D. Johnson, *Teaching Reading Comprehension*.

21. Michael Strange, "Instructional Implications of a Conceptual Theory of Reading Comprehension," *The Reading Teacher*; Keith E. Stanovich, "Toward an Interactive-Compensatory Model of Individual Differences in the Development of Reading Fluency," *Reading Research Quarterly*; H. Levin and E. L. Kaplan, "Grammatical Structure and Reading," in *Basic Studies in Reading* edited by H. Levin and J. Williams; Kenneth S. Goodman, "Unity in Reading," in *Theoretical Models and Processes of Reading*, 3rd ed. Edited by Harry Singer and Robert Ruddell.

22. Michael Strange, "Instructional Implications . . . Reading Comprehension," p. 392; K. Stanovich, "Toward an Interactive . . . Reading Fluency," p. 33–34; D. LaBerge and S. Jay Samuels, "Toward a Theory of Automatic Information Processing in Reading," *Cognitive Psychology*.

23. Michael Strange, "Instructional Implications . . . Reading Comprehension," p. 393; David Rummelhart, *Toward an Interactive Model of Reading*; Richard Rystrom, "Reflections of Meaning," *Journal of Reading Behavior*; Richard Anderson, Rand Spiro, and Mark Anderson, *Schemata as Scaffolding for the Representation of Information in Connected Discourse*.

24. Jana M. Mason, "A Schema-Theoretic View of the Reading Process as a Basis for Comprehension Instruction," in *Comprehension Instruction: Perspectives and Suggestions*, edited by Gerald G. Duffy, Laura R. Roehler, and Jana Mason, p. 28.

25. Durkin, "What is the . . . Reading Comprehension?" p. 27.

26. Jana M. Mason, J. H. Osborn, and B. V. Rosenshine, "A Consideration of Skill Hierarchy Approaches to the Teaching of Reading," Technical Report 42.

27. E. Marcia Sheridan, "A Review of Research on Schema Theory and Its Implications for Reading Instruction in Secondary Reading."

28. Bonnie J. F. Meyer, "Structure of Prose: Implications for Teachers of Reading."

29. Edward Thorndike, "Reading and Reasoning: A Story of Mistakes in Paragraph Reading," *Journal of Educational Psychology*.

30. Nila Banton Smith, "Patterns of Writing in Different Subject Areas," *Journal of Reading*; James M. McCallister, "Using Paragraph Clues as Aids to Understanding," *Journal of Reading*.

31. Earl H. Cheek and Martha Collins Cheek, "Organizational Patterns: Untapped Sources for Better Reading," *Reading World*.

32. Martha D. Collins Cheek, "Organizational Patterns: An Aid to Comprehension," American Reading Forum Proceedings.

33. Barak V. Rosenshine, "Skill Hierarchies in Reading Comprehension," in *Theoretical Issues in Reading Comprehension*, edited by Rand J. Spiro, Bertram C. Bruce, William F. Brewer.

34. John E. Readence and Mary McDonnel Harris, "False Prerequisites in the Teaching of Comprehension," *Reading Improvement*.

35. Miles V. Zintz, *The Reading Process*, pp. 231–32; Frank B. May, *Reading as Communication*, pp. 127–44, 160–73; John N. Mangieri, Lois A. Bader, and James E. Walker, *Elementary Reading*, pp. 66–74.

36. Emerald V. Dechant and Henry P. Smith, *Psychology in Teaching Reading*, 2nd ed., p. 254; Mildred A. Dawson and Henry A. Bamman, *Fundamentals of Basic Reading Instruction*, p. 182.

37. Robert Oakan, Morton Wierner, and Ward Cormer, "Identification, Organization, and Reading Comprehension for Good and Poor Readers," *Journal of Educational Psychology*.

38. Herbert D. Simons, "Linguistic Skills and Reading Comprehension," in *The Quest for Competency in Reading*, edited by Howard A.

Klein, p. 165; F. A. Briggs, "Grammatical Sense as a Factor in Reading Comprehension," in *The Psychology of Reading Behavior*, edited by G. B. Schick, pp. 145–49; Mary Anne Hall and Christopher J. Ramig, *Linguistic Foundations for Reading*, pp. 61–79.

39. James Deese, *Psycholinguistics*, p. 1.

40. Lou E. Burmeister, *From Print to Meaning*, pp. 112–13; Roach Van Allen, *Language Experiences in Communication*, pp. 370–71; Robert Emans, "Use of Context Clues," in *Teaching Word Recognition Skills*, compiled by Mildred A Dawson, pp. 181–87.

41. Barbara D. Stoodt, "The Relationship Between Understanding Grammatical Conjunctions and Reading Comprehension," *Elementary English*.

42. Harris and Smith, *Reading Instruction*, p. 225.

43. Edna L. Furness, "Pupils, Pedagogues, and Punctuation," *Elementary English*.

44. Durkin, *Teaching Them to Read*, p. 431; Josephine Piekarz Ives, "The Improvement of Critical Reading Skills," in *Problem Areas in Reading—Some Observations and Recommendations*, edited by Coleman Morrison, p. 5; Paul C. Burns and Betty D. Roe, *Teaching Reading in Today's Elementary Schools*, p. 218.

45. Helen M. Robinson, "Developing Critical Readers," in *Dimensions of Critical Reading*, edited by Russel G. Stauffer; William Eller and Judith G. Wolf, "Developing Critical Reading Abilities," *Journal of Reading*.

46. David H. Russell, *Children's Thinking*, Chapter 5.

47. Mary Austin and Coleman Morrison, *The First R: The Harvard Report on Reading in Elementary Schools*, Chapter 12.

48. Constance McCullough, "Responses of Elementary School Children to Common Types of Reading Comprehension Questions," *Journal of Educational Research*.

49. Charlotte Agrast, "Teach Them to Read Between the Lines," *Grade Teacher*; Alan R. Harrison, "Critical Reading for Elementary Pupils," *The Reading Teacher*.

50. Agrast, "Teach Them to Read"; Evelyn Wolfe, "Advertising and the Elementary Language Arts," *Elementary English*.

51. Robert R. Nardell, "Some Aspects of Creative Reading," *Journal of Educational Research*.

52. Jerome A. Niles and Larry A. Harris, "The Context of Comprehension," *Reading Horizons*.

53. Molly M. Wilson, "The Effect of Question Types in Varying Placements on the Reading Comprehension of Upper Elementary Students," *Reading Psychology*.

54. Dolores Durkin, "What Classroom Observations Reveal About Reading Comprehension Instruction," *Reading Research Quarterly*; Dolores Durkin, "Reading Comprehension Instruction in Five Basal Reader Series," *Reading Research Quarterly*.

55. Michael Strange, "Instructional Implications . . . Reading Comprehension," pp. 394–97.

56. Dale D. Johnson, "*Journal of Reading*: A Themed Issue on Vocabulary Instruction," *Journal of Reading*, p. 580.

57. Edwin E. Vineyard and Harold W. Massey, "The Interrelationship of Certain Linguistic Skills and Their Relationship with Scholastic Achievement When Intelligence is Ruled Constant," *Journal of Educational Psychology*.

58. Robert B. Ruddell, "Vocabulary Learning: A Process Model and Criteria for Evaluating Instructional Strategies," *Journal of Reading*; Eileen Carr and Karen K. Wixson, "Guidelines for Evaluating Vocabulary Instruction," *Journal of Reading*.

59. Carr and Wixson, "Guidelines for . . . Vocabulary Instruction," *Journal of Reading*.

60. David P. Ausubel, "The Use of Advance Organizers in the Learning and Retention of Meaningful Verbal Material," *Journal of Educational Psychology*.

61. M. F. Graves, C. L. Cooke, and M. J. LaBerge, "Effects of Previewing Difficult Short Stories on Low Ability Junior High School Students' Comprehension, Recall, and Attitudes," *Reading Research Quarterly*.

62. Jean Wallace Gillet and Charles Temple, *Understanding Reading Problems: Assessment and Instruction*, p. 227.

63. R. J. Smith and D. D. Johnson, *Teaching Children to Read*.

64. Patricia L. Anders and Candace S. Bos, "Semantic Feature Analysis: An Interactive Strategy for Vocabulary Development and Text Comprehension," *Journal of Reading*.

65. Anders and Bos, "Semantic Feature Analysis . . . Text Comprehension."

66. Rand J. Spiro and Ann Myers, "Individual Differences and Underlying Cognitive Processes in Reading," in *Handbook of Reading Research*, edited by P. David Pearson, p. 491.

67. Judy A. Barnes, Dean W. Ginther, and Samuel W. Cochran, "Schema and Purpose in Reading Comprehension and Learning Vocabulary from Context," *Reading Research and Instruction*, pp. 16–28.

68. Harry Singer, "Active Comprehension: From Answering to Asking Questions," *The Reading Teacher*.

69. Anthony V. Manzo, "ReQuest Procedure," *Journal of Reading*.

70. Annemarie Sullivan Palinesar, "The Quest for Meaning from Expository Text: A Teacher-Guided Journey," Gerald G. Duffy, Laura R. Roehler, and Jana Mason, eds., *Comprehension Instruction: Perspectives and Suggestions*, pp. 251–64.

71. B. J. F. Meyer, *The Organization of Prose and Its Effects on Memory*; W. Kintsch, *The Representation of Meaning in Memory*; C. H. Frederiksen, "Effects of Task-Induced Cognitive Operations on Comprehension and Memory Processes," R. O. Freedle and J. B. Carroll, eds., *Language Comprehension*

and the Acquisition of Knowledge; J. M. Mandler and M. S. Johnson, "Remembrance of Things Parsed: Story Structure and Recall," *Cognitive Psychology;* D. E. Rummelhart, "Notes on a Schema for Stories," in *Representation and Understanding,* edited by D. G. Bobrow and A. M. Collins; N. L. Stein and C.G. Glenn, "An Analysis of Story Comprehension in Elementary School Children," in *New Directions in Discourse Processing,* edited by R. O. Freedle; P. W. Thorndyke, "Cognitive Structures in Comprehension and Memory of Narrative Discourse," *Cognitive Psychology.*

72. Robert J. Tierney, James Mosenthal, and Robert M. Kantor, "Classroom Applications of Text Analysis: Toward Improving Text Analysis," in *Promoting Reading Comprehension,* edited by James Flood.

73. Nancy Marshall, "Using the Story Grammar to Assess Reading Comprehension," *The Reading Teacher.*

74. Marshall, "Using Story Grammar . . . Reading Comprehension," *The Reading Teacher.*

75. M. A. Bowman, "The Effect of Story Structure Questioning Upon the Comprehension and Metacognitive Awareness of Sixth Grade Students," (Doctoral dissertation, University of Maryland); Gloria M. McDonell, "Effects of Instruction in the Use of an Abstract Structural Schema as an Aid to Comprehension and Recall of Written Discourse," (Doctoral dissertation, Virginia Polytechnic Institute and State University); J. Fitzgerald and D. L. Spiegel, "Enhancing Children's Reading Comprehension Through Instruction in Narrative Structure," *Journal of Reading Behavior.*

76. Marilyn Smith and Thomas W. Bean, "Four Strategies That Develop Children's Story Comprehension and Writing," *The Reading Teacher.*

77. D. Ray Reutzel, "Story Mapping: An Alternative Approach to Comprehension," *Reading World;* I. L. Beck, M. G. McKeown, E. S. McCaslin, and A. M. Burkes, "Instructional Dimensions That May Affect Reading Comprehension: Examples from Two Commercial Reading Programs."

78. Meyer, *The Organization of Prose and Its Effects on Memory.*

79. Jo Anne L. Vacca, Richard T. Vacca, and Mary K. Gove, *Reading and Learning to Read,* p. 218.

80. Durkin, "What Classroom Observations . . . Comprehension Instruction," *Reading Research Quarterly.*

81. George D. Spache and Evelyn B. Spache, *Reading in the Elementary School,* 5th ed., pp. 557–59.

82. Maryann Eeds, "What to Do When They Don't Understand What They Read— Research-Based Strategies for Teaching Reading Comprehension," *The Reading Teacher.*

83. David E. Rummelhart, "Schemata: The Building Blocks of Cognition," in *Theoretical Issues in Reading Comprehension,* edited by Rand J. Spiro, Bertram C. Bruce, and William F. Brewer.

84. Taba, "The Teaching of Thinking," *Elementary English.*

85. Joseph R. Jenkins and Darlene Pany, "Instructional Variables in Reading Comprehension," in *Comprehension and Reading: Research Review,* edited by John T. Guthrie.

86. Dale D. Johnson and Thomas G. Barrett, "Prose Comprehension: A Descriptive Analysis of Instructional Practices," in *Children's Prose Comprehension: Research and Practice,* edited by Carol M. Santa and Bernard I. Hayes.

87. Penny Baum Moldofsky, "Teaching Students to Determine the Central Story Problem: A Practical Application of Schema Theory," *The Reading Teacher.*

88. Joel R. Levin and Michael Pressley, "Improving Children's Prose Comprehension: Selected Strategies That Seem to Succeed," in *Children's Prose Comprehension: Research and Practice*, edited by Carol M. Santa and Bernard I. Hayes.

89. Ruth J. Kurth and M. Jean Greenlaw, "Research and Practice in Comprehension Instruction in Elementary Classrooms," in *Comprehension: Process and Product*, edited by George H. McNinch.

90. Jane Hansen, "An Inferential Comprehension Strategy for Use with Primary Grade Children," *The Reading Teacher*.

91. Ann L. Brown, J. C. Campione, and J. A. Day, "Learning to Learn: On Training Students to Learn From Texts," *Educational Researcher*.

92. Linda E. Gambrell, "Think-Time: Implications for Reading Instruction," *The Reading Teacher*.

93. Roscoe Davidson, "Teacher Influence and Children's Levels of Thinking," *The Reading Teacher*.

94. Elaine Schwartz and Alice Sheff, "Student Involvement in Questioning for Comprehension," *The Reading Teacher*.

■ Other Suggested Readings

Afflerbach, Peter P. "The Influence of Prior Knowledge on Expert Readers' Main Idea Construction Strategies." *Reading Research Quarterly* 25 (Winter 1990): 31–46.

August, Diane L., John H. Flavell, and Renee Clift. "Comparison of Comprehension Monitoring of Skilled and Less Skilled Readers." *Reading Research Quarterly* 20 (Fall 1984): 39–53.

Beck, I. L. and M. G. McKeown. "Learning Words Well: A Program to Enhance Vocabulary and Comprehension." *The Reading Teacher* 36 (1983): 622–25.

Becoming a Nation of Readers: The Report of the Commission on Reading. Washington, D.C.: National Institute of Education, 1985.

Cohen, Ruth. "Self-Generated Questions as an Aid to Reading Comprehension." *The Reading Teacher* 36 (April 1983): 770–75.

Dewitz, Peter, Eileen M. Carr, and Judythe P. Patberg. "Effects of Inference Training on Comprehension and Comprehension Monitoring." *Reading Research Quarterly* 22 (Winter 1987): 99–122.

Dupuis, M. M. and S. L. Snyder. "Develop Concepts Through Vocabulary: A Strategy for Reading Specialists to Use with Content Teachers." *Journal of Reading* 26 (January 1983): 297–305.

Farrar, Mary Thomas. "Why Do We Ask Comprehension Questions? A New Conception of Comprehension Instruction." *The Reading Teacher* 37 (February 1984): 452–56.

Flood, James, (ed.) *Promoting Reading Comprehension.* Newark, Delaware: International Reading Association, 1984.

Fowler, G. L. "Developing Comprehension Skills in Primary Students Through the Use of Story Frames." *The Reading Teacher* 36 (November 1982): 176–79.

Freeman, G. and E. G. Reynolds. "Enriching Basal Reader Lessons with Semantic Webbing." *The Reading Teacher* 33 (March 1980): 677–84.

Gemake, Josephine. "Interactive Reading: How to Make Children Active Readers." *The Reading Teacher* 37 (February 1984): 462–66.

Gordon, C. J. and C. Braun. "Using Story Schemata as an Aid to Reading and Writing." *The Reading Teacher* 37 (November 1983): 116–21.

Greenlaw, M. Jean and Ruth J. Kurth. "Current Research and Analysis of Definitions of Comprehension." In *Comprehension: Process and Product.* Edited by George H. McNinch. Sarasota, Florida: American Reading Forum Yearbook, 1981.

Hansen, Jane. "The Effects of Inference Training and Practice on Young Children's Reading Comprehension." *Reading Research Quarterly* 30 (Summer 1981): 52–64.

Hodges, C. A. "Toward a Broader Definition of Comprehension Instruction." *Reading Research Quarterly* 15 (Winter 1980): 299–306.

Irwin, Judith W., (ed.) *Understanding and Teaching Cohesion Comprehension.* Newark, Delaware: International Reading Association, 1986.

Johnson, Dale D., Susan D. Pittelman, and Joan E. Heimlich. "Semantic Mapping." *The Reading Teacher* 39 (April 1986): 778–83.

Lipson, Marjorie L. "Some Unexpected Issues in Prior Knowledge and Comprehension." *The Reading Teacher* 37 (April 1984): 760–64.

McNeil, John D. *Reading Comprehension, New Directions for Classroom Practice.* Glenview, Illinois: Scott, Foresman, 1984.

Nolte, R. Y., and H. Singer. "Active Comprehension: Teaching a Process of Reading Comprehension and Its Effects on Reading Achievement." *The Reading Teacher* 39 (October 1985): 24–31.

Patching, W., Edward Kameenui, Douglas Carnine, Russell Gersten, and Geoff Colvin. "Direct Instruction in Critical Reading Skills." *Reading Research Quarterly* 18 (Summer 1983): 406–18.

Piccolo, J. Anne. "Expository Text Structure: Teaching and Learning Strategies." *The Reading Teacher* 40 (May 1987): 838–47.

Raphael, T. E. "Teaching Question-Answer Relationships, Revisited." *The Reading Teacher* 39 (February 1986): 516–22.

Reder, Lynne M. "The Role of Elaboration in the Comprehension and Retention of Prose: A Critical Review." *Review of Educational Research* 50 (Spring 1980): 5–53.

Smith, Carl B. "Two Approaches to Critical Thinking." *The Reading Teacher* 44 (December 1990): 350–51.

Smith, Carl B. "Vocabulary Development in Content Area Reading." *The Reading Teacher* 43 (March 1990): 508–509.

Squire, J. R. "In Composing and Comprehending: Two Sides of the Same Basic Process." *Composing and Comprehending.* Edited by J. M. Jensen. Urbana, Illinois: National Conference on Research in English, 1984.

Sundbye, Nita. "Text Explicitness and Inferential Questioning: Effects on Story Understanding and Recall." *Reading Research Quarterly* 22 (Winter 1987): 82–98.

Tharp, Roland G. "The Effective Instruction of Comprehension: Results and Description of the Kamehameha Early Education Program." *Reading Research Quarterly* 17 (Summer 1982): 503–27.

Whaley, J. F. "Story Grammar and Reading Instruction." *The Reading Teacher* 34 (April 1981): 762–71.

Wilhite, Stephen C. "Headings as Memory Facilitators: The Importance of Prior Knowledge." *Journal of Educational Psychology* 81 (March 1989): 115–17.

Zakaluk, Beverly L., S. Jay Samuels, and Barbara M. Taylor. "A Simple Technique for Estimating Prior Knowledge: Word Association." *Journal of Reading* 30 (October 1986): 56–60.

10

Study Skills and Strategies

Just as early reading skills provide a foundation for reading, word identification skills assist word analysis, and comprehension skills improve thinking abilities, so study skills and strategies foster independence in reading. Study skills and strategies are intended to help students use reading skills in their daily activities and content areas. For example, skills such as how to organize information, use reference skills, read maps or tables, and use parts of a book are essential to becoming an independent reader. Thus, learning the proper use of study skills and strategies becomes another important task in the reading process.

This chapter contains a list of the various study skills together with research relevant to each area to assist teachers in planning prescriptive instruction in the content area. In addition, there is a section on selected study strategies that can be effective tools in helping students become more efficient learners.

To provide prescriptive information regarding the development of study skills, ideas for teaching are included along with specific procedures by diagnosing the study skills. Specific questions discussed are:

Why are study skills and strategies important?

What are the study skills?

What information does research provide about the development of study skills?

What are some effective study strategies that students can use to become more efficient learners?

Which diagnostic procedures are most effective in this area?

What are some prescriptive teaching ideas that can be used to develop study skills?

As this chapter is read, the following terms are important to note.

Vocabulary to Know

K-W-L	RAM	Specialized study skills
Organizational skills	REAP	SQRQCQ
PARS	Reference skills	SQ3R
PORPE	RIPS	Study skills
PQRST	SIP	Study strategies

■ The Importance of Study Skills and Strategies

The development of study skills is extremely important because of the high correlation between knowing how to use the skills and success in implementing strategies in content materials. One of the first procedures that students must learn when reading content materials is which skills to use to understand the material. Although there is some emphasis on the development of study skills in basal readers, these skills are not fully developed until students become more involved in reading science, literature, social studies, and other content materials.

Study skills are generally not used so much in pleasure reading as they are in learning situations involving content reading assignments. Quite often, completing these assignments is a task that few students enjoy. Smith summarizes quite well the special situation that exemplifies the use of study skills. He states that this is an assignment made by another person, materials are chosen by someone else, and testing will be conducted by this other person.[1] The other person, of course, is the teacher; however, practically speaking, the one who will benefit from the assignments is the student. The result of these assignments should be the development of specific study skills that become automatic responses used as needed.

Much of the responsibility for learning to use study skills effectively rests with the student; however, it is incumbent upon the teacher to provide the necessary instruction if the learning of these skills is to occur. Unfortunately, instruction in this area often does not occur as frequently or with as much emphasis as is required. If students are to learn the effective use of study skills, they must receive carefully planned instruction in a variety of situations in the different content areas, and be provided appropriate assignments to sharpen these skills.

Although material in which these skills must be used becomes more complex as the level increases, the basic application of the study skills remains unchanged. Thus, application in each of the content areas is the key to efficient use of the study skills.

There are various techniques for teaching the study skills. Perhaps the most effective way to instruct students is to demonstrate the skills, although many teachers use inductive approaches such as inquiry, discovery, and problem solving.[2] An integral part of the instructional process, as previously mentioned, is the application of this skill knowledge to materials. Perhaps the use of content materials for this purpose is most efficient.

Study skills are important because they represent a structure of knowledge that must be transferred from one set of materials to another. The structure is adapted to the content and allows for the consistent application of these skills to various types of content materials. As a result, students learn to apply these skills with some degree of consistency, thus becoming more independent readers.

In an effort to better understand the complex nature of the process involved in studying and learning, teachers may wish to consider several ideas about this complex act. Four major factors that are determining influences on studying have been identified. They include:

1. The nature of the criterion task or goal for which the student is preparing;
2. The nature of the material the student is studying;
3. The cognitive and affective characteristics of the student; and
4. The strategies the student uses to learn the material.[3]

The interaction of these factors in many different ways certainly compounds the difficult task of teaching students how to study.

It is necessary that the student not only be given a purpose for reading by the teacher initially, but also that she develops the skill of learning to establish her personal reason or goal for studying. Students can best acquire this skill through the use of study strategies such as SQ3R, which is discussed later in this chapter.

The second factor affecting studying concerns the materials used by students. Effective content instruction requires the use of textbooks as well as supplementary materials. Because of the special relationship between the use of study skills and the acquisition of knowledge in the various content areas, it is essential that materials carefully be selected and that students understand how the information in the material is organized. Difficulties frequently arise in studying content materials because students are unable to determine which comprehension skills to apply when reading the material. This difficulty results primarily from a lack of understanding of the organization of the material used by the authors. Understanding text structure or organizational patterns is a key to learning the material. For a more thorough discussion on text structure, see chapter 9.

When study skills are discussed, it is not unusual for the primary topic to indicate whether one strategy is more effective than another in helping the student learn the material. Although notetaking, outlining, summarizing, using book parts, and map reading are useful in the study process, research has failed to substantiate the superiority of one technique over another. What it indicates, however, is that the appropriate study strategy with the right material will enable the student to understand the information better, and that if students are taught the use of study strategies, then they must be taught to use the strategy appropriately.[4] Furthermore, research confirms that introducing students who already study effectively to a new strategy, may be harmful rather than helpful.[5] Thus, teachers must know the strengths and weaknesses of their students, so that appropriate instruction in the study skills can be provided.

Other factors that contribute to the difficult task of teaching students how to study effectively have been identified by Graham and Robinson.[6] These include attitudes, cultural background, general knowledge, general health, linguistic knowledge and flexibility, and readiness for study tasks.

Attitudes

Attitudes play an important role in how well students learn. This is particularly true of study skills. Students with positive attitudes typically are more willing to try new or different study strategies. However, students with less positive attitudes about learning often are less willing to attempt something that is new or different. These students are usually the ones who experience difficulty in reading and understanding the various content materials assigned by the teacher.

Furthermore, the teacher's attitude about the effective use of study skills is just as important as the students. In order for students to read content materials successfully, they must understand what is expected of them. If they do not, it is essential that the teacher's objectives and expectations are clearly understood. If the teacher's primary objective in a lesson is that students understand the author's purpose, then this should be indicated to them before they begin to read. An effective means of assisting students having difficulty understanding the author's purpose is to discuss this with them. Active communication between teachers and students is essential to success in learning to use study skills effectively.

Cultural Background

Another important element in helping students to become more adept at studying is to identify and use cultural background attributes. A primary strength of this country is the diverse background of the people in it. Teachers should use this strength as it exists in their classroom to facilitate learning. Utilizing students' cultural strengths within lessons is an effective way to help them learn to use study skills more appropriately. Teachers should understand and use the cultural forces that have already influenced their students' development outside of the classroom. This knowledge of the diverse cultures of the students and their multicultural backgrounds can be used to enrich the classroom environment and instructional procedures. Also, this knowledge of the students' experiences will strengthen the rapport between students and teachers, and enhance learning.

General Knowledge

A third important factor that influences students' ability to apply study skills in learning content materials is general knowledge. This prior knowledge or schemata is composed of ideas and information that students possess as a result of their experiences and insights. Students differ in their cognitive development; thus, it is important for teachers to be aware of these differences. Typically, students will retain information, perceive relationships, and make inferences at various levels primarily because of different experiences, and widely-varying cultural and socioeconomic backgrounds.

General Health

An important factor in developing effective study skills is the general health of students in the teacher's classroom. It is especially important to be aware of any physical problems that students may exhibit, since physically ill students will not be able to achieve at levels equal to their capabilities.

Linguistic Knowledge and Flexibility

Linguistic knowledge and flexibility influences development of study skills. This is evidenced by the ability of fluent readers to demonstrate flexibility in their language, enhancing their application of study skills and learning content materials. However, inexperienced readers have less flexible linguistic strategies available to them in facilitating their application of study skills. Both types of students require assistance from the teacher in either developing new study skills strategies or expanding already learned strategies in order to improve their ability to apply study strategies.

Study Skills Readiness

A final factor to consider when teaching students how to use study skills effectively is their readiness for completing content assignments. In order to acquire information, students must be ready for the task. Appropriate instruction and supervision at school ensures that students are ready to undertake various content assignments; however, a problem may develop when assignments are to be completed at home. Assignments at home require intrinsic motivation that some students may be unable to generate. Students experiencing this type of problem may exhibit these behavioral characteristics: (a) forgetting to complete their homework assignments; (b) inability to use time wisely in which to fit every subject; (c) rarely finishing the assignments they start; or (d) finding it generally difficult to complete school work at home. These students need help in improving their readiness in applying study skills. It may also be advisable to contact these students' parents so that appropriate supervision can be provided at home. Parents could help students construct and use

Figure 10.1
Categories of
Study Skills

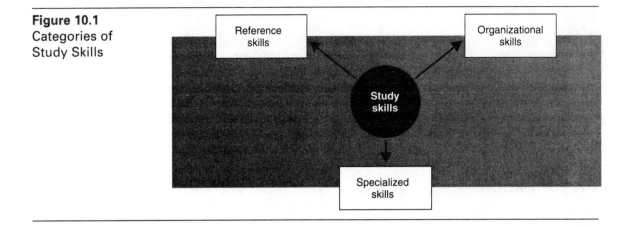

assignment sheets, prepare a study schedule for recording their daily and weekly activities, and organize their study habits. Coordination between parents and teachers is essential in developing effective study habits.

■ Identifying Study Skills

The study skills are divided into three basic categories: reference skills, organizational skills, and specialized study skills (see figure 10.1). Each of these skill areas is discussed in more detail in separate sections of this chapter. In addition to a discussion of each skill category, some research is provided to give insight into the importance of the various areas and findings that must be considered in developing the skills.

Reference Skills

Reference skills are primarily concerned with locating information in various sources. Skills in this category involve learning to use the dictionary and its subskills, using encyclopedias, using specialized reference materials such as the atlas and the almanac, and using the library card catalog or computer terminal.

Obviously, students need to understand the proper use of all the reference skills in order to gain information necessary for the further understanding of content materials. As students become more involved in the content areas in upper elementary school, the middle school, and the junior high school, these skills become more and more important. Students are frequently given assignments requiring them to locate information that can only be found in reference materials. The use of these skills becomes an indispensable tool for acquiring knowledge.

Unfortunately, many students from the upper elementary through the high school levels lack proficiency in using reference skills. Although a summary of British research studies indicates that a majority of students with access to an atlas at home were able to use it to some extent,[7] how many students have an atlas in their home? When these deficiencies occur, little is gained from criticizing prior instruction in the lower grades; it becomes the responsibility of teachers at these upper levels to improve the students' skills.

Even with appropriate instruction, many students will still experience difficulty in using reference materials effectively because of the readability level of much of the material. When students read on lower instructional levels than their grade placement, reference materials written on an even higher level represent a serious obstacle to acquiring information. Thus, teachers must assist students in using reference materials written at levels that most closely meet their students' reading levels.

Bond and Wagner suggest that skill in locating information in reference materials is dependent upon certain abilities: (1) appraisal of the problem, (2) knowledge of appropriate sources, (3) locating a desired source, (4) using the index and table of contents, and (5) skimming.[8]

Because learning to use reference materials is so vital to the learning process and is one of the primary objectives of the upper elementary grades,[9] Nelson recommends closer cooperation between the librarian and the teacher. She also recommends that games, films, and periodicals, such as *Sports Illustrated* and *Hot Rod*, should be used more in teaching reference skills.[10]

A suggestion for improving the students' skill in using the dictionary, in an effort to relieve some of the boredom, is the use of word games featuring limericks and synonyms.[11]

Learning to use reference skills is essential. Instruction in the various content areas places certain demands on students, requiring some degree of expertise in using reference skills. Without these skills, success will be hampered.

Organizational Skills

For some students an even more difficult task than learning to use reference skills is developing organizational skills. These require the ability to synthesize and evaluate the material read so that it can be organized into a workable format. A high level of cognition is required. The skills included in this area deal with developing outlines, underlining important points or key ideas, and taking notes during reading.

The need to outline compels students to locate the main idea in a passage and whatever details are essential to its development. The primary purpose of the outline technique is to help students locate the relevant information in a passage or series of materials. It is often suggested as a technique in studying for exams or preparing material for a research paper. Harris recommends teaching the use of outlines prior to teaching note-taking skills[12] while Hansell found that appropriate training improves the ability to outline.[13]

Harris and Sipay[14] suggest that students should be taught the effective use of outlining by:

1. Discussing the importance of outlining with students.
2. Demonstrating how to outline using previously read material.
3. Giving students a series of graded exercises in outlining and providing assistance in completing this task.

The skill of underlining is another valuable tool for organizing data and gathering information for research papers. An interesting aspect of underlining is that research has clearly indicated its superiority to outlining in gathering information.[15] It is also clear that underlining key words in a passage increases the likelihood that the information will be remembered.[16]

Poostay[17] has recommended that the following instructional sequence be used to assist students to develop and expand their underlining capabilities:

1. Copy a selection of 100–150 words.
2. Preview the selection, then underline key concepts. Include 5–7 key concepts per 100 words.
3. Make copies of the underlined selection for your students.
4. As you read a portion of the selection, have the students point to each underlined concept.
5. Demonstrate and discuss how and why each concept was selected.
6. Read the selection again and ask students to predict the content of the selection using only the underlined concepts.
7. Collect the underlined selection and give out the original source, and ask the students to read it.
8. Use unaided and aided recall strategies to check the students' comprehension of the selection.
9. Allow students to practice on other selections, and then encourage them to use this technique on their own.

Notetaking is the third important skill involved in organizing material. It is helpful when attending classes or perhaps listening to a speaker, because the student learns to write down only the important points. The primary task involved in taking notes is to distinguish relevant from irrelevant information. For taking notes, Hafner suggests the following procedures:

1. List the main points with necessary clarifying statements.
2. List illustrations (graphic and verbal) and experiments useful for clarifying points.
3. List key terms and their definitions.
4. List terms or concepts that need further clarification.[18]

Stahl, King and Henk[19] found that students' notetaking could be enhanced through training and evaluation. They suggested a four-step process that included modeling, practicing, evaluating, and reinforcing.

According to various research studies, notetaking appears to be a useful skill for students to develop as a technique for acquiring important information both in text material and in listening situations.[20]

The importance of these organizational skills cannot be overemphasized. They play a major role in successful reading. Research clearly indicates that training in these skills improves success in content reading, and that many students in the content areas are deficient in these skills.[21]

Specialized Study Skills

The specialized study skills are essential in obtaining as much information as possible from a book or other materials. In this particular skill area, all parts of a book or materials are analyzed to determine what information can be obtained from them and how best to understand the information presented. Some skills included in this area are previewing; scanning and skimming materials; reading maps, tables, graphs, and diagrams; adjusting rate according to material and purpose; and using appropriate study strategies such as SQ3R.

Previewing, scanning, and skimming content materials are valuable tools for learning about the organizational structure of materials, determining whether or not the information is useful, locating details, and determining the main ideas. Research indicates that previewing is especially valuable as an initial step in reading, and that instruction in how to read and interpret subheadings when previewing is essential.[22]

Another very important skill, especially in social studies, science, and math, is concerned with reading maps, tables, graphs, and diagrams. Unfortunately, research does not indicate clearly the order in which these subskills should be presented; however, no one disputes their usefulness.[23]

Adjusting rate according to the material and purpose is a third valuable skill that students must learn. Rate should be adjusted according to the difficulty level of the material and the purpose for which it is being read. For example, students should realize that they do not read a comic book in the same manner or at the same rate as they read their social studies book. Hafner and Jolly suggest that an appropriate rate is the maximum comfortable speed at which one can read and still understand the passage.[24]

A fourth valuable skill in reading content material is using appropriate study strategies such as SQ3R. These strategies are being used more widely by teachers; research indicates that they are being used successfully.[25] Selected strategies will be presented in the following section of this chapter.

Learning the proper use of study skills is essential to the reading process. These skills are particularly vital to comprehension of content materials. Without the ability to organize materials, use the dictionary, outline, understand specialized vocabulary, use parts of a book, read maps and charts, and use the many other skills, learning to read content-related material is a very difficult task.

Study Strategies

Study strategies are, in essence, learning strategies that students should activate when interacting with expository text. The ability to use these strategies effectively can be the determining factor in whether or not students understand the content materials that they are required to read in the school setting. Because of their importance to the learner, this section is devoted to the discussion of selected study strategies that teachers can introduce to their students. In order for students to gain the greatest benefit from these strategies, it is essential that teachers demonstrate and model appropriate usage of these strategies. Also, students should be given ample time to learn how to use these strategies effectively through practice, teacher feedback, and evaluation. When properly used, study strategies should enhance the student's ability to interact with expository material more effectively.

SQ3R One of the most widely used study strategies is SQ3R developed by Robinson. It is especially beneficial when used as a teacher-guided activity in the introduction of a new chapter or a new textbook. It can be used in groups or for the class as a whole. SQ3R comprises the following five steps:

Step 1: S = Survey. The reader surveys the material, giving careful attention to the title, introductory pages, heading, organization of the material, and summary. Following this survey, the reader should try to recall as much information as possible before going on to the next step.

Step 2: Q = Question. As the reader reviews what is remembered from the survey, specific questions should be formulated to be answered as the material is read. These questions assist the reader in establishing purposes for reading.

Step 3: R = Read. With specific questions in mind, and given a purpose by the teacher, the student reads the material to locate answers. It is possible that answers to all of the questions will not be found, and in that case other resources must be sought. In addition, the student should be encouraged to use these unanswered questions to stimulate class discussion.

Step 4: R = Recite. After reading the material, the student should recite the answers to the questions formulated prior to reading. This assists in remembering, and leads the reader to summarize the ideas presented. Recitation will help the reader to become more critical in analyzing the information and possibly question the logic of some of the author's ideas. This recitation is a personal matter; it is not a recitation to the class.

Step 5: R = Review. At this point, the reader reviews the ideas presented in the entire selection and may outline them mentally or on paper. The reader should attempt to fill in the specific details from what was read. If the student cannot review the material in this manner, then assistance is needed in developing the higher-level comprehension skills of interpretive and critical reading.[26]

There are variations of SQ3R for various content areas: the PQRST technique is recommended by Spache for studying science materials, and Fay has proposed the SQRQCQ technique for use in reading mathematics. Both procedures are outlined next.

Science: PQRST

Step 1: P = Preview. Rapidly skim the total selection.

Step 2: Q = Question. Raise questions to guide the careful reading that will follow.

Step 3: R = Read. Read the selection, keeping the questions in mind.

Step 4: S = Summarize. Organize and summarize the information gained from reading.

Step 5: T = Test. Check your summary against the selection to determine if the summary was accurate.[27]

Mathematics: SQRQCQ

Step 1: S = Survey. Read the problem rapidly to determine its nature.

Step 2: Q = Question. Decide what is being asked, what the problem is.

Step 3: R = Read. Read for details and interrelationships.

Step 4: Q = Question. Decide what processes should be used.

Step 5: C = Compute. Carry out the computation.

Step 6: Q = Question. Ask if the answer seems correct, check the computation against the problem facts and the basic arithmetic facts.[28]

PARS A modified and simplified study strategy developed by Smith and Elliot primarily for use with younger students who have limited experience in using study strategies. The steps are:

1. *Preview* the material to get a general sense of movement and organization, i.e., its important headings or concepts.
2. *Ask questions* before reading to make sure that you, as a student, are setting a purpose or purposes that satisfy you and your perception of what the teacher will emphasize.
3. *Read* with those purpose-setting questions in mind.
4. *Summarize* the reading by checking information gained against the pre-established questions.[29]

REAP This study strategy was developed by Eanet and Manzo to be used in reading and content area classrooms. It is intended to develop independence in reading while strengthening thinking and writing skills. In this strategy, students are not required to preview the material or establish questions to guide reading. Since there is no preparation for reading, the emphasis is on reading the material and remembering what the author has said. It is helpful if the student has some previously developed ability to summarize and take notes. The four steps are:

1. *Read.* The student reads to find out what the writer is saying.
2. *Encode.* The writer's message is translated by the student into his own language.
3. *Annotate.* Students write the message in notes for themselves using any one of several forms of annotation such as heuristic, summary, thesis, question, critical, intention, or motivation.
4. *Ponder.* The students think about the author's message and may wish to discuss their findings with others.[30]

K-W-L A study strategy developed by Ogle to enable teachers to assist students in activating prior knowledge when interacting with expository text, and to heighten their interest in reading this material. The three steps are:

1. *K - What I Know.* The students brainstorm in response to a concept presented by the teacher before they read the selection. Teachers should write down these ideas on the board, poster board, or any convenient place in order to use them as a beginning point for discussion. After this, teachers should generate categories from the brainstorming session that will enable students to better understand what they will be reading.
2. *W - What Do I Want to Learn?* Students develop questions that highlight their area of interest as a result of the activities in the first step. Students then read the selection.
3. *L - What I Learned.* After completing their reading selection, students write down what they have learned, check this against their questions, and finish answering any remaining questions.[31]

PORPE This writing-study strategy was developed by Simpson primarily for students to use in learning how to study for essay questions. As students encounter more expository text material, especially in upper elementary and middle school, they also encounter an increased emphasis on the use of essay questions to assess knowledge. Additionally, the current emphasis on qualitative assessment to assess students' knowledge, particularly in the elementary grades, is heavily dependent upon children's writing activities. Thus, it is likely that the use of essay questions for assessment purposes in the elementary grades will increase. The five steps are:

1. *Predicting* potential essay questions that may be asked.
2. *Organizing* key ideas for possible answers.
3. *Rehearsing* the key ideas for possible answers.
4. *Practicing* the recall of key ideas in self-assigned reading tasks.
5. *Evaluating* the completeness, accuracy, and appropriateness of their answers to essay questions as compared to key ideas and possible answers that were studied.[32]

RAM A study strategy developed by Dana to prepare poor readers for reading and sets the stage for the content. The three steps are:

1. *Relax* before beginning to read.
2. *Activate* purpose, attention, and prior knowledge.
3. *Motivate* yourself, as a student, for the reading task.[33]

SIP A study strategy developed by Dana that is designed to help poor readers focus their attention on content while reading. It is effective with both narrative and expository text. The three steps are:

1. *Summarize* the content of each page or naturally divided section of the text.
2. *Imaging* is important because it reminds the students to form an internal visual display of content encountered while reading. It is economical since it adds no time to the reading task, and it provides a second imprint of the text's content.
3. *Predict* while reading. Students should stop after each page or naturally divided section in the text and predict what might happen next. This step usually piques the reader's interest to the extent that many will want to read more to verify their prediction.[34]

RIPS This strategy was designed by Dana to help disabled readers repair comprehension problems while reading. It is especially effective in converting negative impulses toward the text material into a constructive process. The four steps are:

1. *Read on* and then *reread* when necessary. If comprehension breaks down during reading, then students should stop and reread until comprehension improves.

2. *Imaging* is an essential component of this strategy and requires students to image the content in order to provide themselves with a visual imprint of the material. Visual images that do not make sense will cue the readers that comprehension difficulties are continuing.

3. *Paraphrase* the problem section and restate the information in their own words.

4. *Speed up, slow down, and/or seek help.* This step reminds students that during the reading-on and rereading of text, they should possibly speed up or slow down their reading rate. If all else fails, the readers should seek help.[35]

■ Prescriptive Teaching of Study Skills

The last section of this chapter explores two concepts. The first relates to diagnostic procedures for the teachers' use. The second concerns the application of prescriptive techniques to the various study skill areas. Each of these concepts is explored individually in a table format.

Since the importance of diagnosis is evident, the first concept presented concerns the application of appropriate diagnostic procedures to the various skill areas (see table 10.1). Each primary skill is represented, allowing the teacher to use the table efficiently. Unfortunately, the lack of formal diagnostic procedures related to study skills to some extent impedes diagnosis; however, using informal diagnostic procedures does yield much specific information, which is of great value to the teacher.

Since so few diagnostic procedures are available as compared to the other skill areas, all of the study skills are listed together with the appropriate corresponding diagnostic procedures. In some instances, the diagnostic tools specify a particular study skill area that is measured. Those instances are clearly noted in the table.

Table 10.1

Diagnostic Procedures for Evaluating Study Skill Areas

Skill Areas	Procedures
Reference, Organizational, and Specialized Study Skills	Criterion-referenced tests Group Reading Inventory *Iowa Silent Reading Test* (Directed Reading Subtest measuring Dictionary, Library, Locational, Skimming, Scanning, and Encyclopedia skills) *MAT6 Reading Diagnostic Tests* (Skimming, Scanning) Observation checklist *Test of Reading Comprehension*

The diagnostic procedures presented in table 10.1 give information that can be used in diagnosing students' strengths and weaknesses in study skills. When this diagnostic information has been used by the teacher, the next step is the implementation of a prescriptive program.

Prescriptive techniques for use in the classroom are presented in the final portion of this chapter. Each of the major study skill areas is divided according to specific skills, with activities presented to assist teachers in their instructional programs. These ideas are presented in table 10.2.

The preceding table represents an effort to provide diagnostic-prescriptive information in a format that is usable and that will enhance teachers' effectiveness in developing study skills.

Table 10.2

Study Skills

Skill	Prescriptive Technique
Reference Skills	
Use dictionary	Divide the group into teams. Call out a word and see which group can locate the word first. They must give the guide words in order to score a point.
	Give students a pronunciation key from the dictionary and a list of words spelled using the symbols from the pronunciation key. Take turns pronouncing the words using the appropriate accent.
Use encyclopedia	Put various topics on slips of paper and let students select one. Ask them to find the appropriate encyclopedia to locate information on the topic. Then identify five important facts about the topic.
	Play a game with the students taking turns being the librarian. The other students select prepared questions or make up questions to ask the librarian. When the librarian locates the answer in the encyclopedia, another student becomes the librarian.
Use specialized reference materials	Give students cards that tell about a trip they have won. Use an atlas to determine the roads they should take to get to their destination.
	Use questions that students prepare and that can be answered with an almanac. Let a student ask a question and see who can locate the information first. The winner gets to ask the next question.
Use library card catalog or computer terminal	Give assignments that can be answered from the card catalog. Let students work in teams to locate the information requested.
	Ask students to prepare questions that other students may answer using the card catalog. Different classes may exchange their questions and have contests.
Organizational Skills	
Develop outlines	Prepare a large model of an outline, omitting the words. Tape it to the floor or the wall. Give students the information that could complete the outline. Let them fill in the blanks.
	Give students sentence strips containing information that could be put together to form an outline. Ask them to develop the outline. Two groups may compete to see who can finish first. They may then write a story from the outline.

Table 10.2

Continued

Skill	Prescriptive Technique
Underline important points or key ideas	Give each team a short selection and a red pen. Get them to discuss and agree upon the important points that should be remembered and underlined. Use several copies of a selection and ask students to underline the key ideas. Then compare what each student marked. For any points that differ, ask the student to explain why they were underlined.
Take notes during reading	Ask students to take notes as they read by listing important points. Then ask them to use their notes to report what they read to another student. Let them check one another to be sure all important points were covered. Let students read different sections of a chapter and take notes. Then combine the notes to see if the most important information is included as they use the notes to answer questions.
Specialized Study Skills *Use title page*	Give students several title pages and a list of questions that can be answered using the title page. Keep score as to who can answer the most questions. Ask each student to develop one question that can be answered from the title page. Let them ask the question of the class. When all the questions are answered, ask students to work in pairs and design their own title page.
Use table of contents and lists of charts	Play a game in which students give clues to locate information in the table of contents. For example, "I'm looking for the page number for the story, *The Gray Fox.*" Give students a book without the table of contents and ask them to make one to go with the book.
Locate introduction, preface, and foreword	Have a treasure hunt in the classroom to locate books containing an introduction, preface, or foreword. Award one point for each one with an introduction, two points for each preface, three points for each foreword, and four bonus points for a book with all three components. Go through a book containing two or three of these components and develop questions from the information provided. To answer the questions, students must read the information in the book.
Use appendix	Give students materials that refer them to the appendixes in the material. Ask them to follow the reference and locate specific information in the designated appendix. Play "I Am Looking For" by telling the students things that you are looking for. All the information should be located in one of the appendixes in a book that they have.
Identify bibliography and lists of suggested readings	After reading material in a book containing a list of suggested readings, refer the students to this list and ask them to select the two readings that seem most interesting to them and tell why they seem interesting. Ask students to look at the bibliography in a book and find one or more of the materials listed in the bibliography. Then look at the material and determine what the author used from this source in writing the material.
Use glossary and index	Give students a crossword puzzle using words from the glossary in the book. In order to complete the puzzle, the student must use the glossary. Ask students questions that can be answered from a book. However, to answer the questions they must locate the information in the index of the book.

Table 10.2

Continued

Skill	Prescriptive Technique
Use study questions	Direct students to use the study questions to help establish their purposes for reading a material. They may try to answer the questions prior to reading the material and then answer them after they read. Let students read material and develop study questions that would aid other students as they read the material.
Read maps, tables, graphs, and diagrams	Draw a map to be followed as students go on a treasure hunt around the classroom or school. As they reach certain points, other maps are given until they find the one that directs them to the hidden treasure. Get one group in the class to make a graph or table about the class, the weather, or something of interest to the students. Then let this group explain to the others in the class how the information can be read.
Use footnotes, typographical aids, and marginal notes	Give students material containing footnotes and ask them to answer a question from the information in a footnote. For example, "What is the first page of the information that the author used in this reference?" Ask students to make an outline of a chapter using only the words in bold and italic type. Then ask them to read the chapter to see if these were actually the most important ideas.
Preview, skim, or scan materials	Give students a short selection and two questions that can be answered from the selection. Allow them a very short time to skim the material to locate the answer. Ask students to preview a chapter before they read it and list at least two questions that they want to answer as they read the material.
Adjust rate according to material and purpose	Give students two selections to read, one technical and one light narrative. Ask them to choose a selection and tell how quickly they will read it by placing a SLOW or FAST sign on their desk. Prior to each reading activity, ask students why they are reading the material and at what rate the material should be read according to their purpose. Let them keep a log for several days to note the material, the purpose for reading it, and the rate.
Understand general and specialized vocabulary	Develop a vocabulary bank that contains all new words learned in each class. Each card in the bank should contain the word, the definition, and a sentence. If the word is general or relates to every content area, a red line should be placed across the card; if it relates to math, a blue line, and so on for each subject area. Words relating to several areas would have the various definitions and colors on the card. Identify all vocabulary words in each lesson that may cause problems in reading the material. Discuss these words and their meanings as used in the context of the material. Use the newspaper and search for the words to see if they can be used to mean other things.
Use appropriate study strategies such as SQ3R	Make a large sign to hang as a mobile in the classroom to remind the students to use the appropriate study technique as they read. Periodically review the study technique with the students to encourage them to use the procedure correctly. As students are introduced to the different study procedures appropriate to particular content areas, tell them they will have their own codes or formulas that other classes in the school will not know. These formulas, such as SQ3R, will help them read the content material more easily. Then continuously use the "code" language with them to encourage its use.

■ Summary

Study skills provide the essential structure for the acquisition of knowledge from the printed page. The development of these skills is crucial to becoming an independent reader with the ability to comprehend specific information, especially from the various content materials.

The three primary categories of study skills are reference, organizational, and specialized study skills. Various techniques for teaching these skills include demonstration, inquiry, discovery, and problem solving.

Reference skills involve such skills as using the dictionary, encyclopedias, and library card catalog or computer terminal, while organizational skills include outlining, underlining, and notetaking. The third category, specialized study skills, stresses learning skills, such as how to use parts of a book, previewing, skimming, scanning, and study strategies.

Study strategies are in essence learning strategies that students should activate when interacting with expository text. The ability of students to use these strategies may be the determining factor in whether or not they understand the content materials that they are required to read in school.

Diagnostic-prescriptive procedures and techniques were presented in tables to provide specific information to teachers for use in their classrooms.

■ Applying What You Read

You are the language arts teacher for the sixth grade. The students have difficulty in using materials in the library. Which skills would you need to develop, and how would you go about it?

Study strategies are used most often in the content areas. How can the content teacher develop these strategies? Select one content area and some specific study strategies to use as an example.

Design a study skills program that would involve all the content teachers in your school. Decide how diagnostic data will be obtained, and which content areas will be used to develop and review the specific skills.

■ Notes

1. Carl B. Smith, *Teaching in Secondary School Content Subjects*, p. 252.
2. Larry A. Harris and Carl B. Smith, *Reading Instruction: Diagnostic Teaching in the Classroom*, p. 334.
3. Bonnie B. Armbruster and Thomas H. Anderson, "Research Synthesis on Study Skills," *Educational Leadership*, p. 154.
4. Armbruster and Anderson, "Research Synthesis on Study Skills," p. 155.
5. B. Y. L. Wong and W. Jones, "Increasing Metacomprehension in Learning Disabled and Normally-Achieving Students Through Self-Questioning Training."
6. Kenneth G. Graham and H. Alan Robinson, *Study Skills Handbook: A Guide for All Teachers*.
7. Herbert A. Sandford, "Directed and Free Search of the School Atlas Map," *The Cartographic Journal*.
8. Guy L. Bond and Eva B. Wagner, *Teaching the Child to Read*, 4th ed., Chapters 10–11.
9. Ryland W. Crary, *Humanizing the School: Curriculum Development and Theory*, p. 195.
10. Raedeane M. Nelson, "Getting Children into Reference Books," *Elementary English*, pp. 884–87.
11. Mary Louise Labe, "Improve the Dictionary's Image," *Elementary English*.
12. Albert J. Harris and Edward R. Sipay, *How to Increase Reading Ability*, 6th ed., p. 491.
13. T. Stevenson Hansell, "Stepping up to Outlining," *Journal of Reading*.

14. Albert J. Harris and Edward R. Sipay, *How to Increase Reading Ability: A Guide to Developmental and Remedial Methods*, 8th ed., p. 521.

15. James Crewe and Dayton Hullgren, "What Does Research Really Say About Study Skills?" in *The Psychology of Reading Behavior, 18th Yearbook National Reading Conference*, pp. 75–78.

16. James Hartley, Sally Bartlett, and Alan Branthwaite, "Underlining Can Make a Difference—Sometimes," *Journal of Educational Research*.

17. Edward J. Poostay, "Show Me Your Underlines: A Strategy to Teach Comprehension," *The Reading Teacher*, pp. 828–29.

18. Lawrence E. Hafner, *Developmental Reading in Middle and Secondary Schools: Foundations, Strategies, and Skills for Teaching*, p. 176.

19. Norman A. Stahl, James R. King, and William A. Henk, "Enhancing Students' Notetaking Through Training and Evaluation," *Journal of Reading*, pp. 614–23.

20. James W. Dyer, James Riley, and Frank Yekovich, "An Analysis of Three Study Skills: Notetaking, Summarizing, and Rereading," *Journal of Educational Research*; Vincent P. Orlando, "Notetaking vs. Notesaving: A Comparison While Studying From Text," in *Reading Research: Studies and Applications, 28th Yearbook of the National Reading Conference*, edited by Michael L. Kamil and Alden J. Moe, pp. 177–81; Carol A. Carrier and Amy Titus, "Effects of Notetaking Pretraining and Test Mode Expectations on Learning from Lectures," *American Educational Research Journal*.

21. George D. Spache and Evelyn B. Spache, *Reading in the Elementary School*, 4th ed., p. 291.

22. Spache and Spache, *Reading in the Elementary School*, p. 278; J. K. Hirstendahl, "The Effect of Subheads on Reader Comprehension," *Journalism Quarterly*.

23. Spache and Spache, *Reading in the Elementary School*, p. 282.

24. Lawrence E. Hafner and Hayden B. Jolly, *Patterns of Teaching Reading in the Elementary School*, p. 176.

25. Abby Adams, Douglas Carnine, and Russell Gersten, "Instructional Strategies for Studying Content Area Texts in the Intermediate Grades," *Reading Research Quarterly*.

26. Francis P. Robinson, *Effective Study*, 4th ed.

27. George D. Spache, *Toward Better Reading*.

28. Leo Fay, "Reading Skills: Math and Science," in *Reading and Inquiry*, edited by J. Allen Figurel.

29. Carl B. Smith and Peggy G. Elliot, *Reading Activities for Middle and Secondary Schools*, pp. 194–95.

30. Marilyn G. Eanet and Anthony V. Manzo, "REAP—A Strategy for Improving Reading/ Writing/Study Skills," *Journal of Reading*, pp. 647–52.

31. Donna M. Ogle, "K-W-L: A Teaching Model that Develops Active Reading of Expository Text," *The Reading Teacher*, pp. 564–70.

32. Michele L. Simpson, "PORPE: A Writing Strategy for Studying and Learning in the Content Areas," *Journal of Reading*, pp. 407–14.

33. Carol Dana, "Strategy Families for Disabled Readers," *Journal of Reading*, p. 31.

34. Dana, "Strategy Families for Disabled Readers," pp. 31–32.

35. Dana, "Strategy Families for Disabled Readers," p. 32.

■ Other Suggested Readings

Anderson, Thomas H., and Bonnie B. Armbruster, "Studying," in *Handbook of Reading Research* pp. 657–80. Edited by P. David Pearson. New York City, New York: Longman 1984: 657–80.

Ankney, Paul, and Pat McClurg. "Testing Manzo's Guided Reading Procedure." *The Reading Teacher* 34 (March 1981): 681–85.

Blanchard, Jay S. "What to Tell Students About Underlining . . . and Why." *Journal of Reading* 29 (December 1985): 199–203.

Cushenberry, Donald C. "Effective Procedures for Teaching Reference Study Skills." *Reading Horizons* 19 (Spring 1979): 245–47.

Kiewra, Kenneth A. "Acquiring Effective Notetaking Skills: An Alternative to Professional Notetaking." *Journal of Reading* 27 (January 1984): 299–302.

Levin, Joel R., Jill Kessley Berry, Gloria E. Miller, and Nina P. Bartell. "More on How (and How Not) to Remember the States and Their Capitals." *The Elementary School Journal* 82 (March 1982): 379–88.

Moorman, Gary B., and William E. Blanton. "The Information Text Reading Activity (ITRA): Engaging Students in Meaningful Learning." *Journal of Reading* 34 (November 1990): 174–183.

Schilling, Frank C. "Teaching Study Skills in the Intermediate Grades—We Can Do More." *Journal of Reading* 27 (April 1984): 620–23.

Shugarman, Sherrie L., and Joe B. Hurst. "Purposeful Paraphrasing: Promoting a Nontrivial Pursuit for Meaning." *Journal of Reading* 29 (February 1986): 396–99.

Simmers-Wolpow, Ray, Daniel P. Farrell, and Marian J. Tonjes. "Implementing a Secondary Reading/Study Skills Program Across Disciplines." *Journal of Reading* 34 (May 1991): 590–95.

Simpson, Michele L. "The Status of Study Strategy Instruction: Implications for Classroom Teachers." *Journal of Reading* 28 (November 1984): 136–43.

Spires, Hiller A., and P. Diane Stone. "The Directed Notetaking Activity: A Self-questioning Approach." *Journal of Reading* 33 (October 1989): 36–39.

Thelen, Judith. *Improving Reading in Science.* Delaware: International Reading Association, 1983.

Tierney, Robert J., John E. Readence, and Ernest K. Dishner. *Reading Strategies and Practices: A Compendium.* 3rd ed. Boston: Allyn and Bacon, 1990: 282–319.

Wade, Suzanne E., and Ralph E. Reynolds. "Developing Metacognitive Awareness." *Journal of Reading* 33 (October 1989): 6–15.

11

Personal Reading

Up to this point, some teachers continue to perceive prescriptive reading instruction as involving strictly the teaching of individual skills. This is definitely not true in a good diagnostic-prescriptive reading program! A major component that distinguishes a skill-development program from a diagnostic-prescriptive program is personal reading. Until students have the opportunity to use reading skills in a reading situation and choose to read, the program has not fulfilled all of its objectives.

Personal reading development is not included in all classes at some schools. This was vividly pointed out as one of the students eagerly told a class visitor that she was working on compound words in reading. When asked how she used these skills, the student replied, "I don't know, but I get a check mark when I finish the game!" Without personal reading, the word identification, comprehension, and study skills remain fragmented parts that do not contribute to the development of a mature reader.

To provide ideas regarding the incorporation of personal reading into the diagnostic-prescriptive program, this chapter is designed to answer the following questions:

What is personal reading?

Why is personal reading important in a diagnostic-prescriptive reading program?

How is personal reading developed?

How does personal reading relate to other reading instruction?

How can students be motivated to read?

What are some techniques for developing personal reading habits?

As this chapter is read, the following terms are important to note.

Vocabulary to Know

Affective domain	Creative reading	Recreational reading
Bibliotherapy	Personal reading	Sustained silent reading

■ The Importance of Personal Reading

Recreational reading, reading for enjoyment, and application of reading skills are terms sometimes used when referring to personal reading. Regardless of what this crucial area is called, the idea is the same. In personal reading, students **apply all their knowledge to decode words and interpret printed symbols in order to increase their enjoyment and knowledge.**

The importance of personal reading in the reading curriculum is reinforced in the recommendations of *Becoming a Nation of Readers* prepared by the Commission on Reading. Five of the seventeen recommendations given in the report relate to the importance of personal reading. They include:

- Parents should read to preschool children and informally teach them about reading and writing.
- Parents should support school-aged childrens' continued growth as readers.
- Children should spend more time in independent reading.
- Schools should cultivate an ethos that supports reading.
- Schools should maintain well-stocked and managed libraries.[1]

These recommendations not only point to the importance of developing personal reading habits but also say explicitly that the development of such abilities requires effort on the part of parents, teachers, students, and entire school faculties.

Students who have developed the prereading, word identification, comprehension, and study skills, yet do not read to enrich their lives, need prescriptive instruction in personal reading, just as do students who have difficulty in understanding cause-effect relationships. Unless students perceive the learning of reading skills as an aid in reading materials and developing a lifetime habit of reading, then their knowledge is little more than isolated learning and is of little benefit. Therefore, teachers and students should continuously remind themselves that skill knowledge in reading is a *means* of assisting the student to learn the necessary fundamentals in order to develop personal reading habits. *Students learn to read by reading!*

In a diagnostic-prescriptive reading program, teachers and students sometimes become so involved with skills instruction that the application of the knowledge in personal reading becomes secondary. Teachers and administrators who make personal reading the major goal of the school reading program demonstrate to students that reading is more than skill development. This point cannot be overemphasized, as the authors noted in working with approximately sixty second and third graders. When asked to draw a picture of what reading meant to them, two drew a picture of the teacher reading to a class, five drew themselves reading books on their own, and the remainder showed skill development activities ranging from the basal reader groups to doing worksheets! Thus, good prescriptive reading instruction includes reading experiences that are meaningful and that help students want to read.

The following five areas of personal reading are "the skills" included for all students in the prescriptive program (see figure 11.1):

Enjoy and respond to stories and poems read by others.

This is a personal reading habit begun at a very young age, prior to school entrance, as parents read to their children. This is a pleasant experience that initiates enjoyment of the rhythm of language as well as the information from the story. Teachers continue to read to students to broaden their background of experience and motivate them to read on their own.

Read materials for enjoyment.

This includes reading books, comic books, or any material that gives the student pleasure. These materials are usually written at the student's independent reading level.

Read materials to gain information.

Students should appreciate using reading to gain information. This may include using reference materials, reading books and magazines, brochures, or any other printed material.

Learn more about self through reading about others.

As students read, they learn about other people, their joys and sorrows, as well as how they cope in life situations. This knowledge of others not only teaches the students about life, but also helps them learn more about themselves as they face daily life situations. Books that relate to situations a student can identify with often help in dealing with problems or experiences the student is facing.

Figure 11.1

Goals of Personal Reading Skill Development in a Diagnostic-Prescriptive Reading Program

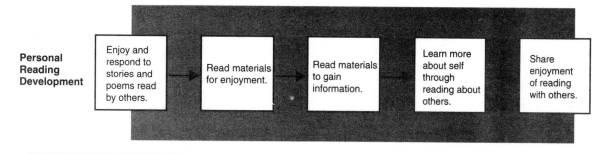

Share enjoyment of reading with others.

The student who has fully developed personal reading habits not only reads, but also shares with others the ideas gained from the materials.

Personal reading is the reading skills of the affective domain. Reading skills in the other areas emphasize the cognitive aspect of learning. In order for students to succeed with the cognitive skills, development of the affective domain is vital.

This includes not only learning to enjoy reading, but also the development of a positive self-image. Pryor suggests that "changing a poor reader's self-concept by bolstering his feeling about himself is perhaps the first step toward improving the academic problem."[2] Additional ideas regarding the interrelationship of self-concept and reading are presented by Quandt.[3] This affective component of reading aids in the development of interest, attitudes, and personal values, as well as in reading for information and enjoyment. These areas are addressed more specifically in the following pages. To know how to develop this area with individual students, teachers use informal measures along with their own knowledge of children to diagnose a student's status in the development of personal reading skills and to provide the proper direction for growth in the affective areas.

■ Motivating Students to Read

Motivating students to read is often a greater challenge to teachers than teaching the cognitive skills in reading. Motivation to learn involves two basic components: interests and attitudes. The importance of motivation, interests, and attitudes becomes readily apparent when one realizes the relationship between motivation (including interests and attitudes) and reading achievement. Den Heyer not only found this relationship to be significant but also learned that the relationship between motivational measures and reading achievement increases consistently with age, with the relationship being well established in the higher primary grades.[4] Walberg and Tsai suggest that the strongest correlates of reading achievement are attitude towards reading, kindergarten attendance, use of English in the home, and stimulating materials in the home environment.[5] Further research has indicated a strong relation between liking/not liking reading and liking/not liking school.[6] With our increased concern about school-dropouts and the war on illiteracy, the teachers and administrators in the school reading programs must acknowledge the importance of motivation!

There is no simple way to motivate students, but much can be done to interest them in reading.

Attitudes can be improved by providing appropriate instruction in an exciting manner, rewarding the student with words of praise, using appropriate techniques, and providing materials that are interesting and written at the appropriate level.

Much research has been conducted regarding students' reading interests.[7] From this vast amount of information, teachers have attempted to select materials based on the age level of the students. Weintraub concluded that no single category of books will give children of the same age what they want to read. Thus, he suggests that each teacher identify the unique reading interests of the students in the classroom and select books with this knowledge in mind.

Moray presented a summary of the research in the area of reading interests. She concludes that:

- Gender is a more important factor than intelligence, race, grade, or economic level in determining reading preferences at each age and grade level.
- At the age of 9 or 10, girls will read books that interest boys, but boys will not read books that interest girls.
- Teachers must be aware of individual student interests, rather than relying on broad generalizations.
- Materials other than textbooks must be included in the reading program, as basals do not contain the variety of stories necessary to meet the identified interests of students.[8]

Although reading interests vary from student to student, in a review of research relating to student's reading interests, Huus found several patterns that may be helpful in motivating students to read. She noted that primary level students like animals, home and family, make-believe, and cowboys as topics, but they also express interests in history and science informational materials. Through the middle years of elementary school, although gender differences in interests appear, both boys and girls like mystery, animals, adventure, comics, and humor. Huus also observed that interests in reading appear to have changed little over the years, and that the factors that affect reading interest are gender, age, literary quality, and the reading program.[9]

Each year the International Reading Association and Children's Book Council have a joint project that evaluates children's books published during the year. From this evaluation, a list of children's favorites are identified and published in the October issue of *The Reading Teacher*. Sebasta evaluated the books selected for "Children's Choices" to determine if they had characteristics that differed from other books not selected by children. He found:

- Plots of the "Children's Choices" are faster paced than those found in books not chosen as favorites.
- Young children enjoy reading about nearly any topic if the information is presented in a specific way. The topic may be less important than interest studies have indicated, as specifics rather than topics seem to underlie the preferences.
- Children like detailed descriptions of settings. They want to know exactly how the place looks and feels before the main action occurs.

- One type of plot structure does not dominate these favorite books. Some stories have a central focus with a carefully arranged cause-and-effect plot, while others have plots that meander with episodes showing no connection.
- Children do not like sad books.
- Many books explicitly teach a lesson.
- Warmth was the most outstanding quality found in the books. Children enjoy books where the characters like each other, express their feelings in things they say and do, and sometimes act selflessly.[10]

If teachers expect students to develop personal reading skills, students need to have interesting materials. These include not only library books, but also magazines, newspapers, and comic books. These materials sometimes interest students in reading; they seem to be more fun to read because they differ from the traditional school reading materials.[11] Developing an interest in some material and allowing the student to complete the material successfully is a motivating experience that will begin to change negative attitudes towards reading. Appendix F contains a selected bibliography of children's books.

Alexander and Filler identified several variables that seem to be associated with attitudes toward reading. These are achievement, self-concept, parents and the home environment, the teacher and classroom environment, instructional practices and special programs, gender, test intelligence, socioeconomic status, and interests.[12] As teachers attempt to improve students' attitudes toward reading, keep these ideas in mind:

- In order to have a positive feeling toward themselves and what they are doing, students need to be successful and commended for their efforts. Reading is no exception. Materials that are appropriate for the students' reading levels assist in developing this positive feeling.
- Teachers' awareness of the students' attitudes toward reading is essential. This can be learned from observation, supplemented with the use of an attitude inventory. Some questions relating to attitude toward reading are included in the interest inventory instrument in appendix C.
- A student's attitude toward reading material affects comprehension of the material. For example, the student who does not like social studies but enjoys science will probably read science material with greater understanding than social studies material.
- Initial attitudes towards reading are formed by parents and the home environment. This factor must be accepted and an effort made to help parents realize the effect of their attitude on the student's progress in reading.

In a study of the effect of home and school on early interest in literature, Morrow found high interest children preferred crayon and paper activities, looked at books more frequently, had more library cards, were read to more often, and watched less television than low interest children. More parents of children in the high interest group held college or graduate degrees and voluntarily read as a leisure time activity. Parents of children in the high interest group read more novels and magazines than did parents of children in the low interest groups.[13] Parental cooperation is extremely important in overcoming negative attitudes toward reading.

Schools can communicate either positive or negative feelings about reading. Teachers who are enthusiastic about reading, classrooms that invite students to read, and a program that stresses reading as an exciting part of the school, greatly assist in the development of positive attitudes toward reading. Flexible grouping and varied instruction are more conducive to improving attitudes toward reading than rigid ability groups.[14]

Teachers must be cautious about making generalizations regarding students' attitudes toward reading. Girls do not necessarily have better attitudes toward reading than boys,[15] just as brighter students do not always have a better attitude than less intelligent students.[16] Moreover, teachers should not assume that students from lower socioeconomic backgrounds are more likely to have negative attitudes toward reading.[17]

Roettger found that high attitude/low performance students viewed reading as important to life survival while low attitude/high performance students perceived reading as a means of personal improvement and academic success. Both groups felt, however, that too little time and concern was given to personal reading in their classrooms.[18]

In order to develop the cognitive reading skills in a meaningful way, students must be motivated to read. This means meeting the interests and improving attitudes toward reading. The following section presents more ideas that can be used in the prescriptive teaching of personal reading.

■ Techniques for Developing Personal Reading

Motivate students to read, persuade students to be excited about reading, improve their attitudes toward reading—how many times do teachers hear these requests! In the area of personal reading, specific skills are not identifiable and assessing specific strengths or weaknesses is very subjective; likewise ways to develop this area are less definite. This is because (1) the behaviors are not easily identifiable, and (2) students respond differently. Teachers find, as they review activity books, that most suggestions are directed toward the development of cognitive skills with few ideas presented for the personal reading area. Yet personal reading is basic to developing good readers.

To assist teachers in developing personal reading, this section presents ideas that can be used in improving the classroom atmosphere through the use of activities, bibliotherapy, and creative reading. Remember to share ideas with parents in order to derive maximum benefit from the school activities.

Classroom Atmosphere

On the first day of school as students go into their classroom, they notice that it is clean and colorful. The bulletin boards invite them into the room and give clues that learning will be fun this year. Book jackets and words indicating that reading is important are displayed throughout the room. In a back corner is a rug with bright cushions scattered around. Several shelves of books, magazines, comic books, and even a newspaper arouse the curiosity of the students. How soon can they go to the corner and stretch out on the floor to read a magazine?

The atmosphere in this room is conducive to the development of personal reading. However, teachers must plan for the students to obtain maximum benefit from these resources. Each student needs time to look at books every day, to expand interests in reading, and to apply the reading skills that are being taught. Reading as a pleasurable activity does not just happen; the teacher provides this opportunity through careful planning, structuring opportunities and instruction, while making it appear to be unstructured learning.

To provide students with opportunities to read and to see others read, many teachers are using USSR (Uninterrupted Sustained Silent Reading), SSR (Substantial or Sustained Silent Reading), or SQRT (Sustained Quiet Reading Time) in their classrooms. This procedure may be used with a total classroom or a total school so as to involve everyone in reading. In attaining this objective, the key to the success is that *everyone* be involved. If the idea is used in a total school, all of the students, teachers, administrators, and staff must observe the time and read some material silently for a designated time per day or at least twice a week. This brief time for silent reading is not a break for the teacher to plan or grade papers, or for the principal to check to see who is following directions. It is a time for reading or looking at printed material. This procedure serves as a motivational tool for many students when it is introduced in a positive manner and allows everyone to participate. The principal may want to read with various classes so students have another adult reading model. After the designated time for reading, the students proceed with their other work unless someone wants to share what was read. This is not a requirement and is done only if initiated by the student and for only a brief period of time.

A classroom teacher may wish to initiate this idea for five minutes one day a week to begin motivating students to read on their own. The time can be increased to a maximum of fifteen minutes as students become more familiar with the procedure, and it may be expanded to include the entire school. This uninterrupted silent reading time is provided to allow students time to experience the joys of silent reading and to begin to develop good reading habits.

A modification of SSR may be used with beginning readers. "Booktime" should be held at the same time each day, beginning with one to five minutes per group and progressing to ten to fifteen minutes. The teacher works with five to seven students at a time and places books, which have been introduced by the teacher as stories are read to the class, into a reading center area. Just as in SSR, the teacher reads while the students read, but she may also answer questions and pronounce words at the students' requests. During "Booktime" the students may read in pairs and talk quietly about the books.[19]

Another inviting way to motivate students to read in their extra time is through the use of a reading area or center in the classroom. This classroom library needs a variety of books displayed in an interesting manner. The center may have some paperbacks in a book rack along with the books borrowed from the school library. The teacher may add a rug and some large pillows to make the area more exciting. The authors have seen many motivating reading centers in classrooms at all levels. Some teachers add old bathtubs or sofas to encourage students to relax as they read. Another idea is to add a tree house in one corner of the room. This may consist of a large tree limb planted in a container with paper leaves on which new words are written. More elaborate tree houses may be made by painting a large tree on the wall and ceiling, then building a small platform where students can sit while they read. Some teachers may build a "reading shack" in their reading area. This is made of a wooden, house-shaped frame covered with chicken wire. Cushions on the floor enable the students to sit comfortably as they read in a more isolated environment.

In addition to a motivating reading area, teachers can enhance the classroom atmosphere by using colorful bulletin boards that encourage students to read. These displays are changed frequently and may be done by students as a way of sharing what they read. Other ideas for motivating students to read are presented by Fennimore, Roeder and Lee, and Johns and Lunt.[20]

The physical classroom atmosphere has a marked effect on student interest in reading. Desk arrangement, grouping procedures, reading centers, and displays can work to encourage or to deter reading progress. Remember that the classroom atmosphere also includes teacher-student relationships, teacher attitude toward reading, and the overall attitude of the teacher concerning the school and the students. An attractive room will not overcome a negative teacher attitude. Thus, the classroom teacher who is positive about learning and shows a feeling of concern about meeting the individual reading needs of each student will have students with positive attitudes about reading. When both students and teachers feel good about where they are, the atmosphere is more conducive to learning!

Bibliotherapy

Bibliotherapy is defined as "getting the right book to the right child at the right time."[21] This procedure is used to help students acquire insight into areas of interest or problems that they may be facing. Bibliotherapy is a way of providing therapy through books. For example, the student whose parents are getting a divorce may get some help in dealing with the problem by reading *It's Not the End of the World*, by Judy Blume (Bantam Press, 1972), or *The Boys and Girls Book About Divorce*, by Richard A. Gardner, M.D. (Bantam Press, 1970), or *Chloris and the Creeps*, by Kin Platt (Dell, 1973). Huck and Kuhn suggest that the three processes in bibliotherapy correspond to the three phases of psychotherapy: identification, catharsis, and insight. In the identification phase, the student associates self with another person. Catharsis is the release of the emotion in some manner. Insight is the emotional awareness to deal with the problem.[22]

The classroom teacher can use bibliotherapy to interest students in reading by guiding them to materials that relate to their particular needs. This motivates them to read more on their own in order to identify with others in similar situations. Thus, bibliotherapy is another way to assist students in developing personal reading.

Studies conducted using bibliotherapy in the classroom tend to be short-term. Tillman found that 14 weeks seemed to be the maximum length of treatment.[23] Such short-term studies have raised questions as to the usefulness of this strategy in changing student attitudes[24]; however, teachers are encouraged to consider this a helpful strategy for select students who are experiencing problems with self and are avoiding reading. In using the strategy, there needs to be a long-term commitment to student development over a period of time—attitudes and personalities do not change quickly! As this strategy is used at school, teachers may find that results occur more quickly when parents are included. Edwards and Simpson found that the use of bibliotherapy with parents and children resulted in opening lines of communication, stimulating parent's interest in their child's reading, increasing the child's interest in recreational reading, and helping the parent and child appreciate the value of reading.[25]

Creative Reading

As the cognitive reading skills are developed, students are encouraged to react to the printed word by expressing their own ideas about what they have read. This expression of feeling is done through dramatics, writing, art, music, or thought. Creative reading is based on an expansion of the cognitive comprehension skills into the affective areas of individual reaction of expression.

Many students expand their personal reading because of the enjoyment of expressing their interpretation about what the author has said. Language arts activities, including creative thinking, are often used to enhance the development of creative reading. Turner and Alexander have suggested:

> A classroom environment in which reading is perceived by the teacher as a creative activity will be more likely to develop in children a view that reading is a fascinating and wonderful adventure. This concept of reading will not easily be lost in later years. But if it is not instilled early in school experiences, it will be even more difficult to gain in upper grades.[26]

Turner and Alexander suggested four areas that need to be considered in developing creative reading:

1. The types of reading materials that provide the best stimulus for creative thinking.
2. Ways of structuring oral questions and discussions to help students think creatively about reading.
3. Reading tasks that open rather than close doors to productive, creative thoughts.
4. Environments that encourage creative behavior.

Teachers must provide opportunities for students to read creatively as another means of developing personal reading. Although creative reading is sometimes viewed as the highest-level cognitive skill, beginning readers enjoy expressing their reaction to the printed word. Activities such as role playing, dramatics, puppetry, composition, pantomime, and dance are used to enhance the development of creative reading skills and to motivate students to read.

Creative dramatics provide excellent ways for teachers to develop reading and language abilities. Creative drama includes dramatic play, pantomime, story dramatization, and sensitivity exercises along with other activities to encourage students to relate new learning to existing knowledge. However, teachers know that creative dramatics does not just happen in the classroom; careful planning is needed. As Prentice and Tabbert emphasized, creative drama is not an unstructured free-for-all, but a structured undertaking in which the teacher sets limits, establishes guidelines, and intervenes when necessary to change the direction of the activity or make suggestions. Further suggestion is given that students be introduced to creative drama slowly and that they be free to proceed at their own pace. Evaluation is an essential part of each activity with teachers asking questions as the process progresses.[27] Research has shown that creative drama enhances reading readiness, vocabulary development, oral reading, comprehension, and self-concept. Miller and Mason suggested that it also can be used to develop comprehension when exercises are given to help students improvise from a storyline by adding characteristics and actions that can be inferred from given information. This process develops comprehension by bringing plot, character, and setting from the written page into the mind of the student.[28]

Another important way of developing an atmosphere of creativity in the classroom is to read aloud to students. Trelease[29] suggested that reading aloud to children is essential to promoting their literacy abilities. He points out that it is not only fun, but simple and cheap. One of the primary benefits of reading aloud is that children are exposed to good books, which in turn serves to enhance independent reading. Other benefits of successful read aloud programs in school districts are that parents become more involved, guest readings are used, and the community as a whole develops a more positive attitude toward reading.

Fostering creativity in the classroom through storytelling is enjoying a rebirth and further enhances the language acquisition and development of children. Peck[30] believes that storytelling in the classroom promotes expressive language development in both speech and written composition. She further states that it also promotes receptive language development in both reading and listening comprehension. Storytelling represents an important venue for learning because with the teacher as the storyteller, students develop skills of effective and critical listening. In addition with the students as the storytellers, there is great opportunity for developing oral and written language.

Strickland and Morrow[31] pursued this theme of children and storytellers and found that research indicated that children are active participants in their learning of language through social contexts, interacting with other children and adults, and actually constructing language as they learn. They also found that storytelling in early grades is an excellent technique of fostering growth in language. They suggest that in order to encourage children to retell stories, it is crucial for the teacher to model storytelling for them. When children are given the opportunity to tell stories, their language development is greatly enhanced. They also become active participants in the creation of language, learn to associate oral language with print, and improve socially through more contact with their peers.

A creative and unique way of encouraging independent reading in the elementary school was suggested by O'Masta and Wolf.[32] The "Reading Millionaires Project" was initiated to enhance literacy in a small elementary school. The primary objective of the program was to reach a schoolwide goal of reading a million minutes at home with all students participating in and contributing to the project. Other objectives included increasing the amount of independent reading by students, fostering a positive attitude toward reading by both students and parents, providing students the opportunity to learn that reading occurs both at home and school, and providing parents with opportunities to interact in a positive manner with their child about reading. The project was monitored through the use of banking methods involving a "Savings Book." The results of the project were encouraging and demonstrated that the amount of reading children engage in at home can be readily increased.

In fostering independent reading, most of the emphasis is placed on using story-based literature. Glazer and Lamme[33] suggested that the genre of picture book editions of single poems can be used to help children appreciate poetry and artwork and to expand their language arts and content area capabilities. In sharing poetry with children, they suggested using oral reading and chanting, adding music or sound effects, highlighting the poet, studying and comparing artwork, creating illustrations, and integrating poetry with content areas.

Personal reading is the application of reading knowledge. Teachers use many techniques to interest students in reading as a personal habit rather than just an assigned task. Materials such as paperback books seem to improve students' attitudes toward reading.[34] Bissett as well as Burger, Cohen, and Bisgaler found that by making books available and encouraging students to read them, the amount of personal reading triples.[35] Bamberger has pointed out that in areas throughout the world where personal reading habits have remained highly developed, the school library is the hub of the curriculum.[36] Thus, teachers who realize the importance of using many strategies and use these strategies to encourage personal reading develop students who enjoy reading. Strickler summarizes personal reading ideas as follows:

- Use the students' interests in planning instruction.
- Assure the students' success in the mastery of reading skills and strategies.
- Help students discover their own purposes for reading.
- Read often to the students.
- Carefully select books for the literature program, using children's literature to supplement the curriculum.
- Be an enthusiastic model of reading habits.
- Fill bookshelves in the classroom.
- Provide time for independent reading.
- Encourage students to read and share what they have read.
- Develop a literature program to help students realize the potential literature has for widening their world.[37]

■ Summary

Personal reading is an integral part of diagnostic-prescriptive instruction. Too much stress on skill development without adequate opportunities for application of these skills makes learning a boring process for students. Personal reading is especially desirable, since one of the primary goals of reading instruction is to enable students to read for pleasure as well as to gain information.

Fostering personal reading in the classroom enables the teacher to develop the affective domain in addition to the skills-oriented cognitive domain. The affective domain is important in developing a student's self-concept and awareness. It also plays a major role in motivating students by using high interest books and a variety of other materials.

Developing personal reading habits is not an easy task. In order to facilitate this task, motivated students are needed; develop students who are excited about reading by building upon their interests. Some techniques for achieving this goal are: enhancing the classroom atmosphere, using bibliotherapy, and encouraging creative reading.

The successful development of personal reading in the classroom provides much needed pleasure for students and certainly increases the effectiveness of the diagnostic-prescriptive reading program. A bibliography of high interest children's books is found in appendix F.

■ Applying What You Read

You have a group of students who seem to be developing their word identification and comprehension skills adequately; however, they are somewhat unenthusiastic about learning to read. Outline a program to develop their personal reading habits.

The atmosphere within a classroom frequently affects learning in either a positive or negative manner. Give some specific examples of how your classroom could be changed to promote a more positive atmosphere toward reading.

Using bibliotherapy in your classroom can exert a positive influence on the students. In order to implement this, go to the library, check out some books, and categorize them according to areas of need so that they are available.

Creative reading allows students to express their own ideas and to interpret what they read. Identify five activities you could do in your classroom to enhance creative reading.

■ Notes

1. *Becoming a Nation of Readers: The Report of the Commission on Reading.* Washington, D.C.: National Institute of Education.
2. Frances Pryor, "Poor Reading—Lack of Self-esteem?" *The Reading Teacher.*
3. Ivan Quandt, *Self-Concept and Reading.*
4. Ken den Heyer, "Reading and Motivation," in *Language and Literacy: The Social Psychology of Reading,* edited by John R. Edwards, pp. 51–65.
5. Herbert J. Walberg and Shiow-Ling Tsai, "Correlates of Reading Achievement and Attitude: A National Assessment Study," *Journal of Educational Research.*
6. Lian-Hwang Chiu, "Children's Attitudes Toward Reading and Reading Interests," *Perceptual and Motor Skills.*
7. Helen M. Robinson and Samuel Weintraub, "Research Related to Children's Interests and to Developmental Values of Reading," *Library Trends;* Stephen Meisal and Gerald G. Glass, "Voluntary Reading Interests and the Interest Content of Basal Readers," *The Reading Teacher;* Samuel Weintraub, "Children's Reading Interests," *The Reading Teacher;* Beta Upsilon Chapter, Pi Lambda Theta, "Children's Interests Classified by Age Level," *The Reading Teacher.*
8. Geraldine Moray, "What Does Research Say About the Reading Interests of Children in the Intermediate Grades?" *The Reading Teacher.*

9. Helen Huus, "A New Look at Children's Interests," in *Using Literature and Poetry Affectively*, edited by Jon E. Shapiro, pp. 37–45.

10. Sam Leaton Sebasta, "What Do Young People Think About the Literature They Read?" *Reading Newsletter*.

11. Constance V. Alongi, "Response to Kay Haugaard: Comic Books Revisited," *The Reading Teacher*.

12. J. Estell Alexander and Ronald Claude Filler, *Attitudes and Reading*, p. 3.

13. Lesley Mandel Morrow, "Home and School Correlates of Early Interest in Literature." *Journal of Educational Research*.

14. Ann Kirtland Healy, "Effects of Changing Children's Attitudes Toward Reading," *Elementary English*.

15. Terry Denny and Samuel Weintraub, "First Graders' Responses to Three Questions About Reading," *Elementary School Journal*.

16. Harlan S. Hansen, "The Impact of the Home Literacy Environment on Reading Attitude," *Elementary English*.

17. M. J. Heimberger, *Sartain Reading Attitudes Inventory*.

18. Doris Roettger, "Elementary Students' Attitudes Toward Reading," *The Reading Teacher*.

19. Laraine K. Hong, "Modifying SSR for Beginning Readers," *The Reading Teacher*; Jim Kaisen, "SSR/Booktime: Kindergarten and 1st Grade Sustained Silent Reading," *The Reading Teacher*.

20. Flora Fennimore, "Projective Book Reports," *Language Arts*; Harold H. Roeder and Nancy Lee, "Twenty-five Teacher Tested Ways to Encourage Voluntary Reading," *The Reading Teacher*; Jerry L. Johns and Linda Lunt, "Motivating Reading: Professional Ideas," *The Reading Teacher*.

21. Sara W. Lundsteen, *Children Learn to Communicate*, p. 216.

22. Charlotte S. Huck and Doris Young Kuhn, *Children's Literature in the Elementary School*, 2nd ed., p. 264.

23. Chester E. Tillman, "Bibliotherapy for Adolescents: An Annotated Research Review," *Journal of Reading*.

24. Frederick A. Schrank and Dennis W. Engels, "Bibliotherapy as a Counseling Adjunct: Research Findings," *Personnel and Guidance Journal*.

25. Patricia A. Edwards and Linda Simpson, "Bibliotherapy: A Strategy for Communication Between Parents and Their Children," *Journal of Reading*.

26. Thomas N. Turner and J. Estill Alexander, "Fostering Early Creative Reading," *Language Arts*.

27. Walter C. Prentice and Jon Charles Tabbert, "Creative Dramatics and Reading: A Question of Basics."

28. G. Michael Miller and George E. Mason, "Dramatic Improvisation: Risk-Free Role Playing for Improving Reading Performance," *The Reading Teacher*.

29. Jim Trelease, "Jim Trelease Speaks on Reading Aloud to Children," *The Reading Teacher*, pp. 200–207.

30. Jackie Peck, "Using Storytelling To Promote Language and Literacy Development," *The Reading Teacher*, pp. 138–41.

31. Dorothy S. Strickland and Lesley Mandel Morrow, "Oral Language Development: Children as Storytellers," *The Reading Teacher*, pp. 260–61.

32. Gail A. O'Masta and James M. Wolf, "Encouraging Independent Reading Through the Reading Millionaires Project," *The Reading Teacher*, pp. 656–62.

33. Joan I. Glazer and Linda Leonard Lamme, "Poem Picture Books and Their Uses in the Classroom," *The Reading Teacher* pp. 102–109.

34. Lawrence F. Lowrey and William Grafft, "Paperback and Reading Attitudes," *The Reading Teacher*.

35. Donald J. Bissett, "The Amount and Effect of Recreational Reading in Selected Fifth Grade Classrooms," in Victor Burger, T. A. Cohen, and P. Bisgaler, *Bringing Children and Books Together*.

36. Richard Bamberger, *Promoting the Reading Habit*.

37. Darryl J. Strickler, "Planning the Affective Component," in *Classroom Practice in Reading*, edited by Richard A. Earle, p. 6.

■ Other Suggested Readings

Beed, Penny L., E. Marie Hawkins, and Cathy M. Roller. "Moving Learners Toward Independence: The Power of Scaffolded Instruction." *The Reading Teacher* 44 (May 1991): 648–55.

Boyle, Owen F., and Suzanne F. Peregoy. "Literacy Scaffolds: Strategies for First- and Second-Language Readers and Writers." *The Reading Teacher* 44 (November 1990): 194–201.

Colvin, Marilyn A., and Elton Stetson. "A Recreational Reading Program for Disabled Readers: It Works!" *Reading Horizons* 20 (Summer 1980): 247–51.

Dupart, Annie. "Encouraging the Transition to Pleasure Reading Among Children 10–12 Years." *The Reading Teacher* 38 (February 1985): 500–503.

Dyson, Anne Haas. "Weaving Possibilities: Rethinking Metaphors for Early Literacy Development." *The Reading Teacher* 44 (November 1990): 202–13.

Fredericks, Anthony D. "Developing Positive Reading Attitudes." *The Reading Teacher* 36 (October 1982): 38–40.

Gray, Mary Jane. "Does the Teacher's Attitude Toward Reading Affect the Attitude Toward Reading Held By the Students?" *Reading Horizons* 21 (Summer 1981): 239–43.

Greaney, Vincent. "Parental Influences on Reading." *The Reading Teacher* 39 (April 1986): 813–18.

Harker, W. John. "Children's Literature and Back to the Basics." *Reading Horizons* 20 (Spring 1980): 159–64.

Martin, Charles B., Bonnie Crammond, and Tammy Safter. "Developing Creativity Through the Reading Program." *The Reading Teacher* 35 (February 1982): 568–72.

Mendoza, Alicia. "Reading to Children: Their Preferences." *The Reading Teacher* 38 (February 1985): 522–27.

O'Bruba, William S. "Reading Through the Creative Arts." *Reading Horizons* 27 (April 1987): 170–77.

Rhodes, Lynn K., and Mary W. Hill. "Supporting Reading in the Home-Naturally: Selected Materials for Parents." *The Reading Teacher* 38 (March 1985): 619–23.

Searls, Donald T., Nancy A. Mead, and Barbara Ward. "The Relationship of Students' Reading Skills to TV Watching, Leisure Time Reading, and Homework." *Journal of Reading* 29 (November 1985): 158–62.

Shannon, Patrick. "Hidden Within the Pages: A Study of Social Perspective in Young Children's Favorite Books." *The Reading Teacher* 39 (March 1986): 656–63.

Spiegel, Dixie Lee. *Reading for Pleasure*. Newark, Delaware: International Reading Association, 1981.

Stevens, Kathleen C. "The Effect of Interest on the Reading Comprehension of Gifted Readers." *Reading Horizons* 21 (Fall 1980): 12–15.

Streeter, Brenda B. "The Effects of Training Experienced Teachers in Enthusiasm on Students' Attitudes Toward Reading." *Reading Psychology* 7 (Summer 1986): 249–59.

Vukelich, Carol. "Parents' Role in the Reading Process: A Review of Practical Suggestions and Ways to Communicate with Parents." *The Reading Teacher* 37 (February 1984): 472–77.

Watson, Jerry J. "An Integral Setting Tells More than When and Where." *The Reading Teacher* 44 (May 1991): 638–47.

12

Teaching Students with Special Needs

As the faculty gathered to review their diagnostic-prescriptive reading program, several of the classroom teachers indicated concern about how the students who were mainstreamed into the regular classrooms as mandated by P. L. 94–142 would fit into the program. Another group was concerned about meeting the needs of several new students who spoke little or no English. During discussions of these two groups of students with special needs, questions about at-risk students were asked repeatedly—questions about students who are considered to have language deficits due to a limited background of experiences.

Because of their concerns about students with special needs in the diagnostic-prescriptive reading program, the teachers decided to investigate several areas in greater detail in order to better meet the individual needs of the learner. As these teachers read and reported back to the faculty, it became evident that students with special needs have always been a concern for the classroom teacher. However, because many of them were taught primarily in a special setting away from the regular classroom, or received special teaching assistance, the classroom teacher did not have a major responsibility in meeting such specialized needs. With the passage of P. L. 94–142, the influx of students with a primary language other than English, and the recognized special language needs of other students, the classroom teacher has become the manager of instruction for a very diverse population. Many teachers do not feel qualified to fill this role. Thus, this chapter presents some ideas on how to provide prescriptive reading instruction to students with special needs. The following questions will be addressed:

Who are the students with special needs?

What effect has the concept of mainstreaming had on diagnostic-prescriptive reading instruction?

How can students who are mainstreamed become involved in diagnostic-prescriptive reading instruction?

How do non-English speaking students affect diagnostic-prescriptive reading instruction?

How are at-risk students involved in the diagnostic-prescriptive reading program?

As this chapter is read, the following terms are important to note.

Vocabulary to Know

At-risk	Hearing-impaired	Non-English speaker
Bilingual	Learning-disabled	Physically handicapped
Educationally different	Mainstreaming	Psychologically handicapped
Emotionally disturbed	Mildly mentally handicapped	Visually impaired
Gifted	Multicultural	

■ An Overview

Many students in our schools have special needs that must be accommodated. These needs range from physical handicaps to gifted. It is imperative for the classroom teacher to be aware of ways to deal with these differences so that students with special needs are integrated into the class diagnostic-prescriptive reading program. In order to address these special needs, it is necessary to identify specific categories of needs that the classroom teacher may encounter.

For clarity, the authors have divided these areas of special needs into three broad categories, with subcategories under each. These broad categories include: students who have (1) educational differences, (2) psychological handicaps, and (3) physical handicaps. Each of these areas is defined, with general suggestions for prescriptive teaching strategies provided for the categories.

Before beginning the discussion of these various categories of students with special needs, it would be useful to examine more closely the definition of mainstreaming and its implications for these students as mandated by P. L. 94–142.

Birch[1] defined mainstreaming as an amalgamation of regular and special education into one system to provide a spectrum of services for all children according to their learning needs. Wang[2] interpreted mainstreaming as the integration of regular and exceptional children in a school setting where all children share the same resources and opportunities for learning on a full-time basis. In fact, it represents an effort to provide the most equitable educational opportunity for all students, including those with special needs. It is further intended to create an environment for students with special needs to associate with other students of their age. The implications for the classroom teacher are clear. Opportunities for all students to improve their reading capabilities must be provided; this implies the wider use of diagnostic-prescriptive instruction. Keep these definitions and implications in mind as the various categories of special needs are discussed in the following pages.

On November 19, 1975, Congress passed P. L. 94–142. The law mandates significant changes regarding the education of children with special needs. The most significant change is the requirement that handicapped children be educated with their nonhandicapped peers as much as possible.

Table 12.1

Public Law 94–142.

General Provisions of Public Law 94–142

PART X—EDUCATION AND TRAINING OF THE HANDICAPPED EDUCATION OF THE HANDICAPPED ACT
Part A—General Provisions
Short Title; Statement of Findings & Purpose
Definitions
Sec. 601.
(a) This title may be cited as the "Education of the Handicapped Act".
"(b) The Congress finds that—
   "(1) there are more than eight million handicapped children in the United States today;
   "(2) the special educational needs of such children are not being fully met;
   "(3) more than half of the handicapped children in the United States do not receive appropriate educational services which would enable them to have full equality of opportunity;
   "(4) one million of the handicapped children in the United States are excluded entirely from the public school system and will not go through the educational process with their peers;
   "(5) there are many handicapped children throughout the United States participating in regular school programs whose handicaps prevent them from having a successful educational experience because their handicaps are undetected;
   "(6) because of the lack of adequate services within the public school systems, families are often forced to find services outside the public school system, often at great distance from their residence and at their own expense;
   "(7) developments in the training of teachers and in diagnostic and instructional procedures and methods have advanced to the point that, given appropriate funding, State and local educational agencies can and will provide effective special education and related services to meet the needs of handicapped children;
   "(8) State and local educational agencies have a responsibility to provide education for all handicapped children, but present financial resources are inadequate to meet the special educational needs of handicapped children; and
   "(9) it is in the national interest that the Federal Government assist State and local efforts to provide programs to meet the educational needs of handicapped children in order to assure equal protection of the law.
"(c) It is the purpose of this Act to assure that all handicapped children have available to them, within the time periods specified in section 612(2)(B), a free appropriate public education which emphasizes special education and related services designed to meet their unique needs, to assure that the rights of handicapped children and their parents or guardians are protected, to assist States and localities to provide for the education of all handicapped children, and to assess and assure the effectiveness of efforts to educate handicapped children".

Hedley suggests several principles to consider in implementing mainstreaming. These are:

1. Work in a consistently congenial and scheduled manner with the child study team.
2. Include parents in the planning and implementation of the individual study program.
3. Stress diagnostic-prescriptive approaches and a more complete knowledge of the dimensions of language assessment.

4. Stress non-biased, non-discriminatory assessment in terms of special disability while assessing reading ability.
5. Commitment to a highly individualized program for the special learner and for the class is necessary.
6. Emphasis on small group instruction, peer-tutoring, parent-tutoring, and the use of the support staff, especially in the classroom is helpful.
7. Openness to task analysis and break-down of instructional tasks for the learner, as well as reduced or changed pace of presentation based on educational need of the student.
8. Openness to using techniques and materials modeled by the special educator and the corrective reading teacher.
9. Stress on greater knowledge of the linguistic and reading processes in terms of cognitive strategies for the special student.
10. Knowledge of what impairs receptive and expressive language.
11. Arrangement of planning periods where the child study team discusses and coordinates instruction for the class as a whole as well as for the exceptional student.
12. Increased awareness of social problems and group dynamics when dealing with exceptional students.
13. Self awareness of attitudes and abilities for working with special students.
14. Emphasis on reduced class size in order to give more individual attention and to do more planning.[3]

■ Educational Differences

Five groups of students comprise an area of special needs arising from educational differences. These can be classified as learning-disabled students; at-risk students; non-English speaking students; mildly mentally handicapped students; and gifted students. Each of these areas is discussed separately in the following pages.

Learning-Disabled (ADD and LD)

In the context of this chapter, learning-disabled refers to the area classified as Specific Learning Disabilities. More and more students are being placed in this category for the purpose of receiving special instruction in the regular classroom as well as in special resource programs.

Several definitions of specific learning disabilities have been offered; however, the most widely accepted definition was proposed by the National Advisory Committee on Handicapped Children in 1968. It states that:

> Children with special (specific) learning disabilities exhibit a disorder in one or more of the basic psychological processes involved in understanding or in using spoken or written language. These may be manifested in disorders of listening, thinking, talking, reading, writing, spelling, or arithmetic. They

include conditions which have been referred to as perceptual handicaps, brain injury, minimal brain dysfunction, dyslexia, developmental aphasia, etc. They do not include learning problems which are due primarily to visual, hearing, or motor handicaps, to mental retardation, emotional disturbance, or to environmental disadvantage.[4]

Although that is the more widely accepted definition of learning disabilities, the U.S. National Joint Committee on Learning Disabilities is urging that this definition be revised to better facilitate the identification and treatment of the individual.[5]

This committee suggested that their definition has several advantages over the federal definition because: (1) it is not concerned exclusively with children; (2) it avoids the controversial phrase basic psychological processes; (3) spelling is not included since it is more logically subsumed under writing; (4) it avoids the use of confusing terms such as perceptual handicaps, dyslexia, minimal brain dysfunction; and (5) it clearly states that learning disabilities may occur in conjunction with other types of handicaps.[6]

Hallahan and Kauffman[7] have grouped the causes of learning disabilities into three primary areas: organic and biological factors which are manifested primarily in the central nervous system dysfunction; genetic factors; and environmental factors.

Gilliland enumerates some characteristics of the learning-disabled student that should provide the classroom teacher with insight into how to meet better their learning needs. These characteristics of learning-disabled students are outlined below.

- Students are usually much better in mathematics than reading.
- Word identification skills are poorly developed in comparison to other reading skills.
- Many students are hyperactive, experiencing difficulty in sitting still while working on a task.
- Concentration on interesting tasks is interrupted because of sounds or movement around them.
- There are difficulties in recognizing likenesses and differences in similar spoken or printed words.
- Students have difficulty in drawing simple shapes.
- Reversals of letters or changes of the order of sounds in a word are symptoms of specific learning disabilities.
- There is some lack of coordination in writing or walking.
- The student tends to repeat the same errors over and over.
- Many students have great difficulty in following directions.
- There is quite a lot of variance in performance in different areas. Mathematics may be very high and reading very low.
- Students experience difficulty in organizing their work.
- Many students are very slow in finishing their work.[8]

Since students with specific learning disabilities are difficult to diagnose and even more difficult to teach, it is imperative that classroom teachers use all their skills to identify these students as soon as possible. However, there are educators who believe that because faulty assumptions have been made, students identified as learning-disabled have not really benefited as much as they could have from the increased emphasis on early identification and intervention. Such assumptions concern the ease of identifying an LD student by trained professionals, the ease of defining the area of learning disabilities, and that intervention naturally follows identification.[9] Thus, in implementing a prescriptive reading program, it is imperative to consider each student's needs and plan accordingly.

In discussing learning disabilities as related to reading, Johnson and Myklebust suggested two types of reading disorders—visual processing and auditory processing.[10] Disorders in visual processing are recognized through

- Visual discrimination difficulties and confusion of similar letters and words,
- Slow rate of perception,
- Letter and word reversals and inversions,
- Difficulty in following and retaining visual sequences,
- Associated visual memory problems,
- Inferior drawings,
- Difficulty in visual analysis and synthesis,
- Marked inferiority of visual skills in relation to auditory skills on diagnostic tests,
- In instructing students with this type of disorder, the teacher should use the auditory skills by teaching sounds and words through association.

Auditory processing disorders are characterized by

- Associated auditory discrimination and perceptual problems that hinder the use of phonetic analysis,
- Difficulty in separating words into their component phonemes and syllables or in blending them into whole words,
- Difficulty in spontaneous recall of the sounds associated with letters or words,
- Disturbances in auditory sequencing, and
- A general preference for visual activities over auditory tasks.

Students with this type of disorder should be taught by using strategies that emphasize the visual recognition of whole words while the auditory skills are being developed.

Perhaps another more debilitating disorder exhibited by many LD students is a short attention span. Students with attention deficits tend to exhibit short attention spans and are easily distracted. This disorder results in losing "attention contact" regardless of the degree of stimulation of the activity in progress[11]. This can be very frustrating to students as well as teachers, since there is an inability to sustain or focus attention on specific activities. Unfortunately, a number of students with learning disabilities experience this problem. Shaywitz and Shaywitz[12] indicated that estimates of the frequency of occurrence of attention deficits in learning-disabled children ranged from as low as thirty-three percent to as high as eighty percent.

The American Psychiatric Association[13] refers to those students having severe difficulty with inattention, hyperactivity, and impulsivity as having an Attention Deficit Hyperactivity Disorder (ADHD). A variation of Attention Deficit Hyperactivity Disorder (ADHD) where hyperactivity is less prevalent is known as Attention Deficit Disorder (ADD). The American Psychiatric Association has identified fourteen behaviors that are symptomatic of Attention Deficit Hyperactivity Disorder (ADHD). Included in these are:

1. Frequently fidgets with hands or feet or squirms in seat.
2. Experiences difficulty in remaining seated when required to do so.
3. Easily distracted.
4. Experiences difficulty in taking turns in games or other group situations.
5. Frequently blurts out answers to questions before they have been completed.
6. Experiences difficulty in following instructions.
7. Experiences difficulty in attending to tasks or play activities.
8. Frequently shifts from one unfinished activity to another.
9. Experiences difficulty in playing quietly.
10. Frequently interrupts others.
11. Experiences difficulty in listening attentively.
12. Frequently talks excessively.
13. Frequently loses things necessary for tasks or activities at school or home.
14. Frequently engages in physically dangerous activities without considering possible consequences.

In order for children to be diagnosed as Attention Deficit Hyperactivity Disorder (ADHD), they must exhibit eight of these preceding behaviors more frequently than normal for children of the same mental age, exhibit these behaviors before seven years of age, and have exhibited these behaviors for at least six months.[14]

In implementing instruction for learning-disabled students, it is essential that the amount of on-task reading time be augmented; increase the amount of direct, supervised instruction the student receives, and be more aware of those students who are falling behind their classmates.[15]

Although teachers may note that learning-disabled students seem to have greater difficulties in one modality than the other, there is no one method of reading instruction that can be suggested for learning-disabled students. Through the use of many techniques in the prescriptive process, the special needs of these students can be met.

Some specific suggestions for teaching learning disabled students are to:

1. Have students participate in plays, dramatizations, and role playing. These types of activities will help develop better and more effective language skills.
2. Provide immediate feedback to students after they have completed an assigned task or activity and reinforce correct responses.

3. Assign tasks in which students will experience success.
4. Use systematic and sequential instruction by carefully planning each reading lesson. It is also important to establish a specific routine with a minimum of changes.
5. Limit the number of concepts and vocabulary that is introduced to the students.
6. Use process writing emphasizing the three stages of planning, drafting, and evaluating and revising.[16]
7. Introduce dialogue journals which involve a written conversation between two writers, usually teacher and student, over a sustained period of time. This process includes the student writing in her journal, the teacher reads and responds to the student's journal, and the teacher and the student discuss the journal.[17]

At-Risk Students

The term at-risk is often used to describe a particular segment of the population of the United States that is thought of as underfed, undereducated, and underprivileged. This group is also often referred to as culturally deprived, culturally disadvantaged, and educationally disadvantaged. An equally descriptive term, societally neglected, is defined by Swanson and Willis to include those children and youth whose experienced environmental, cultural, and economic societal conditions consistently prevent them from realizing their potential within the dominant educational, vocational, and social structures of present society.[18]

These students usually experience great difficulty with reading and communicating orally in the school setting. Part of the problem can be ascribed to environmental factors; however, most of the difficulty is with language acquisition. The language of the at-risk student is typically nonstandard American English, usually dialectical in nature; this creates many problems when these students encounter teachers and the type of reading material used in most schools. Teachers are often unaccustomed to divergent speaking patterns, and students are unaccustomed to the speaking patterns and value system of the teachers. Moreover, these students may receive most of their reading instruction from a basal reader written in standard American English, depicting a way of life that is unfamiliar to the at-risk student. As a result of these and other factors, such students lag behind others who have a wider background of experiences and are better able to cope with the language of the materials and the teacher. This situation creates frustration for the at-risk student and begins a cycle that may perpetuate a lifetime of failure.

To better meet the needs of these students, the teacher must first recognize the characteristics of these students:

- Most are from families below the poverty level.
- Many suffer from malnutrition and diseases such as severe anemia, rickets, and vitamin and protein deficiencies.
- Often these students suffer from retarded physical growth.[19]

Mainstreaming students encourages interaction with age appropriate peers and requires that classroom teachers use a diagnostic-prescriptive process within the class. Photo courtesy of Edward B. Lasher.

The limiting factors for the at-risk students as they develop their reading skills are poor language development, low self-concept, improper nutrition, and lack of motivation. Each of these factors affects the development of any learning capability.

Language development is limited, as these students often come from homes where there is little verbal interaction and few, if any, reading materials. Verbal communication lacks content and is given primarily in brief commands. This language background does not provide the type of stimulation that the student needs for developing good expressive or receptive language skills.

Students from at-risk homes may also have a poor self-concept because of a lack of identity in the home and of recognition in areas that are important to them. These feelings are more prevalent in students from lower socioeconomic levels where positive feelings are often not expressed in the home. When the child with a poor self-concept enters school and is confronted with frustrating language experiences, reading difficulties begin.

An added impediment in teaching the at-risk student is nutritional deprivation or malnutrition. Malnutrition has an effect on both physical and mental development prior to school entrance and continues to retard learning by leaving the student with a physiological need. Until this basic need is fulfilled, maximum learning cannot occur.

All the above factors contribute to a lack of motivation to learn to read. The constant feelings of frustration and failure are reflected by an apathetic reaction to learning. Classroom teachers must attempt to deal with this problem by improving the students' language skills and self-concept, while the school provides nutritious meals. Language skills may be improved through the use of oral language activities throughout the school day. Self-concept can be improved as the student is given learning activities at which he can succeed. These students also need much positive reinforcement. Thus, classroom teachers must make every effort to help these students succeed by:

Carefully introducing vocabulary as well as concepts. Because of these students' limited background experiences, they need more preparation for learning in order to increase the likelihood of success.

Being patient with their language usage. Never ridicule a person's language. Language is essential for expressing emotions and ideas.

Providing an atmosphere conducive to class discussions involving everyone. Involving each student in the learning process improves self-concept, and the students begin to feel that they are an integral part of the class.

Being enthusiastic and receptive in dealing with the students. Enthusiasm is contagious. If the teacher enjoys teaching, the student will enjoy learning.

At-risk children experience a number of problems in the literary learning process which adversely affects their ability to experience success in reading and writing. Two of the more critical factors in this process are engagement and time. Engagement relates to the actual time at-risk children spend on reading and writing; time relates to the amount of time available to the at-risk learner in the instructional setting.

Greenwood[20] found that when at-risk students are given more instructional time to complete tasks and academic engagement is increased, their ability to achieve at higher levels is enhanced.

Another study[21] found that engagement and community were major factors in developing successful literary learning in at-risk students. Here again, engaging in actual reading and writing and developing the belief that they were an integral part of the literate classroom community were keys to unlocking learning for at-risk students.

Developing the at-risk student's language base should be a major focus of any instructional program. Roser, Hoffman, and Farest[22] found that literature units were especially effective in developing literacy in at-risk students. These units consisted of groups of books that had a similar topic, theme, author/illustrator, or genre. The objectives of these literature units were to: (1) offer exposure to a variety of children's books; (2) contribute to a rich literary environment; (3) motivate responsive reading; (4) encourage voluntary reading; (5) expand reading interest; (6) help children grow in language, reading, writing, and thinking; and (7) help children discover their own connections with literature.

Some other specific suggestions for teaching at-risk students are to:

1. Emphasize language-based activities, especially in the early reading stages, so that students become more aware of the relationship between oral language and print. The language-experience approach would be particularly effective with this population.

2. Use reading materials that focus on the cultural heritage of the students, if available. If unavailable, be sure to emphasize the positive aspects of the various cultures in this country. Reading materials that stress cultural diversity should be used.

3. Ignore dialectical differences that occur in oral reading situations when the meaning of the selection is not changed.[23]

4. Motivate students by emphasizing their positive attributes. Use their existing language base to develop more sophisticated language skills.

5. Encourage students to communicate their ideas by emphasizing writing activities that enable them to better understand the relationship between oral language and written language.

Non-English Speaker

This segment of the school population comprises students who do not use American English as their primary language. Included here are Hispanics (Mexican-American, Cuban, Puerto Rican), Vietnamese, Europeans, Asians, and any other group that does not speak American English or uses American English as a secondary language. Obviously, difficulties in communicating orally and learning to read are inherent in these situations.

Students who speak English as a second language may be referred to as bilingual. Those who speak only their native language are monolingual. Lacking English as a primary language, many students who are very capable of learning are unable to do so because of the language barrier. Justin, for example, indicates that almost one million Spanish-speaking students in the Southwest will be unable to go beyond the eighth grade because of the language factor. Cordasco also found similar problems among Puerto Rican students on the East Coast.[24]

Another serious concern to the non-English speaking population is the erosion and, in some cases, complete loss of their cultural identity. Many in this group see the American school system as an instrument of destruction of their culture. Until recently, U.S. education perceived its role as a "melting pot," where the various cultural and language differences were replaced by American standards, mores, and language, thus projecting these students into the mainstream of the American way of life. Although most of these cultural groups want to participate in the American way of life, they also wish to maintain their cultural heritage.

Fortunately, some change of attitude on the part of educators is apparent in the advent of a trend toward providing better educational services to our non-English speaking population. There is a belief that these multicultural groups should not be stripped of their culture, which is experiencing something of a renaissance in multicultural activities—a return to their "roots," a feeling many Americans are experiencing.

In an effort to ensure the right of students to an appropriate education, the U.S. Department of Health, Education, and Welfare has issued guidelines to prevent any type of language discrimination.[25] Another organization, the NEA, has set up a Task Force on Bilingual/Multicultural Education, which defines bilingual education as "A process which uses a pupil's primary language as the principal medium of instruction while teaching the language of the predominant culture in a well-organized program, encompassing a multicultural curriculum."[26]

As classroom teachers attempt to teach reading to monolingual or bilingual students, they should remember that prescriptive instruction must be adapted to individual needs. Furthermore, the same sequence in learning words is used for the non-English speaker as for the English speaker. The students learn first through *listening*, add the word to the *speaking* vocabulary, then use it in *reading*, and finally learn to *write* the word. Employing this procedure, students can learn words more quickly. Perez found that extending practice in oral language skills through the elementary grades appears to increase the likelihood of reading success.[27]

Some other suggestions that the teacher of the non-English speaker should remember are listed below:

- Become familiar with the students' culture so that cultural habits are understood.
- Teach the student some survival words in English, e.g., name, address, restroom, etc.
- Teach sentence formation by speaking in simple sentences.
- Use resources from within the community to help the student. Adults or other students who speak the language can be valuable in teaching English to the student.
- Identify concepts, such as numbers, letters, time, colors, etc., that the student needs to learn. Provide systematic instruction.
- Do not automatically place these students in the low reading group. They probably need to be placed in several groups in order to gain more experience with the language.
- Team the student with another student who acts as a "big sister" in helping the foreign speaker become acquainted with the school.
- Most importantly, use variety in teaching and do not drill the student in phonics. English has sounds that do not exist in other languages; thus, the teacher should not expect Spanish-speaking students to learn immediately the *j* sound, as in *jump*, because this sound does not exist in their native language.

Mildly Mentally Handicapped

As mainstreaming procedures are implemented in the school system, a major trend is to provide Mildly Mentally Handicapped (MMH) students with opportunities to associate with other students of their age. In some systems this includes placing the

MMH student in the regular classroom during some designated class or possibly on a permanent basis. The classroom teacher may also be involved in teaching MMH students whose parents will not allow them to be tested or placed in special classes.

For many years, IQ scores were used exclusively to determine who was mentally retarded with ranges anywhere from 50–55 to 70–75 indicating MMH classification. Recently, the debate over the accuracy of IQ scores, especially in regard to blacks and Hispanics from culturally deficient or different backgrounds, has resulted in the consideration of other criteria along with IQ scores.

Several characteristics of the MMH student which will assist the classroom teacher in providing appropriate reading instruction are highlighted by Kirk:

- Such areas as auditory and visual memory, language use, conceptual and perceptual abilities, and imaginative and creative abilities may develop slowly.
- Academically, the MMH student experiences great difficulty with reading, writing, and spelling activities on entering school. These skills are often not acquired until the student is eight or even eleven years old.
- Progress in school is at one-half to three-quarters the rate of the average student, which is comparable to the student's mental development.
- MMH students often exhibit short attention spans and are easily frustrated; however, this situation improves when instruction is geared to meet the student's needs.
- MMH students often create more behavior problems in school than other students; however, much of this can be alleviated through the use of appropriate instructional techniques. Despite this reputation for disruptive behavior, evidence indicates that there is no significant difference between MMH students' behavior in the classroom and that of educationally handicapped students.[28]

As teachers plan for providing diagnostic-prescriptive instruction to the MMH student, they must recognize that these students need the same basic reading skills presented at a slower rate. Kolstoe has some additional recommendations for presenting learning tasks to the MMH student:

1. The tasks should be uncomplicated. The new tasks should contain the fewest possible elements, and most of the elements should be familiar, so [the student] has few unknowns to learn.
2. The task should be brief. This assures that [the student] will attend to the most important aspect of the task and not get lost in a sequence of interrelated events.
3. The task should be sequentially presented so the learner proceeds in a sequence of small steps, each one built upon previously learned tasks.
4. Each learning task should be the kind in which success is possible.
5. Overlearning must be built into lessons. Drills in game form seem to lessen the disinterest inherent in unimaginative drill.

6. Learning tasks should be applied to objects, problems, and situations in the learner's life environment. Unless the tasks are relevant, the learner has great difficulty in seeing their possible importance.[29]

More specifically, MMH students may benefit from using self-paced, modules,[30] from computer-assisted instruction in learning sight words,[31] and by learning how to compare unknown words that they already have in their sight vocabulary.[32]

Nelson, Cummings, and Boltman[33] suggested some general guidelines for teaching basic concepts to MMH. For example, in presenting concepts at a concrete level, simple objects such as toys and clothing, as well as the children themselves, should be used so that the children are not distracted by a need to learn about unfamiliar objects. At more abstract levels, children should reverse concepts, such as holding a ball above a table and then below a table or by classifying objects according to color and size. Remember that these basic concepts should be taught in conjunction with instruction in reading and writing.

MMH students may also benefit from cooperative learning opportunities. Stevens and Slavin[34] found evidence to suggest that cooperative learning can have a positive impact on the academic performance of mainstreamed students with mild disabilities.

Knowledge of these procedures should assist the classroom teacher in providing appropriate prescriptive instruction for the MMH student.

Gifted

Until recently, gifted students have been neglected. This occurred primarily because many educators believed that these students were quite capable of fulfilling their own needs. Further, concern for the gifted seemed to decrease as a result of the increased interest in providing better educational opportunities for minorities and low socioeconomic groups. However, in the 1970s, there was a renewed concern for providing more appropriate educational experiences for the gifted student.

Just as in the other areas of special needs, it is important to identify at an early age those students exhibiting superior talent in one or more areas and to promote opportunities for developing their potential. To assist identifying these students, it is necessary to define the term *gifted*. The most widely accepted definition of the gifted student was proposed by Marland in 1972. He stated that perhaps as many as three to five percent of the school-age population are gifted and defined this group in the following way:

> Gifted and talented children are those identified by professionally qualified persons who, by virtue of outstanding abilities, are capable of high performance. These are children who require differentiated educational programs and services beyond those normally provided by the regular program in order to realize their contribution to self and society.[35]

Renzulli,[36] on the other hand, believes that this estimate of three to five percent is needlessly restrictive and suggested that fifteen to twenty-five percent of all children may have the ability, motivation, and creativity to exhibit gifted behavior at some time during their school career.

Children capable of high performance include those with demonstrated achievement or potential ability in any of the following areas:

- General intellectual ability
- Specific academic aptitude
- Creative or productive thinking
- Leadership ability
- Visual and performing arts
- Psychomotor ability

This rather broad definition encompasses a larger population and recognizes those students exhibiting talent in areas other than intelligence, as determined by IQ scores; actually, this allows for some affective assessment of what constitutes giftedness.

Classroom teachers may wish to note the following characteristics of giftedness as suggested by Terman and Oden in order to facilitate more individualized learning experiences for such students:

- Gifted students exhibit above-average health and physical characteristics.
- Gifted students are two to four years beyond the average level in school work.
- Mental health problems are rare in the gifted population.
- Contrary to some belief, gifted students interact well with peers.
- Wide ranges of interests are enjoyed by gifted students.
- Gifted students tend to be very successful adults.[37]

In the past, the classroom teacher has been totally responsible for providing instruction to this group of students with educational differences. However, with the renewed interest in the gifted student, school systems are developing programs that should help in meeting these special needs. These programs may be in the form of ability grouping, acceleration to provide more advanced content, enrichment programs to supplement the regular school offerings, and special classes within a school, or perhaps even Saturday sessions.

In the prescriptive reading program, the gifted student follows the same scope and sequence of skills but moves at a faster rate and has more instruction in the higher-level reading skills. Bynum has proposed that curricula activities provide opportunities for students to do some of the following:

- Add breadth and depth to present knowledge.
- Use many instructional media, especially those that free the student from limited content restrictions.

- Develop efficient reading and study skills.
- Raise the conceptual level on which they function and think.
- Use problem-solving techniques.
- Develop and use critical thinking skills.
- Develop and use creative abilities.
- Do independent work.
- Explore, under guidance and independently, many fields of interest.
- Deal with high-level abstractions.
- Converse with students of like abilities.
- Participate in planning learning experiences.
- Apply theory and principles to solving life problems.
- Develop leadership abilities or become effective followers.
- Develop a personal set of values.
- Set and reach immediate and ultimate goals.
- Develop self-discipline and a sense of social responsibility.[38]

Olenchak and Renzulli[39] developed a schoolwide enrichment model needed for gifted students that is comprised of five components:

1. *Curriculum Compacting.* Modifying the regular curriculum in order to eliminate repetition of previously mastered material, upgrade the challenge level of the regular curriculum, and provide time for appropriate enrichment and/or acceleration activities while ensuring mastery of basic skills.
2. *Assessment of Student Strengths.* Develop systematic procedures for gathering and recording information about students' abilities, interests, and learning styles.
3. *Type I Enrichment: General Exploratory Experiences.* Design experiences and activities that expose students to a wide variety of disciplines, visual and performing arts, and any information not ordinarily covered in the regular curriculum.
4. *Type II Enrichment Group Training Activities.* Use instructional methods and materials that are intentionally designed to promote the development of thinking and feeling processes.
5. *Type III Enrichment: Individual and Small Group Investigations of Real Problems.* Develop investigative activities and artistic productions in which the learner assumes the role of a firsthand inquirer. In this stage, students think, feel and act like a practicing professional.

Teachers should remember that the gifted need planned reading instruction to assist in expanding their vocabulary and in using the many ideas these students learn so quickly. They also need opportunities to interact with other students at all levels in order to become adjusted citizens in the school and community.

■ Psychologically Handicapped

Teaching emotionally disturbed or behavior-disordered students is a cause of great concern to educators. Many of these students are quite capable of performing school tasks; however, they are often unable to do so because of psychological problems manifested in deviant or disruptive behavior in the classroom. These students may show great enthusiasm for completing an assigned task, only to suddenly explode into disruptive behavior, creating many problems for the classroom teacher. They may also be totally withdrawn from classroom activities.

Bower has identified some specific behavior patterns of emotionally disturbed students. While the presence of these problems does not always mean that the student has a psychological impairment, their incidence over a long period of time deserves attention. They are:

- Absence of knowledge and skill acquisition in academic and social behaviors not attributed to intellectual capability, hearing and visual status, or physical health anomalies.
- Absence of positive, satisfying interpersonal relationships with adults and peers.
- Frequent instances of inappropriate behavior episodes that are surprising or unexpected for the conditions in which they occur.
- Observable periods of diminished verbal and other motor activity (e.g., moods of depression or unhappiness).
- Frequent complaints of a physical nature, such as stomach aches, soreness in the arm, and general fatigue.[40]

When classroom teachers identify students with these characteristics and refer them for further evaluation, or when they have a student who has already been formally identified as having emotional problems, they must have strategies for dealing with these students in the classroom. Such students follow the same basic procedures in the diagnostic-prescriptive reading program; however, the teacher must adjust teaching strategies to meet the personal needs of a student with a sometimes unpredictable reaction.

Kirk and Gallagher suggest some specific procedures that may be used with the emotionally disturbed student. These include psychodynamic strategies, the psychoeducational strategy, the behavior modification strategy, the developmental strategy, the learning disability strategy, and the ecological strategy.[41] Of these strategies the most useful in the classroom setting seem to be the behavior modification strategy and the learning disability strategy. The behavior modification strategy applies the principles of respondent and operant conditioning, in which the student is rewarded for the desired behavior.

The learning disability strategy is proposed by those who believe that emotional disturbances and learning disabilities are interrelated. This approach attempts to modify behavior by developing a more positive self-concept through successful experiences in school work.

As classroom teachers work with the emotionally disturbed student in the diagnostic-prescriptive reading program, consideration may be given to the basic guidelines outlined below:

- Be sure that instruction is based on the student's needs and interests, and that learning experiences are successful for the student.
- Offer options for learning a specified skill and allow the student to choose.
- Work with other resource persons in the community, such as social workers and psychiatrists, to meet the student's social and academic needs.
- Establish a positive relationship with the student. Teachers must sometimes have a high degree of tolerance for hate and aggressive reactions.
- Provide guidance to help students realize the seriousness of their actions and to take steps toward self-control.
- Learn to "read" the student; try to determine why certain actions or reactions occur. Then try to be empathetic and help the student work out dilemmas.

In the instructional setting, do not restrict yourself to just one approach or to just using one type of reading material, such as basal readers. Instead, vary your approaches, use an integrated reading and writing program with language-based activities and literature to enhance the child's experience base and prior knowledge. D'Alessandro[42] found that using a literature-based reading program with emotionally handicapped children had a very positive impact on the children's self-concept and attitude toward books.

■ Physically Handicapped

Students with physical handicaps include those with disorders of the nervous or musculoskeletal system, the visually disabled, and the hearing impaired. Because this book is limited to addressing the reading needs of students, the authors include under this category only those physical impairments that affect reading performance, namely the visual and hearing disorders. Students with such impairments experience difficulties in performing tasks because of a loss of acuity in either the visual or auditory mode. As a result of these losses, they must receive special assistance from the teacher in performing certain learning tasks. Students with severe losses in vision or hearing are generally referred to more specialized school settings which are better equipped to cope with their special needs than the regular classroom. Thus, the regular classroom teacher will probably not have totally blind or deaf students in the classroom.

Visual Impairments

In discussing visually impaired students, teachers may wish to use the three different types of impairments identified by Barraga. The *blind* students have only light perception or have no vision and learn through Braille or media that do not require vision. Students with *low vision* "have limitations in distance vision but are able to see objects and materials when they are within a few inches or a maximum of two feet away."[43] Barraga's third type of visual impairment is known as *limited vision* and includes students whose vision can be corrected.

Research in the area of the partially sighted or students with low vision suggests that these students do perform in the normal range on standardized tests due to their ability to communicate with others via oral means. Bateman found that the partially sighted students in her study were normally distributed with an average IQ of 100 on the Binet or Wechsler scales. She also found that on the *Illinois Test of Psycholinguistic Ability* the students were normal in the auditory-vocal channel subtests but performed significantly lower on the visual reception, visual association, motor expression, and visual sequential memory subtests.[44] Studies such as that of Demott indicate that there are no differences between sighted and visually impaired students in their understanding of ideas and concepts. He concluded that the visually impaired student, like the sighted, learns words and their meaning through use in the language rather than via direct experience.[45]

Teachers should recognize that research findings indicate that blind students are equal to the sighted in reading comprehension when provided more time to read the tests. Bateman found that partially sighted students in grades two to four

- Were similar to the reading achievement level of sighted students,
- Scored highest on a silent reading test and lowest on a timed oral reading test, and
- Made more reversal errors than the sighted group but either did not differ or made fewer errors in other areas than the sighted.[46]

With this research information, teachers should recognize that educational objectives for the visually impaired are the same as for the sighted student, only the methods and materials must be changed. Lowenfeld suggests three basic ideas for the teacher to consider in teaching the visually impaired.

Concreteness: Students must be provided with objects that can be manipulated and touched in order to learn about their size, shape, weight, etc.

Unifying experiences: Systematic stimulation is necessary in order for the visually impaired to learn how parts relate to the total picture. For example, in order to learn how one part of the neighborhood connects to another the student must be taken to the places and provided explanations. Without adequate vision it is difficult for a person to unify parts into a meaningful whole.

Learning by doing: The visually impaired student must be stimulated by sight, touch, or hearing to become involved with an activity. Thus, visually impaired students must be invited and shown how to become involved in a learning task because they cannot see the learning activity to automatically involve themselves.[47]

Classroom teachers can greatly assist the visually impaired student by providing instruction in listening skills. Because so much of their education comes through listening to information, this area must be strengthened through direct instruction. Additionally, classroom teachers should be aware of special materials and equipment that assist in providing prescriptive instruction in reading.

For the visually impaired student, lighting is one of the most important considerations. Glare and direct sunlight limit vision, while evenly distributed light and appropriate artificial illumination assist the visually impaired reader. These students may also need adjustable desks to assure the right angle of light, gray-green chalkboards that reflect more light, typewriters, dictaphones, record players, magnifying lenses, large-type books, three-dimensional maps, and other specially designed teaching-learning aids.[48]

Classroom teachers should realize that visually impaired students fit into the diagnostic-prescriptive reading program just as other students with specific reading needs. The only difference is that specialized materials and techniques are needed to further assist them. These are provided, along with teaching assistance, by a special teacher who can help the regular teacher and the student to have positive teaching-learning experiences.

Hearing Impairments

As with the visually impaired, hearing-impaired students can be grouped in two basic categories. According to Moores, the following definitions can be used to describe the hearing impaired:

A 'deaf person' is one whose hearing is disabled to an extent (usually 70 dB ISO or greater) that precludes the understanding of speech through the ear alone with or without the use of a hearing aid.

A 'hard-of-hearing' person is one whose hearing is disabled to an extent (usually 35 to 69 dB ISO) that makes difficult, but does not preclude, the understanding of speech through the ear alone, with or without a hearing aid.[49]

The regular classroom teacher is not trained to provide appropriate instruction to the totally deaf student; however, the hard-of-hearing student can function in the classroom with assistance from the classroom teacher who consults with a special teacher. It is important to note that students with a mild to moderate hearing loss are less likely to exhibit significant academic problems than students with more severe deficits, especially over longer periods of time.[50]

The hearing-impaired student suffers handicaps in many developmental areas, with language and related areas, such as reading, being most severely affected. Gentile has found that hearing-impaired students at age eight scored at about grade two in reading and math computation, and at age seventeen the children scored at about grade four in reading and grade six in math computation. These findings are substantiated by similar results in a study by Trybus and Karchmer.[51] Pflaster indicates that the factors that appear to relate more directly to academic performance of hearing-impaired students are oral communication, personality, and linguistic competence.[52]

Although hearing-impaired students seem to do poorly in language-related areas, their intelligence range is like the range for normal children on nonverbal intelligence measures.[53]

In teaching the hearing-impaired student, Kirk and Gallagher note the use of special educational procedures, such as the use of hearing aids, auditory training, speech or lipreading, oral speech remediation, speech development, and language development.[54] Many of these procedures are used by a special teacher and may be adapted for use in the regular classroom. One example is the use of lipreading. Hard-of-hearing students often rely on this procedure to supplement the faint voices they hear. Students learn to see or hear a few clues in a sentence and fill in the gaps from the context. In using lipreading, teachers must be aware that some sounds are more difficult to "read" or hear than others. For example:

- Vowels are more difficult to discriminate by lipreading, but are easier to discriminate through hearing because they are in lower-frequency ranges.
- Consonants such as *s* are in a higher-frequency range and are sometimes more difficult to hear.
- Sounds such as *k*, *h*, and *g* cannot be discriminated visually.

Thus, the teacher must realize that the hard-of-hearing student who uses lipreading may miss some information because of the formation or frequency of the sounds.

Larson and Miller provide a list of suggestions for the classroom teacher to consider in teaching the hearing-impaired student in the classroom:

1. Give the child favorable seating in the classroom and allow him to move to the source of speech within the room; let the child turn around or have speakers turn toward the child, to allow visual contact with anyone who is speaking.
2. Encourage the student to look at the speaker's lips, mouth, and face. Speech-reading should help clarify many of the sounds the child cannot hear.
3. Speak naturally—neither mumbling nor overarticulating. Speak neither too fast nor too slow, too loud nor too soft.
4. Keep hands away from the mouth when speaking, and make sure that books, papers, glasses, pencils, and other objects do not obstruct the visual contact.
5. Take note of the light within the room so that the overhead light or window light is not at the speaker's back. Speech-reading is difficult when light shines in the speechreader's eyes. Try to prevent shadows from falling on the speaker's mouth.

6. Stand in one place while dictating spelling words or arithmetic problems to the group, allowing the hard-of-hearing child to see better, as well as to give a sense of security that the teacher will be there when she looks up.

7. Speak in complete sentences. Single words are more difficult to speech-read than are complete thoughts. Approximately 50 percent of the words in the English language look alike on the lips. Such groups of words are termed *homophenous*. (Examples: *man, pan, ban, band, mat, pat, bat, mad, pad, bad.*) Phrases and sentences placing the word in context help promote visual differentiation among homophenous words.

8. Give the student assignments in advance or give the topic that will be discussed. A list of new vocabulary to be used in an assignment also assists the student. Familiarity may help the child understand the word in context and help promote visual differentiation among homophenous words.

9. Occasionally have the hearing-impaired child repeat the assignment to some other child so you are sure the assignment has been understood.

10. Remember at all times that this is a normal child with a hearing handicap; never single out a hearing-impaired child in front of the group or in any other manner encourage an attitude of being "different."

11. Understand that the child with a hearing loss may tire faster than a child with normal hearing. The demands placed upon a child in speech-reading and listening are greater than for hearing people.

12. Take into consideration that many children hear better on some days than they do on others. Also, children may suffer from tinnitus (hearing noises within the head) which may make them nervous and irritable.

13. Restate a sentence, using other words that have the same meaning, when the hearing-impaired individual does not understand what has been said. The reworded sentence might be more visible. (Example: Change, "Close your book," to "Shut the book," or "Please put your book away now." Look in a mirror and observe the difference.)

14. Encourage the hearing-impaired child to participate in all school and community activities. This child is just as much a part of the environment as any other child.

15. Help the child to accept mistakes humorously. The deaf and the hard-of-hearing resent being the target of laughter just as much as anyone else. Laugh with them, not at them.

16. Encourage an understanding of and interest in the handicap of a hearing-impaired child by the entire group.[55]

In the diagnostic-prescriptive reading program, hearing-impaired students must develop the same basic skills as normal students. These students may learn them more slowly and in different ways because of their difficulty with language, but they can, with the guidance of patient teachers, become adequate readers.

■ Summary

In the diagnostic-prescriptive reading program, the classroom teacher must be aware of the special needs of some students. The goal of this chapter was to help classroom teachers acquire some knowledge of these special needs and ideas on how to deal with them in the reading program.

Students with special needs were divided into three basic types, with specific subcategories under each type. The basic types discussed were—

Students with educational differences, which included learning-disabled, at-risk, non-English speaking, mildly mentally handicapped, and gifted.

Students with psychological handicaps, including emotionally disturbed or behaviorally disordered.

Students with physical handicaps, included in this category are visual and hearing impairments.

In addition to defining and describing the characteristics of each group, ideas for developing prescriptive reading techniques were presented.

Because of the emphasis being placed on mainstreaming, as mandated by P.L. 94–142, the classroom teacher again assumes the primary responsibility for educating all students and must acquire the skills essential for dealing with those students and their special needs in the school reading program.

■ Applying What You Read

In your classroom, you have several students who fit into the special needs category as defined in this chapter. How can they be included in the diagnostic-prescriptive reading program?

Some parents have just been told that their visually impaired children will be mainstreamed into your classroom. How would you explain to them how the children will function in the regular classroom?

You have just been assigned two new students who speak only Vietnamese. What should you do to help them learn English?

■ Notes

1. J. W. Birch, *Mainstreaming: Educable Mentally Retarded Children in Regular Classes.*
2. Margaret C. Wang, "Mainstreaming Exceptional Children: Some Instructional Design and Implementation Considerations," *The Elementary School Journal.*
3. Carolyn N. Hedley, "Mainstreaming and the Classroom Teacher: A Practical Approach," *Reading Horizons.*
4. National Advisory Committee on Handicapped Children, *First Annual Report, Subcommittee on Education of the Committee on Labor and Public Welfare, U.S. Senate,* p. 14.
5. U.S. National Joint Committee on Learning Disabilities, "Revised Definitions of LD," *The Reading Teacher.*
6. U.S. National Joint Committee on Learning Disabilities, "Revised Definitions of LD," *The Reading Teacher.*
7. Daniel P. Hallahan and James M. Kauffman, *Exceptional Children: Introduction to Special Education,* pp. 121–67.
8. Hap Gilliland, *A Practical Guide to Remedial Reading,* pp. 282–83.
9. Carol Strickland Beers and James Wheelock Beers, "Early Identification of Learning Disabilities: Facts and Fallacies," *The Elementary School Journal.*
10. Donald J. Johnson and Helmer R. Myklebust, *Learning Disabilities: Educational Principles and Practices.*
11. Earl H. Cheek, Rona F. Flippo, and Jimmy D. Lindsey, *Reading for Success in Elementary Schools.*
12. S. E. Shaywitz and B. A. Shaywitz, "Attention Deficit Disorder: Current Perspectives," Paper presented at National Conference on Learning Disabilities, Bethesda, MD: National Institutes of Child Health and Human Development, 1987.

13. American Psychiatric Association, *Diagnostic and Statistical Manual of Mental Disorders (DSM-III-R)*, 3rd. ed.

14. Hallahan and Kauffman, *Exceptional Children: Introduction to Special Education*.

15. Gaea Leinhardt, Naomi Zigmond, and William W. Cooley, "Reading Instruction and Its Effects," *American Educational Research Journal*.

16. Ada L. Vallecorsa, Rita Rice Ledford, and Ginger G. Parnell, "Strategies for Teaching Composition Skills to Students with Learning Disabilities," *Teaching Exceptional Children*, pp. 52–55.

17. Martha Gonter Gaustad and Trinka Messenheimer-Young, "Dialogue Journals for Students with Learning Disabilities," *Teaching Exceptional Children*, pp. 28–32.

18. B. Marion Swanson and Diane J. Willis, *Understanding Exceptional Children and Youth*, p. 133.

19. Swanson and Willis, *Understanding Exceptional Children and Youth*, p. 133.

20. Charles R. Greenwood, "Longitudinal Analysis of Time, Engagement, and Achievement in At-Risk Versus Non-Risk Students," *Exceptional Children*, pp. 521–35.

21. JoBeth Allen, Barbara Michalove, Betty Shockley, and Marsha West, "I'm Really Worried about Joseph: Reducing the Risks of Literacy Learning," *The Reading Teacher*, pp. 458–72.

22. Nancy L. Roser, James V. Hoffman, and Cynthia Farest, "Language, Literature, and At-Risk Children," *The Reading Teacher*, pp. 554–61.

23. Donald J. Leu, Jr. and Charles K. Kinzer, *Effective Reading Instruction in the Elementary Grades*, pp. 463–64.

24. Neal Justin, "Culture Conflict and Mexican-American Achievement," *School and Society*; F. Cordasco, "Puerto Rican Pupils and American Education," in *Education and the Many Faces of the Disadvantaged: Cultural and Historical Perspectives*, edited by W. W. Brickman and S. Lehrer, pp. 126–31.

25. Swanson and Willis, *Understanding Exceptional Children and Youth*, p. 154.

26. National Education Association, "America's Other Children-Bilingual Multicultural Education: Hope for the Culturally Alienated," *NEA Reporter*.

27. Eustolia Perez, "Oral Language Competence Improves Reading Skills of Mexican American Third Graders," *The Reading Teacher*.

28. Steven R. Forness, Arthur B. Silverstein, and Donald Guthrie, "Relationship Between Classroom Behavior and Achievement of Mildly Mentally Retarded Children," *American Journal of Mental Deficiency*.

29. Oliver P. Kolstoe, *Teaching Educable Mentally Retarded Children*, 2nd ed., p. 27.

30. David C. Gardner and Margaret Kurtz, "Teaching Technical Vocabulary to Handicapped Student," *Reading Improvement*.

31. M. Lally, "Computer-assisted Teaching of Sight-word Recognition for Mentally Retarded School Children," *American Journal of Mental Deficiency*.

32. Frances M. Guthrie and Patricia M. Cunningham, "Teaching Decoding Skills to Educable Mentally Handicapped Children," *The Reading Teacher*.

33. R. Brett Nelson, Jack A. Cummings, and Heidi Boltman, "Teaching Basic Concepts to Students Who Are Educable Mentally Handicapped," *Teaching Exceptional Children*, pp. 12–15.

34. Robert J. Stevens and Robert E. Slavin, "When Cooperative Learning Improves the Achievement of Students with Mild Disabilities: A Response to Tateyama-Sniezek," *Exceptional Children*, pp. 276–80.

35. Sidney P. Marland, *Education of the Gifted and Talented*, p. 10.

36. J. S. Renzulli, "Dear Mr. and Mrs. Copernicus: We Regret to Inform You. . . ," *Gifted Child Quarterly*, pp. 11–14.

37. Lewis M. Terman and Melita H. Oden, *The Gifted Group and Midlife: Thirty-Five Years' Follow-Up of the Superior Child, Genetic Studies of Genius*.

38. Margaret Bynum, *Curriculum for Gifted Students*.

39. F. R. Olenchak and J. S. Renzulli, "The Effectiveness of the Schoolwide Enrichment Model on Selected Aspects of Elementary School Change," *Gifted Child Quarterly*, pp. 36–46.

40. Eli M. Bower, *Early Identification of Emotionally Handicapped Children in School*, 2nd ed.

41. Samuel A. Kirk and James G. Gallagher, *Educating Exceptional Children*, pp. 406–20.

42. Marilyn D'Alessandro, "Accommodating Emotionally Handicapped Children Through a Literature-based Reading Program," *The Reading Teacher*, pp. 288–93.

43. Natalie Barraga, *Visual Handicaps and Learning*, p. 14.

44. Barbara Bateman, *Reading and the Psycholinguistic Process of Partially Seeing Children*.

45. Richard M. Demott, "Verbalism and Affective Meaning for Blind, Severely Visually Impaired and Normally Sighted Children," *The New Outlook for the Blind*.

46. Bateman, *Reading the Psycholinguistic Process of Partially Seeing Children*.

47. Berthold Lowenfeld, ed. *The Visually Handicapped Child in School*.

48. Kirk and Gallagher, *Educating Exceptional Children*, 3rd ed., p. 268.

49. Donald F. Moores, *Educating the Deaf: Psychology, Principles and Practices*, p. 5.

50. Julia M. Davis, Patricia G. Stelmachovicz, Neil T. Shepard, and Michael P. Gorga, "Characteristics of Hearing-Impaired Children in the Public Schools: Part II-Psychoeducational Data," *Journal of Speech and Hearing Disorders*.

51. A. Gentile, *Further Studies in Achievement Testing, Hearing Impaired Students*; Raymond J. Trybus and Michael A. Karchmer, "School Achievement Scores of Hearing Impaired Children: National Data on Achievement Status and Growth Patterns," *American Annals of the Deaf*.

52. Gail Pflaster, "A Factor Analysis of Variables Related to Academic Performance of Hearing-Impaired Children in Regular Classes," *The Volta Review*.

53. Richard G. Brill, "The Relationship of Wechsler IQ's to Academic Achievement Among Deaf Students," *Exceptional Children*.

54. Kirk and Gallagher, *Educating Exceptional Children*, pp. 213–23.

55. Alfred D. Larson and June B. Miller, "The Hearing Impaired," in *Exceptional Children and Youth: An Introduction*, edited by Edward L. Meyen, pp. 463–65.

■ Other Suggested Readings

Adams, Phyllis J., and Peggy L. Anderson. "A Comparison of Teachers' and Mexican-American Children's Perceptions of the Children's Competence." *The Reading Teacher* 36 (October 1982): 8–13.

Andrews, Jean F., and Jana M. Mason. "Strategy Usage Among Deaf and Hearing Readers." *Exceptional Children* 57 (May 1991): 536–45.

Barnitz, John G. "Orthographics, Bilingualism, and Learning to Read English as a Second Language." *The Reading Teacher* 35 (February 1982): 560–67.

Brooks, C. R., and S. T. Riggs. "WISC-R, WISC, and Reading Achievement Relationships Among Hearing-Impaired Children Attending Public Schools." *The Volta Review* 82 (February/March 1980): 96–102.

Carlton, Mary B., Freddie W. Litton, and Stephen A. Zinkgraf. "The Effects of an Intraclass Peer Tutoring Program on the Sight-word Recognition Ability of Students Who Are Mildly Mentally Retarded." *Mental Retardation* 23 (April 1985): 74–78.

Caton, Hilda, and Earl Rankin. "Variability in Age and Experience Among Blind Students Using Basal Reading Materials." *Visual Impairment and Blindness* 74 (April 1980): 147–49.

Edwards, Patricia A., Kathy Beasley, and Judy Thompson. "Teachers in Transition: Accommodating Reading Curriculum to Cultural Diversity." *The Reading Teacher* 44 (February 1991): 436–37.

Flatley, Joannis K., and Adele D. Rutland. "Using Wordless Picture Books to Teach Linguistically/Culturally Different Students." *The Reading Teacher* 40 (December 1986): 276–81.

Fuchs, Lucy. "Images of Hispanics in 4 American Reading Series." *The Reading Teacher* 40 (May 1987): 848–55.

Gilliland, Hap. "The New View of Native Americans in Children's Books." *The Reading Teacher* 35 (May 1982): 912–17.

Greer, Jeptha V. "At-Risk Students in the Fast Lanes: Let Them Through." *Exceptional Children* 57 (March/April 1991): 390–91.

Hanson, Vickie L., Isabelle Y. Liberman, and Donald Shankweiler. "Linguistic Coding by Deaf Children in Relation to Beginning Reading Success." *Journal of Experimental Child Psychology* 37 (April 1984): 378–93.

Hoge, Robert D., and Robert McSheffrey. "An Investigation of Self-Concept in Gifted Children." *Exceptional Children* 57 (December/January 1991): 238–45.

Howell, Helen. "Language, Literature, and Vocabulary Development for Gifted Students." *The Reading Teacher* 40 (February 1987): 500–505.

Johnson, Lawrence J., and Marleen Pugach. "Peer Collaboration: Accommodating Students with Mild Learning and Behavior Problems." *Exceptional Children* 57 (March/April 1991): 454–61.

Johnson, Roger T., and David W. Johnson. "Building Friendships Between Handicapped and Nonhandicapped Students: Effects of Cooperative and Individualistic Instruction." *American Educational Research Journal* 18 (Winter 1981): 415–24.

Manzo, Anthony V. "Psychologically Induced Dyslexia and Learning Disabilities." *The Reading Teacher* 40 (January 1987): 408–13.

Oliver, J. M., Nancy Hodge Cole, and Holly Hollingsworth. "Learning Disabilities as Functions of Familial Learning Problems and Developmental Problems." *Exceptional Children* 57 (March/April 1991): 427–42.

Quintero, Elizabeth, and Ann Huerta-Macias. "All in the Family: Bilingualism and Biliteracy." *The Reading Teacher* 44 (December 1990): 306–15.

Raynor, Phyllis F. "Development of Programs for Children with Specific Reading Disabilities in the German Democratic Republic." *The Reading Teacher* 39 (May 1986): 912–18.

Sutton, Christine. "Helping the Nonnative English Speaker with Reading." *The Reading Teacher* 42 (May 1989): 684–89.

Varnhagen, Connie K., and Susan R. Goldman. "Improving Comprehension: Casual Relations Instructional for Teaching Handicapped Learners." *The Reading Teacher* 39 (May 1986): 896–904.

Fitting the Parts Together

As teachers consider the concept of diagnostic-prescriptive instruction, the importance of the various steps in the process are apparent. Each of the components in the steps is essential as is the involvement of teachers, parents, and students to the overall effectiveness of the program. As the steps are implemented, careful evaluation is necessary to determine how the parts are blending to form a total diagnostic-prescriptive program that meets the individual learning needs of each student.

The Total Diagnostic-Prescriptive Reading Program

As teachers and administrators initially implement a diagnostic-prescriptive reading program, there is a tendency to follow a step-by-step procedure without seeing a total program emerge. Thus, this chapter is designed to review the essential components of a diagnostic-prescriptive reading program and to show how they fit together to make a total program. This review may serve as a standard for evaluating any diagnostic-prescriptive reading program.

As the concepts presented in this book are summarized in this chapter, note the
following terms.

Vocabulary to Know

Approaches	Direct instruction	Parental involvement
Basal instruction	Emergent literacy	Personal reading
Collaborative learning	Grouping	Prescriptions
Comprehension	Indirect instruction	Record-keeping procedures
Coordination	Individualization	Scope and sequence
Diagnosis	Language-based instruction	Word identification

■ Components of the Diagnostic–Prescriptive Reading Program

In reviewing a total diagnostic-prescriptive reading program, it is necessary to examine the component parts of the program. Each of these constituents must be considered if the effectiveness of the total program is to be evaluated. A weakness in
any one of them results in a program that may not provide maximum learning opportunities for the student. Therefore, faculties continuously assess their programs
and strive to improve. The essential components of the diagnostic-prescriptive
reading program are outlined on the following pages and summarized in table 13.1.

**A scope and sequence of reading skills and knowledge expectations in listening,
speaking, and writing guides the teacher.** As discussed in previous chapters,
teacher knowledge of a hierarchy of reading skills and an understanding of language
development are necessary components of the program because diagnostic-
prescriptive instruction is predicated on the theory of continuous progress for each
student. The students' strengths and weaknesses in various areas are determined so
that the teacher can develop effective prescriptions. Even though a basal reading
series is developed around a planned scope and sequence of skills, teachers may be
unaware of this structure or use it only as outlined in the teacher's manual. Teachers
who do not use basal materials or have a district continuum have to be knowledgeable of reading and language development to guide their instruction. Based on student need, instruction is adjusted by omitting skills that the student knows,
reteaching those that appear to be causing difficulty, and revamping lessons to meet
the reading/language needs of the student.

Diagnosis determines the reading needs of each student. Diagnosing the
strengths and weaknesses of each student in the classroom is vital to the success of
a diagnostic-prescriptive reading program. Determining instructional, independent,

and frustration reading levels, interests, and specific strengths and weaknesses in reading and language is the first step that enables the teacher to locate appropriate materials and to develop prescriptions to meet the needs of the students. These data are obtained through the use of informal and formal testing procedures. Testing procedures represent only one way of obtaining information about students. "Kid watching" or observing students during various reading activities provides excellent diagnostic information. Further, teachers can not allow test scores to influence their judgments more than their observation. The observational data gained is much more informative in providing appropriate instruction than the three scores given for the various reading levels of the student on an IRI.

A variety of materials and teaching techniques are necessary components of prescriptive instruction. As teachers learn about student needs in reading and language through the different diagnostic procedures, they soon realize that there is no one material, approach, or technique that is appropriate for all students. Various approaches, basal and language based instruction, in conjunction with the other approaches described in chapter 6, are essential in prescriptive instruction.

Schools implementing a diagnostic-prescriptive reading program need a variety of materials that accommodate not only the skill needs, but also the interests and learning styles of the students. Using this assortment of approaches and materials, the teacher matches the instructional techniques with the diagnosed student needs. Thus, in a diagnostic-prescriptive reading program, the teacher is the director of the instructional program.

Planned lesson procedures including both direct and indirect teaching strategies are necessary. Teachers organize the reading lessons used for prescriptive instruction. The guided or directed reading lesson format helps the teacher to organize lessons through the use of a specified step-by-step procedure that incorporates the areas important to the development and application of reading skills. By following this process, the teacher is able to provide direct instruction, to interrelate learning for the lesson, and to show students how learning is applied.

This procedure is presented in chapter 6. The steps include:

Readiness: Developing background for the material to be read together with the concepts and vocabulary needed for reading it is the essential first step.

Skill development: The teacher introduces or reviews the skills that students need in order to read the material.

Review: The concepts, vocabulary, and skills should be reviewed to help students relate these to the material to be read. In addition, the teacher and students should establish purposes for reading the material to guide their silent reading.

Guided Reading: With purposes for reading the material clearly established, the student is asked to read the material silently. Following the silent reading, the material is discussed. At this time, the teacher may ask students to read portions aloud as they locate specific information or to identify character moods by verbalizing their statements with appropriate expression.

Follow-up: After the students have read the material and discussed it with others so as to summarize the ideas of the author, some follow-up activities may be done. They may include more skill development in areas of need, or activities to encourage students to extend the information given by the author. Activities such as reading other materials related to the topic or interpreting what has been read through art work or creative writing are some of the things that are done as follow-up. Personal reading habits can be greatly enhanced at this time.

Teachers may deviate from this structured format to give more variety to their reading lessons, to adjust their instruction to different materials or approaches, and to better meet student needs. However, keep this procedure in mind for every lesson so that the necessary elements of a good reading lesson are always present.

A systematic record-keeping procedure helps monitor the progress of the students. The concept of a diagnostic-prescriptive reading program is based on the idea that the teacher knows the reading needs of the students and provides appropriate instruction based on these needs. Thus, the teacher must have a systematic way of recording the strengths and weaknesses of the entire class as well as of individual students.

Teachers sometimes get so involved in record-keeping that they lose sight of teaching. This must not happen. Record-keeping procedures are to help in the instructional program, not interfere with teaching. Schools that have a diagnostic-prescriptive reading program usually have a record-keeping procedure that is used throughout the school. Such continuity enables the school to have a record on each student as progress is made from level to level.

The record-keeping procedure may be based on the hierarchy of reading skills allowing for teacher comments. There are usually two forms, a class profile and an individual student profile. The class profile sheet is a listing of all students in the class with spaces to mark strengths and weaknesses in each area. The teacher uses this sheet to group students by interests, skill needs, or general level of performance. The student profile contains information on the individual student and follows the student throughout school.

Record-keeping procedures are crucial in the diagnostic-prescriptive reading program. Teachers cannot remember the specific needs of every student without some systematic way of noting the information—record keeping is the necessary aid that can be used to guide instruction, confer with parents, and evaluate progress.

Teachers and administrators must commit themselves to meeting the individual reading needs of each student in the school. In the diagnostic-prescriptive reading program, the school staff believes that every student can learn to read and communicates this belief to the students. The staff provides various types of learning experiences to help students overcome weaknesses and to extend their reading performance to their potential level. In this type of reading program, the teachers realize that students read at many different levels and have varying needs. Thus, they use various approaches and materials.

The school atmosphere encourages students to read because the adult models in the school think reading is important; they demonstrate this by reading to the students, and talk about what they read. The teachers motivate the students to read and help them understand how the skills are applied.

In a school where the entire school staff is committed to reading improvement and individual reading needs are considered, students feel good about learning; therefore, they tend to learn more.

Teachers work together to develop good reading habits for each student in all classes. As teachers diagnose specific reading-language needs and record this information for use in providing appropriate prescriptive instruction, the information is shared with all teachers who work with the student. This means that diagnostic information determined by the classroom teacher, the special reading teacher, and the content teacher are combined, so that each teacher provides the most appropriate instruction for each student.

Coordination is an essential ingredient in the diagnostic-prescriptive program. As outlined in chapter 1, many people must work together in order to implement the program. This involves working together to share diagnostic information and to plan for prescriptive instruction. The classroom teacher and the special reading teacher, such as the Chapter I teacher, coordinate the instructional program for the students that they share. This is essential because without such coordination, the two teachers may be working against one another by using different approaches and materials to develop the needed skills. Additionally, time is wasted repeating diagnostic procedures when the information could be shared.

Content teachers are also a part of this coordinated effort. All teachers in a departmentalized situation have responsibilities regarding the development of reading in their content area. This includes determining the strengths and weaknesses in the skills areas and incorporating reading development into their instructional program. The diagnostic data collected by the language arts teacher should be shared with all of the other content teachers. Conversely, the diagnostic information from the various content teachers is shared with the language arts teacher, who may keep the up-to-date diagnostic records on the students. This exchange of information enhances the coordination and planning of joint units and activities.

Planning with the media specialist and guidance counselor greatly assists in the development of personal reading habits. Their encouragement and leadership will guide students into areas of reading that they have not explored.

Students spend time reading as a leisure-time activity and to gain knowledge. One of the major weaknesses of many diagnostic-prescriptive reading programs is the overemphasis on isolated skill development and the virtual exclusion of the importance of language application or personal reading aspects of the program. In a good program, students are encouraged to read materials on their own during their extra time and during planned free reading times. Moreover, students are shown how to read materials to gain information as a variety of different materials are used for instruction.

To enhance reading as a lesiure-time activity, many schools have incorporated Sustained Silent Reading activities as described in chapter 11. Through community efforts, other schools have initiated Reading Is Fundamental (RIF) programs sponsored by the Smithsonian Institute. There are many ways to encourage students to read. Teachers must try continuously to motivate students to develop their personal reading habits because without this aspect of the diagnostic-prescriptive program, reading has no purpose.

Table 13.1

Diagnostic-Prescriptive Reading Instruction

Continuum of Skills	Diagnosis	Prescriptions	Planned Lessons	Record-keeping Procedure
Basis for diagnosis and prescriptions	Identify strengths and weaknesses	Based on diagnosis	Provides format for reading lessons	Based on continuum of skills
	Use variety of instruments	Use variety of approaches and materials	May be adapted as necessary	Record strengths and weaknesses of students

The use of collaborative learning and various grouping procedures helps to meet the needs of the students. In some classrooms, students spend most of their time with the students in their group. If this is the "low" group, these students are immediately labeled and tend to associate primarily with others in their group. Their performance seldom improves because they are expected to be the "low" group. The same is true for the other groups when only achievement grouping is used for instruction. Thus, teachers must use a variety of grouping patterns to enhance learning as well as social development.

Interest groups and skill groups provide some shifts in the composition of groups. At some point instruction must be individualized, and occasionally the entire class may work together on a task. Various grouping procedures are used in a diagnostic-prescriptive program to meet student needs, and students move from group to group as instruction is provided to aid their reading development.

Parents are involved in the program. No diagnostic-prescriptive reading program is fully functional until parents are involved. Parents assist in reading development in many ways. They serve as reading models in the home environment. This has been identified continuously as a significant factor in reading development.

Parents can also assist in reinforcing concepts introduced at school. Teachers involve parents in the development of necessary reading skills when this seems feasible for the student, and when the parent is willing to work with the teacher. Some parents may pressure students to such an extent that more harm than good results. Other parents may determine their own instructional procedures which may confuse the student. These situations exist and teachers must consider them in involving parents. However, do not let this discourage the inclusion of parents in the reading program—they are the crucial link in helping their child realize the importance of

Commitment	Coordination	Personal Reading	Grouping	Parental Involvement
Encourage students to read	Work together to diagnose	Develop lesiure-time reading habits	Use variety of groups	Invite parents into school
Meet individual student needs	Plan together for instruction	Learn to read for information	Aids in organizing and managing the class	Tell them about program
		Use SSR and RIF Motivate students to read	Have flexible groups	Train them to assist

reading. Some parents may prefer to work in the school as volunteers to tutor students or perform clerical tasks for the teacher. They are welcome additions.

When including parents in the reading program, the school faculty needs to consider the development of a training course to help parents understand the program and develop activities that can be used to help their children. Some schools include information regarding child growth and development, and ideas on getting along with children. These programs help parents to feel a part of the school, to meet other parents with similar concerns, and to learn how they can help their children. The total diagnostic-prescriptive program is not functioning properly until parents are welcomed as a part of the school team.

As these points are reviewed, it is very evident that the diagnostic-prescriptive reading program include everyone working together to help develop reading habits necessary for students to become lifetime readers.

■ Summary

The different components of the diagnostic-prescriptive reading program have been summarized in this chapter and in table 13.1. As schools implement a reading program, they must consider all these parts in order to develop a balanced program that meets the needs of all students. These constituents may serve as evaluative criteria as the program is reviewed and revised.

A diagnostic-prescriptive reading program requires faculty commitment and administrative leadership to develop a program that meets the needs of the students. This is not an easy assignment; the rewards of seeing students who enjoy learning because they can read, and the feelings of satisfaction that teachers reflect as they guide these learning experiences, make teaching and learning joyous experiences for all.

■ Applying What You Read

As a reading teacher in a middle school, you are asked to help evaluate a diagnostic-prescriptive reading program. What would you look for?

Ten components of a diagnostic-prescriptive reading program have been identified. Which component do you feel is the most important, and why? How would you rank the others?

■ Other Suggested Readings

Baumann, James F. "Implications for Reading Instruction from the Research on Teacher and School Effectiveness." *Journal of Reading* 28 (November 1984): 109–15.

Crawford, John. "Teaching Effectiveness in Chapter I Classrooms." *Elementary School Journal* 90 (September 1989): pp. 33–46.

Goldenberg, Claude N. "Parents' Effects on Academic Grouping for Reading: Three Case Studies." *American Educational Research Journal* 26 (Fall 1989): 329–52.

Guzzetti, Barbara J., and Robert J. Marzano. "Correlates of Effective Reading Instruction." *The Reading Teacher* 37 (April 1984): 754–58.

Hagin, Rosa A. "Prevention of Reading Problems." *Reading and the Special Learner*. Edited by Carolyn H. Hedley and John S. Hicks. Norwood, NJ: Ablex, 1988.

Hallinger, Philip, and Joseph Murphy. "Characteristics of Highly Effective Elementary School Reading Programs." *Educational Leadership* 52 (February 1985): 39–42.

Heathington, Betty S., and Alexander J. Estill. "Teachers' Perceptions Concerning the Directed Reading Activity." *Reading Improvement* 21 (Summer 1984): 140–44.

Hoffman, Amy R., Patricia Kearney, and Susan Daniels. "Reading Instruction: What We Say and What We Do." *Reading Improvement* 22 (Spring 1985): 64–72.

Hoffman, James V., and William L. Rutherford. "Effective Reading Programs: A Critical Review of Outlier Studies." *Reading Research Quarterly* 20 (Fall 1984): 79–92.

Hunter, Madeline. "A Tri-Dimensional Approach to Individualization." *Educational Leadership* 34 (February 1977): 351–55.

Lofton, Glenda. "Building a Comprehensive Reading Program." In *Reading Research to Reading Practice, 3rd Yearbook of The American Reading Forum*, pp. 33–38. Edited by George H. McNinch. Athens, Georgia: The American Reading Forum, 1983, 33–38.

Rhodes, Lynn K., and Curt Dudley-Marling. *Readers and Writers with a Difference: A Holistic Approach to Teaching Learning Disabled and Remedial Students*. Portsmouth, NH: Heineman, 1988.

Schneider, Barbara L. "Further Evidence of School Effects." *Journal of Educational Research* 78 (July/August 1985): 351–56.

Schubert, Delwyn, and Theodore Torgerson. *Improving the Reading Program*. Dubuque, Iowa: William C. Brown Company Publishers, 1981.

Singer, Harry, John D. McNeil, and Lory L. Furse. "Relationship Between Curriculum Scope and Reading Achievement in Elementary Schools." *The Reading Teacher* 37 (March 1984): 608–12.

Stallings, Jane. "A Study of Implementation of Madeline Hunter's Model and Its Effects on Students." *Journal of Educational Research* 78 (July/August 1985): 325–37.

Strange, Michael C. "Considerations for Evaluating Reading Instruction." *Educational Leadership* 36 (November 1978): 178–81.

Appendixes

Appendix A

Reading Skills List

Prereading Skills

A. Oral Language Skills
1. Recognize word boundaries.
2. Use adequate vocabulary.
3. Understand basic concepts such as colors, shapes, size, direction.
4. Tell about a picture or object.
5. Express ideas in complete sentences.
6. Relate story in sequence.
7. Participate in discussions.

B. Visual-Motor Skills
1. Coordinate eye-hand movements.
2. Execute directionality in coordinated eye-hand movements.
3. Draw specified designs such as circles and lines.
4. Reproduce designated designs, numerals, letters, or words.
5. Reproduce own name in manuscript.

C. Visual Discrimination/Visual Memory Skills
1. Match shapes, objects, and pictures.
2. Recognize likenesses and differences in objects and designs.
3. Recognize likenesses and differences in numerals, letters, and words.
4. Match uppercase and lowercase letters.

5. Identify from memory objects, pictures, or designs briefly presented.
6. Classify objects or pictures.
7. Recognize own name in manuscript.
8. Recognize designated designs, numerals, letters, or words.
9. Match colors.
10. Follow picture, design, letter, or word in sequence.
11. Identify uppercase and lowercase letter symbols.

D. Visual Comprehension Skills
1. Identify details in pictures.
2. Identify missing parts in picture/symbol.
3. Identify sequence of pictures/story from pictures.
4. Identify common characteristics of objects.

E. Auditory Discrimination/Auditory Memory Skills
1. Discriminate among various environmental sounds.
2. Discriminate among different sounds of letters and words.
3. Identify simple everyday sounds.
4. Recognize rhyming words.
5. Follow simple one- and two-step directions.
6. Identify sounds in words.
7. Reproduce simple sounds, letters, and words.

8. Identify beginning sounds in words.
9. Identify ending sounds in words.
10. Identify medial sounds in words.
11. Use rhyming words to complete sentences.
12. Identify syllables in words.

F. Auditory (Listening) Comprehension Skills
   1. Follow directions.
   2. Associate object or picture with oral description.
   3. Identify main idea.
   4. Identify main character.
   5. Identify details in sentence and story.
   6. Identify sequence of events.
   7. Identify relationships such as cause-effect and comparisons.
   8. Interpret descriptive language.
   9. Recognize emotions of characters and story.
   10. Draw conclusions.
   11. Anticipate outcomes.

Word Identification Skills

A. Sight Vocabulary
   1. Identify familiar words, i.e., nouns, verbs, etc.
   2. Identify basic sight words in context.

B. Phoneme-Grapheme Correspondences (Phonics)
   1. Reproduce from memory uppercase and lowercase letter symbols.
   2. Associate concept of consonants with appropriate letters.
   3. Associate concept of vowels with appropriate letters.
   4. Associate sounds and symbols for initial, medial, and final consonant sounds.
   5. Recognize sounds and symbols of variant consonant patterns.
   6. Associate sounds and symbols for initial, medial, and final long and short vowel patterns.
   7. Recognize sounds and symbols of variant vowel patterns.
   8. Blend sounds to form words.
   9. Substitute initial, medial, and final sounds to form new words.

C. Structural Analysis
   1. Recognize compound words.
   2. Recognize contractions and original word forms.
   3. Analyze affixes (suffixes and prefixes) in words.
   4. Recognize inflectional endings.
   5. Divide unknown words into syllables.
      a. Dividing between two consonants
      b. Dividing between single consonants
      c. Dividing with *le* endings
      d. Dividing words with prefixes and suffixes
      e. Dividing words with common endings
   6. Accent appropriate syllables in words.
      a. Accenting first syllable
      b. Accenting compound words
      c. Accenting base word with prefix or suffix
      d. Using primary and secondary accents

D. Contextual Analysis
   1. Use picture clues to determine unknown words.
   2. Use context clues to determine unknown words.
      a. Sentence sense (missing word) clue
      b. Synonym, antonym, and homonym clue
      c. Familiar expression clue
      d. Comparison and contrast clue
      e. Words and multiple-meaning clue
      f. Summary clue

Comprehension Skills

A. Literal Skills
   1. Understand concrete words, phrases, clauses, and sentence patterns.
   2. Identify stated main ideas.
   3. Recall details (who, what, when, where, how).
   4. Remember stated sequence of events.
   5. Select stated cause-effect relationships.
   6. Contrast and compare information.
   7. Identify character traits and actions.
   8. Interpret abbreviations, symbols, and acronyms.
   9. Follow written directions.
   10. Classify information.

B. Interpretive (Inferential) Skills
1. Predict outcomes.
2. Interpret character traits.
3. Draw conclusions.
4. Make generalizations.
5. Perceive relationships.
6. Understand implied causes and effects.
7. Identify implied main ideas.
8. Interpret figurative language.
9. Interpret meaning of capitalization and punctuation in a selection.
10. Understand mood and emotional reactions.
11. Interpret pronouns and antecedents.
12. Understand author's purpose and point of view.
13. Construe meaning by signal words.
14. Understand meaning of abstract words.
15. Summarize information.
16. Recognize implied sequence.
17. Use context clues to determine meaning.
    a. Synonym, antonym, and homonym clue
    b. Familiar expression clue
    c. Comparison and contrast clue
    d. Words and multiple meaning clue
    e. Summary clue
18. Synthesize data.

C. Critical Reading Skills
1. Identify relevant and irrelevant information.
2. Interpret propaganda techniques.
3. Perceive bias.
4. Identify adequacy of materials.
5. Understand reliability of author.
6. Differentiate facts and opinions.
7. Separate real and unreal information.
8. Understand fallacies in reasoning.

Study Skills

A. Reference Skills
1. Use dictionary.
   a. Alphabetical order and guide words
   b. Pronunciation symbols
   c. Accent marks
   d. Syllabication
2. Use encyclopedias.
3. Use specialized reference materials such as the atlas and almanac.
4. Use library card catalog.

B. Organizational Skills
1. Develop outlines.
2. Underline important points or key ideas.
3. Take notes during reading.

C. Specialized Study Skills
1. Use title page.
2. Use table of contents and lists of charts.
3. Locate introduction, preface, and foreword.
4. Use appendix.
5. Identify bibliography and lists of suggested readings.
6. Use glossary and index.
7. Use study questions.
8. Read maps, tables, graphs, and diagrams.
9. Use footnotes, typographical aids, and marginal notes.
10. Preview, skim, or scan materials.
11. Adjust rate according to material and purpose.
12. Understand general and specialized vocabulary.
13. Use appropriate study strategies such as SQ3R.

Appendix B

Published Informal Reading Inventories

Analytical Reading Inventory
Mary Lynn Woods & Alden J. Moe
Charles E. Merrill, 1989
Grade range: 1–9   Forms: 3

Basic Reading Inventory
Jerry Johns
Kendall/Hunt, 1991
Grade range: PP-8   Forms: 3

Classroom Reading Inventory
Nicholas J. Silvarali
William C. Brown, 1990
Grade range: PP-8   Forms: 4

Ekwall Reading Inventory
Ed Ekwall
Allyn and Bacon, 1986
Grade range: PP-9   Forms: 4

Informal Reading Inventory
Paul Burns & Betty Roe
Houghton Mifflin, 1989
Grade range: PP-12   Forms: 4

Sucher-Allred Reading Placement Inventory
Floyd Sucher & Ruel Allred
Economy, 1985
Grade range: PP-9   Forms: 2

Appendix C

Interest and Attitude Inventory

Name: _____ Date: _____

Grade in School: _____ Age: _____ Teacher: _____

I. Family
  1. Do you have brothers or sisters? _____ brothers _____ sisters

   Are they older or younger? _____ older _____ younger

   What kinds of activities do you like to do with them? _____

   _____

  2. Who lives in your home with you? _____

  3. What do you like to do with _____ ? _____

   _____

4. Do you help with chores at home? _____

    What do you do to help? _____

    _____

5. When you have time at home to spend just like you want, what do you like to do? _____

    _____

II. Self
1. What would you like to be when you grow up? _____

    _____

2. Why do you want to be a _____ ? _____

3. What do you like most about yourself? _____

    _____

4. If you could change anything about yourself, what would it be? _____

    _____

5. What do you like best about your home or family? _____

    _____

    What do you like least about your home or family? _____

    _____

6. Do you have an area at home to go and be alone? _____ Where? _____

    _____

7. I am happy when _____

8. I really get excited when _____

9. My greatest worry is _____

10. The best thing that ever happened to me was _____

    _____

11. When I was younger _____

    _____

12. I am really afraid when _____

III. Reading/Language
  1. Given a choice, which do you like the best: writing, reading, talking, listening to stories, or

       drawing? _____

       Why? _____

  2. Do you have any books of your own to read at home? _____ What are the names of some

       of them? _____

       _____

  3. What is the name of your favorite book? _____

       _____ Why? _____

  4. Does someone read to you at home? _____ What kinds of stories do you like for them to

       read? _____

       Why? _____

  5. Do you read to someone at home? _____ Who? _____

       What do you like to read to them? _____

  6. Given a choice of the following, which would you prefer to do?

       watch television _____

       play with Nintendo games _____

       watch videos _____

       read a book _____

       go to the mall _____

       visit the zoo _____

       go to the library _____

       play with a friend _____

  7. Do you ever read magazines? _____ Comics? _____

       Newspapers? _____

8. How important do you think it is to learn to read?

Very important _____

A little _____

Not at all _____

9. I would love to read if _____

OR

I love to read when _____

10. Reading _____

IV. School
1. Do you like school? _____

What is your favorite subject? _____

Why? _____

What is your least favorite subject? _____

Why? _____

2. What did you enjoy most about school during the past year? _____

_____

3. Do you ever get into trouble at school? If so, what kind? _____

_____

4. When do you do your homework? _____

Where do you do it? _____

Is anyone available to help you with your homework? _____

Who? _____

5. Do you have a set time to go to bed on school days? _____

_____

6. School would be better if only _____

_____

V. Friends
    1. Do you have a best friend? _____ Why is this person your best friend? _____

    _____

    2. What do you enjoy doing most with your friends? _____

    _____

    3. Would you rather play with a friend or be by yourself? _____

    Why? _____

    4. I wish that _____ was my friend because _____

    _____

    5. I wish that my friends _____

VI. Interests
    1. Your favorite indoor games/activities are _____

    2. Your favorite outdoor games/activities are _____

    3. Do you like sports? _____ What sports do you like best? _____

    _____

    4. Do you have any after-school activity such as team practice, music lessons, tutoring, etc.? ____

    _____ What do you think about these activities? _____

    _____

    5. Do you have any hobbies or collections? _____ What are they? _____

    _____

    6. Do you have any pets at home? _____ What kind? _____

    What do you do to help care for it/them? _____

    OR

    If you don't have any pets, what kind of pet would you like to have? _____

    _____ Why? _____

    7. If you could have three wishes and they might all come true, what would you wish for? _____

    _____

    _____

8. What do you usually like to do after school? _____

    When it rains? _____

    On Saturdays? _____

    In the summer? _____

9. Who do you admire the most? _____

    Why? _____

10. What are your favorite TV programs? _____

11. Do you like to go to the movies? _____ What is your favorite movie? _____

    _____

12. Do you like videos? _____ How often do you watch one? _____

VII. Firsthand Experiences
    Have you been

    to the zoo? _____   to a farm? _____

    to the circus? _____   to summer camp? _____

    on an airplane? _____   to a swimming pool? _____

    on a train? _____   to the grocery store? _____

    to the beach? _____   to a shopping center/mall? _____

    to the mountains? _____   on a long vacation trip? _____

    on a boat? _____   to a restaurant? _____

VIII. Now that I have asked you these questions, is there something else you would like to tell me about yourself?

Appendix D

Observation Checklist for Reading

Name _____ Grade _____ Age _____

Teacher _____ Date _____

A. General Skills

____ 1. Reads in spare time

____ 2. Shares with others

____ 3. Works well independently and in groups

____ 4. Seeks help when needed

____ 5. Has varied interests

____ 6. Assumes leadership role when appropriate

____ 7. Has good rapport with teacher

____ 8. Accepts responsibility

____ 9. Organizes time efficiently

____ 10. Other _____

B. Oral Reading Skills

____ 1. Pronounces words accurately

____ 2. Enunciates words in a natural speaking voice

____ 3. Uses pleasing voice skills (rate, pitch, expression)

____ 4. Uses correct phrasing

____ 5. Reads fluently

____ 6. Holds book correctly

____ 7. Reads without pointing to words

_____ 8. Does not lose place while reading

_____ 9. Recognizes and uses appropriate punctuation

_____ 10. Reads without repeated words or phrases

_____ 11. Reads without making omissions or additions of words

_____ 12. Other _____

C. Silent Reading Skills

_____ 1. Holds book correctly

_____ 2. Reads without moving head

_____ 3. Reads without pointing to words

_____ 4. Does not vocalize

_____ 5. Uses no lip movement

_____ 6. Reads at a steady rate

_____ 7. Other _____

D. Listening Skills

_____ 1. Listens to follow directions

_____ 2. Listens for different purposes

_____ 3. Listens to remember sequence of ideas

_____ 4. Listens to answer questions

_____ 5. Listens to understand main ideas

_____ 6. Listens to predict outcomes

_____ 7. Listens to summarize

_____ 8. Listens when someone reads or speaks

_____ 9. Other _____

E. Prereading Skills

Oral Language Skills

_____ 1. Participates freely and easily in discussions

_____ 2. Speaks in complete sentences

_____ 3. Expresses experiences

_____ 4. Uses an adequate vocabulary

_____ 5. Develops sequence of ideas in conversation

_____ 6. Uses descriptive words and phrases

_____ 7. Describes simple objects

_____ 8. Relates words and pictures

_____ 9. Other _____

Visual Perception Skills

_____ 1. Notes similarities in objects and words

_____ 2. Classifies objects into appropriate categories

_____ 3. Identifies from memory what is seen briefly

_____ 4. Recalls items in sequence

_____ 5. Recognizes likenesses and differences in objects and words

_____ 6. Matches picture parts

_____ 7. Matches numbers

_____ 8. Recognizes upper and lowercase letters

_____ 9. Matches words

_____ 10. Recognizes geometric shapes

_____ 11. Recognizes colors

_____ 12. Recognizes own name

_____ 13. Reproduces numerals, letters, and words

_____ 14. Other _____

Auditory Perception Skills

_____ 1. Identifies and differentiates between common sounds

_____ 2. Differentiates sounds of loudness, pitch, and sequence

_____ 3. Identifies rhyming words

_____ 4. Hears differences in environmental, letter, and word sounds

_____ 5. Imitates sound sequences

_____ 6. Repeats words and sentences in sequence

_____ 7. Hears beginning, medial, and final sounds

_____ 8. Other _____

Visual-Motor Skills

_____ 1. Develops left-to-right eye movement

_____ 2. Coordinates hand-eye movement

_____ 3. Other _____

F. Word Identification Skills

Sight Vocabulary

_____ 1. Recognizes words in isolation

_____ 2. Recognizes words in context

Phonetic Analysis

_____ 1. Identifies initial consonant sounds in words

_____ 2. Identifies medial consonant sounds in words

_____ 3. Identifies final consonant sounds in words

_____ 4. Substitutes initial consonant sounds to form new words

_____ 5. Substitutes medial consonant sounds to form new words

_____ 6. Substitutes final consonant sounds to form new words

_____ 7. Identifies vowel sounds in initial position

_____ 8. Identifies vowel sounds in medial position

_____ 9. Identifies vowel sounds in final position

_____ 10. Substitutes vowel sounds in initial position to form new words

_____ 11. Substitutes vowel sounds in medial position to form new words

_____ 12. Substitutes vowel sounds in final position to form new words

Structural Analysis

_____ 1. Recognizes compound words

_____ 2. Recognizes contractions

_____ 3. Recognizes base (root) words

_____ 4. Recognizes suffixes

_____ 5. Recognizes prefixes

_____ 6. Identifies common word endings

_____ 7. Divides words into syllables

_____ 8. Accents appropriate syllables when sounding out words

_____ 9. Recognizes possessive forms of nouns

_____ 10. Knows common rules for forming the plural of nouns

_____ 11. Other _____

Contextual Analysis Skills

_____ 1. Uses context to read unfamiliar words and to gain meaning

_____ 2. Other _____

G.   Comprehension Skills

Literal Skills

_____ 1. Reads for detail (who, what, when, where, why)

_____ 2. Reads for the main idea

_____ 3. Reads for a purpose

_____ 4. Reads to follow directions

_____ 5. Reads to follow sequence of events

_____ 6. Understands cause-and-effect in stories

_____ 7. Identifies meanings of words, phrases, and sentences

_____ 8. Identifies character traits

_____ 9. Understands the sense of the sentence

_____ 10. Other _____

Interpretive Skills

_____ 1. Reads to interpret illustrations

_____ 2. Reads to draw conclusions

_____ 3. Reads to make generalizations

_____ 4. Reads to get implied meaning

_____ 5. Reads to understand author's purpose

_____ 6. Interprets and appreciates figurative language

_____ 7. Understands writing style and literary quality of material

_____ 8. Makes inferences

_____ 9. Predicts outcomes

_____ 10. Recognizes mood of the story

_____ 11. Identifies character feelings and actions

_____ 12. Uses punctuation to interpret author's message

_____ 13. Other _____

Critical Skills

_____ 1. Differentiates between real and unreal

_____ 2. Determines propaganda in material

_____ 3. Identifies relevant and irrelevant information

_____ 4. Notes qualifications of the author

_____ 5. Reads to evaluate and judge

_____ 6. Distinguishes between fact and opinion

_____ 7. Discerns the attitudes of the writer

_____ 8. Other _____

H. Study Skills

_____ 1. Alphabetizes words by _____ 1, _____ 2, _____ 3, _____ 4, _____ 5 letters

_____ 2. Finds words using guidewords in dictionary

_____ 3. Locates main entry for a word containing an inflectional ending or suffix

_____ 4. Uses the key in a dictionary to pronounce words

_____ 5. Outlines a paragraph

_____ 6. Outlines a chapter

_____ 7. Develops an outline using several sources

_____ 8. Summarizes a paragraph

_____ 9. Summarizes a chapter

_____ 10. Synthesizes information from several sources

_____ 11. Skims or scans material when appropriate

_____ 12. Locates information using an encyclopedia

_____ 13. Locates information using the card catalog

_____ 14. Locates information using the table of contents

_____ 15. Locates information using an index

_____ 16. Locates information using an appendix

_____ 17. Locates information using a glossary

_____ 18. Locates information using an atlas

_____ 19. Interprets diagrams

_____ 20. Interprets charts and tables

_____ 21. Interprets maps

_____ 22. Adjusts rate of reading according to material and purpose for reading

_____ 23. Other

I. Other Observations

_____

_____

_____

Appendix E

Interpretive Report

I. *STUDENT DATA*
Student's Name: Claudia
Date of Birth: August 23, 1975
Sex: Female
Age: Eleven Years, Three Months
School: Central Middle
School District: Central   Grade: 5.3
Parents: Mr. & Mrs. Joe Smith
Home Phone: unlisted
Address: Central, Florida
Examiner: Susan Hunter
Dates Tested: September 20, 1986; September 21, 1986; October 19, 1986; October 20, 1986; October 22, 1986; and October 24, 1986

II. *BACKGROUND INFORMATION*
Family, Birth and Developmental History
Claudia is an eleven-year, three-month-old female who lives with her parents in Central, Florida. Claudia is one of four children. She was the second born. She has an older brother, Paul, age seventeen. Claudia has a younger brother, Neil, age eight and a younger sister, Jackie, age seven. The four children attend school in Central, Florida.

Claudia's mother, Diane Smith, works in the home. Joe Smith, Claudia's father, is employed by the Department of Public Transportation. Mr. and Mrs. Smith completed their education through the eleventh grade. The Smith family lives in a rural environment and at the present time falls into the lower socioeconomic class.

According to Mrs. Smith, Claudia was a full-term baby with no reported complications during pregnancy or delivery. Claudia accomplished all developmental tasks at an appropriate age. Mrs. Smith stated that Claudia was a healthy child, except for colds and one case of pneumonia, which occurred at the age of two. Claudia was hospitalized two days during the case of pneumonia. According to Mrs. Smith, Claudia has suffered no serious illnesses or accidents that would affect current educational performance.

Social History
Claudia is a friendly and happy child. She has a close relationship with her parents and siblings. Claudia enjoys visiting neighbors in her rural community and especially enjoys visiting relatives in Tallahassee, Florida. According to Claudia's mother, Claudia has good relationships with her teachers and peers. Claudia presently exhibits no behavioral problems in the home, school, or neighborhood in which she lives.

Claudia's firsthand experiences have been limited. According to Claudia, she has been to the zoo and on a picnic. She has not had opportunities to visit a museum or a circus; she has never been on a boat or airplane; she has not had the experience of family vacations.

Educational History
Claudia is presently attending Central Middle School located in Central, Florida. Prior to her enrollment in Central Middle School, she attended Central Elementary and Lee Elementary. Claudia attended Lee Elementary in the first, second, and third grade. While at Lee Elementary, Claudia repeated the first grade. Claudia did not attend kindergarten.

Currently, Claudia is making average or above average grades (on her level of functioning), except in spelling. Claudia reported that she made a "D" in spelling on her last progress report. Presently, Claudia's grades in other subject areas are as follows: "C" in reading; "C" in English; "B" in social studies; "B" in math; and "B" in physical education. According to Claudia, her favorite subjects are spelling and English. She stated that math was difficult for her and that it was her least favorite subject.

Physical Factors

Claudia's vision and hearing were recently screened at her school. Hearing was found to be within normal limits. Claudia failed the vision screening at her school and was referred to a local clinic for further evaluation. At the local clinic, it was found that Claudia had good visual acuity and no vision problems that would interfere with educational functioning.

General Behavior During Testing

Claudia was eager to be tested. She appeared to enjoy the attention provided by the examiner.

Since the examiner has known Claudia for three years, rapport had already been established. Throughout the testing sessions, Claudia was attentive and appropriately active. She did appear to lack self-confidence. Claudia completed all activities easily and allocated adequate time on most tasks.

Overall, Claudia's performance during the testing sessions was not hindered by any significant interfering factors. It is the examiner's opinion that the test results obtained are representative of her skills and abilities.

III. *DIAGNOSIS*

Test Data

Test Administered: *Durrell Analysis of Reading Difficulty*

Test Date: *October 24, 1986*

SUBTEST	GRADE LEVEL/POSITION	
Oral Reading	2H	Comprehension: Good
Silent Reading	2M	Comprehension: Good
Listening Comprehension	3	Comprehension: 100%
Word Recognition	3H	
Listening Vocabulary	3H	
Word Analysis	3H	
Spelling	4M	
Identifying Sounds in Words	3M	

Test Administered: *Stanford Diagnostic Reading Test—Green Level*

Test Dates: *October 19, 1986; October 20, 1986*

SUBTEST	RAW SCORE	% ile	STANINE	GRADE EQUIVALENT
Auditory Vocabulary	22/40	15	3	3.3
Auditory Discrimination	28/36	24	4	2.2
Phonetic Analysis	12/36	8	2	2.0
Structural Analysis	43/60	18	3	3.3
Comprehension	45/60	20	3	3.5

Test Administered: *Slosson Oral Reading Test*

Test Date: *September 21, 1986*

Present Grade: 5.1 Raw Score: 94/200 Reading Level: 4.7

Test Administered: *Slosson Intelligence Test*

Test Date: *October 22, 1986*

Chronological Age: 11–2
Mental Age: 9–2
Intelligence Quotient: 82

Test Administered: *Sucher-Allred Reading Placement Inventory*
Test Date: September 20, 1986

Word Recognition	3^1
Independent Level	1
Instructional Level	2^1
Frustration Level	2^2

Analysis and Interpretation of Data

The *Elementary Interest Inventory*, developed by Patti Russell, Martha Collins, and Earl Cheek for use in reading diagnosis, was administered to Claudia on September 20, 1986. The *Elementary Interest Inventory* is a questionnaire individually administered to acquire information relative to home and school relationships, interests, and firsthand experiences.

In the area of Home Relationships, Claudia reported that she enjoys outdoor sports with her brothers and sister (e.g., football, baseball). She also enjoys helping her mother in the home with cooking and cleaning. Claudia stated that she enjoys watching television during her spare time.

In the Personal Life area of the *Elementary Interest Inventory*, Claudia stated that she wanted to be a teacher because she enjoys "little children." Claudia reported that she worries about failing tests at school and that she wants to do better in math. When she wants to be alone, Claudia said that she would go for a walk down the lane. Claudia enjoys receiving gifts from friends and family, especially a gift of money.

The third section of the *Elementary Interest Inventory* provides questions relative to Reading. Claudia stated that she enjoys reading the *Readers Digest*, which can be found in her home. Claudia said that she did not like to read very much and later contradicted herself by saying "I like it," (i.e., reading). Reportedly, Claudia reads when she has nothing else to do but she did feel reading was important.

When asked questions relative to school, Claudia indicated that she did like school. Her favorite subject is spelling and her least favorite subject is math. She stated that school would be better "if there were fewer children in the classroom."

The Peer Relationship section of the *Elementary Interest Inventory* revealed that Claudia does have a best friend, Sarah. Claudia did express concern about other children getting into trouble at school. According to Claudia, she does not like to have friends who fight at school.

When answering the questions from the Interest section of the *Elementary Interest Inventory*, Claudia indicated she liked jumping rope, playing school, and enjoyed the sport of basketball. She does not have any after-school activities or hobbies. Claudia indicated that she admired her mother and father. Claudia did say, that more than anything else, she wished for money. Her firsthand experiences have been limited. Claudia does go with her mother to the store and has been to the zoo and on a picnic with her class. No other experiences were reported by her.

In the Unaided Question section of the *Elementary Interest Inventory*, Claudia indicated material needs when asked to tell the examiner something else about herself.

Durrell Analysis of Reading Difficulty

The *Durrell Analysis of Reading Difficulty* was administered on October 24, 1986. This test consists of several subtests that are used to evaluate various aspects of a student's reading ability.

The Oral Reading subtest consists of timed passages. Following the reading of the passages, the student is asked several comprehension questions. Claudia obtained a grade equivalent of 2 High on this subtest. Claudia's comprehension was good overall. Claudia evidenced many repetitions when reading the passages orally. She also ignored ending punctuation. Claudia consistently left off endings of words, for example, the "ing," "ed," and "ly." Claudia's comprehension on three of the passages was 100%. On passage 2A, Claudia attained 81%

comprehension. The analysis of the Oral Reading subtest reveals Claudia's ability to use context, which can be considered an area of strength.

The Silent Reading subtest is timed, just as the Oral Reading subtest. Immediately following the reading of the passages, the student is asked to provide the examiner with memories from the passages. Claudia attained a median grade equivalent of 2 Middle on this subtest.

As on the Oral Reading subtest, comprehension on the Silent Reading subtest can be considered "good" overall. It should be noted that Claudia remembered the first passage read, 1A, just as it was presented in the test booklet. When presented with short reading passages, Claudia has excellent retention. This strength should be utilized in planning a prescription and during the instruction stage. Claudia was observed moving her lips and head while reading silently. As the passages increased in length and difficulty, Claudia's memory for content did decrease.

Claudia obtained a grade equivalent of 3.0 on the Listening Comprehension subtest. The Listening Comprehension subtest consists of passages read to the student by the examiner. Immediately following the readings, the student must answer several comprehension questions. At grade level 3.0, Claudia attained 100% comprehension. The fourth grade passage proved difficult for Claudia. She received credit at this level for only two questions. This resulted in a 25% comprehension score at the fourth grade level.

On the Word Recognition/Word Analysis subtest the student is required to first recognize words that are flashed; if the student misses the word flashed, an opportunity is provided for analysis of the word. This subtest revealed a flash score of 3 High and an analysis score of 3 High. Claudia appears to have limited word-analysis skills and is slow in sounding out words. She does try hard and is persistent, which appears to be a strength. She does know the sounds of initial consonants, but when presented with words having three or more syllables, a breakdown in her skills is clearly evident. Claudia exhibited difficulty with vowel and consonant sounds within words.

The *Listening Vocabulary* subtest provides a measure of the number of words the student understands in speech. Since the words in this subtest are the same as the ones used in the Word Recognition/Word Analysis subtest, a direct raw score comparison can be determined between listening vocabulary and the student's ability to read these words (Donald D. Durrell and Jane H. Catterson, 1980). On the Listening Vocabulary subtest, Claudia attained a score of 3 High. Claudia evidenced a direct correlation between her score on the Word Recognition/Word Analysis subtest and the Listening Vocabulary subtest. She achieved a grade equivalent of 3 High on both tests.

The Sounds in Isolation subtest reveals the student's ability to elicit the sounds of letters, blends, digraphs, phonograms, and affixes. Claudia did well with the sounds of letters. She knew the sounds of several blends and digraphs. Those blends and digraphs presenting difficulty for Claudia are as follows: /fl/, /sk/, /th/, /tr/, and /gr/. Some phonograms and affixes also presented difficulty. Recognition of final affixes appears to be Claudia's weakest area.

Claudia received her highest score on the *Durrell Analysis of Reading Difficulty* in the area of spelling. She attained a grade equivalent of 4 High. Words were dictated from List 1 and List 2. On List 1, Claudia spelled ninety percent of the words correctly. On List 2, she spelled only fifty percent of the words with accuracy. Claudia has a definite weakness spelling words with three or more syllables. Claudia again proved that she knows the initial consonant sounds and most initial digraphs.

On the Identifying Sounds in Words subtest, Claudia received a score of 93% or a grade equivalent of 3 Middle. When hearing spoken words, Claudia has a strength in identifying the written words that have the same beginning and ending sounds.

Overall, on the *Durrell Analysis of Reading Difficulty*, Claudia appears to be functioning at a solid third grade level in reading. Claudia is functioning below her expected level when considering her grade placement and chronological age.

Stanford Diagnostic Reading Test (Green Level)
The *Stanford Diagnostic Reading Test (Stanford)* was administered on October 19, 1986 and October 20, 1986. The *Stanford* can be administered individually or with a group of students. For this particular case study, the *Stanford* was administered to two students simultaneously. The Green Level, which covers grades 2.6 to 5.5, was used with Claudia. The *Stanford* provides the examiner with percentiles, stanines, and grade equivalents.

On subtest one, Auditory Vocabulary, Claudia identified twenty-two of the forty items. This subtest contains vocabulary items covering reading, math, social studies, the arts and other areas. On this subtest, the child has to only identify a word that best suits the sentence, which is dictated by the examiner. The Auditory Vocabulary raw score of twenty-two yielded a percentile of fifteen, a stanine of three, and a grade equivalent of 3.3. This subtest revealed that Claudia is functioning below average in auditory vocabulary.

The Auditory Discrimination subtest requires the student to discriminate vowels and consonants. Twenty-eight out of thirty-six items were discriminated correctly. Claudia did a better job of discriminating consonants than vowels. Ending sounds again presented much difficulty for Claudia. She attained a grade equivalent of 2.2 on this subtest, which places her in the fourth stanine or low average range.

The Phonetic Analysis subtest revealed a definite weakness. Claudia's total raw score was twelve out of a possible thirty-six. She received a grade equivalent of 2.0 and fell in the second stanine. On this subtest, the student has to read a word with an underlined grapheme and then find another word with the same sound. This subtest is timed. Claudia experienced difficulty with consonant clusters, consonant digraphs, short vowels, and long vowels. Phonetic analysis appears to be a definite weakness.

The Structural Analysis subtest is divided into two sections. The first part of the Structural Analysis subtest measures the student's skill in identifying the first syllable in two syllable words. On the second section of this subtest, the student must

blend elements together to make words. Claudia did better with structural analysis than phonetic analysis. Claudia's score on the Word Division section was only one point less than the score on Blending. Overall, she attained a grade equivalent of 3.3, which places her in the third stanine. Claudia had difficulty determining the first syllable in the following words: "surely," "forget," "future," "report," "pirate," "station," "picnic," "pretend," and "elect." Claudia does not appear to know the rules of dividing words into syllables. On the blending section of this subtest, Claudia evidenced difficulty with affixes.

Claudia obtained her highest score on the *Stanford* in the area of comprehension. The Comprehension subtest revealed a grade equivalent of 3.5. The Reading Comprehension subtest consists of Part A and Part B. In Part A, the student must read a sentence or two and choose a word(s) that completes the sentence. The child must use literal and inferential comprehension skills in choosing the correct answer. The second part of the comprehension subtest consists of short paragraphs. The student must read the passages and then choose the correct answers for the questions that follow. Literal and inferential questions are provided. Claudia appears to have as much difficulty with literal comprehension questions as she has with inferential type questions. Approximately one-half of her errors occurred when answering literal questions. The other fifty percent of her errors occurred when answering inferential questions.

Slosson Oral Reading Test (SORT)
The *Slosson Oral Reading Test (SORT)* was administered on September 21, 1986. The SORT is composed of ten word lists ranging from the primer level to the high school level. The reading level obtained from the SORT is representative of median school achievement. The SORT consists of two hundred words. Claudia pronounced ninety-four (94) of the two hundred (200) words correctly, which yielded a reading level of 4.7. Her grade level at the time of testing was 5.1. The SORT indicates her expanded vocabulary to be a relative strength. Since Claudia exhibits a weakness in phonetic analysis and a weakness in

structural analysis, she was unable to decode the new words on the *SORT*. She had a tendency to guess and did not even attempt several of the words on the lists past the fifth grade level. Words containing three or more syllables again presented difficulty for Claudia as evidenced by the following errors: "enforce" for "interfere"; "intation" for "importance"; "medication" for "malicious"; "invitor" for "inventory"; and "excends" for "excellence." Claudia was able to decode the first and second syllable of some of the words.

Slosson Intelligence Test (SIT)

The *Slosson Intelligence Test (SIT)* is designed for use in screening. An intelligence quotient is obtained from this test. The *SIT* is an individually administered test. The *SIT* was administered to Claudia on October 22, 1986 and yielded an intelligence quotient of 82, which places her in the low average range. She attained a mental age of 9–2, which is two years below her chronological age.

Claudia's major areas of weakness were in math and vocabulary. Claudia could not tell the examiner the following: the number of feet in a specific number of yards; the number of pints in a gallon; or one-half of thirty-six. In the area of vocabulary, Claudia did not know the meaning of "dungeon," "inventory," or "scarce." A few of Claudia's errors appeared on judgment reasoning. She could not explain how a clock differs from a calendar, or how a crayon is different from a pencil. Overall, the *SIT* indicates that Claudia is in need of vocabulary development and remedial assistance in the area of mathematics.

Sucher-Allred Placement Inventory

The *Sucher-Allred Reading Placement Inventory (Sucher)* was administered on September 20, 1986. The *Sucher* is made up of a word recognition subtest and an oral reading subtest. The words and passages begin with primer level through grade nine. Following the passages on the oral reading section are comprehension questions that the child or student must answer when asked by the examiner. The *Sucher* provides an Independent Level of reading, an Instructional Level of reading, and a Frustration Level of reading. It also provides

the examiner with a grade equivalent for word recognition. On the word recognition subtest, Claudia attained a 3^1 grade equivalent. Claudia made one error on List C (2.1 reader) and two errors on List D (2.2 reader). She read "disease" for "decided," "nod" for "nodded," and "single" for "signal." Claudia achieved 90% accuracy on List E (3.1 reader), 53% accuracy on List F (3.2 reader), and 27% accuracy on List G (grade 4 reader). She again demonstrated difficulty with vowel sounds. This was evidenced by errors made on the following words: "desk" for "dusk" and "cokepit" for "cockpit."

The Oral Reading section of the *Sucher* revealed an independent reading level of first grade. Claudia had four word recognition errors at this level. Her errors consisted of one mispronunciation, one omission, one insertion, and one substitution. Claudia did well on the comprehension questions, missing only one-half of one question out of a total of five questions, which resulted in a ninety percent comprehension score.

Claudia's instructional level on the *Sucher* was determined to be a 2^1 grade equivalent. Claudia exhibited eight word recognition errors and had a comprehension score of eighty percent. Claudia's breakdown is occurring on word recognition. Most of her errors were determined to be mispronunciations. She had one omission and one insertion. Claudia had difficulty with the sight words "will" and "should." She consistently read "oh or ohl" for "owl."

The frustration level for Claudia occurred with Selection D, or the 2^2 grade level. Her word recognition errors increased to twelve. Her comprehension dropped to sixty percent. Claudia mispronounced ten words, had one omission, and had one insertion. She consistently read "Peter" for "Pete." She experienced difficulty with the sight words "it" and "had." She read "I" for "it" and "have" for "had." The inference questions presented the most difficulty for Claudia.

Claudia was allowed to read Selection E, grade 3^1 even though her frustration level had been determined with the previous passage. She again did well in the area of comprehension, missing a total of one question. Claudia exhibited eighteen word recognition errors while reading this passage. Claudia appears to be using context well, as evidenced by the ninety percent comprehension score.

Synthesis
In summary, Claudia is functioning below level for her present grade placement and chronological age. Use of context when reading appears to be one area of strength. Claudia does not exhibit the characteristics of being a visual or auditory learner. Claudia's phonetic analysis and structural analysis skills are weak. Since she has limited word-analysis capabilities, utilization of context should be considered in her plan of instruction. Claudia also evidenced a weakness in vocabulary. Overall, Claudia has many weaknesses in the area of reading. These weaknesses need to be addressed through prescriptive reading instruction.

IV.   *PRESCRIPTION*
Claudia's weaknesses in reading can best be met through the use of a variety of approaches. Because of her present age and grade level, intensive instruction in phonics and word analysis are not recommended. Use of a third grade basal reader in conjunction with other approaches is the recommended strategy. A multi-sensory approach and/or the language-experience approach should be coupled with the use of the basal reader. Claudia's reading prescription should also include vocabulary building and language development.

The language-experience approach will provide reading material that has been extracted from the student's spoken language. The language-experience approach includes the following steps:
- discuss experiences common to the student (a stimulus such as a field trip is desirable)
- prepare the student(s) by having the ideas summarized
- provide time for sharing ideas
- read each idea as it is written
- read the story with the student
- discuss the story and point out particulars
- make copies of stories
- on days that follow, the story should be reread and ideas and vocabulary should be discussed.

The language-experience approach would be an appropriate method for the following reasons: several learning modalities will be used; the information will be of interest to Claudia; oral language skills will be addressed; and vocabulary development will be emphasized.

The multi-sensory approach also should be an effective means of teaching Claudia. This approach utilizes several channels of learning. The senses of vision, hearing, touch, and muscle movement are incorporated into this approach. The VAK (visual-auditory-kinesthetic) method is recommended. The student will follow the following steps when using this approach:
- Tracing: The student will trace a written word and say the entire word as it is traced. The student will do this until the word can be traced from memory. The student will then write the word, saying the word as it is written.
- Writing Without Tracing: Once the student is familiar with the word, she will write it from memory without any tracing.
- Recognition in Print: The student will be allowed to look at the word, will be told the word, will pronounce the word, and will write it from memory.
- Word Analysis: The student will be taught to look for the familiar parts of a word and try to identify new words from known parts.

Claudia's vocabulary can be increased by teaching homonyms and synonyms for words already known to her. Claudia should also be taught dictionary skills in order that she may become proficient in looking up the meanings of new and/or unknown words. Language stimulation should also be one phase of Claudia's prescription. Providing her with experiences she has never had (e.g., a trip to a museum or historical southern home) is another recommended avenue for her development.

With the appropriate prescription and instruction, Claudia's reading level should increase. She is a motivated child and is always eager to learn. During the instruction phase, periodic monitoring is recommended. Pre-testing and post-testing should be utilized in order to determine achievement of established goals and objectives.

Appendix F

Children's Choices

This is a list of "Children's Choices" published annually by the International Reading Association in *The Reading Teacher*. These titles represent some of the selections chosen from 1989–91. For additional titles, see the October issues of *The Reading Teacher*.

All Ages

Beauty and the Beast. Marie LePrince de Beaumont; trans. by Richard Howard. Ill. by Hilary Knight. Simon & Schuster.

Can You Match This?: Jokes about Unlikely Pairs. Rick Walton and Ann Walton. Ill. by Joan Hanson. Lerner.

Chocolate Dreams. Arnold Adoff. Ill. by Turi MacCombie. Lothrop.

Clowning Around!: Jokes about the Circus. Rick Walton and Ann Walton. Ill. by Joan Hanson. Lerner.

Earthlets as explained by Professor Xargel. Jeanne Willis. Ill. by Tony Ross. Dutton.

The Empty Pot. Demi. Ill. by the author. Holt.

Fossil Follies!: Jokes about Dinosaurs. Rick Walton and Ann Walton. Ill. by Joan Hanson. Lerner.

The Gift of the Willows. Helena Clare Pittman. Ill. by the author. Carolrhoda.

Guppies in Tuxedos: Funny Eponyms. Marvin Terban. Ill. by Giulio Maestro. Clarion.

Her Seven Brothers. Paul Goble. Ill. by the author. Bradbury.

I Known an Old Lady Who Swallowed a Fly. Retold by Glen Rounds. Ill. by the author. Holiday House.

If You're Not Here, Please Raise Your Hand: Poems About School. Lalli Dakos. Ill. by G. Brian Karas. Four Winds.

Jumbo the Boy and Arnold the Elephant. Dan Greenburg. Ill. by Susan Perl. Harper.

Little Penguin's Tale. Audrey Wood. Ill. by author. HBJ.

Oh, the Places You'll Go! Dr. Seuss. Ill. by the author. Random House.

Oh, That's Ridiculous! Selected by William Cole. Ill. by Tomi Unger.

Seasons. Poetry selected by Alberto Manguel. Ill. by Warabe Aska. Doubleday.

Swan Lake. Margot Fonteyn. Ill. by Trina Schart Hyman. Gulliver.

Young Merlin. Robert D. San Souci. Ill. by Daniel Horne. Doubleday.

Beginning Independent Readers

Alexander's Midnight Snack: A Little Elephant's ABC. Catherine Stock. Ill. by the author. Clarion.

Cave Boy. Cathy East Dubowski. Ill. by Mark Dubowski. Random House.

Esther's Trunk. Jez Alborough. Ill. by the author. Warner.

Fish Eyes: A Book You Can Count On. Lois Ehlert. Ill. by the author. HBJ.

Good Hunting, Blue Sky. Peggy Parish. Ill. by James Watts. Harper.

The Guy Who Was Five Minutes Late. Bill Grossman. Ill. by Judy Glasser. HarperCollins.

Harry's Bath. Harriet Ziefert. Ill. by Seymour Chwast. Bantam.

Hello, House! Linda Hayward. Ill. by Lynn Munsinger. Random House.

Henry and Mudge in the Sparkle Days. Cynthia Rylant. Ill. by Sucie Stevenson. Bradbury.

A Hundred Million Reasons for Owning an Elephant (Or at Least a Dozen I Can Think of Right Now). Lois G. Grambling. Ill. by Vickie M. Learner. Barron's.

I Like Me! Nancy Carlson. Ill. by the author. Viking.

In the Haunted House. Eve Bunting. Ill. by Susan Meddaugh. Clarion.

The Mixed-Up Mice Clean House. Robert Kraus. Ill. by the author. Warner.

My Mom Made Me Go to Camp. Judy Delton. Ill. by Lisa McCue. Delacorte.

My Perfect Neighborhood. Leah Komaiko. Ill. by Barbara West-man. HarperCollins.

Never Spit on Your Shoes. Denys Cazet. Ill. by the author. Orchard.

Oscar Got the Blame. Tony Ross. Ill. by the author. Dial.

Pigs at Home. Ron and Atie Van Der Meer. Ill. by the authors. Aladdin.

Ronald Morgan Goes to Bat. Patricia Reilly Giff. Ill. by Susanna Natti. Viking.

The Silly Book. Babette Cole. Ill. by the author. Doubleday.

Some Bodies in the Attic: A Spooky Pop-Up Book. Design and paper engineering by Keith Moseley. Ill. by Andy Everitt-Stewart. Grosset & Dunlap.

"Stand Back," Said the Elephant, "I'm Going to Sneeze!" Patricia Thomas. Ill. by Wallace Tripp. Lothrop.

Where's Peter Rabbit? Beatrix Potter. Ill. by Colin Twinn. Viking.

Who Goes Out on Halloween? Sue Alexander. Ill. by G. Brian Karas. Bantam.

Who's Sick Today? Lynne Cherry. Ill. by the author. Dutton.

The Winter Duckling. Keith Polette. Ill. by Clovis Martin. Milliken.

A Zoo in Our House. Heather Eyles. Ill. by Andy Cooke. Warner.

Younger Readers

Anna Marie's Blanket. Joanne Barkan. Ill. by Deborah Maze. Barron's.

The Adventures of Underwater Dog. Jan Wahl. Ill. by Tim Bowers. Grosset.

Airmail to the Moon. Tom Birdseye. Ill. by Stephen Gammell. Holiday House.

Aliens for Breakfast. Jonathan Etra and Stephanie Spinner. Ill. by Steve Bjorkman. Random House.

All I See. Cynthia Rylant. Ill. by Peter Catalanotto. Orchard.

Amelia Bedelia's Family Album. Peggy Parish. Ill. by Lynn Sweat. Greenwillow.

The Baby Blue Cat Who Said No. Ainslie Pryor. Ill. by the author. Viking.

Because of Lozo Brown. Larry L. King. Ill. by Amy Schwartz. Viking.

Best Enemies. Kathleen Leverich. Ill. by Susan Condie Lamb. Greenwillow.

The Best Friends Club: A Lizzie and Harold Story. Elizabeth Winthrop. Ill. by Martha Weston. Lothrop.

Blackberry Ramble. Thacher Hurd. Ill. by the author. Crown.

Blow Me a Kiss, Miss Lilly. Nancy White Carlstrom. Ill. by Amy Schwartz. HarperCollins.

The Boy and the Ghost. Robert D. San Souci. Ill. by J. Brian Pinkney. Simon & Schuster.

Bye Bye Baby. Janet Ahlberg and Allan Ahlberg. Ill. by the authors. Little, Brown.

Charlie Anderson. Barbara Abercrombie. Ill. by Mark Graham. McElderry.

The Cherry Pie Baby. Kay Chorao. Ill. by the author. Dutton.

Chicka Chicka Boom Boom. Bill Martin, Jr. and John Archambault. Ill. by Lois Ehlert. Simon & Schuster.

The Completed Hickory Dickory Dock. Jim Aylesworth. Ill. by Eileen Christelow. Atheneum.

Crazy Clothes. Niki Yektai. Ill. by Sucie Stevenson. Bradbury.

Dad's Car Wash. Harry A. Sutherland. Ill. by Maxie Chambliss. Atheneum.

Daniel's Dog. Jo Ellen Bogart. Ill. by Janet Wilson. Scholastic.

The Day the Dragon Came to School. Marie Tenaille. Ill. by Violayne Hulne. Alladdin.

Dinosaur Garden. Liza Donnelly. Ill. by the author. Scholastic.

The Dinosaur Who Lived in My Back-yard. B. G. Hennessy. Ill. by Susan Davis. Viking.

The Dragon Nanny. C. L. G. Martin. Ill. by Robert Rayevsky. Macmillan.

Eagle-Eye Ernie Comes to Town. Susan Pearson. Ill. by Gioia Fiammenghi. Simon & Schuster.

Earrings. Judith Viorst. Ill. by Nola Langer Malone. Atheneum.

Even That Moose Won't Listen to Me. Martha Alexander. Ill. by the author. Dial.

Five Little Ducks. Raffi. Ill. by Jose Aruego and Ariane Dewey. Crown.

Five Little Monkeys Jumping on the Bed. Retold by Eileen Christelow. Ill. by the author. Clarion.

The Frog. Pat Paris. Ill. by the author. Simon & Schuster.

Go to Sleep, Nicholas Joe. Marjorie Weinman Sharmat. Ill. by John Himmelman. Harper.

The Good-Bye Book. Judith Viorst. Ill. by Kay Chorao. Atheneum.

Good-bye Sammy. Liza Ketchum Murrow. Ill. by Gail Owens. Holiday House.

Grandma Gets Grumpy. Anna Grossnickle Hines. Ill. by the author. Clarion.

Granny Is A Darling. Kady MacDonald Denton. Ill. by the author. McElderry.

The Gunnywolf. A Delaney. Ill. by the author. Harper.

Harold's Runaway Nose. Harriet Sonnenschein. Ill. by Jurg Obrist. Simon & Schuster.

Herbie Hamster, Where Are You? Terence Blacker. Ill. by Pippa Unwin. Random House.

Horrible Harry in Room 2B. Suzy Kline. Ill. by Frank Remkiewicz. Viking.

I Meant to Clean My Room Today. Miriam Nerlove. Ill. by the author. McElderry.

If I Had Long, Long Hair. Angela Elwell Hunt. Ill. by L. Diane Johnson. Abingdon.

The Jacket I Wear in the Snow. Shirley Neitzel. Ill. by Nancy Winslow Parker. Greenwillow.

Jenny and the Tooth Fairy. Jean Richardson and Mike Dodd. Ill. by Mike Dodd. Oxford University Press.

Jessica. Kevin Henkes. Ill. by the author. Greenwillow.

Good-bye Sammy. Liza Ketchum Murrow. Ill. by Gail Owens. Holiday House.

Johnny Appleseed. Steven Kellogg. Ill. by the author. Morrow.

Just a Daydream. Mercer Mayer. Ill. by the author. Golden.

Over the Steamy Swamp. Paul Geraghty. Ill. by the author. Gulliver.

Pig Surprise. Ute Krause. Ill. by the author. Dial.

P. J. Funnybunny in the Perfect Hiding Place. Marilyn Sadler. Ill. by Roger Bollen. Golden.

Plateo's Big Race: A Tiny Dinos Story about Learning. Guy Gilchrist. Ill. by the author. Warner.

Porker Finds a Chair. Sven Nordqvist. Ill. by the author. Carolrhoda.

Rainy Day Kate. Lenore Blegvad. Ill. by Erik Blegvad. McElderry.

Rap. Keith Elliot Greenberg. Ill. with photographs. Lerner.

Rotten Ralph's Show and Tell. Jack Gantos. Ill. by Nicole Rubel. Houghton.

Sheep on a Ship. Nancy Shaw. Ill. by Margot Apple. Houghton.

Skip to My Lou. Adapted by Nadine Bernard Westcott. Ill. by the author. Joy Street.

The Stick-in-Bed Birthday. Linda Wagner Tyler. Ill. by Susan Davis. Viking.

Tacky the Penguin. Helen Lester. Ill. by Lynn Munsinger. Houghton.

Thanks a Lot, Triceratot: A Tiny Dinos Story about Helping Others. Guy Gilchrist. Ill. by the author. Warner.

Three Cheers for Errol! Babette Cole. Ill. by the author. Putnam.

Tree Trunk Traffic. Bianca Lavies. Ill. with photos by the author. Dutton.

The Umbrella Day. Nancy Evans Cooney. Ill. by Melissa Bay Mathis. Philomel.

A Visit from Dr. Katz. Ursula K. Le Guin. Ill. by Anne Barrow. Atheneum.

The Wedding of Brown Bear and White Bear. Martine Beck. Ill. by Marie H. Henry. Little, Brown.

Well, I Never! Susan Pearson. Ill. by James Warhola. Simon & Schuster.

We're Going on a Bear Hunt. Michael Rosen. Ill. by Helen Oxenbury. McElderry.

What If the Shark Wears Tennis Shoes? Winifred Morris. Ill. by Betsy Lewin. Atheneum.

Who's Afraid of the Big Bad Wolf? Retold by Tony Bradman. Ill. by Margaret Chamberlain. Aladdin.

The Wolf Who Cried Boy. Jeffrey Dinardo. Ill. by the author. Grosset.

You Are Much Too Small. Betty D. Boegehold. Ill. by Valerie Michaut. Bantam.

Middle Grades

Ace: The Very Important Pig. Dick King-Smith. Ill. by Lynette Hemmant. Crown.

The Adventures of Ratman. Ellen Weiss and Mel Friedman. Ill. by Dirk Zimmer. Random House.

Anna Banana: 101 Jump-Rope Rhymes. Joanna Cole. Ill. by Alan Tiegreen. Morrow.

Amazing Lizards. Trevor Smith. Ill. by Colin Woolf, Julie Anderson, and John Hutchinson. Knopf.

Animal Camoflauge: A Closer Look. Joyce Powzyk. Ill. by the author. Bradbury.

As: A Surfeit of Similes. Norton Juster. Ill. by David Small. Morrow.

The Bathwater Gang. Jerry Spinelli. Ill. by Meredith Johnson. Little, Brown.

The Believers. Rebecca C. Jones. Arcade.

Beyond the Ridge. Paul Goble. Ill. by the author. Bradbury.

Brutus the Wonder Poodle. Linda Gondosch. Ill. by Penny Dann. Random House.

Buzz Beamer's Radical Sports. Bill Hinds. Ill. by the author. Sports Illustrated/Little, Brown.

Catwings. Ursula K. Le Guin. Ill. by S. D. Schindler. Orchard.

The Christmas Coat. Clyde Robert Bulla. Ill. by Sylvie Wickstrom. Knopf.

The Class Trip (Sweet Valley Twins Super Edition #1). Created by Francine Pascal. Bantam.

Cleaver of the Good Luck Diner. James Duffy. Scribners.

Crayons. Henry Pluckrose. Ill. with photographs by Chris Fairclough. Watts.

The Doll in the Garden: A Ghost Story. Mary Downing Hahn. Clarion.

Following the Mystery Man. Mary Downing Hahn. Clarion.

The Fourth Grade Wizards. Barthe DeClements. Viking.

Fresh Brats. X. J. Kennedy. Ill. by James Watts. McElderry.

Fudge-a-Mania. Judy Blume. Dutton.

The Ghost in Tent 19. Jim O'Connor and Jane O'Connor. Ill. by Charles Robinson. Random House.

The Ghosts of Hungryhouse Lane. Sam McBratney. Ill. by Lisa Thiesing. Holt.

The Great School Lunch Rebellion. David Greenberg. Ill. by Maxie Chambliss. Bantam.

Just My Friend and Me. Mercer Mayer. Ill. by the author. Golden.

Just One Tooth. Miriam Nerlove. Ill. by the author. McElderry.

The Lady with the Alligator Purse. Adapted by Nadine Bernard Westcott. Ill. by the adapter. Joy Street.

Little Grunt and the Big Egg: A Prehistoric Fairy Tale. Tomie dePaola. Ill. by author. Holiday House.

Little Rabbit Foo Foo. Michael Rosen. Ill. by Arthur Robins. Simon & Schuster.

The Long Blue Blazer. Jeanne Willis. Ill. by Susan Varley. Dutton.

Mama Went Walking. Christine Berry. Ill. by Maria Cristina Brusca. Holt.

Mathilda the Dream Bear. Nicholas Heller. Ill. by the author. Greenwillow.

Max's Chocolate Chicken. Rosemary Wells. Ill. by the author. Dial.

Merry Christmas, Bigelow Bear. Dennis Kyte. Ill. by the author. Doubleday.

Miss Eva and the Red Balloon. Karen M. Glennon. Ill. by Hans Popel. Simon & Schuster.

Mother Halverson's New Cat. Jim Aylesworth. Ill. by Toni Goffe. Atheneum.

Mouse Paint. Ellen Stoll Walsh. Ill. by the author. HBJ.

Not Like That, Like This! Tony Bradman. Ill. by Joanna Burroughes. Oxford University Press.

"Not Now!" Said the Cow. Joanne Oppenheim. Ill. by the Chris Demarest. Bantam.

Oh No, It's Waylon's Birthday! James Stevenson. Ill. by the author. Greenwillow.

The Great Yellowstone Fire. Carole G. Vogel and Kathryn A. Goldner. Ill. with photographs. Sierra Club/Little, Brown.

Giants of the Air: The Story of Commercial Aviation. David Jefferis. Ill. by Terry Hadler, Ron Jobson, and Michael Roffe. Watts.

The Girl Who Invented Romance. Caroline B. Cooney. Bantam.

Gray Boy. Jim Arnosky. Lothrop.

Hail to the Chief!: Jokes about the Presidents. Diane Burns and Clint Burns. Ill. by Joan Hanson. Lerner.

Haunted Houses. Lewann Sotnak. Ill. by Robert Andrew Parker. Crestwood House.

The High Rise Glorious Skittle Skat Roarious Sky Pie Angel Food Cake. Nancy Willard. Ill. by Richard Jesse Watson. HBJ.

If You Made a Million. David M. Schwartz. Ill. by Steven Kellogg. Lothrop.

I Thought You Were My Best Friend. Ann Reit. Scholastic.

Jenny Archer, Author. Ellen Conford. Ill. by Diane Palmisciano. Little, Brown.

Jessie's Wishes. Sally Wittman. Ill. by Emily Arnold McCully. Scholastic.

The Jet Age: From the First Jet Fighters to Swing-Wing Bombers. David Jefferis. Ill. by Terry Hadler, Ron Jobson, and Michael Roffe. Watts.

A Job for Jenny Archer. Ellen Conford. Ill. by Diane Palmisciano. Little, Brown.

Kirsty Knows Best. Annalena McAfee. Ill. by Anthony Browne. Knopf.

Mail-Order Kid. Joyce McDonald. Putnam.

The Makeover Summer. Suzanne Weyn. Avon.

Margaret Ziegler Is Horse-Crazy. Crescent Dragonwagon. Ill. by Peter Elwell. Macmillan.

Meg MacKintosh and the Mystery at Camp Creepy. Lucinda Landon. Ill. by the author. Joy Street.

Merry Christmas, Festus and Mercury. Sven Nordqvist. Ill. by the author. Carolrhoda.

Merry-Go-Round: A Book about Nouns. Ruth Heller. Ill. by the author. Grosset & Dunlap.

Mummy Knows Best (A Mummy Dearest Creepy Hollow Whoooooooo Dunnit?). Robert Kraus. Ill. by the author. Warner.

Ms. Wiz Spells Trouble. Terence Blacker. Ill. by Toni Goffe. Barron's.

My Buddy, the King. Bill Brittain. Harper.

The Mysterious Cases of Mr. Pin. Mary Elise Monsell. Ill. by Eileen Christelow. Atheneum.

No Bean Sprouts, Please! Constance Hiser. Ill. by Carolyn Ewing. Holiday House.

O'Diddy. Jocelyn Stevenson. Ill. by Sue Truesdell. Random House.

On the Road with New Kids on the Block. Nancy E. Krulik. Ill. with photographs. Scholastic.

One Sister Too Many. C. S. Adler. Macmillan.

Orp and the Chop Suey Burgers. Suzy Kline. Putnam.

Park's Quest. Katherine Paterson. Lodestar.

Peace Begins with You. Katherine Scholes. Ill. by Robert Ingpen. Sierra Club/Little, Brown.

The Phantom of Creepy Hollow (A Mummy Dearest Creepy Hollow Whoooooooo Dunnit?). Robert Kraus. Ill. by the author. Warner.

Shira: A Legacy of Courage. Sharon Grollman. Doubleday.

The Show-and-Tell War and Other Stories About Adam Joshua. Janice Lee Smith. Ill. by Dick Gackenbach. Harper.

Slime Time. Jim O'Connor and Jane O'Connor. Ill. by Pat Porter. Random House.

Sly, P. I.: The Case of the Missing Shoes. Cathy Stefanec-Ogren. Ill. by Priscilla Posey Circolo. Harper.

The Stupids Take Off. Harry Allard and James Marshall. Ill. by James Marshall. Houghton.

Supposes. Dick Gackenbach. Ill. by the author. Gulliver.

Third Grade Is Terrible. Barbara Baker. Ill. by Roni Shepherd. Dutton.

The Tiny Parents. Ellen Weiss and Mel Friedman. Knopf.

Twenty Ways to Lose Your Best Friend. Marilyn Singer. Ill. by Jeffrey Lindberg. HarperCollins.

Vampires Don't Wear Polka Dots—or Do They? Debbie Dadey and Marcia Thornton Jones. Scholastic.

Wayside School Is Falling Down. Louis Sachar. Ill. by Joel Schick. Lothrop.

The Witch's Handbook. Malcolm Bird. Ill. by the author. Aladdin.

*Adapted from Children's Choices (1989–91). *The Reading Teacher* (October/1989–91). Reprinted with permission of the International Reading Association.

Appendix G

Construction of an Informal Reading Inventory

An IRI consists of a series of graded passages of approximately 100 to 200 words. Passages at the lower levels, such as preprimer, may have fewer than 100 words, while passages at the upper levels, such as senior high, may have more than 200 words. These passages may be selected from graded basal reading series that are unfamiliar to the student, from children's books whose readability level has been determined by the publisher or by the teacher, or from any other graded materials the teacher wishes to use.

Task 1

(Optional) *Select a list of words that can be used to assess the student's sight vocabulary level.* This first step assists in determining an approximate level at which to begin to administer the graded reading selections. A teacher may use word lists that are already developed and leveled, such as the *Dolch Basic Sight Word List* or the *Slosson Oral Reading Test.* The teacher may prefer to prepare a word list using words from the basal reader or a graded word list such as the Harris-Jacobson *Basic Reading Vocabularies.*

To develop a word list from a basal or another more extensive list of words, select at random about twenty words from each level of the basal (preprimer through the highest available level), or from each grade indicated on the word list. These words should be typed by level on a sheet for teacher use and placed individually on index cards for student use. Remember, such a list only measures sight vocabulary. It does *not* measure the most important area of reading—comprehension.

Task 2

Obtain two passages of approximately 100 to 200 words for each readability level (preprimer through senior high school). One of the passages will be used to assess oral reading skills, and the second selection will be used to measure silent reading proficiency.

Sample Questioning Patterns for Assessing Selected Comprehension Skills

Literal Questions

Details	What color is the house?
Cause-effect situations	Why was the store owner angry?
Sequence	What happened first in the story?
Main idea	What was this story about?
Character traits and actions	How did Bob act when he saw his bicycle?

Interpretive Questions

Predict outcomes	How do you think the story ended?
Figurative language	What does "laughed his head off" mean in this story?
Mood and emotional reaction	How did Mary feel when she saw Kristy?
Author's purpose and point of view	How did the author feel about pollution?
Abstract words	What ideas in the paragraph help demonstrate the concept of democracy as it is known in the United States?

Critical Reading Questions

Fallacies in reasoning	What words or ideas in the story seem to stereotype Wendy?
Facts and opinions	What is the writer's opinion of the use of nuclear energy?
	What facts are given to substantiate this opinion?
Relevant and irrelevant information	What information would be necessary to make plane reservations for a trip to California?

It is essential to select passages that will interest students, regardless of age. Remember that you may have a seven-year-old who reads at an eighth-grade level or a fourteen-year-old who reads at a second-grade level. Obviously, if a student's interest in the content of the material is high, a more accurate and complete diagnosis is likely. High interest content has a greater effect on increasing comprehension instructional level than on increasing word recognition instructional level. High interest materials have a greater effect for boys than for girls, as well as on average and below average readers when compared to above average readers. Therefore, examine the material being used for the IRI to be sure that the passages are as interesting as possible; you will obtain better results from the inventory.

Task 3

Develop comprehension questions for each of the passages. After the series of graded passages has been chosen and the readability level of each passage determined, the next step is to develop a series of comprehension questions for each passage. It is strongly suggested that a minimum of five and a maximum of ten questions be used. Although using ten questions requires more teacher time, the greater number ensures a more precise evaluation of the students' comprehension.

Questions should measure the three levels of understanding: literal, interpretive, and critical. Samples of various types of questions are provided in the above chart.

In developing questions for the IRI, there are certain guidelines to keep in mind. To expedite the process, it is best to read the passages and prepare as many questions as possible, then classify each question in the light of the skill being measured. Following this classification, select the best questions to sample adequately the students' performance at each of the three levels of comprehension, as well as their proficiency in the specific skills. The questions can then be tested with selected students to determine their quality. Poor questions should be replaced with others from the list.

Summary Record Sheet

Student Name: _____ Date _____
Administrator: _____ Levels Used: __ ; __ ; __ ; __ ; __ ; __ :

Words Missed (Oral Reading)

Level _____	Level _____	Level _____	Level _____	Level _____	Level _____
S–U	S–U	S–U	S–U	S–U	S–U

Comprehension Check (Oral Reading)

Level _____	Level _____	Level _____	Level _____	Level _____	Level _____
1. _____	1. _____	1. _____	1. _____	1. _____	1. _____
2. _____	2. _____	2. _____	2. _____	2. _____	2. _____
3. _____	3. _____	3. _____	3. _____	3. _____	3. _____
4. _____	4. _____	4. _____	4. _____	4. _____	4. _____
5. _____	5. _____	5. _____	5. _____	5. _____	5. _____
6. _____	6. _____	6. _____	6. _____	6. _____	6. _____
7. _____	7. _____	7. _____	7. _____	7. _____	7. _____
8. _____	8. _____	8. _____	8. _____	8. _____	8. _____
9. _____	9. _____	9. _____	9. _____	9. _____	9. _____
10. _____	10. _____	10. _____	10. _____	10. _____	10. _____
S–U	S–U	S–U	S–U	S–U	S–U

Observation Notes on Oral Reading: _____

_____

_____

_____

_____

_____

Task 4

Develop response sheets for use while administering the inventory. The teacher needs response sheets on which to record the student errors made during the administration of the IRI. These sheets may have various formats, ranging from a one-page sheet with blanks for recording errors to copies of each page of the inventory, on which the teacher marks oral reading errors and other responses. Combining the latter with the single-page response sheet as a summary is preferable.

The single-page response sheet should provide spaces to record information such as:

• Student's name
• Name of person administering the inventory
• Date of administration

Words Asked (Silent Reading)

Level _____	Level _____	Level _____	Level _____	Level _____	Level _____
S–U	S–U	S–U	S–U	S–U	S–U

Comprehension Check (Silent Reading)

Level _____	Level _____	Level _____	Level _____	Level _____	Level _____
1. _____	1. _____	1. _____	1. _____	1. _____	1. _____
2. _____	2. _____	2. _____	2. _____	2. _____	2. _____
3. _____	3. _____	3. _____	3. _____	3. _____	3. _____
4. _____	4. _____	4. _____	4. _____	4. _____	4. _____
5. _____	5. _____	5. _____	5. _____	5. _____	5. _____
6. _____	6. _____	6. _____	6. _____	6. _____	6. _____
7. _____	7. _____	7. _____	7. _____	7. _____	7. _____
8. _____	8. _____	8. _____	8. _____	8. _____	8. _____
9. _____	9. _____	9. _____	9. _____	9. _____	9. _____
10. _____	10. _____	10. _____	10. _____	10. _____	10. _____
S–U	S–U	S–U	S–U	S–U	S–U

Observation Notes on Silent Reading: _____

_____

_____

_____

_____

Independent Level: _____
Instructional Level: _____
Frustration Level: _____

- Levels of the IRI passages used during oral reading
- Responses to the comprehension questions following oral reading—the simplest procedure to use is a plus and minus for right and wrong responses
- Words asked during silent reading
- Responses to the comprehension questions following silent reading

- A summary of oral and silent reading word errors
- A summary of comprehension question responses
- Special notes and comments
- The independent, instructional, and frustration level of the student

A sample one-page response sheet is given. Response sheets of the second kind should show copies of the passages that the student is reading, together with the comprehension questions directly following the passage. As the student reads, the teacher makes appropriate marks and comments on the sheet. This information may then be transferred to the one-page response sheet if both are being used.

Task 5

Type the passages that the student will read. If the passages are written by the teacher or taken from materials that may be inconvenient to use, each should be typed on a separate sheet or a large index card.

Type and spacing should be appropriate to the student; for example, a primary type and double-spaced line are used for the younger student.

Following these five steps very closely will greatly assist the teacher in constructing an IRI. But what happens after construction? The two most important events are left: administration and interpretation. These must occur almost simultaneously; therefore, they are discussed at length in chapter 2.

Glossary

Accent. The part of a word that receives stress when it is spoken.

Achievement groups. A system in which students are divided into several groups based upon their demonstrated ability and aptitude.

Acronyms. Abbreviations that consist of the first letter (or letters) of each word in a phrase, i.e., Nabisco from National Biscuit Company.

Advance organizer. A type of outline that is written at a higher level of abstraction than a normal summary; it forms a framework to aid text reading.

Affective domain. That part of the taxonomic hierarchy that involves the feelings, emotions, and attitudes of a student.

Affix. A prefix or suffix added to a word to change its meaning.

Analysis. The evaluation of data to form a basis for decision making.

Analytic phonics. A method that begins with teaching an entire word and then teaching the sounds within a word.

Approaches. Different techniques used to provide reading instruction.

Assessment. The procedures and methods used to evaluate the progress that a student makes in skill development.

Assessments. Informal and formal evaluation of performance in an identified area.

At-risk. Children and youth whose experienced environmental, cultural, and socioeconomic conditions prevent them from realizing their potential within the current dominant educational, vocational, and societal structures.

Attitude inventory. The rating forms used to assess a student's feelings toward reading.

Auditory discrimination. The ability to differentiate between a variety of sounds.

Auditory memory. The ability to recall the differentiation between a variety of sounds.

Automaticity. The reaction to print without conscious attention to the behavior. In word identification, this means providing a correct pronunciation of the word without consciously decoding the word.

Basals. Textbooks used in the elementary grades with the primary purpose of introducing students to reading skills in a sequential order.

Basal instruction. Reading instruction which uses the basal and the specific procedure as outlined in the accompanying teacher's manual.

Basal reader approach. An approach to reading instruction which uses the basal and follows basal instruction. This approach includes the development of specific reading skills in a specified order and uses books, workbooks, and other materials as designed by the publisher.

Bibliotherapy. Encouraging a student to read a particular book that will help him gain insight into areas of interests or to problems that he may be facing.

Bilingual. Students who speak two or more languages, with English often being the second language.

Bookhandling. A strategy for helping students learn about a book by teaching them to identify the front and back, author/illustrator, table of contents, index, etc. to aid them in obtaining the most information from the document.

Booksharing. Strategies which encourage students to share books read with peers. The sharing can be through the creative use of character plays, dress-ups, interviews, etc.

Cause-and-effect relationships. A comprehension skill that requires the reader to determine what event was precipitated by another event in the story.

Cloze procedure. An informal diagnostic technique consisting of a 250–300 word passage from which every fifth word is deleted. Its primary purposes are to determine the students' instructional and independent reading levels, as well as their ability to use context when reading.

Cognitive development. The growth of the intellect.

Collaborative learning (cooperative learning). A type of intraclass grouping technique that emphasizes group dynamics within a classroom setting by stressing shared learning experiences to reach a common goal or to solve a common problem.

Comparisons. The ability to determine which ideas are alike and in what way they are alike.

Compound words. Words that are composed of two or more shorter words that have independent meanings.

Comprehension. The understanding of the meaning of the printed word in relation to personal experiences and the context of the information.

Computer-assisted instruction. Reading instruction which uses computer software to provide learning experiences.

Concepts. Abstract ideas generalized from several pieces of related specific information. They are theories, ideas, views, or goals.

Consonant cluster. The occurrence of two or more consonant sounds that represent one or more sounds. Also called consonant blends or digraphs.

Consonants. The letters *b, c, d, f, g, h, j, k, l, m, n, p, q, r, s, t, v, w, x, y,* and *z.*

Content Reading Inventory. An informal diagnostic procedure which uses content materials such as textbooks to assess the student's skill in reading content information.

Context clue. Words other than the word being read that aid in obtaining the meaning or recognizing an unknown word.

Contextual analysis. The use of the meaning of a phrase, sentence, or passage, in conjunction with other word identification skills to decode an unknown word or to derive meaning from a word or passage.

Continuous diagnosis. The ongoing process of continuously updating previous diagnostic data.

Contractions. A combination of two words from which one or more letters have been replaced by an apostrophe.

Contrasts. The ability to determine which ideas are different and in what ways they differ from each other.

Coordination. The cooperation of classroom teachers, reading specialists, and content teachers to ensure the success of the total school reading program.

Correlation. The degree of relationships between two variables expressed by the coefficient of correlation, which extends along a scale from 1.00 (a perfect positive relationship) through 00.00 (no relationship) to −1.00 (a perfect negative relationship).

Creative reading. A type of reading in which the reader reacts to the printed word by expressing her own ideas about what has been read.

Criterion-referenced tests. Tests based on objectives that contain the specific conditions, outcomes, and criteria that are expected for satisfactory completion of the task.

Critical reading. The process of analyzing and evaluating what is read.

Critical skills. Comprehension skills that require the reader to make an evaluation or judgment of the material read.

Cross-age tutoring. An instructional format in which an older student works with a younger student in an effort to improve the reading skills of the younger student.

Data. Information that has been gathered about a specific subject from a variety of sources.

Diagnosis. The act of determining the nature of a problem through careful examination and study.

Diagnostic-prescriptive instruction. A process in reading whereby the individual strengths and weaknesses are identified through various diagnostic procedures, and appropriate instruction is provided based upon that diagnosis.

Dictation. The process whereby a person (usually a student when using language experience) tells information to the teacher to write in order to transfer information from speech to print.

Direct instruction. The conscious interaction between the teacher and student in which new information is presented via teacher demonstration and teacher-student discussion.

Directed learning activity. An instructional plan for use in content instruction which includes these basic steps: identify learning skills, determine concepts, assess students, outline teaching strategies which include the introduction of concepts and vocabulary, purposes for reading, reading of information and discussion, and reteaching.

Directed reading activity. An instructional plan based on these five basic steps: readiness, skill development, review, guided reading, and follow-up.

Discourse analysis. The analysis of syntax in text materials in order to enhance reader comprehension.

Eclectic approach. A method of teaching reading that stresses a variety of approaches based on individual students needs, learning styles, and interests.

Educationally different. This category includes mentally handicapped students, learning disabled students, and gifted students.

Emergent literacy. The development of the language process for success in the school environment and the exploration of the home as a primary source of instruction and influence on literacy before formal school instruction is begun.

Emotionally Disturbed. Students who are socially maladjusted, manifest inappropriate behavior, suffer periods of diminished verbal and motor activity, or have frequent complaints of a physical nature including general fatigue, which interferes with their success in learning situations.

Environment. The home and school climate which affects learning both positively and negatively.

Environmental Print. Familiar symbols within the environment which encourage children to associate labels and words, i.e., McDonald's, toothpaste, red six-sided signs say STOP.

Facilities. The materials, physical features, and physical arrangement of the classroom.

Figurative language. Language that is rich in comparisons, similes, and metaphors.

Formal diagnostic procedures. The standardized techniques used by teachers and reading specialists to learn more about students' strengths and weaknesses in reading.

Frustration level. The level at which a student has extreme difficulty in pronouncing words and comprehending the material.

Gifted. Students who exhibit superior talent in one or more areas.

Grade equivalent. A score derived from the raw score on a standardized test, usually expressed in terms of a grade level divided into tenths.

Grade level. The actual grade in which a student is enrolled.

Grade placement. The level at which a student is placed for instruction.

Graded basal series. A group of readers published by a specific company and intended for sequential use during the elementary years.

Group achievement tests. Tests administered to a large number of students simultaneously which measure the depth of a student's knowledge of various broad areas of the curriculum.

Group-administered formal tests. Diagnostic procedures that include diagnostic reading tests, achievement tests, and intelligence tests designed to be administered to a large number of students simultaneously and that have been standardized with populations of students.

Group diagnostic tests. Diagnostic instruments that are administered to many students simultaneously and provide the teacher with in-depth information.

Group survey tests. Diagnostic instruments that are administered to many students simultaneously, providing scores for vocabulary, comprehension, and sometimes the rate of reading for each student.

Grouping. Any of a variety of methods by which a classroom of students is subdivided for appropriate reading instruction.

Grouping procedures. The methods and criteria used to combine students for instruction. These include achievement grouping, skills grouping, interest grouping, and cross-age or peer grouping.

Hearing-impaired. Students who have auditory processing impediments that make it difficult for them to function in the classroom.

Hesitations. Pauses of more than five seconds between words during the administration of an Informal Reading Inventory.

Heterogeneous. A word taken from the Greek term meaning different. Used in reading instruction to describe a randomly formed group.

Homogeneous. A word taken from the Greek term meaning same. Usually used in reading instruction to define a group formed on the basis of similarities of knowledge.

Independent level. The level at which students read for recreational purposes. The material is easy enough to read quickly with maximum comprehension.

Indirect instruction. The interaction between the student and learning resources (other students or materials) to further extend or review information gained via direct instruction.

Individual auditory discrimination tests. Instruments administered to a single student to determine his ability to distinguish likenesses and differences in sounds.

Individual diagnostic reading tests. Instruments that provide the most thorough diagnosis of a student's reading problems by incorporating various subtests that aid the teacher in identifying specific reading strengths and weaknesses.

Individual intelligence tests. Tests given to a single student in order to predict the level of proficiency that may be expected from his performance of a specific activity.

Individual oral reading tests. Instruments administered to a student by asking her to read aloud in order for the teacher to note such errors and difficulties as mispronunciations, omissions, repetitions, substitutions, unknown words, and sometimes hesitations.

Individualization. Students are given assignments based on their own instructional level and are engaged in tasks that meet their specific needs.

Individualized instruction. Instruction is geared to the instructional level of each student, so that every student is working on an assignment to meet his/her specific needs.

Individualized reading approach. A teaching technique based on Olson's philosophy about child development, i.e., one that promotes the concepts of seeking, self-selection, and pacing.

Individually-administered formal tests. Diagnostic instruments designed for use with a single student. These tests can be categorized as oral reading tests, diagnostic reading tests, auditory discrimination tests, auditory and visual screening tests, and intelligence tests.

Inflectional ending. A word ending that, when added to a root word, denotes tense, number, degree, gender, or possession.

Informal diagnosis. The use of nonstandardized techniques by teachers in order to determine their students' strengths and weaknesses in reading.

Informal Reading Inventory. A compilation of graded reading selections with comprehension questions to accompany each selection. This inventory is individually administered to determine the student's strengths and weaknesses in word recognition and comprehension.

Insertions. Words that do not appear on the printed page, added by the reader during the administration of an Informal Reading Inventory.

Instructional level. The reading level at which a student can read the material, but has some difficulty with recognition of words and comprehension, so that a teacher is required to assist him.

Integrated instruction. A crucial component of the diagnostic-prescriptive program that involves the simultaneous implementation of reading, writing, expressive and receptive language, studying, researching and using content strategies in the classroom.

Interactive model. A theory of the reading process, developed by Rummelhart, that postulates that the reader and the text work in concert to reveal the meaning of the passage.

Interest groups. An organizational plan by which students with similar interests are allowed to work together in order to explore their mutual interests in greater depth.

Interest inventory. An inventory used to measure a student's likes, dislikes, and areas of enjoyment, in order to explore her mutual interests in greater depth.

Interpretation. An in-depth evaluation of data by which the strengths and weaknesses of each student are examined, along with an exploration of the underlying causes for poor test results.

Interpretive comprehension. The process of assimilating information in an effort to infer the author's meaning.

Interpretive skills. Comprehension skills that involve comprehending the inner meanings of the material read.

Invented spelling. Children's use of their sound-symbol knowledge to write words representing the message they wish to communicate, i.e., I LV U (I love you).

K-W-L. A study strategy developed by Ogle to enable teachers to assist students in activating prior knowledge when interacting with expository text, and to heighten their interest in reading this material.

Language-based instruction. The development of listening, speaking, reading, and writing through learning activities which coordinate these areas and encourage the use of children's literature, invented spelling, group discussions, etc.

Language development. The increase of quantity, range, and complexity of language production as children grow.

Language experience approach. A method in which instruction is built upon the use of reading materials created from the spoken language of the student, written initially by the teacher just as the student speaks.

Learning-disabled. Students who exhibit a disorder in one or more of the basic neurological or psychological processes involved in understanding or in using spoken or written language.

Listening comprehension. The recall or recognition of ideas understood after hearing information.

Literal skills. Basic level comprehension skills such as recalling details, finding the main idea, or interpreting symbols and acronyms. This area of comprehension involves the recognition or recall of text information.

Literature-based reading. The use of children's books as the primary classroom reading material for the development of the reading-language process.

Mainstreaming. The act of integrating students with special needs into a normal classroom situation.

Management. The total process of selecting, organizing, and presenting classroom materials to the students.

Mean. The average of a set of numbers derived by taking the sum of the set of measurements and dividing it by the number of measurements in the set.

Median. The central number in a set, above and below which an equal number of scores fall.

Mildly mentally handicapped. Students with an I.Q. range of 55 to 80 who have slow auditory and visual memory, conceptual and perceptual ability, and imaginative and creative ability.

Miscomprehension. Performance in which students frequently misunderstand questions and give different answers instead of **wrong** answers.

Miscues. Any responses during oral reading that deviate from those anticipated.

Mispronunciations. Words that are called incorrectly in the oral reading process or during an Informal Reading Inventory.

Multicultural. The segment of the population that has cultural values reflective of two or more cultures.

Multi-sensory approach. A teaching technique that involves the senses of touch and muscle movement, along with vision and hearing.

Naturalistic assessment. The use of observation, student work, and actual performance in language-related activites to evaluate performance in reading and language.

Non-English speaker. The segment of the school population who do not use America's English as their primary language.

Normal curve. The bell curve which has more scores at the mean or median and a decreasing number in equal proportions at the left and right of the center.

Objective-based tests. Tests based on specific objectives, but for which no predetermined criteria for achievement are provided.

Observations. Teacher analysis of a student's knowledge, traits, behaviors, attitudes, and interactions, as part of the ongoing diagnostic program.

Omissions. Words that are left out by the reader during the administration of an Informal Reading Inventory.

Oral language. An area of emergent literacy that emphasizes the development of speaking skills, including vocabulary and syntactical ability.

Organization. The instructional design used to manage groups in a classroom situation effectively.

Organization patterns. The manner in which textual material is written. In content writing, these patterns appear as enumeration, relationship problem solving, and persuasion.

Organizational skills. A category of study skills that involves the ability to synthesize and evaluate material read so that it can be arranged into a workable format.

Parental Involvement. A facet of the total school reading program wherein parents act as reading models and are actively involved in their child's learning.

PARS. A modified study strategy developed by Smith and Elliot primarily for use with younger students. The steps are: preview, ask questions, read, and summarize.

Peer tutoring. An instructional format that involves students who are in the same grade level working together. These students do not have the same reading level or mastery of the same reading skills.

Percentile. The percentage score that rates a student relative to the percentage of others in a group who are below his score. Percentiles cannot be averaged, added together, subtracted, or treated arithmetically in any manner.

Personal reading. The use of all reading skills by the student in order to develop reading into a leisure-time activity. Personal reading combines all the cognitive skills with a positive attitude towards reading.

Phoneme-grapheme correspondences. The association of specific sounds with specific symbols in beginning reading instruction.

Phonemic awareness. The awareness of sounds as important units of words.

Phonic analysis. The process of using letter sounds to pronounce an unknown word.

Physically handicapped. Referring to students with disorders of the nervous system, musculoskeletal system, visual impairments, or hearing impairments.

Picture clue. A clue to an unknown word that appears in the form of a picture in the text.

PORPE. A writing-study strategy developed by Simpson primarily for students to use in learning how to study for essay questions. The steps are: predicting, organizing, rehearsing, practicing, and evaluating.

Portfolios. The systematic collection of materials, observation, and student work for use in evaluating changes in student performance in reading and language.

PQRST. A study strategy developed by Spache for studying science materials. The steps are: preview, question, read, summarize, and test.

Prefix. A word component that is attached to the beginning of the root word to change its meaning.

Prereading. The stage of language development in which children are aware of the importance of print in the reading process, are developing the association of sounds with letters, and are experimenting with language to change meanings. These are the emergent literacy activites which precede the formalization of reading.

Prereading skills. The basic skills necessary for developing a foundation that will enable a student to master higher-level reading skills and to learn to read. These skills include oral language development, visual perception, listening comprehension, and visual-motor development.

Prescription. A specific direction that is recommended following a careful diagnosis.

Prescriptive instruction. Reading instruction provided to meet the diagnosed reading needs of each student. It is based on the principles of teamwork, application of reading skills, positive self-concept, no one best way, varied approaches, a hierarchy of skills, continuous diagnoses, and flexible instruction.

Prior knowledge. The knowledge structures that readers bring to a written text.

Psychologically handicapped. Referring to students who are emotionally disturbed or suffer from a behavior disorder.

Questioning. A primary strategy for developing student comprehension of reading materials. Ideally a wide range of question types is employed, including those generated by the student.

RAM. A study strategy developed by Dana to prepare disabled readers for reading. The three steps are: relax, activate, and motivate.

Range. The distance between the largest and smallest numbers in a set.

Raw Score. An untreated test score usually obtained by counting the number of items correct. It is the basis for determining all the derived scores.

Readability. The determination of the approximate grade level at which various materials are written.

Reading/language process. The processes used to communicate information via speaking, listening, reading, and writing. In reading process, students learn to identify printed symbols and associate meaning with those symbols in order to understand ideas conveyed by the writer. This is part of the language process.

REAP. A study strategy developed by Eanet and Manzo to be used in reading and content area classrooms. The steps are: read, encode, annotate, and ponder.

Reciprocal questioning. A procedure in which teacher and student take turns asking each other questions about a passage they have both read.

Reciprocal teaching. A form of reading instruction in which students engage in an interactive dialogue. Instruction includes generating questions, summarizing, predicting, and clarifying, all of which are modeled by the teacher.

Record-keeping procedures. A system by which a teacher keeps track of the reading needs of the student in order to provide the appropriate ongoing instruction.

Recreational reading. Reading done by a student for enjoyment and personal satisfaction.

Reference skills. Skills that are concerned with locating information in various sources.

Relevant and irrelevant information. A critical reading skill that requires the reader to determine whether the author's evidence or examples are germane to the subject matter at hand.

Reliability. A term that refers to the consistency with which the test agrees with itself or produces similar scores when readministered over a period of time by the same individual.

Repetitions. Words that are reread during the administration of an Informal Reading Inventory.

Retelling. A strategy used to determine a student's understanding of information read without the use of questions. This strategy asks students to tell the information read according to what they remember when this retelling is followed by probes (questions) to gain additional information.

RIPS. A study strategy developed by Dana to help disabled readers repair comprehension problems while reading. The steps are: reading on and then rereading, imaging, paraphrasing, and speeding up, slowing down, and/or seeking help.

Schema. A theory of comprehension that states that to understand information the reader uses what is in his mind, and adds to his store of information when new, related information is read.

Scope and sequence. The identification and orderly presentation of the reading skills to be taught at each level from kindergarten to the highest level.

Semantic mapping. A strategy that visually displays the relationship among words and helps to categorize them.

Sight words. The words that students see most frequently in reading and recognize instantly without using other decoding skills.

Signal words. Connectors such as conjunctions, that help the reader to understand the meaning of a passage i.e., therefore, however, in addition, and, etc.

Skill development. The process of teaching reading through instruction of individual skills in some systematic sequence.

Skills groups. The use of reading skills for the purpose of student placement in an individual situation.

SIP. A study strategy developed by Dana to help disabled readers to focus their attention on content while reading. The steps are: summarizing, imaging, and predicting.

Specialized study skills. A category of study skills that involves analyzing all parts of a book or material to determine what information can be obtained from it and how best to understand the information presented.

SQRQCQ. A study strategy developed by Fax for use in reading mathematics. The steps are: survey, question, read, question, compute, and question.

SQ3R. A study strategy developed by Robinson, which involves these five steps: survey, question, read, recite, and review.

Standard deviation. A term used to describe the variation of scores from the mean, a condition that varies with the range in a set of scores.

Standard score. A raw score expressed in some form of standard deviation unit. Standard scores can be dealt with arithmetically and are easier to interpret than raw scores.

Stanine. A type of standard score that is based upon a nine point scale with a mean of five and a standard deviation of about two.

Story grammar. A framework for specifying the organizational structure of a narrative. Sometimes it is called a story structure.

Story structure. The components of a story including the plot, setting, characters, main events, etc. which can be identified to aid in comprehension.

Structural analysis. The word identification skill that stresses the analysis of word structure for purposes of pronunciation as well as comprehension.

Structured overview. A way of representing the conceptual vocabulary of written material as a visual pattern, in order to enhance an awareness of the way in which the concepts are related. It may be used initially or in review.

Study skills. The higher-level reading skills that require the application of many other reading skills.

Study strategies. Essential learning strategies that students should activate when interacting with expository text.

Substitutions. Words that are given as replacements for the actual printed word during the administration of an Informal Reading Inventory.

Suffix. A word part that is attached to the end of the root word to change its meaning.

Summarizing. Organizing interpreted data into a compact format that makes it easily accessible for classroom use.

Sustained silent reading. A classroom activity wherein everyone is required to read some material silently for a designated period of time.

Syllables. Parts of a word that are combined to form the entire word. Each syllable has one vowel sound.

Synthesis. The ability to form a point of view after reading several sources of information.

Synthetic phonics. A method that presents the isolated sounds in a word, then blends them to form the entire word.

Taxonomy. A hierarchy of the learning processes, classified from lowest to highest; categorizing.

Teacher effectiveness. A concept that identifies the characteristics of teachers who are effective in helping students learn, as compared to those who are not as successful.

Text structure. A framework for specifying the organizational structure of expository texts.

Use of material. The matching of available classroom teaching instruments to diagnosed student needs.

Validity. The extent to which a test measures what it is designed to measure.

Variant patterns. Vowel combinations in words that represent a unique sound or do not follow rules typically taught about decoding different sounds of unknown words.

Visual comprehension. A prereading skill that comprises interpretive tasks necessary for understanding the visual stimuli presented in reading materials.

Visual discrimination. The ability to differentiate between printed symbols.

Visual memory. The ability to recall the differentiation of printed symbols.

Visual-motor skills. A prereading skill that includes such understandings as eye-hand coordination, direction, and drawing specific designs using circles and lines.

Visually impaired. Describes a student who is blind, has limited vision, or has low vision that prevents him from functioning normally in a classroom situation.

Vowels. The letters *a, e, i, o, u,* and sometimes *y* and *w.*

Whole language assessment. The evaluation of language performance through student work in language activities such as story retelling, invented spelling, discussions, and bookhandling.

Word boundaries. A prereading subskill that involves recognizing the spacing between words in oral language.

Word identification. The use of prior memory or a decoding process by the reader to assist in the identification of words and the association of meaning with the identified symbols.

Word recognition inventories. Graded lists of words pronounced by a student in order for a teacher to learn more about her word recognition skills.

Writing. The communication of a message using symbols to represent ideas. The writing process involves several stages including the initiation of an idea, the development of the idea using words/sentences, editing this initial development, and finalization of the written product.

Bibliography

Adams, Abby, Douglas Carnine, and Russell Geisten. "Instructional Strategies for Studying Content Area Texts in the Intermediate Grades." *Reading Research Quarterly* 18 (Fall 1982): 27–55.

Adams, Marilyn J. *Beginning to Read: Thinking and Learning About Print*. Urbana-Champaign, IL: University of Illinois, 1990.

Adams, M. J., and A. W. F. Huggins. "The Growth of Children's Sight Vocabulary: A Quick Test with Educational and Theoretical Implications." *Reading Research Quarterly* 20 (Spring 1985): 262–81.

Agrast, Charlotte. "Teach Them to Read Between the Lines." *Grade Teacher* 85 (November 1967): 72–74.

Ahead Designs. *Create with Garfield*. Allen, TX: Developmental Learning Materials, 1987.

Alexander, J. Estill, and Ronald C. Filler. *Attitudes and Reading*. Newark, DE: International Reading Association, 1976.

Allen, JoBeth, Barbara Michalove, Betty Shockley, and Marsha West. "I'm Really Worried about Joseph: Reducing the Risks of Literacy Learning." *The Reading Teacher* 44 (March 1991): 458–72.

Allen, M. "Relationship Between Kuhlmann-Anderson Intelligence Tests and Academic Achievement in Grade IV." *Journal of Educational Psychology* 44 (1944): 229–39.

Allen, Roach Van. *Language Experiences in Communication*. Boston: Houghton Mifflin Company, 1976.

Allen, Roach Van. "The Language-Experience Approach." *Perspectives on Elementary Reading*. Edited by Robert Karlin. New York: Harcourt Brace Jovanovich, Inc., 1973.

Allington, Richard L., and Anne McGill-Franzen. "Word Identification Errors in Isolation and in Context: Apples vs. Oranges." *The Reading Teacher* 33 (April 1980): 795–800.

Alongi, Constance V. "Response to Kay Haugaard: Comic Books Revisited." *The Reading Teacher* 27 (May 1974): 801–03.

Amanda Stories. Los Angeles, CA: Voyager Company, 1989.

American Psychiatric Association. *Diagnostic and Statistical Manual of Mental Disorders (DSM-III-R)*. 3rd ed. Washington, D.C.: American Psychiatric Association, 1987.

Ames, W. S. "The Development of a Classification Schema of Contextual Aids." *Reading Research Quarterly* II (1966): 57–82.

Anders, Patricia L., and Candace S. Bos. "Semantic Feature Analysis: An Interactive Strategy for Vocabulary Development and Text Comprehension." *Journal of Reading* 29 (April 1986): 610–16.

Anderson, Richard C., Elfrieda H. Hiebert, Judith A. Scott, Ian A. G. Wilkinson, and Members of the Commission on Reading. *Becoming a Nation of Readers: The Report of the Commission on Reading*. Washington, D.C.: National Institute of Education, 1985.

Anderson, Richard, Rand Spiro, and Mark Anderson. *Schemata as Scaffolding for the Representation of Information in Connected Discourse*. Center for the Study of Reading, Technical Report No. 24. Champaign, University of Illinois, Urbana-Champaign, 1977.

Armbruster, Bonnie B., and Thomas H. Anderson. "Research Synthesis of Study Skills." *Educational Leadership* 39 (November 1981): 154.

Armstrong, Robert J., and Robert F. Mooney. "The Slosson Intelligence Test: Implications for Reading Specialists." *The Reading Teacher* 24 (January 1971): 336–40.

Arnold, Richard D. "Class Size and Reading Development." *New Horizons in Reading*. Edited by John E. Merritt. Newark, DE: International Reading Association, 1976.

Ashby-Davis, Claire. "Cloze and Comprehension: A Qualitative Analysis and Critique." *Journal of Reading* 28 (April 1985): 585–89.

Asher, S. "Topic Interest and Children's Reading Comprehension." *Theoretical Issues in Reading Comprehension*. Edited by R. Spiro, B. Bruce and W. Brewer. Hillsdale, NJ: Lawrence Erlbaum, 1980.

Athey, Irene. "Reading Research in the Affective Domain." *Theoretical Models and Processes of Reading*. 3rd ed. Edited by Harry Singer and Robert B. Ruddell. Newark, DE: International Reading Association, 1985.

Aukerman, Robert D. *Approaches to Beginning Reading*. 2nd ed. New York: John Wiley & Sons, 1984.

Aukerman, Robert D. *Reading in the Secondary School Classroom*. New York: McGraw-Hill, Inc., 1972.

Austin, Mary, and Coleman Morrison. *The First R: The Harvard Report on Reading in Elementary Schools*. New York: The Macmillan Company, 1963.

Ausubel, David P. "The Use of Advance Organizers in the Learning and Retention of Meaningful Verbal Material." *Journal of Educational Psychology* 51 (1960): 267–72.

Baghban, Marcia. *Our Daughter Learns to Read and Write: A Case Study from Birth to Three*. Newark, DE: International Reading Association, 1984.

Bailey, Mildred H. "The Utility of Phonic Generalizations in Grades One Through Six." *The Reading Teacher* 20 (February 1967): 413–18.

Baldwin, R. Scott, Ziva Peleg-Bruckner, and Ann H. McClintock. "Effects of Topic Interest and Prior Knowledge on Reading Comprehension." *Reading Research Quarterly* 20 (1985): 497–504.

Balsam, M., and C. Hammer. *Success with Reading*. New York: Scholastic, 1985.

Bamberger, Richard. *Promoting the Reading Habit*. Paris: UNESCO Press, 1975.

Barnes, Judy, Dean W. Ginther, and Samuel W. Cochran. "Schema and Purpose in Reading Comprehension and Learning Vocabulary from Context." *Reading Research and Instruction* 28 (Winter 1989): 16–28.

Barraga, Natalie. *Visual Handicaps and Learning*. Belmont, CA: Wadsworth Publishing Company, 1976.

Barrett, Thomas C. "The Relationship Between the Measures of Pre-reading Visual Discrimination and First-grade Achievement: A Review of the Literature." *Reading Research Quarterly* I (Fall 1965): 51–76.

Barrett, Thomas, and R. Smith. *Teaching Reading in the Middle Grades*. Reading, MA: Addison-Wesley, 1976.

Bateman, Barbara. *Reading and the Psycholinguistic Process of Partially Seeing Children*. Arlington, VA: Council for Exceptional Children, 1963.

Baumann, James F. "Teaching Third-grade Students to Comprehend Anaphoric Relationships: The Application of a Direct Instruction Model." *Reading Research Quarterly* XXI (Winter 1986): 70–90.

Beck, I. L., M. G. McKeown, E. S. McCaslin, and A. M. Burkes. *Instructional Dimensions That May Affect Reading Comprehension: Examples from Two Commercial Reading Programs*. Pittsburg, PA: University of Pittsburgh, Learning Research and Development Center, 1979.

Beers, Carol S., and James W. Beers. "Early Identification of Learning Disabilities: Facts and Fallacies." *The Elementary School Journal* 81 (November 1980): 67–76.

Berger, Eugenia H. *Parents as Partners in Education: The School and Home Working Together*. 3rd ed. New York: Macmillan Publishing Co., 1991.

Bergeron, Bette S. "What Does the Term Whole Language Mean? Constructing A Definition from the Literature." *Journal of Reading Behavior* (Summer 1990): 301–29.

Beta Upsilon Chapter, Pi Lambda Theta. "Children's Interests Classified by Age Level." *The Reading Teacher* 27 (April 1974): 694–700.

Birch, J. W. *Mainstreaming Educable Mentally Retarded Children in Regular Classes*. Reston, VA: Council for Exceptional Children, 1974.

Bissett, Donald J. "The Amount and Effect of Recreational Reading in Selected Fifth-grade Classrooms." Ph.D. Dissertation, Syracuse University, 1969.

Blanchard, Jay S. *Computer-Based Reading Assessment Instrument*. Dubuque, IA: Kendall/Hunt, 1985.

Blanchard, Jay S., and Claire J. Rottenberg. "Hypertext and Hypermedia: Discovering and Creating Meaningful Learning Environments." *The Reading Teacher* 43 (May 1990): 656–61.

Bloom, Benjamin, et al. *Taxonomy of Educational Objectives—Handbook I: The Cognitive Domain*. New York: David McKay Company, Inc., 1956.

Bloomfield, Leonard, and Clarence L. Barnhart. *Let's Read: A Linguistic Approach*. Detroit, MI: Wayne State University Press, 1961.

Boehm, Ann E. *Examiner's Manual: Boehm Test of Basic Concepts-Revised*. San Antonio, TX: Psychological Corporation, Harcourt Brace Jovanovich, 1986.

Bond, Guy, and Robert Dykstra. *Final Report, Project No. X-001*. Washington, D.C.: Bureau of Research, Office of Education, U.S. Department of Health, Education, and Welfare, 1967.

Bond, Guy L., and Robert Dykstra. "The Cooperative Research Program in First Grade Reading Instruction." *Reading Research Quarterly* II (Summer 1967): 5–141.

Bond, Guy, and Eva B. Wagner. *Teaching the Child to Read*, 4th ed. New York: Macmillan, 1966.

Bormuth, John. "The Cloze Readability Procedure." *Elementary English* 45 (April 1968): 429–36.

Bower, Eli M. *Early Identification of Emotionally Handicapped Children in School*, 2nd ed. Springfield, IL: Charles C. Thomas, 1969.

Bowman, M. A. "The Effect of Story Structure Questioning Upon the Comprehension and Metacognitive Awareness of Sixth Grade Students." Ph.D. Dissertation, University of Maryland, 1980.

Boyd, R. D. "Growth of Phonic Skills in Reading." *Clinical Studies in Reading III*, pp. 68–87. Edited by Helen M. Robinson, Supplementary Educational Monographs, No. 97. Chicago: University of Chicago Press, 1969.

Brackett, G. *Super Story Tree*. New York: Scholastic, 1989.

Braun, Carl. "Interest-loading and Modality Effects on Textual Response Acquisition." *Reading Research Quarterly* 4 (Spring 1969): 428–44.

Briggs, F. A. "Grammatical Sense as a Factor in Reading Comprehension." *The Psychology of Reading Behavior*. Edited by G. B. Schick. Milwaukee: National Reading Conference, 1969.

Brill, Richard G. "The Relationship of Wechsler IQ's to Academic Achievement Among Deaf Students." *Exceptional Children* 28 (February 1962): 315–21.

Bristow, Page S., John J. Pikulski, and Peter L. Pelosi. "A Comparison of Five Estimates of Instructional Level." *The Reading Teacher* 37 (December 1973): 273–79.

Britton, J. *Language and Learning*. Miami, FL: University of Miami Press, 1970.

Bromley, Karen D'Angelo. "Buddy Journals Make the Reading-Writing Connection." *The Reading Teacher* 43 (Novmeber 1989): 122–29.

Brountas, Maria. "Whole Language Really Works." *Teaching Pre K–8* (November/December 1987): 57–60.

Brown, Ann L., J. C. Campione, and J. A. Day. "Learning to Learn: On Training Students to Learn from Texts." *Educational Researcher* 10 (1981): 14–21.

Brown, Linda L., and Rita J. Sherbenou. "A Comparison of Teacher Perceptions of Student Reading Ability, Reading Performance, and Classroom Behavior." *The Reading Teacher* 34 (February 1981): 557–60.

Brown, Virginia L., Donald D. Hammill, and J. Lee Wiederholt. *Manual: Test of Reading Comprehension, Revised Edition*. Austin, TX: Pro-Ed, 1978.

Bruckerhoff, Charles. "What Do Students Say About Reading Instruction." *The Clearing House* 51 (November 1977): 104–7.

Burger, Victor, T. A. Cohen, and P. Bisgaler. *Bringing Children and Books Together*. New York: Literary Club of America, 1956.

Burmeister, Lou E. *From Print to Meaning*. Reading, MA: Addison-Wesley, 1975.

Burns, Jeanne M. "A Study of Experiences Provided in the Home Environment Associated with Accelerated Reading Abilities as Reported by Parents of Intellectually Superior Preschoolers." Ph.D. Dissertation, Louisiana State University, 1986.

Burns, Jeanne M., and Martha D. Collins. "Parent Perceptions of Factors Affecting the Reading Development of Intellectually Superior Accelerated Readers and Intellectually Superior Nonreaders." *Reading Research and Instruction* 26 (Summer 1987): 239–46.

Burns, Paul C., and Betty D. Roe. *Teaching Reading in Today's Elementary Schools.* 2nd ed. Chicago, IL: Rand McNally College Publishing Company, 1980.

Bussis, Anne M., and Edward A. Chittenden. "Research Currents: What the Reading Tests Neglect." *Language Arts* 64 (March 1987): 302–08.

Bynum, Margaret. *Curriculum for Gifted Students.* Atlanta, GA: State Department of Education, 1976.

Canney, George, and Robert Schreiner. "A Study of the Effectiveness of Selected Syllabication Rules and Phonogram Patterns for Word Attack." *Reading Research Quarterly* XII (1976–77): 102–24.

Carey, Robert F. "Toward a More Cognitive Definition of Reading Comprehension." *Reading Horizons* 20 (Summer 1980): 293.

Carr, Eileen, and Karen K. Wixson. "Guidelines for Evaluating Vocabulary Instruction." *Journal of Reading* 29 (April 1986): 588–95.

Carrier, Carol A., and Amy Titus. "Effects of Notetaking, Pretraining and Test Mode Expectations on Learning from Lectures." *American Educational Research Journal* 18 (1981): 385–97.

Carroll, John B., Peter Davies, and Barry Richman. *Word Frequency Book.* New York: American Heritage Publishing Company, Inc., 1971.

Cassidy, Jack. "Cross-Age Tutoring and the Sacrosanct Reading Period." *Reading Horizons* 17 (Spring 1977): 178–80.

Cazden, Courtney B. "Contexts for Literacy; In the Mind and in the Classroom." *Journal of Reading Behavior* 14 (1982): 413–27.

Chall, Jeanne. *Learning to Read: the Great Debate.* New York: McGraw Hill Book Co., 1967.

Cheek, Earl H., and Martha Collins-Cheek. "Organizational Patterns: Untapped Sources for Better Reading." *Reading World* 22 (May 1983): 278–83.

Cheek, Earl H., Rona F. Flippo, and Jimmy D. Lindsey. *Reading for Success in Elementary Schools.* New York: Holt, Rinehart, and Winston, 1989.

Child Study Committee on the International Kindergarten Union. *A Study of the Vocabulary of Children Before Entering First Grade.* Washington, D.C.: The International Kindergarten Union, 1928.

Chiu, Lian-Hwang. "Children's Attitudes Toward Reading and Reading Interests." *Perceptual and Motor Skills* 58 (June 1984): 960–62.

Chomsky, Carol. "Approaching Reading Through Invented Spelling." *Theory and Practice of Early Reading,* pp. 43–65. Edited by L. B. Resnick and P. A. Weaver. Hillsdale, NJ: Erlbaum, 1979.

Chomsky, Carol. "Stages in Language Development and Reading Exposure." *Harvard Educational Review.* (February 1972): 1–33.

Chomsky, Carol. *The Acquisition of Syntax in Children from 5 to 10.* Cambridge, MA: MIT Press, 1969.

Chomsky, Noam. *Language and Mind.* Enl. ed. New York: Harcourt Brace Jovanovich, Inc., 1972.

Christie, James F. "Syntax: A Key to Reading Comprehension." *Reading Improvement* 17 (Winter 1980): 313–17.

Clark, Ann D., and Charlotte J. Richards. "Auditory Discrimination Among Economically Disadvantaged and Nondisadvantaged Preschool Children." *Exceptional Children* 33 (1966): 259–62.

Clarke, Barbara K. "A Study of the Relationship Between Eighth Grade Students' Reading Ability and Their Social Studies and Science Textbooks." Unpublished doctoral dissertation, Florida State University, 1977.

Clarke, L. K. "Invented versus Traditional Spelling in First Graders' Writing: Effects on Learning to Spell and Read." *Research in the Teaching of English* 22 (October 1988): 281–309.

Clark, M. *Young Fluent Readers.* London: Heinemann Educational Books, 1978.

Clay, Marie. *The Early Detection of Reading Difficulties: A Diagnostic Survey.* Aukland, New Zealand: Heinemann Educational Books, 1972.

Clymer, Theodore. "The Utility of Phonic Generalizations in the Primary Grades." *The Reading Teacher* 16 (January 1963): 252–58.

Cohen, Elizabeth G. "Expectation States and Interracial Interaction in School Settings." Edited by R. H. Turner and J. F. Short. *Annual Review of Sociology* 8 (1982): 209–35.

Collins-Cheek, Martha D. "Organizational Patterns: An Aid to Comprehension." American Reading Forum Conference Proceedings, 1982.

Collins, Martha D. "Evaluating Basals: Do They Teach Phonics Generalizations." *Evaluation in Reading—Learning—Teaching—Administering. Sixth Yearbook of the American Reading Forum.* Edited by Donovan Lumpkin, Mary Harshberger, and Peggy Ransom. Muncie, IN: Ball State University Press, 1986.

Collins, Martha D. "How Do Three-Year Olds Select Favorite Books." Paper presented at the College Reading Association, Philadelphia, PA, October 1989.

Collins, Martha D. "Reading Interests of Five-Year Olds: Effects of Language Development." In process.

Cordasco, F. "Puerto Rican Pupils and American Education." *Education and the Many Faces of the Disadvantaged: Cultural and Historical Perspectives.* Edited by W. W. Brickman and S. Lehrer. New York: Wiley, 1962.

Cosmic Osmo, 1990. Menlo Park, CA: Activision, Cyna Software.

Courtney, Brother Leonard. "Methods and Materials for Teaching Word Perception in Grades 10–14." *Sequential Development of Reading Abilities,* pp. 42–46. Edited by Helen M. Robinson. Supplementary Educational Monographs, No. 90. Chicago, IL: University of Chicago Press, 1960.

Crary, Ryland W. *Humanizing The School: Curriculum Development and Theory.* New York: Alfred Knopf, 1969.

Crewe, James, and Dayton Hullgren. "What Does 'Research' Really Say about Study Skills?" *The Psychology of Reading.* 18th Yearbook National Reading Conference, 1969.

Dale, Edgar, and Jeanne Chall. "A Formula for Predicting Readability." *Educational Research Bulletin* (January 21, 1948): 11–20, 28.

D'Alessandro, Marilyn. "Accommodating Emotionally Handicapped Children Through a Literature-based Reading Program." *The Reading Teacher* 44 (December 1990): 288–93.

Dallmann, Martha, Roger L. Rouch, Lynette Chang, and John J. DeBoer. *The Teaching of Reading.* 4th ed. New York: Holt, Rinehart and Winston, Inc. 1974.

Dana, Carol. "Strategy Families for Disabled Readers." *Journal of Reading* 33 (October 1989): 31–32.

Davidson, Roscoe. "Teacher Influence and Children's Levels of Thinking." *The Reading Teacher* 22 (May 1969): 702–04.

Davis, Julia M., Patricia G. Stelmachovicz, Nell J. Shepard, and Michael P. Gorga. "Characteristics of Hearing-Impaired Children in the Public Schools: Part II—Psychoeducational Data." *Journal of Speech and Hearing Disorders* 46 (May 1981): 130–37.

Dawson, Mildred A., and Henry A. Bamman. *Fundamentals of Basic Reading Instruction.* New York: David McKay Co., 1959.

Dechant, Emerald V., and Henry P. Smith. *Psychology in Teaching Reading.* 2nd ed. Englewood Cliffs, NJ: Prentice-Hall, Inc., 1977.

Deese, James. *Psycholinguistics.* Boston: Allyn and Bacon, Inc., 1970.

DeGrella, Jeanne B. *Creating A Literate Classroom Environment. Resources in Education.* Nevada: ERIC Document Reproduction Service, ED 312 610, 1989.

Demott, Richard J. "Verbalism and Affective Meaning for Blind, Severely Visually Impaired and Normally Sighted Children." *The New Outlook for the Blind* 66 (January 1972): 1–25.

den Heyer, Ken. "Reading and Motivation." *Language and Literacy: The Social Psychology of Reading.* Vol. 1. Edited by John R. Edwards. Silver Spring, MD: Institute of Modern Languages, 1981.

Denny, Terry, and Samuel Weintraub. "First Graders' Responses to Three Questions About Reading." *Elementary School Journal* 66 (May 1966): 441–48.

DeSanti, Roger J. "Concurrent and Predictive Validity of a Semantically and Syntactically Sensitive Cloze Scoring System." *Reading Research and Instruction* 28 (Winter 1989): 29–40.

Deutsch, Cynthia P., and Shirley C. Feldman. "A Study of the Effectiveness of Training for Retarded Readers in the Auditory Skills Underlying Reading." Title VII, Project No. 1127 Grant, U.S. Department of Health, Education, and Welfare, Office of Education. New York: Medical College, 1966.

Deutsch, Martin, et al. *Communication of Information in the Elementary School Classroom.* New York: Institute for Developmental Studies, New York Medical College, 1964.

Dickerson, Dolores P. "A Study of Use of Games to Reinforce Sight Vocabulary." *The Reading Teacher* 36 (October 1982): 46–49.

Dixon, Carol N. "Selection and Use of Instructional Materials." *Teaching Reading in Compensatory Classes*, pp. 104–13, 187–91. Edited by Robert C. Calfee and Pricilla A. Drumm. Newark, DE: International Reading Association, 1979.

Doyle, C. "Creative Applications of Computer Assisted Reading and Writing Instruction." *Journal of Reading* 32 (December 1988): 236–39.

Dreyer, Hal. "Rx for Pupil Tutoring Programs." *The Reading Teacher* 26 (May 1973): 180–83.

Duffelmeyer, Frederick A., and Barbara Blakelly Duffelmeyer. "Are IRI Passages Suitable for Assessing Main Idea Comprehension?" *The Reading Teacher* 42 (February 1989): 358–63.

Duffelmeyer, Frederick A., Susan S. Robinson, and Susan E. Squire. "Vocabulary Questions on Informal Reading Inventories." *The Reading Teacher* 43 (November 1989): 142–48.

Duffy, Gerald G. *Teacher Effectiveness Research: Implications for the Reading Profession*. East Lansing, MI: ERIC Document Reproduction Service, ED 204 344, 1981.

Duffy, Gerald G., and Laura R. Roehler. *Improving Classroom Reading Instruction: A Decision Making Approach*. 2nd edition. New York: Random House, 1986.

Dunn, N. E. "Children's Achievement at School-Entry as a Function of Mothers' and Fathers' Teaching Sets." *Elementary School Journal* 81 (1981): 245–53.

Durkin, Dolores. "An Earlier Start in Reading." *Elementary School Journal*.

Durkin, Dolores. *Children Who Read Early: Two Longitudinal Studies*. New York: Teacher's College Press, 1966.

Durkin, Dolores. "Dolores Durkin Speaks on Instruction." *The Reading Teacher* 43 (March 1990): 472–76.

Durkin, Dolores. "Reading Comprehension Instruction in Five Basal Reader Series." *Reading Research Quarterly* 16 (1981): 515–44.

Durkin, Dolores. *Teaching Them to Read*. 3rd ed. Boston, MA: Allyn and Bacon, Inc., 1978.

Durkin, Dolores. *Teaching Young Children to Read*. 4th ed. Boston, MA: Allyn and Bacon, Inc., 1987.

Durkin, Dolores. "What Classroom Observations Reveal About Reading Comprehension Instruction." *Reading Research Quarterly* 15 (1978–79): 481–533.

Durkin, Dolores. "What Is the Value of the New Interest in Reading Comprehension?" *Language Arts* 58 (January 1981): 27.

Durrell, Donald D., and Jane H. Catterson. *Durrell Analysis of Reading Difficulty: Manual of Directions*. New York: The Psychological Corporation, 1980.

Durrell, Donald D., and Helen A. Murphy. "The Auditory Discrimination Factor in Reading Readiness and Reading Disability." *Education* 73 (May 1963): 556–60.

Dyer, James W., James Riley, and Frank P. Yekoich. "An Analysis of Three Study Skills: Notetaking, Summarizing, and Rereading." *Journal of Educational Research* 73 (1979): 3–7.

Dykstra, Robert. "Auditory Discrimination Abilities and Beginning Reading Achievement." *Reading Research Quarterly* I (Spring 1966): 5–34.

Dykstra, Robert. "Summary of the Second Phase of the Cooperative Research Program in Primary Reading Instruction." *Reading Research Quarterly* IV (Fall 1968): 49–70.

Dyson, Anne H. "N Spell my Grandmama: Fostering Early Thinking about Print." *The Reading Teacher* 38 (December 1984): 262–71.

Eanet, Marilyn G., and Anthony V. Mazo. "REAP—A Strategy for Improving Reading/Writing/Study Skills." *Journal of Reading* 19 (May 1976): 647–52.

Eberwein, Lowell D. "The Variability of Readability of Basal Reader Textbooks and How Much Teachers Know About It." *Reading World* 18 (March 1979): 259–72.

Educational Products Information Exchange. *Report of a National Study of the Quality of Instructional Materials Most Used by Teachers and Learners*. Technical Report 76, New York: E.P.I.E. Institute, 1977.

Edwards, Patricia A., and Linda Simpson. "Bibliotherapy: A Strategy for Communication Between Parents and Their Children." *Journal of Reading* 30 (November 1986): 110–18.

Eeds, Maryann. "Bookwords: Using a Beginning Word List of High Frequency Words from Children's Literature K–3." *The Reading Teacher* 38 (January 1985): 418–23.

Eeds, Maryann. "What to Do When They Don't Understand What They Read—Research-Based Strategies for Teaching Reading Comprehension." *The Reading Teacher* 8 (February 1981): 565–75.

Edlesky, C., K. Draper, and K. Smith. "Hookin' 'em in at the Start of School in a 'Whole Language' Classroom." *Anthropology and Education Quarterly* (Winter 1983): 257–81.

Ekwall, Eldon E. *Diagnosis and Remediation of the Disabled Reader.* Boston, MA: Allyn and Bacon, Inc., 1976.

Ekwall, Eldon E. "Informal Reading Inventories: The Instructional Level." *The Reading Teacher* 29 (April 1976): 662–65.

Ekwall, Eldon E. "Should Repetitions Be Counted as Errors?" *The Reading Teacher* 27 (January 1974): 365–67.

Ekwall, Eldon E., and James L. Shanker. *Diagnosis and Remediation of the Disabled Reader.* 2nd ed. Boston, MA: Allyn and Bacon, Inc., 1983.

Eller, William, and Judith G. Wolf. "Developing Critical Reading Abilities." *Journal of Reading* 10 (December 1966): 192–98.

Emans, Robert. "The Usefulness of Phonic Generalizations Above the Primary Grades." *The Reading Teacher* 20 (February 1967): 410–25.

Emans, Robert. "Use of Context Clues." *Reading and Realism.* Edited by J. Allen Figurel. Newark, DE: International Reading Association, 1969.

Emans, Robert. "Use of Context Clues." *Teaching Word Recognition Skills.* Compiled by Mildred A. Dawson. Newark, DE: International Reading Association, 1971.

Emans, Robert, and Gladys Mary Fisher. "Teaching the Use of Context Clues." *Elementary English* 44 (1967): 243–46.

Evans, M. A., and T. H. Carr. "Cognitive Abilities, Conditions of Learning, and Early Development of Reading Skill." *Reading Research Quarterly* 20 (Spring 1985): 327–50.

Evertson, Carolyn M., and Linda M. Anderson. "Beginning School." *Educational Horizons* 57 (Summer 1979): 164–68.

Farr, M., ed. *Advances in Writing Research Vol. 1, Children's Early Writing Development.* Norwood, NJ: Albex, 1985.

Farr, Roger, ed. *Iowa Silent Reading Test: Manual of Direction.* New York: Harcourt Brace Jovanovich, Inc., 1973.

Farr, Roger. "Trends: A Place for Basal Readers Under the Whole Language Umbrella." *Educational Leadership* 46 (November 1988): 86.

Farr, Roger C., George A. Prescott, Irving H. Balow, and Thomas P. Hogan. *MAT6 Reading Diagnostic Tests: Teacher's Manual.* San Antonio, TX: The Psychological Corporation, Harcourt Brace Jovanovich, 1986.

Farris, P. J., and D. Kaczmarski. "Whole Language, a Closer Look." *Contemporary Education* 59 (Winter 1988): 77–81.

Fay, Leo. "Reading Study Skills: Math and Science." *Reading and Inquiry.* Edited by J. Allen Figurel. Newark, DE: International Reading Association, 1965.

Fennimore, Flora. "Projective Book Reports." *Language Arts* 54 (February 1977): 176–79.

Fernald, Grace M. *Remedial Techniques in Basic School Subjects.* New York: McGraw-Hill, 1943.

Fidell, Rachel, and Estelle A. Fidell, eds. *Children's Catalog.* 13th ed. Bronx, NY: H. W. Wilson Company, 1976.

Fisher, C. W., N. N. Filby, R. Marliave, L. S. Cahen, M. M. Dishaw, J. E. Moore, and D. C. Berliner. *Teaching Behaviors, Academic Learning Time, and Student Achievement: Final Report of Phase III-B, Beginning Teacher Evaluation Study.* San Francisco, CA: Far West Educational Laboratory for Educational Research and Development, 1978.

Fitzgerald, J., and D. L. Spiegel. "Enhancing Children's Reading Comprehension Through Instruction in Narrative Structure." *Journal of Reading Behavior* 15 (1983): 1–17.

Fitzgerald, Jill, Dixie Lee Spiegel, and James W. Cunningham. "The Relationship Between Parental Literacy Level and Perceptions of Emergent Literacy." *Journal of Reading Behavior* 23 (1991): 191–213.

Flesch, Rudolf F. "A New Readability Yardstick." *Journal of Applied Psychology* 32 (June 1948): 221–33.

Flesch, Rudolf F. *Why Johnny Can't Read and What You Can Do About It.* New York: Harper and Row, 1955.

Fogarty, Joan L., and Margaret C. Wang. "An Investigation of the Cross-age Peer Tutoring Process: Some Implications for Instructional Design and Motivation." *The Elementary School Journal* 82 (May 1982): 451.

Forness, Steven R., Arthur B. Silverstein, and Donald Guthrie. "Relationship Between Classroom Behavior and Achievement of Mildly Mentally Retarded

Children." *American Journal of Mental Deficiency* 84 (November 1979): 260–65.

Frederiksen, C. H. "Effects of Task-Induced Cognitive Operation on Comprehension and Memory Processes." *Language Comprehension and the Acquisition of Knowledge.* Edited by John B. Carroll and Roy O. Freedle. New York: Halsted Press, 1972.

Fry, Edward. "The New Instant Word List." *The Reading Teacher* 34 (December 1980): 284–89.

Fry, Edward B. *Elementary Reading Instruction.* New York: McGraw-Hill Book Company, 1977.

Fry, Edward B. "Fry's Readability Graph: Clarifications, Validity, and Extension to Level 17." *Journal of Reading* 21 (December 1977): 242–52.

Furness, Edna L. "Pupil, Pedagogues, and Punctuation." *Elementary English* 37 (1960): 184–89.

Gall, M. D., B. A. Ward, D. C. Berliner, L. S. Cahen, K. A. Crown, J. D. Elashoff, G. C. Stanton, and P. H. Winne. *The Effects of Teacher Use of Questioning Techniques on Student Achievement and Attitude: Stanford Program on Teacher Effectiveness, A Factorially Designed Experiment on Teacher Structuring, Soliciting, and Reading.* San Francisco, CA: Far West Laboratory for Educational Research and Development, 1975.

Gambrell, Linda E. "Think-Time: Implications for Reading Instruction." *The Reading Teacher* 34 (November 1981): 143.

Gardner, David C., and Margaret Kurtz. "Teaching Technical Vocabulary to Handicapped Students." *Reading Improvement* 16 (Fall 1979): 252–57.

Gates, Arthur I. *A Reading Vocabulary for the Primary Grades.* New York: Teachers College, Columbia University, 1926.

Gates, Arthur I., Anne S. McKillop, and Elizabeth C. Horowitz. *Gates-McKillop-Horowitz Reading Diagnostic Tests.* 2nd ed. Manual of Directions. New York: Teachers College Press, 1981.

Gaustad, Martha Gonter, and Trinka Messenheimer-Young. "Dialogue Journals for Students with Learning Disabilities." *Teaching Exceptional Children* 23 (Spring 1991): 28–32.

Geissal, Mary Ann, and June Knafle. "A Linguistic View of Auditory Discrimination Tests and Exercises." *The Reading Teacher* 31 (November 1977): 134–41.

Gemake, Josephine. "Interference of Certain Dialect Elements with Reading Comprehension for Third Graders." *Reading Improvement* 18 (Summer 1981): 183–89.

Gentile, A. *Further Studies in Achievement Testing, Hearing Impaired Students.* Annual Survey of Hearing Impaired Children and Youth. Washington, D.C.: Gallaudet College, 1973.

Gillet, Jean Wallace, and Charles Temple. *Understanding Reading Problems: Assessment and Instruction.* Boston, MA: Little, Brown and Company, 1982.

Gilliland, Hap. *A Practical Guide to Remedial Reading.* Columbus, OH: Charles E. Merrill Publishing Company, 1978.

Glass, Gerald G., and Elizabeth H. Burton. "How Do They Decode? Verbalizations and Observed Behaviors of Successful Decoders." *The Reading Teacher* 26 (March 1973): 645.

Glazer, Joan I., and Linda Leonard Lamme. "Poem Picture Books and Their Uses in the Classroom." *The Reading Teacher* 44 (October 1990): 102–9.

Gleitman, Lila R., and Paul Rozin. "Teaching Reading by Use of Syllabary." *Reading Research Quarterly* VIII (1973): 447–83.

Goodman, Kenneth S. "A Linguistic Study of Cues and Miscues in Reading." *Elementary English* 42 (1965): 639–43.

Goodman, Kenneth S. "Behind the Eye: What Happens in Reading." *Theoretical Models and Processes in Reading.* 2nd ed. Edited by Harry Singer and Robert Russell. Newark, DE: International Reading Association, 1976.

Goodman, Kenneth S. "Let's Dump the Up-tight Model in English." *Elementary School Journal* 69 (October 1969): 1–13.

Goodman, Kenneth S. "The 13th Easy Way to Make Learning to Read Difficult: A Reaction to Gleitman and Rosin." *Reading Research Quarterly* VIII (1973): 484–93.

Goodman, Kenneth S. "Unity in Reading." *Theoretical Models and Processes in Reading.* 3rd. ed. Edited by Harry Singer and Robert Russell. Newark, DE: International Reading Association, 1985.

Goodman, Kenneth S., and Catherine Buck. "Dialect Barriers to Comprehension Revisited." *The Reading Teacher* 25 (October 1973): 6–12.

Goodman, Yetta M. "Kid Watching: An Alternative to Testing." *National Elementary School Principal* 57 (June 1978): 41–45.

Goodman, Yetta, and Carolyn L. Burke. *Reading Miscue Inventory*. New York: Richard Owen Publishing Company, Inc., 1982.

Goodman, Yetta M., and Kenneth S. Goodman. "Spelling Ability of a Self Taught Reader." *The Elementary School Journal* 64 (1963): 149–54.

Graham, Kenneth G., and H. Alan Robinson. *Study Skills Handbook: A Guide for All Teachers*. Newark, DE: International Reading Association, 1984.

Grant, Linda, and James Rothenberg. *Charting Educational Futures: Interaction Patterns in First and Second Grade Reading Groups*. Washington, D.C.: National Institute of Education, April 1981.

Graves, Donald H. *Writing: Teachers and Children at Work*. Exeter, NH: Heinnemann Educational Books, 1983.

Graves, M. F., C. L. Cooke, and M. J. LaBerge. "Effects of Previewing Difficult Short Stories on Low Ability Junior High School Students' Comprehension, Recall, and Attitudes." *Reading Research Quarterly* 18 (1983): 262–76.

Gray, William S. *On Their Own in Reading: How to Give Children Independence in Analyzing New Words*. Rev. ed. Chicago: Scott, Foresman, 1960.

Gray, William S. "Reading and Physiology and Psychology of Reading." *Encyclopedia of Educational Research*. Edited by E. W. Harris. New York: Macmillan, 1960.

Greenwood, Charles R. "Longitudinal Analysis of Time, Engagement, and Achievement in At-Risk Versus Non-Risk Students." *Exceptional Children* 57 (May 1991): 521–35.

Gundach, J. B., F. M. Scott McLane, and G. D. McNamee. "The Social Foundations of Children's Early Writing Development." *Advances in Writing Research: Vol. 1, Children's Early Writing Development*, pp. 1–58. Edited by M. Farr. Norwood, NJ: Albex, 1985.

Guszak, Frank J. "Teacher Questioning and Reading." *The Reading Teacher* 21 (December 1967): 227–34.

Guthrie, Frances M., and Patricia M. Cunningham. "Teaching Decoding Skills to Educable Mentally Handicapped Children." *The Reading Teacher* 35 (February 1982): 54–59.

Guthrie, John J. "Effective Teaching Practices." *The Reading Teacher* 35 (March 1982): 766–68.

Guzzetti, Barbara J., and Robert J. Marzano. "Correlates of Effective Reading Instruction." *The Reading Teacher* 37 (April 1984): 754–59.

Hafner, Lawrence. *Developmental Reading in Middle and Secondary Schools: Foundations, Strategies, and Skills for Teaching*. New York: Macmillan Publishing Company, Inc., 1977.

Hafner, Lawrence E., and Hayden B. Jolly. *Patterns of Teaching Reading in the Elementary School*. New York: Macmillan Publishing Company, Inc., 1972.

Hajek, E. "Whole Language: Sensible Answers to the Old Problems." *Momentum* 15 (May 1984): 39–40.

Hall, Mary Anne. *Teaching Reading as a Language Experience*. 3rd ed. Columbus: Charles E. Merrill Publishing Company, 1989.

Hall, Mary Anne. *The Language Experience Approach for Teaching Reading*. 2nd ed. Newark, DE: International Reading Association, 1978.

Hall, Mary Anne, and Christopher J. Ramig. *Linguistic Foundations for Reading*. Columbus, OH: Charles E. Merrill Publishing Company, 1978.

Hallahan, Daniel P., and James M. Kauffman. *Exceptional Children: Introduction to Special Education*. Englewood Cliffs, NJ: Prentice-Hall, 1991.

Haller, Emil J., and Sharon A. Davis. "Does Socio-Economic Status Bias the Assignment of Elementary School Students to Reading Groups." *American Educational Research Journal* (Winter 1980): 409–18.

Halliday, M. A. K. *Learning How to Mean: Exploration in the Development of Language*. London: Edward Arnold, 1975.

Hancock, J. "Learning with Databases." *Journal of Reading* 32 (April 1989): 582–89.

Hanna, Paul R., and James I. Moore. "Spelling—From Spoken Word to Written Symbol." *Elementary School Journal* 53 (1953): 329–37.

Hansell, T. Stevenson. "Stepping up to Outlining." *Journal of Reading* 22 (December 1978): 248–52.

Hansen, Harlan S. "The Impact of the Home Literacy Environment on Reading Attitude." *Elementary English* 46 (January 1969): 17–24.

Hansen, Jane. "An Inferential Comprehension Strategy for Use with Primary Grade Children." *The Reading Teacher* 34 (March 1981): 665–69.

Hardman, Patricia K., Judith A. Clay, and Allan D. Liberman. "The Effects of Diet and Sublingual Provocative Testing on Eye Movements with Dyslexic Individuals." *Journal of the American Optometric Association* 60 (January 1989): 10–13.

Hargis, Charles H., and Edward F. Gickling. "The Function of Imagery in Word Recognition Development." *The Reading Teacher* 31 (May 1978): 870–73.

Harlin, Rebecca, and Sally Lippa. "Emergent Literacy: A Comparison of Formal and Informal Assessment Methods." *Reading Horizons* 30 (Spring 1990): 209–23.

Harris, Albert J. "Practical Applications of Reading Research." *The Reading Teacher* 29 (March 1976): 559–65.

Harris, Albert J., and Milton D. Jacobson. *Basic Elementary Reading Vocabularies*. New York: The Macmillan Publishing Company, Inc., 1972.

Harris, Albert J., Blanche Serwer, and Laurence Gold. "Comparing Approaches in First Grade Teaching with Disadvantaged Children Extended into Second Grade." *The Reading Teacher* 20 (May 1967): 698–703.

Harris, Albert J., and Edward R. Sipay. *How to Increase Reading Ability*. 6th ed. New York: David McKay Company, Inc., 1975.

Harris, Albert J. and Edward R. Sipay. *How to Increase Reading Ability: A Guide to Developmental and Remedial Methods*. 8th ed. New York: Longman Publishing Company, 1985.

Harris, Albert J., and Edward R. Sipay. *How to Increase Reading Ability*. 9th ed. New York: Longman Publishing Company, 1990.

Harris, Larry A. "Interest and the Initial Acquisition of Words." *The Reading Teacher* 22 (January 1969): 312–14, 362.

Harris, Larry A., and Carl B. Smith. *Reading Instruction: Diagnostic Teaching in the Classroom*. 3rd ed. New York: Holt, Rinehart, and Winston, 1980.

Harris, Larry A., and Carl B. Smith. *Reading Instruction: Diagnostic Teaching in the Classroom*. 4th ed. New York: Macmillan Publishing Company, Inc., 1986

Harrison, Alan R. "Critical Reading for Elementary Pupils." *The Reading Teacher* 21 (1967): 244–52.

Harste, J. C., C. I. Burke, and V. A. Woodward. *Children, Their Language and World: Initial Encounters with Print*. Bloomington, IN: Indiana University, 1981.

Hartley, James, Sally Bartlett, and Alan Branthwaite. "Underlining Can Make a Difference—Sometimes." *Journal of Educational Research* 74 (March/April 1980): 218–24.

Hays, Warren S. *Criteria for the Instructional Level of Reading*. Tucson, AZ: ERIC Document Reproduction Service, ED 117 665, 1975.

Healey, Ann Kirtland. "Effects of Changing Children's Attitudes Toward Reading." *Elementary English* 40 (November 1963): 255–57, 279.

Heath, Shirley B. *Ways with Words: Language, Life, and Work in Communities and Classrooms*. New York: Cambridge University Press, 1983.

Heath, Shirley B., and C. Thomas. "The Achievement of Preschool Literacy for Mother and Child." *Awakening to Literature*. Edited by H. Goelman, A. A. Oberg, and F. Smith. Exeter, NH: Heinemann, 1984, pp. 51–72.

Hedley, Carolyn N. "Mainstreaming and the Classroom Teacher: A Practical Approach." *Reading Horizons* 21 (Spring 1981): 189–95.

Heimberger, M. J. *Sartain Reading Attitudes Inventory*. Pittsburgh, PA: ERIC Document Reproduction Service, ED 045 291, 1970.

Helgren-Lempesis, Valerie A., and Charles T. Mangrum II. "An Analysis of Alternate-Form Reliability of Three Commercially-Prepared Informal Reading Inventories." *Reading Research Quarterly* XXI (Spring 1986): 209–15.

Henk, William A. "Reading Assessments of the Future: Toward Precision Diagnosis." *The Reading Teacher* 40 (May 1987): 860–70.

Hiatt, Diana Buell. "Time Allocation in the Classroom: Is Instruction Being Shortchanged?" *Phi Delta Kappan* 61 (December 1979): 289–90.

Hiebert, E., and C. Adams. "Fathers' and Mothers' Perceptions of Their Preschool Children's Emergent Literacy." *Journal of Experimental Child Psychology* 44 (August 1987): 25–37.

Hiebert, Elfreida H., and Jacalyn Colt. "Patterns of Literature-Based Reading Instruction." *The Reading Teacher* 43 (October 1990): 14–20.

Hiebert, E. H. "An Examination of Ability Grouping for Reading Instruction." *Reading Research Quarterly* XVIII (1983): 232–55.

Hillerich, Robert L. "The Truth About Vowels." *Insights Into Why and How to Read*. Edited by Robert Williams. Newark, DE: International Reading Association, 1976.

Hillerich, Robert L. "Vowel Generalizations and First Grade Reading Achievement." *Elementary School Journal* 67 (1967): 246–50.

Hillerich, Robert L. "Word Lists: Getting It All Together." *The Reading Teacher* 27 (January 1974): 353–60.

Hirstendahl, J. K. "The Effect of Subheads on Reader Comprehension." *Journalism Quarterly* 45 (1968): 123–25.

Hittleman, Daniel R. "Seeking a Psycholinguistic Definition of Readability." *The Reading Teacher* 26 (May 1973): 783–89.

Holland, Howard K., and Armand J. Galfo. *An Analysis of Research Concerning Class Size*. Richmond, VA: State Department of Education, 1964.

Hong, Laraine K. "Modifying SSR for Beginning Readers." *The Reading Teacher* 34 (May 1981): 888–91.

Huck, Charlotte S., and Doris Young Kuhn. *Children's Literature in the Elementary School*. 2nd ed. New York: Holt, Rinehart, and Winston, 1968.

Hudson, J., and J. Haworth. "Dimensions of Word Recognition." *Reading* 17 (1983): 87–94.

Huey, Edmund B. *The Psychology and Pedagogy of Reading*. New York: Macmillan and Company, 1908.

Huus, Helen. "A New Look at Children's Interests." *Using Literature and Poetry Affectively*. Edited by Jon E. Shapiro. Newark, DE: International Reading Association, 1979.

Ives, Josephine Piekarz. "The Improvement of Critical Reading Skills." *Problem Areas in Reading—Some Observations and Recommendations*. Edited by Coleman Morrison. Providence, RI: Oxford Press, Inc., 1966.

Jagger, Angela. "On Observing the Language Learner: Introduction and Overview." *Observing the Language Learner*. Edited by Angela Jagger and M. Trika Smith-Burke. Newark, DE: International Reading Association, 1985.

Jastak, J., S. Bijou, and S. Jastak. *Wide Range Achievement Test*. New York: The Psychological Corporation, 1976.

Jenkins, Joseph R., and Darlene Pany. "Instructional Variables in Reading Comprehension." *Comprehension and Reading: Research Review*. Edited by John T. Guthrie. Newark, DE: International Reading Association, 1981.

Jobe, Fred W. *Screening Vision in Schools*. Newark, DE: International Reading Association, 1976.

Johns, Jerry L. *Computer-based Graded-word Lists*. Dekalb, IL: Northern Illinois University, 1988.

Johns, Jerry L., Rose M. Edmond, and Nancy A. Mavrogenes. "The Dolch Basic Sight Vocabulary: A Replication and Validation Study." *The Elementary School Journal* 78 (September 1977): 31–37.

Johns, Jerry L., and Linda Lunt. "Motivating Reading: Professional Ideas." *The Reading Teacher* 28 (April 1975): 617–19.

Johns, Jerry L., and Anne Marie Magliari. "Informal Reading Inventories: Are the Betts Criteria the Best Criteria?" *Reading Improvement* 26 (Summer 1989): 124–32.

Johnson, Dale D. "Journal of Reading: A Themed Issue on Vocabulary Instruction." *Journal of Reading* 29 (1986): 580.

Johnson, Dale D. "The Dolch List Re-examined." *The Reading Teacher* 24 (February 1971): 449–57.

Johnson, Dale D., and Thomas G. Barrett. "Prose Comprehension: A Descriptive Analysis of Instructional Practices." *Children's Prose Comprehension: Research and Practice*. Edited by Carol M. Santa, and Bernard I. Hayes. Newark, DE: International Reading Association, 1981.

Johnson, Dale, and Alden Moe with James Bauman. *The Ginn Word Book for Teachers*. Lexington, MA: Ginn and Company, 1983.

Johnson, Dale D., Richard J. Smith, and Kenneth L. Jensen. "Primary Children's Recognition of High Frequency Words." *The Elementary School Journal* 73 (December 1972): 162–67.

Johnson, Donald J., and Helmer R. Myklebust. *Learning Disabilities: Educational Principles and Practices*. New York: Gruen and Stratton, 1967.

Johnson, Robert T., and David W. Johnson. "Action Research: Cooperative Learning in the Science Classroom." *Science and Children* 24 (October 1986): 31–32.

Jongsma, Eugene R. "The Cloze Procedure: A Survey of the Research." Bloomington, IN: Indiana University, August, 1971.

Jongsma, Kathleen S., and Eugene A. Jongsma. (Reviewers). "Test Review: Commercial Informal Reading Inventories." *The Reading Teacher* 34 (March 1981): 697–705.

Jonz, John. "Another Turn in the Conversation: What Does Cloze Measure?" *TESOL Quarterly* 24 (Spring 1990): 61–83.

Jorm, Anthony F. "Effect of Word Imagery on Reading Performance as a Function of Reading Ability." *Journal of Educational Psychology* 69 (February 1977): 46–54.

Juel, Connie. "Comparison of Word Identification Strategies With Varying Context, Word Type and Reader Skill." *Reading Research Quarterly* XV (1980): 358–76.

Juel, Connie, and B. Holmes. "Oral and Silent Reading of Sentences." *Reading Research Quarterly* XVI (1981): 545–68.

Justin, Neal. "Culture Conflict and Mexican-American Achievement." *School and Society* 98 (1970): 27–28.

Kalmbach, James R. "Getting at the Point of Retellings." *Journal of Reading* 29 (January 1986): 326–33.

Kaplan, Sandra Nina, Jo Ann Butom Kaplan, Sheila Kunishima Madsen, and Bette K. Taylor. *Change for Children*. Pacific Palisades, CA: Goodyear Publishing Company, Inc., 1973.

Karlsen, Bjorn, Richard Madden, and Eric F. Gardner. *Stanford Diagnostic Reading Test: Manual for Administering and Interpreting*. New York: Harcourt Brace Jovanovich, Inc., 1976.

Kaster, L. A., N. L. Roser, and J. V. Hoffman. "Understandings of the Forms and Functions of Written Language: Insights from Children and Parents." *Research in Literacy: Merging Perspective, 36th Yearbook of the National Reading Conference*. Edited by J. E. Readance and R. S. Baldwin. Rochester, NY: National Reading Conference, Inc., 1987, pp. 85–92.

Kaufman, Maurice. *Perceptual and Language Readiness Programs: Critical Reviews*. Newark, DE: International Reading Association, 1973.

Kean, M., A. Summers, M. Ravietz, and I. Farber. *What Works in Reading*. Philadelphia, PA: School District of Philadelphia, 1979.

Keegan, Suzi, and Karen Shrake. "Literature Study Groups: An Alternative to Ability Grouping." *The Reading Teacher* 44 (April 1991): 542–47.

Kierstead, Janet. "Outstanding Effective Classrooms." *Claremont Reading Conference Forty-Eighth Yearbook*. Claremont, CA: Claremont Reading Conference, 1984.

King, Ethel M., and Muehl Siegmar. "Different Sensory Cues as Aids in Beginning Reading." *The Reading Teacher* 19 (December 1965): 163–68.

Kirk, Samuel A., and James J. Gallagher. *Educating Exceptional Children*. 3rd ed. Boston, MA: Houghton Mifflin Company, 1979.

Koenke, Karl. "A Comparison of Three Auditory Discrimination-Perception Tests." *Academic Therapy* 13 (March 1978): 463–68.

Kolker, Brenda, and Paul N. Terwilliger. "Sight Vocabulary Learning of First and Second Graders." *Reading World* 20 (May 1981): 251–58.

Kolstoe, Oliver P. *Teaching Educable Mentally Retarded Children*. 2nd ed. New York: Holt, Rinehart, and Winston, 1976.

Kounin, J. S. *Discipline and Group Management in Classrooms*. New York: Holt, Rinehart, and Winston, 1970.

Knapp, Michael I., and Brenda J. Turnbull. "Better Schooling for the Children of Poverty Alternatives to Conventional Wisdom." *Study of Academic Instruction for Disadvantaged Students: What Is Taught, and How, to the Children of Poverty: Interim Report from a Two-Year Investigation, Vol. 1*. Prepared by Michael S. Knapp et al. Washington, D.C.: U.S. Department of Education, Office of Planning, Budget and Evaluation, 1991.

Kucera, Henry, and Francis W. Nelson. *Computational Analysis for Present-Day American English*. Providence, RI: Brown University Press, 1967.

Kuchinskas, Gloria, and M. C. Radenchich. *The Literary Mapper*. Gainesville, FL: Teacher Support Software, 1990.

Kuchinskas, Gloria, and M. C. Radenchich. *The Semantic Mapper*. Gainesville, FL: Teacher Support Software, 1986.

Kulik, C. C., and J. A. Kulik. "Effects of Ability Grouping on Secondary School Students: A Meta-Analysis of Evaluation Findings." *American Educational Research Journal* 19 (1982): 415–28.

Kurth, Ruth J., and M. Jean Greenlaw. "Research and Practice in Comprehension Instruction in Elementary Classrooms." *Comprehension: Process and Product*. Edited by George H. McNinch. First Yearbook of the American Reading Forum. Athens, GA: The American Reading Forum, 1981.

Labbo, Linda D., and William H. Teale. "Cross-age Reading: A Strategy for Helping Poor Readers." *The Reading Teacher* 44 (February 1990): 362–69.

Labe, Mary Louise. "Improve the Dictionary's Image." *Elementary English* 48 (March 1971): 363–65.

LaBerge, D., and S. Jay Samuels. "Toward a Theory of Automatic Information Processing in Reading." *Cognitive Psychology* 6 (1974): 293–323.

Lahey, Benjamin, and Ronald Drabman. "Facilitation of the Acquisition and Retention of Sight-word Vocabulary Through Token Reinforcement." *Journal of Applied Behavior Analysis* 7 (Summer 1974): 307–12.

Lally, M. "Computer-Assisted Teaching of Sight-Word Recognition for Mentally Retarded School Children." *American Journal of Mental Deficiency* 85 (January 1981): 383–88.

Lange, Bob. "Readability Formulas Second Looks, Second Thoughts." *The Reading Teacher* 35 (April 1982): 858–61.

Larson, Alfred D., and June B. Miller. "The Hearing Impaired." *Exceptional Children and Youth: An Introduction*. Edited by Edward L. Meyen. Denver, CO: Love Publishing Company, 1978.

Lehr, Fran. "Direct Instruction in Reading." *The Reading Teacher* 39 (1986): 706–09.

Leichter, H. J. "Families as Environments for Literacy." *Awakening to Literacy*. Edited by H. Goelman, A. A. Oberg, and F. Smith. Exeter, NH: Heinemann, 1984, pp. 38–50.

Leinhardt, Gaia, Naomi Zigmond, and William W. Cooley. "Reading Instruction and Its Effects." *American Educational Research Journal* 18 (Fall 1981): 356–58.

Leu, Donald J., Jr., and Charles K. Kinzer. *Effective Reading Instruction in the Elementary Grades*. Columbus, OH: Merrill Publishing Company, 1987.

Levin, Harry, and E. L. Kaplin. "Grammatical Structure and Reading." *Basic Studies in Reading*. Edited by H. Levin and J. Williams. New York: Basic Books, 1970.

Levin, Harry, and J. Watson. "The Learning of Variable Grapheme-to-Phoneme Correspondences: Variations in the Initial Consonant Position." *A Basic Research Program on Reading*. U.S. Office of Education Cooperative Research Project No. 639. Ithaca, NY: Cornell University, 1963.

Levin, Joel R., and Michael Pressley. "Improving Children's Prose Comprehension: Selected Strategies That Seem to Succeed." *Children's Prose Comprehension: Research and Practice*. Edited by Carol M. Santa and Bernard I. Hayes. Newark, DE: International Reading Association, 1981.

Liebert, Robert E., and John K. Sherk. "Three Frostig Visual Perception Sub-tests and Specific Reading Tasks for Kindergarten, First, and Second Grade Children." *The Reading Teacher* 24 (November 1970): 130–37.

Lipa, Sally. "Test Review: Diagnostic Reading Scales." *The Reading Teacher* 38 (March 1985): 664–67.

Loban, Walter. *The Language of Elementary School Children*. Urbana, IL: National Council of Teachers of English, 1963.

Lowenfield, Berthold, ed. *The Visually Handicapped Child in School*. New York: John Day Co., 1973.

Lundsteen, Sara W. *Children Learn to Communicate*. Englewood Cliffs, NJ: Prentice-Hall, Inc., 1976.

MacGinitie, Walter H., and Ruth K. MacGinitie. *Gates-MacGinite Reading Tests Teacher's Manuals*. Chicago, IL: Riverside Publishing Company, 1989.

McBroom, Maude, Julia Sparrow, and Catherine Eckstein. *Scale for Determining a Child's Reader Level*. Iowa City, IA: Bureau of Publications, Extension Division, State University of Iowa, 1944.

McCallister, James M. "Using Paragraph Clues as Aids to Understanding." *Journal of Reading* 8 (October 1965): 11–16.

McCullough, Constance. "Responses of Elementary School Children to Common Types of Reading Comprehension Questions." *Journal of Educational Research* 51 (September 1957): 65–70.

McDonell, Gloria M. "Effects of Instruction in the Use of an Abstract Structural Schema as an Aid to Comprehension and Recall of Written Discourse." Ph.D. Dissertation, Virginia Polytechnic Institute and State University, 1983.

McFeely, Donald C. "Syllabication Usefulness in a Basal and Social Studies Vocabulary." *The Reading Teacher* 27 (May 1974): 809–14.

McGee, Lea M., and Donald J. Richgels. *Learning How to Mean: Exploration in the Development of Language.* Boston, MA: Allyn and Bacon, Inc., 1990.

McKenna, Michael C. *Computer Assisted Reading Achievement.* Burlington, NC: Southern Micro Systems.

McKenna, Michael C., and Dennis J. Kear. "Measuring Attitude Toward Reading: A New Tool for Teachers." *The Reading Teacher* 43 (May 1990): 626–39.

McKenna, Michael C., and Kent Layton. "Concurrent Validity of Cloze as a Measure of Intersentential Comprehension." *Journal of Educational Psychology* 82 (June 1990): 372–77.

McLaughlin, Harry G. "SMOG Grading—A New Readability Formula." *Journal of Reading* 12 (May 1969): 639–46.

McNeil, J. D., and E. R. Keislar. "Value of the Oral Response in Beginning Reading: An Experimental Study Using Programmed Instruction." *British Journal of Educational Psychology* 33 (1963): 162–68.

Magic Slate. Pleasantville, NY: Sunburst Communications, 1985.

Mandler, J. M., and M. S. Johnson. "Remembrance of Things Passed: Story Structure and Recall." *Cognitive Psychology* 9 (1977): 111–51.

Mangieri, John N., Lois A. Bader, and James E. Walker. *Elementary Reading.* New York: McGraw-Hill Book Company, 1982.

Mangieri, John N., and Michael S. Kahn. "Is the Dolch List of 220 Basic Sight Words Irrelevant?" *The Reading Teacher* 30 (March 1977): 649–51.

Manning, Marilyn M., and Gary L. Manning. "Early Readers and Nonreaders from Low Socioeconomic Environments: What Their Parents Report." *The Reading Teacher* 38 (1984): 32–34.

Manzo, Anthony V. "ReQuest Procedure." *Journal of Reading* 13 (1969): 123–26.

Marland, Sidney P. *Education of the Gifted and Talented.* Washington, D.C.: U.S. Office of Education, 1972.

Marshall, Nancy. "Using Story Grammar to Assess Reading Comprehension." *The Reading Teacher* 36 (March 1983): 616–20.

Martin, Jeanne, and Carolyn M. Evertson. *Teachers' Interactions with Reading Groups of Differing Ability Levels.* Washington, D.C.: National Institute of Education (March 1980).

Marzano, Robert J., Norma Case, Anne DeBooy, and Kathy Prochoruk. "Are Syllabication and Reading Ability Related?" *Journal of Reading* 19 (April 1976): 545–47.

Mason, George E. *Language Experience Recorder Plus.* Gainesville, FL: Teacher Support Service, 1987.

Mason, Jana M. "A Schema-Theoretic View of the Reading Process as a Basis for Comprehension Instruction." *Comprehension Instruction: Perspectives and Suggestions.* Edited by Gerald G. Duffy, Laura R. Roehler, and Jana Mason. New York: Longman, 1984.

Mason, Jana M., and J. Allen. "A Review of Emergent Literacy with Implications for Research and Practice in Reading." *Review of Research in Education.* Edited by E. Z. Rothkopf. Washington, D.C.: American Educational Research Association, 1986.

Mason, Jana M., J. H. Osborn, and B. V. Rosenshine. "A Consideration of Skill Hierarchy Approaches to the Teaching of Reading." *Technical Report 42.* Champaign, IL: University of Illinois, 1977.

Mavrogenes, Nancy A., Earl F. Hanson, and Carol K. Winkley. "A Guide to Tests of Factors that Inhibit Learning to Read." *The Reading Teacher* 19 (January 1976): 343–58.

Maxwell, Martha. "Readability: Have We Gone Too Far?" *Journal of Reading* 21 (March 1978): 525–30.

May, Frank B. *Reading as Communication.* Columbus, OH: Charles E. Merrill Publishing Company, 1982.

Meisal, Stephen, and Gerald G. Glass. "Voluntary Reading Interests and the Interest Content of Basal Readers." *The Reading Teacher* 23 (April 1970): 655–59.

Mersereau, Y., M. Glover, and M. Cherland. "Dancing on the Edge." *Language Arts* 66 (February 1989): 109–18.

Meyer, Bonnie J. F. "Structure of Prose: Implications for Teachers of Reading." Research Report No. 3. Tempe, AZ: Arizona State University, Department of Educational Psychology, 2.

Meyer, Bonnie J. F. *The Organization of Prose and Its Effect on Memory.* Amsterdam: North Holland, 1975.

Miller, G. Michael, and George E. Mason. "Dramatic Improvisation: Risk-Free Role Playing for Improving Reading Performance." *The Reading Teacher* 37 (November 1983): 128–31.

Miller, John W., and Michael McKenna. *Teaching Reading in the Elementary Classroom.* Scottsdale, AZ: Gorsuch Scarisbrick, 1989.

Moacdieh, Chris. "Grouping for Reading in the Primary Grades: Evidence on the Revisionist Argument." Paper presented at the Annual Meeting of the American Educational Research Association, Los Angeles, CA: April 13–17, 1981.

Moldofsky, Penny Baum. "Teaching Students to Determine the Central Story Problem: A Practical Application of Schema Theory." *The Reading Teacher* 36 (1983): 740–45.

Montessori, Maria. *The Secret of Childhood.* New York: Ballantine Books, 1966.

Moores, Donald F. *Educating the Deaf: Psychology, Principles and Practices.* Boston, MA: Houghton Mifflin Company, 1978.

Moray, Geraldine. "What Does Research Say about the Reading Interests of Children in the Intermediate Grades?" *The Reading Teacher* 31 (April 1978): 763–68.

Morrice, Connie, and Maureen Simmons. "Beyond Reading Buddies: A Whole Language Cross-age Program." *The Reading Teacher* 44 (April 1991): 572–79.

Morrow, Lesley Mandel. "Home and School Correlates of Early Interest in Literature." *Journal of Educational Research* 76 (March/April 1983): 221–30.

Morrow, Lesley Mandel. *Literacy Development in the Early Years.* Englewood Cliffs, NJ: Prentice Hall, 1989.

Morrow, Lesley Mandel. "Relationships Between Literature Programs, Library Corner Designs, and Children's Use of Literature." *Journal of Educational Research* (July/August 1982): 339–44.

Mosenthal, Peter B. "The Whole Language Approach: Teachers Between a Rock and a Hard Place." *The Reading Teacher* 42 (April 1989): 628–29.

Mullis, Ina V. S., and Lynn B. Jenkins. *The Reading Report Card, 1971–1988: Trends from the Nation's Report Card.* Princeton, NJ: National Assessment of Educational Progress, (January 1990).

Musgrave, G. R. *Individualized Instruction.* Boston, MA: Allyn and Bacon, Inc., 1975.

Nardelli, Robert R. "Some Aspects of Creative Reading." *Journal of Educational Research* 50 (March 1957): 495–508.

National Advisory Committee on Handicapped Children. *First Annual Report, Subcommittee on Education of the Committee on Labor and Public Welfare, U.S. Senate.* Washington, D.C.: U.S. Government Printing Office, 1986.

National Education Association. "America's Other Children—Bilingual Multicultural Education: Hope for the Culturally Alienated." *NEA Reporter* 15 (1976): 13.

Nelson, Joan. "Readability: Some Cautions to the Content Area Teacher." *Journal of Reading* 21 (April 1978): 620–25.

Nelson, Raedeane M. "Getting Children into Reference Books." *Elementary English* 50 (September 1973): 884–87.

Nelson, R. Brett, Jack A. Cummings, and Heidi Boltman. "Teaching Basic Concepts to Students Who Are Educable Mentally Handicapped." *Teaching Exceptional Children* 23 (Winter 1991): 12–15.

Neuman, Susan B. "Effect of Teaching Auditory Perceptual Skills on Reading Achievement in First Grade." *The Reading Teacher* 34 (January 1981): 422–26.

Newman, Judith M., and Susan M. Church. "Myths of Whole Language." *The Reading Teacher* 44 (September 1990): 22.

Niles, Jerome A., and Larry A. Harris. "The Context of Comprehension." *Reading Horizons* 22 (Fall 1981): 33–42.

Ninio, A. "Picture Book Reading in Mother Infant Dyads Belonging to Two Subgroups in Israel." *Child Development* 51 (1980): 587–90.

Oakan, Robert, Morton Wierner, and Ward Cormer. "Identification, Organization, and Reading Comprehension for Good and Poor Readers." *Journal of Educational Psychology* 62 (1971): 71–78.

Oakland, Thomas D. "Auditory Discrimination and Socioeconomic Status as Correlates of Reading Ability." *Journal of Learning Disabilities* 2 (June 1969): 325–29.

Ogle, Donna M. "K-W-L: A Teaching Model that Develops Active Reading of Expository Text." *The Reading Teacher* 39 (February 1986): 564–70.

Ohnmacht, D. C. "The Effects of Letter Knowledge on Achievement in Reading in the First Grade." *Reading Research Revisited*. Edited by L. M. Gentile, M. L. Kamil, and J. S. Blanchard. Columbus, OH: Charles E. Merrill Publishing Co., 1983, pp. 141–42.

Olenchak, F. R., and J. S. Renzulli. "The Effectiveness of the Schoolwide Enrichment Model on Selected Aspects of Elementary School Change." *Gifted Child Quarterly* 33 (Winter 1989): 36–46.

Ollila, Lloyd. "Reading: Preparing the Child." *Reading: Foundations and Instructional Strategies*. Edited by Pose Lamb and Richard Arnold. Belmont, CA: Wadsworth Publishing Company, 1976.

Olson, Arthur V., and Clifford L. Johnson. "Structure and Predictive Validity of the Frostig Developmental Test of Visual Perception in Grades One and Three." *Journal of Special Education* 4 (Winter–Spring 1970): 49–52.

Olson, Willard C. *Child Development*. Boston, MA: D.C. Heath and Company, 1949.

O'Masta, Gail A., and James M. Wolf. "Encouraging Independent Reading Through the Reading Millionaires Project." *The Reading Teacher* 44 (May 1991): 656–62.

Orlando, Vincent P. "Notetaking vs. Notehaving: A Comparison While Studying from Text." *Reading Research: Studies and Applications. Twenty-eighth Yearbook of the National Reading Conference*. Edited by Michael L. Kamil and Alden J. Moe. Clemson, SC: National Reading Conference, 1979, pp. 177–81.

Otto, Wayne. "Evaluating Instruments for Assessing Needs and Growth in Reading." *Assessment Problems in Reading*. Edited by Walter H. MacGinitie. Newark, DE: International Reading Association, 1973.

Otto, Wayne, and Robert Chester. "Sight Words for Beginning Readers." *The Journal of Educational Research* 65 (1971): 425–43.

Pallinesar, Annemarie Sullivan. "The Quest for Meaning from Expository Text: A Teacher-Guided Journey." *Comprehension Instruction: Perspectives and Suggestions*. Edited by Gerald G. Duffy, Laura R. Roehler, and Jana Mason. New York: Longman, 1984.

Paradis, Edward. "The Appropriateness of Visual Discrimination Exercise in Reading Readiness Materials." *Journal of Educational Research* 67 (February 1974): 276–78.

Parker, Francis W. *Talks on Pedagogies*. Chicago, IL: Kellog, 1984.

Pearson, P. David, and Linda Fielding. "Research Update: Listening Comprehension." *Language Arts* 59 (September 1982): 617–29.

Pearson, P. David, and Dale Johnson. *Teaching Reading Comprehension*. New York: Holt, Rinehart, and Winston, 1978.

Peck, Jackie. "Using Storytelling to Promote Language and Literacy Development." *The Reading Teacher* 43 (November 1989): 138–41.

Perez, Eustolia. "Oral Language Competence Improves Reading Skills of Mexican American Third Graders." *The Reading Teacher* 35 (October 1981): 24–29.

Persell, C. *Education and Inequality: The Roots and Results of Stratification in American Schools*. New York: Free Press, 1977.

Peterson, P., L. Wilkinson, and M. Hallinan. *The Social Context of Instruction: Group Organization and Group Processes*. New York: Academic Press, 1984.

Pflaster, Gail. "A Factor Analysis of Variables Related to Academic Performance of Hearing-Impaired Children in Regular Classes." *The Volta Review* 82 (February/March 1980): 71–84.

Pikulski, John. "The Validity of Three Brief Measures of Intelligence for Disabled Readers." *Journal of Educational Research* 67 (October 1973): 67–68, 80.

Pikulski, John. "A Critical Review: Informal Reading Inventories." *The Reading Teacher* 28 (November 1974): 141–51.

Pikulski, John. "Informal Reading Inventories (Assessments)." *The Reading Teacher* 43 (March 1990): 514–16.

Pikulski, John J., and Irwin S. Kiroch. "Organization for Instruction." *Teaching Reading in Compensatory Classes.* Edited by Robert C. Calfee and Pricilla A. Drum. Newark, DE: International Reading Association, 1979, pp. 72–86, 187–91.

Pikulski, John J., and Timothy Shanahan. "Informal Reading Inventories: A Critical Analysis." *Approaches to the Informal Evaluation of Reading.* Edited by J. Pikulski, and T. Shanahan. Newark, DE: International Reading Association, 1982.

Plattor, Emma E., and Ellsworth S. Woestehoff. "Specific Reading Disabilities of Disadvantaged Children." *Reading Difficulties: Diagnosis, Correction and Remediation.* Edited by William Durr. Newark, DE: International Reading Association, 1970.

Plessas, G., and C. R. Oakes. "Prereading Experiences of Selected Early Readers." *The Reading Teacher* 18 (1964): 241–45.

Poostay, Edward J. "Show Me Your Underlines: A Strategy to Teach Comprehension." *The Reading Teacher* 37 (May 1984): 828–29.

Prentice, Walter C., and Jon Charles Tabbert. "Creative Dramatics and Reading: A Question of Basics." Grand Forks, N.D.: University of North Dakota, Center for Teaching and Learning, 1978.

Price, L. "How Thirty-Seven Gifted Children Learned to Read." *The Reading Teacher* 30 (1976): 44–49.

Pryor, Frances. "Poor Reading—Lack of Self-Esteem?" *The Reading Teacher* 28 (January 1975): 359.

Psychological Corporation, The. *1987 Catalog: Tests and Services for Educators.* San Antonio, TX: The Psychological Corporation, Harcourt Brace Jovanovich, 1987.

Purves, A. C., and Richard Beach. *Literature and the Reader: Research in Response to Literature, Reading Interests, and the Teaching of Literature.* Urbana, IL: National Council of Teachers of English, 1972.

Quandt, Ivan. *Self-Concept and Reading.* Newark, DE: International Reading Association, 1972.

Radencich, Marguerite C. "Test Review: Gray Oral Reading Tests-Revised and Formal Reading Inventory." *Journal of Reading* 30 (1986): 136–39.

Rankin, Earl F., and Betsy M. Overholzer. "Reaction of Intermediate Grade Children to Contextual Clues." *Journal of Reading Behavior* 1 (Summer 1969): 50–73.

Readance, John E., and Mary McDonnell Harris. "False Prerequisites in the Teaching of Comprehension." *Reading Improvement* 17 (Spring 1980): 18–21.

Reeves, Harriet Ramsey. "Individual Conferences— Diagnostic Tools." *The Reading Teacher* 24 (February 1971): 411–15.

Reid, D. Kim, Wayne P. Hresko, and Donald D. Hammill. *Manual: The Tests of Early Reading Ability.* 2nd ed. Austin, TX: Pro-Ed, 1989.

Reinking, David. *The Comprehension Connection.* St. Louis, MO: Milliken, 1987.

Renzulli, J. S. "Dear Mr. and Mrs. Copernicus: We Regret to Inform You . . ." *Gifted Child Quarterly* 26 (Winter 1982): 11–14.

Reutzel, D. Ray. "Story Mapping: An Alternative Approach to Comprehension." *Reading World* 24 (December 1984): 18–25.

Reutzel, D. Ray, and Robert B. Cooter, Jr. "Organizing for Effective Instruction: The Reading Workshop." *The Reading Teacher* 44 (April 1991): 548–55.

Reutzel, D. Ray, and P. M. Hollingsworth. "Whole Language and the Practitioner." *Academic Therapy* 23 (March 1988): 405–16.

Rich, S. J. "Restoring Power to Teachers: The Impact of 'Whole Language'." *Language Arts* 62 (November 1985): 717–24.

Richards, J. C., J. P. Gipe, and B. Thompson. "Teachers' Beliefs About Good Reading Instruction." *Reading Psychology* No. 1 (1987): 1–6.

Rickelman, Robert J., and William A. Henk. "Telecommunications in the Reading Classroom." *The Reading Teacher* 43 (February 1990): 418–19.

Ridley, Lia. "Enacting Change in Elementary School Programs: Implementing a Whole Language Perspective." *The Reading Teacher* 43 (May 1990): 640–46.

Robeck, Mildred C., and John A. R. Wilson. *Psychology of Reading: Foundations of Instruction.* New York: John Wiley and Sons, Inc., 1974.

Robinson, Francis P. *Effective Study.* 4th ed. New York, Harper and Row, 1970.

Robinson, Helen. "Developing Critical Readers." *Dimensions of Critical Reading.* Edited by Russell G. Stauffer. Newark, DE: University of Delaware, Proceedings of the Annual Education and Reading Conference, 1964.

Robinson, Helen, and Samuel Weintraub. "Research Related to Children's Interests and to Developmental Values of Reading." *Library Trends* 22 (October 1973): 81–108.

Roeder, Harold H., and Nancy Lee. "Twenty-five Teacher Tested Ways to Encourage Voluntary Reading." *The Reading Teacher* 27 (October 1973): 48–50.

Roettger, Doris. "Elementary Students' Attitudes Toward Reading." *The Reading Teacher* 33 (January 1980): 451–53.

Roney, R. Craig. "Background Experience Is the Foundation of Success in Learning to Read." *The Reading Teacher* 38 (November 1984): 196–99.

Rosenblatt, Louise M. "Towards a Transactional Theory of Reading." *Journal of Reading Behavior* 1 (1969): 31–49.

Rosenholtz, S. J. "Modifying a Status-Organizing Process of the Traditional Classroom." *Pure and Applied Studies in Expectation States Theory.* Edited by J. Berger and M. Zelditch, Jr. San Francisco, CA: Jossey-Bass Publishing Company, 1984.

Rosenshine, Barak V. "Skill Hierarchies in Reading Comprehension." *Theoretical Issues in Reading Comprehension.* Edited by Rand J. Spiro, Bertram C. Bruce, and William F. Brewer. Hillsdale, NJ: Lawrence Erlbaum Associates, 1980.

Rosenshine, Barak V., and David C. Berliner. "Academic Engaged Time." *British Journal of Teacher Education* 4 (1978): 3–16.

Rosenshine, Barak, and Robert Stevens. "Classroom Instruction in Reading." *Handbook of Reading Research.* Edited by David Pearson with R. Barr, M. L. Kamil, and P. Mosenthal. New York: Longman, 1984.

Roser, Nancy L., James V. Hoffman, and Cynthia Farest. "Language, Literature, and At-Risk Children." *The Reading Teacher* 43 (April 1990): 554–61.

Ross, Ramon. "A Look at Listeners." *Elementary School Journal* 64 (April 1964): 369–72.

Rothman, Robert. "NEAP Board Adopts Blueprint for 1992 Reading Test." *Education Week*, 14 March 1990, p. 4.

Ruck, L. V. "Some Questions About the Teaching of Syllabication Rules." *The Reading Teacher* 27 (March 1974): 583–88.

Ruddell, Robert B. *Reading-Language Instruction: Innovative Practices.* Englewood-Cliffs, NJ: Prentice-Hall, 1974.

Ruddell, Robert B. "Vocabulary Learning: A Process Model and Criteria for Evaluating Instructional Strategies." *Journal of Reading Behavior* 29 (April 1986): 581–87.

Rummelhart, David E. "Schemata: The Building Blocks of Cognition." *Theoretical Issues in Reading Comprehension.* Edited by Rand J. Spiro, Bertram C. Bruce, and William F. Brewer. Hillsdale, NJ: L. Erlbaum Associates, 1980.

Rummelhart, David. *Toward an Interactive Model of Reading.* Center for Human Information Services, Technical Report No. 56. San Diego, CA: University of California, 1976.

Rummelhart, David E. "Understanding Understanding." *Understanding Reading Comprehension*, pp. 1–20. Edited by James Flood. Newark, DE: International Reading Association, 1984.

Rupley, William H., and Timothy R. Blair. "Specification of Reading Instructional Practices Associated with Pupil Achievement Gains." *Educational and Psychological Research* 1 (1981): 161–69.

Russell, David H. *Children's Thinking.* Boston, MA: Ginn and Company, 1956.

Rystrom, Richard, "Reflections of Meaning." *Journal of Reading Behavior* 9 (Summer 1977): 193–200.

Samuels, S. Jay. "Automatic Decoding and Reading Comprehension." *Language Arts* 53 (March 1976): 323–25.

Sanders, Norris M. *Classroom Questions—What Kinds?* New York: Harper and Row, 1966.

Sandford, Herbert A. "Directed and Free Search of the School Atlas Map." *The Cartographic Journal* 71 (December 1980): 83–92.

Sauffer, Russel G. *The Language-experience Approach to the Teaching of Reading.*

Schell, Leo M. "Teaching Structural Analysis." *The Reading Teacher* 21 (November 1968): 133–37.

Schell, Leo M. "The Validity of the Potential Level Via Listening Comprehension: A Cautionary Note." *Reading Psychology* 3 (1982): 271–76.

Schell, Leo M., and Robert E. Jennings. "Test Review: Durrell Analysis of Reading Difficulty (3rd Edition)." *The Reading Teacher* 35 (November 1981): 204–10.

Schickedanz, J. A., and M. Sullivan. "Mom, What Does U-F-F Spell?" *Language Arts* 61 (January 1984): 7–17.

Schieffelin, Bambi B., and Marilyn Cochran-Smith. "Learning to Read Culturally/ Literacy Before Schooling." *Awakening Literacy.* Edited by H. Goelman, A. A. Oberg, and F. Smith. Exeter, NH: Heinemann, 1984.

Schrank, Frederick A., and Dennis W. Engels. "Bibliotherapy as a Counseling Adjunct: Research Findings." *Personnel and Guidance Journal* 60 (November 1981): 143–47.

Schwartz, Elaine, and Alice Sheff. "Student Involvement in Questioning for Comprehension." *The Reading Teacher* 29 (November 1975): 150–54.

Schwartz, Robert M., and Keith E. Stanovich. "Flexibility in the Use of Graphic and Contextual Information by Good and Poor Readers." *Journal of Reading Behavior* 13 (Fall 1981): 263–69.

Searls, Evelyn F. *How to Use WISC-R Scores in Reading/ Learning Disability Diagnosis.* Newark, DE: International Reading Association, 1985.

Sebasta, Sam Leaton. "What Do Young People Think about the Literature They Read?" *Reading Newsletter,* no. 8. Rockleigh, NJ: Allyn & Bacon, Inc., 1979.

Shannon, Patrick. "Some Subjective Reasons for Teachers' Reliance on Commercial Reading Materials." *The Reading Teacher* 35 (May 1982): 884–89.

Shaywitz, S. E., and B. A. Shaywitz. "Attention Deficit Disorder: Current Perspectives." Paper presented at the National Conference on Learning Disabilities, Bethesda, MD: National Institutes of Child Health and Human Development, 1987.

Sheridan, E. Marcia. *A Review of Research on Schema Theory and Its Implications for Reading Instruction in Secondary Reading.* South Bend, IN: ERIC Document Reproduction Service, ED 167 947, 1978.

Simons, Herbert D. "Linguistic Skills and Reading Comprehension." *The Quest for Competency in Reading.* Edited by Howard A. Klein. Newark, DE: International Reading Association, 1972.

Simpson, Michele L. "PORPE: A Writing Strategy for Studying and Learning in the Content Areas." *Journal of Reading* 29 (February 1986): 407–14.

Singer, Harry. "Active Comprehension: From Answering to Asking Questions." *The Reading Teacher* 31 (May 1978): 901–08.

Singer, Harry. "Teaching Word Recognition Skills." *Teaching Word Recognition Skills.* Edited by Mildred A. Dawson. Newark, DE: International Reading Association, 1971.

Singer, Harry. "Theoretical Models of Reading." *Journal of Communications* 19 (1969): 134–56.

Singer, Harry, and Robert Ruddell, eds. *Theoretical Models and Processes of Reading.* 3rd ed. Newark, DE: International Reading Association, 1985.

Singer, Harry S., Jay Samuels, and Jean Spiroff. "The Effect of Pictures and Contextual Condition on Learning Responses to Printed Words." *Reading Research Quarterly* 9 (1973–74): 555–67.

Sipay, Edward R. *Sipay Word Analysis Tests.* Cambridge, MA: Educators Publishing Service, Inc., 1974.

Slater, Mallie. "Individualized Language Arts in the Middle Grades." *The Reading Teacher* 27 (December 1973): 253–56.

Slaughter, Helen B. "Indirect and Direct Instruction in a Whole Language Classroom." *The Reading Teacher* 42 (October 1988): 30–34.

Slavin, Robert. *Cooperative Learning.* New York: Longman, 1983.

Slosson, Richard L. *Slosson Oral Reading Test.* East Aurora, NY: Slosson Educational Publications, Inc., 1990.

Smith-Burke, M. Trika. "Classroom Practices and Classroom Interaction during Reading Instruction: What's Going On?" *The Dynamics of Language Learning: Research in Reading and English.* Edited by James R. Squire. Urbana, IL: National Conference on Research in English, ERIC Clearinghouse on Reading and Communication Skills, 1987, pp. 226–65.

Smith, Carl B. *Teaching in Secondary School Content Subjects.* New York: Holt, Rinehart, and Winston, Inc., 1978.

Smith, Carl B., and Peggy G. Elliot. *Reading Activities for Middle and Secondary Schools.* New York: Holt, Rinehart, and Winston, Inc., 1979.

Smith, Frank. *Psycholinguistics and Reading.* New York: Holt, Rinehart, and Winston, Inc., 1973.

Smith, Frank. *Understanding Reading: A Psycholinguistic Analysis of Reading and Learning to Read.* 4th ed. Hillsdale, NJ: L. Erlbaum Associates, 1988.

Smith, Henry P., and Emerald V. Dechant. *Psychology in Teaching Reading.* Englewood Cliffs, NJ: Prentice-Hall, Inc., 1961.

Smith, Marilyn, and Thomas W. Bean. "Four Strategies that Develop Children's Story Comprehension and Writing." *The Reading Teacher* 37 (December 1983): 295–301.

Smith, M. Cecil. "A Longitudinal Investigation of Reading Attitude Development from Childhood to Adulthood." *Journal of Educational Research* 83 (March/April 1990): 215–29.

Smith, Nila Banton. *American Reading Instruction,* 3rd ed. Newark, DE: International Reading Association, 1974.

Smith, Nila Banton. "Patterns of Writing in Different Subject Areas." *Journal of Reading* 8 (October 1965): 31–37.

Smith, R. J., and D. D. Johnson. *Teaching Children to Read.* Reading, MA: Addison-Wesley, 1980.

Snow, C. E. "Literacy and Language: Relationships During the Preschool Years." *Harvard Educational Review* 53 (May 1983): 165–89.

Snyder, Geraldine V. "Learner Verification of Reading Games." *The Reading Teacher* 34 (March 1981): 686–91.

Spache, George D. *Diagnostic Reading Scales.* Revised. Monterey, CA: CTB/McGraw-Hill, 1972.

Spache, George D. *Diagnostic Reading Scales, Examiner's Manual.* Monterey, CA: CTB/McGraw-Hill, 1973.

Spache, George D. *Diagnostic Reading Scales.* Technical Bulletin. Monterey, CA: CTB/McGraw-Hill, 1973.

Spache, George. *Toward Better Reading.* Champaign, IL: Garrard Press, 1963.

Spache, George, and Evelyn B. Spache. *Reading in the Elementary School,* 4th ed. Boston, MA: Allyn and Bacon, Inc., 1977.

Spache, George, and Evelyn B. Spache. *Reading in the Elementary School,* 5th ed. Boston, MA: Allyn and Bacon, Inc., 1986.

Spiro, Rand J., and Ann Myers. "Individual Differences and Underlying Cognitive Processes in Reading." *Handbook of Reading Research.* Edited by P. David Pearson. New York: Longman, 1984.

Squire, James R. "Introduction: A Special Issue on the State of Assessment in Reading." *The Reading Teacher* 40 (April 1987): 724–25.

Stahl, Norman A., James R. King, and William A. Henk. "Enhancing Students' Notetaking Through Training and Evaluation." *Journal of Reading* 34 (May 1991): 614–23.

Stahl, Steven A., Michael G. Jacobson, Charlotte E. Davis, and Robin L. Davis. "Prior Knowledge and Difficult Vocabulary in the Comprehension of Unfamiliar Text." *Reading Research Quarterly* 24 (Winter 1989): 27–43.

Stallings, J. A., and D. Kaskowitz. *Follow-through Classroom Observation Evaluation, 1972–1973.* Menlo Park, CA: Stanford Research Institute, 1974.

Stanovich, Keith E. "A Call for an End to the Paradigm Wars in Reading Research." *Journal of Reading Behavior* 3 (1990): 221–31.

Stanovich, Keith E. "Toward an Inter-active Compensatory Model of Individual Differences in the Development of Reading Fluency." *Reading Research Quarterly* XVI (1980): 34–35, 42–45.

Stauffer, Russell G. *The Language-experience Approach to the Teaching of Reading.* New York: Harper and Row, 1970.

Stein, N. L., and C. G. Glenn. "An Analysis of Story Comprehension in Elementary School Children." *New Directions in Discourse Processing.* Edited by R. O. Freedle. Norwood, NJ: Ablex, 1979.

Stern, Paula R., and Richard Shavelson. "The Relationship Between Teachers' Grouping Decisions and Instructional Behavior: An Ethnographic Study of Reading Instruction." Paper presented at the Annual Meeting of the American Educational Research Association, Los Angeles, CA, April 13–17, 1981.

Stevens, Kathleen C. "The Effect of Background Knowledge on the Reading Comprehension of Ninth Graders." *Journal of Reading Behavior* 12 (Summer 1980): 451–54.

Stevens, Robert J., and Robert E. Slavin. "When Cooperative Learning Improves the Achievement of Students with Mild Disabilities: A Response to Tateyama-Sniezek." *Exceptional Children* 57 (December/January 1991): 276–80.

Sticht, Tom G., L. J. Beck, R. N. Hanke, G. M. Kleiman, and J. H. James. *Auding and Reading: A Developmental Model*. Alexandria, VA: Human Resource Research Organization, 1974.

Stoodt, Barbara D. "The Relationship Between Understanding Grammatical Conjunctions and Reading Comprehension." *Elementary English* 49 (1972): 502–4.

Strange, Michael. "Instructional Implications of a Conceptual Theory of Reading Comprehension." *The Reading Teacher* 33 (January 1980): 392.

Strickland, Dorothy. "Black Is Beautiful vs. White Is Right." *Elementary English* 49 (1972): 220–24.

Strickland, Dorothy S., and Lesley Mandel Morrow. "Assessment and Early Literacy." *The Reading Teacher* 42 (April 1989): 634–35.

Strickland, Dorothy S., and Lesley Mandel Morrow. "Emerging Readers and Writers: Sharing Big Books." *The Reading Teacher* 43 (January 1990): 342–43.

Strickland, Dorothy S., and Lesley Mandel Morrow. "New Perspectives on Young Children Learning to Read and Write." *The Reading Teacher* 42 (October 1988): 70–71.

Strickland, Dorothy S., and Lesley Mandel Morrow. "Oral Language Development: Children as Storytellers." *The Reading Teacher* 43 (December 1989): 260–61.

Strickland, Dorothy S., and Lesley Mandel Morrow. "Reading, Writing, and Oral Language." *The Reading Teacher* 42 (December 1988): 240–41.

Strickler, Darryl J. "Planning the Affective Component." *Classroom Practice in Reading*. Edited by Richard A. Earle. Newark, DE: International Reading Association, 1977.

Success with Writing. New York: Scholastic, 1988.

Sulzby, Elizabeth. "Children's Emergent Reading of Favorite Storybooks: A Developmental Study." *Reading Research Quarterly* 22 (Summer 1985): 458–81.

Swanson, B. Marian, and Diane J. Willis. *Understanding Exceptional Children and Youth*. Chicago: Rand McNally College Publishing Company, 1979.

Taba, Hilda. "The Teaching of Thinking." *Elementary English* 42 (May 1976): 534.

Taylor, Denny. *Family Literacy*. Exeter, NH: Heinemann, 1983.

Taylor, Stanford E., Helen Frackenpohl, and Catherine White. *A Revised Core Vocabulary: A Basic Vocabulary for Grades 1–8, An Advanced Vocabulary for Grades 9–13*. Huntington, NY: Educational Development Laboratories, 1969.

Taylor, Wilson L. "Cloze Procedure: A New Tool for Measuring Readability." *Journalism Quarterly* 30 (Fall 1953): 415–33.

Teale, William, Elfrieda Hiebert, and Edward Chittenden. "Assessing Young Children's Literacy Development." *The Reading Teacher* 40 (April 1987): 772–77.

Teale, William H. "Home Background and Young Children's Literacy Development." *Emergent Literacy: Writing and Reading*. Edited by W. H. Teale and E. Sulzby. Norwood, NJ: Ablex, 1987, pp. 173–206.

Teale, William H. "Positive Environments for Learning to Read: What Studies of Early Readers Tell Us." *Language Arts* 55 (November/December 1978): 922–32.

Teale, William, and Elizabeth Sulzby. *Emergent Literacy: Writing and Reading*. Norwood, NJ: Ablex, 1987.

Terman, Lewis M., and Melita H. Oden. *The Gifted Group on Midlife: Thirty-Five Years' Follow-up of the Superior Child, Genetic Studies of Genius, Vol. 5*. Stanford, CA: Stanford University Press, 1959.

The Children's Writing and Publishing Center. Fremont, CA: The Learning Company, 1989.

The Manhole, 1990. Menlo Park, CA: Activision, Mediagenic.

Thorndike, Edward. "Reading and Reasoning: A Study of Mistakes in Paragraph Reading." *Journal of Educational Psychology* 8 (1971): 323–32.

Thorndike, Robert L. *The Concepts of Over and Underachievement*. New York: Teachers College Press, Columbia University, 1963.

Thorndyke, P. W. "Cognitive Structures in Comprehension and Memory of Narrative Discourse." *Cognitive Psychology* 9 (1977): 77–110.

Tibbetts, Sylvia-Lee. "How Much Should We Expect Readability Formulas to Do?" *Elementary English* 50 (January 1973): 75–76.

Tierney, Robert J., James Mosenthal, and Robert M. Kantor. "Classroom Applications of Text Analysis: Toward Improving Text Analysis." *Promoting Reading Comprehension*. Edited by James Flood. Newark, DE: International Reading Association, 1984.

Tillman, Chester E. "Bibliotherapy for Adolescents: An Annotated Research Review." *Journal of Reading* 27 (May 1984): 713–19.

Trelease, Jim. "Jim Trelease Speaks on Reading Aloud to Children." *The Reading Teacher* 43 (December 1989): 200–207.

Trybus, Raymond J., and Michael A. Karchmer. "School Achievement Scores of Hearing Impaired Children: National Data on Achievement Status and Growth Patterns." *American Annals of the Deaf* 122 (April 1977): 62–69.

Turner, Thomas N., and J. Estill Alexander. "Fostering Early Creative Reading." *Language Arts* 52 (September 1975): 786.

U.S. National Joint Committee on Learning Disabilities. "Revised Definition of LD." *The Reading Teacher* 35 (November 1981): 134–35.

Vacca, J. Anne L., Richard T. Vacca, and Mary K. Gove. *Reading and Learning to Read*. Boston, MA: Little, Brown and Company, 1987.

Valencia, Shelia W. "Alternative Assessment: Separating the Wheat from the Chaff." *The Reading Teacher* 44 (September 1990): 60–61.

Valencia, Shelia W. "A Portfolio Approach to Classroom Reading Assessment: The Whys, Whats, and Hows." *The Reading Teacher* 43 (January 1990): 338–40.

Vallecorsa, Ada L., Rita Rice Ledford, and Ginger G. Parnell. "Strategies for Teaching Composition Skills to Students with Learning Disabilities." *Teaching Exceptional Children* 23 (Winter 1991): 52–55.

Veatch, Jeanette. *Individualizing Your Reading Program*. New York: G. P. Putnam's Sons, 1959.

Vignocchi, Nello. "What Research Says About the Effect of Class Size on Academic Achievement." *Illinois School Research and Development* 17 (Spring 1981): 51–54.

Vinyard, Edwin E., and Harold W. Massey. "The Interrelationship of Certain Linguistic Skills and Their Relationship with Scholastic Achievement When Intelligence Is Ruled Constant." *Journal of Educational Psychology* 48 (1957): 279–86.

Wade, Suzanne E. "Using Think Alouds to Assess Comprehension." *The Reading Teacher* 43 (March 1990): 442–51.

Walberg, Herbert J., and Shiow-Ling Tsai. "Correlates of Reading Achievement and Attitude: A National Assessment Study." *Journal of Educational Research* 78 (January/February 1985): 159–67.

Wang, Margaret C. "Mainstreaming Exceptional Children: Some Instructional Design and Implementation Considerations." *The Elementary School Journal* 81 (March 1981): 195–221.

Wardhaugh, Ronald. "Syl-lab-i-ca-tion." *Elementary English* 43 (November 1966): 785–88.

Watson, D. J. "Defining and Describing Whole Language." *The Elementary School Journal* 90 (November 1989): 129–41.

Waugh, Ruth F., and K. W. Howell. "Teaching Modern Syllabication." *The Reading Teacher* 29 (October 1975): 20–25.

Wepner, Shelley B. "Holistic Computer Applications in Literature-based Classrooms." *The Reading Teacher* 44 (September 1990): 12–19.

Wheeler, H. E., and Emma A. Howell. "A First Grade Vocabulary Study." *Elementary School Journal* 31 (September 1930): 52–60.

Whitehurst, F. Falco, C. J. Lonigan, J. E. Fischal, B. D. DeBaryshe, M. C. Valdez-Manchaca, and M. Culfield. "Accelerating Language Development through Picturebook Reading." *Developmental Psychology* 24 (July 1988): 552–59.

Wiederholt, J. Lee. *Formal Reading Inventory*. Austin, TX: Pro-Ed, 1985.

Wiederholt, J. Lee, and Brian R. Bryant. *Manual: Gray Oral Reading Tests-Revised*. Austin, TX: Pro-Ed, 1986.

Wiederholt, J. Lee, and Brian R. Bryant. *Manual: Gray Oral Reading Tests–Revised.* Austin, TX: Pro-Ed, 1992.

Williams, Joanna P. "Successive vs. Concurrent Presentations of Multiple Grapheme-Phoneme Correspondences." *Journal of Educational Psychology* 59 (1968): 309–14.

Wilson, Molly M. "The Effect of Question Types in Varying Placements on the Reading Comprehension of Upper Elementary Students." *Reading Psychology* 1 (Spring 1980): 93–102.

Winkley, Carol. "Which Accent Generalizations Are Worth Teaching?" *The Reading Teacher* 20 (December 1966): 219–24, 253.

Wixson, Karen K. "Level of Importance of Postquestions and Children's Learning from Text." *American Educational Research Journal* 21 (1984): 419–33.

Wolfe, Evelyn. "Advertising and the Elementary Language Arts." *Elementary English* 42 (January 1965): 42–44.

Wong, B. Y. L., and W. Jones. "Increasing Metacomprehension in Learning Disabled and Normally Achieving Students Through Self-Questioning Training." Burnaby, B. C. Canada: Simon Fraser University, 1981: Mimeographed.

Wood, Karen D. "Free Associational Assessment: An Alternative to Traditional Testing." *Journal of Reading* 29 (November 1985): 106–11.

Wood, Martha, and Mavis Brown. "Beginning Readers' Recognition of Taught Words in Various Contextual Settings." *Reading Research: Studies and Applications. Twenty-eighth Yearbook of the National Reading Conference.* Edited by Michael L. Kamil and Alden J. Moe. Clemson, SC: National Reading Conference, 1979, pp. 55–61.

Woodcock, Richard W. *Woodcock Reading Mastery Tests-Revised: Manual.* Allen, TX: DLM Corporation, 1987.

Yaden, David B., Jr., and Lea M. McGee. "Reading as a Meaning Seeking Activity: What Children's Questions Reveal." In *Thirty-third Yearbook of the National Reading Conference,* pp. 101–9. Edited by Jerry Niles. Rochester, NY: National Reading Conference, 1984.

Zabrucky, Karen, and Hilary Horn Ratner. "Effects of Reading Ability on Children's Comprehension Evaluation and Regulation." *Journal of Reading Behavior* 21 (March 1989): 69–83.

Zintz, Miles V. *The Reading Process.* Dubuque, IA: Wm. C. Brown Company Publishers, 1980.

Index